D0762100

RIOT IN THE CITIES

RIOT IN THE CITIES

An Analytical Symposium on the Causes and Effects

Edited by

Richard A. Chikota and Michael C. Moran

Fairleigh Dickinson University Press

Rutherford · Madison · Teaneck

Library of Congress Catalogue Card Number: 74-76132

Associated University Presses
Cranbury, N. J. 08512

In its original form, this symposium was first published as Vol. 45, Numbers 3 and 4 of the Journal of Urban Law, with the following Editors and Staff:

ISSUE EDITORS	STAFF
Richard A. Chikota	Dennis R. Pollard
Marsel S. Greenia	David T. Coyle
Michael C. Moran	Eugene Eickholt
Gerald D. Ducharme	Ruthanne Gartland
Lawrence G. Campbell	Elliot Glicksman
Melvine Merzon	Frederick Lauck
	Vera Massey Jones
	Thomas M. Powers

SBN 8386 7443 7

Printed in the United States of America

CONTENTS

ARTICLES

RIOT IN THE CITIES

Introduction

PAUL P. HARBECHT, S.J.*

THE major need is to generate new will—the will to tax ourselves to the extent to meet the vital needs of the nation.[1]

The articles that follow center on the relationship of law to the problems raised by the civil disorders—some call them riots, others rebellion—that occurred in the summer of 1967. Law, however, is not created out of, nor does it operate in a vacuum. If ours is a racist society, and we have all the evidence we need to know that it is, it should not surprise us to learn that we have laws that are in substance and in application, discriminatory. What we are determines what we do.

For a long time non-Americans have been willing to admit that they and their society were not perfect. But we have taken heart from the ideals on which our country was founded, ideals wonderfully embodied in our Constitution. We have been humble about it all, even eager to admit that we fell short of our ideals in practice—but then doesn't everyone? What we are now faced with, and with shock, is that we are so far short of our ideals that our shortcomings may well make our way of life no longer viable. The issue we face can be put simply enough: if we wish to keep our affluence where it is and the way it is, we will have to give up some of our ideals. The South Africans have made this choice. All men in that country are not equal and if the whites can

* Dean University of Detroit School of Law; A.B. Loyola, Chicago; LL.B. Georgetown; S.J.D. Columbia.

1. Report of the National Advisory Commission on Civil Disorders 23 (Bantam 1968).

maintain their power, all men are not going to be equal. If, on the other hand, we wish to pursue our ideals of freedom and equality, we are going to have to redistribute our affluence. Thus far we have shown little willingness to do this.

Thus far, since the problems of poverty and social degradation have been brought clearly to light, our effort has been to solve our problems of poverty and race without disturbing the positions of power and the possession of affluence. Vast outlays of wealth will be necessary to care for the juvenile offender, to rebuild the ghettos, to fight crime, to do, in short, those million things in a thousand places that our commissions, our reports, our professors and our leaders of the poor have all told us are absolutely essential.

Of course wealth alone will not do the trick. We need a "new will" as the President's Commission states. With that new will all the remedial action will become possible; without it, not even the wealth will be forthcoming.

We should make no mistake about the size of our problem. It is not a mere accident that nearly a fifth of our people either have not broken into our system or have been spewed out of it, or that they should be exploited after they have fallen by the wayside. The millions of poor and the victims of racial prejudice are merely the cost of running our country in the way we have chosen. We have said, if a man cannot work (and often this implies skills we have not made available to him), then neither let him eat. We have put a modern gloss on this good scriptural doctrine because we no longer let him starve to death, at least not quickly.

Competition is a basic rule of our system. The race is to the swift. Naturally, in the struggle to keep up, some are going to come last. Naturally, they are going to be the mentally ill, the black, the Indian, the Puerto Rican, anyone who, by nature or by the exclusionary rules we establish, cannot compete.

We are materialistic. We tend to determine a man's worth by what he has or what he can produce. And we have an accurate measure for this, too. It is the market place. It is not just any production that counts. The production has to be marketable; people must be willing to part with money for what a man can do or what he does is worthless.

Self-reliance is another basic quality an American must have to gain our respect. If he needs help, particularly if he is lacking in the cardinal virtues of thrift, industry, cleverness in managing his money, then he deserves to be out-traded, to live in a ghetto. If a man cannot get off the dole, he is morally inferior and we owe him nothing, though, in our charity, we may give him enough to survive.

This is the name of the game in America, this is the system. Unfortunately those who cannot or will not play the game, who do not fit the system are taking advantage of some of our own rules. They are speaking up, they are marching to Washington. Some are even threatening to throw all our rules out the window.

At this point we have a choice, we can bend all of our efforts to equip them to play the game, to learn to operate within the system or we can change some of our rules. To do the former is impossible. These are the rejects of the system as it now functions. Even to try to integrate these people into the system must result in changing that system. More wisely we could choose to subject our system, and therefore ourselves to some serious scrutiny. Surely a system which operates at such a high cost of human misery, a system that is so exclusive, can be improved upon.

To speak this way, is to invite being tagged with the pejorative labels we have ready to hand, socialism, communism, planned economy, etc. We have, however, a problem before us that will not be frightened off by names, and we can no longer indulge the warm feeling that nobody has really done anything wrong, we just have not pursued the American way hard enough nor long enough.

An introduction should be brief. I end with some questions that will, I hope, remain with the reader after he has perused or studied the writers who follow. What kind of a society lives with a fifth of its people suffering in poverty when it has at hand the means to relieve that suffering? What kind of society places a higher priority on a space program than it does upon the needs of the mentally ill and the aged? What kind of society is it that neglects almost entirely training and care of its juvenile delinquents? What kind of society reserves for its business and commerce its greatest subsidies and accords the least support to its poor, its sick, its weak and stricken members?

Is it the kind of society whose members would seriously ask, "Am I my brother's keeper?"

First Amendment Freedoms and the Politics of Mass Participation:

Perspective on the 1967 Detroit Riot

JOHN W. SMITH* AND LOIS H. SMITH**

> *There are no single answers or easy assumptions to make about Detroit's riot. Such simplistic approaches are too often part of American thinking.*†

> *I would like to say at the outset, sir, that we found no single cause for the disturbance that occurred in Los Angeles.*††

INTRODUCTION

WHAT perspective should one take in looking at a civil disturbance, such as the 1967 summer Detroit destruction?

Attorneys have their own definition of the situation: they saw the temporary demise of the rule of law and through the smoke could foresee crowded court dockets, rights, claims, bonds, and settlements.

From the point of view of a policeman or soldier it was a question of law enforcement and reestablishing order.

From the viewpoint of most civil administrators it was largely a matter of coordinating Balkanized local governments into a united front to plan for rebuilding, to budget special and emergency funds for the impacted area, and to organize renovation or renewal programs as well as to relocate the displaced.

As seen by the rioters in the streets, at the time, the destruction might have appeared as a holiday from morals, an opportunity to steal what they deemed unassigned, unowned store stock, and to capitalize on someone else's capital in a community temporarily tolerant of such bargains-for-the-asking.

Insurance men saw in the looting client policies, claims, adjustors' estimates, probable increased costs for riot coverage and ultimately partial cancellation at renewal time.[1]

---

* A.B. Northwestern University, M.A. The University of Michigan. Assistant Professor of Political Science, Indiana University of Pennsylvania. The author wishes to acknowledge the IUP central research fund for providing a grant to do a search of the literature and to messieurs Cecil Eubanks, Clifford DuRand and James Reiley for reading an earlier draft.

** A.B. 1964, J.D. 1967 University of Detroit. Member, State Bar of Michigan. The authors absolve Indiana University of Pennsylvania and the three readers from any responsibility for the contents.

† Jerome Cavanagh, Mayor of Detroit, in 1967 testimony before the National Advisory Commission on Civil Disorders.

†† John A McCone, Chairman of California Governor Brown's Commission on the Los Angeles Riots, in 1967 testimony before the Senate Judiciary Committee.

1. *See generally, Hearings on S.J. 102* Before the Senate Comm. on Commerce, 90th

Sociologists might see this same disturbance in terms of collective behavior, a temporary loss in a sense of community or an attempt to establish a sense of belonging, perhaps as a manifestation of alienations, or racial tension.[2]
relation to the fortunes of elected political leaders, including President Johnson, for he sent federal troops; Governor Romney, for his actions were seen in light of his aspirations to become President; and Mayor Cavanagh, for he made strenuous efforts to make the central city a pace setter in the use of federal funds to revamp the core area.

The question of which one of these perspectives is proper clearly begs the question. For this question presupposes there is one single, superior or preferred perspective. Each of these orientations has a logical and partial claim to validity; however, none of them can make a pretense to explaining totally the causes or cures of such a complex event. It is axiomatic that such a multifaceted, involved event is not susceptible to *single factor analysis.* The Detroit riot was a week-long commotion in a geographically dispersed area including a string of outbursts in the surrounding state communities of Pontiac, Grand Rapids, Saginaw, Muskegon, Benton Harbor, Kalamazoo, and Albion. There were also destructive, publicized preludes, *inter alia* in Los Angeles, Newark and Cleveland. Oversimplifying the reasons and remedy for this type of event is spurious, and a fundamental logical fallacy; it is a reductionism.[3]

Reasoning of the Right, Left, and Center

Only the extreme ideological perspectives advance one factor explanations. Of far right groups presently in the United States, the John Birch Society is a chief representative. For them there is a facile reason for all such disturbances, viz. it is a conspiracy headed by "The Organization" and dedicated to the promulgation of communism by nefarious means.[4] The riots are politically meaningful for they are controlled

Cong., 1st Sess., ser. 90-24 (1967); also Sengstock, *Mob Action: Who Shall Pay the Price?*, U. Det. J. of Urban L. 407 (1967) and articles cited therein; City of Detroit Mayor's Development Team Report to Mayor Jerome P. Cavanagh, Oct. 26, 1967, Book I, Summary of Recommendations. A Report by The President's National Advisory Panel on Insurance in Riot-Affected Areas: Meeting The Insurance Crisis of Our Cities, (1968).

2. R. Turner and L. Killian, Collective Behavior, (1957); *e.g.*, N. Smelser, Theory of Collective Behavior (1963); Seeman, *On the Meaning of Alienation*, 24 Am. Soc. Rev. 784 (1959); *e.g.*, G. E. Simpson and J. M. Yinger, Racial and Cultural Minorities: An Analysis of Prejudice and Discrimination, 497 (1958).

3. "We must watch ourselves closely when we mention causes or offer solutions, for we have a strong tendency to oversimplify through seizing upon only one of many possibilities." W. Little et. al., Applied Logic, 10 (1955).

4. The official guide to the Society suggests three methods whereby the Communists take over: infiltration and propaganda, "fermenting internal civil war," and inducing us into "gradual surrender." R. Welch, The Blue Book of the John Birch Society, 24-5

and inspired. This "John Birch Society reasoning" seems to be that Negroes are incapable of such riotous actions of their own volition: in this they are similar to a 1794 defense argument that:

> . . . a negro slave was not in point of law, such a person as could be capable of committing this offense, being under the direction and control of his master.

The holding, running contrary to this argument, seems more plausible and rather germane seventeen decades later:

> The Court . . . were clearly of opinion, that a negro was, in contemplation of law, such a person as was capable of committing a riot, in conjunction with white men. . . Besides, it is evident, that a negro was one who was capable of committing an injury. . . . it was not necessary, men should be possessed of civil rights, to make them amenable to justice for those offenses.[5]

Indeed, the whole John Birch Society emphasis on a conspiratorial theory of history has been noted as a symptom of a mentality in search of the historic key which will unlock the name of the true clandestine power group—the few—who manipulate the many.[6] In addition to communists, of course, there are others who have been accused of such *sub rosa* manipulation, especially Jews and Jesuits.[7]

On the other end of the ideological spectrum, the left, credence is also given to a simple, single factor at the base of the riots. The Marxists too find their explanation necessary and sufficient. Riots are caused by the inherent conflict in capitalism between the exploiting bourgeoise and the downtrodden proletariat who are forced to attack with violence,

---

(1961). Referring to "the Watts Rebellion," Gary Allen, writing in the official journal of the Society, notes that the whole Los Angeles uprising was "planned, engineered, and integrated" by "some forty to fifty Negroes sent by the Communists . . ." Allen, *The Plan to Burn Los Angeles*, AM. OPINION, 1 (1967).

5. State v. Thackam and Mayson, 1 S.C. (1 Bay) 358 (1794).

6. The John Birch view on the alarming Communist conspiracy is at the base of this group. "You may think I am an alarmist. Frankly I am. For in my opinion, based on many years of intensive study of the methods, the progress, and the menace of the Communist conspiracy, there is ample reason for extreme alarm; and I hope to make you alarmists too." Welch, however, would say the group is also positive: "I have tried to establish fundamental and permanent objectives, much broader than the fight against the Communist conspiracy, because I am convinced that these ultimate long-range objectives are more important than the defeat of the Communist conspiracy." Those objectives, "as officially stated, will be to promote less government, more responsibility, and a better world." R. WELCH, *supra* note 4 at 29, 126, 131. The difficulty with this conspiratorial view of history as an absolute monomania is briefly pointed out in the very critical account by B. R. EPSTEIN & A. FOSTER, REPORT ON THE JOHN BIRCH SOCIETY, 6, 16, 24-5 (1966).

7. Secret influential groups holding power over the masses' destiny; this is the simple, single-minded, easily digested scapegoat approach to explanation. *See* H. ARENDT, THE ORIGINS OF TOTALITARIANISM 94, 108 (2d ed. 1958); J. S. CURTISS, AN APPRAISAL OF THE PROTOCOLS OF ZION (1942).

the only way they can, the base and superstructure of capitalistic domination, perhaps fittingly epitomized in the indominable member of the John Birch Society who is an exploiting local merchant.

In all fairness it must be noted that mainstream *leaders* who claim to have investigated the riots have not found documentation supporting conspiratorial explanations,[8] Representative William Cramer, chief proponent of the anti-riot bill, to the contrary notwithstanding.[9] Conservatives do not attribute the riots to such communist manipulation.[10] Liberals also find a variety of causes.[11]

---

8. The Presidential Commission on Civil Disorders reported the riots were not a black-power conspiracy. Detroit's Mayor Cavanaugh testified to the Commission on August 16: "I would say from the evidence we have now that the influence of the conspirators was very small." Det. News, Aug. 20, 1967, § A, at 20, col. 1. The Senate Permanent Subcommittee on Investigations supposedly has found "no evidence of a national conspiracy . . ." Mears, *Probers Find No Civil Disorder Conspiracy Clues*, Indiana Evening Gazette, Sept. 28, 1967, at 13, col. 2. The official California investigation on the Watts Riots found such extreme and emotional statements unsupported or disproved. REPORT BY THE GOVERNOR'S COMM. ON THE LOS ANGELES RIOTS—AN END OR A BEGINNING, (1965). This was recently reaffirmed by the Commission's chairman, John A. McCone, "We found no evidence that Communist agents had anything to do with starting the riots in Watts in 1965. We did find some subversive elements were in it after it started, and this is customary for them. We found no evidence, otherwise." *S. Hearings on H.R. 421*, pt. 2, 90th Cong., 1st Sess., 668 (1967). The New Jersey Commission, *infra* note 170, at 144 states "The evidence presented to the Commission does not support the thesis of a conspiracy or plan to initiate the Newark riot."

9. The information which lends credence to the position that riots in many instances are well planned, highly organized undertakings by certain groups or individuals who are using interstate facilities to carry on the business of inciting urban warfare is overwhelming, in my opinion.

> Despite the overwhelming evidence of outside influences in many of these riots, including statements by mayors, journalists who observed the riots and others, it appears that some continue to adhere to the belief that the riots are parochial, and spontaneous, and that a Federal law making it an offense to travel in or use a facility of interstate commerce to incite a riot would be unnecessary, ineffective and an usurpation of State and local police powers.

In a very anti-Birch reference he carefully distinguishes himself from Robert Welch:

> But, unless this Government recognizes the very real possibility that subversive elements are active in at least exploiting some of the riots, if not instigating them, and that a pattern has been set and a blueprint being followed, we can expect many more years of violence and bloodshed in the streets of America.

S. Hearings on H.R. 421, pt. 2, 90th Cong., 1st Sess., 763, 769, 774 (1967).

10. Senator Strom Thurmond (R.,S.C.) said that there "are five chief causes of these riots. These five causes have wreaked havoc upon the fabric of America. The roots I think are to be found in communism, false compassion, civil disobedience, the court decisions, and the criminal instinct that lies repressed in the heart of every man." *S. Hearings on H.R. 421*, pt. 1, 90th Cong., 1st Sess., 19 (1967).

Senator Herman Talmadge (D., Ga.) suggests:

> what we have witnessed in city after city is without a doubt a creature of the misguided philosophy that there is no moral or legal obligation to obey all the laws all the time, but only some of the laws some of the time . . . We have seen the fruits of this disrespect for authority and law and order in city after city, community after community throughout America.

112 CONG. REG. S15657 (daily ed. July 20, 1966).

11. Senator Steven Young (D.,Ohio) suggests:

> Mr. President, no individual—not a Rap Brown nor a Stokely Carmichael—no one—could cause what happened in Detroit and Newark this year or in Watts two years ago, just as no one individual could have stopped what occurred in the 13 colonies in 1776. Those very foolish short-sighted persons who say that the rioting

Whether of the right, left, or center, most *lay people* tend to attribute the causes of the riot in proportion to their antagonism or tolerance towards Negroes:

> Respondents who are relatively antagonistic toward Negroes tend to view the riot as the result of outside "agitation", to believe the riot hurt the Negro's cause, and to suggest punitive solutions to the problem. Conversely, respondents who are tolerant in their general attitudes toward Negroes tend to see the causes of the riot in such sources as white prejudice and discrimination against Negroes or lack of employment and educational opportunities, are more likely to believe the riot helped the Negro's cause, and are more likely to suggest ameliorative solutions to the problem, such as full civil rights for Negroes and increased educational and economic opportunities.[12]

To date, one of the most serious sociological studies denies that the disturbances have been organized, but it grants as a distinct possibility that the riots may become organized.[13]

In sum, it is possible to analyze the riots in terms of a single factor or a variety of factors, some of which are immediate and tangible, while other factors are more remote in time and concern background conditions. The second alternative set of explanations is more congruous to social scientific investigation.

> resulted from the war on poverty are 100 per cent wrong. Poverty, not the war on poverty, was the basic cause of this rioting.

112 CONG. REC. S13749 (daily ed. Sept. 27, 1966).

Senator Kuchel (R.,Cal.) lists the causes of agitation and disorder as: "discrimination, poverty, inadequate housing, unemployment, and the general economic and emotional depression that persists in these areas." 112 CONG. REC. S11739 (daily ed. June 6, 1966).

The highest placed federally appointed Negro, a man in President Johnson's Cabinet, also stresses long-term factors:

> Three out of four Americans now live in urban areas. It is simply a cruel fact that it is in the core of cities where blight and decay are found in the greatest magnitude, where housing is worst, unemployment is highest, schools are oldest, where park and recreation facilities are least likely to be found, and where better medical and social welfare programs are needed most.
>
> It is also here that minority groups, particularly Negroes, are too often confronted by closed housing markets within the cities, and by suburban walls of privilege around the cities. It is hardly surprising, then, that these are environments of poverty, ignorance, disease, and violence.

Robert C. Weaver, Secretary of HUD, *S. Hearings on S. 3509 and S.J. Res. 187*, pt. 1, 89th Cong., 2d Sess., 87 (1966).

Governor Romney, in a televised address in the aftermath of the riots, asked "Why did it happen?" He replied, "There is no single response, but in my judgment, these are among the reasons . . . . " He then catalogued eighteen specific "deficiencies in our society and our personal attitudes and endeavors that have built up the situation which resulted in the havoc of the Detroit riot." Among the causes are failure to support responsible Negro leadership, Negro poverty amidst a generally affluent society, urban renewal which has acted as Negro renewal, flight to the suburbs, and the friction between Negroes and the predominantly Caucasian police force. Det. News, July 31, 1967 §C at 20, cols. 2-3.

12. Cohen, *The Los Angeles Riot Study*, 12 SOCIAL WORK 17 (1967).

13. John P. Spiegel, Statement Presented to the Senate Judiciary Comm., Aug. 29, 1967, p. 7, mimeo:

The Prism

The perspective of both *de facto* participants of the disturbances and most *post facto* analysis is always through a partial and disproportioned vantage point or prism, as it were. In the case of the participants, events are colored through the prism of their first-hand experiences; after-the-fact analysts generally view events through categories established through their professional training. Philosophers of history and those who study the sociology of knowledge probably spend more time than anyone trying to establish how best to view, record, and explain these events.[14] A distillation of some of their deliberations would divulge at least one major conclusion: description and explanation are a function of how one chooses or simply assumes to define the situation.[15]

Hence, with all reporters of the 1967 summer events in Detroit there will be this prismatic effect, this definition of situation, which in turn is caused by differences in their relation to the location of the event, and the kind of reality toward which the reporter has been trained to be sensitive. Consequently any single discussion will be limited to events in a certain space and time and through a view point limited by personal background and experience.

This article, too, is therefore limited in perspective. What is of concern is the disturbance as a legal-political event. What have the courts formally declared are the boundaries of individual and mass participation? What political benefits, if any, can be found in the disturbances? What are the democratic percepts which govern our thinking on the role of violence? How do these events illustrate the general problem of meaningful and constructive participation in an industrial, urban society? Finally, how have the violent disturbances effected political leadership?

I realize that this committee is considering legislation in the area of the prevention of riots based upon the assumption that riots are stimulated by outside agitators who cross state boundaries. I must say that our findings in no way support this proposition.

Lieberson & Silverman, *The Precipitants and Underlying Conditions of Race Riots*, 30 Am. Soc. Rev. 897 (1965) Posit:

> [R]iots are more likely to occur when social institutions function inadequately, or when grievances are not resolved, or cannot be resolved under the existing institutional arrangements. . . . The failure of functionaries to perform the roles expected by one or both of the racial groups, cross-pressures, or the absence of an institution capable of handling a community problem involving inter-racial conflict will create the conditions under which riots are most likely.

Apparently the July 1968 Glenville ghetto riot in Cleveland, Ohio was planned. *See* Time, Aug. 2, 1968, p. 12.

14. *E.g.*, R. G. Collingwood, The Idea of History, 249 ff (1946); The Varieties of History, esp. 290 ff (F. Stern, ed. 1957); W. Walsh, Introduction to Philosophy of History, esp. 100 ff (1951); K. Mannheim, Ideology and Utopia: An Introduction to the Sociology of Knowledge, (1936).

15. The idea behind definition of situation was first developed by the sociologist W. I. Thomas; *see* An Introduction to the History of Sociology, 800-801 (H. E. Barnes ed. 1948).

It will be the burden of this article to inspect these questions on the role of mass activity in a constitutional democracy under rule of law. We do not lay claim to a definitive study, but within the spirit of a multi-analytic framework, we hope to shed a proportioned light on two significant elements in the larger and many-sided discussion.

> *The constitutional guarantee of liberty implies the existence of an organized society maintaining public order, without which liberty itself would be lost in the excess of anarchy.**
>
> *But when a legislature undertakes to proscribe the exercise of a citizen's constitutional right to free speech, it acts lawlessly; and the citizen can take matters in his own hands and proceed on the basis that such a law is no law at all.***
>
> *The power of a state to abridge freedom of speech and of assembly is the exception rather than the rule and the penalizing even of utterances of a defined character must find its justification in a reasonable apprehension of danger to organized government. The judgment of the legislature is not unfettered. The limitation upon individual liberty must have appropriate relation to the safety of the state. Legislation which goes beyond this need violates the principle of the Constitution."****

Having inquired into the perspectives which one could assume in looking at the riots, and having noted what possible cause or causes contemporary analysts contend produced the riots, we turn our attention to rules which the courts say govern permissible from impermissible forms of individual and group or mass participation.

Behind the court rules, pounded out case by case, there stand two commonly held major assumptions. The first is that there are no absolute rights which accrue to either the individual or the state. This means that neither should the individual be totally free from state restraint nor should the state be wholly free from individual restraint. The one produces anarchy, the other produces totalitarianism. This is a juristic premise which is often articulated in cases which decide where to draw the line on permissible as opposed to impermissible individual or group action in light of the Bill of Rights. Consider two expressions of this position:

> We have never held that such freedoms [First Amendment freedoms] are absolute. The reason is plain. . . "Civil liberties, as guaranteed by the Constitution, imply the existence of an organized society maintaining public order without which

* Cox v. Louisiana, 379 U.S. 554 (1965).
** Poulos v. New Hampshire, 345 U.S. 423 (1953) (Douglas & Black, JJ., dissent).
*** Herndon v. Lowry, 301 U.S. 258 (1937).

liberty itself would be lost in the excesses of unrestrained abuses."[16]

[T]he freedom of speech which is secured by the Constitution does not confer an absolute right to speak, without responsibility, whatever one may choose, or an unrestricted and unbridled license giving immunity for every possible use of language and preventing the punishment of those who abuse their freedom . . . .[17]

This position, that freedoms are not absolute, is commonly but not universally held. On the present Supreme Court, Associate Justice Black is the most persistent opponent.[18] The second assumption is that rights are not sharply distinct but are blended, common, and inseparable. Again, consider two examples of this postulate:

It was not by accident or coincidence that the rights to freedom in speech and press were coupled in a single guaranty with the rights of the people peaceably to assemble and to petition for redress of grievances. All these, though not identical, are inseparable. They are cognate rights, and therefore are united in the First Article's assurance.[19]

It is beyond debate that freedom to engage in association for the advancement of beliefs and ideas is an inseparable aspect of the "liberty" assured by the Due Process Clause of the Fourteenth Amendment, which embraces freedom of speech.[20]

Doctrines

Without absolutes there can be no ultimate benchmarks. Hence, the courts' rules are based on a variety of doctrines which generally follow from the aforesaid assumptions. These doctrines serve as the most nearly attainable set of stable criteria.

The first doctrine concerns *pre-facto* punishment of citizen participants. This is the area of censorship. Just as the common law doctrine states that a man is assumed innocent until proven guilty, so too a person is assumed free to participate until it is proven that the action is legally impermissible. This is *the doctrine of prior restraint* or previous prohibition. Judge Fuld, in a New York case concerned with the use of school buildings by a folk singer, states the general case:

[T]here is no power in government under our Constitution to exercise prior restraint of expression of views, unless it is demonstrable on a record that such expression will immediately and irreparably create injury to public weal. . . .[21]

16. American Communications Ass'n, C.I.O. v. Douds, 339 U.S. 399 (1950).
17. Whitney v. California, 274 U.S. 371 (1926).
18. Black, *The Bill of Rights*, 35 N.Y.U.L. Rev. 865 (1960).
19. Thomas v. Collins, 323 U.S. 530 (1945).
20. NAACP v. Alabama, 357 U.S. 460 (1958).
21. East Meadow Comm'y Concerts Ass'n v. Board of Educ., 18 N.Y.2d 129, 219 N.E. 2d 175 (1966). *See also* Times Film, Corp. v. Chicago, 365 U.S. 43 (1961).

On the other hand, it is possible from a California case to say a school board may require a prior statement of legal purpose before granting permission to a group that might be criminal syndicalists: thus we have the corollary "Not all prior restraints are, *ipso facto,* unconstitutional."[22] Nevertheless, the jurists have been consistent in suggesting that "The main purpose of such Constitutional provisions was to prevent previous restraint . . . ."[23] The immunity persists, however, only "so long as it [the action] is not harmful in its character when tested by such standards as the law affords."[24] The standards of the law, in turn, must be posited upon a real problem of inciting to violence and the law must deal directly with the abuse, while "the rights themselves must not be curtailed."[25] In specific application this means a Louisiana civil rights leader who wishes to speak publically need not present his ideas first to police authorities for their consideration and approval.[26] It also means an Alabama civil rights leader who wishes to parade need not secure a permit from a city commissioner who has power of judgment over the possible "public welfare, peace, safety, health, decency, good order, morals, or convenience" of the event, because this also is an imposition and an invidious restraint.[27] With regard to New York City, authorities cannot deny a park speaking permit based on general discretionary criteria just because the man has an obnoxious and unpopular set of views, even though he might recreate what news reports said in the past were hysteria conditions, and even if he is an American Nazi who someday might be assassinated.[28] These same public authorities cannot act differently to a Baptist minister because an official decided on the basis of past performance, the speaker will denounce other religious beliefs.[29] It would seem then that the possible threat of a wrong is not sufficient ground for prevention: it is better, as in the case of the Wisconsin sheriff, to wait until the protesters have actually engaged in the physical violation of the law, and not before then.[30] As we will note in the last two sections of this article, this doctrine certainly does not put a premium upon tranquility. It makes of democracy a forum for a wide latitude of views.

---

22. ACLU v. Board of Educ., 28 Cal. Rptr. 704, 379 P.2d 8 (1963).

23. *In re* Porterfield, 28 Cal. 2d 91, 168 P.2d 713 (1946). *See also* Thornhill v. Alabama, 310 U.S. 88 (1940); Buxom v. Riverside, 29 F. Supp. 3 (S.D. Cal. 1939); Barton v. Bessemer, 234 Ala. 20, 173 So. 626 (1937); People v. Talley, 332 P.2d 447 (Super. Ct. 1958); and People v. Armentrout, 118 Cal. App. 761, 1 P.2d 556 (Super. Ct. 1931).

24. People v. Arnold, 127 Cal. App. 2d 844, 273 P.2d 712 (Super. Ct. 1954).

25. People v. Garcia, 37 Cal. App. 2d 753, 98 P.2d 270 (Super. Ct. 1939). *See also* Norton v. Ensor, 269 F. Supp. 533 (D. Md. 1967).

26. Cox v. Louisiana, 379 U.S. 557 (1965).

27. Shuttlesworth v. Birmingham, 180 So.2d 114 (1965).

28. Rockwell v. Morris, 12 App. Div. 2d 272, 211 N.Y.S.2d 25 (1961).

29. Kunz v. New York, 340 U.S. 290 (1951).

30. State v. Givens, 28 Wis. 2d 109, 135 N.W.2d 780 (1965).

The next doctrine concerns the courts' assumption of good-will or valid intention on the part of the legislature. This is *the doctrine of the presumption of constitutionality.* For example, as stated in the very important anarchy case in 1925, *Gitlow v. New York:* "Every presumption is to be indulged in favor of the validity of the statute."[31] Indeed, whenever possible, the courts will interpret statutes so as to avoid unconstitutional results.[32] And the courts do not act to strike down a statute unless it appears to be unconstitutional beyond a reasonable doubt.[33] In areas other than civil liberties, such as an interesting Wisconsin case of 1910, where a statute is made to cover certification of a party petition, it is even possible for the court to "consider 'the surrounding circumstances, the existing condition of things, the evils to be remedied, the objects to be attained' " and to "look at the whole and every part of the statute and the apparent intention derived from the whole, to its subject matter, to its effects and consequences, and to its reason and spirit" before rendering the implied intent.[34] But, presumption of validity narrows in scope when a statute appears to limit the use of a constitutionally protected right.[35] This is so because standards of permissive vagueness are relatively more strict in first amendment issues, and, within the confines of rights cases, decisions are to be resolved in favor of protecting the right against state encroachment.[36] According to Associate Supreme Court Justices Brennan,[37] Douglas,[38] and Harlan,[39] the states' power to "sweep" too broadly through protected freedoms can be judicially curtailed.[40]

Another test which the courts have employed is *the doctrine of bad tendency,* which was employed by Sanford in the 1925 criminal anarchy case, *Gitlow v. New York.*[41] This is not a libertarian thesis,

31. 268 U.S. 668 (1925). *See also* State v. Mills, 278 Ala. 188, 176 S.2d 884 (1965); State Fed'n of Labor v. McAdory, 246 Ala. 1, 18 S.2d 810 (1944); *Ex parte* Porterfield, 63 Cal. App. 2d 518, 147 P.2d 15 (1944); Barr v. Cardell, 173 Iowa 18, 155 N.W. 312 (1915); and State v. Klapprott, 127 N.J.L. 395, 22 A.2d 877 (1941).

32. United States v. C.I.O., 335 U.S. 106 (1948).

33. State v. Laundy, 103 Ore. 443, 204 P. 958 (1922).

34. State v. Phelps, 144 Wis. 1, 128 N.W. 1044 (1910). *See also* Milwaukee County v. Carter, 258 Wis. 139, 45 N.W.2d 90 (1950); Neacy v. Board of Sup'rs, 144 Wis. 210, 128 N.W. 1063 (1910); and State v. Frear, 142 Wis. 320, 125 N.W. 961 (1910).

35. Dunne v. United States, 138 F.2d 137 (8th Cir. 1943).

36. NAACP v. Button, 371 U.S. 415 (1963).

37. *Id.* at 433.

38. Griswold v. Connecticut, 381 U.S. 485 (1965).

39. NAACP v. Alabama, 377 U.S. 307 (1964).

40. Supreme Court Associate Justices Reed and Douglas would say when the sweep is built into every portion of the statute then the whole statute is null and void. This does not mean partial, but total invalidity. Beauharnais v. Illinois, 343 U.S. 280 (1952) (Reed & Douglas, JJ. dissent). *Accord,* State v. Junkin, 85 Neb. 1, 122 N.W. 473 (1909).

41. 268 U.S. 652 (1925).

and the suggestion is that it is not success, but intent and tendency, which suffice to make an act a crime. This doctrine allows the court to consider the circumstances in which the act occurs: hence Sanford's dictum that "a state, in the exercise of its police power, may punish those who abuse this freedom by utterances inimical to the public welfare, tending to corrupt public morals, incite to crime, or disturb the public peace, is not open to question."[42] The authors agree with Eubanks that this case is difficult to apply because of its imprecise language.[43] It is interesting to note that Holmes in *Gitlow*[44] dissented from Sanford's opinion, suggesting that eloquence and desire which have strong tendencies are the stuff of successful change and ought to be given a hearing.

Nevertheless, the doctrine has persisted and has been invoked against those who threaten to speak on the overthrow of organized government by unlawful means.[45] During World War II, in New Hampshire, a case arose which reached the Supreme Court and the high bench invoked a direct tendency corollary. They decided that words spoken in public places such as "damn racketeer" or "damn Fascist" have a direct tendency to violence, and thus are a crime: the Supreme Court decided there was no substantial infringement on protected First Amendment rights.[46] An indirect use of this doctrine of bad tendency was in the celebrated *John Kasper Case*[47] which arose out of Kasper's defilement of a restraining order to cease speaking against a desegregation order to integrate the Clinton, Tennessee High School with twelve Negroes. The Sixth Circuit Court of Appeals upheld the lower court criminal contempt citation on grounds that Kasper's speech was calculated to cause resentment to the law of the land, the desegregation order.

In the main, however, the bad tendency test has not been employed. Several cases have overt references against the position and covert retreat from the position is dominant. The most striking statement of this opposition, although not the most important, comes from the New Jersey Court of Chancery:

> Our law does not prohibit the public expression of unpopular views. It is lawful to advocate, for instance, the establishment of a dictatorship in America, or a soviet form of government, or an hereditary monarchy, or the abolition of religious free-

42. *Id.* at 667.
43. Letter from Cecil Eubanks to the authors, March 29, 1968.
44. Note 41 *supra.*
45. Stromberg v. California, 283 U.S. 359 (1931).
46. Chaplinsky v. New Hampshire, 315 U.S. 568 (1942) (Fighting Words Doctrine) *cf.* notes 155, 156.
47. Kasper v. Brittain, 245 F.2d 92 (6th Cir. 1957).

> dom, or other changes in our political, economic, or social system, no matter how unwise or shocking. If lawless elements in the community instead of ignoring such propaganda, or meeting it by sound argument, resort to riot, it is the duty of police to protect the lawful assemblage and to repress those who unlawfully attack it.[48]

The United States Supreme Court has been firm in its rejection of the doctrine since the beginning of World War II on three separate occasions, the first two of which deal with injunctions against labor picketing where violence is in the background.[49] On the third occasion, in 1948, in a 5-4 major free speech decision written by Justice Douglas, the Court said a Chicago ordinance curbing free speech, when a talk only *tended* to break the peace, was an infringement on protected rights.[50] We may conclude from this review of the doctrine's history that it is receding, but not a dead letter.

A milder form of the preceding doctrine, also propounded by Holmes, is *the doctrine of clear and present danger*. The full context of the phrase in its original source is:

> The question in every case is whether the words used are used in such circumstances and are of such a nature as to create a clear and present danger that they will bring about the substantive evils that Congress has a right to prevent. It is a question of proximity and degree.[51]

The doctrine is not general in scope, but applies only to the staking out of areas of permissible prohibitions or restraints on individuals by the state where first amendment rights are concerned. It was never intended to be a test for all regulatory statutes, as in the case of controlling labor union activity.[52]

The complete history of this phrase is carefully traced by Professor Corwin,[53] from its inception as a dictum in 1919, through its first appearance twenty years thereafter as a majority opinion in Herndon v. Lowry,[54] to its extensive misuse by Learned Hand of the Second Circuit in the *Dennis* case,[55] and by four of the Justices in *Dennis* on

48. American League of Friends v. Eastmead, 116 N.J. Eq. 487, 174 A. 157 (1934).

49. Cafeteria Employees Local 302 v. Angelos, 320 U.S. 293 (1943) and Milk Wagon Drivers Local 753 v. Meadowmoor Dairies, 312 U.S. 287 (1941).

50. Terminiello v. Chicago, 337 U.S. 1 (1948).

51. 249 U.S. at 52 (1919).

52. A.F.L. v. Mann, 188 S.W.2d 276 (Tex. Civ. App. 1945).

53. Corwin, *Bowing Out 'Clear And Present Danger,'* 27 N.D. Law 325 (1952).

54. 301 U.S. 242.

55. United States v. Dennis, 183 F.2d 201 (2d Cir. 1950). Hand added that "in each case the court must ask whether the gravity of the 'evil,' discounted by its improbability, justifies such invasion of free speech as is necessary to avoid the danger."

appeal the following year.[56] The noted authority's conclusion was that the doctrine had become an encrusted "cliché."[57] Corwin was of the opinion that the *Dennis* holding produced *"a declaration of independence by the Court from the tyranny of a phrase."*[58] What could be retained from the doctrine was that legislation limiting first amendment rights must be so designed as to demonstrate a valid, potential, and direct abuse to the well being of the state, such as activities which deter the public welfare, disrupt the public peace, or criminally incite.[59]

Since *Dennis,* the frequency with which the doctrine has been invoked has been decreasing. As recently as 1962, the Court has used the phrase to reverse a Georgia Court of Appeals conviction of a sheriff who issued press releases comparing the judges who tried him to the Ku Klux Klan.[60] However, it is important to observe the doctrine did not serve as justification for repressing free speech, but rather for elaborating the protected right's scope. Other courts also persist in invoking the doctrine. For example, the Supreme Court of South Carolina in 1962 used it as a collateral argument in the Claffin College and South Carolina State College Negro student protest case.[61] Also, in the same year, a federal district court cited the phrase in a CORE twelve store picket case in Baton Rouge, Louisiana. But the reference to the Holmesian formula was accomplished amidst several other appeals, including invocation to the reasonable man and the need to balance potential rights, as over and against equal protection of the rights of all citizens to use the public ways and streets.[62]

Two state cases in this decade point out the continued if diminished relevancy of the doctrine. In one a white supremacist party in Maryland, the National State Rights Party, was enjoined from meeting when Negro defendants in the immediate vicinity were being tried on rape charges, on grounds the party meeting was a clear and present danger. On the other hand, the injunction of the lower circuit court for a stay of ten months was denied as being beyond a reasonable period of danger.[63] In the other case, which arose out of a self-appointed Marxist Harlem speaker's citation for conspiracy to riot, the court squarely

---

56. Dennis v. United States, 341 U.S. 494 (1951).
57. Corwin, *supra* note 53 at 357.
58. *Id.* at 358.
59. 268 U.S. 652.
60. Wood v. Georgia, 370 U.S. 375 (1962).
61. State v. Brown, 240 S.C. 357, 126 S.E.2d 1 (1962).
62. Clemmons v. CORE, 201 F. Supp. 737 (E.D. La. 1962).
63. Carroll v. President and Comm'rs of Princess Anne, 247 Md. 126, 230 A.2d 452 (1967).

based its argument on the clear and present danger test.[64] It is important to know that Epton, the Harlem Marxist, spoke out during the 1964 Harlem summer riot.

In the main, the courts are receding from the doctrine of clear and present danger, relying on it less frequently, and when invoking it, do so with less singleness and confidence. Corwin was correct when he suggested that the Court has curtailed the doctrine but has not suddenly abandoned it, for the Court "prefers the tactics of rear guard action to those of outright retreat."[65]

The next doctrine is set out as a thesis so that it can be compared to its antithesis, which will be presented below. Before labeling and discussing this doctrine, however, the authors must state two caveats. The first is that although most jurists eschew blanket statements and absolutes in the realm of judging protected rights, it is possible that some jurists will be dogmatic and subtle and assert that one category is ipso facto of higher value than another, all things being equal. The other warning is that although most significant doctrines are authoritatively promulgated by the Supreme Court, for this Court alone is not bound by *stare decisis*,[66] it is possible that some inferior courts have been "creative and adoptive." This is so because not all decisions are or can be reviewed by the high bench.[67] The next doctrine then, is both a blanket statement and one developed *sub rosa,* outside the sanctioning domain of the Supreme Court: it is, to indulge in a neologism, *the doctrine of first amendment subordination.*

Although the following citations are not complete, because no key number system could pick up the strand of thought, the string of authority marshalled below appears conclusively to demonstrate that at least one federal court and several state courts have attested to the idea. The federal case on point, a 1956 Smith Act conviction,[68] contains the thesis that the societal value of speech, must, on occasion, be subordinated to other values and considerations. The point is not developed; indeed it is not strenuously argued and may well be judged an *obiter dictum.* It is in turning to the state courts that we find ample evidence of the doctrine. In a 1948 California decision a jurist suggests public individuals have a right to passage on sidewalks which is *superior* to any rights of a crowd to obstruct the sidewalk to listen to a speech.[69]

64. People v. Epton, 19 N.Y.2d 496, 227 N.E.2d 829 (1967).

65. Corwin, *Bowing Out 'Clear And Present Danger,' supra* note 58.

66. Douglas, *Stare Decisis,* 4 THE RECORD 152-79 (1949).

67. That explains why political scientists have conventionally been limited observers of the law: their research and literature is far too confined to the United States Supreme Court. IMPACT AND FUNCTIONS IN A LOCAL POLITICAL SYSTEM 1-3 (1967).

68. United States v. Lightfoot, 228 F.2d 861 (7th Cir. 1956).

69. Ex parte Bodkin, 86 Cal. App. 2d 208, 194 P.2d 588 (Dist. Ct. App. 1948).

A 1924 Indiana Supreme Court decision suggests that the rights of individuals are subordinate to the welfare of the general public.[70] In 1903, the Nebraska Supreme Court asserted that exercise of the police power intended as a reasonable regulation is valid even though it may effect incidentally some constitutionally protected right.[71] Several New York decisions have relied on this doctrine: for example in 1921, similar to the California case above, the court felt a man addressing an assembly, *ipso facto*, has a subordinate right to someone traveling along the walk.[72] Another New York case has suggested all individual rights should be used in subordination to the rights of others,[73] and yet another decision declared that an assembly may be regulated in the name of police powers and that assembly rights must be exercised in subordination to general comfort and convenience.[74] Pennsylvania courts on three occasions[75] appeared to have resolved the dilemma of protecting order vis-à-vis promoting change in favor of order by saying that the police power is a paramount right, superior to the bill of rights, and speech-assembly provisions must be exercised in subordination to any such reasonable rules that appear. It fell to Chief Justice Eggleston of the Supreme Court of Appeals of Virginia in two cases decided in 1967[76] to expound formally the heretofore vague doctrine. First amendment speech and assembly rights are subordinate to the greater rights of the general public interest and the general comfort and convenience.

The antithesis of subordinate rights is, logically, superordinate rights. This position also has been propounded, and it is based on the assumption that some rights are more fundamental to an ordered liberty than others.[77] If these rights are truly fundamental and other

---

70. Thomas v. Indianapolis, 195 Ind. 440, 145 N.E. 550 (1924).

71. Anderson v. State, 69 Neb. 686, 96 N.W. 149 (1903). It is impossible to reconcile the Anderson case with a decision eighteen years later from New York where it was asserted: "The ordinance [an anti-littering ordinance designed to prevent commercial and business advertising matter] within reasonable limits is a proper one, and should be sustained, but no city ordinance, no matter how worthy its intendment, should be permitted in any way to curtail any of the fundamental rights of the citizen." People v. Johnson, 117 Misc. 133, 191 N.Y.S. 750 (Ct. Gen. Sess. 1921).

72. People v. Atwell, 232 N.Y. 96, 133 N.E. 364 (1921). *See also* People v. Kieran, 26 N.Y.S.2d 291 (Nassau County Ct. 1940).

73. Meltex v. Livingston, 208 Misc. 1033, 145 N.Y.S.2d 858 (New York County Sup. Ct. 1955).

74. People v. Richards, 177 Misc. 912, 31 N.Y.S.2d 457 (Nassau County Dist. Ct. 1941).

75. Wortex Mills v. Textile Union, 369 Pa. 359, 85 A.2d 851 (1952) [*Cf.* Buckley v. Meng, 35 Misc.2d 467, 230 N.Y.S.2d 924 (Sup. Ct. 1962) which predicates the opposite paramount value]; Commonwealth v. Widovich, 295 Pa. 311, 145 A. 295 (1929); and Commonwealth v. Egan, 113 Pa. Super. 375, 173 A. 764 (1934).

76. York v. Danville, 207 Va. 665, 152 S.E.2d 259 (1967) and Thomas v. Danville, 207 Va. 656, 152 S.E.2d 265 (1967).

77. Palko v. Connecticut, 302 U.S. 319 (1937).

rights are derivative, secondary, or tertiary, then it follows these basic rights ought to be specially honored. According special place to certain rights means advocating *the doctrine of preferred position.* Just as Professor Corwin traced the intellectual history of the clear and present danger doctrine, so too, in *Kovacs v. Cooper,*[78] Justice Frankfurter accounts chronologically for the development of the preferred position from 1937 to 1949. In strong but perceptive terms in a concurring opinion, Justice Frankfurter suggested that this doctrine is a potentially mischievous phrase because it implies that any statutory regulation of communication tends to be presumptively invalid. The genesis of the phrase is disputed, but no constitutional scholar can avoid mentioning the heralded[79] footnote four of *United States v. Carolene Products Co.* of 1938,[80] written by Justice Stone. The doctrine first assumed a majority stance in *Kovacs,* and was used, for example, in the 1939 hand bill cases,[81] and a 1943 decision which suggested first amendment freedoms *in toto* are in a preferred position.[82] In addition to Frankfurter's suggestion that the doctrine leads to presumptive invalidity there is a second implication. As McKay comments favorably: championing the preferred position doctrine embodies "the principled response of a judiciary alert to its highest duty . . . through assiduous striving after the blessing of liberty."[83] Pursuit of this doctrine puts the court in the active role of guaranteeing first amendment rights against any encroachment whenever an issue of this species is brought to their attention. This goal is accomplished by narrowing the presumption of constitutionality[84] and putting the burden of proof on the state to demonstrate the rule is imminently needed to forestall a concrete danger.

The middle ground between the above two doctrines is neither supremacy for public powers nor for first amendment freedoms. The golden mean falls in between, and this would be a balancing and harmonizing of powers and rights without recourse to absolutes, decided in the context of the particular case, and adjudged by reasonable men of good will. *The doctrine of balancing necessary public power and individual rights* conjures up the metaphor of weighing equities, an already familiar and symbolic representation of the courts' function. Examples of what might be balanced include an Ohio municipality's

---

78. 336 U.S. 90 (1949).

79. The most detailed history and analysis of the footnote appears in A. MASON, THE SUPREME COURT: PALLADIUM OF FREEDOM 151-61 (1962).

80. 304 U.S. 144 (1938).

81. Schneider v. Irvington, 308 U.S. 147 (1939).

82. Murdock v. Pennsylvania, 319 U.S. 105 (1943).

83. McKay, *The Preference for Freedom,* 34 N.Y.U. L. REV. 1182 (1959).

84. *E.g.* Gibson v. Legislative Investigation Comm., 126 So.2d 129 (Fla. 1960). *See also* C. BLACK, THE PEOPLE AND THE COURT 21 ff. (1960).

interest in aesthetics vis-à-vis the right of a private property owner to put up a political sign;[85] or a Brooklyn police officer's duty to tell a speaker to move on because of possible disorderly conduct vis-à-vis the speaker's right to collect a congregation about him on a public street and sidewalk even if he thereby interferes with persons passing by;[86] or a Greenwich Village police officer's responsibility to give a summons for littering to a protester who has set up a four foot square table on a sidewalk close to the curb vis-à-vis the protester's right to condemn American foreign policy in Viet Nam where disinterested pedestrians were able to pass by unimpeded and without serious inconvenience;[87] or a Virginia state court's power to issue an injunction directed at Negro non-violent picketers preventing them from marching, because by massive occupancy of approaches to a theatre they excluded everyone from it, vis-à-vis the Negroes' right to protest and inform the public and public officials of their grievance;[88] or California's power to restrict picketing because it publicized labor disputes illegally under the Hot Cargo and Secondary Boycott Act passed in the wake of the economic and social problems arising in the aftermath of the Second World War vis-à-vis the union members' right to exercise protected forms of speech when they believed the actual and immediate emergency from the post war period had subsided;[89] or the power of Milwaukee's City Housing Authority to require tenant certification of non-subversive leanings vis-à-vis the tenants' fear of being suppressed from free and uninhibited speech;[90] or the power of Mississippi high school officials to ban "One Man One Vote" and "SNCC" buttons on the grounds of hampering school activities vis-à-vis the students' right to protected speech;[91] or

85. Peltz v. South Euclid, 11 Ohio St. 2d 128, 288 N.E.2d 320 (1967). The property owner won!

86. People v. Friedman, 277 N.Y. 682, 14 N.Y.S.2d 389 (Magis. Ct. 1939). The defendant was found guilty because the policeman did not act capriciously or unreasonably in light of heavy traffic.

87. People v. Strauss, 48 Misc. 2d 1006, 266 N.Y.S.2d 431 (New York Crim. Ct. 1965). Strauss was found not guilty because, in context, he had a right to free expression and did not impede public safety or convenience.

88. Baines v. Danville, 337 F.2d 579 (4th Cir. 1964). In a brilliant and lengthy decision Circuit Judge Haynsworth said what is required is mutual accommodation of the rights of the public and those rights of protestants which are guaranteed by the first amendment. *Id.* at 587. The Negroes' appeal for cessation of the temporary restraining order was granted because the possibility for violence had changed for the better.

89. *Ex parte* Blaney, 30 Cal. 2d 643, 184 P.2d 892 (1947). The unions won and by so doing exposed the statute's rationale to a full scrutiny for vagueness (which it was), violating prior restraint (which it was), being partially invalid (the entire statute infringed and therefore was entirely void), and timeliness (the statute was not valid since the immediate crisis had passed).

90. Lawson v. Milwaukee Housing Auth., 270 Wis. 269, 70 N.W.2d 605 (1955). The tenant won because the possible harm from suppression of speech outweighed any threatened evil from members of subversive organizations.

91. Burnside v. Byars, 363 F.2d 744 (5th Cir. 1966). The students' right was upheld because authorities could not prove any reason to tip the balance in favor of the neces-

the duty of Georgia officials to enforce an anti-trespass statute vis-à-vis the right of a twenty-three year old Ohio sociologist protesting a Georgia restaurant owner's race exclusion policy;[92] or the power of Alabama's Governor to interfere with the advanced planned Selma protest march along U.S. Highway 80 by a large group trying to demonstrate their grievances when the Governor must insure the safety and convenience of people who travel along the road vis-à-vis Mrs. Williams, Martin Luther King and members of the Southern Christian Leadership Conference who have a protected right to petition peacefully for redress of grievances;[93] or New Hampshire's police power to curb offensive and annoying words such as "scab" vis-à-vis the citizen's right to speak and distribute his ideas when, where and how he chooses;[94] or whether the city of Portsmouth, New Hampshire has power to regulate the place of religious meetings on public park ground vis-à-vis the Jehovahs' Witnesses' right to exercise the protected First Amendment Freedom of religion provision.[95]

In conclusion one can say of these seven doctrines that the courts have a variety of tests which overlap and represent shades of latitude toward state power, some of which contradict others, thus providing a multitude of possible boundaries for court determination of permissible individual and group participation. No one doctrine dominates in all the cases but some are of more historic than contemporary importance.

Time, Place and Manner

In addition to court derived doctrines to decide what constitutes permissible expressions of first amendment rights, the jurists have also derived a common law set of distinctions over certain conditions which

---

sity for the rule for carrying out the school's teaching or disciplinary function. The rule was arbitrary and unreasonable.

92. United States v. Grimes, 229 F. Supp. 289 (N.D. Ga. 1964). Grimes lost his appeal for habeas corpus because even a segregation-minded Georgia restaurant owner has a right to his property, and any balancing right of the protester to demonstrate is cancelled when free speech passes certain boundaries.

93. Williams v. Wallace, 240 F. Supp. 100 (N.D. Ala. 1965). Restraining order against Wallace was issued; the marchers' right was upheld; and a woman from Detroit was murdered along the way. Justice Johnson balanced the extent of the Negroes' right to demonstrate against the enormity of the wrongs Negroes had suffered. The justice hence entered the dialogue over the merits of the case, going into the percentage of Negro voter registration in Dallas county, where Selma is located, rather than remaining aloof from the merits and only passing on the procedural questions involved. Whether one agrees or disagrees with the decision, it is apparent that the court's balance was improperly based on substantive considerations. In the authors' opinion the case is bad law, not because of the holding, but because of the presence of non-procedural considerations.

94. State v. Dyer, 98 N.H. 59, 94 A.2d 718 (1953). Case remanded for jury determination.

95. State v. Derrickson, 97 N.H. 91, 81 A.2d 312 (1951). The answer is that First Amendment rights may be reasonably and nondiscriminatively regulated in order that the constitutional rights of others may be protected.

give these freedoms limited validity, based upon peculiar context. For example, the abstract freedom of assembly is always protected, but the actually exercised freedom to meet without a parade permit in Florence, South Carolina may be impermissible in context.[96] Propriety may or may not prevail, and context alone determines the answer.

It is axiomatic that certain events can be curtailed on Sunday[97] and this is a typical example of a time limitation on the exercise of even protected rights. Another example is that certain activities are curbed on election day.[98] War time emergencies can create curbs on the free exercise of otherwise protected rights, including the right to the writ of habeas corpus.[99] Emergency conditions force curbs on freedoms, even for a category of citizens such as Japanese Americans.[100] Pending riots might justify curbs on free speech.[101] Past picketing with violence might curb future rights to picket.[102] Groups might legitimately be forced to wait twenty-four hours from the time of securing a permit to march before actually taking to the street in order to give the city time to prepare for the event.[103] Ten months suspension of activities on the other hand is apparently too long a cooling off period.[104] Hearings by a judicial investigating body may justify temporary curbs on the freedom to protest.[105] The most important conclusion which can be drawn from these diverse conditions is that no one rule suffices to cover all contingents, and post facto judicial determination in context seems the only salutary means of finding an answer.

It is also axiomatic that there are certain instances when discretion demands silence or the curbing of protected freedoms, the most obvious being a citizen in the armed forces, who *ipso facto* comes under the umbrage of an entirely different set of canons of conduct, namely military law.[106] There are several other place restrictions which allow for the curbing of otherwise protected freedoms, including marching on streets which have another and perhaps more primary function,[107]

---

96. Florence v. George, 241 S.C. 77, 127 S.E.2d 210 (1962).
97. Braunfeld v. Brown, 366 U.S. 599 (1961).
98. *E.g.* N.D. CENT. CODE 16-20-16 (1960).
99. U.S. CONST. art. I, § 9, cl. 2.
100. Korematsu v. United States, 323 U.S. 214 (1944).
101. Griffon v. CORE, 221 F. Supp. 899 (E.D. La. 1963).
102. Steiner v. Oil Workers Local 128, 19 Cal. 2d 676, 123 P.2d 20 (1942).
103. Commonwealth v. Hessler, 141 Pa. Super. 421, 15 A.2d 486 (1940).
104. Note 63, *supra*.
105. People v. United Mine Workers, 70 Colo. 269, 201 P. 54 (1921).
106. "So far as military personnel are concerned, offenses are punished by a system of courts-martial under regulations prescribed by Congress. Articles of War were adopted for the Army by Congress in 1789, and for the Navy in 1800. In 1950 these two statutes, as amended, were replaced by the Uniform Code of Military Justice, setting up a single system for all the armed services." C. H. PRITCHETT, AMERICAN CONSTITUTIONAL ISSUES 186 (1962).
107. Walker v. Birmingham, 388 U.S. 307 (1967); Commonwealth v. Surridge, 265

but not highway construction sites.[108] A public park is a place which comes under peculiar regulation,[109] as well as a company owned town,[110] a courthouse square,[111] a governor's mansion[112] and the White House.[113] It stands to reason a prison environment is a special place[114] and so is a jail yard,[115] and the premises of a fire house.[116] A foreign embassy[117] and the United Nations area[118] pose the problem of freedom to picket relative to the inherent powers of the President to conduct foreign affairs. Universities are a special place for the exercise of freedoms because of their role to probe,[119] and high schools pose other problems.[120] Finally, a private club,[121] a private restaurant catering to the public,[122] and areas zoned for residential use pose special problems.[123] What can be concluded from these diverse examples is that some areas are more amenable to public gatherings and free exchange, whereas other places are designed and protected from the full blast of public controversy.

Finally, it is axiomatic that the mode of exercise of first amendment freedoms has much to do with whether the right is ultimately protected: for example, speech can be communicated in a whisper or electronically magnified through high decibel loud speakers, and the latter has come under police power restraint.[124] Communication of ideas by lecture is certainly different than mail.[125] An anonymous

Mass. 425, 164 N.E. 480 (1929) and Ex parte Heffron, 179 Mo. App. 639, 162 S.W. 652 (1914).

108. Davidson v. Carpenters Council, 356 Mich. 557, 97 N.W.2d 11 (1959).

109. Commonwealth v. Abrahams, 156 Mass. 57, 30 N.E. 79 (1892).

110. Marsh v. Alabama, 326 U.S. 501 (1946).

111. Hamer v. Musselwhite, 376 F.2d 479 (5th Cir. 1967).

112. Flores v. Denver, 122 Colo. 71, 220 P.2d 373 (1950) and Pope v. State, 192 Misc. 587, 79 N.Y.S.2d 466 (Ct. Cl. 1948). The Pope case deals with Governor Dewey when he was delivering an address at Liverpool.

113. Scott v. District of Columbia, 184 A.2d 849 (Mun. Ct. App. 1962). 40 U.S.C. § 193g (1964) was used to pick up the Ressurrection City marchers in June, 1968.

114. Roberts v. Pepersack, 256 F. Supp. 415 (D. Md. 1966).

115. Adderley v. Florida, 385 U.S. 39 (1966).

116. Application of Hooker, 208 Misc. 188, 143 N.Y.S.2d 750 (Sup. Ct. 1955).

117. Frend v. United States, 100 F.2d 691 (D.C. Cir. 1938).

118. People v. Carcel, 2 Misc.2d 827, 150 N.Y.S.2d 436 (Magis. Ct. 1956).

119. Sigma Chi. Fraternity v. Regents of Univ. of Colorado, 258 F. Supp. 515 (D. Colo. 1966); Webb v. State Univ. of New York, 125 F. Supp. 910 (N.D. N.Y. 1954); Goldberg v. Regents of Univ. of California, 57 Cal. Rptr. 463, 370 P.2d 313 (1967) and Samson v. Trustees of Columbia Univ., 101 Misc. 146, 167 N.Y.S. 202 (Sup. Ct. 1917).

120. Danskin v. San Diego Unified School Dist., 28 Cal. 2d 536, 171 P.2d 885 (1946); Steele v. Sexton, 253 Mich. 32, 234 N.W. 436 (1931) and Pare v. Donovan, 54 Misc. 2d 194, 281 N.Y.S.2d 884 (Sup. Ct. 1967).

121. Gallaher v. American Legion, 154 Misc. 281, 277 N.Y.S. 81 (Sup. Ct. 1934).

122. Walker v. State, 220 Ga. 415, 139 S.E.2d 278 (1964).

123. *See* Kamin, *Residential Picketing and The First Amendment*, 61 Nw. U.L. Rev. 216-31 (1966).

124. Brinkman v. Gainesville, 83 Ga. App. 508, 64 S.E.2d 344 (1951).

125. Lamont v. Postmaster General, 381 U.S. 301 (1965) and Heilberg v. Fixa, 236 F. Supp. 405 (N.D. Cal. 1964).

publication is a different mode of expression than one which contains the name of the sponsor.[126] The courts have also drawn distinctions where the communication has been carried on by kite flying,[127] literature distribution by door to door doorbell ringing,[128] literature distribution by broadcasting handbills which later litter the place of distribution,[129] protest by flag desecration,[130] picketing for labor[131] and nonlabor purposes,[132] sit-ins[133] and lay-ins,[134] and wearing black arm bands.[135] Manner of protected speech also varies if one selects to protest by using a banner,[136] or speaking while loitering in a public place,[137] or even giving legal advice in public to a group.[138] The ingenuity of mode of presentation has yielded unique ways of expression, and certainly manner of conveyance must be considered by the court in evaluating whether the communication falls within the permissible purview of protected rights.

Permissible Encroachment

Court decisions declaring the boundaries of permissible individual and group participation are not only based on doctrines and considerations of time, place, and manner, but are also based on the one constitutionally defined crime, which is treason,[139] and five types of statutes which outlaw sedition,[140] espionage,[141] insurrection,[142] conspiracy against the selective service,[143] and criminal syndicalism.[144] All

126. State v. Freeman, 143 Kan. 315, 55 P.2d 362 (1936) and Smith v. Higinbothom, 187 Md. 115, 48 A.2d 754 (1946).

127. People v. Yolen, 49 Misc. 2d 470, 267 N.Y.S.2d 925 (1966).

128. Martin v. Struthers, 319 U.S. 141 (1943) and Mogadore v. Coe, 197 N.E.2d 570 (1963).

129. Wolin v. Port Auth., 268 F. Supp. 855 (S.D.N.Y. 1967); Milwaukee v. Kassen, 203 Wis. 383, 234 N.W. 352 (1931); *In re* Anderson, 69 Neb. 686, 96 N.W. 149 (1903) and People v. Hess, 198 Misc. 913, 103 N.Y.S.2d 582 (Police J. Ct. 1950).

130. Commonwealth v. Karvonen, 219 Mass. 30, 106 N.E. 556 (1914). This case proclaims that preventing the carrying of a red flag is not unlawfully depriving persons of their liberty; whereas Allen v. District of Columbia, 187 A.2d 888 (Ct. App. 1963) claims carrying a red flag was within the protection of the First Amendment and did not constitute disorderly conduct.

131. Hardie-Tynes Mf'g Co. v. Cruse, 189 Ala. 66, 66 S. 657 (1914).

132. Hubbard v. Commonwealth, 207 Va. 673, 152 S.E.2d 250 (1967).

133. Bell v. State, 227 Md. 302, 176 A.2d 771 (1962).

134. Note 132, *supra*.

135. Tinker v. Des Moines Comm'y School Dist., 258 F. Supp. 971 (S.D. Iowa 1966).

136. Watters v. Indianapolis, 191 Ind. 671, 134 N.E. 482 (1922).

137. Phifer v. Birmingham, 42 Ala. App. 282, 160 So. 2d 898 (1964).

138. NAACP v. Harrison, 202 Va. 142, 116 S.E.2d 55 (1960).

139. U.S. Const. art. III, § 3, cl. 1.

140. *E.g.* Smith Act, 18 U.S.C. §§ 2384, 2385 (Supp. 1966).

141. *E.g.* Espionage Act, 12 U.S.C. §§ 1,2 (1917).

142. *E.g.* Ga. Ann. Code ch. 26, § 901-904 (1953).

143. Selective Training and Service Act, 50 U.S.C.A. Appendix § 311 (1940).

144. *E.g.* Ohio Rev. Code §§ 2923.12-15 (1967).

of these forms of participation fall beyond the pale of protected rights and all are punishable.

Special mention needs to be made of syndicalism. This was the belief in industrial violence advocated by the Industrial Workers of the World, the so-called Wobblies or IWW's. The movement had its most adherents in the second decade of the present century and was led by such colorful figures as Big Bill Haywood. The group's intellectual leader, a French former engineer and neo-Marxian polemist Georges Sorel, who is the subject of sustained attention in Part III of this article, gave the advocates of the one big industrial union ample philosophic justification for raw violence. Cases decided against the Wobblies, who were primarily western lumbermen, miners, and agricultural workers, have not been adequately studied by intellectual historians and thus the court material has never been evaluated for twentieth century American law and political thought.[145] The IWW's goals include going after improved worker's benefits with any means available, including sabotage. They clearly employed techniques which go beyond permissible boundaries of protected rights.

Courts *always* assume[146] the redress of grievances is possible through the rule of law, and violence is therefore *never* justified. The authors will leave this assumption and pick up the strand of thought in a later section, speculating what events follow if the courts' assumption is inadequate.

The courts have held classes of people cannot be bound to second class forms of participation because of a particular position or station in society or the economy. Political parties abiding by the rule of law cannot be restrained.[147] Ordinary citizens cannot be bound to inferior forms of participation because of the discretion of a mayor,[148] or a chief of police.[149] Nor can labor pickets,[150] an interest group,[151] or a minister[152] be cataloged separately. It was also held that registered foreign agents[153] who have signed under the provisions of the Foreign

---

145. The leading historian of Wilson makes no reference to the IWW movement in the otherwise comprehensive A. LINK, WOODROW WILSON AND THE PROGRESSIVE ERA: 1910-17 (1954). Typical of the other works in the field is the survey of writings by Berthoff, *The Working Class* in THE RECONSTRUCTION OF AMERICAN HISTORY, ch. 7 (J. Higham, ed. 1962).

146. People v. Cox, 66 Cal. App. 287, 226 P.14 (Dist. Ct. App. 1924).

147. Field v. Hall, 201 Ark. 77, 143 S.W.2d 567 (1940) and In re Garrabad, 84 Wis. 585, 54 N.W. 1104 (1893).

148. Buffalo v. Till, 192 App. Div. 99, 182 N.Y.S. 418 (Sup. Ct. 1920).

149. Trujillo v. Walsenburg, 118 P.2d 1081 (1941) and Edgewater v. Cox, 123 N.J.L. 212, 8 A.2d 375 (1939).

150. Reno v. Second Judicial Dist. Ct., 59 Nev. 309, 95 P.2d 994 (1939).

151. Myerson v. Samuel, 74 F. Supp. 315 (E.D. Pa. 1947).

152. Coughlin v. Chicago Park Dist., 364 Ill. 90 4 N.E.2d 1 (1936).

153. United States v. Peace Information Center, 97 F. Supp. 255 (D.D.C. 1951).

Agents Registration Act of 1938[154] are not singled out for special consideration.

In two cases[155] the Supreme Court has suggested that *fighting words* do not fall under the halo of protected rights. The state is permitted to encroach upon these expressions because they lead to violence. It is possible to imagine the problems caused by Negroes who might be brought in to break a union strike.[156]

Related to the withdrawal of court protection where fighting words are spoken or printed, is the problem of an assembly held under potential assault from outsiders. The general rule is that assemblies are allowable when persons of reasonable courage agree to meet.[157] Thus, Paul Robeson, the famous Negro singer and communist, has a right to assemble to discuss national issues feeling free from potential assault because he can assume police protection of his Constitutional rights.[158] When a speaker at an assembly, however, incites the group to riot, the protective cover falls away.[159] Likewise, labor unions and business establishments have the same right to assemble when there is no reason to anticipate a disturbance, and the police are compelled to make the speaker's words and not the listener's agitation the basis for permitting the assembly to continue.[160]

Expression of views cannot be suppressed because they are merely unpopular,[161] unorthodox,[162] immoderate,[163] or disconcerting.[164] One man's expression cannot be abridged because another man tries to stage a riot or police officers are fearful of a breach of peace: this would be yielding to intimidation if it were allowed.[165] The state cannot suppress views simply to conserve what public officials deem to be desirable conditions.[166] Protected freedoms are therefore to be preserved from frontal attack and from stifling by more subtle forms of interference.[167]

In sum, the state's powers are there to preserve and not prevent

---

154. Foreign Agents Registration Act, 52 Stat. 631 (1938) amended by 56 Stat 248 (1942), as amended 22 U.S.C. 611 (Supp. 1941-1943).

155. Chaplinsky v. New Hampshire, 315 U.S. 568 (1942) and Cantwell v. Connecticut, 310 U.S. 296 (1940).

156. *See* Weiner, *Negro Picketing for Employment Equality,* 13 HOWARD L.J. 275 (1967).

157. State v. Butterworth, 104 N.J.L. 579, 142 A. 57 (1928).

158. Robeson v. Fanelli, 94 F. Supp. 62 (S.D.N.Y. 1950).

159. Kasper v. State, 326 S.W.2d 664 (1959).

160. Neelley v. Farr, 61 Colo. 485, 158 P. 458 (1916) and Jordahl v. Hayda, 1 Cal. App. 696, 82 P. 1079 (Ct. App. 1905).

161. Hurwitt v. Oakland, 247 F. Supp. 995 (N.D. Cal. 1965).

162. State v. Woodruff, 13 So. 2d 704 (Fla. 1943).

163. Application of Cassidy, 268 App. Div. 282, 51 N.Y.S.2d 202 (1944).

164. Brown v. Stillwater, 149 P.2d 509 (Okla. Crim. App. 1944).

165. Sellers v. Johnson, 163 F.2d 877 (8th Cir. 1947).

166. CORE v. Douglas, 318 F.2d 95 (5th Cir. 1963).

167. Bates v. Little Rock, 316 U.S. 516 (1960).

the exercise of free expression so long as it is consonant with a broadly viewed definition of rule of law. Unfortunately the state has not always broadly viewed the free expression of acts.

II

> *Watts may be symbolic for this nation in its lesson of riot and the subsequent responsiveness of community, a state and a nation in overcoming root causes found in unemployment and its accompanying exigencies.**
>
> *One of the paradoxes of the largely nonviolent protest movement is that some of its great victories have come as a consequence of violence: the brutal treatment of freedom riders led to the ICC order desegregating transportation facilities . . . .***

The common law adversary process of case-by-case decision-making is always slow; it is also usually after the fact in its judgment.[168] To prevent violence from occurring and to study such disturbances *in toto* we must turn from the judiciary to legislative investigations, blue ribbon citizen panels, and *ad hoc* administrative studies.

The most predictable response after a riot or any major violent calamity is a formal investigation. These post mortems are designed either to clarify or quietly bury the event in delayed, bland, or permanently postponed reports. These reports (and this remark is generally valid for any area of formal inquiry) will either be specific and narrowly confined, or generic and broadly coordinated. Again, the reports may be descriptive and read like a scenario-of-events-without-comment, or they may be analytic and reform inspired. In turn, the reception of these reports can be either filed and forgotten or well-thumbed and used as the basis for an overhauling. As both the New Jersey and National Advisory Commission mention, few students of statecraft realize how frequently it is that royal commissions, task force reports, blue ribbon panels, and bureau investigations generate little if any change because they are suppressed, not printed, not read or distributed ineffectively.

More man hours have been spent analyzing each of the riots from Watts to the present than there were hours of rioting. The Watts revolt of 1965 was the subject of a report by the McCone Committee,

---

* Harold E. Simmons, Deputy Director, Program Development, California State Department of Social Welfare, in 1967 testimony before the Senate Committee on Education and Welfare.

** A. Osofsky, The Burden of Race (1967).

168. For a discussion of the courts as a decision-making body for solving conflict see Aubert, *Courts and Conflict Resolution*, XI J. of Conflict Resolution 41 (1967).

under the sponsorship of California Governor Brown.[169] Similarly, the Newark riot and the string of smaller disturbances is the subject of a report written by a group impanelled by Govornor Hughes.[170] The 1967 Detroit riot was or has been studied by Cyrus Vance[171] and the Mayor's Development Team.[172] The Philadelphia Negro high school riot of 1967 is under study by the United States Justice Department.[173] The United States Civil Rights Commission prior to 1967 held enlightened hearings in Cleveland and Newark,[174] and although not connected with the riot investigations *per se,* they shed a great deal of light on background conditions.

There are also general investigations into the riots as a group. The highest level of these is the President's Commission on Civil Disturbances which was ordered in the wake of the Detroit riot.[175] The

---

169. Report by the Governor's Commission, *supra* note 7. The Presidential Task Force to Coordinate the Los Angeles Rehabilitation Program issued an interim report but no final report. This is a classical example of a never-completed study; it is discussed in *Hearings Before the Senate Subcomm. on Executive Reorganization of the Comm. on* Governmental Relations, 89th Cong., 2d Sess., pt. 12, at 2491 (1966).

170. Report for Action: Governor's Select Commission on Civil Disorder (1968). One of their chief themes is taken up in Part V of this essay: "The burden of responsibility weighs most heavily on those in positions of leadership, power and with control over the resources that will be needed to produce tangible results." See also N.Y. Times, Sept. 3, 1967 § 1, at 33, cols. 1-2 and Feb. 11, 1968 § 1, at 1, cols. 2-3 ff. Consider the following excerpt from Governor Hughes' August 8, 1967 letter to the Commission, reproduced at 201: "For example, consider the situation of Newark, the scene of an American disaster which has shocked the nation, as portrayed in its application under the Federal Model Cities law, by other sources:

Among the nation's largest cities with a population upwards of 400,000 people, it has the heaviest tax burden in the nation; it has the sharpest shifts in population; it has the highest crime rate per 100,000 population; it has the highest rate of substandard housing; it has the highest rate of venereal disease; it has the highest rate of increase of tuberculosis; it has the highest rate of maternal mortality and the second highest rate of infant mortality; it is second highest in population density, and second highest in birth rate; it is seventh in the absolute number of drug addicts."

171. Final Report of Cyrus Vance, Special Assistant to the Secretary of Defense, Concerning the Detroit Riots, July 23 through August 2, 1967, mimeo, Release from the Office of Asst. Sec. of Defense for Public Affairs, Sept. 12, 1967. This report and secret policy memos stemming from Vance's experience have been very influential in preparations for 1968 riots. N.Y. Times, April 14, 1968 § 1, at 1, cols. 2-3.

172. City of Detroit Mayor's Development Team Report, *supra* note 1, in three books.

173. The Justice Department Community Relations Service has operations in 35 cities in an effort to improve race relations and prevent racial crisis; they also investigate and make recommendations. See N.Y. Times, Oct. 22, 1967 § I at 4, col. 1.

174. Cleveland on April 1-7, 1966 and Newark on Sept. 11-12, 1962. Testimony is subdivided into discussions of housing, education, employment, health, welfare, and police-community relations. For the most recent statistical summary on Negroes in these regards *see* U.S. Depts. of Labor and Commerce, Social and Economic Conditions of Negroes in the United States, BLS Rep. no. 332, Current Population Reports, Series P-23, No. 24 (1967).

175. Report of the National Advisory Commission on Civil Disorders (1968). All citations herein are to the March 2, 1968 advance copy. Their basic conclusion has been well publicized: "Our nation is moving toward two societies, one black, one white—separate and unequal." SUM-2. "[w]hite society is deeply implicated in the ghetto. White institutions created it, white institutions maintain it, and white society condones it."

assignations of Senator Kennedy and Dr. King led President Johnson to appoint a commission to study violence in America.[175a] The Republican governors studied and then proposed a sixty point riot plan.[176] Congress is especially concerned: the House Un-American Activities Committee[177] and the House Armed Services Committee[178] are investigating; in the Senate, messieurs McClellan,[179] Clark,[180] Ribicoff,[181] and Eastland[182] are delving into various aspects of the riots.

In addition to these governmentally sponsored studies, which generally have subpoena power, several academic institutions are compiling data, especially the growing number of urban research centers.[183] Even a private association has spent time in an analysis of the riots.[184] Finally, Congress has passed and the President has signed

SUM-4. This is reinforced by their analysis of basic causes at SUM-23 ff. "The civil disorders of 1967 involved Negroes acting against local symbols of white American society . . . rather than against white persons." SUM-13. In this context and all others the eleven members were careful not to label the disorders race riots. Twelve grievances were identified and ranked into three levels of relative intensity: the three most significant being police practices, unemployment and underemployment, and inadequate housing. SUM-17 & 18. What the group did not evaluate was how rational the rioters were, since at SUM-9 concerning Detroit's riot they state ". . . A spirit of carefree nihilism was taking hold." Although Daniel P. Moynihan is only quoted directly once in the report the authors feel his influence is extensive on the subjects of employment and family structure. In the authors' opinion the chief deficiency is the report's deemphasis on "meaningful involvement of ghetto residents in shaping policies and programs which affect the community," which is buried in Chapter 10, SUM-40. It is noteworthy that the panel which was unanimous and contained Herbert Jenkins, a police officer, cautioned against destructive weapons, which they said, "have no place in densely populated urban communities." SUM-47. As the elixir which will overcome future riots the choice is "a policy which combines ghetto enrichment with programs designed to encourage integration of substantial numbers of Negroes into the society outside the ghetto." SUM-59. In brief, "The major goal is the creation of a true union—a single society and a single American identity." SUM-61. The immediate goals should be improved employment, education, public welfare, and housing. A major recommendation was the enactment and enforcement of a "federal open housing law to cover the sale and rental of all housing, including single family homes." SUM-75.

175a. 4 Weekly Comp. Pres. Docs. 915 (1968); Exec. Order No. 11,540.

176. Det. News, Aug. 11, 1967 § A, at 1, cols. 1-3.

177. *Hearings on Subversive Influences in Riots, Looting and Burning Before the Comm. on Un-American Activities of the House of Representatives*, 90th Cong., 1st Sess., pts. I, II, III (1968).

178. *Hearings Before Special Subcomm. to Inquire into the Capability of the National Guard to Cope with National Disturbances* of the House Comm. on Armed Services, 90th Cong., 1st Sess., (1967).

179. *Hearings Before the Permanent Subcomm. on Investigations* of the Senate Comm. on Government Operations, 90th Cong., 1st Sess., several parts (1967).

180. *Hearings Before the Subcomm. on Employment, Manpower, and Poverty* of the Senate Comm. on Labor and Public Welfare, 90th Cong., 1st Sess., several parts (1967).

181. *Hearings Before the Subcomm. on Executive Reorganization* of the Senate Comm. on Government Operations, 89th Cong., 2d Sess., several parts (1966).

182. *Hearings on H.R. 421* Before the Senate Committee on the Judiciary, 90*th* Cong., 1*st* Sess., several parts (1967).

183. *See* A Directory of Urban Research Study Centers prepared by the Subcomm. on Urban Affairs of Joint Comm. on the Economy, 90*th* Cong., 1*st* Sess., Aug. 1967.

184. The Free Press, a Detroit Newspaper, plus the Urban League and Henry Ford II sponsored a study by Dr. Nathan S. Caplan of the University of Michigan's Institute for

into law[185] an Urban Studies Fellowship Program which in time will generate still more analysis.

Given the ideological prism of personnel on some of these investigating committees it is not difficult to assert that solons Eastland and Tuck, the latter being sub-committee chairman of the House Un-American Activities Committee, have seen a thread of red whereas Senators Ribicoff and Clark, along with the Civil Rights Commission, have found multiple causation based in large measure on background conditions. But nevertheless the analytic reports have been clearly written and concerned with generic, big, issues. They have focused on the need for broadly based, coordinated, and sustained reforms, fundamental to overhauling the center city.

The Squeaky Wheel

What has happened since some of these reports were filed?

The civic associations, which generally produce spurious issues,[186] confronted root issues, such as open housing.[187] Large businesses, which earlier escaped the high taxes of the center city for suburban industrial parks, suddenly discovered they could employ more city Negroes.[188] Planning and transportation authorities, which heretofore had not given serious attention to subway and bus routes for Negro ghetto dwellers, dramatically found these areas needed immediate attention.[189]

Social Research. See. Det. Free Press, Oct. 25, 1967 § A at 16, cols. 5-7. Professor Jack Walker is presently doing research on the topic, The Ann Arbor Center for Urban Studies is also investigating.

185. 78 Stat. 803 (1964), 20 U.S.C. § 811 (supp. 1967). This act really was a three year extension of the law. By renewal time 38 universities were participating. For President Johnson's comments see 3 Weekly Comp. of Pres. Docs. 28 Aug., 1190, 1967. For House Action see 113 Cong. Rec. 123, H 9985 (daily ed. Aug. 7, 1967).

186. The point is worth belaboring. Consider the two following rather typical serious comments: "With rare unanimity, political scientists who have examined the way decisions are reached at the local level agree that the practice is more one of problem-avoiding than of problem-solving." Montgomery, *Notes on Instant Urban Renewal*, Trans-Action, Sept., 1967, p. 10. "In lieu of really significant problems (which often cannot be made into "good program material" because of their significance), the civic association atmosphere tends to produce spurious problems." E. C. Banfield, Political Influence C. 10 (1961).

187. The Hudson Committee advocacy of open housing and their October "pilgrimage" to Lansing, the State Capitol, to present their views, proves that with a crisis the bland diet of civic associations can be made meaty. See N.Y. Times Nov. 19, 1967, § I at 57, cols. 1-2.

Root issues have been exposed before, however, as in the 1919 Chicago race riots, but the exposure had no lasting effect. *See* A. I. Waskow, From Race Riot to Sit-in Ch. 5 (1967).

188. Complete documentation of this point falls outside the scope of this essay. No Congressional study of the scope or effectiveness of these efforts has been undertaken. It is doubtful that as many as 17,900 Negroes in two years were employed from the Watts area after the riot of 1965 due to a special corporation set up to reduce high Negro unemployment; see *Senate Hearings on H.R. 421*, 90*th* Cong., 1*st* Sess., pt. 2, 652-3 (1967).

189. Washington, D.C.'s subway system was being designed without a stop in a predominately Negro area. This was corrected by Negro protest. The Watts area, without effective bus transportation in most of the south-central Los Angeles district prior to the

Urban renewal programmers, who were often more preoccupied with removing Negroes from condemned areas than relocating them in adequate surrogate housing, were dramatically confronted by the need to renew the very areas into which the displaced Negroes moved.[190] Police officers, who for so long contended that they were not guilty of police brutality toward Negroes, suddenly found public officials proposing neighborhood police liaison offices.[191] Social agencies, which had both small eleemosynary and rehabilitation operations, began to pour resources into the impacted area in larger and more conspicuous programs.[192] Blighted and vacant lots, eye sores and uninspirational to generations of ghetto dwellers, were discovered, beautified, and made into recreation areas.[193]

Mayors too looked at their cities in a new light. For the first time they began to see advantages in cooperation with suburbs. They proposed coordination of services during emergencies, thus bidding for the gradual consolidation of authorities which presently are so artificially scattered by municipal jurisdictions.[194] Detroit's mayor found he must have better plans for emergencies and therefore placed contingent control operations in a state of readiness. The mayor also suggested an increased number of Negroes on the police and fire departments and proposed increased equipment allocations.

Congress too took cognizance of the riots and acted on long pending legislation. The House, which laughed down the rat control bill,[195] reversed itself and through a rider passed an authorization

---

1965 riot, now has improved bus routes due to a HUD grant according to Secretary Robert C. Weaver's testimony on *Senate Hearings on S. 3509 and S.J. Res. 187*, pt. 1, 89*th* Cong., 2*d* Sess. 95 (1966).

190. GREER, URBAN RENEWAL AND AMERICAN CITIES, *et passim* (1965). See 44 U. DET. J. URBAN L. 169 (1966). The New Jersey Commission, *supra* note, at 60-61 makes these points. The President's Commission, *supra* note, at 17-170 lightly mentions it.

191. Strichartz Report, *supra* note, at Book One. Four forms of "Citizen Participation and Communication" reform were suggested: police neighborhood communications units, police neighborhood information and referral centers, a citizens assistance agency, and a public television demonstration program. The New Jersey Commission, *supra* note, at 17 suggests a central complaint bureau which "would receive all complaints against city agencies." These are variations on the ombudsman.

192. Cohen, *supra* note 2, at 15.

193. Watts will have a strip farm for fresh fruits and vegetables along transmission lines of the Los Angeles Department of Water and Power. 12th Street in Detroit will have play areas and tree-shaded shopping plazas in part due to efforts by the Cotillion Club.

194. Cavanagh proposed a mutual aid fire fighting pact between Detroit and its suburbs after 41 suburbs sent equipment to the riot area. If billed the city would have to pay $200,000. Eight Pittsburgh suburbs have also proposed a mutual assistance pact to handle emergencies such as a riot. Det. News, Aug. 18, 1967, § A, at 10, col. 1. Indiana Evening Gazette, Oct. 11, 1967, § I, at 6. col. 3.

195. Mr. Gross: Does the gentleman imply that with the passage of this $40 million bill we are then going to embark upon rat killing around the world? The gentleman spoke of city rats? What about country rats?

Mr. Broyhill: But I think the most profound statement the gentleman made is the fact

bill.[196] The war on poverty, funded through the Office of Economic Opportunity, was continued.[197] Rent supplements were continued.[198] Model cities money was allocated.[199] And, above all, the 90th Congress, Second Session passed the 1968 Civil Rights Law, the Anti-Riot and Open Housing bill, in the wake of Martin Luther King's assassination.[200]

These positive actions by local groups, the mayor's office, and the Congress were not fortuitous. The old adage is substantially correct: the squeaky wheel gets the most grease. All these groups were educated by dramatic confrontation. They responded to crisis events with dispatch, proving once again that violence is often a propitious occasion for reform.

In brief, the rioters have reaped rewards and not reprisals. The whole Negro community substantially gained by the rioting of a small percent of the Negroes. Violent actions produced what Negro petitions did not.

Professor Roy Pierce, a specialist on contemporary France, has often observed that the post-war Republic had too much, not too little, stability. Coalition cabinet personnel may have whirled through the eddying waters of the Fourth Republic, but the basic political problems persisted after every administration turnover. With the coming of deGaulle, pent up problems cascaded into perspective as the wide-open flood gates of the new regime took power. So too with Negro-related

---

that it does set up a new bureau and sets up possibly a commissioner on rats or an administrator of rats and a bunch of new bureaucrats on rats. . . . Mr. Speaker, I think the "rat smart thing" for us to do is vote down this rat bill "rat now."

Mr. Latta: How about snake bite cases? If we are going to start eradicating all the rats—how about snakes in the West? How about bugs?

Mr. Berry: Mr. Speaker, it surprises me somewhat that no one has rallied to the defense of the rat during the discussion of this bill before the House spend $40 million over the next 2 years for local rat control programs. Certainly there must be someone who sees this as a threat to a species of wildlife.

After the bill was defeated . . .

Mr. Kupperman: Mr. Speaker, I have seen rat-infested areas and buildings in the slums of the city of New York. Adjoining the congressional district which it is my honor to represent, is the congressional district represented by Adam Clayton Powell. One might say that I am serving as the interim voluntary Congressman for that area. Mr. Speaker, I have seen some of the conditions which exist there. If you were a hard-working father coming home from work to find one of your children bitten by a rat, you might very well start a small riot yourself. Mr. Speaker, I am ashamed of the vote today on this question." Excerpts from 113 CONG. REC. H. 9114-9119 (daily ed. July 20, 1967).

196. The bill was H 6418, considered Sept. 20, 1967, two months after the first bill was defeated.

197. 1968 estimated OEO appropriations totaled $1,860,000,000, year ending June 30, 1968.

198. 1968 estimated appropriations of $6,000,000, year ending June 30, 1968.

199. 1968 estimated appropriations of $150,000,000, year ending June 30, 1968.

200. H 2516, Pub. L. No. 90-284 (April 11, 1968). On April 30, 1968, Rev. James Groppi again proved the squeaky wheel principle, *see* MILWAUKEE, WIS. CODE § 109-1 (1968).

problems in mid-Twentieth Century America: although Negro aspiration for a full measure of equality was partially precipitated by the courts, starting with *Brown v. Board of Education*,[201] the basic problems still persisted. The judicial phase gave way to a legislative phase, but the basic problems still persisted. Negro aspirations during this period were taking a more forceful and direct action approach, including boycotts, sit-ins, wade-ins, and pray-ins. With each cautious Negro action there was a Caucasian reaction, and on balance the reach was favorably disposed towards acceding to Negro aspirations. But the basic problems persisted. Now the flood gates, occasioned by the riots, are wide open, and commendable or not, whether opened by design or chance, black violence has been met by a benign white response.

In sum, the riots from Watts through Detroit have been of positive political benefit to the Negro drive toward equal status in American society. This does not mean further riots will be so rewarded. Certainly there is some threshold of tolerance after which repression sets in. But, to date, the crisis-producing politics engendered by the riots has forced root issues to the fore and has nurtured the aims of the proponents of change.

III

> *Effort rapidly to persuade a large group is likely to involve violence.**
>
> *Democracy involves a reliance on time and tentative effort. . . . Democracy again, is a matter of discussion and the collaboration of many minds.***
>
> *Violence is not the first thought but the last, the final effort to solve an otherwise insoluble problem in a crude manner.****

Violence can be catalogued into individual and group or mass efforts. We are concerned only with mass violence in this essay. Again, mass violence can be subdivided into international disputes, such as war for example, and intranational or domestic violence.[202] In this article we are concerned only with domestic mass violence. This topic has not been either systematically or deeply studied by students of statecraft except for studies of revolutions.[203] This gap in political in-

---

201. 347 U.S. 483 (1954).

* Q. WRIGHT, A STUDY OF WAR 252 (1964).

** E. BARKER, REFLECTIONS ON GOVERNMENT 127 (1958).

*** C. MERRIAM, POLITICAL POWER 219 (1964).

202. On the distinction between-group and within-group conflict see Marwell, *Conflict over Proposed Group Actions: A Typology of Clevage* 10 J. OF CONFLICT RESOLUTION 427 (1966).

203. The same point is made by S. WOLIN, POLITICS AND VISION 220 (1960). One serious attempt at studying violence which has been relied upon by Martin Luther King

vestigation is akin to the absence of systematic knowledge among biologists as to the nature of mammal decomposition. In both cases the reason is probably the same: the subjects are unpleasant and even repugnant. But this does not reflect on the significance of either violence in politics or decomposition in biology.

The purpose of this section of the essay will be to survey briefly some of the more salient ideas on mass domestic violence in the corpus of Western political thought, no matter how repulsive the ideas, and to relate this body of speculation to the current American crisis over urban riots.

Theory

Classical Greek thoughts on the nature of mass domestic violence stem from the assumption that a head of state will actively use violence as frequently as necessary to keep his *polis* integrated and responsive to his decrees. This assumption about the tyrant has not substantially altered since it was first formulated in Western thought. Plato devotes a relatively large section of his writings to the activities of the tyrant.[204] Tyranny violates the ideal of a just state, no matter how stable a regime it may be. The appetites of the tyrant are drunkenness, lust, passion, and a general disharmony of parts. Jealously, faithlessness, injustice, friendlessness, and impiety prevail. Tyrants do not subject themselves to the laws. This corresponds with our contemporary notion that tyrants exercise rule of man whereas constitutional communities live under the rule of law. Greeks attached a stigma to the tyrant; his actions are reprehensible.

Aristotle follows his mentor's line of thought. The tyrant uses an "iron hand." This curiously anticipates Bismarck's use of the phrase "blood and iron" and Stalin's chosen pseudonym, which designates "man of steel." For Aristotle, the tyrant uses violence as an instrument

---

and his followers is R. Niebuhr, Moral Man and Immoral Society Ch. 9 (1948). See a recent apology for violence in S. Lynd & T. Hayden, The Other Side (1967). Tom Hayden, coauthor of the above mentioned book, was active in Newark prior to the 1967 summer riot and has subsequently defended the rioters at a panel on "The Legitimacy of Violence" and a book Rebellion in Newark (1967). Hayden, although he studied political thought under James Meisel at The University of Michigan, is more of a radical activist than a dispassionate student of statecraft. *See* N.Y. Times, Dec. 17, 1967 § I at 16, col. 1 for a brief report on the panel.

The only people studying violence on a sustained basis are the conflict-resolution social scientists. They generally employ news reported data and manipulate their data with rotated factor matrix methods plus game theory. Their chief publication is J. of Conflict Resolution. For a list of many of the variables they use see Feierabend & Ferierabend, *Aggressive Behaviors Within Politics, 1948-1962: A Cross-National Survey* 10 J. of Conflict Resolution 249 (1966).

204. Plato, The Republic Book IX, 575.

in his own hands, and he who exercises it is the most corrupt practitioner of statecraft.[205]

Christian thought adds a great deal to a discussion of violence. From Christ's beatitudes we read that the meek are blessed and shall inherit the earth; the peace-makers are also blessed and shall be called the sons of God.[206] Christ may have used violent means, however, for he cast the money changers out of the temple.[207] Thus, one interpretation of Christ's life suggests there is both legitimate and illegitimate violence.

St. Paul, author of much of the New Testament, issued his attitude on citizen violence toward the state in his letter to the Romans. Since "there is no authority except from God," then "he who resists the authorities resists what God has appointed, and those who resist will incur judgment."[208] In the same chapter he argues against reveling, or rioting, as it is variantly translated. Such an absolute citizen duty to rulers, because rulers have power from above, is grist for the mill from those who advocate submission to all *de facto* political power. To balance this doctrine of submission, at least one theologian has elected to emphasize Paul's admonition that a citizen is free to reject worldly authority when it becomes a terror against the workers of Christian good.[209]

The interpretation of the Christian position derives a great deal from subsequent church leaders. For example, St. Thomas took a direct stand in his works on the issue of tyrants and resistance to them. St. Thomas agreed with Plato and Aristotle: tyranny is the wretchedest form of rule. Yet the people under a tyranny ought to suffer a mild tyranny, for by disrupting it through coercion a worse calamity might befall them. He suggests that apostolic teaching instructs people to suffer a "forward master" with grace and forebearance. The cruelty of tyrants should never be banished by a private act of violence such as assassination. If, however, the tyrant owes his initial position to the multitude, then that tyrant can "be disposed or have his powers restricted."[210] This is a long way from the stoic position of passive acquiescence and turning the other cheek. It is also one of the first signs in occidental thought that followers are morally justified in exercising violence against leaders.

Machiavelli, often called the first modern political philosopher,

---

205. ARISTOTLE, THE POLITICS Book IV, 1295a; Book V, 1313a ff.

206. MATT. 5:5,9; LUKE 6:27-30.

207. MATT. 21:12; MARK 11:15; LUKE 19:45; JOHN 2:14.

208. ROMANS 13:2-3.

209. C. Anderson Scott, *Romans*, in THE ABINGTON BIBLE COMMENTARY 1161 (Eiselen *et al.* eds., 1929). The late theologian was Dunn professor of New Testament, Westminster College, Cambridge. ACTS 5:17-29 has been omitted from this entire discussion.

210. ST. THOMAS AQUINAS, LETTER TO THE KING OF CYPRUS ON KINGSHIP ch. 6 par. 24 ff.

who wrote in the opening of the 16th Century, certainly heralded a turning point in western thought on speculation concerning the role of both mass domestic and foreign violence. In a Machiavellian state the prince could impose his will upon the people with the use or threat of violence. Machiavelli looked upon this controlled violence, however, not as inherently good or evil, but as a separate fact.[211] In a newly acquired principality in particular, the prince could not possibly avoid the name of cruel. Machiavelli is well known as the advocate of as much violence as was necessary in the domestic affairs of decadent polities. And because men are not of good will and do not keep faith it is not obligatory to be honest: indeed a wise prince realizes he must become a beast. The prince ought to emulate the lion insofar as it defends against the wolves, and to emulate the fox so as to defend against the snares.[212] Under a truly republican polity the violence of wolves is not needed, but under most political communities violence must be employed in a manipulated and controlled manner to keep the populace in its subordinated position.[213] The newness in Machiavelli's thinking is his honest opinion on the proper use of violence as an instrument of calculated policy. Perhaps the dead horse does smell, but the stench must not obliterate the use of the power.

One hundred and twenty years later in England, the issue of employing violence in domestic politics was again squarely confronted. John Locke, the radical liberal, spoke on behalf of those who would do violence to a transgressing legislature. Where a breach of promise by the rulers is poignantly felt by the ruled then the rulers "forfeit the power the people had put in their hands for quite contrary ends, and it devolves upon the people . . . ."[214] Locke advocates unequivocally the right to rebel, by force if necessary. He was fully aware of his hypothesis which he said lay "a ferment for frequent rebellion."[215] For the first time here was a thinker who prepared an apology for morally condoning violence against an abusive ruler. St. Thomas laid the groundwork but in the secular and dominant tradition it is Locke who fully prepared the justification.

Now, of course, it is well known that the Lockian invocation to arms to overthrow a tyrannical leader was employed by the Americans in their cause against the British. Thomas Jefferson in the Declaration of Independence, "the world's greatest editorial," used the Locke-

---

211. F. Pollock, An Introduction to the History of the Science of Politics 43 (1960).
212. Machiavelli, The Prince ch. 17.
213. *Id.* at ch. 18.
214. Locke, Two Treatises on Government, Second Essay, ch. XIX, par. 222 ff.
215. *Id.* at par. 224.

derived dictum that when, in the course of human events, it becomes necessary, and after deliberating seriously, a group must violently object to a ruler's unjust administration. For Jefferson this idea of salubrious violence was not a passing or flashy justification; it was a staple in his thinking. Ten years after the great proclamation he wrote "I hold it that a little rebellion, now and then, is a good thing."[216] His position proclaiming the need for periodic violence in order that "the tree of liberty be watered with the blood of patriots and tyrants"[217] reinforces his consistent conviction that a country needs either metaphoric or real bloodshed to keep the body politic vital.

The author with whom Westerners most closely associate the advocacy of mass violence is the 19th Century theorist, Karl Marx.[218] For Marx society is eventually cut into two classes, the exploited proletariat and the exploiting bourgeoise who control the means of production. Change occurs through a struggle between the two classes, a dialectical confrontation of thesis with antithesis, out of which arises a higher synthesis. This theory is similar to the story of the regeneration of the Phoenix which is born out of the fire of its own ashes. This is an all encompassing theory of historical explanation based on epochs of civilization, in turn based upon economic development of the era. Marxian thought is a rejection of inevitable violent helical progress culminating in a classless society where the state has withered away. Violence will be eliminated only in this final culmination, for any state is an instrument of force in the hands of the smaller class. For Marx change is not crescive or fully obtainable through reforms: important change must be brought on by crisis and struggle.

Although the Fabian Socialists of England suggested that they could work within the context of democratic procedures to build their better world through legal means, the communistic Marxians vehemently deny this. The self-appointed interpreters of this mantle of communistic Marxism are Lenin, Stalin, Mao, and Ho Chi Minh. The critical point about this wing of the communistic socialist cause is that violence can be manipulated. Right reason will not free workers from chains: workers will prevail only by emancipating themselves from the chains by force. Morality is not fundamentally an issue between the Fabians and the communists for to a communist the advocacy or use of violence against the state is inevitable.

Finally, early in this Century Georges Sorel, the French syndicalist, gave sustained attention to the utility of sabotage as a *modus operandi*

---

216. The Life and Selected Writings of Thomas Jefferson 431 (A. Koch and W. Peden eds. 1944).

217. Letter to William Stevens Smith, Nov. 13, 1787.

218. K. Marx, Capital: A Critique of Political Economy, *et passim.*

in industrial relations between workers and their exploiting employers. Sorel's engineering background gave him a certain precision in his social thinking which compelled him to be rather systematic and brutal. For example, he employs the following distinction in his *magnum opus*: "[W]e should say, therefore that the object of force is to impose a certain social order in which the minority governs, while violence tends to be the destruction of that order."[219] This "new school" does not rely on parliamentary tactics like the Fabians, but advocates "violence as the most efficacious means of obtaining concessions."[220] Violence is useful as a means of inspiring fear in the middle class. Indeed, the workers are astonished at "the timidity of the forces of law and order in the presence of a riot . . ." Sorel thus calls for the intimidation of the law abiding. He calls for the abandoning of "old official, Utopian and political tabernacles" and for the attainment of a vital course based upon calamity and carnage. He demands immediate provocation by the workers when they want more; he calls for swift and direct attack; he pleads for emotion and an abandonment of logic. This violence must be a motive force in history and should be hailed as "the ethics of the producers."[221]

It is fitting at this juncture of the essay to explain Sorel's most heralded notion. Sorel formulated a tangent idea which he labeled *the myth of the general strike*. This myth is designed to be a mass commitment for all the proletariat to believe in. It is to signify the future unfolding of events comfortable to the workers. The details of this unfolding are unimportant. In fact, the prophesy might not be true, but no matter, for this too is not the essence of the idea. The myth of the general strike in Sorel's words is a "body of images capable of evoking instinctively the sentiments which correspond to the different manifestations of the war . . ."[222] It is a rallying call for the class war. It is designed to produce a vision and a community enthusiasm "without whose cooperation no morality is possible."[223] Sorel has come a long way from the ideas of Plato and the Christian thinkers in his attitude toward violence. Truth gives way to myth. Emotion supersedes logic. Leaders yield to followers. It is noteworthy that this communist-inspired thinker with his theory of violence-as-a-social-force had a strong appeal to the Italian fascism of Mussolini, although Sorel himself never was a fascist.

With greater sophistication today we know that much of what Sorel

219. G. Sorel, Reflections on Violence 195 (T. E. Hulme, trans., 1941).
220. *Id.* at 140, 70, 69.
221. *Id.* at 127.
222. *Id.* at 294.
223. *Id.* at 133, 135-136, 139, 294.

was developing with his idea of the myth of the general strike is now catalogued the self-fulfilling prophesy. His formulated myth required simplified ideas and a symbol to which people could respond emotionally. The myth is not important per se, but only as a star to which the masses can hitch their aspirations for a more pure tomorrow.

In this Sorelian context *Black Power*, the shibboleth of some of the Negroes active in present American racial demonstrations, is defined as an irrational rallying call to action, neither automatically associated nor disassociated from the advocacy of violence. What the action is designed to accomplish when *Black Power* arrives is not and perhaps cannot be so much an objective goal as it is something vague which can be believed in with intense emotional commitment. After all, to be intelligible, words must have some conventional referent or benchmark; *Black Power* has no agreed upon conventional context. It is only a vacuum-word with emotional magnetism.

Merriam,[224] Cassirer[225] and Barker[226]-American, German and English students of politics—have reflected on the nature of such emotional appeals to empty low-level symbols in the light of our experiences in World War II. They found a large measure of the irrational in these calls. Merriam saw these self-fulfilling symbols as forward-looking, fixing on vague, unattained group aspirations. Cassirer suggested these myths are expressions of emotions, that they were appeals to social and not individual experience, and that they produce "violent concussion that may shake our cultural and our social order to its very foundation." Barker said such mythological symbols appeal vaguely to a brotherhood, something super-personal, and promise a soothing future hazily perceived. The English poet W. H. Auden[227] summarized all these observations commendably when he wrote

By the water's edge
The unthinking flood, down there, yes, in his
Proper place, the polychrome Oval
With its kleig lights and crowd engineers,
The mutable circus where mobs rule
The arena with roars, the real world of
Theology and horses, our home because
In the doubt-condemning dual kingdom
Signs and insignia decide our cause,

---

224. C. Merriam, Systematic Politics 81-93 (1945). For the most elaborate discussion by an American political scientist see M. Edelman, The Symbolic Uses of Politics ch. 6, Language and the Perception of Politics, 114 ff. (1964). See also R. MacIver, The Web of Government, Part One (rev. ed., 1965).

225. E. Cassirer, The Myth of the State 52, 57 ff., 374 (1946).

226. E. Barker, Reflections on Government ch. 5 *et passim.* (1942).

227. W.H. Auden, The Age of Anxiety 39 (1946-7).

Fanatics of the Egg or Knights sworn to
Die for the Dolphin, and our deeds wear
Heretic green or orthodox blue,
Safe and certain.

In essence *Black Power,* like heretic green or orthodox blue, is empty and void of tangible meaning. *Black Power* is like an empty vessel, a container ready to be filled with whatever meaning suits the leader of the movement at-the-moment.[228]

NON-VIOLENCE

No survey of violence would be complete without a study of non-violence. It has long amazed the authors that there is no separate English antonym for violence. Peace is the opposite of war. Force, at least according to Sorel, is the exercise of sanguine power by the governing minority, whereas violence is sanguine power exercised by the exploited majority.

Non-violence has a long history and has been advocated by a variety of thinkers. There are two traditions involved, one religiously motivated and the other secular. The Quakers, Mennonites, Amish and other sects profess non-violence out of Christian conscience. Leo Tolstoy and his followers also developed a non-violent Christian-based attitude.[229] The secular tradition is also well developed. The Reverend Martin Luther King was essentially in this lineage, having derived his inspiration less from the Bible and church history than from Indian nationalist M. K. Gandhi.[230] It may be countered that "Mahatma," Gandhi's title, means great religious one. It may also be countered that King knew of the Hindu emphasis of respect for all

228. One of the first book reviews of STOKLEY CARMICHAEL & CHARLES HAMILTON, BLACK POWER: THE POLITICS OF LIBERATION IN AMERICA (1967) ended with this observation: "In the absence of more detailed political frameworks and ideologies for Black Americans, some students of the struggle are likely to conclude, after reading this book, that Black Power is not much more than an organizing vehicle and a scare phrase." N.Y. Times, Dec. 10, 1967 § 7, at 67, col. 2. As the cynical politician said: platforms are to run on, not stand by. In a post-King assassination article Hamilton admitted "it is virtually impossible to come up with a single definition satisfactory to all." N.Y. Times, April 14, 1968 § 6, at 23, col. 1.

229. H. TROYAT, TOLSTOY (1967). This is one of the most neglected thinkers and movements in Western political thought. Virtually none of the major American political treatises so much as mention the author-moralist. research needs to be done to determine the relative importance of this man's moral-political thought.

230. On King's awareness of and attitude toward non-violent direct action see KING, STRIDE TOWARD FREEDOM ch. VI (1958); KING, WHY WE CAN'T WAIT ch. II, pt. III (1963); KING, STRENGTH TO LOVE ch. 17 (1963). Rathburn, *Martin Luther King: The Theology of Social Action,* 20 AM. Q. 38 (1968) is in conflict with present interpretation. Also THE SUPREME COURT REVIEW: 1965, 168 (Kurland, ed., 1965), gets directly to the point. The early sit-in movement, which was rather spontaneous, became equipped with rather elaborate scholarly justification, often of Indic origin. For example, Howard University, a Negro school in Washington, D.C., as early as 1962 taught a course in the Philosophy and Methods of Non-Violence, N.Y. Times, March 11, § 1 at 60, col. 1.

life. But in turn Gandhi was inspired by those portions of Henry David Thoreau which talk of peaceful non-violence as a form of civil disobedience. Thoreau, it must be remembered, was not overly impressed by conventional Christianity. In turn, Thoreau was influenced by his naturalistic philosophy and by the holy Hindu books which had been recently translated into English.[231] It is easier to say that secular non-violence has an honorable legacy of East-West passage.

There are many volumes which describe non-violence in action and there are several volumes on satyagraha, or soul force.[232] The moral to these books is clear; non-violence requires a great deal of discipline and self-restraint on behalf of those against whom the non-violence is directed. Its adherents have never been in numerical ascendancy. The Indian nationalist movement, based to a large extent on Gandhi's leadership and ideas, was successful and stands as a monument to the efficacy of moral intimidation. But the reader must never forget that the nationalist movement degenerated into bloodshed during the 1947 Indian-Pakistan partition, and occasioned the largest loss of life since the end of the Second World War. Moreover, we must remember that Aden also overcame British colonial status, but by the effective implementation of a terrorist campaign and corporal intimidation.

We will acknowledge that the aforementioned survey of Western political philosophers' ideas on domestic mass violence is partial and leaves out a number of ideas and thinkers such as John of Sailsbury, George Buchanan, Juan de Mariana, Jonathan Mayhew, Hegel, Arendt, de Tocqueville, Simmel, and his student Coser, plus such recent thinkers as Blankston, Lasswell, Kaplan, Liewan, and Tanter.[233] However cursory, what is apparent from this survey is that violence occasionally is deemed morally admissible by some thinkers. Violence is thus thought of as a proper instrument for dealing with tyrants. Although inconsistent and occasionally obscure, our Western heritage does not forbid the use of violence by rational men who are not easily perturbed; indeed, under certain conditions it is encouraged. The Marxists and

---

231. The best discussion of the much traveled idea and Gandhi's contributions are contained in SHARMA, MAHATMA GANDHI: A DESCRIPTIVE BIBLIOGRAPHY (New Delhi: S. Chand & Co. 1955). Unfortunately the book is full of errors and is definitely not definitive.

232. The most extensive list in all languages, including nine tongues in all, is DESHPANDE, GANDHIANA: A BIBLIOGRAPHY OF GANDHIAN LITERATURE (Ahmedabad: Navajivan Publishing House 1948). The most complete, documented and mature study of Gandhi's philosophy, such as it was, is DHAWAN, THE POLITICAL PHILOSOPHY OF MAHATMA GANDHI (Ahmedabad: Navajivan Publishing House 1951). The most readily available analysis of his philosophy is J. BONDURANT, CONQUEST OF VIOLENCE: THE GANDHIAN PHILOSOPHY OF CONFLICT (1958). DIWIHAR, SATYAGRAHA IN ACTION: A BRIEF OUTLINE OF GANDHIJI'S SATYAGRAHA CAMPAIGNS (1949) is also instructive for historical perspective.

233. *See* Tanter and Midlarsky, *A Theory of Revolution*, 11 J. OF CONFLICT RESOLUTION 264 (1967) for various typologies of revolution.

syndicalists are not the only champions of violence: St Thomas Aquinas, Locke, and Jefferson all developed their hypotheses which "ferment frequent rebellion."

Practice

From the theory of violence we turn to the practice. The United States has been a violent-ridden nation since its inception. As Charles Merriam,[234] the University of Chicago political scientist, stated in the last days of World War II:

> Those who wish to accept the cult of violence may find on the pages of history enough of fire and sword to occupy all their reading hours and confirm them in their conviction of the inevitability of violence in social change. But a student of government will indicate alternative possibilities while not denying war and riot their relaxation in volcanic hours of smoke and death.

The pages of United States history do at times read like a story of war and riot. But before indicating alternative ways to resolve conflict we must look squarely at our violent past to assess the magnitude of fire and sword which has produced our present world.

It is often said that the state is that institution which ultimately has a monopoly on the legitimate use of violence. Society acknowledges this through the police, and the military. We justify violence on the grounds of defending against someone else's use of violence. Most Western nations have departments of defense and offices of public safety but never departments of offense or offices of state violence.

Linguists tell us that it is possible to determine the general significance of an idea or event in a culture by counting the number of synonyms and near equivalent terms. By this criterion domestic mass violence is quite prominent, for English lexicons contain ten such terms. Alphabetically, these manifestations are 1.) *civil war,* such as the war between the states in the 1860's, which was the most costly event in men and property in American history. 2.) *Coxey's Armies,* such as those unruly veteran protest demonstrations on Washington during the 1890's. 3.) *mobs,* including Ku Klux Klan lynchings, which were the initial cause for the formulation of the National Association for the Advancement of Colored People.[235] 4.) *mutinies,* which is the word

234. C. Merriam, Systematic Politics, 247-248 (1945).

235. A. Link, American Epoch, 30 (1955) ". . . in August 1908, an anti-Negro riot occured in Springfield, Illinois, within half a mile of Lincoln's home, and humanitarians in the North at last awoke to the imminent threat of southernizing their section. The following February, on Lincoln's birthday, the young Negro rebels and a distinguished group of white educators, clergymen, editors, and social workers met in New York City and organized the National Association for the Advancement of Colored People . . ."

employed by some to characterize protests against Korean and Viet Nam War conscription regulations. 5.) *raids,* such as John Brown's celebrated attack on Harper's Ferry in the name of the abolitionist cause. 6.) *rebellions,* such as the Whiskey Rebellion by Western Pennsylvania farmers, which historians say augmented the cause for a strong central government in the minds of many contemporary people; and the Dorr's Rebellion in Rhode Island, a dispute which ultimately went to the Supreme Court and culminated in the promulgation of the doctrine of political questions.[236] 7.) *revolt, protest* or *uprising* against authority, such as many of the Negroes in the Watts section of Los Angeles label the 1965 summer events.[237] 8.) *revolutions,* of which the War of Independence against the British Crown is the most obvious and the abortive Revolutionary Action Movement, RAM, plot in Philadelphia being the most recent. 9.) *riots,* the Detroit incident here under review being the most costly American experience in lives and property. 10.) some *labor strikes,* at least those such as the Pullman strike of 1877, the Colorado Coal strike of 1914, The Haymarket labor protest of the 1880's, the Little Steel Strike in Chicago of the late 1930's, and the Kohler strike of the 1950's.[238]

Reviewing these ten classifications convinces us of the persistence, relative frequency, and rather prominent role of domestic mass violence in the United States. We see three additional conclusions. Some of these events are labeled haphazardly. Why do Watts Negroes say the 1965 uprising was a revolt? Was it seen by the participants as a protest against the constituted community—the whites who dominated Watts from outside? What is the difference between a mob and a riot? Often we suspect there is none. The mass media initially captioned the Detroit events as a riot and their initial term prevails. Does this mean historians of 2067 must follow this choice of terms? They probably will for want of a more precise vocabulary or sustained interest in the serious lexical problem of classifying the genus-species relationships which are being developed by conflict resolution social scientists. Another conclusion we find in the above list of actual violent occurances is a commentary on the continuing dispute over the cause or

---

For a general discussion of defining a mob for the purpose of drafting legislation see Sengstock, *supra* note 1 at 427-431.

236. Luther v. Borden, 16 U.S. (7 How.) 1 (1849). *See* POST, THE SUPREME COURT AND POLITICAL QUESTIONS (1936).

237. Cohen, *supra* note 11, at 20. *Cf.* Life, July 28, 1967, p. 14B ". . . the Watts riot —or the "revolt" as it is locally, and I think correctly, known . . . ."

238. Kamin, *Residential Picketing and the First Amendment,* 61 NW. U.L. REV. 216-217 (1966) discusses the Haymarket tragedy and the Little Steel Strike in light of regulation of picketing and crowd-handling problems. The VANCE REPORT, *supra* note, at 104 ff. and 131 ff. lists incidents since 1838 when federal troups were called in and requested. There are 17 separate years listed, some with several outbreaks.

causes of such events. To what extent, for example, were the railroad strikes of 1877 the handicraft of agitators who planned their action rather than the outpouring of spontaneous social unrest or turmoil? This is the same question our generation is asking about Detroit events, and the same answers are proffered.[239] Is all violence caused by a John Brown or an H. Rap Brown? Many would say no. These events have a multiplicity of causes and no man, no matter his charm or press, may be so played up or should be so flattered and elevated in significance. It seems to us that the mono-causists again have the worst of the argument. Finally, this list of ten forms of domestic mass violence partially clarifies the controversy over the issue of calculated versus semi-spontaneous events. On the one hand the revolutionary and civil wars were planned and rationalized. On the other hand KKK lynching mobs and the two rebellions mentioned above do not evidence any considerable forethought or after-the-fact justification. Some violence is based upon premeditated procedure; it is both planned and conspiratorial, whereas other violence is more nearly felt reaction to immoderate action; it is both crude and spontaneous. In any case, violence *ipso facto* is not necessarily a conspiracy supported by elaborate philosophical proscriptions.

Analysis

Theory shows how violence can be justified. Historical facts demonstrate some men have used violence without meditation. What we need is an analytic scheme which will describe the limits of present theory and account for the amount of logic which can be marshalled in the defense of violence. It is only when we put our thoughts in order that we have a chance of acting with reason, and not emotionally. We submit below the outline of an analytic scheme to clarify the issue. We find at least six dimensions to domestic mass violence. The continua proposed are tentative and not mutually exclusive.[240] Any one dimension may be most emphasized by a group or author and almost all the combinations have been advocated.

---

239. S. Lens, Radicalism in America (1966). Rummel, *Dimensions of Conflict Behavior Within Nations, 1946-1959,* 10 J. of Conflict Resolution 71 (1966).

240. C. Merriam, Politcal Power 168 (1946) goes into a brief but brilliant diagnosis of the use of violence. These ideas and the six-fold continua here proposed need further elaboration.

Tanter's nine measures of domestic conflict, *supra* note—at 62 are useful because they can be delimited empirically. His categories are 1.) number of assassinations; 2.) number of general strikes; 3.) presence or absence of guerilla warfare; 4.) number of major government crises; 5.) number of purges; 6.) number of riots; 7.) number of revolutions; 8.) number of anti-government demonstrations; and 9.) number of people killed in all forms of domestic violence.

A. Violence is either looked upon as irrational fate, an eternal, unpleasant, and altogether unavoidable condition which is to be suffered, or it is a condition which should be rationally pursued and employed as an instrument of policy.

B. Violence is either a weapon in the leader's arsenal, or it is a tool which should be used by followers against nefarious and uncompromising leaders.

C. Violence is either a tool of last resort to be used once or infrequently, or it is to be used as a *modus operendi,* in the style of the Mao-Mao terrorists. For example, some might contend Americans are essentially peaceful; others would say Americans have a proclivity to violence.

D. Violence is either a morally justifiable act, "when in the course of human events it becomes necessary," or as the contemporary communists say, "as an act of revolutionary morality," or it is an immoral tactic which taints the end by the use of nefarious means, or it is amoral action.

E. Violence is either used to achieve secession from the group or institution against whom it is aimed, or it is a protest for admission.

F. Violence is either for the purpose of creating a new leadership order, or it is for the purpose of contesting lack of access by those who have grievances, or it is designed to reinforce an existing access structure which is often static and rigid and has developed a high "grievance level."[241]

These six dimensions of domestic mass violence are summarized thus:

1. passive, irrational . . . active, rational
2. leader's weapon . . . follower's tool
3. single event . . . occasional event . . . *modus operendi*
4. moral . . . immoral . . . amoral
5. separate . . . integrate
6. overturn access . . . modify access . . . defend access

Application

The utility of this scheme will be more obvious once it is applied to familiar material.[242] In Plato's thought, violence is labeled irrational,

241. We have attempted to tie in these six continua with the excellent research of the Lemberg Institute. See especially their Six City Study—A Survey of Racial Attitudes in Six Northern Cities: Preliminary Findings, mimeo, p. 6 (June, 1967). Dimension F-6 is also stressed by L. A. Caser, Continuities in the Study of Social Conflict 83, 101-3 (1967). Their four stages of precipitating event, confrontation, roman holiday, and war are easily applied to most riots and certainly to Detroit's July disturbance.

242. For more exhaustive but less rewarding analysis of precipitating events in 76 race riots, exclusive of housing riots, see Lieberson & Silverman, *supra* note 13.

and he said it was used by tyrants against followers, as a *modus operendi* if necessary. Violence is immoral because it is unjust and out of harmony with balanced passions. As Plato saw it, violence is used to integrate the polity by the tyrant. It is an instrument in maintaining the *status quo* and denying subordinates any access to power. The emphasis in Platonic thought is on the fourth dimension: tyrannies are morally repugnant.

A second application of this scheme will further clarify the dimensions: the American Civil War was a sequence of actively perpetrated violent acts by leadership groups on both sides who realized it would take an extensive number of battles to gain a moral peace. The Confederacy fought for a separate nation:[243] the North fought to make the nation indivisible. For the North, in part, the war served as a means of abolishing slavery, whereas for the South it was a defense of their peculiar way of life. As articulated in the Gettysburg address, Lincoln would emphasize the fifth dimension: "Now we are engaged in a great civil war, testing whether that nation, or any nation so conceived and so dedicated, can long endure."

Many other facets of Plato's thought and the Civil War could be studied in the light of this scheme: suffice it to say that both are made somewhat more clear.

The chief burden of this article is to shed light on the Detroit disturbance as a legal-political event. Since we have submitted a general conceptual scheme for the analysis of domestic mass violence we have a burden to apply the scheme to the riot. Our analysis is as follows:

First, for the most part for citizens of Detroit and the other communities hit by the riot, the events caught their attention because regular work schedules were interrupted by curfews and cancelled shifts. The majority were non-participants[244] and looked upon the

---

243. It was Texas v. White, 74 U.S. (7 Wall.) 700 (1868) which legally decided the question of whether secession, in point of law, was constitutionally possible.

244. In the Watts riot of 1965 only 15% of the residents of the impacted area participated. Cohen, *supra* note 12, at 15. Also note the following:

"The typical rioter in the summer of 1967 was a Negro, unmarried male between the ages of 15 and 24 in many ways very different from the stereotypes. He was not a Southern migrant. He was born in a Northern state and was a life-long resident of the city in which the riot took place. Economically his position was about the same as his Negro neighbors who did not actively participate in the riot.

"Although he had not, usually, graduated from high school, he was somewhat better educated than the average inner-city Negro, having at least attended high school for a time.

"Nevertheless, he was more likely to be working in a menial or low status job as an unskilled laborer. If he was employed, he was not working full time and his employment was frequently interrupted by periods of unemployment.

"He feels strongly that he deserves a better job and that he is barred from achieving it, not because of lack of training, ability, or ambition, but because of discrimination by employers.

events as irrational, including most Negroes and most of the publically elected Negro leaders such as Detroit Democratic Representatives Conyers and Diggs. Secondly, a small but active minority used the disruption for economic gain, for stealing and looting, and it was a still smaller minority which committed acts of arson, sniping, and sabotage to revenge felt wrongs. The pre-dawn Sunday events which triggered the riots were not led; leaders came after the commotion grew and events were covered in the mass media. Third, the riots were protracted over several days and locations and therefore were composed of a series of events, but no one seriously thought of making the riots a daily business.[245] Fourth, a majority of the rioters, who were a small proportion of the population, *appear* to have looked upon their actions as neither a moral expression of pent up problems (just revenge) nor immoral (stealing is wrong), but as amoral (a chance to do something). Fifth, the dimension of separation or integration does not apply because none of the participants claim to have championed any profound ideas, and the call to *Black Power* seems to be a Sorelian myth of the general strike. Most emphasis might be placed on the sixth dimension, since Negro participants in Detroit and Watts often said they wanted to intimidate whites into the realization that past Negro protests fell on deaf ears.

But a caution must be made: since these events were neither highly led nor prepared as a moral crusade this sense of "loud protest" can be too facilely developed into a theory for action which was not in fact all that present. This is not to deny theory may follow the action. Inasmuch as the Detroit riots are interpreted some semblance of "reason" will surely always be invented.[246] We must be cautious, however, in positing reason where there was only emotion, and systematic cause where there was only random, personal meaning.

"He rejects the white bigot's stereotype of the Negro as ignorant and shiftless. He takes great pride in his race and believes that in some respects Negros are superior to whites. He is extremely hostile to whites, but his hostility is more apt to be a product of social and economic class than of race; he is almost equally hostile toward middle-class Negroes.

"He is substantially better informed about politics than Negroes who were not involved in the riots. He is more likely to be actively engaged in civil rights efforts, but is extremely distrustful of the political system and of political leaders." REPORT OF THE NATIONAL ADVISORY COMMISSION ON CIVIL DISORDERS, *supra* note 175, at 2-50 to 2-52.

245. This capacity to keep up the frenzy of the reign of terror in the crisis period (cf. C. BRINTON, THE ANATOMY OF REVOLUTION 255 (1965) reminds one of Lord Halifax's comment through the character of a trimmer that "Temporal things will have their weight in the World, and tho zeal may prevail for a time, and get the better in a Skirmish, yet the war endeth generally on the side of Flesh and Blood, and will do so until mankind is another thing than it is at present."

246. Every reign of terror is followed by a thermidor reaction, a convalescence from the fervor of revolution, a revulsion against the men who made the terror, and a return to old habits in daily life. C. BRINTON, *supra* note 245, at 235, 205.

*Yet Mr. Shriver was told time and time again by the people in Watts that "if you come in and build us a medical facility we will burn it down. If we participate in the building of this facility it will serve the purposes of this community."**

*Violence and voting are incompatible techniques.** Negroes must be encouraged to play a larger role in determining how their own problems are to be solved and in responding with a sense of participation and responsibility within the framework of an orderly and dynamic society.****

Riots are a destructive form of participation. Within any functioning democracy there are other forms of participation, alternate forms which are constructive. This section of the article is an inquiry into the forms and degree of participation which citizens of a democracy can and do exercise.

The classical Greek distinction concerning participation was over the number of people who ruled, either the one, the few, or the many. Each of these types had a healthy and a diseased condition, thus making six possible types. One Twentieth century thinker, Robert Michels,[247] insisted strongly there is an iron law of oligarchy in political parties, making democratic government neither rule by the one nor the many, but by the few.

To this simple trichotomy we may add the classical distinction between direct and indirect participation. The Greek city-states, Swiss cantons, and New England town meetings all are examples of direct mass participation. Rousseau[248] and Gandhi[249] had visions of returning to this form of statecraft with its face-to-face community. Their ideals were impractical, however, for the size of modern nation state and the scale of modern urban industrial life necessitates an indirect scheme of democracy.

This means the mass of the electorate is confined in its mode of participation: not everyone can go to Lansing, Michigan or Washington D.C. to legislate. The many must therefore make voting for representatives the *sine qua non* of their political participation.

This voting is either viewed as a duty or a right. In at least one

---

* Bertrand Harding, Deputy Director, Office of Economic Opportunity in 1966 Senate Hearings.

** C. MERRIAM, SYSTEMATIC POLITICS (1945).

*** Joseph L. Hudson Jr., Chairman of the New Detroit Committee in an October 1967 speech to the United Fund.

247. R. MICHELS, POLITICAL PARITES: A SOCIOLOGICAL STUDY OF THE OLIGARCHICAL TENDENCIES OF MODERN DEMOCRACY, 377 ff. (Eden & Cedar Paul trans. 1915).

248. ROUSSEAU, THE SOCIAL CONTRACT BOOK III.

249. B. S. SHARMA, GANDHI AS A POLITICAL THINKER 91-93 (Allahabad: Indian Press (Publications) Private Ltd. 1956).

other democracy—Australia[250]—it is a duty, and qualified electors who fail to vote without good cause are required to pay the state for not exercising their franchise. In the United States, on the other hand, voting is not deemed to be a duty. Indeed, until recently there were poll taxes imposed upon voters. With the elimination of first the national poll tax[251] and then the state poll tax[252] the nation is ambivalent in its attitude toward the franchise. Registration laws are now the major depressants on voting turnout.[253] In any case what is clear is that this does not favor a voting stimulant. The present nature of the franchise implies citizenship in good standing, a recognition of maturity on the voter's part, and the assumption that the voter is responsible for his or her own actions and those of the community.

Citizens, however, can participate in ways other than voting. Voting is the species of the genus participation. Political participation generally is "taking part in making the basic decisions as to what are the common goals of one's society and as to the best ways to move toward these goals."[254] Thus citizen participation can be sub-divided into responding and instituting administrative matters[255] and the more conventionally assumed political activity *per se*. Although political activity is more apparent, a significant amount of citizen activity is spent ordering and requesting bureaucratic action. Reluctance to go to the police station is perhaps as bad a sign for democracy as reluctance to go to the polling booth. And it is as important that the station or the booth is available as it is that it is actually utilized. Someone may wish to avail themselves of a service or right only sporadically, yet to be a first class citizen he must always find it available.

Unfortunately, for an extended period of over a decade the political science profession nearly equated participation with voting. Due in part to the statistical nature of voting data and to newly acquired methodological skills the profession rushed into the research field and gathered material, processed it, and reported their findings in several major studies and with impressive insight.[256] In reporting their results

---

250. Australia's requirement is a positive obligation written into statutes at both federal and state level. For the federal provision see the 1899 Commonwealth Electoral Act, § 128A. *Also see Crisp, Compulsory Voting in Australia* 6 PARLIAMENTARY AFFAIRS (1953).

251. U.S. CONST. amend. XXIV.

252.Harper v. Virginia State Bd. of Elections 383 U.S. 663 (1966).

253. Kelley *et. al., Registration and Voting: Putting First Things First* 61 AM. POL. SCI. REV. 373-374 (1967).

254. J.C. DAVIES, HUMAN NATURE IN POLITICS 23 (1963).

255. This topic is not well researched: Citizen attitude toward bureaucrats is better researched for India than for the United States: see S. J. ELDERSVELD *et. al.*, THE CITIZEN AND THE ADMINISTRATION IN A DEVELOPING DEMOCRACY (1968), esp. chs. 1 and 7.

256. A few of the major volumes are P. LAZARSFELD *et. al.*, THE PEOPLE'S CHOICE (1944); B. BERELSON *et. al.*, VOTING: A STUDY OF OPINION FORMATION IN A PRESIDENTIAL

they employed such phrases as "voter participation" rather than describing voting as one aspect of participation. One excellent study contains this rather typical clause: "differences in participation which appear to vary with different election appeal . . . ."[257] The error is understandable but nevertheless serious: by participation they mean a voter turnout.

Both voting and registration in turn are not the only categories of participation. Currently the span of participatory events which students of political science see is slowly widening to embrace a larger number of activities. A reaction to voting studies has set in. Voting is now viewed as a significant but limited activity. As the two authors who have synthesized the field—Lane and Milbrath[258]—suggest, participation also includes everything from using party bumper stickers and attending political rallies to contributing money and running for office.[259] Milbrath has suggested and reworked a theory that forms of participation fall along a continuum.[260] The bandwagon to generic studies of participation is upon us, aided in part by the very influential Almond and Verba five nation comparative study of participation.[261] The most recent announcement of Ph. D. dissertations lists fifteen

---

CAMPAIGN (1954); A. CAMPBELL *et. al.*, THE VOTER DECIDES (1954); A. CAMPBELL *et. al.*, THE AMERICAN VOTING BEHAVIOR (Burdick & Brodbeck, eds., 1959); and A. CAMPBELL *et. al.*, ELECTIONS AND THE POLITICAL ORDER (1966).

257. Robinson & Standing, *Some Correlates of Voter Participation: The Case of Indiana* 22 J. OF POLITICS 110 (1960). To insure the reader this not a straw man argument, consider the following: "The data on political participation will refer to the percentage of registrants who exercised their political franchise by voting for a presidential candidate." Glantz, *The Negro Voter in Northern Industrial Cities* 13 W. POL. Q. 1001 (1960).

258. R. LANE, POLITICAL LIFE: WHY AND HOW PEOPLE GET INVOLVED IN POLITICS (1959); L. MILBRATH, POLITICAL PARTICIPATION: HOW AND WHY DO PEOPLE GET INVOLVED IN POLITICS? (1965). One other general work on the topic exists: it is APPROACHES TO THE STUDY OF POLITICAL PARTICIPATION (S. Rokkan, ed. 1962). See also LIPSET, POLITICAL MAN (1960).

259. Excellent investigations by the University of Michigan Detroit Area Study conducted over the years have yielded important information on the nature of behavior patterns in the metropolis. For our study, in particular, the Winter 1960-1961 study, No. 870, by Warren Miller and Donald Stokes, is important; it concentrated on "Group Influences on Political Behavior" and asked respondents about their participation in a variety of conventionally designated categories such as using buttons or stickers for candidates, contributing or soliciting contributions for a candidate or party, membership in a group, handing out leaflets, voting, attending partisan and union sponsored rallies, and receiving campaign information in the mail, Items 83-91. Due to sophisticated sampling techniques however, the sample or N (Number from the universe being sampled) was 419. Since this was a limited study of union affiliates no direct use of this data could be made in the present study. The 1951-1952 DAS, No. 104, asked questions on social participation, Items 34-38, specifically questioning respondents whether they talked or wrote about the recent campaign, their registration performance, and their party performance. These were not found useful due to the confined nature of the questions and the 16 year time lapse.

260. L. MILBRATH, *supra* note at 18 and L. Milbrath, *Political Participation in the States* in POLITICS IN THE AMERICAN STATES 28 (H. JACOB AND K. N. VINES, eds. 1965).

261. G. ALMOND & S. VERBA, THE CIVIC CULTURE: POLITICAL ATTITUDES AND DEMOCRACY IN FIVE NATIONS (1963).

studies in the area.[262] There are even two texts using participation and conflict resolution themes,[263] and what more important sign of arrival could one ask for?

But even these current generic definitions of participation are inadequate. The new studies still have a lingering positivistic bias. Their euphemisms for power, such as decision-making or political process, still hide part of the full spectrum.[264] We agree with the critics of the community power studies who say these studies employ an elitist theory and emphasize "functions of the system as a whole; there is no longer a direct concern with human development."[265] Walker, one of Dahl's few critics, we think is correct when he argues that the community power studies make solidarity so important marginal men are not really viewed as citizens of the state.[266] Kariel, the most lyrical of the critics, sums up the point:

> Yet, because "functionality" or "success" or "stability" are not sufficient criteria for taking the measure of a political order, the relevance of the prevailing empirical approach remains limited.[267]

Milbrath, an avowed positivist, is very open in acknowledging this criticism: he is not concerned with marginal activities because "[t]hey are, almost by definition, extraordinary rather than normal . . ."[268] The empiricists stop short of studying the psychological good which can come even from unsuccessful forms of participation, such as failing attempts at securing a primary nomination. Few of the new studies mention boycotts, for example, even though this is mass participation through selective buying habits to gain a political end.[269] Even

---

262. Three dissertations on participation and civil rights, two of these at Northwestern, the former school of Milbrath and the present location for Greer; four on participation in the countries of Mexico, India, Brazil, and Kenya; three on student participation in Indonesia, the Philippines, and Venezuela; two University of Minnesota dissertations inspecting general patterns; two on psychological aspects, one of which is being done at Northwestern; and an evaluation of non-participation at Johns Hopkins. 61 AM. POL. SCI. REV. 846 ff. (1967). *See also* the special issue on *Students and Politics* 97 DAEDALUS 1-341 (1968).

263. D.D. NIMMO & T. UNGS, AMERICAN POLITICAL PATTERNS: CONFLICT AND CONSENSUS 111 (1967) divide citizen activity into "opinion-holding, political leadership, voting, partisan activity, and group membership." R. DAHL, PLURALIST DEMOCRACY IN THE UNITED STATES: CONFLICT AND CONSENT (1967).

264. *Cf.* S. WOLIN, POLITICS AND VISION 220-221 (1960). "All that can be said with confidence is that euphemisms for power and violence have not been dispelled by positivism."

265. Walker, *A Critique of the Elitist Theory of Democracy* 60 AM. POL. SCI. REV. 288 (1966).

266. *Id.*, at 291.

267. H. KARIEL, THE PROMISE OF POLITICS 83 (1966).

268. L. MILBRATH, *supra* note 260, at 27.

269. Cf. Walker, *supra* note 265, at 295 "[L]ittle attention has been directed to the great social movements which have marked American society in the last one hundred

though sit-ins from Greensboro on have made major inroads on community discrimination habits, and more direct-action techniques are being employed every year, empiricists have generally left this segment out of their research designs and theoretical constructs.[270] They have been oblivious to such events as the procession of nearly 800 racial demonstrations in 70 days following the 1963 Birmingham street demonstrations.

Positivists have neglected the extreme forms of participation. They have neglected to do research on the riot and the boycott. They have neglected the feeling of the poor and the many Negroes who have few if any group affiliations which would give them a sense of responsibility in the greater community.[271] What happens to those who feel they have no stake in society and have no way to participate but by rioting?[272] What happens to those whose dignity and personal development are stunted for want of any general democratic mode of participation? By their own philosophical tenets the positivists neglect "egalitarianism, individual participation, and personal experience as genuine goods" in and of themselves.[273] None of the positivists are asking the question of how pressing it is to the slum dweller that he is incapable of contributing suggestions as to how his own public life ought to be led.

Specifically, what must be done is an investigation of such agencies as the Office of Economic Opportunity's Community Action Program's attempt to develop, conduct, and administer "with the maximum feasible participation of residents of the areas and members of the group served."[274] Empirical studies must investigate on what grounds Whitney Young of the Urban League can say of the OEO: "We feel that there has been more representation, more democratic participation

---

years." Dahl's reply to this was "Well defined social movements—the anti-slavery movement of the pre-Civil War period or the agrarian discontent of the 1880's and the 1890's—are comparatively rare in the United States."

270. *Cf.* Dahl, *Further Reflections on "The Elitist Theory of Democracy"* 60 AM. POL. SCI. REV. 304 (1966).

271. For a discussion of the group approach to the study of politics see Smith, *Regulation of National and State Legislative Lobbying* 43 U. DET. L.J. 668-669 (1966).

272. The most eloquent statement of the problem we have seen in print is that of John B. Turner, Chairman of the Division on Social Policy and Action of the National Association of Social Workers and Commissioner of the New York City Department of Welfare:

> The strength and freedom derived by most citizens out of participation and affiliation with groups is virtually unexperienced by the poor. Numerous studies and surveys have documented the restricted participation of the poor in groups which are concerned with promoting a better life for them in a material way. Organization is an accepted and encouraged way of life except when it comes to the poor.

Hearings on H. R. 8311 Before the House Comm. on Education and Labor, 90th Cong., 1st Sess., pt. 3 at 1613 (1967).

273. H. KARIEL, *supra* note 267, at 53.

274. 78 Stat. 516 (1964), 42 U.S.C. § 2781(a)(3) (Supp. 1967).

of the Negro in the poverty programs than in any other program of the departments of government."[275] We need to know whether riots can be partially reduced by multipurpose service centers in poor housing areas so that residents can present their grievances on a face-to-face basis.

Students of urban politics must go beyond conventional governmental institutions and study what functions, if any, are performed by block clubs, of which there are over 1,400 in Detroit. To study participation fully we must study what impact there was on the 1,000 persons who were informally consulted on the Virginia renewal plaza project in the burned-out 12th Street area. The study would assess what sense of belonging this implanted in the people as well as any tangible planning modifications.

We already know how such community consultant groups are circumvented and degraded. We know, as Dr. Kenneth Clark of the City College of New York points out, that "almost invariably political conversationalists intervened to truncate or to control or to restrict the extent of community action. . ."[276] It may well be true as he goes on to assert that "We did not calculate that for the poor the chief consequences of the culture of poverty is a kind of human stagnation, acceptance, defeat, which made meaningful involvement more verbal than real."[277] Empirical studies may even be able to verify this assertion in a score of cases. However, his human stagnation is not the point. The point is that in a democracy every citizen, whether or not in poverty, every man, whether or not he is white, is as important as everyone else in the eyes of the law. Yes, some people might be circumvented, but what counts is that the community design ways in which to engage the poor and the defeated to place their own aspirations and priorities in front of decision-making bodies, so that they can participate in making their own political future. Whatever the present facts might be, this is the goal or perhaps the myth of our egalitarian society.

There is a most damaging criticism to this suggestion for an equalitarian society with widespread political participation. Mass participation might well lead to a *mass society*, to a society ripe for manipulation by a Hitler.[278] This is the poetic nightmare conjured up by W. H. Auden who speaks of crowd engineers and of a kingdom where "signs

---

275. *Hearings on H.R. 8311* Before the House Comm. on Education and Labor, 90th Cong., 1st Sess., pt. 3 at 2286 (1967).

276. *Hearings Before the Subcomm. on Executive Reorganization* of the Senate Comm. on Government Operations, 89th Cong., 2d Sess., pt. 13 at 2759 (1966).

277. *Id.*

278. "For Hitler had grasped a truth which had eluded Papen, the dilettante, that the key to power no longer lay in the parliamentary and presidential intrigues . . . but, outside, in the masses of German people." A. BULLOCK, HITLER: A STUDY IN TYRANNY 119 (1958).

and insignia decide our cause."[279] This is the specter which the social philosopher William Kornhauser discusses, namely, "that insofar as a society is a mass society, it will be vulnerable to political movements destructive to democratic institutions. . ."[280] By a mass society he means a community where "elites are readily accessible to influence by non-elites and non-elites are readily available for mobilization by elites."[281] In a mass society people have become estranged from their traditions and fellow creatures; they lack intermediate group association and are in search of a maximum leader. They find him: he is a man who fills the dual voids of authority and community with charismatic leadership and totalitarian party.[282] Such a mass society has too much participation. It is full of estranged men in a state of guided but seemingly spontaneous frenzy. The criticism of mass participation then is that the state might deteriorate into irrational and unbridled mob action. It would often be violent action, similar to the Red Guard Movement in the present Chinese Peoples' Republic, populated by true believers[283] who find their only purpose in uniting with the crowd, and their only happiness in self-sacrifice and rejection of traditional values.[284]

The criticism of mass participation deteriorating into a manipulated mass society is potentially valid, but not irrevocably so. *The query is* what quality as well as what quantity of participation. Non-participation is a multifaceted category.[285] For those whose contribution to statecraft would only be forced and never sincere, there would be no reason to force them into activity. And those who feel content with the system to the point of lethargy are probably better not moved. But for other non-participants it is a question of uneasy apathy, of cheerless acceptance. What may be needed for them is a system which nurtures participation. It appears from research studies that some who do not now concern themselves with the public business do so out of a sense of powerlessness, or low efficacy.[286] These are the people who would otherwise constructively contribute: these are the people for whom a suitable environment must be prepared.

---

279. W. H. AUDEN, *supra* note 227.
280. W. KORNHAUSER, THE POLITICS OF MASS SOCIETY 5 (1959).
281. *Id.*, 39.
282. H. ARENDT, *supra* note 7, at 808-811 (1958).
283. E. HOFFER, THE TRUE BELIEVER 57-118 (1951).
284. This is a variation on a theme by J. ORETA Y GASSET, THE REVOLT OF THE MASSES (1932); E. FROMM, ESCAPE FROM FREEDOM (1941); H. ARENDT, *supra* note 7. For all of these people "the social landscape has been flattened out" by the mass society and its erosion of the conventional political terrain: H. KARIEL, *supra* note, at 58.
285. Rosenberg, *Some Determinants of Political Apathy* 18 PUB. OPINION Q. 349-366 (1954).
286. C. MERRIAM AND H. GOSNELL, NON-VOTING (1924); A. CAMPBELL *et al.*, THE AMERICAN VOTER ch. 5, *Voting Turnout* 89-115 (1960).

And in what ways can we thus escape from a manipulated mass politics into a healthy polity with greater active acceptance? The answer is that there are a variety of ways, including long term solutions such as more quality education, employment opportunity, and more family stability. The city can engage the people in their own locations by decentralizing decision-making. Three of the cities have already begun to see the logic in "working with rather than for the people."[287] The centralized plans will still be created, but by advocate planners with prior, not *post facto* concurrence. The planning will be with the people in small and large block sessions, school district hearings, picnics, and by letters, brochures, advisory committees, resident staff town hall forums, and building caucuses. The planning and consultation will be through improvement associations, property owners' associations, merchant associations, regional chambers of commerce, tenant councils, high school parents' community associations, mothers' playground protective and improvement associations, and such peak associations in Detroit as the Congress of Grass Roots Organization (CONGRO), the New Detroit Committee, Urban Community Resources, Inc., the Committee for Neighborhood Conservation and Improved Housing, and the Model Cities Citizens Governing Board.[288]

It is acknowledged that decentralization is feasible. The local residents and merchants do not want a gesture; they want to cooperate in a fundamental way. The two immediate past Secretaries of Health, Education, and Welfare, who were responsible for much of the activity concerning the cities, are agreed that decentralization is important and must be implemented. Mr. Ribicoff said "It is disillusioning that those responsible for these programs [in reference to urban-federal joint projects] never even bother talking to the people so vitally involved."[289]

---

287. The phrase was suggested by an OEO recipient from San Francisco, California in testimony before Senator Clark's mobil Subcommittee. A West Oakland, California witness was on target although factually inaccurate when he said "We understand our Constitution; it says it is 'For the people and by the people.' But this program was got together and the poor people are tired of people planning for them and not planning with them." An East Oakland woman active in neighborhood organizations put the case in concrete terms: "[T]hey are learning their rights and how to participate in things within our community organization. We are learning zoning and planning . . . and how to actually go downtown and rock those people out . . . ask for those things that normal citizens would except the city fathers to do." *Hearings Before the Subcomm. on Employment, Manpower, and Poverty* of the Senate Comm. on Labor and Public Welfare, 90th Cong., 1st Sess., pt. 11 at 3447, 3455, and 3462.

288. The North Minneapolis, Minnesota Pilot Center area of 52,000 residents is a case in point. According to Paul Gilje, Research Director for the Citizens League, a non-partisan citizens good government organization in the twin cities, over a seven week period made almost 7,000 contacts, excluding distribution of 18,000 brochures and special newspapers. The cooperating agencies include the OEO, HUD, Bureau of the Budget, HEW, state, county, and city agencies, plus private settlement houses.

On April 21, 1968 HEW established a Coordinator for Citizen Participation to aid voluntary citizen groups. HEW, Office of Education Press release T87.

289. *Hearings Before the Subcomm. on Executive Reorganization* of the Senate Comm. on Government Operations, 89th Cong., 2d Sess., pt. 12 at 2573 (1966).

Mr. Gardner was even more forthright: "You cannot pre-package a solution in Washington and hand it to a community. You must, to a considerable degree, supply them with the ingredients that they can put together, working with the Federal representatives at the local level."[290]

Detroit politicians and those in other metropolitan areas will agree to decentralization of decision-making and pre-plan consultation for three practical reasons. First, they will still have final authority. In Detroit, for example, the Common Council will have ultimate approval of most community-based decisions. Secondly, the politicians realize this decentralized trend is relatively important, both for national political parties and city non-partisan politics. In addition to the amateur Democratic clubs which were so richly spawned during the late Adlai Stevenson's two presidential campaigns, there are a host of reform-minded and improvement groups whose sound has been heard sufficiently to make the politician realize there are votes behind the voices.[291] Third, since the riots in various cities even more local community associations are springing up. For example, in Detroit the Linwood, North Virginia Park, Dexter-Lodge, and Clairmont-Detroit River groups have all activated themselves.[292]

The whole thrust toward more quality participation is to make meaningful the literal definition of democracy, viz. rule by the people. The people will feel they have a place in the scheme of things and a sense of determining their own destiny. The consent of the governed is facilitated by community involvement. With diffuse authority, albeit with central city supervision, the people will be able to participate in a continual dialogue with their governors. The bureaus will no longer be able to tell the citizens what their problems are. Election will be supplemented, but not supplanted, by continuous contacts, and the result ought to be higher morale. Impersonal, technical, and fast-moving urban life will be made more nearly individual, more specifically applicable to the citizen to articulate governmental officials.

Scott Greer summarized his study on urban political participation with these words:

> [T]he participation of the average individual in democratic society is a somewhat bizarre experience . . . it is difficult to

290. *Senate Hearings on S. 3509 and S.J. Res. 187*, pt. 1, 89th Cong., 2d Sess., pt. I at 279 (1966).

291. S. A. MITCHELL, ELM STREET POLITICS (1959); J. Q. WILSON, THE AMATEUR DEMOCRAT: CLUB POLITICS IN THREE CITIES (1966).

292. Interview with Mr. Carl Almblad, Detroit City Planning Commissioner, Oct. 13, 1967. HUD Model Cities Program Deputy Director John A. Briggs suggested "the most important innovations in this program may come through new ways for citizens to join with local officials in making decisions."

> make a case for the widespread importance of the democratic process for most people, except in the home and friendship circle.[293]

Then the processes of statecraft must be brought down to the geo-political level of the home, the block club, and the neighborhood.

A Somber Ending

We cannot end without a somber and unpleasant fact. Although meaningful increases in the quality and quantity of political participation can and will transpire within the cities, both for Negroes and whites, this activity will not be sufficient in itself to prevent riots. There are no nostrums or palliatives in such complex affairs. Indeed, the most startling finding to report is that as the poor are exposed to the rich and as Negroes are exposed to white living conditions there may well be more tension.[294] The contrast of the affluence and amenities of the middle class whites to the Negroes' own conditions will accentuate differences. Exposing the contrasts only yields stronger desires, and this means stronger tensions.

The price of increased participation by the poor, whatever their color, will and is generating tension for rapid change. The rising expectations of the North are generally more apparent than in the South, especially the rural South, for it is in the North that there is the most contact on an equal basis between the races and the classes.[295]

But who ever said democracy is a placid way of life or that increasing the scope of the *demos* who can partake in the governing of society will reduce the problems of statecraft? So long as all factions of the *demos* agree to participate through lawful means, and those means are open to all, the bracing effects of more participation ought to be beneficial.

---

293. Greer, *Individual Participation in Mass Society in* Approaches to the Study of Politics 341 (R. Young, ed. 1958).

294. There cannot be any formal proof of this, but consider the following: "Nobody can plan for the inner city but inner city people. If they don't, you will have another explosion." Detroit News, Nov. 15, 1967 § C, at 2, col. 5.

The Deputy Director, Program Development, California State Department of Social Welfare, Mr. Harold E. Simmons: "Some believe tensions are even greater in Watts and Hunters Point because of the nearness to more affluent areas which by contrast to poverty accentuate one's sensitivity to this difference." *Hearings on H.R. 8311* Before the Comm. on Education and Labor, 90th Cong., 1st Sess., pt. 3 at 2025 (1967).

295. Consider the following assertion about southern conditions: "There would seem to be a critical point, at about 30 per cent Negro, where white hostility to Negro political participation becomes severe." *Social and Economic Factors in Negro Voter Registration in the South* 57 Am. Pol. Sci. Rev. 29 (1963).

Using the data bank of Matthews and Prothro referred to above, John Orbell, an Ohio State University political scientist, postulated "that proximity to the dominant white culture increases the likelihood of protest involvement" of southern college students. He also states that "Conservative Southern claims that the progress of integration will only

> *It is an intriguing question how much strife might have been spared and how much understanding might have been engendered, had the elective branches of the government provided the leadership with which they are charged and, as subsequent events proved, of which they are capable when pressed.**
>
> *Was this the only true history of the times, a mood blared by trumpets, trombones, saxophones, and drums, a song with turgid, inadequate words?***

Both a legal and political analysis of the Detroit riot have led us to a dominant observation: *it concerns the role of Negro leadership.* One of the most dramatic moments of the five day period occurred on the first day, Sunday morning, July 23. Negro Democratic Representative John Conyers spoke to a milling crowd on 12th Street.[296] With a bullhorn Conyers said to the crowd "Take it easy brother, I assure you we are in touch with the police. Please disperse . . ." According to a very perceptive eye-witness account, Conyers moved to the top of a parked vehicle and spoke further, but was forced to stop as rioters broke bottles on the curb and rocks flew around him.[297]

Fellow Negro Democratic Congressman Diggs, from another Detroit District, was no more successful in pacifying the crowds. Negro Hubert Locke, at the time on leave from Wayne State University and acting as an Administrative Assistant to the Police Chief, could do nothing either with the ignited throng.

Why couldn't these three highly placed Negro public officials, two of whom were elected a year before, do anything to snap a quiet victory from the jaws of the riot? Timing alone made rational dialogue that Sunday morning and noon improbable. But even before that day Negro leaders had not been conspicuously successful in constructively organizing as a political minority group so as to present their grievances through conventional political channels.

In fact, throughout the United States Negro leadership is not pro-

---

bring an increase of Negro assertiveness seem quite plausible from the present theoretical position." Orbell, *Protest Participation Among Southern Negro College Students* 61 AM. POL. SCI. REV. 446, 456 (1967).

* H.J. ABRAHAM, FREEDOM AND THE COURT (1967).

** R. ELLISON, INDIVISIBLE MAN (1952).

296. Mayor Cavanagh's suggestion that 12th Street, about 20 percent of which was destroyed, be renamed, is unwise. We cannot erase a memory by purging a name. Watts Negroes took pride in their sectional designation within the Los Angeles community because of the fame and infamy of the 1965 disturbance.

The Virginia Park Rehabilitation Citizens Committee is working in cooperation with the Detroit Housing Commission in planning the rebuilding of the area. This demonstrates two of this article's major themes: rioters are rewarded with more attention, and the plan has an excellent chance of passage and success due to neighborhood involvement. The grassless lots will be made profitable by grasroots efforts. *See* New York Times, Dec. 10, 1967, § I at 157, col. 3.

297. Det. News, Aug. 1, 1967, § B at 3, col. 5.

portionately as successful as its white counterpart. Although Negroes account for approximately eleven percent of the total population,[298] they only constitute approximately one percent of Congress.[299] Negroes as a race are therefore underrepresented over ten times their proportionate number in Congress. The Supreme Court may have said that there should be one man, one vote as nearly as practicable,[300] but this doctrine applies to all citizens by area, not to all groups by race.

Until the 1967 off-year campaigns the same disproportionate underrepresentation was true for mayoral positions. Presently Washington, D.C. has an appointed Negro mayor while Cleveland, Ohio along with Gary, Indiana and Flint, Michigan have elected Negro mayors.

All these Congressional and mayoral positions are in the North and only one of the prominently elected Negroes is a Republican, *viz.* Senator Brooke of Massachusetts. The deep South still has not produced a state-wide elected Negro official.[301] Mississippi, for example, with 43 percent of its population Negro, the highest concentration in the nation, has one Negro, Robert Clark, in the Jackson Legislature. And his election was unsuccessfully challenged January 2, 1968, just as Julien Bond's position was in the Georgia State Legislature.[302]

North or South, this chasm of elected Negro leadership is only partially due to discrimination in registering and voting.[303] Negroes

---

298. Philip M. Hauser, Demographic Factors in the Integrating of the Negro, Exhibit 201 of *Hearings Before the Subcomm. on Executive Reorganization* of the Senate Comm. on Government Operation, 89th Cong., 2d Sess., pt. 14 at 3001 (1966). "[T]hus by 1960, Negroes constituted slightly above one-tenth (10.6 percent) of the total population."

299. For the Senate: 1/100 = 1%. Senator Brook, Mass. For the House: 5/435 = approx. 1% Reps. Hawkins, Cal.; Nix, Pa.; Dawson, Ill.; Conyers and Diggs. Mich.; Powell is not included as he was not seated for the 90th Congress.

According to Hauser, *id.*, at 3004, "Six states in the North and West (California, Illinois, Michigan, New York, Ohio and Pennsylvania) absorbed 72 percent of all Negro net in-migration between 1910 and 1950. Between 1950 and 1960, the same six states absorbed 68 percent of all net in-migration of nonwhites." With the exception of Ohio these are the states with Negro House representation. The Spanish-speaking population has been left out of this study, but they are not rioting so they do not get substantial billing.

300. Wesberry v. Sanders 376 U.S. 7-8 (1964).

301. Elected Negro politicians are not numerous North or South. In the South most are first generation and in Louisiana, e.g. "there are no full time politicians in the State." D.C. THOMPSON, THE NEGRO LEADERSHIP CLASS 93 (1963).

302. Bond v. Floyd 385 U.S. 116 (1966).

303. Voting by virtue of "grandfather clauses," white primaries, or gerrymandering is no longer the problem: it is settled law. *See* THE NEGRO VOTES C. Aiken ed. (1962) for a compilation of court cases.

> It is widely believed by students of Negro politics that the low rate of voter registration by southern Negroes is partly the result of a lack of leadership. Only when there is a pool of educated and skillful leaders whose means of livelihood is not controlled by whites can sufficient leadership and political organization develop to ensure a relatively high rate of Negro registration in the South. Our data support[s] this line . . . of argument. Matthews & Prothro, *Social and Eco-*

as a group lack the educated leadership of skillful wordsmiths who can organize and appeal to the mass citizenry, white as well as black. And it is quality leadership more than any of a host of other factors which the Negroes need to develop for their race. Leadership is the *sine qua non* of politics,[304] more important than numbers, more potent than ideas, more effective than access, more valuable even than money. Leadership alone can orchestrate an organization, recruit members, clarify a blaring but unscored idea, create access, and produce wealth.

Negroes no longer accept white leadership: black pride requires black leaders. The NAACP may have been founded by Caucasians but the association will surely not now be led by them. SNCC has also evolved, in this case from Christian biracial origins in 1960 into an exclusively secular Negro group. Saul Alinski may be a consultant to Negro urban ghetto dwellers but he cannot and does not aspire daily to lead them.

Democracy is postulated on the assumption people and groups will look out for their own welfare; self-help is self-rule. That is why three commentators can judge the riots as ultimately a positive sign.[305] The entelechy or vital force directing the life of a democracy is control over one's destiny. In turn group assertiveness is the condition upon which the group basis of politics rests, that collectivities wishing recognition

---

nomic Factors in Negro Voter Registration in the South, 57 AM. POL. SCI. REV., 32 (1963). *See* also their book: D. MATTHEWS & J. W. PROTHRO, NEGROES AND THE NEW SOUTHERN POLITICS (1967) which contains a modified version of the above article.

304. The Negro community has witnessed the emergence of the "Talented Tenth" projected by W. E. B. DuBois, but find that this group, (sic.) which has grown beyond the 10 percent envisioned, has tended to operate in the more traditional ways and has lost touch with the plight of the 35-40 percent of the Negro population whose pervasive concern is not status frustration, but rather economic frustration.[3]

Footnote three reads as follows: "DuBois' thesis was that if the upper 10 percent of the Negro group could receive college education, as contrasted with Booker T. Washington's emphasis on elementary and vocational training, they would serve as a leadership group to help pull up the masses." COHEN, *supra* note 11at 18.

305. *Hearings Before the Subcomm. on Executive Reorganization* of the Senate Comm. on Government Organization, 89th Cong., 2d Sess., pt. 12 at 2499 and 2500 (1966): from the NATION, December 20, 1965, Exhibit 175, *The Language of Watts,* by Stanley Sanders:

> To a people who have always been acted upon, rarely doing anything for itself or to communicate outside, the riots were a bold departure from a long tradition of inertia. Admittedly, the fact that the activity was destructive is not irrelevant, but it is less important than the fact that rioting is for the Negro in Watts a form of expression. No one understands his problem or bothers to care. Few of his local leaders have the imagination or vision to articulate his special feelings to the outside world.

Governor Rockefeller of New York said "There have been a lot of changes recently in the racial situation and a number of forces have been unleashed, but they're part of the forces of progress." Indiana Evening Gazette, Aug. 24, 1967, § I, at 3, cols. 5-7.

Whitney Young, of the Urban League, said:

> The fact that Negro citizens are protesting or even rioting, as senseless as I think riots are, at least it says that they have not completely given up; that they do

seek that recognition. Negroes are beginning to take their destiny into their own hands, albeit with the wrong tools. The point to be emphasized is Negro desire for recognition, not the present Negro tools for demanding that recognition. The goal is praiseworthy, the procedure is galling.

But, you will object, Negroes need not be recognized as a group, but as individuals. This is true, and this is the eventual goal of an individualistic community, but if Negroes *qua* Negroes are repressed, then Negroes *qua* Negroes must organize.

But, you will object further, Caucasians will look after Negroes. The United States is a nation of virtual representation. This is not true, however, for such Senators as Stennis of Mississippi. Mississippi Negroes are functionally represented through the NAACP and the factional Freedom Democratic Party, not through the white supremist Democratic party, or the moribund Republican party. If the Evers brothers do not organize the Negro in Mississippi, who shall pay attention to Negro demands?

In abstract theory, Negroes *per se* need not be elected to office to insure Negroes equal protection of the law. In practice, both racial and ethnic groups develop identification and come to the aid and succor of fellow group members. The test of this, if one is needed, is found among ethnic identifiable members of Congress. Let a Greek-American from North Carolina write Representative Kyros of Maine and he will reply, not because the writer is a constituent but because he was a Greek. Again, let a North Dakota Pole write Representative Roman Pucinski of Illinois, and the chances are that solon will answer the correspondence.[306] It all resolves to this: white leadership cannot be a successful surrogate for popularly elected Negro representation because of the nature of pluralistic American group identification and representation.

Non-elected Negro leaders abound: Whitney Young of the Urban League, Roy Wilkins of the NAACP, Ralph Abernathy of the Southern Christian Leadership Conference, Robert Weaver of the Department of Housing and Urban Development, and the Negro businessmen of the Cotillion Club in Detroit and the Detroit Negroes' City—Wide Citizens Action Committee.[307] But non-elected officials do not have

---

> believe that if they take certain action that something will happen and at least they feel in America they have a right to fight for freedom and I think this is a great asset.

Hearings on H.R. 8311 Before the House Comm on Education and Labor, 90th Cong., 1st Sess., pt. 3 at 2284 (1967).

306. There is a large body of literature in political science on ethnic group politics, *see e.g.* Cornwells, *Bosses, Machines, and Ethnic Groups*, 353 ANNALS 27-39 (1964). The New Jersey Commission, *supra* note at 162, recognized the need for more Negro politicians in heavily Negro areas.

307. For a public opinion poll breakdown of Negro popularity among Negroes see W. BRINK & L. HARRIS, THE NEGRO REVOLUTION IN AMERICA ch. 7 (1963).

political power; at best they have influence.[308] Laws are made by elected legislators and laws are most fully enforced by elected chief administrators. There are proportionately too few Negro elected officials who pass and police the laws. And long ago Negroes learned they could not accept the good will and self-restraint of the whites; they must control their own political destiny.

Perhaps Representative Conyer's near stoning and ridicule by fellow Negroes is an indication that even with popularly elected Negroes tension will not automatically subside. Unless these officials truly represent their fellow members and establish rapport, they may themselves be the target of riots.[309] For example, Flint, Michigan will not be immune to another riot simply because it has a Negro chief administrator.[310] As a larger proportion of the Negro community be-

308. The king has power when he tells his henchmen to act. The king's mistress has influence when she bends the ear of the king, who tells the henchmen. Professional political science literature is highly dependent on Lasswell's assertion that "The study of politics is the study of influence and the influentials." POLITICS: WHO GETS WHAT, WHEN, AND HOW 13 (1958). C. MERRIAM, POLITICAL POWER 136-142 (1964) lists violence as the most repellent quality of power. The so-called community power literature follows up the Lasswellian dictum that politics is the study of influence. For a study of Atlanta, Georgia see M. K. JENNINGS, COMMUNITY INFLUENTIALS, esp. ch. 2 (1965). This study supplants in many ways the earlier study of Atlanta by F. HUNTER, COMMUNITY POWER STRUCTURE (1953). For the power literature which overlaps the influence literature, see the early formulation by C. MERRIAM, *supra* this note, B. GROSS, THE LEGISLATIVE STRUGGLE ch. 8 (1953), and A. ROSE, THE POWER STRUCTURE: POLITICAL PROCESS IN AMERICAN SOCIETY chs. 1-2 (1967).

309. *See* N.Y. TIMES, Oct., 1, 1967, § I at 68, col. 4. The best empirical evidence on factors which contribute to summer urban and dominantly Negro riot conditions is being collected by the Lemberg Center for the Study of Violence, Brandeis University, Waltham, Mass. Starting with May, 1968, they are publishing the RIOT DATA REVIEW.

310. It is true of course that by our saying Flint is not immune from a riot, we are developing a condition which may precipitate riotous conditions: this is the *self-fulfilling prophecy* principle, that saying makes it so. Just as newspapers reporting the riot fan the the flames of the holocaust, so too any statement of the possibility of riot adds credence to the potential event and makes it an overt speculation. It does not follow from this, however, that newsmen should stop writing of violence nor that social scientists should eschew the study of violence and the conditions which foster it. For a discussion of the self-fulfilling prophecy see R. K. MERTON, SOCIAL THEORY AND SOCIAL STRUCTURE ch. 11 (1957) and Kautsky, *Myth, Self-fulfilling Phophecy, and Symbolic Reassurance in the East-West Conflict*, 9 J. OF CONFLICT RESOLUTION 1-17 (1965). For a lawyer's account of this same point see Ernst, *Free Speech and Civil Disobedience* 3 AM. CRIMINAL L.Q. 15 (1964). Consider the following: "An acute societal pressure in favor of rule by muscle is our mass media, believed by our people either to act from bias, or useable for publicity, the more outlandish the more fruitful." *Id.* at 16.

News coverage may indeed have substantially increased the scope of the Newark and Detroit riots, fanning the flame in a string of towns surrounding the major outbreak. The Mayor of Milwaukee was particularly put out by television coverage of the open housing marches. Newspaper and radio coverage of curfew and liquor bans was not accurate in Detroit according to Det. News, Aug. 3, 1967, § C at 7, cols. 1-5.

Columbia University Graduate School of Journalism held a two-day conference on the mass media and race relations. One conclusion was that reporters had a responsibility not to create a crisis by reporting it out of context. Some thought there was a very real danger of creating "leaders by giving an inordinate amount of TV time" to some colorful spokesmen. *See* NEWSWEEK, Oct. 30, 1967, p. 60. The University of Missouri School of Journalism conference report, RACE AND THE NEWS MEDIA, P. Fisher & R. Lowenstein, eds.

comes militant it is possible Negro mainstream politicians may lose their appeal, especially to young male Negroes, and thereby lose the utility of a group-hero in high places.[311] Mr. Conyers, in other words, must not only be a qualified man trained in democratic procedures and nurtured in non-violent political tactics; he must appeal to Negroes who want to identify with him and respect him.

In sum, the indispensable key to the potential riotous black urban areas is responsible, popular, elected Negro leadership. The courts *ipso facto* abhor violent actions because of their deep-set major juristic premise that the rule of law is a solution for every conceivable community problem; change can always be peaceful and politically manageable because the procedures for change, the political branches, are always available and run by men of good will. On the other hand, politics in America is deeply set with the premise that when a group is denied access to participate in the conduct of statecraft, it becomes necessary to take to the streets. If a group is not adequately represented and counseled with, and cannot correct the wrong, then it is free to do violence to the system. This is the legitimization of violence which was historically traced in Part III. If it is the group's own fault that it is not participating in the official decision-making processes, then violence may erupt but without that violence being meaningful. The efficient and ultimate escape from this violence is neither judicial punishment of the rioters nor legislative punishment for leaders who use interstate commerce to incite riots. The solution must be positive: it must be the development of a democratically oriented and politically sensitive high quality Negro political leadership.

Development, however, takes time.

1967) went to print before the Detroit and Newark riots of 1967 and subsequently deals only with the Watts riot news coverage. The whole topic needs re-thinking.

The VANCE REPORT, *supra* note 171, at 49 carefully points out that rumors are an important element of a riot and could be offset by the identification of authorative sources of information and the development on a priority basis of reliable news bulletins.

311. On the status of increasing Negro militancy by an empirically oriented sociologist see G. MARX, PROTEST AND PREJUDICE: A STUDY OF BELIEF IN THE BLACK COMMUNITY (1967).

The Emerging General Theory of Civil Disobedience Within the Legal Order

ROBERT H. FREILICH*

THE CONCEPTUAL SETTING OF THE PROBLEM

> *The nature of conscience is sometimes to obey and sometimes to disobey. If society is going to exist in dependence upon man's moral nature, on his ability to choose the right course from the wrong—on his conscience—then society is also going to have to recognize man's right and duty to follow his conscience even if this leads to civil disobedience.*[1]
>
> *The use of civil disobedience is a step away from civilization; a step toward the substitution of private for institutional solution of disputes; a step back toward the substitution of violent for non-violent methods of resolving private and public issues. Its use seems particularly anomalous for anyone who is sincerely working for peace.*[2]

CIVIL disobedience is at the center of a maelstrom in contemporary American life. There is no aspect of our national scene which is free from the pervading influence of the forces set in motion by the practice of civil disobedience.[3] Nor, as shown by the conflicting com-

---

* Professor of Law, University of Missouri at Kansas City School of Law; A.B., University of Chicago; LL.B. Yale Law School; M.I.A. Columbia University. The author gratefully acknowledges the help and encouragement of Professor Wolfgang Friedmann, Columbia Law School, Professor Ernest Nagel of Columbia University, and Judge Charles Breitel of the New York Court of Appeals, through the Seminar on Legal Philosophy at Columbia University in which the author participated as a J.S.D. candidate, 1967-1968.

1. Freeman, *Moral Preemption Part I: The Case for the Disobedient*, 17 HASTINGS L.J. 425, 437 (1966).

2. Duffy, *Civil Disobedience*, 40 OHIO BAR, 781, 787 (1967).

3. America today is torn by the conflict in Vietnam which has led to the refusal to pay taxes, the refusal to submit to the draft, conscientious objection, picketing and obstructing of military research and manufacturing firms, "peace" demonstrations, and marches. Students who have played a large role in the anti-Vietnam cause have also participated in free speech movements on campuses across the country, leading in some cases to vulgar excesses (Berkeley filthy speech movement). The racial question has stimulated "sit-ins," "camp-ins," and numerous forms of law-breaking, legal protest, and dissent in combatting legal and social forms of segregation and discrimination in the South and North. The cities have seen the refusal of poverty groups to submit to the intolerable conditions of slum life leading to rent-strikes against bad housing, and demonstrations against welfare and police abuses. In medical science grave questions of civil disobedience have arisen in connection with birth control and contraception, abortions, heart and organ transplants, unauthorized autopsies and euthanasia. The list is by no means exclusive.

See on the student protest movement: Newfield, *The New Student Radicals*, CURRENT, July, 1965; LIPSET & WOLIN, THE BERKELEY REVOLT (1965); *Hearings, Subcommittee of the Judiciary Committee, U.S. Senate*, 89th Cong., at 17, May 17, 1965. On the extension of civil rights civil disobedience to all forms of American behavior, *see* OPPENHEIMER &

ments of both legal and non-legal writers on the subject, can one readily discern any agreement on what civil disobedience is; what its effect will be on democratic society and institutions; and finally what place it has within the structure of our legal order.[4] To some civil disobedience represents a resort to violent means of resolving disputes; to others its very definition excludes violence as having a place; some see it as a calling upon conscience, morality, and higher law; while others believe that the concept embodies only the destruction of the public order and disrespect for law. In attempting to resolve antinomies created by the interlocking values of order and justice, dogmatic answers are given which have little relationship to the ceaseless change of law in response to underlying moral and social values.[5]

The recent death of the Reverend Dr. Martin Luther King has focused attention as never before on the value and meaning of civil disobedience in American life. Threatened by the chaos of urban riots, the preachings of black militants, and the terrorism of white racists, millions of Americans may now understand Dr. King's message that only through nonviolent action can the ever deepening stream of violence, discrimination, and hatred in American life be diverted and altered. The followers of Dr. King now appear more ready than ever to continue his work[6] and to participate meaningfully in marches and

---

LAKEN, A MANUAL FOR DIRECT ACTION, STRATEGY AND TACTICS FOR CIVIL RIGHTS AND ALL OTHER NON-VIOLENT PROTEST MOVEMENTS (1965); on the extension of the protest movement to the slum and housing conditions of the cities, *see Tenant Rent Strikes*, 3 COLUM. J. of L. AND SOCIAL PROBLEMS 1 (1967).

On the moral, ethical, legal and sociological considerations of medical transplants, innovations, and genetic experiments, public hearings were held in Washington, D.C. on March 8, 1968, by the Senate Government Research Subcommittee. Dr. Christian Barnard, the noted South African heart specialist testified at the hearings that the ethics of organ transplants must be left to the medical profession. "You are seeing ghosts where there are no ghosts." New York Times, Mar. 9, 1968, at 3, col. 6.

4. Allen, Civil Disobedience and the Legal Order 36 U. CINC. L. REV. 1-38, 175-195 (1967). Dean Allen of the University of Michigan Law School in his recent articles has made a penetrating and scholarly review of the conflicts and problems in coming to grips with the concept and practice of civil disobedience. The diversity of responses are also well represented by numerous legal articles: *From Seisin to Sit-In*, 44 BUFF. L. REV. 435 (1964); *Civil Disobedience-A Threat to Our Law Society* 51 A.B.A.J. 645 (1965); *Civil Disobedience and the Law, A Symposium*, 3 AM. CRIM. L. Q. 11 (1964); *Is There A Jurisprudence of Civil Disobedience?* 5 ILL. C.L.E. 71 (1967); *Right of Protest and Civil Disobedience* 41 IND. L.J. 228 (1966); *Civil Rights Yes—Civil Disobedience No.*, 13 LA. B.J. 229 (1966); *Riots of 1964, The Causes of Racial Violence*, 40 N. D. LAW. 552 (1965); *Demonstrators and A Constitutional Rule of Law* 14 U.C.L.A. L. REV. 454 (1967); *Law, Speech & Disobedience* 202 THE NATION 357 (1966).

5. A writer in the *New Yorker* magazine once wrote that in passing by a small church outside of London, he noticed a sign containing the thought for the day: "Between scepticism on the one hand and dogmatism on the other hand, there is a middle way, which is our way, open minded certainty." A great deal of what is written about civil disobedience will conform to this clever and witty aphorism.

6. New York Times, Ap. 6, 1968, at 25. col.1. Abernathy Takes Civil Rights Post Held By Dr. King and Pledges Nonviolence.

camp-ins on behalf of the Negro.[7] The President and national leaders have called for and won passage of the 1968 Civil Rights Act which will insure a federal fair housing provision as a testimonial to the contribution that Dr. King's theories have made to the American way of life.[8]

The great question of the utility of civil disobedience has also been brought to light in the ever mounting dissent to the Vietnam War. The United States government has now brought the fundamental moral and philosophical issue of the Vietnam War into the courts. By indicting the Chaplain of Yale University, William Sloane Coffin Jr., Dr. Benjamin Spock, and others for allegedly conspiring to persuade young men to violate the draft laws, the government has raised the question that goes back to Plato and beyond: "How far can the individual go in opposing government"?[9] In fact, the co-defendants make no effort to hide their anti-draft activities. They are deliberately violating the law as a form of anti-war protest and are willing to be imprisoned for expressing their opinions as strongly as they could.[10] The defendants contend that under higher law, the war is morally wrong, and that they are acting within the American constitutional system through non-violent challenge to the war policy.

The question of order and stability raised by civil disobedience is not serious if the non-violent means are confined to small groups of individuals. But where the moral uncertainty of a law or policy has spread to a large segment of society, the question of the efficacy and value of the law itself is raised. In preserving the rule of law a government must adapt its laws to changing social and ethical values. Greater problems arise when the means to challenge a law go beyond civil disobedience, and amount to the use of violence, interference with the rights of third persons and ultimately resistance.

---

7. New York Times, Oct. 24, 1967, at 33, col. 5, Dr. King Suggests 'Camp-In' In Cities.

8. Hunter, *Dr. King's Death Is Expected to Spur Rights Bill*, N.Y. Times, Ap. 6, 1968 at 25, col. 6.

9. Reston, *The Legal and Moral Issues of the War*, N.Y. Times, Sunday, Jan. 7, 1968.

10. Graham, *The Law, Case Against Spock et al.*, N.Y. Times, Jan. 14, 1968, at 8E col. 1. The defendants are charged with violating the Selective Service Act of 1940 which makes it a felony, punishable by up to five years imprisonment, to hinder the administration of the draft law or to counsel or aid and abet a draft registrant to violate his duties under the draft law. Similar prosecutions were made of Eugene V. Debs in W. W. I and Dean Larry Gara of Bluffton College during the Korean War. Legally, draft protesters may not appeal to the constitution since the Supreme Court decision in *Schenck v. United States* 249 U.S. 47 (1919) when Justice Holmes, speaking for a unanimous court, said that such activities constitute "a clear and present danger" and are not protected by the First Amendment. *But see* United States v. O'Brien, 36 U.S.L. Week 4469 (1968) dissenting opinion of Douglas J. that such activity is not proscribed during peacetime.
During W. W. I, 3, 989 men refused to be conscripted, including Professor Mackintosh of the Yale Divinity School, to fight in "unjust" wars and were confined to military imprison-

Commentators have stated that the practice of civil disobedience will in fact lead to the use of these extreme forms of behavior antithetical to a democratic system.[11] Equally cogent arguments are made that if we suppress the use of civil disobedience and resort to conscience and morality in opposing existing law, the frustrations and tensions of the people opposing the laws will be diverted instead to the very forms of resistance society seeks to avoid.[12] If reforms are inevitable to preserve society, and if the lawful forms of dissent may not be adequate to disturb or raise the conscience of the public to reform the laws, then perhaps the resort to civil disobedience looms large as a tool to evoke change in a democratic society.

The danger of resistance is a real one. In recent months the frustrations over the war in Vietnam have led many to ignore civil disobedience and instead proceed directly from "dissent to resistance."[13] Thus, recent incidents have involved the use of masses of students and "mobile tactics" to interfere with draft centers, divert the needs of thousands of police, and stop the Secretary of State from speaking in New York;[14] while in other incidents priests and ministers have poured blood on Baltimore draft files.[15]

Yet by no means are the majority of Americans, including students, who oppose the war in Vietnam, predisposed towards resistance as a solution. In a recent poll of Harvard University seniors, 22 percent of those polled stated they would leave the country or go to jail rather than be inducted, while 61 percent said they would serve if they could

---

ment and encampment. J. W. Holmes, *Disobedience To Law, Is it Ever Justifiable*, The Community Pulpit, Series 1929-1930, No. 10.

11. *See* note 49 infra.

12. *See* note 19 infra.

13. Reston, *Washington: From Dissent to Resistance*, New York Times, Nov. 1, 1967:

> The trend of the young militants in American Politics is now clearly moving from peaceful dissent to physical resistance. The large majority of protesting university students may still be satisfied with legal demonstrations but the minority militants are not and increasingly the minority is trying to substitute violent defiance for the majority's peaceful disobedience.

14. *See* flyer, From Dissent to Resistance, Nov. 20, 1967, Sponsored by The Resistance at Columbia University, calling for mobile tactics on "Stop the Draft Week" at the New York draft center, Dec. 4-8, 1967, a tactic that failed but led to sporadic acts of violence and the diverting of thousands of police.

See New York Times, Oct. 24, 1967, at 1, col. 1, reciting the blocking of military research sites by students:

> To many of the students the tactic of physically blocking the institute's entrance signified their feeling that opponents of American foreign policy must move "from dissent to resistance" a theme enunciated frequently by leaders of the Washington demonstration—"We have realized how little influence people have on decisions made in their name" said one student, "People have seen that acts of dissent have not fazed the government in the slightest".

See New York Times, Nov. 10, 1967, Bigart—"Leaders of Rusk Demonstration,—the resistance activists—were controlled at the outset by marshals who wore blue and orange armbands and commands were passed through a bullhorn."

15. New York Times, Oct. 28, 1967, at 5, col. 3.

find no legitimate way of avoiding the draft.[16] Similar findings have been made of the Negro community in their attitudes toward urban riots.[17]

While the general view is that this is a serious but transitory phenomenon which will ease when the war ends, others view it as a fundamental challenge to our social order. They propose a politics of stability, and encourage those who are seeking a new set of priorities to employ civil disobedience in resisting the status quo. We must not lead our younger generation into an abyss by failing to provide alternative solutions to resistance and by refusing to recognize sincere moral and conscientious objection to our legal and social norms. The question has been raised: "How can you put morality into criminal law, if you make criminals out of those who most actively follow conscience?"[18]

It will be the purpose of this article to cut away much of the overgrowth of confusion in this area and to delineate both definitionally and from emerging practice and legal institutions, the nature of civil disobedience and its relationship to the legal order. One can trace the beginnings of a general theory of civil disobedience within the legal order vis-à-vis the universally accepted precondition that every legal order must contain a minimum but essential degree of efficacy and societal acceptance. The boundaries and limitations of the doctrine are shaped on the one hand by the expanding concept of lawful dissent and constitutionally protected civil liberties, and on the other hand by the practical limitations of morality, conscience and non-violence—its essential attributes.

Definitions of Civil Disobedience

In a recent article, thirteen writers, philosophers and sociologists could come to no common agreement on a definition of civil disobedience.[19] The closest thread that runs through the discussion is that civil disobedience is to be distinguished from "dissent" and lawful agitation and argument on the one hand, and "resistance," including covert and surreptitious actions and the provocation and perpetration of violence, on the other hand. Civil disobedience must also be distinguished from a dissociation from society. It constitutes a violation of a legal norm, rule or regulation in the specific sense rather than a

16. New York Times, Jan. 15, 1967.

17. Report of the National Commission on Civil Disorders 128 (Bantam Books, Inc. ed. 1968); *See also After the Riots: A Survey*, Newsweek, Aug. 21, 1967 at 18-19.

18. *Clark v. United States* 236 F.2d 13 (9th Cir. 1955), *cert. den.* 352 U.S. 882 (1956); Freeman, *A Remonstrance for Conscience,* 106 U. Pa. L. Rev. 806 (1958).

19. *A Baker's Dozen of Writers Comment On Civil Disobedience*, 1967, New York Times, Nov. 26, 1967, at 27 (Magazine).

rejection of the system as a whole. In that sense it is a paradox for one purports to act in the general good to remove a law that has as its own warrant supposed utility for the greater good.[20]

The paradox is further heightened by the general agreement that while the legal system cannot logically permit law breaking,[21] the term civil disobedience can have meaning only if one generally assumes that the system itself, as distinguished from the norm disobeyed, is entitled to obedience.[22] Therefore, it cannot be immediately assumed that the question is one of morals only and not of law. A democracy cannot be maintained by passive obedience to all law[23] nor by men unwilling to take to the streets when ordinary debate is discouraged or ineffectual.[24]

Civil disobedience can, therefore, be defined as the deliberate and open violation of law with intent, within the framework of existing government to protest a wrong or accomplish some betterment in society.[25] This definition is usually supplemented by the appeal of the disobedient to either natural law,[26] religious belief,[27] morality or con-

---

20. Keeton, *The Morality of Civil Disobedience*, 43 TEX. L. REV. 507 (1965)

21. Brown, *Civil Disobedience*, 58 J. PHILOSOPHY 669, 672 (1961).

22. *Supra* note 19 at 128, *Civil Disobedience is Justified by Vietnam* by Herbert C. Kelman.

23. *See* BOUCHER, ON CIVIL LIBERTY, PASSIVE OBEDIENCE AND NONRESISTANCE, A VIEW OF THE CAUSES AND CONSEQUENCES OF THE AMERICAN REVOLUTION 496 (1797) [Reprinted in I THE PEOPLE SHALL JUDGE 173 (1945); GUSTAV RADBRUCH, RECHTSPHILOSOPHIE, THE LEGAL PHILOSOPHIES OF LASK, RADBRUCH AND DABIN, 224, (1950). In both cases an earlier view that "the law is the law" and justified absolute obedience to the positive law, was proved historically incorrect and Radbruch subsequently came to recognize the need for certain enactments to give way to justice, through the use of disobedience and even resistance, citing as his example the moral lawlessness of the positive laws enacted by the Nazi government in Germany.

24. Walter Lippmann, *N.Y. Herald Tribune*, Oct. 26, 1965, at 26 col. 6: "When debate by those who have a right to know is discouraged we must not be surprised that these great matters are then taken to the teach-ins and into the streets".

See also, THE OCCASIONAL SPEECHES OF JUSTICE OLIVER WENDELL HOLMES 6-7 Howe ed. 1962): "A man must share the passion and action of his time at the peril of being judged not to have lived."

25. Keeton, *supra* note 20 at 508; Allen, *supra* note 4 at 9. MILLER, NON-VIOLENCE—A CHRISTIAN INTERPRETATION, 71 (1964) "Civil disobedience or civil resistance is a form of non-violent direct action that involves breaking the law."

26. *See* Cohen, *The Essence and Ethics of Civil Disobedience*, The Nation, Mar. 16, 1964, 257, 260:

> It [natural law] has its roots deep in the history of Western thought—in Cicero and Aquinas and Hooker and Grotius and Locke, in Jefferson and a host of others who have sought to justify conduct by virtue of its harmony with some antecedently established superhuman moral law, usually divine.

See also MacGuigan *Civil Disobedience and Natural Law*, 11 CATH. LAW. 118 (1965) an excellent source for the historical and philosophical background of civil disobedience, commencing with Plato (death of Socrates), Aristotle, the Maccabees, Sts. Augustine and Aquinas, the middle ages and the modern church. MacGuigan states that the positivist is concerned by hypothesis with the validity and legality of law, not its efficacy. "In that sense the question of obedience to law is solely for the natural lawyer." *See also, Contemporary Civil Disobedience: Selected Early and Modern Viewpoints*, 41 IND. L. J. 477 (1966).

27. KELSEN, WHAT IS JUSTICE, (1957). Of the concept of love thy enemy, forming the central theme of the New Testament and around which the moral justification for denying the positive law is based, Kelsen states:

science,[28] or the invalidity of the challenged law under a higher statute, constitutional mandate[29] or international legal norm.[30] In this definition we stress the following elements: 1.) we are not dealing with evasion of the law, for the conduct must be open and public in order to appeal to the conscience of the community;[31] 2.) there must be an insistence on moral justification and conscience, with rational objectives larger than narrow self-interest;[32] 3.) the intent is not to foster lawlessness, but to uphold the legal order and employ all the democratic procedures of dissent, protest, and redress of grievances;[33] 4.) the violator must be willing to accept legal punishment which not only dramatizes the alleged wrong, but invokes the community's sense of injustice;[34] and 5.) all forms of violence and interference with rights of third persons must be avoided.[35]

> This is indeed a revolutionary doctrine. Not only because it is incompatible with the existing law but because the demand to love one's enemy is beyond human nature and the love of God is justice only in a transcendental sense. From the point of view of human reason, Jesus' teaching is not a solution of the problem of justice as a problem of a social technique for the regulation of human relations; it is rather the dissolution of this problem. For it implies the request to abandon the desire for justice as conceived of by man.

28. Freeman, *Civil Liberties—Acid Test of Democracy*, 43 MINN. L. REV. 511 (1959); Freeman, *A Remonstrance for Conscience* 106 U. PA. L. REV. 806 (1958).

29. Black, *The Compatibility of Civil Disobedience* 43 TEX. L. REV. 492 (1965); PRACTICING LAW INSTITUTE, THE COMMUNITY AND RACIAL CRISES (1966) at 89, McKay, *Laws Governing Demonstrations and Other Forms of Protest.*

30. *See* Freeman, *The Case for the Disobedient*, 17 HASTINGS L. J. 425, 427 (1966) in which a brief sketch is drawn of the principles of international law emanating from the Nuremberg trials. *See United States v. Ohlendorf* 4 TRIALS OF WAR CRIMINALS BEFORE THE NUREMBERG MILITARY TRIBUNALS 1 (1949).

31. The most famous American civil disobedient, Henry David Thoreau wrote:

> No citizen need resign his conscience to the legislator. The only obligation which I have a right to assume is to do at any time what I think right—A very few—men serve the state with their consciences also and so necessarily resist it for the most part.

THOREAU, ON CIVIL DISOBEDIENCE (1847), in AESTHETIC PAPERS 189-211 (Elizabeth P. Peabody, ed. 1849).

32. "Those only can take up civil disobedience, who believe in willing obedience even to irksome laws imposed by the state so long as they do not hurt their conscience or religion and are prepared equally willingly to suffer the penalty of civil disobedience." M. K. Ghandhi, Young India, Nov. 3, 1921. *See also* Lovell, *Direct Action*, New Left Review, London, Mar.-Apr. 1961, at 16: "If you do an act of civil disobedience, are prepared to go to jail or take some kind of personal risk, you show that there is something more serious to the business than being just out for your own ends."
For an outstanding exposition on the role of conscience in the history of civil disobedience, see Freeman, *A Remonstrance for Conscience.* 106 U. PA. L. REV. 806 (1958).

33. McKay, *Protest and Dissent*, UTAH L. REV. 20 (1966).

34. From Plato's description of Socrates willingness to pay even the price of death for his civil disobedience to the present day of Mahatma Ghandhi, the conscientious lawbreaker is not only willing but glad to pay the penalty of his act in witness of the truth which he would serve: "By paying the penalty we give an obedience to the law not less exacting than that of conformity to its terms. By disobeying and accepting the penalty, we recognize the authority of the government." J. H. Holmes, Disobedience to Law, Is It Ever Justifiable? The Community Pulpit, Series 1929-1930, No. 10.

35. Dwight MacDonald, *Legal Protest Is No Longer Tactically Effective*, *supra* note 13 at 130: "The limits of civil disobedience? By definition they fall short of violence, since it is an illegal tactic within the framework of, if not legality, at least the civis, an attempt

In finding the place of civil disobedience in the legal order some importance must be attached to the ways in which conscientious law violation may be practiced. If law violation were to be continuously and irrationally applied it would destroy the system itself. Consequently, the methods which are adopted must be suitable to the purpose intended.[36] Civil disobedience has been associated throughout history with movements of non-violence and the use of non-violent coercion to obtain ends.[37]

The various forms of non-violence have been classified as:[38]

Persuasion

1. By Argument.
2. By Suffering: (a) inflicted by opponent (non-resistant martyrdom) (b) self-inflicted (hunger strike).

Non Violent Coercion

1. Indirect Action:—withdrawal from voluntary cooperation with opponent (strike, boycott, non-cooperation).
2. Political Actions Through Institutions and Culture—combining partisan persuasion and impersonal coercion of law and established traditions. This involves the threat of force or "legitimated violence" by courts, police, etc.
3. Social Coercion: (a) ostracism; (b) collective pressure through passive resistance.

Most of these forms of non-violence are perfectly compatible with maintenance of the legal order. Ghandhi himself recognized that passive resistance or non-cooperation was more passive than civil disobedience, which he characterized as the performing of acts to compel a response by a dominant group, where it takes the form of arrest and/or violation of law.[39] Ghandhi distinguished his form of civil disobedience, "satyagraha" (love-force) from orthodox passive resistance which he claimed was based on simple expedience (the eschewing of violence because of mere lack of numbers).[40] Civil disobedience aims at the securing of rights by the suffering of the resister—not of the persons resisted. It is through the moral transference to society at

---

to demonstrate to our fellow citizens, that our common interests demand such a repudiation of the letter in order to preserve the spirit."

36. "Civil disobedience is a very potent weapon. But everyone cannot wield it. For that one needs training and inner strength. It requires occasions for its use." I PYARELAL, MAHATMA GHANDHI, THE LAST PHASE 25 (1956).

37. MILLER, NON-VIOLENCE—A CHRISTIAN INTERPRETATION (1964).

38. C. CASE, NON-VIOLENT COERCION 397 (1923). For similar references see SEIFERT, CONQUEST BY SUFFERING, THE PROCESS AND PROSPECTS OF NON-VIOLENT RESISTANCE (1965) and LYND, NON-VIOLENCE IN AMERICA, A DOCUMENTARY HISTORY (1966).

39. MacGuigan, *Civil Disobedience and Natural Law* 11 CATH. LAW. 118 (1965).

40. KUPER, PASSIVE RESISTANCE IN SOUTH AFRICA (1956).

large that the purposes are achieved short of any breakdown of the social order.[41]

Associated with the concept of civil disobedience is the correlative notion of obedience to the state, and in a democratic state to the rule of law.[42] The necessity of political obedience arises from man's need to live with his fellows. Since social life is an essential condition of existence, so too is obedience to the rules whereby that social life is made possible. Law and order are but the minima of social requirements, and individual decisions violating these requirements cannot be permitted. But modern man demands that the state secure obedience only to the degree that governmental decisions embody the largest possible measure of social experience based upon satisfaction of needs. This view emphasizes the duty of the state in securing obedience. Thus, while stability and order are essential for peaceful allegiance, obedience can only be enforced when the mass of society is in some sort of agreement with the law.[43] The desire for peaceful government is not one, however, that will be satisfied at any cost. There may come a time when men are willing to endure disobedience and disorder rather than continue to submit to the denial of their claims.[44] Constitutional government can never be an end in itself—it commands obedience only so long as its blessings are not too high a price for law and order, and where the latter are deemed necessary at any cost, men will respond.[45]

It is as a safety valve for the democratic system, where frustrations and discriminations exist which cannot be redressed in the normal course of events, that civil disobedience emerges as a viable alternative to violence and revolution. Failing this choice and leaving open only lawful forms of dissent may not lead to reform soon enough.[46] With

---

41. MacGuigan, *supra* note 39.

42. "The case for the rule of law needs no more elaborate defense than does the case for civilization." Allen, *supra* note 4 at 14.

43. XI ENCYCLOPEDIA OF THE SOCIAL SCIENCES, *Political Disobedience* 415 (1963).

44. H. LASKI, THE STATE IN THE NEW SOCIAL ORDER (1922).

45. Dickinson, *Social Order and Political Authority*, 23 AMERICAN POLI. SCI. REV. 293 (1929).

46. In FREEDOMS, COURTS, POLITICS AND STUDIES IN CIVIL LIBERTIES 233 (1965), Lucius J. Barker recites the following segments of speeches by President Kennedy:

> Speech, June 19, 1963
> "The venerable code of equity law commands "for every wrong, a remedy." But in too many communities, in too many parts of the country, wrongs are inflicted on Negro citizens for which no effective remedy of law is clearly and readily available. State and local laws may even affirmatively seek to deny the rights to which these citizens are fairly entitled—and this can result only in decreased respect for the law and increased violations of law—In short the result of continued inaction will cause leadership to pass from the hands of reasonable and responsible men to the purveyors of hate and violence, endangering domestic tranquility . . . .
> Speech, June 11, 1963
> "Difficulties over segregation and discrimination exist in every city, in every State of the Union, producing in many cities a rising tide of discontent that threatens

this in mind we can now explore civil disobedience within the American system.

The Emerging Theory

The Legal Order and Social Effectiveness

For those writers who see society as relatively stable and operating within a well-defined system of positive laws, civil disobedience usually constitutes an immediate danger to society threatening the breakdown of law and order. It acts as a stimulus to violence and is a denial of basic democratic operative procedure. Lawyers constantly ask—at what point will civil disobedience stop once its force is put into motion?[47] The overwhelming body of American lawyers are disposed to deny any validity to a theory of civil disobedience within the legal order.[48] An authority has described this position as one of Gertrude Stein logic—a law, is a law, is a law—[49] but the viewpoint is expressed with serious alarm for the maintenance of our institutions and liberty.[50]

In analyzing the problem in this manner considerable difficulty is engendered by a failure to recognize that the legal order is not one which exists independently of the moral and social values of society.[51] Though lawyers generally agree that the law is subject to change, most tend to assert that its reform, while inevitable, should proceed

---

> public safety. We are confronted primarily with a moral issue and it is as clear as the American constitution . . . .

See also MYRDAHL, THE AMERICAN DILEMMA (1944) for a brilliant study of the conflict between American ideals and conscience and the failure of the rule of law to bring justice to the Negro.

47. PRACTICING LAW INSTITUTE, THE COMMUNITY AND RACIAL CRISES (1966), *Laws Governing Racial Demonstrations and Other Forms of Protest* by Robert McKay, at 89.

48. *See* Powell, *A Lawyer Looks at Civil Disobedience*, 23 WASH. & LEE L. REV. 205 (1966); Whittaker, *Will Civil Disobedience Lead to Chaos in Our Society*, TRIAL, 10 (Dec.-Jan. 1965); and other articles by nationally known lawyers and jurists: Leibman, *Civil Disobedience: A Threat to our Law Society* 51 A.B.A.J. 645 (1965); Freund, *Civil Rights and the Limits of Law*, 14 BUFFALO L. REV. 199 (1964); Tweed, Segal & Packer, *Civil Rights and Disobedience to Law, A Lawyer's View* 36 N.Y.S.B.J. 290 (1964), Waldman, *Civil Rights—Yes; Civil Disobedience—No*, 37 N.Y.S.B.J. 331 (1965); Fuchsberg, Editorial in TRIAL 8 (Dec.-Jan. 1965).

49. Freeman, *Moral Preemption Part I: The Case for the Disobedient*, 17 HASTINGS L.J. 425 (1966).

50. Powell, *A Lawyer Looks at Civil Disobedience*, 23 WASH. & LEE L. REV. 205, 231 (1966): "History has demonstrated that once a society condones organized defiance of law and due process, it becomes increasingly difficult to protect its institutions and to safeguard liberty."

51. *See* Smith, *The Development of the Right of Assembly—A Current Socio—Legal Investigation*, 9 WM. & MARY L. REV. 359, 376 (1967):

> Order, viewed from the standpoint of sociology, has its roots not in a universal law of nature, nor in the establishment of a form of recognized external authority, but instead, in the very social experience of the individual himself.

See also LANDIS, SOCIAL CONTROL 24-35 (1939); *See generally* Benoit—Smullyan, Status, Status Types and Status Interpretation 9 Am. Soc. Rev. 151 (1944).

within the orderly processes of the legal system.[52] Ordinarily the antinomy between order and justice[53] results in common agreement that the preservation of order is necessary before any other values of life can be achieved.[54] The proposition that a system of rule by law is to be preferred to a system of private use by force is likely to find few opponents.[55]

The meaning of "rule of law", however, is far from clear. Those who are most vague about its meaning often regard the rule of law as an absolute necessity that must be preserved at all costs; whereas those who attempt to clarify the meaning seldom express either alarm about inroads into the rule of law or the possibilities for enlarging its role.[56]

One of the earliest positivists in English jurisprudence, Austin, avoided the circuity of defining law by law, since his central concept of law was that of a sovereign issuing commands, the effectiveness of which lay not in brute strength or power, but in a habit of obedience of the bulk of society.[57] From this principle of effectiveness, Austin and his followers were disturbed by the possibility of a lack of obedience in the event of conflict between law and morality: "Here we touch upon the most difficult of questions. If the law is not what it ought to be; if it openly combats the principle of utility, ought we to obey it? Ought we to violate it?"[58]

---

52. *See* Hart, The Concept of Law 89 (1961), for a discussion of the rules of recognition, the attributes of the legal system which develop the institutional machinery for judicial process, the creation of rules and change.

53. Hall, *From Legal Theory to Integrative Jurisprudence*, 33 U. Cinn. L. Rev. 153, 172 (1964).

54. Thus Hart, in *Positivism and the Separation of Law and Morals*, 71 Harv. L. Rev. 593, 622-623 (1958) states: "Such rules [forbidding the use of violence, establishing order and constituting the minimum forms of property] are so fundamental that if a legal system did not have them there would be no point in having any other rules at all."

55. Davis, Administrative Treatise, § 1.08 *Supremacy of Law or Rule of Law* (1958).

Aristotle was the one of the first to uphold this principle: "The rule of law is preferable to that of any individual." III Politics 139 (Davis ed. 1916).

"If the rule of law is a synonym for law and order, most states have achieved it and it is a universally recognized principle." Jennings, The Law and the Constitution 44 (4th ed., 1952).

The principle has been recognized by our Supreme Court:

> But from their very own experience and their deep reading in history, the Founders knew that Law alone saves a society from being rent by internecine strife or ruled by mere brute power, however, disguised. Civilization involves subjection of force to reason and the agency of this subjection is law.

Frankfurter, J., concurring in *United States v. United Mine Workers* 330 U.S. 258 (1947).

56. Davis, *supra* note 55 at 53.

57. Austin, The Province of Jurisprudence Determined (Library of Ideas ed. 1954). Thus Fuller in *American Legal Philosophy at Mid-Century* 6 J. Leg. Ed. 457, 581-585 states that Austin believed in "rule backed force" rather than "force backed rules" *see* I Austin, Lectures on Jurisprudence 276 (1879).

58. Bentham, Principles of Legislation, The Theory of Legislation 65 (Ogden ed. 1931); Markby, Elements of Law 4-5 (5th ed. 1896) states:

> Austin's followers also saw clearly the necessity for morals. Positive laws, as Austin has shown, must be legally binding, and yet a law may be unjust—he has

Austin, accordingly, called upon judges and legislators to respond to the growing needs of society as revealed by the standard of utility to better keep the rule of law within the willing obedience of the citizenry.[59]

Legal theorists have tended to deprecate the position of the positivists as being ethically neutral and divorced from reality.[60] Sociological jurists have generally been more interested in the law's efficacy than have natural jurists, but both attack the empty formalism or validity of the law of the positivists.[61] MacGuigan states:

> Efficacy and justice . . . are concerned with the content of a legal rule: a law is efficacious when it is actually being obeyed by the people whose conduct it aims to govern, and it is just when it should be obeyed by them. . . . [Thus for the natural lawyer] the ultimate question . . . "what is law?" has as a counterpart . . . "should this law be obeyed?" For the most part philosophers do not contest whether disobedience is legitimate—only to determine when it is legitimate and when it is not."[62]

Present day natural law philosophers tend generally to believe that there are too many precedents to deny the ethical, spiritual, and moral validity of civil disobedience. The popular attitude that exalts peace and order in society almost as an absolute, expressing strong disapproval of any form of disobedience to lawful authority, is emphatically rejected.

Modern theorists now accept the principle that a valid law must be efficacious and constitute a positive norm of the legal order. Thus, the refusal to recognize a law may render such a law or the legal system ineffective, just as custom may be a tool in creating law.[63]

---

admitted that law itself may be immoral in which case it is our moral duty to disobey it.

59. II AUSTIN, LECTURES ON JURISPRUDENCE 641 (5th ed. 1885). Thus Hart in his article, *Positivism and the Separation of Law and Morals,* 71 HARV. L. REV. 593 (1958) disputes the view taken by other contemporary legal theorists—Fuller, *Human Purpose and Natural Law* 53 J. PHILOSOPHY 697 (1953); Brecht, *The Myth of Is and Ought,* 54 HARV. L. REV. 811 (1941) and Friedmann, LEGAL THEORY 294-95 (3d ed. 1953)—that Austin spoke only for the authority of the national state and that his theories weakened resistance to state tyranny. *See* RADBRUCH, DIE ERNEUERUNG DES RECHTS 595 (1947). Hart states, in fact, that Austin did understand the nature of law as having its roots in the social life and obedience of the people.

60. STONE, THE PROVINCE AND FUNCTION OF LAW 49 (1950), but this position has been sharply controverted. *See* Morison, *Some Myths About Positivism,* 68 YALE L.J. 212 (1958).

61. MacGuigan, *Civil Disobedience and Natural Law,* 52 KY. L.J. 346 (1964).

62. *Id.*

63. KELSEN, THE GENERAL THEORY OF LAW AND STATE (1961). An attack upon the "basic" norm would be revolution (at 118) yet Kelsen states as his "principle of minimum effectiveness":

> Every single norm loses its validity when the total legal order to which it belongs loses its efficacy as a whole. The efficacy of the entire legal order is a necessary condition for the validity of every single norm of the order. (119)—

Within the legal system there is a constant conflict between the norms and their acceptance. Fuller has simply stated that the stability of a legal system requires the laymen's acceptance of the rules as being essentially right.[64] In subsequent writing Fuller has been even more emphatic:

> All this amounts to saying that to be effective . . . a written constitution must be accepted, at least provisionally not just as law but as good law. . . . [T]o be effective it requires not merely the respectful deference we show for an ordinary legal enactment but that willing convergence of effort we give to principles in which we have an active belief.[65]

American legal theorists have long accepted the wedding of law to social reality. Holmes' admonition that the law is founded on experience, not logic, was followed by the social engineering of Pound, the doctrines of the legal realists and functionalists of the thirties, and those who espouse the social development of law today.[66] Whether the formulation of law be considered the product of actual observance, growth of customs and the living law of groups and communities as espoused by Savigny and Ehrlich, or as the authoritative commands or hierarchies of the positivists, as theorized by Kelsen and Austin, the differences are only relative and each stresses the fundamental concept of the efficacy of the law.[67] The legal system thus finds itself in a movement between maximum and minimum morality and social values—between incorporation into law of those moral conditions which are crucial to the survival of the legal structure and the transformation of all or most of the social norms of the community into legal norms.[68]

> Within a legal order which is itself efficacious there may occur isolated norms which are valid and which are not efficacious, that is are not obeyed and not applied even when the conditions which they themselves lay down for their application are fulfilled. But even in this case efficacy has some relevance to validity. If the norm remains permanently inefficacious, the norm is deprived of its validity by 'desuetudo'. 'Desuetudo' is the negative legal effect of custom. A norm may be annulled by custom, viz., by a custom contrary to the norm, as well as it may be created by custom.—Thus a norm is a valid legal norm if—(b) it has not been annulled either in a way provided for by that legal order or by way of desuetudo or by the fact that the legal order as a whole has lost its efficacy.

64. FULLER, THE LAW IN QUEST OF ITSELF 90-91 (1940).

65. Fuller, *Positivism and Fidelity to Law*, 71 HARV. L. REV. 630, 642 (1958).

66. *See* Pound, *The Need for a Sociological Jurisprudence* 19 GREEN BAG 607 (1907); Dror, *Prolegomon to a Social Study of Law* 13 J. LEG. ED. 131 (1961); CARDOZO, THE GROWTH OF THE LAW (1924). Fuller has in fact equated the American legal realists as the inheritors of the Austininian tradition. FULLER, THE LAW IN QUEST OF ITSELF 45 (1940). As to the modern approach:

> The common characteristic of the approach was and remains the view that—the law—cannot begin and end with the logical deduction of general principles from the judicial opinions of decided cases. Law is an instrument of social change as well as for social stability. Goldstein, *Educational Planning at Yale*, 21 U. MIAMI L. REV. 520 (1967).

67. FRIEDMANN, LEGAL THEORY 15 (5th ed. 1967).

68. Strawson, *Social Morality and Individual Ideal* 37 J. PHILOSOPHY 1 (1961).

The principle of efficacy therefore impels the conclusion that when there are serious cleavages between groups in society and the existing legal order, the very preservation of order and integrity may require that civil disobedience be considered as a viable alternative to violent resistance. For unlike violence, resistance, or revolution, which deny the legitimacy of the system itself, civil disobedience seeks change within the system to make it truly efficacious for all of society. Civil disobedience only denies the legitimacy or application of specific laws, policies, or practices within the framework of the existing system. Those who engage in civil disobedience are usually deeply committed to the values on which the system is based, regarding various laws and actions as unlawful precisely because they are inconsistent with these values and procedures.[69]

The relationship of civil disobedience to law, morality, and social change has been well stated by Professor Wolfgang Friedmann in his latest work on legal theory:

> Unless a minimum of conformity between legal order and social effectiveness is maintained by the various processes of legal evolution, a revolution will ultimately destroy the existing legal order and substitute a new one. When the feudal order that tied peasants to the land was no longer acceptable, the peasants fled to the free cities and eventually the feudal order collapsed. When a majority of Negroes no longer accepts legal, economic or social inferiority to a white minority within a legal order and the change of the legal system through legislative, administrative and judicial reforms fails to keep pace with the change of moral pressure, a revolution will ultimately displace the former order.[70]

Lawyers too often fail to understand that certain crucial issues are not simply legally oriented, but involve moral and social question of the highest order. The law itself must be adaptable to accommodate the demands of these interests while preserving the values of which the law itself is the guardian.

---

69. *See* Kelman, *Civil Disobedience Is Justified by Vietnam*, N.Y. Times, Nov. 26, 1967, at 128 (Magazine). William Buckley, writing in the same issue has suggested "deportation" as the solution for the individual's right to refuse to go along with his community, reminding us of the statement that Plato has Socrates make: "If any man of the Athenians is dissatisfied with us, he may take his good and go away whithersoever he pleases; we give that permission to every man (Crito, XIII)." It is unlikely that such solutions are seriously offered for our Negro population or other substantial dissatisfied elements of our population. *See Contemporary Civil Disobedience: Selected Early and Modern Viewpoints* 41 Ind. L.J. 477, 482 (1966). It seems that the efficacy of the law must be resolved within our own system.

70. Friedmann, *supra* note 67 at 44.

Alternatives to Violence

An underlying criticism of civil disobedience is the blanket condemnation that its use leads directly to, and, is a primary cause of, riot, violence, and disorder. A characteristic statement of this position follows:

> Possibly the most serious aspect of the expanding use of protest methods in the name of civil disobedience is the resulting incitement to mob violence. No one knows the extent to which the doctrine of disobedience, and especially the widespread resort to the streets, has contributed to the general deterioration of respect for law and order and specificially to major outbreaks—such as riots in Harlem, Rochester, Philadelphia, Chicago and Watts. Yet few objective observers would deny that the contribution has been significant. . . . Can we reasonably expect throngs in the streets to understand and observe subtle differences between peaceful protest, disorderly conduct and mob violence.[71]

One of the difficulties inherent in statements of this genre is that they are usually based on similar unsupported statements in other newspapers and periodicals.[72] Yet the general evidence of American history furnishes support for the opposite conclusion that violence, resistance, and rebellion have long been a trait of the American people and that civil disobedience may offer a clear alternative to the resort to violence as a solution to legal and social reforms.

Riots and rebellions have occurred many times in American history[73] quite independently of any widespread notions of civil diso-

---

71. Powell, *A Lawyer Looks at Civil Disobedience*, 23 WASH. & LEE L. REV. 205, 225-26 (1966).

72. Thus, of the three sources which Powell cites as authority for this statement, two are unsupported conclusionary affirmations:

1.) "For example, Charles E. Rice; Professor of Law, Fordham University wrote that a 'contributing factor' to the first Watts riot was the anarchic effect of the campaign of nonviolent civil disobedience," N.Y. Times, Aug. 29, 1965 (letter to editor);

2.) "Arthur Krock, in discussing causes of racial riots, cited: 'The preachment of Dr. Martin Luther King that individuals have a right to select the laws they will obey—,' New York Times Service, as published in Richmond Times Dispatch, April 17, 1966; while the third can hardly be described as a resort to civil disobedience, but instead a perfect example of exhortations to violence:

3.) "John A. McCone, who headed the California Commission to investigate the 1965 riots, commented on the reoccurrence of rioting in Watts, March, 1966: 'A contributing cause [to the initial riot] was the continuing exhortation of some leaders of the civil rights movement for *extreme* action—The commission itself made the following finding as to the 'aggravating events' causing the Watts riots: "Throughout the nation, unpunished violence and disobedience to law were widely reported and almost daily there were exhortations here and elsewhere, *to take the most extreme and even illegal remedies* —" Report of Governor's Commission on the Los Angeles Riots, Dec. 2, 1965 pp. 4, 85."

73. *See* Note, *Riot Control and the Use of Federal Troops*, 81 HARV. L. REV. 638 (1968); B. RICH, THE PRESIDENTS AND CIVIL DISORDER (1941), *Civil Disobedience In the Civil Rights Movement; To What Extent Protected and Sanctioned* 16 W. RES. L. REV. 711

bedience. The Boston tea party, Shay's Rebellion, The Whisky Insurrection, Fries Rebellion, and South Carolina's resistance to the tariff law are striking examples of violence in response to tax laws.[74] The conflict between labor and capital produced innumerable incidents of riot, violence and disorder;[75] while the depression set off waves of violence in rural areas over mortgage foreclosures.[76] More recently we have witnessed the violent Detroit riots during World War II and the summer of 1967[77] and the series of riots and fireburning in many cities across the country as the aftermath of the death of Dr. Martin Luther King.[78]

Mass violence is only one aspect. America has been plagued by an alarming increase in the number of violent crimes committed. Reports of the Federal Bureau of Investigation show that every major city in the United States is facing a "crime wave" and that even for cities with populations of only 250,000 to 500,000, average increase for crimes of all kinds is up 20 percent for the first nine months of 1967.[79] No doubt the reasons for the rapid increase are manifold, but certainly among them is the constant deprivation of our poor and minority groups in the nation's slums, and the frustrations and tensions of the younger generation, reflected in an increasing use of drugs.[80]

Recently a week long symposium was held at Northwestern University. The theme was intended to span the whole spectrum of violence in American life—in political action, societal behavior, and communi-

---

(1965); U.S. ADJUTANT-GENERAL, FEDERAL AID IN DOMESTIC DISTURBANCES 1787-1903, S. Doc. No. 209, 57th Cong., 2d Sess (1903); Comment, *Federal Intervention in the States for the Suppression of Domestic Violence: Constitutionality, Statutory Power and Policy* 1966 DUKE L.J. 415.

74. *See* MINOT, HISTORY OF THE INSURRECTION IN MASSACHUSETTS (1810) (Shay's rebellion); BALDWIN, THE WHISKEY REBELS (1939); DAVIS, THE FRIES REBELLION (1899); OGG, THE REIGN OF ANDREW JACKSON (1919) (South Carolina resistance). For a general history of violence in early American history, *see* OFFICE OF THE J.A.G., FEDERAL AID IN DOMESTIC DISTURBANCES, S. Doc. No. 263, 67th Cong. 2nd Sess. (1921-1922).

75. ADAMIC, DYNAMITE—THE STORY OF CLASS VIOLENCE IN AMERICA (1931); YELLEN, AMERICAN LABOR STRUGGLES (1936); BERMAN, LABOR DISPUTES AND THE PRESIDENTS OF THE UNITED STATES, (1924); 4 PERLMAN & TAFT, LABOR MOVEMENTS—HISTORY OF LABOR IN THE UNITED STATES 1896-1932 (1935).

76. HALL, READINGS IN JURISPRUDENCE 1006 (1938); *Farm Crisis Rises: Law Breaks Down*, N.Y. Times, Jan. 22, 1933.

77. The history of the Detroit riots of 1943 is contained in SHOGAN & CRAIG, THE DETROIT RACE RIOT (1964), while an account of the current 1967 riots is contained in the following newspaper articles: N.Y. Times, July 24, 1967, at 1, col. 6; *id.* July 25, 1967, at 1, col. 8; *id.* July 30, 1967, § 1, at 1, col. 2; *id.* July 30, 1967, § 1, at 1, col. 3.

78. *Army Troops in Capitol as Negroes Riot; Guard Sent into Chicago, Detroit, Boston; Many Fires Set* N.Y. Times, April 6, 1968 at 1, col. 8.

79. N.Y. Times, Jan. 22, 1968, at 21, col. 1. The same report of the F.B.I. showed that the figures for the City of Buffalo, New York were up 22.8 percent over a similar period in 1966 and that the figure for robberies were actually up 165 percent in 1967 over 1966.

80. For the story of the use of L.S.D. and other hallucinatory and addictive drugs and incidence of crime, see Bieser, *Drugs and the Law. Who Pays for the Trip,* 36 U. CINN. L. REV. 39 (1967).

cation through the media and the arts. Dr. Leslie Fiedler, novelist and critic, stated that Americans are violent people and that this nation has been built on a series of violent actions. He justified violence even in the arts: "Violence is everywhere, and always at the heart of human affairs. Violence within art shows us the violence within ourselves. It purges us, moves us and leaves us feeling calm."[81]

It is the deprived status of the minority groups in American society that gives rise to disruptive social pressures and to high crime rates.[82] The National Advisory Commission on Civil Disorders,[83] appointed by the President to study the disorders of the summer of 1967 (including the Detroit riot),[84] concluded that the causes of racial disorder are imbedded in a massive tangle of social, economic, political and psychological issues and circumstances arising out of the historical pattern of Negro-White relations but that the most fundamental cause is the racial attitude and behavior of white Americans toward black Americans.[85]

Similarly the Moynihan Report[86] through the most detailed study of the statistics of unemployment and poverty, the wage system, welfare, delinquency and crime, has established that three centuries of injustice have brought about deep seated structural distortions in the life of the Negro American and that a national effort must be directed toward strengthening the Negro family unit.[87] The Moynihan Report echoed the previous findings of the Negro sociologist, E. Franklin Frazier, that family disorganization has been partially responsible for a large amount of juvenile delinquency and adult crime among Negroes.[88] Nor is this suggestion a recent thought or phenomenon in our society. In a remarkable speech to the inmates of the Cook County Jail in 1902, Clarence Darrow suggested that there was a direct correlation between

---

81. Crowther, *Students Cheer Talk of Violence*, N.Y. Times, Jan. 22, 1968, at 18, col. 3.

82. Bazelon, *Law Morality and Civil Liberties*, 12 U.C.L.A. L. REV. (1964); HANDLER, RACE AND NATIONALITY IN AMERICAN LIFE (1944); MYRDAHL, THE AMERICAN DILEMMA (1944).

83. REPORT OF THE NATIONAL ADVISORY COMMISSION ON CIVIL DISORDERS 2 (Bantam Books, Inc., ed. 1968):

"What white Americans have never fully understood—but what the Negro can never forget—is that white society is deeply implicated in the ghetto. White institutions created it, white institutions maintain it and white society condones it."

84. Executive Order 11365 (July 29, 1967).

85. REPORT, *supra* note 83 at 203: "Race prejudice has shaped our history decisively in the past; it now threatens to do so again. White racism is essentially responsible for the explosive mixture which has been accumulating in our cities since the end of World War II."

86. Report of the office of Policy Planning and Research, United States Department of Labor. The Negro Family: The Case for National Action (March, 1965).

87. *See* RAINWATER & YANCY, THE MOYNIHAN REPORT AND THE POLITICS OF CONTROVERSY 94 (1967).

88. Frazier, *Problems and Needs of Negro Children and Youth Resulting from Family Disorganization*, J. NEGRO ED. 276-77 (1950).

the social and economic conditions of the slums and the rate of crime.[89] There can no longer be any question that there is a sharp relationship between unemployment, poverty, and crime; and that crimes of violence are overwhelmingly associated with poverty.[90] Yet we must not facilely be led to believe that socio-economic factors are the sole causes of crime. The rise in crime not only in the United States, but in prospering countries of Europe, in absolute figures, belie that.[91] In his message to Congress on Civil Rights in 1968, President Johnson adverted to the known fact that lawlessness renders the people of the ghettos as its primary victim and:

> In that crowded ghetto, human tragedies and crime increase and multiply. Unemployment and educational problems are compounded . . . Lawlessness must be punished—sternly and promptly. But the criminal conduct of some must not weaken our resolve to deal with the real grievance of all those who suffer discrimination. . . . Last summer our nation suffered the tragedy of urban riots. Lives were lost; property was destroyed. No people need or want protection—the effective non-discriminatory exercise of the police power—more than the majority of slum dwellers, like better schools, housing, and job opportunities, improved police protection is necessary for better conditions of life in the central city today. It is a vital part of our agenda for urban America.[92]

Substantial unanswered questions are raised when men seek to foster moral prescriptions and solutions which are not based on real conditions.When our society sets the rules for the poor to live with, how can we expect them to comply when they lack the training or capacity to do so! We need a probing awareness of the conditions of physical and mental life which are essential to foster respect for, and the ability to comply with, the standards of law and morality we have adopted. There must be a legal commitment to social responsibility.[93]

---

89. ATTORNEY FOR THE DAMNED, CLARENCE DARROW, in his own words, edited by Arthur Weinberg, (1957) at 3.

90. CONANT, SLUMS AND SUBURBS (1961); HOLLINGSHEAD & REDLICH, SOCIAL CLASS AND MENTAL ILLNESS (1958); Preamble, Economic Opportunity Act of 1964, 78 Stat. 508 (1964). Similar findings have been made between the relationship of mental retardation and crime to poverty and substandard living conditions, PRESIDENT'S BOARD ON MENTAL RETARDATION 61-62 (1963).

91. Breitel, *Criminal Law and Equal Justice*, 1966 UTAH L. REV. 1. (Associate Justice, New York Court of Appeals); RADZINOWICZ, THE NEED FOR CRIMINOLOGY 29 (1965).

92. *Message to Congress on Civil Rights*, N.Y. Times, Jan. 25, 1968, at 22, col. 2. That Negroes are much more likely to be the victims of violence and lack of order can hardly be disputed. *See* Silberman, *The City and the Negro*, Fortune, Mar., 1962 at 88-89.

93. Bazelon, *supra* note 82 at 19-20. Justice Bazelon (U.S. Court of Appeals, D.C. Circuit) hypothesizes that most problems concerning the responsibility of society come down to a question of the proper or improper allocation of resources, material and emotional. We must, therefore stop treating the physical and mental derelicts of our streets as criminals—the drunkards, vagrants, chronic alcoholics, petty thieves, drug

If the trend to violence in America is seen as an independent trait of our society, linked with the socio-economic conditions that aggravate the resort to violence, then the perspective of non-violent, civil disobedience is clearly an alternative to violence. Civil disobedience constitutes a totally differing theme in American history, anti-authoritarian in concept, and based upon the American conscience and belief in morality, which seeks to support not destroy the basic ideals of our way of life:

> Except for the brief period of the Puritan oligarchy, American thinkers have also been largely free of the appeal to authority and revelation. One of their dilemmas has been to square their basic non-conformism with the stability required by property, investment and law. . . . American thinkers have been at their best in their anti-authoritarianism, in the dicta of Jefferson and Madison on freedom of thought, in the pamphleteering of the Jacksonians, in Calhoun's plea for a veto power by which political minorities could hold their place, in Thoreau's doctrine of "civil disobedience," in the thunderbolts of Henry Demarest Lloyd against Standard Oil, in Brooks Adams' gloomy predictions of "centralization and decay," in William James' "pluralistic universe," in Justice Holmes' "can't help's," in Veblen's polemics against "absentee owners."[94]

The Quakers in England and early America helped establish the right against self-incrimination by refusing to testify against conscience,[95] as well as the liberties of freedom of religion and conscience.[96] Jefferson was able to explain: "The rights of conscience we never submitted, we could never submit. We are answerable for them to our God."[97] American history has had its abolitionists; Ralph Waldo Emerson and the doctrine of "Man The Reformer"; the Progressive

---

addicts and prostitutes—and begin to treat them as sick individuals, according to their needs. Hall, *The Law of Arrest in Relation to Social Problems*, 3 U. CHI. L. REV. 345, 368 (1936). Similarly with the insane, Durham v. United States 214 F.2d 862 (D.C. Cir. 1954), we must make the behavioral sciences relevant to the law. The law is making vast strides in this direction. In accord with the brilliant treatise of Professor Ernest Nagel, THE METHODOLOGY OF THE SOCIAL SCIENCES (1961), there has been increasing use of empirical and behavioral studies in law. Law schools have added social scientists to their law facilities and "the two-way traffic between law and social sub-group is only beginning." David Riesman, Talk at Harvard Sesquicentennial (1967). *See* 44 DEN. L.J. Fall 1967 for a special issue devoted entirely to the relationship of law and the social sciences.

94. LERNER, AMERICA AS A CIVILIZATION, THE ANGLE OF VISION 718 (1957) Madison, in fact, supported "factionalism" as the key to American life and liberty (THE FEDERALIST, No. 10.)

95. *See* DOUGLAS, AN ALMANAC OF LIBERTY 236 (1954).

96. TREBOR, THE FLUSHING REMONSTRANCE (1957) published on the 300th anniversary of its declaration.

97. JEFFERSON, NOTES ON VIRGINIA (1801); *see* KONVITZ, FUNDAMENTAL LIBERTIES OF A FREE PEOPLE (1957).

movement; women's suffrage; the anarchists of the early industrial era; the conscientious objectors of both World Wars and the Civil War draft resistance; the post-World War II peace, disarmament, and Vietnam movements; the Civil Rights movement, and many more.[98] These movements have not been led by the underprivileged, the illiterate, or the poor of our society, but rather reflect the response of the education community of America—the publishers, professors, and university students who have been playing a leading role in this historical movement.[99] These movements have acted as the conscience of America, and through them, rather than the violence or existence of masses of men, has come the steady reform of law which is the genius of American democracy and the touchstone of our pluralistic society.

In a similar vein, many of our leading politicians and statesmen have recognized the growing need for civil disobedience and non-violent behavior as a force to stimulate change in the legal system and to counteract the resort to violence. The New York Times editorially has stated:

> The men and women who picketed peacefully in front of the Whitehall Induction Center here yesterday and at other induction centers across the country, were acting within a democratic tradition. So were even those who chose to carry their protest a step further, in acts of non-violent civil disobedience, courting arrests which they were prepared to accept peacefully. They deserve respect for having the courage of their convictions, from those of us who do not share these convictions and from those who prefer to express their own disagreement with public policies in less dramatic ways.
>
> But if war objectors are to earn the respect of others without which protest is futile and self-defeating—they must recognize that dissent in a free society involves responsibilities as well as rights. These include the responsibility to respect the rights of others, which in turn implies the responsibility to observe public order; the responsibility to avoid violence; the responsibility to accept gracefully whatever penalties society may impose through the judicial process for violation of its laws, as did Socrates, Thoreau and Ghandhi.[100]

---

98. A complete history of non-violence in America has been published by Professor Stoughton Lynd, NON-VIOLENCE IN AMERICA: A DOCUMENTARY HISTORY, edited by Stoughton Lynd (1966). An excellent study of the role of conscience in American life is FREEMAN, A REMONSTRANCE FOR CONSCIENCE, 106 U. PA. L. REV. 806 (1958), and recently much illumination on civil disobedience in American history has been shed by Dean Allen in *Civil Disobedience and the Legal Order*, 36 U. CINN. L. REV. 175 (1967).

99. Freeman, *Moral Preemption: The Case for the Disobedient* 17 HASTINGS L.J. 425 (1966).

100. Editorial, *The Responsibility of Dissent*, N. Y. Times, Dec. 5, 1967.

Thus, while some Negro leaders were advocating violence, Dr. Martin Luther King, in testimony before the President's National Advisory Commission on Civil Disorders, urged a camp-in in cities:

> We have got to find a kind of middle road between riots and timid supplication of justice, a program of escalating non-violence to the dimensions of civil disobedience. . . . We need a method of dislocating the functioning of a city without destroying life and property. The time has come, if we can't get anything done, to camp in Washington and stay till the Federal Government and Washington does something.[101]

It has long been recognized that mere dissent is insufficient to move a complacent majority to necessary social and legal reforms. After the initial moderate successes of a protest movement, the leadership is pressed on to achieve abiding and substantial gains. However, the use of incessant speeches and continual picketing does not inconvenience the majority and protests are and can be ignored. It is at this point that civil disobedience becomes a necessary alternative to a violent response.[102] Even the most controversial of subjects, the "Black Power" movement, has been termed by Professor Charles Hamilton of Roosevelt College as a "clear alternative" to violence.[103] Rioting, he claims, stems from suppressed rage induced by long oppression and the lack of political power to improve the conditions that fan the anger. Black power in its most elemental form seeks to establish political and economic power for the Negro minority.

The technique of civil disobedience is the use of non-violence,[104]

---

101. N. Y. Times, Oct. 24, 1967, at 33, col. 5.

102. *See* Practicing Law Institute, The Community and Racial Crises 89 (1966).

103. Janson, *A Theorist Terms Black Power "clear alternative" to Violence*, N. Y. Times, January 22, 1968. *See* also George Romney's speech to Dartmouth College, Oct. 30, 1967 (N. Y. Times, Oct. 31, 1967) in which he praised "sit-ins and peaceful demonstrations —[which] build up our sympathy and our realization of the irregularities which exist" but condemned violence and the lawless character of militant protestors. The chairman of the New York City Human Rights Commission, William Booth, has stated that the term used by the white community "crime in the streets" is nothing more than a euphemism for Negro, that the crime in the streets talked about is 10 percent of the crime in this country. The other 90 percent, he said, consists of sale of narcotics to slum children, and consumer and credit frauds against poverty groups. Booth called for new federal legislation: "We have a duty to make people realize they don't have to tear down the structure, the structure can change within itself." *See* Caldwell, *City Aide Assails Johnson on Crime*, N. Y. Times, Jan. 22, 1968.

104. *See*, Mannheim, Diagnosis of Our Time 13 (1944) for the conclusion that the old symbols of revolution in modern society are obsolete barricades and that new techniques of totalitarian government eliminate effective opposition. The unique spirit of civil disobedience is the ability to achieve victory without violence. "We must meet violence with nonviolence—we must love our white brothers no matter what they do," King, Stride Toward Freedom: The Montgomery Story 11 (1958), "No other method ever achieved so much in so short a period of time." New South, July 1961 at 9. Thus, Ghandhi made "Ahimsa" (literally "non injury") the central article of his faith Speeches and Writ-

which because of its inherent self-limitations, is socially realistic in a democratic society.[105] Civil disobedience is predicated upon openness of society, a lack of surreptitious and covert movements. Its very success depends upon the strategic use of negotiation, demands, time limits, publicity, and demonstrations as preliminary steps.[106] Since the goal is the attainment of social and legal goals, the use of education and modern communication methods is essential for the formation of effective public opinion for support.[107] Society therefore has an inherent control over its use, and this leads in turn to limitations upon techniques and strategies which are useful to civil disobedience.

Because civil disobedience stops short of violence, it offers a positive active channel for the frustration of the minority.[108] We are grate-

---

INGS OF MAHATMA GHANDHI, 346 (4th ed., Madras, 1933). While Ghandhi believed in nonviolence as a creed and called off his 1919 campaign because of sporadic acts of violence, it was sufficient for its success that most Indians accepted it as a workable strategy. BONDURANT, CONQUEST OF VIOLENCE, THE GHANDHIAN PHILOSOPHY OF CONFLICT, 103 (1958). Nonviolence is successful because in accepting punishment (suffering), and thus working within the social and legal system, one advances a good cause as nothing else. M. K. GHANDHI, NONVIOLENT RESISTANCE 315 (1961). The larger the jail sentences, the more effective and successful the movement, *i.e.*, suffragettes. STEVENS, JAILED FOR FREEDOM 16 (1920). Thus Sidney Hook in his Work, THE PARADOXES OF FREEDOM (1962), says that one can defend civil disobedience within a democratic society: "only if he willingly accepts the punishment entailed by his defiance of the law, only if he does not seek to escape or physically resist it" (id. at 117) and that this willingness to accept the punishment arouses second thoughts in the majority on the law's justice and wisdom (*id.* at 119) and serves as "a moral challenge and educational reinfluence on the attitudes of the majority" (*id.* at 119).

105. SEIFERT, CONQUEST BY SUFFERING: THE PROCESS AND PROSPECTS FOR NONVIOLENT RESISTANCE 16 (1955).

106. SHRIDHARANI, WAR WITHOUT VIOLENCE, A STUDY OF GHANDHI'S METHODS 5 (1939).

107. Ghandhi, himself, believed that the method is justified only when it is related to important ends. "It must be a supplement to education, negotiation, political and economic action: SEIFERT, *supra* 105 at 131. The use of the term "truth force" by Ghandhi (satyagraha) symbolizes the important role that is played by the use only of socially acceptable ideas which can be used openly to win over public support. Truth is used as a weapon.

108. Both Thoreau and Ghandhi recognized that there is *always* an incidental risk of violence in the use of civil disobedience. The risk of violence by those who do not comprehend the proper use of nonviolent resistance would be present in any event in any form of human behavior. One of the best explanations is contained in MILLER, NONVIOLENCE: A CHRISTIAN INTERPRETATION 44 (1964):

> For the realist, at least, there are limits of possibility and usefulness within which any method or principle must be regarded, and nonviolence is no exception. Its distinctive merit is not that it keeps the incidence of violence on the level of the status quo, nor that it reduces it below that level; but that in most cases it produces less violence than would be the case if the struggle were waged by violent means. By the very fact of choosing to engage in nonviolent struggle instead of holding to an inert passivity in some quiet nook, we remove nonviolence from the category of the absolute and involve ourselves in existential risk with all its consequences . . . .
>
> The core of nonviolence is imbedded in personal conduct, specifically in the nonviolent person's capacity to absorb violence without retaliating. Without this there can be no such thing as nonviolent tactics and strategy, which are only nonviolent to the extent that the leaders, cadres and masses make them so by their conduct. Not every act of nonviolence can be expected to be perfect, but it must

ful to scholars at the University of Michigan for several studies suggesting that the number of violent crimes declines in Negro communities deeply involved in conducting direct action protests, at least so long as that activity continues.[109] The studies also show that if non-violent responses are to be encouraged and successful, there is a reciprocal obligation on the part of those invested with the police power to recognize it as such and to adjust their responses. So long as the police continue to use desperate rear guard actions against decisions upholding the rights of the accused,[110] utilize "alley courts," "dogs," and "offensive weapons,"[111] then so long will various segments of American society see the police as the enforcer of the majority. Respect for law and order will decay,[112] and hostility towards the police increase.[113] The role of the police must be *positive*. Equal law enforcement, greater fact finding, and above all, communication with the public and an understanding of the varied responses which the public will take must be sought. We will see subsequently that the police have a constitutional obligation to protect demonstrators and speakers against violence on the part of third person observers. If civil disobedience does reduce the incidence of violence, then the police have a duty to understand it and act in moderation towards it, at least to the extent of not encouraging the proponents of violence. There are many occasions when the use of the police in meeting civil disobedience is totally uncalled for and in fact constitutes a provocation to violence.[114]

Thus, the first and essential limitation indicates that civil disobedience cannot effectively be used against totalitarian regimes who will meet non-violent moral force with non-legal physical force. It is within a democratic framework that the government recognizes that civil disobedience constitutes a measure of the utility of the society's norms and a challenge to reform within the system. The experience of

---

at least meet the minimum requirement of nonretaliation—and as much of the rest as the individual is capable of.

109. Solomon, Walker, O'Connor & Fishman, *Civil Rights Activity and Reduction in Crime Among Negroes* 12 ARCHIVES GENERAL PSYCHIATRY 227 (1965), reported in Edwards, *Order and Civil Liberties: A Complex Role For the Police* 64 MICH. L. REV. 47 (1965) and Allen, *Civil Disobedience and the Legal Order,* 36 U. CINN. L. REV. 1, 31 (1967). The authors of the Solomon study report: Such emotional expression, when it occurs in a framework of community organization may reduce the need for aggressive outbursts of a violent sort, thus reducing the incidence of such crimes," *id.* at 236.

110. Kamisar, *Public Safety v. Individual Liberties—Some "Facts" and "Theories,"* 53 J. CRIM. L., C & P.S. 171 (1962).

111. Edwards, *supra* note 109.

112. SILBERMAN, CRISES IN BLACK AND WHITE 53 (1964); LOMAX, THE NEGRO REVOLT 72 (1962).

113. SHAPIRO & SULLIVAN, RACE RIOTS, NEW YORK 40-41 (1964).

114. *See* N. Y. Times, Oct. 28, 1967, at 33, col. 3, in which college authorities were severely criticized for calling in police at a minor Brooklyn College sit-in leading to a violent confrontation.

South Africa has demonstrated that non-violent means cannot be used successfully against determined undemocratic methods and policies.[115]

Fears about the size of groups practicing civil disobedience are unfounded. Increase of size may actually become a handicap as the group tends to include those who are not fully committed, and fear and anxiety is raised in onlookers. Smaller groups are capable of supporting the necessary intensity of conviction which allows for the greatest self-sacrifice and progress. Because the movement is inherently linked to public opinion, the method cannot be used indiscriminately. It must relate to an idea whose time has come and represent an equation between the demands of the disobedient and the cultural and historical trends and beliefs of society at large, ideas capable of sustaining wide public support. Thus, there must be a comparative status of participants who have common goals and work within the same structure. Finally, there will always be a self-limitation by reason of the quality and type of leadership and those willing to follow. Few leaders are capable of dealing effectively with their own resisters, together with their opponents. Neither groups nor leaders will ever be totally successful in obtaining enough persons who are willing to sustain continuous suffering and punishment unless there are deep-seated grievances awaiting articulation.[116]

Beyond all of the strategies and techniques and the alternatives which non-violence presents, there is a deep philosophical support for its use. While the Supreme Court fashions rules for the use of first amendment freedoms which generally revolve about conduct which is non-violent and does not interfere with the rights of third persons, western philosophy since Kant has been concerned with harmonizing moral freedom and duty with juridical relations. Kant's contribution was his categorical imperative: "Act according to a maxim which can be adopted at the same time as a universal law of human conduct"[117] which reveals itself again in his universal principle of all laws as:

> The Law is the whole of the conditions under which the voluntary actions of any one person can be harmonized with the voluntary actions of every other person in accordance with a universal law of freedom.[118]

For Kant, ethical motivation, being dependent upon reason and conscience, was a superior kind of motivation and he recognized that the

115. *See, South Africa, Part I, The Survivalists*, The New Yorker, Jan. 27, 1968 p. 65 (describing the failure of the Liberal party to change the policy of apartheid by non-violent means and the methods used by the government to destroy the party.)

116. *See* Seifert, *supra* note 105 for a complete articulation of the limitations of nonviolent resistance.

117. Kant, Philosophy of Law 34 (Hastie trans. 1887)

118. *Id.* at 45.

law could not deal with such internal relations. Therefore, the law had to be structured carefully so as to preserve the maximum of moral freedom for the individual. Compulsion or juridical sanction could only be justified against an individual when it was used to restrain violence or that individual's interference with another person.[119]

The principle has been carried forward by Neo-Kantian's, such as Stammler, who project as the ultimate ideal freedom of the will. Stammler develops the principle that everyone who is expected to assume legal obligations acquires a right to participate in the community and that right limits his obligations. There is a spirit of community cooperation governed by a principle that every legal demand must be maintained in such a manner that the person obligated may be his own neighbor.[120] In this context the Negro struggling for equal rights replies as did Americans in revolutionary days "You ask me to protect a legal system which accords me no rights, Sir this is a two-way street!"[121] Conditioned by the ethical precepts of non-violence and the neighborly concept of non-interference with a third person's rights, civil disobedience is at least philosophically consistent with the highest standards of our society.

Morris Cohen has pointed out that speculations by philosophers in the metaphysical world must be balanced by hard prudent action in the real world.[122] Civil disobedience, at least by the use of non-violence, purports to furnish the model by which that aim can be accomplished within the legal system.

Constitutional and Legal Framework

Commencing with the Civil Rights movement in 1960, a whole new series of challenges was laid down by the use of civil disobedience to test the legality of widespread practices of racial segregation and discrimination.[123] These actions were challenges to both public and private discrimination, and the demonstrators were usually subjected to arrest and conviction for crimes of trespass and disorderly conduct.[124]

---

119. *Id.* at 28, 36. Kant's ideal was for the law to protect the freedom of the will so as to preserve moral choices for man which can have consequences in the real world.

120. STAMMLER, THE THEORY OF THE JUST LAW 155-63 (Husik trans. 1925).

121. *See* Freeman, *The Case For the Disobedient,* 17 HASTINGS L. J. 425, 434 (1966).

122. COHEN, REASON AND LAW 26 (1950). "[M]en like Kant . . . who make most of metaphysical freedom, leave us rather little of the freedom that we do care about."

123. *See, Sit-Ins and the Civil Rights Act,* 32 TENN L. REV. 294 (1965). "Sit-ins" became expanded to "stand-ins," "wade-ins," "pray-ins," "mill-ins" and other forms of protest demonstrations.

124. *State v. Goldfinch* 241 La. 958, 132 So.2d 860 (1961). Since the *Civil Rights Cases,* 109 U.S. 3 (1883), the state courts have uniformly seen this as involving individual action, while the federal courts have seen it as state action, involving the fourteenth amendment. *See* Wright, THE SIT-IN MOVEMENT, 9 WAYNE L. REV. 445 (1963).

In a series of sweeping decisions, however, the Supreme Court, with respect to sit-ins on private property to protest private discrimination, reversed nearly every conviction.[125] As a *result* of their civil disobedience, the statutes and practices the demonstrators had violated were declared unconstitutional. To some legal commentators such demonstrations do not constitute civil disobedience. They argue that under the supremacy clause these individuals are attempting to invalidate state and local statutes and ordinances in conflict with a higher national law which must be obeyed.[126] However, this concept is, at most, a semantic differentiation, because at the time of the violation the act of the demonstrator was deliberate civil disobedience. Rather than suggest that the Court decided that the "violation" was not civil disobedience, I submit that the Court may be approaching the position that civil disobedience *is* a lawful exercise of a constitutional prerogative.[127] Moreover, such an interpretation would provide an answer for those cases in which civil disobedience would have been a violation of constitutional standards because of an absence of "state action," but for the passage of a statute which made similar future actions lawful (especially the sit-in demonstrations made lawful by the Civil Rights Act of 1964).[128] Nor would such an interpretation mean that any subse-

---

125. Boynton v. Virginia 364 U.S. 454 (1960) was the first major decision on sit-ins. In Peterson v. City of Greenville, 373 U.S. 244 (1963); *Lombard v. Louisiana*, 373 U.S. 267 (1963), Avent v. North Carolina, 373 U.S. 375 (1963), Gober v. City of Birmingham, 373 U.S. 374 (1963) and Shuttlesworth v. City of Birmingham, 373 U.S. 262 (1963), all decided on the same day, sit-in convictions for trespass were struck down because of city ordinances commanding segregation and statements of city officials, police officers, and state practices. Earlier in *Garner v. Louisville*, 368 U.S. 157 (1961) and Thompson v. Louisville, 362 U.S. 199 (1960), convictions had been reversed for lack of evidence. In 1948, the Court in Shelley v. Kraemer, 334 U.S. 1 (1948) ruled that state adjudication of private interests constituted "state action," but the Court has been reluctant to apply this approach broadly. By 1964, the Court had reversed four more trespass convictions because of state accommodations law, county board of health regulations, or action of municipal officials. Robinson v. Florida, 378 U.S. 153 (1964); Griffin v. Maryland, 378 U.S. 130 (1964); Boule v. Columbia, 378 U.S. 347 (1964) and Bell v. Maryland, 378 U.S. 226 (1964).

126. See Black, *The Problem of Compatibility of Civil Disobedience with American Institutions of Government*; 43 TEX. L. REV. 492 (1965). To some, civil disobedience can be an appeal only to moral principle or natural law, but not to higher positive law or the law of a governmental organ, for that is obedience to law. DIXON, UNDERSTANDING JUDICIAL REACTION TO PROTEST BEHAVIOR, COMMUNITY AND RACIAL CRISES 95 (1966). This approach is reminiscent of the discussion of Kelsen's views of the positive law as constituting a "hierarchy of norms" and if there is a contradiction between a higher and lower norm, then it entails only the significance that the latter was never a valid norm of the legal system. See KELSEN, THE GENERAL THEORY OF LAW AND STATE 114-17 (Wedberg Trans, 1961). *See also* Wyzanski, *On Civil Disobedience*, the Atlantic, Feb. 1968, p. 58.

127. The Supreme Court has in several different contexts recognized the principle that non-violent constitutional change is a basic premise and underlying principle of our constitutional system. See Freeman, *Civil Liberties, Acid Test of Democracy*, 43 MINN. L. REV. 511 (1959); Dennis v. United States 341 U.S. 494 (1951); Yates v. United States, 354 U.S. 298 (1957).

128. Civil Rights Act of 1964, § 201 (b), tit. II, Public Accommodations, 42 U.S.C. § 2000 a-2 c (1964). The act was held to be a constitutional exercise under the Commerce

quent violations would be outside of the scope of civil disobedience. A decision by the Supreme Court does not become frozen into changeless law, and such decisions may themselves be reversed either by a subsequent decision of the Court,[129] by statute,[130] or by constitutional amendment.[131] Southern officials may again and again test the meaning of *Brown v. Board of Education.*[132] However, any challenge to a final decision of the Court which is calculated to delay or avoid enforcement of the law would, of course, be in a different category and subject to contempt.[133]

Fundamental to any understanding of the judicial reaction to civil disobedience is the requirement that one must violate a criminal law in order to challenge its validity. Equity will not intervene through either injunction or declaratory judgment to prevent the enforcement of a criminal law or to obtain a ruling if there is no actual controversy. Thus, the Supreme Court refused to hear two "test" cases of Connecticut's anti-contraception statute,[134] until a violation of the law was actually committed and a criminal conviction obtained, at which point the Court declared the statute unconstitutional.[135] However, the Court will protect a person from criminal prosecution when he advocates violating a criminal law in order to test its validity in Court.[136] Civil

Clause in Heart of Atlanta Motel v. United States, 379 U.S. 241, (1964) and Katzenbach v. McLung 379 U.S. 294, (1964). Of greatest interest, however, was the Court's finding in Hamm v. City of Rockhill 379 U.S. 306 (1964) in which the Court decided that violations occuring prior to passage of the act abated even though they were non-federal convictions. Thus, civil disobedience accomplished its basic purpose of legal reform, and was recognized as lawful conduct by a subsequently adopted statute even though there was no reversal on the merits of the violation. Two dissenting justices could find no such intent on the part of Congress "to ratify massive disobedience to law" (*id.* at 328, Justice White dissenting).

129. Thus the separate but equal doctrine of Plessy v. Ferguson 163 U.S. 537 (1896) was reversed by Brown v. Board of Ed., 347 U.S. 483 (1954).

130. Civil Rights Act of 1964 42 U.S.C. § 2000 (1964); Article 7A, New York, Real Property Actions and Proceedings Law § 770 (1965), provided a legal basis for tenants' rent strikes which had no legal sanction prior to passage of the law. *See, Harlem Goes to War Against the Slumlords,* Saturday Evening Post, Feb. 29, 1964, p. 71; *Tenant Rent Strikes,* 3 COLUM. J. L. & SOCIAL PROBLEMS 1 (1967); Enforcement of Municipal Housing Codes, 78 HARV. L. REV. 801 (1965).

131. The XIII amendment to the U.S. Constitution, invalidating Dred Scott v. Sanford, 60 U.S. 393 (1857).

132. 349 U.S. 294 (1955). See Griffin v. School Bd., 377 U.S. 218 (1964); Calhoun v. Latimer, 377 U.S. 263 (1964), *i.e.,* Justice Black's comment in *Griffin, (Id.* at 229): [T]here has been entirely too much deliberation and not enough speed."

133. The conduct of Governors Wallace and Barnett would, in the university desegregation cases, fit under that mold. *See* Tweed, Segal & Packer, *Civil Rights and Disobedience To Law,* 36 N.Y.S.B.J. 290 (1964). A contrary result might obtain if the order disobeyed were an injunction order not yet appealed. Dixon, UNDERSTANDING JUDICIAL REACTION TO PROTEST BEHAVIOR, COMMUNITY AND RACIAL CRISES (1966) p .95.

134. Tileston v. Ullman, 318 U.S. 44 (1943); Poe v. Ullman, 367 U.S. 497 (1961).

135. Griswold v. Connecticut 381 U.S. 479 (1965). *See* McKay, *Protest and Dissent,* 1966 UTAH L. REV. 20, and Aptheker v. Secretary of State, 378 U.S. 500 (1964).

136. Keegan v. United States, 325 U.S. 478 (1945); Okamoto v. United States, 152 F.2d 905 (10th Cir. 1945).

disobedience is thus encouraged by the courts, although the legal doctrine is not without attack for distorting the fundamental issues before the Court.[137]

It is in the area of public demonstrations, marches, meetings, and picketing that the Court has moved to validate civil disobedience, so long as it is conducted in a non-violent manner and does not interfere with the rights of third persons. In a series of cases the Court has upheld the right of demonstrators to peacefully assemble, and the mere "possibility" of violence is not sufficient to vitiate the right.[138] In *Garner v. Louisiana* Chief Justice Warren established and accepted the rule:

> . . . that peaceful conduct, even though conceivably offensive to another class of the public, is not conduct which may be proscribed by Louisiana's disturbance of the peace statutes without evidence that the actor conducted himself in some outwardly unruly manner.[139]

The right of assembly is authorized in mass demonstrations in front of a courthouse[140] and even in a public library,[141] but will not be authorized where it actually creates an interference with security pro-

---

137. In an excellent article, *The Firstness of the First Amendment*, 65 YALE L.J. 464, 478 (1956) Professor Edward Cahn wrote:

> It has been very difficult for First Amendment theory to move beyond this point. From the beginning, the Supreme Court has declined to determine questions of constitutionality unless the person seeking the decision could show he had legal standing to sue. When the rights in issue pertain to the First Amendment, the court has expected to hears appeals from the individuals who were molested in their worship, or arrested for their speech. . . .If a person's own rights had been injured, he could sue, otherwise not. . . .
>
> In either event, it would always be the individual or group of individuals on one side, speaking on behalf of freedom and the community, officially or tacitly on the other side. . . .
>
> These circumstances, proper though they were for jurisdictional purposes established a badly distorted social background for First Amendment litigation. . . .Whoever might come before them as spokesman for First Amendment freedom was required to be an individual; ergo his interest was to be labelled "an individual interest" of one kind or another. On the other hand, whoever might appear for the government was automatically dubbed the spokesman of a public or social interest. See Frank, *The Lawyers Role in Modern Society*, 4 J. PUB. L. 8, 11 (1955) for the statement that lawyers are still taken in by the jargon of such "weighing the interests."

A.B.A., THE CANONS OF PROFESSIONAL ETHICS, canon 32, encourages the violation of law to test its validity against higher law. Until a statute has been construed and interpreted by competent adjudication, the lawyer is free to advise as to its validity, and, conscientiously as to its meaning and intent. *See* McKay, *Laws Governing Demonstrations and Protest*, The Community and Racial Crises (1966) p. 91: "Thus to determine the validity of a law-some protest, disobedience or even lawlessness is not necessarily condemned."

138. Edwards v. South Carolina, 372 U.S. 229, 237 (1963); Cox v. Louisiana, 379 U.S. 536 (1965); Henry v. City of Rock Hill, 376 U.S. 776 (1964); Wright v. Georgia, 373 U.S. 284 (1964).

139. Garner v. Louisiana, 368 U.S. 157 (1961).

140. Edwards v. South Carolina, 372 U.S. 229 (1963); Cox v. Louisiana, 379 U.S. 536 (1965) (2000 students).

141. Brown v. Louisiana, 383 U.S. 131 (1966).

visions of a state, such as a demonstration in front of a jailhouse door.[142] The Court will not sanction the obstruction of public passageways unless the ordinance itself has been discriminatorily enforced,[143] and will look to the imminence of violence and danger at every aspect of the proceeding.[144] However, the Court stated in *Edwards v. South Carolina* that mass demonstrations are presumptively legal and constitute an exercise of basic constitutional rights in their most pristine form.[145]

Similarly, in the area of free speech, the doctrine of "clear and present danger" was enunciated by the Court for the first time in *Schenck v. U.S.*[146] and has been followed ever since. It requires the utmost present danger of an immediate riot, or violent overthrow of the state, to pass the constitutional test.[147] The speech itself must bring about a condition of unrest with respect to actual listeners who are called to riot.[148] The Court has sanctioned many forms of activity including refusal to salute the flag, condemning war and the draft and distributing literature, and recruiting members for the Communist Party.[149] Advances have also been made in permitting criticism of public officials and preventing libel and slander suits unless malice can be shown.[150]

Viewed in the light of the constitutional reforms of the past few decades, the legality of so many forms of civil disobedience activity becomes apparent. It is only when the activity approaches violence or interference with the rights of others that the constitutional protection is lost. Thus, the Supreme Court stated in *Board of Education v. Barnette*:

> The freedom asserted [violation of law requiring salute of the flag] by these appellees does not bring them into collision with

142. Adderley v. State of Florida, 385 U.S. 39 (1966). For two recent and illuminating articles on the right of assembly—*see* 21 ARK. L. REV. 250 (1967) and *Right to Demonstrate*, 45 N. CAR. L. REV. 724 (1967). The *Adderley* decision, while enunciated over the protests of a vigorous dissent, nevertheless stands for the proposition that, in matters of *conduct*, interference with either public or private property will not be tolerated.

143. Poulous v. New Hampshire, 345 U.S. 395 (1953); Cox v. New Hampshire, 312 U.S. 569 (1941); Lovell v. Griffin, 303 U.S. 444 (1938).

144. Edwards v. South Carolina, 372 U.S. 229, 244 (1963).

145. *Id.* at 235.

146. 249 U.S. 47 (1919).

147. Feiner v. New York, 340 U.S. 315 (1951); Dennis v. United States 341 U.S. 494 (1951).

148. *See* KONVITZ, EXPANDING LIBERTIES, FREEDOM'S GAINS IN POST WAR AMERICA 294 (1966).

149. *See* Brennan, *The Supreme Court and the Meiklejohn Interpretation of the First Amendment*, 78 HARV. L. REV. 1 (1965); Emerson, *Towards a General Theory of the First Amendment*, 73 YALE L.J. 877 (1963); Kalven, *The Concept of the Public Forum*, 1965 SUP. CT. REV. 1.

150. New York Times v. Sullivan, 376 U.S. 254 (1964); Time, Inc. v. Hill, 385 U.S. 374 (1967).

> rights asserted by any other individuals . . . The refusal of these persons to participate in the ceremony does not interfere with or deny rights of others to do so. Nor is there any question in this case that their behavior is peaceable and orderly. The sole conflict is between authority and the rights of the individual.[151]

Thus, while there is feverish activity on the part of the states to pass riot control statutes,[152] and a Negro revolutionary has been convicted of conspiring to riot and violating the criminal anarchy statute in the Harlem riots of 1964,[153] the first amendment will protect the non-violent civilly disobedient in the streets. Furthermore, there is in fact an affirmative obligation on the part of the police to protect assemblers and speakers from threatened violence.[154]

Moreover, civil disobedience need not be directed only at particular unjust laws. If statutes and ordinances valid on their face are administered in an unfair and discriminatory manner, the courts have long fashioned a remedy under the fourteenth amendment equal protection clause.[155] Who therefore can say that it is a violation of school attendance laws when massive protests are held against de facto segregation of an entire city's school system, when federal courts may direct schools to end de facto segregation and school boards may have an affirmative duty not only to avoid intentional discrimination but to promote racial balance.[156] Such a concept finds support in Yale Law Professor, Charles Black, who believes that massive civil disobedience may be called for to bring down a state government when all of the laws are directed in fact against the Negro.[157]

Recent events have brought into focus the draft card burning cases in which appellants have contended that draft card burning was

---

151. 319 U.S. 624, 630 (1943).

152. *See* Helman, *A Statutory Reassessment, Inciting to Riot,* 72 CASE & COMMENT, 26 (Nov.-Dec. 1967); *Riot Control and The Use of Federal Troops,* 81 HARV. L. REV. 638 (1968).

153. People v. Epton, 19 N.Y.2d 496 (1967). The case was refused on appeal by the Supreme Court "for want of a substantial Federal question." N.Y. Times, Jan. 23, 1968.

154. *See* Hague v. C.I.O. 307 U.S. 496 (1939) where Justice Roberts stated that street meetings must be accorded a special kind of protection, commented upon in Smith, *The Development of the Right of Assembly—A Current Socio-Legal Investigation,* 9 W. & MARY L. REV. 359, 370 (1967).

155. *See* Yick Wo v. Hopkins, 118 U.S. 356; Snowden v. Hughes, 321 U.S. 1 (1944); Williamson v. Lee Opt. Co., 348 U.S. 483 (1955); Matter of DiMaggio v. Brown, 19 N.Y.2d 283 (1967).

156. McKay, *Racial Protest, Civil Disobedience and the Law,* ARTS & SCIENCES 273, (Winter, 1964). *See* King, *The Civil Rights Struggle in the U.S. Today* 20 RECORD. SUPP. 5, 24 (1965)—Where the Rev. Martin Luther King extends civil disobedience to violation of other than unjust laws "to call attention to overall injustice."

157. Black, *The Problem of Compatibility of Civil Disobedience with American Institutions of Government* 43 TEX. L. REV. 492 (1965) (appealing to the higher constitutional law of the nation).

"symbolic speech' and that any statute prohibiting this form of activity was unconstitutional.[158] Considerable surprise was engendered when the Solicitor-General stressed only the argument that the law admittedly was passed as a "symbol of public authority" to prevent widespread draft resistance, and not as a technique to make certain that registrants carried their draft cards at all times (although the law had been upheld on the latter ground and ruled unconstitutional on the former).[159] In another recent case the United States Court of Appeals for the District of Columbia has ruled that American citizens may violate a State Department ban on travel to foreign restricted areas, since present federal statutes do not give the State Department the right to control a person's travel.[160] These decisions have demonstrated the continuing vitality of civil disobedience in effectuating legal and social reform. Perhaps of greatest significance is the recent recognition being afforded to the role of conscience within the concept of civil disobedience.[161] The Supreme Court has stated its vital role well in *Girouard v. United States*:

> The struggle for religious liberty has through the centuries been an effort to accommodate the demands of the State to the conscience of the individual. The victory for freedom of thought recorded in our Bill of Rights recognizes that in the domain of conscience there is a moral power higher than the State. Throughout the ages men have suffered death rather than subordinate their allegiance to God to the authority of the State.[162]

---

158. The statute, 79 Stat. 586, as amended 50 U.S.C. § 462 (b) (Supp. I, 1965) was indeed prompted by anti-draft demonstrations including burning draft cards. [*See* 2 U.S. CODE CONG & AD. NEWS 2889 (1965)]. Two courts have rejected the first amendment argument [United States v. Smith, 249 F. Supp. 515 (S.D. IOWA *aff'd*, 368 F.2d 529 (8th cir. 1966); United States v. Miller, 249 F. Supp. 59 (S.D.N.Y., 1965) *aff'd*, 367 F.2d 72 (2d cir. 1966), *cert. denied*, 386 U.S. 911 (1967)] while the third rejected the argument, but was reversed on appeal by the First Circuit Court of Appeals, *O'Brien v. United States* 376 F.2d 538 (1st Cir. 1967). The court of appeals maintained the conviction for failing to carry the draft card at all times, but ruled the statute for draft card burning unconstitutional on the ground of symbolic speech. The decision of the First Circuit was subsequently reversed by the Supreme Court in United States v. O'Brien (May 27, 1968) 36 U.S.L. Week 4469 (1968). The Court held: "This Court has held that when "speech" and "non-speech" elements are combined in the same course of conduct, a sufficiently important governmental interest in regulating the nonspeech element can justify incidental limitations on First Amendment freedoms." "Symbolic Speech" has been previously upheld—"red flag"—Stromberg v. California, 283 U.S. 359 (1931); picketing—Thornhill v. Alabama, 310 U.S. 88 (1940); Amalgamated Food Emp. U. Local 590 v. Logan Valley Plaza, 88 S. Ct. 1601 (1968) (picketing of shopping center—constitutionally protected); and sit-ins, Garner v. Louisiana, 368 U.S. 157 (1961).

159. See Graham, *High Court Hears Draft Card Issue*, N.Y. Times, Jan. 25, 1968, at 1, col. 5.

160. *See, Passport Denial Curbed By Court*, N.Y. Times, Dec. 21, 1967. at 1, col. 2. The appeal was brought by Staughton Lynd after he had violated the ban by travelling to North Vietnam and was convicted by the lower court.

161. *See* Freeman, *A Remonstrance for Conscience*, 106 U. PA. L. REV. 806 (1958).

162. 328 U.S. 61, 68 (1946).

We have seen that aside from the question of acts of civil disobedience being legally sustained by the courts, a fundamental concept of non-violent disobedience is the willingness to accept punishment. This concept can only have true meaning if the courts themselves are willing to recognize the presence of conscience as a factor in their treatment of the civilly disobedient. There can be little doubt that within the framework of the legal system significant relief is afforded. This relief is mainly found in the discretion vested in authorities within the system: Prosecutors refusing to bring charges or bringing charges in a lesser degree; grand juries refusing to indict; juries refusing to convict; appellate courts dismissing charges for innocuous technicalities; judges awarding probation, suspended sentences, youthful offender treatment, and other forms of discretionary treatment.[163] The alleviation of punishment may not be of crucial importance, for it is the acceptance of punishment and the ensuing suffering that acts as the moral transference in persuading society of the depth of the social and legal change required. Of greater importance is the future significance of the initial conviction. If society continues to recognize moral and conscientious motivation, then conviction for such motives should not entail the sanctions meted out to ordinary criminals. In dealing with recidivist statutes and a host of other secondary treatment questions the nature of the offense and the intent of the disobedient should be considered.

These issues are of particular concern for men of high courage who enlist in causes of conscience and who seek admission in professions where high moral fitness is the usual applicable standard.[164] The Supreme Court faced this issue in a case involving the denial of an application to the bar because the applicant had been charged with violating the Neutrality Act of 1917 for joining the army of a foreign state and for arrests on charges of "criminal syndicalism" in connection with a strike.[165] The applicant had never been convicted of any crime and the Court concluded:

> [E]ven if it be assumed that the law was violated, it does not seem that such offense indicated moral turpitude—even in 1940. Many persons in this country actively supported the Spanish Loyalist Government. During the prelude to World War II, many idealistic young men volunteered to help causes they believed right. . . . Few Americans would have regarded

---

163. See Allen, *Civil Disobedience and the Legal Order*, 36 U. CINN. L. REV. 16 (1967).

164. Koenigsberg v. State Bar, 353 U.S. 252, 263 (1956); *see* Reich, *The New Property*, 73 YALE L. J. 733 (1964) where admission to the Bar is treated as a property right.

165. Schware v. Board of Bar Examiners, 353 U.S. 232 (1956).

> their conduct as involving moral turpitude. In determining whether a person's character is good, the nature of the offense which he has committed must be taken into account.[166]

The Court directed that the applicant be admitted.

In a recent case the California Supreme Court directed the admission of an applicant to the bar over the refusal of the Committee of Bar Examiners.[167] The applicant had been arrested six times for picketing and participating in "sit-ins" at various business establishments believed to follow discriminatory business or hiring practices. He was convicted twice of misdemeanor charges. The applicant admitted to the Committee that he believed in civil disobedience and might well as an attorney take part in civil rights demonstrations. The court stated:

> It should be emphasized that petitioner explicitly repudiated violent civil disobedience and that all of the demonstrations he participated in were peaceful. The sincerity of petitioner's beliefs in non-violent civil disobedience and his high motivation in this regard are unchallenged by respondent. His sentiments on the qualified right of civil disobedience, however controversial, are shared, not only by large numbers of idealistic youth who have similarly demonstrated peacefully throughout our nation in recent years to protest suppression of the rights of Negroes, but also by some legal scholars and other eminent people . . .
>
> We do not believe that petitioner's participation in the civil disobedience here shown can be characterized as involving moral turpitude. If we were to deny to every person who has engaged in a "sit-in" or other form of non-violent civil disobedience, and who has been convicted therefor, the right to enter a licensed profession, we would deprive the community of the services of many highly qualified persons of the highest moral courage. This should not be done.[168]

In a case involving conscientious objection, it has been held that deliberate violation of the Selective Service Act because of moral scruples, resulting in a felony conviction, was not an "infamous" crime under Section 1 of Article II of the California Constitution, so as to deprive the objector of his right to vote.[169] New York has similarly held that a claim of exemption from military service on conscientious grounds does not justify exclusion from the bar.[170]

---

166. *Id.* at 242.

167. Hallinan v. Committee of Bar Examiners, 65 Cal.2d 447, 421 P.2d 76 (1966), commented upon in 55 CAL. L. REV. 899 (1967) and 13 HOWARD L. J. 445 (1967).

168. *Id.* at 461, 421 P.2d at 86-87.

169. *Otsuka v. Hite*, 64 Cal.2d 596, 414 P.2d 412 (1966).

170. Application of Steinbugler, 297 N.Y. 713, 77 N.E.2d 16 (1947); Koster v. Holz, 3 N.Y.2d 639, 148 N.E.2d 287 (1958).

A recent article makes an interesting analogy between civil disobedience and a civil contract. The author asserts that the right to disobey a law for deeply held moral principles and to accept punishment for the disobedience should correspond to the right to disavow a contract and to pay damages for the breach.[171]

The development of the law in this area has proceeded on three separate levels: Civil disobedience has been recognized as a valid method of testing the validity of the law within the federal system; it has through an ever-expanding concept of constitutional guarantees quickened the pace of legal and social reform; and, finally, in developing an alternative to violence, it has offered society the opportunity to respond to the punishment and suffering of its practitioners, thus effectively strengthening the legal system. While the obligation to obey the law has not been diminished, the effectiveness of the entire social and legal system has been strengthened by the slow but definitive emergence of a legal theory establishing civil disobedience within the legal order.

Conclusion

We have now come full cycle in our exploration of civil disobedience. From these searchings we have seen that civil disobedience can be an indispensable technique for the efficacious functioning of our legal and social order. The practice of civil disobedience and the use of nonviolence, in fact rests on the foundation of the legal system and functions within that system. The courts are beginning to recognize use of civil disobedience. Such an exploration does indeed lead to the conclusion that the law is shaping an emerging general theory of civil disobedience whose outlines are now visible and the substance of which is being constructed. This theory rests on confidence in the viability of our social and legal order.

Our own society at home will be rent by internecine strife in the coming years over the demands of our minority groups for full and equal shares in our national society. The inability of Negroes, lacking the channels of communication, influence and appeal which would enable them to escape the ghetto life, has led to frustrations of powerlessness and to the conviction that there is no effective way except violence as a means of redress and a way of moving the system.[172] It is the

171. De Boisblanc, *The Dilemma of the Disobedient; A Solution*, 42 Ind. L. J. 521 (1967). Where, of course, a law to be obeyed becomes so inefficacious that the bulk of society refuses to obey, then the contract becomes "voidable."

172. Report of the National Advisory Commission on Civil Disorders 205 (Bantam Books ed. 1968). The Report states: "More generally, the result is alienation and hostility towards the institutions of law and government and the white society which controls them. This is reflected in the reach toward racial consciousness and solidarity reflected in the slogan "Black Power."

white society that must bear much of the blame for this posture of violent response. The National Advisory Commission on Civil Disorders took full note of this fact in its report:

> A climate that tends toward the approval and encouragement of violence as a form of protest has been created by white terrorism directed against non-violent protest, including instances of abuse and even murder of some civil rights workers in the South; by the open defiance of law and federal authority by state and local officials resisting desegregation; . . . This condition has been reinforced by a general erosion of respect for authority in American society and reduced effectiveness of social standards and community restraints on violence and crime. This in turn has largely resulted from rapid urbanization . . . The atmosphere of hostility and cynicism is reinforced by a widespread perception among Negroes of the existence of police brutality and corruption and of a "double standard" of justice and protection—one for Negroes and one for Whites.[173]

The response of the leadership community to the riots must cause concern among Negroes that the white community is perpetrating a showdown of violence in an attempt to seal off the Negro community. Instead of responding to the urban crises with funds and legislation to deal with the social and economic problems of the ghetto, which the National Commission Report states is of the highest priority for national action,[174] we see report after report calling for the repeated use of the National Guard to control riots.[175] The Institute for Defense Analysis, engaged in research for the defense department, has recommended a thorough investigation of an assortment of non-lethal weapons on the market that could be used in riot control including chemical, pain, and gas guns.[176] Instead of social legislation promoting fair housing opportunities the State legislatures have seen fit to pass numerous laws against riots and rioters, usually categorizing the offenses as felonies.[177] The National Institute of Municipal Law Officers has published a major report on riots which includes a bibliography of over fifty articles, journals and reports that appeared after the Detroit riot of 1967, dealing with riot control.[178]

---

173. *Id.* at 204.

174. *Id.* at 2.

175. *See* Note, *Riot Control and the Use of Federal Troops*, 81 HARV. L. REV. 638 (1968) and 8 THE MUNICIPAL ATTORNEY, no. 12, Dec. 1967, p. 196 "More Use of National Guard in Riots Urged."

176. REPORT, *supra* note 172 at 196.

177. 8 THE MUNICIPAL ATTORNEY, no. 11, Nov. 1967, p. 178.

178. See Treanor, *Riots and Municipalities*, report no. 152, National Institute of Municipal Law Officers, p. 34 (1968).

This cycle of responses must be stopped or it will lead ultimately to destruction of the American system. It requires a deeper understanding by all Americans that only sustained non-violent responses can lead to solution of the problems ahead. Perhaps the violent deaths of Dr. Martin Luther King and Senator Robert F. Kennedy will catalyze a new moral commitment by the American people.

Our hope is that we can avoid the bloody violence which we have witnessed as so much a part of American history and encourage our society to seek its goals through the use of democratic, moral, and conscientious methods.

Neither will the world stand still while we grope for solutions of our national problems at home. Archibald MacLeish, himself a great institution of America, has written that we have also failed to grasp the true significance of our leadership role in the international community. In a series of essays written over a period of twenty years and recently published, Mac Leish states that we have failed to understand not only the nature of the world we are in and helped to make, but also the nature of the revolution sweeping over the globe, and have therefore maneuvered ourselves into a position of hostility to change, and isolated ourselves from other peoples and nations and from the moral issues of our time.[179]

We have no shortage of goals—world peace, economic justice, human rights—what we lack is an appreciation of the acceptable and necessary means of arriving there. The new nations of the world as well as our own people are demanding rapid development of their human and physical resources. Survival of the free world may very well depend on our ability to accelerate social progress more rapidly than our competitors, not to sanctify order at the price of justice so as to keep entrenched vested interests. One of the directions in which both ethics and action is most likely to move in this century will come from Ghandhian "ahimsa" (love) and satyagraha (civil disobedience).[180] America must be prepared and willing, to embrace those concepts and practices which will move our society and the world forward, while preserving our democratic way of life. Civil disobedience may be at the forefront of this ethical and conscientious way of life.

---

179. A CONTINUING JOURNEY, ESSAYS AND ADDRESSES, by Archibald Mac Leish, (1968).
180. BURTT, MAN SEEKS THE DIVINE 481-524 (1957).

Children of the Detroit Riots:
A Study of Their Participation and Their Mental Health†

RICHARD KOMISARUK, MD* AND CAROL E. PEARSON, MD**

INTRODUCTION

ON July 23, 1967 an outbreak of activity began in the Twelfth Street section of the City of Detroit. It spread within the next few days in all directions to include all parts of the City in which Negro people live. It is the purpose of this article to explore what we will term, for convenience, the Detroit Riots, from a demographic and geographic standpoint, as well as from a psychological and clinical point of view.

The subjects of the research with which this study is concerned are the almost seven hundred juveniles who were brought to the Wayne County Juvenile Court Youth Home during the week of the violent activity.[1] These juveniles comprise less than one-fifth of all persons arrested during the riots. Although it is possible that certain considerations distinguish these youngsters from others in the community who were not arrested, it was not possible for us to develop a matching sample of children who would serve as controls for the clinical and psychological parts of our study in spite of concerted efforts.

The failure of our efforts to obtain a control group was attributable to a pervasive suspicion on the part of those approached that involvement in such a study would render them susceptible to police retaliation. In spite of this deterrent, we feel that some important information has been obtained from this research effort, and that certain conclusions and inferences can be, at least tentatively, drawn from this material.

---

† The opinions expressed are those of the authors, and are not necessarily the views of the Wayne County Juvenile Court or its staff.

* M.D. 1958, Wayne State University, Detroit, Mich.; Director, Clinic for Child Study, Wayne County Juvenile Court; Clinical Instructor, Dep't. Psychiatry, Wayne State University Medical School.

** B.S. 1952; M.D. 1956, University of Michigan; Consultant in Child Psychology Wayne State University Medical School, Wayne County Juvenile Court, Children's Center of Metropolitan Detroit; Clinical Instructor, Dep't. Psychiatry, Wayne State University Medical School.

1. It should be noted that the statements that are being made regarding arrested youngsters in no way include the apparently small number who participated in arson or sniping. None of the arrested youngsters admitted to either of these offenses. Our comments as to the normality of the participation in the riots, therefore, do not explain participation in these two offenses.

The impression of psychopathology may be erroneously conveyed by any discussion of psychodynamic characteristics of individuals or groups. Preparatory to any further presentation, it should be noted that the investigators involved in this study did not accept the premise that participation in the riot activity was in itself evidence of psychopathology.

The Clinical Approach

The sample of youngsters who were studied clinically was taken from the entire group of 673 arrested children. Discharges from the Youth Home of the arrested youngsters began on Thursday, July 27, 1967. The testing began on Tuesday, August 1, 1967. The first group tested was composed of the last seventy children to leave the Youth Home. There were several possible reasons for the delay in discharge from the Youth Home. One was a record of previous offenses of considerable length and severity not necessarily related to the riot; a second was the nature of the charge levelled at the youngster; and third was a difficulty in locating a person parentally responsible for the child to retrieve him from the Youth Home.

The second group of seventy children who were tested was selected by a table of random numbers from all of the arrested youngsters except for the seventy tested initially.

A summary of the psychological testing is reported as follows by Dr. Patricia Carpenter, Chief Psychologist, Wayne County Juvenile Court Clinic for Child Study:

> The study was designed in cooperation with Dr. Richard Komisaruk, Director of the Clinic for Child Study, Dr. Carol E. Pearson, a psychiatric consultant at the Clinic, Dr. Sidney B. Jenkins, Clinical Director, Psychiatric Division of the Wayne County General Hospital, Dr. Herman M. Schornstein, Associate Director of the Clinic for Child Study, and the psychology staff.
>
> We decided to use three instruments: a multiple choice questionnaire (see Appendix A) that would assess conscious attitudes and values, and a sentence completion test (see Appendix B) and figure drawings to appraise more unconscious material. This battery was administered initially to seventy boys in the Youth Home, randomly divided into groups of ten. The administrators, in teams of two, were varied as to race and sex, on the assumption that this might have some bearing on the results. The second group of seventy boys was selected on a truly random basis, and was tested in similar fashion in the Clinic Building, adjacent to the Youth Home. Youngsters tested were assured of anonymity. Data as to age,

father's and mother's occupation, school grade, number of police contacts, jobs held, area of residence and other demographic data were included in the initial part of the questionnaire. Instructions for the drawings were simply to "draw a picture of a person." The items were administered in this order, with subjects assured that their responses would have no bearing on court decisions about them.

The results of the questionnaire portray the average youngster queried in the survey as fifteen to seventeen years old, living in either rented or owned home (about half and half), enrolled in school, being supported by the father's or mother's job, born in Detroit, having had a job, and having been involved with the police less than four times.

He was picked up for looting, expressed little hostility against neighborhood store owners, had close white friends, and felt white people were "like anyone else," although they "did not understand Negroes," and that the police were often unfair and sometimes brutal while the soldiers just did their jobs. The most important thing about the riot was that "everyone went crazy and followed other people," and "riots can be stopped most effectively by giving Negroes equal rights with whites in every area and educating people to understand one another." He feels that because of the riots, "Negroes will be hated more," but on the other hand, "something will be done to help them." Poor Negroes who became successful, achieved this through getting an education, and the best avenues of success for a poor Negro are to become a professional or go into legitimate business. The Vietnam War is regarded as wrong, and most feel it should be stopped; and there is a general feeling that education is the best way to get ahead, and is an important life goal. In addition, most feel Negroes can best get their rights through education. The most popular Negro leaders, nationally and locally, are Dr. Martin Luther King and Reverend Nicholas Hood [Detroit Common Council], respectively; Senator Robert Kennedy is the most popular white national leader, with Governor George Romney as the most popular locally. Most claimed to have heard nothing recently about Mayor Jerome Cavanagh, but when queried about his personal problems and difficulties with the police, most felt sorry for him. The kind of man perceived as an ego ideal is either "kind, gentle and helps others," or "fun-loving guy." The person felt closest to is, by a large majority, "mother."

Although there are few group differences between the boys interviewed in the Youth Home (the first group) and those who came in from outside, there are some suggestive interesting trends. For example, boys in the Youth Home as compared with boys who came in later from outside, tended more frequently to pick Elijah Muhammad as the most admired Negro leader; they also more often felt Negroes could best obtain their rights through violent action. They more often chose as a life goal "to be respected like a man," and more frequently felt closer to their fathers or a peer than to their mothers. These differences may reflect time perspective, in that the Youth Home group was questioned right after the riot, or the fact that many of the Youth Home group were accused of more serious offenses or had more extensive delinquent records.

There appear to be no differences between groups in terms of sex and/or color of examiner, although there is a slight tendency for more hostility to be expressed in the groups where the two examiners were Negro males.

The material in the sentence completion tests and the drawings portray a varied picture of youths who range from those who obviously wish to conform and please white authority figures (perhaps the majority) to militant and angry boys who espouse "black power" slogans. Many boys are reflective and intense in their analysis of the riot and the place of Negroes in the community. For example, *being a Negro in Detroit* is described at one extreme as "the worst thing that ever happened to me," "being a slave," and on the other hand as "like having a house full of gifts," or "proud." *Life ahead looks* "bad; people will have to pay because of the riot," or "like rain ahead," or "pretty mean." *A real man* "works for his money," or "is one who speaks for his rights." *It hurts when* "you see a friend hurt." *Riots can be* "death," or "no games to start," or "heartbreaking." *White people are* "nothing," or "people like anyone else," or "my friends" *I dream about* "the riots," or "a better world in which to live." *After the riot I want most* "to be free," or "peace," or "not to have another start up again." What comes through along with the evasion, the defensiveness and the bitterness, is the hope that somehow things will be better, that the future may be salvaged through education and effort, and that some white people at least are potential allies in the struggle for a fuller life. Themes frequently expressed both in the sentences and on the drawings are the importance of strength and manliness, the supportive function of women, both mothers, and girlfriends, the desire for some positive, idealistic goals, and the importance of education and status strivings.

In general, the results suggest 1.) that the average youth involved in the riot, as assessed by our sample, is oriented toward educational and achievement goals (for example, he is still in school and has held jobs), and looks to them to improve the position of the Negro and gain greater economic and social advantage for himself; 2.) he is sympathetic to moderate leaders (such as Dr. Martin Luther King) who advocate similar goals; 3.) he has an ideal of manhood which includes gentleness and protectiveness; and 4.) he lacks pathological hostility or sexual identification problems, although his self-esteem is somewhat impaired, and he tends to be impulsive and over-dependent. This last impression was based on ratings of the sentence completion tests and the figure drawings.

His intellectual level appears somewhat below average, but in view of the social and educational deprivation he has experienced, this seems to reflect less a real deficit than one more cultural blemish. Although embittered and militant revolutionaries exist in our sample, they are apparently as yet in the minority. One may speculate, of course, that some of these youngsters are consciously fearful and, therefore, suppress their true feelings.[2]

There seems to be an awareness of the different ideologies relevant to the civil rights movement which seems incompatible with the lack of identification with the more outspoken radical leaders as evidenced by the questionnaire results. By extension it would seem that the ideas which underlie the riot activity have been effectively promulgated by the leadership, although the personalities of some of the radical leaders themselves are not taken by the youngsters as ego ideals. This is in contrast with revolutionary movements in the past in which personal demagoguery of individuals has been the *sine qua non* of the effectiveness of the movement.[3]

A question is raised as to who the actual leaders of the riot activity are.[4] Must we assume that avowed civil rights leaders precipitate riot activity? Is it not more likely that the spontaneous combustion of smoldering resentment and hostility gave rise to participation in the riot by average Negro citizens, some of whom assumed roles of leadership?

There had been considerable newspaper publicity regarding Mayor Jerome P. Cavanagh's difficulties in the control of the Detroit Police Force prior to the riots. Exemplary of this problem was the "blue flu," a flagrant absenteeism on the part of numerous police

---

2. Interviews by authors from August through October, 1967 tend to substantiate this point.

3. Fidel Castro in Cuba; Patrice Lumumba in the Congo.

4. Louis Lomax makes an explanatory point in his discussion of Mrs. Parks and the emotional basis of her instigation of the Montgomery bus boycott: There have been scores of attempts to discover why Mrs. Parks refused to move. The local white power structure insisted that the NAACP had put her up to it, but this charge was quickly disproved. The extremists spread the word that Mrs. Parks was a communist agent, that the whole thing had been hatched in the Kremlin; that rumor collapsed under the weight of its preposterousness. The truth is that Mrs. Parks was a part of the deepening mood of despair and disillusionment that gripped the American Negro after World War II. The only way to account for Mrs. Parks is to say that she was a part of the times; that, at long last, her cup ran over. L. Lomax, The Negro Revolt 81 (1962).

officers who were attempting to obtain improvements in salary and working conditions. The adverse publicity was such that the Mayor emerged as being ineffectual in handling the crisis. It had been widely believed that the past popularity of Mayor Cavanagh was instrumental in the relative freedom from riot activity which had characterized the Detroit area in recent years. In fact, it has been generally accepted that Mayor Cavanagh owed his first election to his popularity with the Negro voters. In the light of this, the responses to questions 27 through 29 (see Appendix A) concerning Mayor Cavanagh are of some interest. The response to the first question suggests either ignorance of his difficulties, or denial of their significance.

A question may be raised as to the validity of the questionnaire responses. Although the administration of the questionnaire was handled in such a way that youngsters were guaranteed anonymity, it is certainly possible that some of them maintained the vain hope that certain responses might expedite their release from the Youth Home. However, responses to some of the questions concerning the police tend to refute this possibility (see Appendix A # 8). The popular response was that they were brutal.[5]

With respect to personality characteristics of the boys who were tested, certain values, such as kindness, gentleness, and the usual "boy scout morality" are taken as ideal personality traits. The incompatibility between these espoused ideals and participation in violent activity must be understood in terms of the complexity of the issue.

These espoused ideals are revered in the white American culture along with a respect for competitiveness and aggressiveness, especially in boys. These latter traits are so highly prized in the white culture for white males that their insufficiency is viewed with alarm and concern about adequacy of sexual identity.[6] These same highly prized traits are considered eminently threatening when encountered in Negro males to the point that they are punished and discouraged in various ways rather than rewarded.[7] There are certain token exceptions as exemplified by recent racial integration of most sports activities.

More or less passive values have provided for many Negro youngsters a protective way of life which has served to conceal and bind the unconscious feelings which emerge when conditions allow for a breakthrough. In our interviews with a number of families, this point came

---

5. Rinella, *Police Brutality and Racial Prejudice: A First Close Look*, 45 U. Det. J. of Urban L. —, — (1968).

6. O. Fenichel, The Psychoanalytic Theory of Neurosis 178 (1945).

7. Powdermaker, *The Channeling of Negro Aggression by the Cultural Process*, 48 Am. J. Soc. 754 (1943).

through very clearly: the veneer of passive acceptance of the status quo ante was easily shattered by a militant discontent approaching overt hostility which appeared with minimal stimulation.

Another kind of objection to our study can be raised with respect to the lack of control groups to compare with our sample of arrested youngsters. An available basis of comparison is the delinquent population that we see at the Wayne County Juvenile Court Clinic for Child Study. It is the impression of the psychological team that the group of youngsters arrested during the riots exhibited a somewhat higher level of personality integration as indicated by a more appropriate masculine identification, less dependency, and generally higher level of maturity.

Some consideration of the psychiatric interviews with the families of the arrested youngsters is in order. Ten families were interviewed in their homes by the authors. These families were selected at random from the group of names made available to us. For the most part, the families were notified several days in advance of the planned interview, and it was requested that the youngster under consideration be present. In most instances, the mother and son were seen jointly. Certain other family members were sometimes intermittently present. In two cases, the father and son were seen together.

The median age of the boys seen was sixteen. In only one case was there demonstrable evidence of psychopathology which took the form of slight mental retardation, requiring placement in a special class. In that case it seemed that there was an organic basis for the retardation in terms of the child's early developmental history. It was in keeping with the other findings that few of the boys had had previous contact with the juvenile court. None of the youngsters seen had histories of either significant emotional disturbance or delinquent behavior. An important general question is raised as to what kinds of inhibiting forces prevented participation in the riots when these normal youngsters found the attraction to riot activity irresistible.

In this small sample, the range of socio-economic levels was complete. There was a considerable variety of family constellations, most of which consisted of mother, stepfather and children. This was also characteristic of the larger sample.

Most of the interviews began with expressions of apology for the riots and the youngster's participation in them. Questioning readily unmasked, however, a fund of aggression which revealed a strong identification with the spirit of the riot activity. This, we suspect, may reflect the vicarious use that the mother made of her son's active involvement. It was clear that the families did not vilify the children because of riot participation in spite of any expression of chagrin and dismay over the riots. Thus, within the family, participation was considered neither abnormal nor inappropriate.

An additional comment on the change in the expressed attitude which occurred during the interview is that in many of the families there is a considerable ambivalence towards the riot and towards violent activity generally. Thus, the contradiction of the initially expressed attitude to what later emerged does not reflect falseness so much as a mixture of feelings. Feelings which are identified with aggression and hostility tend to be, for various reasons, suppressed and submerged.

In several instances, mothers who had come originally from the southern United States made comments which compared life in the South invidiously with their lot in Detroit. This attitude could be essentialized as "it isn't so good here, but it's a hundred times better than the way it is in the South. People who complain about things here should see what it's like in the South, and then they wouldn't complain so much."

Again, within a short time, negative feelings regarding the situation of a Negro would emerge even among these people who expressed superficial content. An area in which dissatisfaction was especially intense concerned education of their children. Here, the recognition of the often second-rate opportunities which the children were receiving was universal. There was a prevalent impression that education in a racially mixed school would be better. To this end, some of the parents had attempted to arrange transfers of their children. In any event, the dissatisfaction with schools opened the door to the considerable amount of aggression that prevailed throughout the interviewed group in all instances.

One of the interview fathers expressed a curious and possibly widely prevalent impression of the white power structure. He felt that the entire court system was corrupt because it was possible to accomplish almost any end through well placed payments to the controlling powers. Accordingly, he had paid his attorney (a Negro) what we consider an exorbitant fee for arranging the release of his son from detention. This was accomplished at a time when most of the youngsters were being released on the signature of their parents without legal assistance. This father compared his experience to previous contacts the family had had with law enforcement bodies in which he was convinced that payoffs and bribery were *de rigueur*. He stated these "facts" with a kind of smiling acknowledgment which was in no way counteracted by the hesitancy of the interviewers in accepting the validity of his contentions.

Reference is frequently made to the matriarchal qualities of Negro family life.[8] In the larger group of youngsters that we studied, absence of the natural father was a frequent finding. In the interviewed families, the impression was clearly conveyed that the mother played a vital part in the overall operation of the family. At times, her role was clearly dominant over that of her husband. Many of the mothers were employed gainfully, some of them at jobs which command a nominal respect. Although the item concerning personal respect was not popularly checked on the attitudinal questionnaire,[9] it has become the impression of the interviewers that trans-racial lack of respect for the role of the Negro male was a motivating factor in the unrest that both preceded and, apparently, succeeds the riot. This is compatible with our previously expressed comments concerning the suppression of aggression in the Negro male, and is exemplified by the often menial jobs made available to him. As menial and disagreeable as the jobs which are available to the adult Negro male are, those within the reach of the Negro adolescent male are even more degrading. There is a realistic attitude of hopelessness and pessimism concerning job aspirations in spite of some recent attempts to equalize employment opportunities.

Often, the adolescent Negro male feels a compelling need to earn money in order to obtain certain material things which are not supplied by the family. This need is particularly acute in those families in which the father is absent, and the youth is the nominal male head of the family. For these youths, failure to obtain adequate employment often contributes to a festering resentment which qualifies as one of a set of factors necessary for the spontaneous combustion which we feel triggered the riot.[10]

The high likelihood of her son being exposed to humiliating experiences often leads the Negro mother to be particularly protective of him in an effort to preserve his feelings of self-respect.[11] During the riot, the interviewed participants often had been left alone following vehement warning by their mothers against participation in the riot. It seemed that, although at a conscious level the mothers did not want their sons involved, unconsciously they may well have been desirous

8. *See*, D. MOYNIHAN, THE NEGRO FAMILY: THE CASE FOR NATIONAL ACTION (1965).
9. Appendix A #33e.
10. *See*, Employment Figures according to age and color for city of Detroit.
11. Observation of mothers in interviews described in article.

of this very behavior. For the mothers, this could be viewed as another vicarious avenue toward attainment of self-respect. Thus, it is important to consider this in terms of the unconscious use which the mother makes of her son towards the attainment of some of her personal goals. It appears that a Negro mother prizes assertive behavior in her sons as much as her white counterpart.

THE DEMOGRAPHIC APPROACH

Information was made available to us concerning the ages, genders, school grades, residences and criminal charges of the 673 children who were admitted to the Youth Home between July 23 and 30.[12] To study the meaning of these statistics, several techniques were employed.

First, a map was devised in which the residence locations of all juveniles detained in the Youth Home during the riots were designated by pins. The purpose of this map was to discover any unusual clustering or sparseness. The results indicate very clearly that the residence locations of these youngsters follows the pattern of distribution of Negro families in the City of Detroit.

The riots of 1943, which we believe had a dynamic meaning and mechanism completely different from that of the current disorder, were confined to relatively small areas of the City.[13] The Negro community of those years was likewise confined to a small area of the City, and there was a constricted Negro ghetto which simply no longer prevails. This is not intended to suggest that true housing integration exists in any part of Detroit. It simply means that the Negro community has enlarged and spread in an amoeboid pattern.

There are considerable variances in the socio-economic status of various neighborhoods within the Negro community. Compared economically, they range from destitute to upper middle income and sociologically from marked depression to considerable "upward mobility." The fact that the distribution of residences of arrested youngsters is as diffuse as it is, and as devoid of clustering and unusual grouping, indicates to us quite clearly that economic and sociologic poverty were *not* significant factors in the participation of youngsters in the rioting.

The area in which the riots broke out is contained in the Tenth Precinct, which is included in what is known as the inner city. It is

---

12. We suspect that the relatively large number of youngsters who were arrested and were thus available for our investigation tends to negate the objection to the lack of experimental controls.

13. A. LEE & N. HUMPHREY, RACE RIOT 25-27 (1943).

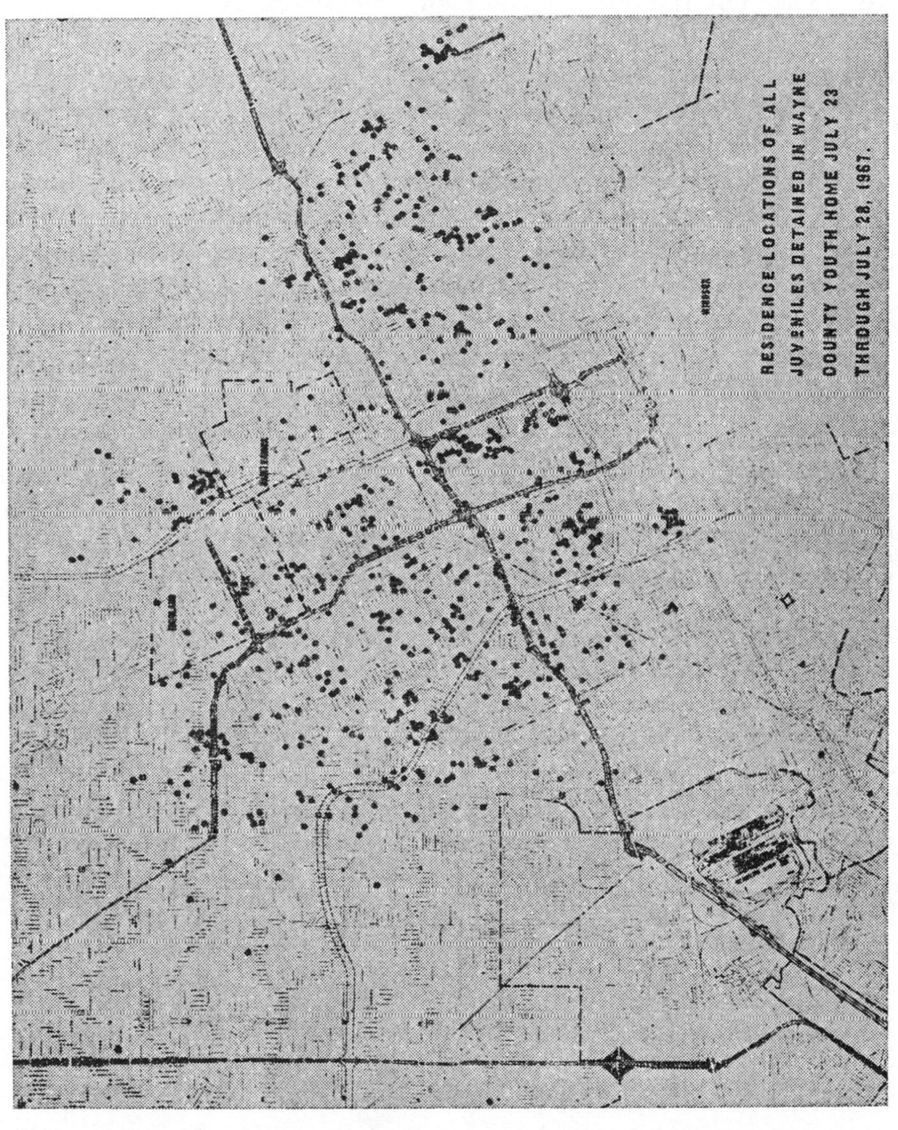
RESIDENCE LOCATIONS OF ALL
JUVENILES DETAINED IN WAYNE
COUNTY YOUTH HOME JULY 23
THROUGH JULY 28, 1967.

primarily a residential section. Part of Twelfth Street, which runs through the Tenth Precinct, was, at least prior to the riot, a center for business—both legitimate and otherwise. There were numerous bars and other entertainment spots along the street. Along a half mile stretch of Twelfth Street, prostitution was open and rampant at all hours of the day and night. Various other forms of illegal activity were also regularly engaged in on Twelfth Street. The immediate incident which triggered the riot was the raiding of an established "blind pig" at the northernmost end of this district.

It is of interest to note that the Tenth Precinct ranked fifth in number of arrests of juveniles. In contrast to this, the Tenth Precinct exceeded all other precincts in residences of arrested youngsters with ninety-eight of 627, but forty-two of these ninety-eight were apprehended in some precinct other than the Tenth. This discrepancy between precinct of residence and precinct of arrest, perhaps suggesting an exodus to safer ground, was not seen to this degree in any of the other precincts studied. This is compatible with an impression which had been garnered in years past; namely, that the activities in the Twelfth Street area predominantly involved adults.[14]

Statistical totals concerning children who were arrested during the riots are as follows:[15]

	Boys	Girls
Negro	600	27
White	41	3

The age distribution of these children is as follows:

Age	Boys	Girls
16	275	9
15	170	7
14	95	5
13	54	6
12	25	1
11	15	1
10	9	1
9	1	0

14. An example of the exclusion of juveniles from criminal activity in the Twelfth Street area was the relative infrequency of juvenile prostitutes there. There had been three separate areas of the city in which streetwalkers were regularly observed. The prostitute under seventeen years of age might be arrested in either of the areas other than Twelfth Street. In addition, these child-prostitutes tended not to be involved in the same type of commercial arrangement prevalent among older prostitutes; that is, they were usually not in cooperation with a pimp.

15. Table computed at Wayne County Juvenile Court.

Their school status is as follows:

Grade	Boys	Girls
12	24	2
11	99	3
10	122	4
9	111	3
8	65	8
7	44	2
6	22	—
5	9	—
4	11	1
Special Classes	56	3
Boys' Training School	3	GTS 2
Job Corps	1	—
Highland Park Comm'y College, 2d year	1	—
Wayne County Training School	—	1
Vista Maria (Delinquent Girls)	—	1
Out of School	74	—
Unknown	2	1

Charges were pressed against 673 of the arrested juveniles. A breakdown according to criminal charge is as follows:

Sodomy	1
Possession of whiskey	1
Possession of knife	2
Indecent liberties	2
Felonious assault	2
Drunk and disorderly	2
Robbery—unarmed	2
Assault with intent to murder	2
Reckless driving	2
Assault and unarmed robbery	2
Attempted arson	2
Lodger	3
Arson	4
Disturbing the peace	6
Unauthorized driving away automobile	10
Inciting to riot	13
Possession of stolen property	46
Breaking and entering	52
Violation of curfew	75
Entering without breaking, and looting	424
Total	673

Nineteen of the youngsters arrested had residences, at the time of the arrest, outside the external boundaries of Detroit. There is no community outside of Detroit which contributed any significant number of youngsters to the total arrested.

The City of Detroit contains two enclaves—Hamtramck and Highland Park. Both of these communities consist of a hodgepodge of industrial and residential sectors. There has been a small, stable Negro population in Hamtramck for many years. On the other hand, comparatively few Negroes lived in Highland Park prior to World War II.[16] Only four youngsters residing in Hamtramck were arrested during the riots, as compared to seventeen from Highland Park. The number of arrests in these communities was thirteen and sixteen, respectively.

On the demographic map, Hamtramck is conspicuous by the sparseness of pins contained therein, as compared to Highland Park and the adjacent sections of Detroit. It is tempting to speculate that the age and stability of the Negro community in Hamtramck contributed to the paucity of Hamtramck youngsters arrested. However, two additional factors must be considered. One is the reported high degree of vigilance on the part of the Hamtramck Police, and the other is the peculiar logistic difficulties in ingress and egress to and from that City by major arteries.

A comparable and interesting demographic artifact seems to have occurred in a small neighborhood in the southwest part of Detroit which forms a narrow peninsula bounded by several suburbs. This part of Detroit is approximately two miles long and a mile wide. The suburbs to the west and north of it are exclusively white. The suburbs to the south of it are predominantly Negro at their junction with Detroit. The part of Detroit under discussion is a racially mixed neighborhood which is between thirty-five and fifty percent Negro in occupancy, and which has existed as a Negro community in the area for some years. The area is considered one of the more stable integrated sections of the City, although this does not imply any true cultural admixture.

It can again be speculated that the relative freedom from riot activity in that area, both in terms of arrests there, as well as children from the area having been arrested, can be accounted for in terms of stability. However, we are advised that a drawbridge over a major artery regulating traffic in and out of that neighborhood was lifted during much of the riot activity.[17]

One might infer that in each illustration, ostensible integration resulted in decreased participation in the riot. However, in each instance, physical containment undoubtedly played a major part in the control of the violence to the extent that the significance of the integration factor is questionable.

Discussion

Some comparisons between the 1967 and 1943 Detroit riots are in order. A psychoanalytic interpretation of the 1943 riot was advanced

---

16. Detroit Housing Commission, Detroit Real Property Survey (1938).
17. Conversation with several unidentified police officers.

by Dr. Richard Sterba.[18] In his discussion of the unconscious origins of prejudice against Negroes, he points out that the Negro may be experienced by the white person either as an ominous newcomer comparable to the unwelcome younger siblings in the family constellation, or as a threatening father, according to the model of the Oedipus complex.[19] He cites extensive clinical material which tends to establish these points.[20] He suspected, but could not verify through clinical experiences with Negro patients, that equal and opposite psychodynamic influences were brought to bear in the vehement hatred that Negroes felt towards white people. Exemplary of these psychodynamic influences at that time were:

1.) The initial triggering events of the riot, vis-à-vis the allegation of sexual attack by members of one race on the other, had much in common with the prevalent lynchings of the century preceding the riot; and
2.) particular selection of automobiles, in important psychological as well as economic symbol for the community, as objects of the destruction.[21]

The bulk of the outright violence during the 1943 riots was inflicted on Negro individuals, as opposed to business places, by whites. There was frequent spontaneous formation of gangs dedicated to the purpose of attacking and dispatching hated individuals; the activities of these gangs followed the usual principles of mob psychology.[22] This, too, must be contrasted with the 1967 events in which group activity was conducted in a markedly different way, and was directed at more abstract goals; attacks were addressed toward the "establishment" rather than persons.

It is difficult to account for the 1967 riots in terms of unconscious factors extrapolated into group psychological principles. A crucially important distinction between the two riots is simply that there was minimal white participation in the 1967 riots. We characterize the 1967 riots as a Negro revolt against the power structure.

Many explanations have been put forth as to the psychological and political basis of the 1967 riots. These explanations range from a conspiracy theory[23] to a kind of simplistic racist view of the Negro as an

18. 1 R. Sterba, Psychoanalysis and the Social Sciences 411-27 (1947).
19. *Id.* at 413, 419.
20. *Id.*
21. *Id.* at 420.
22. Race Riot, *supra* note 13, at 72-74, ch. 6.
23. Prof. Edward Lurie, Department of History, Wayne State University in a personal interview stated that the Detroit Riots represented a complex causative mosaic. This pattern, he maintains, is not explainable through simple reference either to the Detroit

ingrate and an interloper.[24] It is our contention that the riots were caused by the spontaneous combustion of several ingredients which have been present for many years.

The most striking latent sentiment which was expressed in all of our material is the Negro's resentment of the social and cultural position into which he is forced by the dominant white community, and the corresponding insensibility of the white community to this situation. The widespread participation in the riots by Negro youngsters whom we studied which transcended all social and economic strata, establishes quite firmly, in our view, that this social malaise is experienced by all Negroes.

We have suggested above that the Negro mother, however matriarchal, has encouraged her son to express not only his manhood but also her abiding resentment of the derogation of Negroes.

The lack of personal identification on the part of the young Negro men with acknowledged spokesmen for the "black power" movement, in many ways is indicative of their health. That is, they are not inspired so much by an external stimulus, as by internal pressure which is only mobilized and, to some extent, liberated by the ideological expressions of the activist leadership. This is compatible with our observation that the youngsters who were arrested during the riot were appreciably more mature, stable, and better established along the road to psychosexual maturity as men than the group of youngsters who are routinely brought into the Youth Home because of delinquent behavior not connected with the riot.

A question arises as to the influence of progress in the civil rights movement during the past generation on the potentiation of riot activity. Robert Waelder addresses this point in his book, *Progress and Revolution*,[25] in which he states that:

> Revolutions seem to occur most frequently just after conditions have markedly improved, and while they are continuing to improve. . . . Poverty, oppression or, in more scientific terms, a low position in the hierarchies of power, income, status and safety can not, in themselves, be sufficient cause for revolt since such conditions have existed everywhere for long periods of time without generating revolution or revolutionary unrest.[26]

---

situation or the condition of the Negro. He posits a conception of civil disturbances that links our recent urban crises to broad patterns of national political and economic activity, as well as problems of national scope in terms of foreign relations. Included in his conception is an influence attributable to syndicated crime.

24. Comments made on television by citizens of Detroit during the riot.
25. R. Waelder, Progress and Revolution—A Study of Issues of Our Age (1967).
26. *Id.* at 219-20.

Waelder quotes Alexis deTocqueville who posited that, "patiently endured so long as it seemed beyond redress, a grievance comes to appear intolerable once the possibility of removing it crosses men's minds."[27] Waelder states further that, "The theory of the revolution of rising expectations appears to be an important, perhaps crucial, contribution to the understanding of revolution, particularly in an age of progress."[28] Furthermore:

> Revolutionary sentiment may appear not when the people are most downtrodden, but rather when their fortunes are rising—and rising fast, for that matter. . . . Resentment, and with it revolutionary sentiment, is a function of the social distance between rich and poor, though not in the sense employed by the popular theory: the greater the distance, the greater the resentment; but in precisely the opposite sense: the smaller the distance, the greater the resentment. . . . Negro resentment in the United States, for instance, rose to a revolutionary level only recently, after there had been steady improvement, far beyond what competent observers like Mr. Gunnar Myrdal had expected only twenty years earlier."[29]

Nathan Wright, Jr., in *Black Power and Urban Unrest,*[30] speaks of the median family income of white and non-white families from 1947 to 1963. In 1947, the median white family income was $3,157, and the median non-white family income was $1614 per year.[31] In 1963, the incomes had risen so that the median white income was $6,548, and the median non-white income was $3,465.[32] The percentage increase of median incomes of non-white relative to white families was negligible:

> Every American, no matter how unfortunate his condition, may be better off than the workers in the rice fields of China. Yet, a man's lively sense of his own impoverishment and denial must be measured chiefly in terms of what he perceives in relation to things that are close at hand. The American Negro feels what the economic statistics reveal: In his efforts toward progress in relation to white America, he has come up against a stone wall upon which—in large characters which are to him unmistakably and compellingly clear—he reads the word FRUSTRATION! Hence, Watts . . . and what may yet lie beyond.[33]

---

27. *Id.* at 227, quoting ALEXIS DETOCQUEVILLE, THE OLD REGIME AND THE FRENCH REVOLUTION 176 (1955).
28. WAELDER, *supra* note 25, at 229.
29. *Id.* at 225.
30. N. WRIGHT, BLACK POWER AND URBAN UNREST (1967).
31. *Id.* at 48.
32. *Id.* at 49.
33. *Id.* at 50.

Waelder corroborates this view in his statements regarding the revolutionary impulse:

> The revolutionary impulse may well be said to stem from frustration. . . . Frustration is experienced relative to a standard that varies with time, place, and circumstances. The frustrated ambition of an aristocrat or an intellectual may have a higher revolutionary potential than the hunger of a peasant.[34]

On self-respect and respect by others, Wright makes the following comments:

> Undoubtedly, the most crucial part of black self-development is the building of black men's self-respect. . . . In this endeavor, we have gone so far as to adopt the white American disdain for all that pertains to blackness. The sad fact is that in America black people have been taught that to be like other Americans they must come to hate themselves. And this we all too often do with tragic vengeance. Doubtless, many Negroes decry black power because of a cultural perception of incongruity between "power" and "blackness." Negroes are culturally conditioned to see themselves as childlike, immature, and powerless. . . . How can we love our neighbors, when we do not love and respect ourselves?
>
> An eminent young Negro psychiatrist writes: "The Negro community's high rate of crimes of violence, illegitimacy, and broken homes can be traced in part to the Negro's learned self-hatred, as well as to his poverty." He believes that the kind of so-called integration which white people have offered to the black community, "may have negative effects upon the Negro, and may undermine his obvious need for strong, positive group identification. No man can instill pride and self-respect in another man. The same is true with ethnic groups. . . . Instead of hating ourselves—as any group which dwells on its weaknesses might do—we must accentuate the positive aspects of who and what we are."[35]

Two important questions remain to be dealt with. The first is concerned with the appropriateness of psychiatric exploration of the riot issue generally. Is the role of the psychiatrist entirely one of diagnostic exclusion of psychopathology in the participants?

We contend that there is psychopathology of a serious type inherent in the situation which has given rise to the riots. This psychopathology exists principally in the minds of the white community, and it takes the form of inconsistency in the white man's perception of the

34. WAELDER, *supra* note 25, at 233-34.

35. WRIGHT, *supra* note 30, at 63-64, quoting in part Poussaint, Our Sunday Visitor, Oct. 23, 1966, p. 1.

Negro. The roots of this disorder undoubtedly stem from some of the unconscious psychological forces which have been outlined by Sterba[36] and others.[37] There is a fundamental failure of the white culture to identify and adjust the aggressive drive towards Negroes in the same way that most other unjust hostility is held in check.[38] The white youngster is presented with a peculiar inconsistency in his childhood development when he recognizes that the attitude towards the Negro is an exception to the usual Golden Rule which governs his everyday behavior. The white child does not acquire this necessarily from direct statements of sentiment by his parents who may be making a concerted effort to train the child in such matters as racial equality. He does, however, come to recognize the societal derogation of Negroes from his daily life experiences.

Schooling for the Negro child has only very recently included information of a positive nature concerning the Negro and his role in history. Positive associations concerning Negroes generally are few and far between in the education of the white child. This statement does not except the sentimentalized versions of the Negro success stories in which the attainments have been reached because of masochistic humility on the part of the Negro.[39] In such literature, the derogatory tone and attitude remain transparently obvious, and contribute to the educational conditioning of the child in the sense that it considerably widens the gap between the white youngster and his Negro counterpart. The white youngster is, after all, expected to express himself more or less assertively in order that he may effectively compete in the white society.

A curious kind of counter-stereotyping probably exists within the Negro community in its attitude towards white society. This stereotyping certainly may, at times, interfere even with the thrapeutic relationship between a psychotherapist whose race differs from that of his patient,[40] in that it can be and is used in a defensive manner. This defense is very difficult to contend with clinically, and has led many therapists to the belief that all therapeutic endeavors in racially mixed combinations such as these are doomed to failure.[41]

The black separatist movement derives much of its fervor from this kind of racial generalization, coupled with a vindictive pleasure in

---

36. STERBA, *supra* note 18, at 413.
37. F. FANON, BLACK SKIN, WHITE MASKS 31-38 (1967).
38. WRIGHT, *supra* note 30, at 26-27.
39. WRIGHT, *supra* note 30, at 157, 159.
40. Grier, *When the Therapist is Negro: Some Effects on the Treatment Process*, 123, AM. J. OF PSYCHIATRY 1587 (June, 1967).
41. Often cited in case conferences in which there is a mixed patient-therapist unit.

retaliation against aggressive abuse of the Negro. Concerning this point, the Negro seems to experience real pleasure in sensing how frightened the white community is. In our studies, the most abjectly sorrowful and apologetic Negroes whom we interviewed—even those who seemed completely at odds with the purposes of the riot—hastened to assure us that there was undoubtedly going to be further riot activity, and that it was going to be more destructive and bloody than what had already occurred.

This leads to the second clinical question which has to do with prognosis. It has been said, with considerable assuredness by many authorities, that there is going to be more revolutionary activity in the near future.[42] Certainly the historical precedent for this is well established. More important, all of the ingredients necessary for the spontaneous combustion remain substantially as they were prior to the 1967 riots.[43] We suspect that the inflammability may have actually increased for various reasons, not the least of which is the success of the previous efforts.

Are there any steps that can be taken at this time to provide a remedy for the conditions which make possible and necessary the Negro Revolt? We feel that the only answer lies in therapeutic education—principally directed at the children of the white community. Obviously, control of riot damage is a matter which would necessitate the most effective use of police facilities. It should be noted parenthetically that the police need assistance in handling the psychological elements involved in their work with the Negro community. Past efforts have been unsuccessful, and there is an alarming pendulum swing in the direction of increased opportunity for offensive and abusive handling of black citizens by police, e.g. pending "stop and frisk" legislation.

Educational efforts with the white community will not produce immediate results. The failure to initiate a sweeping change in the attitude of the white community toward the Negro, however, can only result in a perpetuation of this situation into a ceaseless series of revolutionary sorties with a limitless potential for destruction.

The same kind of educational efforts must also be afforded the Negro youngster in order that he may develop the self-respect, ethni-

---

42. D. Moynihan in White Paper discussion of riot activity.
43. 1. Failure to be treated with respect
    2. Failure to obtain equal opportunity in selection of employment
    3. Failure of "Open Housing Legislation"
    4. Failure of public school system to meet educational needs of inner city students.

cally and personally, which is a prerequisite to his commanding respect and true acceptance in an integrated community.

An additional alteration essential to the improvement of these overall conditions is that the Negro middle-class be able to contend more effectively with the ambivalence which it currently experiences. This ambivalence is derived from a wish to continue the pursuit of racial integration countered by identification with the black separatist revolutionary movement. Human energy can only be effectively mobilized if this ambivalence is resolved in a constructive manner. Of course, such a resolution is dependent in turn on the elimination of the oppressive derogation which Negroes continue to experience, in however subtle a manner, at the hands of the white community.

Conclusion

We have presented a twofold view of the participation in the Detroit riot by juveniles. Statistically, it is obvious that there was no correlation between socio-economic status and participation in the riot. Residence in a pseudo-integrated community did not in itself decrease participation. Of 673 arrests, 641 were Negro males in the age group of fifteen to seventeen years. The greatest number (424) were arrested for entering without breaking and looting.

Clinically, we found from a random sample of youths selected from the arrested group that the average youngster was fifteen to seventeen years of age, living with and supported by his family, and with no record of major delinquent activity. The most significant finding was that this average youth lacks pathological hostility or sexual identification problems. The impression of the psychological team was that the group of youngsters arrested during the riots exhibited a somewhat higher level of personality integration as indicated by a more appropriate masculine identification, less dependency, and a generally higher level of maturity than the delinquent population that we normally see at the Wayne County Clinic for Child Study.

Clinical psychiatric interviews revealed that although the youths had been warned by their mothers to avoid the riot areas, they were subsequently left alone. We suspect that at an unconscious level, riot participation was not condemned but sanctioned by the mothers, though at a conscious level the reverse was true. The aggressive behavior encountered in the riots was more in keeping with the white American culture which places great emphasis on aggressive behavior in the male than with the heretofore passive behavior stereotypically ascribed to the American Negro.

Appendix A

RIOT QUESTIONNAIRE

Popular responses are marked with (*). If the second most popular choice was close to the first, it is marked (#).

NO. ____ AGE ____ GRADE IN SCHOOL ____ NO. IN HOUSEHOLD ____

IS FATHER PRESENT? ____ IS MOTHER PRESENT? ____ STREET & CROSS STREET ____

OWN OR RENT HOME ____ NO. OF BEDROOMS ____ SOURCE OF INCOME ____

1. Father's Job
   Kind of Job
2. Mother's Job
   Kind of Job
3. ADC or Welfare
4. Other

Have you ever had a job?______ If yes, what kind and when?______

How long have you lived in Detroit?__________

Where were you Born?________

Have you ever been involved with police or Juvenile Court before? No____ Yes____ How many times?________

1. What are you in here for?

   #A. Curfew violation.
   *B. Looting.
   C. Shooting.
   D. Burning.
   E. Other (specify).

2. During the riot, I saw burning—Yes____ No____

   If yes, I felt

   *A. Sad.
   B. Excited.
   *C. Scared.
   D. Happy.
   E. Angry.

3. During the riot, I saw people killed or hurt—Yes____ No____

   If yes, I felt

   A. Sad.
   B. Excited.
   C. Scared.
   D. Happy.
   E. Angry.

4. During the riot, I saw Looting—Yes____ No____

   If yes, I felt

   A. Sad.
   *B. Excited.
   C. Scared.
   D. Happy.
   E. Angry.

5. How do you get along with neighborhood store owners?
   *A. They were always nice to me.
   B. They charged too much.
   C. They cheated us.
   D. Didn't care about them either way.
   #E. They were mostly okay.

6. How do your parents feel about your behavior during the riot?
   A. They don't care.
   *B. They're pretty mad.
   C. They did the same things.
   D. They don't want me home.
   E. They forced me to take things.

7. If you are Negro, how do your parents feel about white people?
   A. They hate them.
   *B. Some are alright.
   C. They're like anyone else.
   D. You can't trust them.
   E. No particular way.

7A. If you are white, how do your parents feel about Negro people?
   A. They hate them.
   B. Some are alright.
   C. They're like anyone else.
   D. You can't trust them.
   E. No particular way.

8. The Police
   *A. Were unfair.
   *B. Just did their jobs.
   C. Weren't strict enough with rioters.
   #D. Were brutal.
   E. Handled things very well.

9. The Soldiers
   A. Were unfair.
   *B. Just did their jobs.
   C. Weren't strict enough with rioters.
   D. Were brutal.
   E. Handled things very well.

10. Teenagers arrested in the riot should all
   A. Be released.
   B. Be released except for the ones involved in burning or killing.
   C. Be sent to the training school.
   D. Should have parents punished.
   E. Should help clean up the mess.

11. The Youth Home people have treated you
    *A. Badly.
    B. Fairly well.
    C. Unfairly.
    D. Very well.
    E. No particular way.

12. During the riot, you heard rumors
    A. Most of which weren't true.
    B. Many of which were proved to be true.
    C. Which made you do things you would not have done otherwise.
    D. Which scared you.
    *E. Which had no effect on you.

13. What do you think is most important about the riot?
    A. Negroes don't have a fair shake here and should have their own community.
    B. Planning & organization from outside Detroit.
    *C. Everybody went crazy and followed other people.
    D. Planning & organization from inside Detroit.
    E. It's because Negroes hate whites.

14. The government can stop riots by
    A. Severely punishing all rioters.
    *B. Giving Negroes equal rights with whites in every area.
    C. Giving money, government positions & jobs to Negroes.
    D. Providing jobs & income to everyone.
    *E. Educating people to understand one another.

15. Because of the riots
    A. Negroes will be liked better.
    #B. Something will be done to help Negroes.
    C. Negroes will make the whites do what the Negroes want.
    *D. Negroes will be hated more.
    E. Nothing will happen.

16. Negroes in other cities
    *A. Are better off than those in Detroit.
    B. Are worse off than those in Detroit.
    C. Are the same as those in Detroit.
    D. Are the same, but have better jobs.
    E. Are the same, but live in nicer places.

17. Negroes who used to be poor, but now are successful
    A. became successful by playing up to white people.
    B. made it to the top on their own.
    C. don't help the poor Negroes.
    *D. became successful by getting an education.
    E. Got rich by cheating poor Negroes.

18. The best way for a poor Negro to make it is
    A. In the rackets.
    B. In the sports field.
    C. In show business.
    *D. To become a professional man.
    E. To go into legitimate business.

19. The only way to get what you want is
    A. To fight for it.
    B. To take it.
    C. You can't.
    D. Get a good job.
    *E. Get a good education.

20. The Viet Nam War
    #A. Is necessary.
    *B. Is wrong & should be stopped.
    C. Is a way of killing Negroes.
    D. Is taking money away from poor people in the USA.
    E. Should be stepped up.

21. You stay poor
    A. If your skin is black.
    B. If your family is poor.
    C. Even if you work.
    D. If you're strictly honest.
    *E. If you don't fight for things.

22. Pick the Negro leader you admire most:
    A. Stokely Carmichael
    *B. Dr. Martin Luther King
    C. Adam Clayton Powell
    D. Elijah Muhammad
    E. Senator Edward Brooke

23. Pick the local Negro you admire most:
    A. Albert Cleage [Black Power]
    B. John Conyers [U.S. Rep. D.]
    C. James Del Rio [Mich. Rep. D.]
    *D. Rev. Nicholas Hood [Det. Common Council]
    E. Waymon Dunn [Inner City Block Club Leader]

24. Negroes can best get their rights by
    A. Non-violent resistance.
    B. Violent action.
    C. Legislation.
    D. Persuasion and example.
    *E. Education.

25. The white leader you admire most is

    A. Ronald Reagan.
    B. President Johnson.
    C. George Wallace.
    D. Fidel Castro.
    *E. Robert Kennedy.

26. The local white leader you admire most is

    #A. Mayor Cavanagh.
    *B. Governor Romney.
    C. Mary Beck [Det. Common Council].
    D. Walter Reuther.
    E. Rev. David Gracie [Civil Rights leader].

27. What have you heard about Mayor Cavanagh recently?
    A. That he wants to get more money for the poor.
    B. That he helps Negroes.
    C. That he's got trouble with his wife.
    D. That he's got trouble with the Police Department.
    *E. Nothing.

28. If you heard about the Mayor's troubles with his wife,

    A. Are not to be trusted.
    B. Are always against Negroes.
    *C. Are like anybody else.
    #D. Are O.K., but don't understand Negroes.
    E. Are better than Negroes.

29. If you heard about the Mayor's trouble with the Police Dept.

    #A. It didn't make any difference.
    B. It made me think less of him.
    C. That's the way politicians are.
    *D. He's still a good guy.
    E. The police are out to get him.

30. If you are Negro, do you have any close white friends?

    Yes______ No______

    If you are white, do you have any close Negro friends?

    Yes______ No______

31. White people

    A. Are not to be trusted.
    B. Are always against Negroes.
    *C. Are like anybody else.
    #D. Are O.K., but don't understand Negroes.
    E. Are better than Negroes.

32. Negroes
    A. Are not to be trusted.
    B. Are always against whites.
    *C. Are like anybody else.
    D. Are O.K., but don't understand white people.
    E. Are better than whites.

33. If you could have what you wanted in life, it would be
    A. Money.
    B. A good job and education.
    C. People who love you.
    *D. Justice for Negroes.
    E. To be respected like a man.

34. The kind of man you want to be is
    A. Tough and strong.
    B. Knows how to get what he wants from people.
    C. Rich and successful.
    *D. King, gentle and helps others.
    E. A fun-loving guy.

35. The person you feel closest to is
    *A. Mother.
    B. Father.
    C. Sister or brother.
    D. Friend (indicate sex) Male____ Female____.
    E. Other (indicate age and sex)
    Male____ Age____: Female____ Age____.

Appendix B

SENTENCE COMPLETION TEST ADMINISTERED TO RIOT PARTICIPANTS

*indicates popular response

1. Life ahead looks
2. The people I hate are
3. A cool guy is
4. Going on a trip is
5. When I'm lonely, I
6. Being a Negro in Detroit is
7. Poor people always
8. Seeing a fire burn
9. When I get high
10. A real man
*11. You can't trust *no one.*
12. When I think of my father
13. You get in trouble if
14. Most of all I need
15. Policemen are

16. I want to be a
17. It hurts when
18. Your best friend
19. Looting stores can be
*20. I could kill someone if *they kill any of my kin folks.*
21. Riots can be
22. My mother and I
23. White people are
24. It scares me when
25. I feel ashamed of
26. A good person will
27. I dream about
*28. Smart guys always *end up losing.*
29. I admire most
30. After the riot I want most

The Dynamics of Recent Ghetto Riots†

JAMES R. HUNDLEY, JR.*

INTRODUCTION

The ghetto riot is a specific case of what sociologists call "crowd" behavior: "The mob, murderous or destructive; the rioting crowd, whether angry or triumphant; crowds engaged in orgies of joy, grief, or religious fervor; audiences which go wild; groups in panic; clusters of gawking spectators—all of these and many other types are manifestations of the crowd."[2]

This article will deal with three major aspects of riots as a type of crowd. It will examine the *general conditions* which precede riot outbreaks, the *immediate or proximate conditions* which are critical in providing the catalyst for particular riots, and the *internal dynamics* or main events and behaviors which occur during the course of riots. The analysis is based mainly on research on the five Negro ghetto riots reported below, but also on conclusions and observations reported in the sociological literature.

† *Editor's Note:* In August of 1968 James R. Hundley, Jr. presented this paper at the Annual Meeting of the American Sociological Association in San Francisco. Because Professor Hundley was fully aware of the terminal nature of his condition, his desire in this—his final—paper was to record and synthesize his observations into a general framework for understanding riots. While Professor Hundley also desired to document completely the relationship of his ideas and findings to those in the research literature as well as to document the empirical bases of his conclusions by his own research data, his illness and death prevented the fullest incorporation of these features into the paper. On November 3, 1967, Mr. Hundley died of cancer at age 28. Thus, the paper is necessarily impressionistic and heuristic, rather than being a fully documented, definitive, research report. While the ideas are those Dr. Hundley originally presented, reorganization and shortening of the paper have been necessary to prepare it for publication and several references have been added to the original version. Colleagues and students of Dr. Hundley at Michigan State University helped to prepare the manuscript for publication.

* Late Assistant Professor, Department of Sociology, Michigan State University.

1. Analysis of Dr. Hundley's research materials continues under the auspices of the sponsors of his research, Michigan State University's School of Police Administration and the National Center on Police and Community Relations.

2. R. TURNER & L. KILLIAN, COLLECTIVE BEHAVIOR 83 (1957).

During the summers of 1966-1967, three researchers spent three weeks interviewing on the west side of Chicago; the Hough area of Cleveland; the west side of Lansing, Michigan; Newark, New Jersey; and Detroit, Michigan. A total of one hundred and fifty interviews of one-to-three hours each were tape recorded with informants in these communities. Our informants were selected on the basis of two criteria: they witnessed the riot activity for a substantial period of time and/or were familiar with the riot area prior to its outbreak. Many respondents fit both criteria. First, contacts were generally made through the Negro news media, sanctioned Negro leadership, and grass-roots community organizations. Clearly, the most useful informant when entering a city was the Negro newsman who, in the course of his job, became familiar with the ghetto area, knew its prior conditions, and could move freely through the area while the rioting was occurring.

Before going into the field in the summer of 1966, an interview schedule was prepared based on many of the notions of Smelser, Turner and Killian.[3] Questions were relatively unstructured and open-ended to allow respondents to provide information in their own words. By tape-recording the information from first hand observers immediately after the riot, it was possible to capture as nearly as possible the reality of those outbreaks. The data are, thus, more direct than mass media reports and other printed documents which have supplied the source of information for most of the past research on riots and crowd behavior, but they still lack the definitiveness of systematic, direct observation.

Analysis and interpretation of the data are far from complete at this time. In this article the attempt is to impart a somewhat comprehensive understanding of the dynamics of riots as revealed by this research. The present analysis is thus characterized more by scope than by depth. Specific interview materials (quotations), statistics compiled from the interviews, and statistics on structural conditions in the cities are not presented here, but will appear in subsequent reports. This report summarizes, collapses, and synthesizes general impressions derived from this experience of interviewing. This analysis must, consequently, be regarded as speculative and tentative.

The General Conditions Promoting a Riot Outburst

Five major general causes of crowd outbursts have been identified, each of which must be present in any social situation before a riot can

3. N. Smelser, Theory of Collective Behavior especially pp. 47-269 (1963); Turner & Killian, *supra* note 2, especially pp. 83-161. For a further comparison of the theoretical approaches of Smelser and Turner & Killian see, J. Hundley, Jr., A Test of Theories in Collective Behavior: The National Farmers' Organization (NFO), 1965 (unpublishd Ph.D. thesis, Columbus: The Ohio State University), especially pp. 15-86.

occur. First, potential participants in a crowd must perceive that a crisis exists. The essence of the perceived crisis in the Negro ghetto is that the residents see a gap between the conditions in which they find themselves and what they feel conditions ought to be. The nature of the crisis in ghetto communities revolves around the historic lack of racial equality in the United States, excessive discrimination, a poor educational system, a lack of jobs, poor housing, insufficient welfare systems, and so forth. Ghettoites increasingly use middle-class, white, suburban situations as a point of comparison for evaluating their own situations, and in such comparisons they are clearly relatively deprived.[4]

The second major causal factor in ghetto outbursts is that those involved perceive that the legitimate channels for bringing about change are closed. They see no other way to redress their grievances. White-sanctioned Negro leadership is perceived as those elected officials who respond to the needs of the party or structure and not to the needs of the people they are elected to represent. Urban Negro ghettos seem to place little confidence in the elected officials who could, but do not, represent them. Elected officials are called "Uncle Toms" and, in fact, may be perceived as having taken an office or residential address in the ghetto only in order to be elected. In order to become effective, ghetto residents may have to become a part of a political machine, which inhibits their ability to reflect the community sentiment. Civil rights' groups and other organizations are potential channels for bringing about change in any ghetto. The most striking fact about our recent research was that the various civil rights' organizations were scarcely organized in any of the ghetto areas. Most people admitted that these organizations had very little rapport with the ghetto residents. Apparently, civil rights' organizations find it difficult to organize even in the so-called middle class areas. There are, of course, very good reasons for the lack of formal organizations in the ghetto. The ghettoite is characterized by high in-migration and low levels of education, factors which work against the organization of effective local groups.

The third necessary ingredient to produce a situation conducive to ghetto rioting is the existence of hope in the potential riot participants that rioting will somehow produce a change in present conditions. Many ghettoites express a feeling that they are at their "wits end," "at the end of the line," they "have taken all that they can take," and "Why not riot?" Something beneficial may result from it. Implicit in the statements made by riot participants is the hope that "whitey" will have to respond. He has failed to respond to the needs of the Negro in

4. For an interesting analysis of the role of relative comparisons in the creation of dissatisfactions see, Davies, *Toward a Theory of Revolution*, 27 American Sociological Rev., 1, 5-19 (Feb., 1962).

the past, and to some the only hope left is to force him to respond by rioting.

A fourth condition that must be present before a riot will erupt is that the people must be able to come in close contact. One can expect more crowds in high population density areas. Rioting tends to occur on warm nights, but it is not because the participants are necessarily more irritable. Warm nights and crowded conditions find people out on the stoops or in the streets where they will be more likely to converge on some abnormal event that might occur. Riots tend to occur on week-ends and in the evenings since large numbers of people who are disengaged from normal daytime activities and restraints are more likely to come together and participate in the crowd behavior.

Finally, the fifth major condition that exists is a substantial breakdown in previously accepted relationships between police and community. One of the most glaring conditions in American cities today is a feeling on the ghettoite's part that he has been subjected to discriminating police tactics. The ghettoite is convinced that police are overly brutal, not polite, disrespectful and that Negroes are often arrested indiscriminately and without justification.[5] Many cases of police harassment and intimidation are reported on the part of various people knowledgeable of the ghetto. To what extent these charges are true is quite difficult to determine. Clearly, however, at the heart of most recent ghetto riots is disdain and hatred for the local police department. The Negro ghettoite feels he has no effective channel or adequate legal representation for lodging a complaint against a police officer. Either the sentence imposed on an erring police officer is too light, or no penalty is invoked at all. Normal police grievance procedures are complicated and time consuming. Usually, the ghettoite has not collected sufficient evidence as defined by the police department to prove any misconduct, nor is the typical ghettoite sophisticated enough to see the charge through proper legal channels.[6] The significance of these facts is that respect for law enforcement, as practiced in the ghetto, has eroded and open hostility toward the police is common-place.

How do these general conditions relate to the increasingly rapid rise in the number of riots in America today? Two major factors are suggested: First, the crisis as perceived by Negroes is becoming more acute, and the gap between ghetto living and the white middle class is perceived as increasing.[7] New welfare programs are not closing the

---

5. P. Meyer, The People Beyond 12th Street: A Survey of Attitudes of Detroit Negroes After the Riot of 1967 8-9 (1967) (Sponsored by the Detroit Urban League).

6. For some further evidence on this point see, Report of the National Advisory Commission on Civil Disorders 310 (Bantam Books ed., 1968).

7. For evidence that such perceptions are based on fact see, Moynihan, *The Crisis in Welfare*, 10 The Public Interest, 3-29 (Winter, 1968).

gap as hoped. As our respondents related to us, many programs simply have not reached the grass-roots level. Even if money was available, there is a general lack of knowledge and of skilled personnel to develop the various kinds of programs that are needed to eradicate the slum. A major factor in the heightening of the crisis is that more people are declaring that the condition of the Negro is intolerable and must change immediately. Various advocates of the Black Power philosophy, both in SNCC and in other informal local organizations, have been giving the lower class Negro a rationale for engaging in violence.

The second major factor for the increasing rate of riots from 1966 to 1967, is the growing belief on the part of ghettoites that a riot will bring attention to ghetto problems. As riots occur in one city and the results are communicated, it is perceived that either having a riot or the threat of a riot is a good way to get the immediate attention of various political officials who in the past have been hesitant to act.

The analysis thus far has identified five general conditions promoting riots. Several other reasons have been recently suggested for the increasing high rate of riots. However, these general conditions can be found in most large metropolitan areas. The attempt in the following section is to identify the causes indicating why a riot erupts at a particular time and place.

The Immediate Conditions Producing a Riot

Four main factors seem to be responsible for producing a riot in a ghetto at a particular time. These include:

1. the creation and transmission of rumors offering a riot as one solution or as a possibility,
2. the occurrence of a given event which typifies the kinds of complaints and grievances that a community has,
3. the convergence of large numbers of people around a precipitating event, and
4. the communication of specific grievances throughout the forming crowd so that definite courses of action emerge and are followed among a substantial number of the converging crowd.

Interviews with knowledgeable informants who had their "ears to the ghetto," made it clear that they had picked up a number of cues indicating that a riot was likely to break out at any time. They noticed an increasing number of rumors that something was going to happen.[8] At various times reports were heard that a riot was going to break out

8. For a discussion of the role of rumor in crowd behavior see, R. Turner, *Collective Behavior*, in Handbook of Modern Sociology 397-409 (R. Faris, ed. 1964).

at a certain time at a certain place. There was a noticeable increase in discussions about police, white merchants, slum lords, etc. Also noticed was the fact that informal leaders were increasingly sanctioning the notion that something ought to be done now, or "we ought to blow the place up." What these informants are alluding to is the fact that the ghetto community is talking more and more about recent experiences and past events that typify their unfavorable position and the extreme nature of the crisis. This involves a heightening of hostility toward objects in the community that they dislike and the development of a one-sided, extreme definition of certain people who are perceived as responsible for their plight. Among these various definitions is the increasing talk that one of the solutions is to "get out of hand" and riot.

When this communication of hostility and dissatisfaction reaches a certain height, some event usually occurs which typifies the kinds of mal-treatment received by the ghettoites. This may be an arrest in which there is an alleged brutality, *e.g.*, Newark; a heated debate among some officials and a ghettoite, *e.g.*, Chicago; the raiding of an after hours bar, *e.g.*, Detroit. The significance of this event is that it immediately focuses the attention on an overt act of suppression that is met with open hostility not because of the act itself, but because it is representative of a long history of such acts.

Another significant aspect of the precipitating event is that it invokes a substantial convergence of people to the scene of the event. Large numbers of people are in the vicinity, they hear about the event, and come to investigate. They come for many reasons. At this point of convergence, many feel that they have been wronged and that something must be done about the situation. These people may also bring their friends. Other people come who hear about the event and are simply curious. Others come because they are simply passing through the neighborhood and see a large throng of people. Others may be there as instigators or agitators who are attempting to start a riot. Finally, it is clear, particularly in the ghetto, that large numbers of people come to exploit the situation and use the emerging crowd as a cover for normally deviant activities. Other people come because they see it as their role to control potential deviant outbursts. These may be police, city officials; and church, civic, and local leaders. From this conglomerate of people, the riot develops.

The fourth and final specific factor that tends to produce a full-fledged riot is the communication among the mass that something wrong has happened and something must be done immediately to right the wrong. Various rumors are passed through the crowd, suggested courses of action begin to emerge, action is taken, and it is on.

THE INTERNAL DYNAMICS OF RECENT CROWD BEHAVIOR

The Keynoting Process

Now that the preconditions for a riot have been met, and a crowd has gathered, what starts the crowd going? What kinds of interaction-mechanisms solidify the crowd and generate certain purposes?

In the initial phase of a riot, Turner and Killian identify a little understood process called keynoting.[9] This process is defined as the offering of a suggestion for positive action among large numbers of people in an ambiguous situation. A popular contention, supported by Turner and Killian, states that the initial direction of a crowd is determined by the first speakers who can determine the direction of the crowd. This idea comes from an image of the crowd as being highly suggestible and subject to manipulation.[10] We offer some alternative notions to this idea. In the first place, our data indicate that a large number of suggestions are offered from certain informal leaders who come to the fore during the creation of the crowd. These suggestions are usually not offered from one main speaker area, but from clusterings of people in various locations at the initial crowd scene. The most typical case is a sequence of the most verbal speakers who offer a variety of alternatives. They speak successively and the crowd selects one or two of them. In fact, the crowd tends to split and follow different paths of action that have been suggested to them by these speakers.

Who are these ghettoites who tend to be leaders? They are not generally unknown, anonymous individuals. There is a very definite tendency for the more verbal speakers in the ghetto to take the leadership, especially those with a certain amount of either informal or formal status in local organizations or informal groups. In each city studied there emerged an active, self-appointed leadership made up of the most verbal Negroes who were present both prior to and during the riots.

The Evolving Riot Activities

Recent ghetto riots occur over a substantial number of hours and days. In the first few hours, a course of action may develop which evokes or demands a response by the police or city officials. Official response results in new courses of crowd action. For example, the initial incident in the Chicago riot last year was whether or not a water hydrant would be left running for the youths' enjoyment. Con-

9. TURNER & KILLIAN, *supra* note 2 at 117 and 197.
10. G. LE BON, THE CROWD (1965).

sequently, early leaders demanded that city officials come to the scene and promise better recreational facilities, especially swimming pools and sprinkler attachments. However, once the police had arrested a number of crowd participants rather indiscriminately, the crowds' purpose was to storm the police station, demanding retribution by releasing their blood brothers from jail. In Cleveland, the initial purpose was to correct the transgressions of a white bar owner who reportedly had been calling Negroes vulgar names. In the later stages, the main activity became burning down dilapidated houses that had been condemned for urban renewal but had not been removed. These examples indicate how crowd focuses shift, relative to the responses that city officials and police display toward prior action.

A crowd moves on courses of action in the early stages when behavioral deviations go unpunished by the various social control personnel in the area. These may be deviations of informal norms such as extreme statements, vehement conversation, threats, and simply walking into the street, or deviations of various legal norms such as window-breaking, looting, burning, and sniping. A crowd starts on courses of action suggested by certain leaders, but facilitating these actions are crowd participants who are not punished by either the crowd, the existing institutions in the ghetto, or the police. Once these deviations have occurred a sufficient number of times, they tend to become normative and expected as common behaviors of the crowd.

Once the crowd begins to engage in various behaviors through the process of keynoting and because deviations go unpunished, other subsequent factors help determine the specific activities of the rioters. Previous grievances that have been talked about in the community for some period of time represent pre-dispositions to act on the part of the crowd. The verbalized conclusions of the community rumor process, and the heightening of hostility prior to the riot, determine the magnitude and kind of activities. There are heterogenous complaints which result in multiple goals by various segments of the rioting crowd.

Emergent Norms

Once various sections of the crowd deviate and develop a course of action, these behaviors tend to be normative and expected. In this sense, the various acting segments of a crowd hold a creative and emergent set of norms that are guiding their behavior. The crowd sets up its own notion of right and wrong.[11] This notion of right or wrong may be an idea that the Negro needs to be treated with respect

11. For a more general discussion of the emergence of norms in crowd behavior see, TURNER & KILLIAN, *supra* note 2 at 394-97.

by police, and that he should not be arrested for "just hanging around and watching the crowd." The emergent norm may be the notion that the Negro section should be allowed to have sprinklers on the fire hydrant just as other city areas have. The crowd may believe that city officials have done nothing about urban renewal and, therefore, want to burn down all the old blighted buildings. The norm may be that white businessmen exploit the Negro, and the only way to solve this is to burn them out completely. At various times, these emergent norms of the crowd tend to be violated either by white passers-by, outside residents in the community, fire departments, or police departments. When these emergent norms are violated, that person or agency may be selected for attack.

The Limits of Deviation

A variety of factors help determine the specific activities of a rioting crowd, but what limits the deviations of a crowd? Crowd behavior is in great part a process of interaction between various participants who are attempting to control the situation and those rioters who continue to adhere to the new norms. Various social control agencies, including police, older ghetto residents, religious and welfare officials, and others, may exert control influences to limit the deviations among a rioting crowd. A second limiting factor is the in-group norms of the rioting recruits. These may be the sparing of Negro-owned businesses, failing to attack women, children, and nuns, or not burning residential homes.

The Crowd Structure

Since crowd behavior is group behavior, an important question is: "What is the group structure of the emerging crowd and how does it change over time?" The early stages of crowd behavior exhibit a rudimentary division of labor. It involves a rather simple relationship between an active core of crowd participants and a relatively passive audience of people who are just standing around watching. Noticeable physical space can separate the active core from the passive audience. Quite soon, however, the active core can be divided into the keynoters or activists and their nearby supporters. How is it determined, then, who will be in the active core or in the passive audience? Who will tend to be the activists and who will tend to be the supporters? To answer these questions, we need to examine again the motivations or the reasons people give for coming to the crowd. It is reasonable to expect that the activists are recruited from those who are aggrieved as well as from the instigators and the exploiters. Many of the supporters are friends of the aggrieved, the instigators, and the exploiters. The curious make up the greater portion of the relatively passive audience. Many exploiters and instigators remain in the passive audience or play a supportive role until the opportune time for their deviant purposes becomes apparent.

Once the rioting crowd begins to act along certain lines, the division of activity becomes quite complicated. In recent ghetto riots, the sequence starts with rock and bottle throwing directed toward police and business establishments. This is then followed by looting. The looting is followed by burning. The window breakers tend to be the more active people, whereas, looters tend to be drawn from a wider range of the population. Early looting of the stores tends to occur in situations where social control agencies have been hesitant to act for some time. Generally, it is after the malicious damage, looting, and burning that the first incidents of sniping are reported.

Our data indicate that most of the brick throwing, early looting, and burning is done by teenage and early twenty-year-old groups of from 5-to-20 individuals. These groups tend to stay together and, in some cases, develop a system of task-sharing. In Chicago, for example, it was noted that large numbers of teenagers would sit under trees near housing developments and rest while other teenage gang members were out engaging in riot activity. Other people reported gangs of teenagers being demarcated by turbans, white shirts, or no shirts. It was also noticed that gangs would tend to stay in certain areas, indicating that they had divided up the turf. These data support Smelser's notion that the degree of organization of crowd behavior depends upon the amount of prior organization that is recruited to the scene of the crowd.[12] Usually, as time progresses, certain groups engage in violent acts while other groups try to make contact with city officials to obtain promises for a redress of grievances.

In the initial hours of a riot, the crowd is usually characterized by a representative group of ghettoites who verbalize specific concessions and changes desired. The later stages of the life cycle involve larger numbers of instigators and exploiters who use the breakdown of social control and the advantage of the emergent norms to engage in looting, burning, sniping, etc. A final observation is that the curious or the passive audience decreases over the life of a crowd, which facilitates the cessation of the riot. It is no accident that the most extreme form of deviation in ghetto riots—shooting and sniping—usually oc-

12. SMELSER, *supra* note 3 at 255.

curs late on the first night, or the second and third night. A passing curious audience provides little support for these deviations. There is some indication in our data that snipers are associated with instigative and/or exploitive groups.

The Interaction Between the Crowd and Social Control Agencies

In the beginning stages of crowd formation, the presence or absence of police officers can have various effects. In most instances, the very presence of the police creates an event, provides a point of focus, and draws people together among whom rumor can be easily transmitted. In other cases, sending too few officers to a scene results in actions being uncontrolled because not enough policemen are available to break the developing crowd structure. We suggest that if the police activity is seen by the rioters as legitimate, then the presence of small quantities of police will not precipitate a riot. However, even if the original police activity is viewed as legitimate, but the policemen are observed as being rude, impolite, unfair, or brutal, then these activities can precipitate a riot. It appears that the police officers, in their attempt to enforce a higher authority, are perceived by ghetto residents more as a causal factor than a deterrent of riot behavior.

One of the puzzles of recent ghetto riots is why, in some cases, the total withdrawal of police simply enhances riot activity. The success of police withdrawal is contingent upon officers or officials contacting the legitimate leaders of the ghetto community and in allowing them to exert social control. Legitimate leaders will not attempt to exert this control unless police or city officials make immediate concessions or promises. The failure to make immediate concessions reinforces the ghettoites perceptions of the white structure's reluctance to respond, and creates a situation of social suicide for any Negro leader who attempts to approach the crowd with promises of a better tomorrow.

Particularly in the early stages of a riot, police forces are incapable of controlling the situation and resort to observation of riot activities. The very presence of the police, who do not exert control, further promotes the emergence of norms which allow deviant activity. In fact, we have reports of policemen weakly chasing looters, chiding observers, or driving back and forth among looters shouting verbal insults. These non-control activities encourage and promote still more hostile behavior.

Lohman outlines five ways to prevent and control crowds. These recommendations are to isolate the crowd, divide it into small units, create diversions, remove individuals involved in the precipitating event, and remove crowd leaders without force.[13] These basic principles are generally not heeded by police departments. For example, policemen tend to stay around even when a crowd starts to form, and do not quickly remove or isolate individuals involved in the precipitating incident. Police do not take into account the communication process in a crowd and fail to divide it into small units. Instead, they attack along a frontal line much like a military operation.

Other factors determine the length of recent ghetto riots besides the activities of the police. The sooner help comes from outside control agencies, the sooner a riot stops. Prior to Detroit, the national guard had been amazingly successful in controlling crowd behavior immediately upon their arrival. Apart from the sheer force of numbers, calling in the national guard indicates the success of rioters, since they have beaten the "boys in blue." The sooner the larger community seeks out real ghetto leaders and satisfies their grievances, the sooner a riot stops. The more exploiters and instigators in a ghetto, the more likely a riot is to occur and of long duration. Finally, the greater degree of normalcy that is maintained within the ghetto community, the more likely a riot will remain small or cease.

Summary, Implications for Law Enforcement

The following are discussed tentatively as the general conditions which underlie the occurrence of riots: 1.) the perception of a crisis in achieving aspirations, 2.) the perception that legitimate channels for bringing about changes are blocked, 3.) hope on the part of ghettoites that rioting will bring about changes, 4.) the possibility that large numbers of people can interact under conditions of reduced social control, and 5.) the breakdown of accepted social control mechanisms. The main factors suggested as being responsible for producing a riot at a particular time and place are: 1.) the presence of rumors of a riot, 2.) an event which typifies grievances and complaints, 3.) the physical convergence of large numbers of people around this event, and 4.) the arousal of a sense of indignation in the crowd, and the emergence of suggested courses of action for immediate redress. The process by which a crowd develops into a riot involves 1.) keynoting or the formation of consensus around suggestions for action, 2.) hostile, deviant acts which go unpunished, and 3.) the emergence of focused hostility as a norm for the crowd, and norms for the types of deviant activities the crowd will sanction. Rioting crowds develop definite group structure, which

13. J. Lohman, The Police and Minority Groups 80-86 (1947).

suggests the possibility of predictable methods for relating to and controlling such crowds by police and others.

Because riot control is such a pressing, immediate need, some additional closing comments on the problem of police–ghetto relations are in order. New and creative approaches to the problems of police and the ghetto are sorely needed. Some kind of credible reviewing mechanism needs to be established to restore faith that police departments will handle grievances of maltreatment, insolence, and brutality. Whether this be a civilian review board, or some variation of this, is not as important as the fact that the community have confidence in what ever mechanism is created. There is a predominant orientation among police departments that the way of solving complicated social problems is by the use of force—more policemen, with more riot helmets, and more sawed-off shotguns. This orientation certainly results in treating symptoms rather than basic causes. There needs to be more policemen recruited from the ghetto, and in many cities more Negro policemen. Some kind of combination of police and social work is particularly needed among older adults as well as among youth. The police find themselves in a position of really not knowing the community, its leaders, or many of its problems. Putting the policeman back on the beat where he comes to know intimately an area might be one partial solution. Also, the policemen assigned to a ghetto need to be rigidly scrutinized. Police departments reflect the society from which they draw recruits—a society which is predominately biased and bigoted toward the Negro. When this predisposition is put together with a policeman's experience of constantly handling the deviant Negro, it results in policemen who personally become very bitter toward all Negroes. Finally, training in riot control techniques based on past research and experience rather than traditional myths is needed. Too many policemen create a scene or incident unknowingly. Sirens blasting and lights flashing, policemen come noisily into a situation and create an event which causes the convergence of people. Other times, they use force indiscriminately and too quickly. Many times, police attack leaders and certain parts of the crowd without breaking up the crowd structure throughout.

The problem of riots must, however, be dealt with in a context which is much broader than that of law enforcement. The basic causes of riots lie deep in our social structure. Negroes increasingly find it impossible to achieve their aspirations by individual and legitimate channels of mobility. Frustrations accumulate and intensify in an environment of threat, distrust, and fear. The ghetto riot is an expression of the intensity of these frustrations.

Detroit 1967:
Racial Violence or Class Warfare?

JEROME R. CORSI

ON July 31, 1967, Governor George Romney attempted to summarize the preceeding days of violence in Detroit. His summary explicitly emphasized the unique nature of this riot:

> Exactly what was the Detroit riot?
> —It was integrated looting, with whites and Negroes both taking part, sometimes side by side; and the looting was conducted by a small minority of the population of both races. . . .
> —It produced an integrated effort to restore law and order, with Negro and white both working for peace, again side by side.[1]

Beginning in the summer of 1964, with urban violence during the national presidential campaign, the nation was faced with summer after summer of "racial" rioting. The summer of 1965 would see violence in Watts from August 11-18. In 1966, there would be twenty such incidents, the most prominent occurring in Cleveland's Hough area between July 18-24.[2] By 1967, the nation was conditioned to expect similar outbreaks.

Perhaps the easiest way to comprehend complex phenomena is to stereotype. If such a process includes both the simplification necessary to generalize, and a detailed attention to exceptions, the process can be a valuable method of understanding. If, however, we fail to adequately account for detail which does not conform to a general pattern of analysis, the process of stereotyping begins to jeopardize true understanding.

The racial violence during the years 1964-1967 has followed some similar lines: predominantly Negro looting, burning, and sniping; violence contained predominantly within Negro sections of the city; white involvement largely limited to participation in police and fire forces. If George Romney's analysis of the rioting in Detroit is correct, we must modify the current stereotype of present racial violence.

The Detroit violence in the summer of 1967 is constantly analyzed as merely another example of the typical racial violence witnessed

1. Governor George Romney, Address to the National Association of County Officials, July 31, 1967.
2. For a detailed list of these outbursts, see: *Major Riots, Civil-Criminal Disorders*, in PERMANENT SUBCOMM. ON INVESTIGATIONS OF THE U.S. SEN. COMM. ON GOV. OPERATIONS, RIOTS, CIVIL AND CRIMINAL DISORDERS, 90th Cong., 1st Sess. 15 (1967).

recently. The President's National Advisory Commission on Civil Disorders includes the Detroit riot entirely within the context of current racial violence: "The summer of 1967 again brought racial disorders to American cities, and with them shock, fear and bewilderment to the nation. The worst came during a two-week period of July, first in Newark and then in Detroit."[3] Even Governor Romney, in assessing the causes for the violence heavily emphasized causes and cures dealing specifically with Negroes.[4] It is the intent of this article to carefully reevaluate the significance of what happened in Detroit during the summer of 1967.

The Question of Poverty and Race: Its Relevance to Detroit 1967

In 1964, President Johnson declared a "war against poverty" in the United States. The country was enjoying one of the most sustained periods of economic progress ever recorded. In the midst of this affluence, the affliction of those in a lower standard of living was intolerable. In the same year, the Council of Economic Advisers (CEA) detailed the problem and established the elimination of poverty as a national goal:

> There will always be some Americans who are better off than others. But it need not follow that "the poor are always with us." In the United States today we can see the misery and degradation that have been the age-old fate of man. Steadily rising productivity, together with assistance, has been eroding mass poverty in America. But that process is far too slow. It is high time to redouble and to concentrate our efforts to eliminate poverty.[5]

The nation was challenged to understand and eliminate one of the oldest ailments of man.

Defining poverty presents a difficult task. It can be defined as the inability to provide for basic human needs. However, poverty is a relative consideration. If it is true that "there will always be some Americans who are better off than others," changing norms and standards may at times dictate that some who can provide basic necessities may yet be considered "poor." As middle class "affluence" becomes more readily attainable, it may become increasingly more difficult to tolerate standards of living which can provide for necessities but perhaps

3. Nat'l. Advisory Comm'n. on Civil Disorders, Summary of Report, Report of the National Advisory Commission on Civil Disorders 1 (1968).

4. Romney, *supra* note 1.

5. Council of Economic Advisers, The Annual Report of the Council of Economic Advisers 55 (1964).

little more. A "Great Society" striving to provide basic physical needs for all must recognize the problem of relative deprivation in the context of rising expectations.

The various attempts to establish poverty levels have primarily relied upon the subsistence definition. In their 1964 *Annual Report,* the CEA established a family poverty level at an annual money income from all sources of $3,000 (before taxes and in 1962 prices).[6] This level was calculated to provide an "acceptable minimum" for the provision of necessities.[7]

In 1962, there were 47 million families in the United States. Using the $3,000 poverty level, the CEA calculated that 9.3 million families, one-fifth of the total, comprising more than 30 million persons, had total money incomes below $3,000. Various types of families were more likely to be poor than others. Nonwhite families were one of the most afflicted groups.[8] Of the poor families, 22 percent were headed by nonwhites. However, nearly one-half of all nonwhite families were poor. While poverty in the United States crossed racial lines, the predominance of poverty among the nonwhite portion of the population has lent definite racial tones to any consideration of the question.

Realizing the need for greater sophistication in establishing a poverty level, the Social Security Administration developed a more complex index. The calculation of this index begins with the Department of Agriculture's estimation of the amount of money needed to purchase food for a minimum adequate diet. This food budget is the lowest that can be devised to supply all essential nutrients using foods readily accessible in the U. S. market (with customary regional variations accounted for). The poverty line is then calculated at three times

---

6. *Id.* at 57-59.

7. This poverty level included detailed calculations on expected budget expenditures. Of the 3,000, one-third was to be spent on food (thus, an annual budget of 3,000 for a 4-person family would provide about $5 per person per week for food). Of the remaining $2,000, an estimated $800 was allocated for housing (rent or mortgage payments, utilities, and heat). This left only $1,200 (less than $25 per week) for clothing, transportation, school supplies and books, home furnishings and supplies, medical care, personal care, recreation, insurance, and everything else. The Council concluded with the understatement: "Obviously it does not exaggerate the problem of poverty to regard $3,000 as the boundary." *See Id.* at 57.

8. One of the major problems in analyzing government data for racial consideration has been the utilization of the undifferentiated category "nonwhite." Daniel P. Moynihan faced this difficulty in dealing with similar data. Where possible, he used more specific racial data. Where this was unavailable he utilized the nonwhite data as if it referred only to Negroes. In 1960, Negroes were 92.1% of all nonwhites. The remaining 7.9% was made up largely of Indians, Japanese, and Chinese. Analysis of various economic criteria (employment, family stability, etc.) indicates that these groups are in a better position than Negroes when analyzed along the same criteria. Thus the use of statistics on nonwhites generally understates the magnitude of the Negro difficulties. This article will also follow this procedure. *See* U.S. DEP'T OF LABOR, OFFICE OF POLICY PLANNING & RESEARCH, THE NEGRO FAMILY: THE CASE FOR NATIONAL ACTION 4 (1965).

the food budget (slightly smaller proportions for one- and two-person families) on the assumption that a family spending this large a proportion of their total income on food will be living at a very inadequate level.[9]

In 1966, the CEA began utilizing the Social Security Administration's definition of poverty.[10] While the results of this index indicate a substantial drop in the incidence of poverty between 1959 and 1966, the data still reveals that the nonwhite segment of the population is over-proportionately represented in the ranks of the poor. In 1966, while only 15.3 percent of all nonfarm white households were poor, a total of 37.5 percent of all nonfarm, nonwhite households were in the same category.[11]

The indices for measuring poverty are somewhat arbitrary. Little detailed attention has been devoted to establishing a substantial index based not on subsistence but on relative deprivation.[12] However, for the purposes of the analysis here the precise number of poor is not a

---

9. The derivation of the Social Security Administration poverty index is a very detailed procedure. For more than 30 years, the food plans prepared by the Department of Agriculture have served as a guide for estimating costs of food needed by families of different composition. The Department of Agriculture translates the criteria of nutritional adequacy set forth by the National Research Council into quantities and types of food compatible with the preference of American families as identified in food composition studies. The Department then calculates cost estimates by examining average prices based on the assumption that all meals are prepared at home from foods purchased at retail. The further translation of the food plan analysis into a poverty index involves three steps: 1.) since the food plans show estimated costs separately for individuals in 19 age-sex classes, and since these must be further adjusted for family size, it is necessary to define the family size and composition prototypes for which food costs are then calculated; 2.) it is necessary to decide how much additional income should be allowed for items other than food; and, 3.) the cash needs of farm families must be further distinguished from the cash needs of comparable nonfarm units. Each of these additional steps requires detailed analysis of relevant data and studies. *See* testimony of Robert M. Ball as reprinted in U.S. Sen. Comm. on Finance SOCIAL SECURITY AMENDMENTS OF 1967, 90th Cong. 1st Sess. 316-32 (1967).

10. The Social Security Administration has realized that the subsistence definition of poverty is insufficient. Thus, some attempt has been made to establish an index along the lines of relative deprivation analysis. A group identified as "low income" includes those above the poverty line but without incomes providing an acceptable standard of living. Application of this index added another 13.5 million persons to the already 32.7 million in the poverty classification in 1965. The CEA has not reported this second index in its poverty analysis. *See* Robert Ball *Id.*

11. A household is defined as the total of families and unrelated individuals. COUNCIL OF ECONOMIC ADVISERS, THE ANNUAL REPORT OF THE COUNCIL OF ECONOMIC ADVISERS 143 (1968).

12. In 1959, the Bureau of Labor Statistics calculated budgets based upon estimates of the total cost of a representative list of goods and services necessary to maintain a "modest but adequate" (not a minimum subsistence) level of living in a large city. For the 20 cities analyzed, the modest but adequate budget for a "city workers' family" averaged $6,083. See U.S. DEP'T OF COMMERCE, BUREAU OF THE CENSUS, STATISTICAL ABSTRACT OF THE UNITED STATES 359 (1963). Utilizing this index, the A. Philip Randolph Institute estimated that in 1964, 47 million Americans lived above poverty limits of $3,130 for a multiple-person family and $1,540 for an unattached individual but below the "modest but adequate" standards. *See* A. PHILIP RANDOLPH INSTITUTE, A "FREEDOM BUDGET" FOR ALL AMERICANS 36 (1966).

central issue. As the CEA argued when first introducing its $3,000 poverty mark:

> No measure of poverty as simple as the one used here, would be suitable for determining eligibility for particular benefits or participation in particular programs. Nevertheless, it provides a valid benchmark for assessing the dimensions of the task of eliminating poverty, setting the broad goals of policy, and measuring our past and future progress toward their achievement.[13]

The benchmark provided by the indices discussed here clearly demonstrates that the nonwhite segment of the population is disproportionately poor.

This conclusion alone, however, does not completely explain why the question of poverty in our nation has become so intertwined with the question of racial deprivation. To more fully appreciate this, a second dimension of analysis is necessary. The Bureau of the Census, under the direction of the Office of Economic Opportunity, directed its efforts toward designating areas of major poverty concentrations within large metropolitan areas. A poverty index based on census tract data was developed and applied to all tracts in the 101 standard metropolitan statistical areas (SMSA's) with a 1960 population of 250,000 or more.[14] As a result, "Poverty Areas" were identified in 100 of the 101 SMSA's with a 1960 population of 250,000.[15]

---

13. C. E. A., 1964, *supra* note 5 at 58.

14. Poverty Areas were determined by first ranking census tracts according to the relative presence of each of five equally weighted poverty-linked characteristics, and then combining these rankings into an overall measure, the "poverty index." The five characteristics were: 1.) percent of families with money incomes under $3,000 in 1959; 2.) percent of children under 18 years old and not living with both parents; 3.) percent of males 25 years old and over with less than 8 years of school completed; 4.) percent of unskilled males (laborers and service workers) in the employed civilian labor force; and, 5.) percent of housing units dilapidated or lacking some or all plumbing facilities. After each tract had been ranked by the index, those in the lowest quartile were designated as "poor" tracts. To obtain evaluations of neighborhood concentrations of poverty, the following poverty area definition was utilized: 1.) any area with five or more contiguous poor tracts regardless of the number of families contained within; 2.) any area of one to four contiguous poor tracts, containing an aggregate of 4,000 or more families; or, 3.) any area of one or two contiguous tracts not ranked in the lowest quartile that was completely surrounded by poor tracts (in some cases, areas of three or four contiguous tracts, not themselves poor but surrounded by poor tracts, were included in the neighborhood after analysis of their characteristics; this was not done, however, for areas of five or more contiguous tracts not themselves poor but surrounded by poor tracts). The original analysis was done on the basis of 1960 census data. The analysis was subsequently updated on the basis of information on urban renewal activities received from local renewal agencies. BUREAU OF THE CENSUS, U.S. DEP'T OF COMMERCE, CHARACTERISTICS OF FAMILIES RESIDING IN "POVERTY AREAS": MARCH 1966, Series P-23, No. 19 1966.

15. The original determinations and the subsequent urban renewal adjustments resulted in the designation of 193 poverty areas in the 100 SMSA's. These poverty areas comprised approximately 22% of the 20,915 tracts in SMSA's with a population of 250,000 or more. No major concentration of poverty was identified in the Davenport-Rock Island-

A detailed analysis of these poverty areas reveals that the nonwhite segment of the population disproportionately resides within these areas.[16] Of the 24,506,000 families within SMSA's, with a 1960 population of 250,000 or more, a total of 22,025,000 or 89.9 percent were white, while 2,481,000 or 10.1 percent were nonwhite. However, the nonwhite segment of the population was distributed more heavily within poverty areas. Thus, of the 4,795,000 families within poverty areas, a total of 3,016,000 or 62.9 percent were white, while a total of 1,779,000 or 37.1 percent were nonwhite. The white segment of the population was more heavily represented in nonpoverty areas. Thus, of the 19,711,000 families outside poverty areas, a total of 19,009,000 or 96.4 percent, were white, while 702,000 or only 3.6 percent were nonwhite.

This disproportionate distribution of white and nonwhite families leads to the conclusion that an individual in a nonwhite family is more likely to find himself within a poverty area, while an individual in a white family is likely to reside outside the poverty areas. Thus, 71.1 percent of all nonwhite families in SMSA's, with a 1960 population of 250,000 or more, resided within poverty areas. At the same time, only 13.7 percent of all white families within these SMSA's resided within poverty areas.

Simply residing within a poverty area, however, does not necessarily lead to the conclusion that the individual or family is itself poor. A further analysis of poor families indicates that not only are white families more likely to reside outside poverty areas, while nonwhite families are more likely to reside within poverty areas, but also that poor white families are likely to reside outside of these areas, while poor nonwhite families are likely to reside within them. Of the 2,187,000 poor white families, only 30.8 percent resided within poverty areas, while 69.2 percent resided outside the areas. At the same time, of the total 857,000 poor nonwhite families, 81.0 percent resided within these areas, while only 19.0 percent resided in other areas.

This analysis indicates even further why the issues of race and poverty become closely interrelated. The nonwhite segment of the population is overrepresented in the poverty areas of our major SMSA's. The poor nonwhite family finds itself trapped within these poverty areas while a greater number of poor white families are able to escape them. The disproportionate number of total nonwhite families residing

Moline, Iowa-Ill., SMSA. BUREAU OF THE CENSUS, U.S. DEP'T OF COMMERCE, POVERTY AREAS IN THE 100 LARGEST METROPOLITAN AREAS, 1960 CENSUS OF POPULATION SUPPLEMENTARY REPORT PC (S1)-54 (1967).

16. The poverty area analysis from the 1960 SMSA data is drawn from BUREAU OF THE CENSUS, POVERTY AREAS IN THE 100 LARGEST METROPOLITAN AREAS, *Id.*

in the poverty areas leads to the further conclusion that even those nonwhite families above the poverty level find it more difficult than comparable white families to move from these areas.

In March, 1966, the Bureau of the Census conducted a "follow-up" study of families residing in poverty areas.[17] The same conclusions were evident. The nonwhite segment of the population was overrepresented in poverty areas. While nonwhite families comprised about 12 percent of all families in major SMSA's during March, 1966, they constituted 42 percent of all families living in poverty areas and only six percent of all families in nonpoverty areas. Secondly, a nonwhite family was more likely to find itself within a poverty area than was a white family. In March, 1966, more than one-half (57 percent) of all nonwhite families residing in SMSA's of 250,000 or more lived in poverty areas, compared only one-tenth of all white families. Finally, poor nonwhite families are more likely to reside within poverty areas than are poor white families. Close to two-thirds of all nonwhite families below the poverty level lived in poverty areas in March, 1966, as compared with only one-fifth of all white families below the poverty level.

There is a definite correlation between the two dimensions of analysis so far advanced. Regardless of which poverty level is utilized, the nonwhite segment of the population is disproportionately poor. These findings immediately lend substance to the charge that the nonwhite individual in the United States faces discrimination. He faces continual barriers in jobs, in education, etc. which trap him in poverty.[18] But furthermore, discrimination in housing and the reluctance of white individuals to live in a predominantly nonwhite area impose a physical trap upon the nonwhite in the United States.[19]

On a further level, this analysis of poverty and race leads to a consideration of how predominantly nonwhite areas are formed. It is not sufficient to understand that nonwhites are disproportionately poor and that nonwhites disproportionately inhabit poverty areas. We must further comprehend the dynamic process of the formation of predominantly nonwhite areas which trap the poor, as well as the more

17. The poverty area analysis from the March 1966 study is drawn from CHARACTERISTICS OF FAMILIES RESIDING IN "POVERTY AREAS": MARCH 1966, *supra* note 14.

18. That nonwhite families in poverty are less likely to escape poverty than comparable white families is indicated in the 1965 CEA ANNUAL REPORT. A study of incomes of the same families in two successive years shows that 76% of nonwhite families with incomes below $3,000 in the first year remain there the successive year. C. E. A., THE ANNUAL REPORT OF THE COUNCIL OF ECONOMIC ADVISERS 164 (1965).

19. That the situation of a predominantly Negro section of a major city establishes a vicious circle by further reinforcing the detrimental effects of discrimination has been thoroughly substantiated. For two excellent studies see: R. WEAVER, THE NEGRO GHETTO (1948); and a later similar study: K. CLARK, DARK GHETTO: DILEMMAS OF SOCIAL POWER (1965).

affluent sections of the nonwhite population, and are avoided by much of the poor segment of the white population.

Perhaps one of the most detailed studies specifically on the question of Negro urban residential location is the one conducted by Karl and Alma Taeuber.[20] The Taeubers thoroughly analyze the process of Negro movement into previously white areas and the complex process of segregation which subsequently results.[21]

The Taeubers' analysis indicates that the first Negroes likely to move into a previously predominantly white area are likely to be higher-status Negroes. A second resulting pattern is to be expected, *viz.*, a gradual exodus of whites. First, the high-status whites will leave, only to be followed by their middle class counterparts. The Taeubers noted that this process was somewhat impeded by the tight housing market of the decade 1940-1950. However, by 1960, these general trends were quite obvious as the suburbanization process accelerated. The Taeubers note the change that occurred within mixed areas as the higher-status whites began to leave:

> [D]uring 1950-1960, high-status whites living in mixed areas, who desired and could afford alternative housing, took advantage of newly available opportunities. The "catching-up" period of adjustment of housing to changing needs and incomes depleted racially mixed areas of much of their high-status white population. Whites living in mixed areas became a more homogeneous low-status group, so that correlations be-

---

20. K. Taeuber & A. Taeuber, Negroes in Cities: Residential Segregation and Neighborhood Change (1965).

21. The Taeubers have constructed a classification scheme for analyzing racial change in census tracts with 250 or more nonwhites in the terminal year of the decade under consideration. Four major types of areas were identified: 1.) established Negro Areas: all tracts in which nonwhites made up 90% of the total population in both the initial and terminal years of the decade (these tracts may have become all-Negro as a result of succession from an earlier stage of being all-white or they may have been initially settled by Negroes); 2.) stable interracial areas: tracts in which both the white and nonwhite populations had a change of fewer than 100 persons and less than 10% between the initial and terminal years of the decade; 3.) consolidation areas: all remaining tracts in which the percentage nonwhite increased between the initial and terminal years; and, 4.) displacement areas: tracts in which the percentage nonwhite decreased over the decade. The type of area most relevant to the analysis here of nonwhite movement into previously white areas is the consolidation area. Consolidation tracts are further subdivided: a.) succession tracts: tracts where a nonwhite population increase occurred while the white population decreased (there were 250 or more nonwhites in the initial and terminal year of the decade); b.) invasion tracts: again a nonwhite population increase occurred while the white population decreased, however, here there were fewer than 250 nonwhites in the initial year of the decade and more than 250 in the terminal year; c.) growing tracts: here the nonwhite population increases while the white population increases or remains stable, however, the nonwhite population increases at a faster rate than the white population; and, d.) declining tracts: the nonwhite population decreases or remains stable while the white population decreases, however, the nonwhite population decreases at a slower rate than the white population. Taeuber Study, *Id.* at 105-14.

tween white and Negro status measures for these mixed tracts diminished.[22]

In fact, the Taeubers found that along some status measures, the Negroes in these areas surpassed the remaining white population:

> [T]he processes of racial succession were often accompanied by a lessened tendency for the whites and Negroes in mixed areas to resemble one another in educational and occupational status . . . . [I]t appears that by 1960 Negroes had moved from a situation in which they were markedly inferior to whites to one where color differentials had narrowed. In fact, in the case of measures of education and home-ownership, Negroes now tend to surpass whites living in these areas.[23]

This analysis of the dynamics of racial change adds a further element to the consideration of the question of poverty and race. Not only are nonwhites disproportionately poor and disproportionately residents of poverty areas, but those whites who remain in predominantly Negro areas tend themselves to be low-status.[24]

The questions of poverty and race are perhaps separable. However, the considerations raised here clearly demonstrate the extensive interrelation of the two questions. Poverty as an economic class consideration cuts across both white and nonwhite segments of the population. The higher incidence of poverty among nonwhites clearly lends a racial element to any discussion of poverty in the United States. The further residential association of some poor whites with nonwhite residential areas extends the analysis of these poor whites from merely questions of poverty to an intimate identification with the more extensive problems of racial bias and discrimination.

These general considerations on the questions of poverty and race

22. *Id.* at 187.

23. *Id.* at 186.

24. The Taeubers note that the pattern described here is subject to significant regional differences. In Northern and border cities, the general pattern is that areas where the Negro population is of high occupational or educational status are also those where Negroes comprise a relatively lower proportion of the population. Areas where the Negro population is of low socioeconomic status tend to have a higher proportion nonwhite. In Southern cities, however, it is more common for areas with high-status Negroes to be predominantly Negro areas, while low-status Negroes live in racially mixed residential areas. To a large extent, the Taeubers attribute this distinction to historical peculiarities of racial residential segregation in Southern cities yet a further element of analysis is introduced. "Old" Southern cities which developed before the Civil War (such as Baltimore and Washington) have had large increases in Negro population. The most important source of additional dwellings for Negroes has been the transfer of existing units from white to Negro occupancy. In this process, the resultant changes resemble those described for Northern cities. "New" Southern cities which developed after the Civil War (such as Atlanta and Dallas) have provided for an increasing Negro housing demand by additional residential construction rather than unit transfer from white to Negro. The subsequent slower growth of the Negro population within these newer Southern cities has permitted this type of adaptation to continue. *Id.* at 189-194.

are applicable to Detroit. Data from the 1965 Transportation and Land Use Study (TALUS) conducted in the Detroit area indicates that poverty disproportionately affects the nonwhite segment of the city.[25] For the entire SMSA,[26] a total of seven percent of the 30,269 white families surveyed had annual incomes under $3,000, while 25.2 percent of the 5,113 nonwhites surveyed were in the same income category. For the city of Detroit itself, 18.9 percent of the 1,116 white families surveyed had annual incomes below $3,000, while 25.9 percent of the 4,506 nonwhite families surveyed were in the same classification.

A further indication of the relative deprivation of nonwhite families is derived from median income analysis. For the entire SMSA, the median income level of the white families surveyed was $9,164, while the median income level of the nonwhite families surveyed was only $5,641. Though the difference in median income levels was still present for the city of Detroit, the disparity was considerably less. The median income level for the white families surveyed in the city was $6,846, while the median income for the nonwhite families surveyed was $6,405.

The Bureau of the Census has provided poverty area data on specific SMSA's.[27] The data for the Detroit SMSA follows the same pattern as the analysis for the entire U.S. The following conclusions about the Detroit SMSA are evident:

1. The nonwhite segment of the population was disproportionately represented in the ranks of the poor. Of the 943,586 families in the SMSA, a total of 817,575 (86.7 percent) were white, and 125,911 (13.3 percent) were nonwhite. However, of the 112,310 poor families in the SMSA, 67,236 (59.9 percent) were white, while 45,074 (40.1 percent) were nonwhite.
2. The nonwhite segment of the population was disproportion-

---

25. From August, 1965, to February, 1966, a study was conducted in seven counties of Southeastern Michigan (Wayne, Oakland, Macomb, Monroe, Washtenaw, St. Clair, and Livingston). This work was conducted to obtain data necessary for developing a comprehensive 1990 transportation and land use plan for the counties under consideration. The Transportation and Land Use Study (TALUS) was conducted by the Center for Urban Studies of the University of Michigan, Dearborn Campus. TALUS surveyed every 25th household in the urbanizing parts of the region, providing a 4% sample of 93% of TALUS area households. The purpose of the survey was two-fold: 1.) to provide an accurate picture of all travel behavior within the region on an average week-day; and, 2.) to obtain information on the social, economic, and demographic characteristics of the population. The data from the TALUS study referred to here was obtained from Irving J. Rubin, TALUS Director. While complete data from the study is not yet available, the following preliminary report was submitted: I. RUBIN, CHARACTERISTICS OF THE WHITE AND THE NEGRO POPULATION IN THE DETROIT METROPOLITAN AREA, released December 29. 1967.

26. The Detroit SMSA data is comprised of statistics from Wayne, Oakland, and Macomb Counties.

27. BUREAU OF THE CENSUS, *supra* note 15.

ately represented in poverty areas. While the nonwhite portion of the population was 13.3 percent of the total, nonwhite families constituted 58.4 percent of the 145,199 families living in the poverty areas. At the same time, the nonwhite families constituted only 5.2 percent of the 798,387 families living outside the poverty areas.

3. A nonwhite family was thus more likely to reside within a poverty area than was a white family. Of the 817,675 white families in the SMSA, only 7.4 percent resided in poverty areas. Of the 125,911 nonwhite families, 67.3 percent resided in these areas.
4. Finally, poor nonwhite families were more likely to reside in poverty areas, while poor white families more easily escaped these areas. Of the 67,236 poor white families, only 17.9 percent resided in poverty areas. Of the 45,074 poor nonwhite families, 75.7 percent resided in the poverty areas.

As was the case with the general analysis, an analysis of the dynamics of racial change in selected Detroit areas furthers the understanding of the interrelation between poverty and race. Two specific areas have been chosen for analysis: these areas correspond to the major violence areas during the 1967 summer riot. (See Maps A and B).[28] The census data from the 1940, 1950, and 1960 population censuses reveals the degree of change which has occurred within these two areas. (See Tables 1 and 2).[29]

An analysis of the change in racial composition of these census tracts clearly shows the nature of the racial changeover in the areas.[30]

---

28. Following the riot in July, 1967, the Detroit Urban League and the Detroit Free Press combined efforts to survey the attitudes of Negroes in the "riot area." Two riot areas were chosen for analysis. On the west side, the area is bounded by McNichols Rd. on the north, Michigan Ave. on the south, Livernois Ave. on the east, and the corporation limits of Highland Park and the Lodge Freeway on the west. On the East Side, the area is bounded by Gratiot Ave. and Harper Ave. on the north, Jefferson Ave. on the south, East Grand Blvd. on the east, and Conner Ave. on the west. These are the "riot areas" chosen for specific analysis in this paper. While violence was reported in a somewhat wider area (including the southern portion of Hamtramck), these two specific areas are felt to have included the scenes of the major portion of the violent activity. P. MEYER, DETROIT URBAN LEAGUE, A SURVEY OF ATTITUDES OF DETROIT NEGROES AFTER THE RIOT OF 1967 (1967).

29. The statistical information on census tracts is drawn from: U.S. DEP'T OF COMMERCE, BUREAU OF THE CENSUS, POPULATION AND HOUSING: STATISTICS FOR CENSUS TRACTS (DETROIT, MICH., AND ADJACENT AREA) (1942); U.S. DEP'T OF COMMERCE, BUREAU OF THE CENSUS, U.S. CENSUS OF POPULATION: CENSUS TRACT STATISTICS (DETROIT, MICHIGAN AND ADJACENT AREA), vol. III, ch. 17 (1952); and, U.S. DEP'T OF COMMERCE, BUREAU OF THE CENSUS, U.S. CENSUSES OF POPULATION AND HOUSING; CENSUS TRACTS (DETROIT, MICH. STANDARD METROPOLITAN STATISTICAL AREA), Final Report PHC (1)—40 (1962).

30. The census tract data can be analyzed according to the classification scheme developed by the Taeubers. In 1940, only one census tract in either area contained 250 or more Negroes. By 1950, the West Side Riot Area contained 10 census tracts (35.7% of all tracts in the Area) with 250 or more Negroes. Of these tracts, 9 were "invasion" tracts and

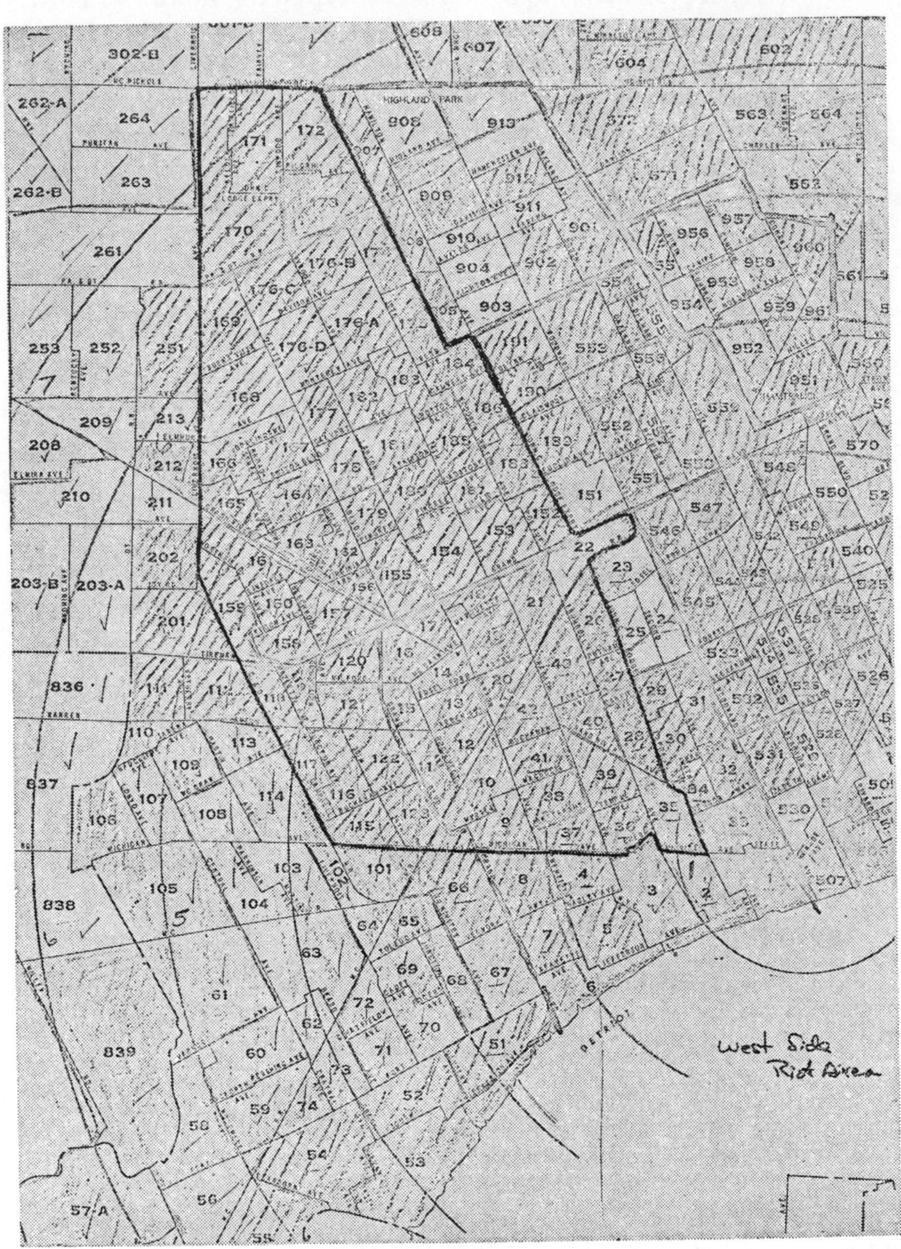

MAP A

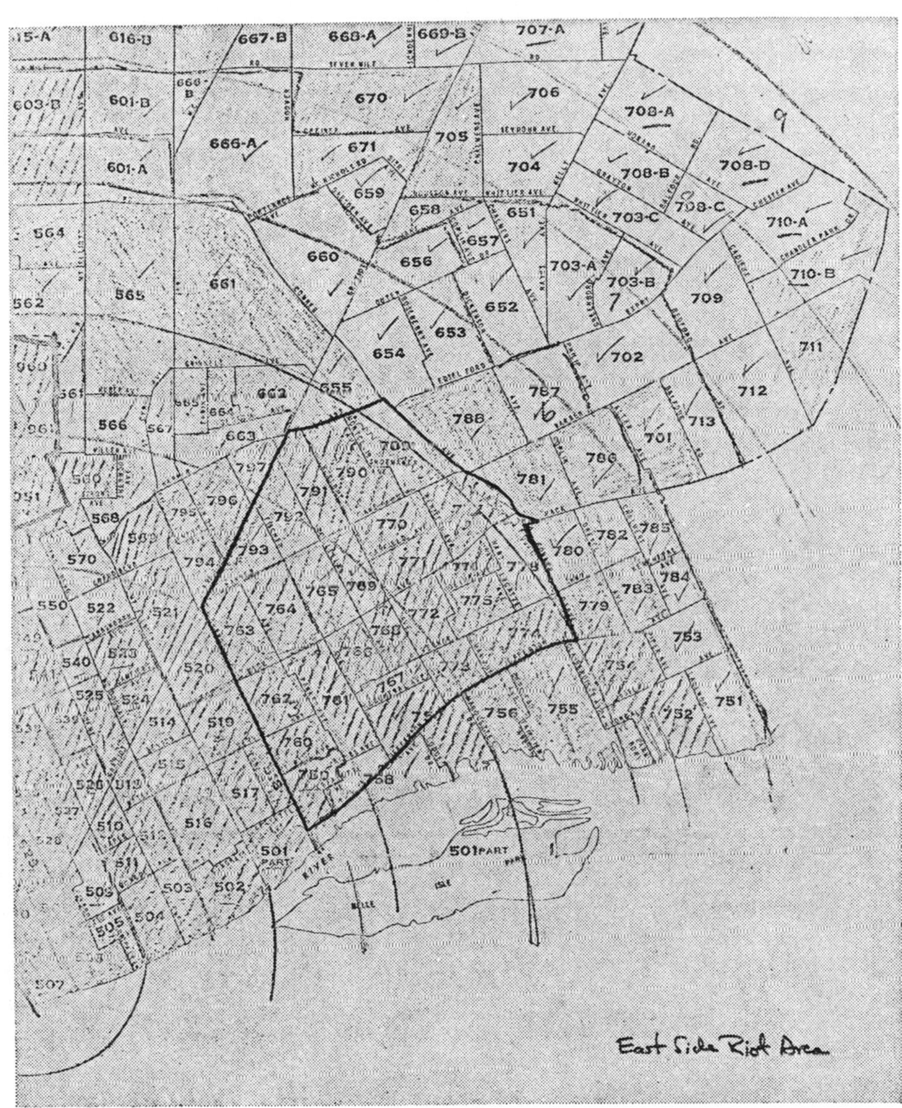
East Side Riot Area
667-B
668-A
669-B
707-A
601-B
670
706
708-A
666-A
671
705
704
708-B
708-D
601-A
659
658
651
703-C
708-C
710-A
660
656
657
703-A
703-B
710-B
661
652
709
653
654
702
711
712
662
787
788
713
701
566
663
790
786
781
797
791
796
795
770
782
785
568
793
780
570
794
779
765
769
771
784
783
522
764
772
774
763
753
540
520
761
762
767
756
755
751
514
519
752
760
517
516
501 PART
503
502
504
501PART

MAP B

TABLE 1
WEST SIDE RIOT AREA

	1940 Census				1950 Census						1960 Census					
Census Tract	# White	% White	# Negro	% Negro	# White	% White	Changes	# Negro	% Negro	Changes	# White	% White	Changes	# Negro	% Negro	Changes
152	3,958	99.6	6	0.2	3,476	93.3	– 6.3	321	6.2	+ 6.0	1,305	41.1	–52.2	1,842	58.0	+51.8
153	9,151	99.8	12	0.1	7,103	86.3	–13.5	1,113	13.5	+13.4	1,465	18.0	–68.3	6,621	81.5	+68.0
154	7,205	99.7	17	0.2	6,120	95.4	– 4.3	291	4.5	+ 4.3	1,211	19.0	–76.4	5,150	80.8	+76.3
155	5,921	99.9	6	0.1	5,637	99.2	– 0.7	37	0.7	+ 0.6	646	11.0	–88.2	5,227	88.7	+88.0
156	1,957	99.8	3	0.2	1,780	99.6	– 0.2	2	0.1	– 0.1	344	18.3	–81.3	1,519	80.9	+80.8
162	3,844	100.0	—	0.0	3,504	99.9	– 0.1	2	0.1	+ 0.1	696	17.7	–82.2	3,223	81.9	+81.8
163	4,912	100.0	—	0.0	4,858	99.6	– 0.4	9	0.2	+ 0.2	1,737	39.6	–60.0	2,630	60.0	+59.8
164	6,749	100.0	1	0.0	5,850	99.6	– 0.4	12	0.2	+ 0.2	1,391	23.9	–75.5	4,431	76.0	+75.8
165	3,578	99.9	2	0.1	3,273	99.8	– 0.1	3	0.1	—	2,009	73.6	–26.6	709	26.0	+25.9
166	4,863	99.9	3	0.1	4,322	99.9	—	2	0.04	– 0.06	1,692	39.5	–60.4	2,581	60.3	+60.26
167	4,450	99.7	6	0.1	3,975	99.1	– 0.6	15	0.4	+ 0.3	1,488	37.6	–61.5	2,464	62.2	+61.8
168	5,924	99.4	36	0.6	5,659	99.1	– 0.3	34	0.6	—	2,159	40.1	–59.0	3,178	59.0	+58.4
169	4,710	99.7	14	0.3	5,082	99.8	+ 0.1	9	0.2	– 0.1	2,138	46.7	–53.1	2,416	52.8	+52.6
174	3,391	76.5	1,041	23.5	1,876	45.2	–31.3	2,252	54.3	+30.8	298	13.1	–32.1	1,970	86.6	+32.3
175	4,729	99.5	15	0.3	4,236	95.1	– 4.4	187	4.2	+ 3.9	803	26.8	–68.3	2,178	72.7	+68.5
176	27,289	99.6	94	0.3	24,448	97.8	– 1.8	529	2.1	+ 1.8	5,653	23.3	–74.5	18,587	76.5	+74.4
177	4,444	99.6	14	0.3	4,112	99.1	– 0.5	34	0.8	+ 0.5	855	21.9	–77.2	3,034	77.7	+76.9
178	5,707	99.8	12	0.2	5,611	99.4	– 0.4	25	0.4	+ 0.2	2,028	46.3	–53.1	2,330	53.2	+52.8
179	4,357	99.9	5	0.1	4,004	99.2	– 0.7	26	0.6	+ 0.5	205	5.3	–93.9	3,693	94.6	+94.0
180	7,488	99.8	15	0.2	5,906	89.9	– 9.9	646	9.8	+ 9.6	309	4.7	–85.2	6,257	95.2	+85.4
181	4,001	98.6	51	1.3	3,704	96.9	– 1.7	103	2.7	+ 1.4	1,448	43.5	–53.4	1,852	55.6	+52.9
182	3,608	99.5	14	0.4	3,304	99.4	– 0.1	19	0.6	+ 0.2	363	11.3	–88.1	2,835	88.4	+87.8
183	4,207	99.7	13	0.3	4,153	98.3	– 1.4	65	1.5	+ 1.2	1,173	28.3	–70.0	2,942	71.0	+69.5
184	5,204	99.8	10	0.2	4,798	98.9	– 0.9	41	0.9	+ 0.7	1,361	30.2	–68.7	3.113	69.0	+68.1
185	4,838	99.4	27	0.5	2,919	65.8	–33.6	1,511	34.0	+33.5	340	8.3	–57.5	3,756	91.3	+57.3
186	3,262	98.7	37	1.1	2,484	81.4	–17.3	559	18.3	+17.2	537	19.7	–61.7	2,187	80.1	+61.8
187	6,555	99.8	14	0.2	4,291	74.1	–25.7	1,485	25.7	+25.5	54	1.0	–73.1	5,179	98.9	+73.2
188	5,127	97.3	133	2.5	2,118	47.9	–49.4	2,297	52.0	+49.5	302	7.3	–40.6	3,788	92.1	+40.1

TABLE 2
EAST SIDE RIOT AREA

Census Tract	1940 Census # White	% White	# Negro	% Negro	1950 Census # White	% White	Change	# Negro	% Negro	Change	1960 Census # White	% White	Change	# Negro	% Negro	Change
757	7,345	99.4	34	0.5	7,191	99.3	− 0.1	40	0.6	+ 0.1	4,570	71.3	−28.0	1,821	28.4	+27.8
758	3,335	98.3	50	1.5	3,701	98.9	+ 0.6	32	0.9	− 0.6	3,599	97.1	− 1.8	102	2.8	+ 1.9
759	6,241	99.5	14	0.2	6,096	95.3	− 4.2	260	4.1	+ 3.9	3,418	62.8	−32.5	1,990	36.6	+32.5
760	4,386	99.6	16	0.4	3,696	97.9	− 1.7	84	2.1	+ 1.7	1,674	41.7	−56.2	2,321	57.9	+55.8
761	2,877	96.5	105	3.5	2,867	93.8	− 2.7	190	6.2	+ 2.7	1,714	58.1	−35.7	1,224	41.5	+35.3
762	5,994	98.9	64	1.1	5,320	90.3	− 8.6	556	9.4	+ 8.3	1,404	23.2	−67.1	4,636	76.7	+67.3
763	7,292	99.6	20	0.3	6,859	94.1	− 5.5	423	5.8	+ 5.5	1,847	28.2	−65.9	4,669	71.3	+65.5
764	5,291	99.2	40	0.8	5,138	98.1	− 1.1	99	1.9	+ 1.1	2,309	39.9	−58.2	3,014	59.8	+57.9
765	5,867	96.9	189	3.1	4,874	86.9	−10.0	725	12.9	+ 9.8	1,261	23.2	−63.7	4,182	76.8	+63.9
766	4,450	99.4	25	0.6	4,176	97.8	− 1.6	87	2.0	+ 1.4	1,032	25.2	−72.6	3,059	74.7	+72.7
767	3,142	99.8	6	0.2	2,898	96.3	− 3.5	109	3.6	+ 3.4	1,004	35.9	−60.4	1,766	63.1	+59.5
768	3,771	96.1	155	3.9	3,078	82.2	−13.9	669	17.9	+14.0	787	21.4	−60.8	2,875	78.3	+60.4
769	4,677	98.7	64	1.3	4,077	90.3	− 8.4	430	9.5	+ 8.2	1,205	29.9	−60.4	2,811	69.8	+60.3
770	4,521	95.0	238	5.0	3,581	82.1	−12.9	774	17.7	+12.7	1,365	33.8	−48.3	2,651	65.7	+48.0
771	5,621	99.9	7	0.1	4,065	77.2	−22.7	1,195	22.7	+22.6	1,132	22.4	−54.8	3,903	77.2	+54.5
772	5,403	99.7	15	0.3	4,920	99.5	− 0.2	20	0.4	+ 0.1	2,001	41.5	−58.0	2,812	58.4	+58.0
773	4,278	100.0	—	0.0	4,115	99.7	− 0.3	10	0.2	+ 0.2	2,158	54.6	−45.1	1,791	45.4	+45.2
774	5,772	99.3	11	0.2	4,951	98.6	− 0.7	38	0.8	+ 0.6	3,452	82.5	−16.1	709	17.0	+16.2
775	4,414	99.5	20	0.5	3,861	98.6	− 0.9	56	1.4	+ 0.9	2,492	74.9	−23.7	813	24.4	+23.0
776	3,255	99.9	4	0.1	2,879	97.7	− 2.2	69	2.3	+ 2.2	1,677	66.9	−30.8	809	32.3	+30.0
777	2,040	99.0	19	0.9	1,967	96.3	− 2.7	74	3.6	+ 2.7	1,148	67.5	−28.8	542	31.8	+28.2
778	749	100.0	—	0.0	703	100.0	—	—	0.0	—	459	75.4	−24.6	150	24.6	+24.6

In 1940, both areas were predominantly white areas. Of the 28 census tracts in the West Side Riot Area, a total of 27 (96.4 percent) were 90 percent or more white-populated; of the 22 census tracts in the East Side Riot Area, all were in the same classification.

In the years between the 1940 and 1950 censuses, racial change was somewhat noticeable in both areas. By 1950, of the 28 census tracts in the West Side Riot Area, only 21 (75 percent) were 90 percent or more white-populated; of the 22 census tracts in the East Side Riot Area, 18 (81.8 percent) were 90 percent or more white-populated. Negro movement into these areas had definitely begun; however, by 1950, the Negro residence within these areas was hardly substantial.

The dramatic change within these areas occurred between 1950 and 1960. What had been relatively stable white-populated areas up until 1950, now underwent a large influx of Negroes accompanied by a corresponding outflow of white residents. In the West Side Riot Area, by 1960, there were no census tracts with a white population of 90 percent or more. What in percentage terms had been a relatively small Negro residential percentage before 1960, was shown by the 1960 census to have grown substantially. In the West Side Riot Area, the percentage of the total population which was Negro had increased 50 percentage points or more in 26 (92.9 percent) census tracts. In the East Side Riot Area, the percentage of the total population which was Negro had increased 50 percentage points or more in 12 (54.6 percent) census tracts.

An examination of the total population statistics for each of these two areas yields a somewhat stronger impression of the nature of the change in racial composition within these areas. In the West Side Riot Area, of the 163, 030 total inhabitants in 1940, 99 percent were white, while only one percent were Negro; by 1950, of the 150,232 total inhabitants, 92.3 percent were white, while only 7.7 percent were Negro; but by 1960, of the 139,702 total inhabitants, 24.3 percent were white, while 75.7 percent were Negro. In the East Side Riot Area, of the 101,823 total inhabitants in 1940, 98.9 percent were white, while only 1.1 percent were Negro; by 1950, of the 97,226 total inhabitants, 93.9

1 was a "succession" tract (this is the tract which had 250 or more Negroes in 1940). By 1950, the East Side Area contained 8 census tracts (36.4% of all tracts in the Area) with 250 or more Negroes. All of these tracts were invasion tracts. By 1960, the West Side Riot Area contained 24 census tracts (85.7% of all tracts in the Area) with 250 or more Negroes. Of these tracts, 14 were invasion tracts, 9 were succession tracts, and one was a "declining" tract. By 1960, the East Side Riot Area contained 20 census tracts (91.0% of all tracts in the Area) with 250 or more Negroes. Of these tracts, 12 were invasion tracts and 8 were succession tracts. By 1960, 5 West Side Riot Area census tracts were 90% or more Negro. This analysis further illustrates the degree of racial change evident in the two riot areas. TAEUBER STUDY, *supra* note 20 at 105-14.

percent were white, while only 6.1 percent were nonwhite; again, by 1960, of the 90,058 inhabitants, 46.0 percent were white, while 54 percent were Negro.

In both areas, the total white population was definitely decreasing while the Negro population was increasing. That the total Negro and white population for each area was a diminishing total over the three censuses indicates that the decline of the white population occurred at a faster rate than the increase of the Negro population. By 1960, Negroes in each area constituted a majority of the total Negro and white population.

The TALUS study included an analysis of the "Area of Civil Disturbance" which very closely corresponds to the area chosen here for the West Side Riot Area.[31] The analysis of the white and nonwhite residents of this area of civil disturbance in 1965 corroborates the further analysis by the Taeubers on the dynamics of racial change.

By 1965, assuming that previous trends continued, the population of this area would be expected to be more and more solidly Negro. In such a situation, the Negro segment of the population would be expected to be of somewhat higher status than the white segment of the population remaining in the area. The TALUS survey indicates that of the 271 white households interviewed, 32.9 percent had incomes annually of less than $3,000; of the 1,441 nonwhite households interviewed, 19.5 percent had annual incomes of less than $3,000. These findings show definite differences from the TALUS income findings previously mentioned for the entire Detroit SMSA because more nonwhite households were below the annual income level of $3,000 than were white households. Within the area of the civil disturbance, there were more poor white households than nonwhite households.

Other TALUS findings demonstrate significant differences between the white and nonwhite residents. The nonwhite residents were more likely than the white residents to be married; 67.1 percent of the nonwhites interviewed were married, compared with only 38.3 percent of the whites. The nonwhite residents were more likely to be employed than were the white residents of the area: 80.7 percent of the nonwhites reported employment, while only 47.3 percent of the whites reported a similar status. The nonwhite residents were more likely to own automobiles: 29.6 percent of the nonwhites interviewed did not own a car, compared to 51.5 percent of the whites interviewed.

This general portrait of the population in the area of the civil

31. The Talus "Area of Civil Disturbance" is bounded by W. McNichols on the north, Livernois on the west, W. Grand Blvd. on the south and Woodward and Highland Park City Limits on the east. Rupin, *supra* note 25.

disturbance does indicate a somewhat higher status Negro population than white population. As such, the analysis completes the picture of racial change within the area: A Negro movement into the area began, the white population left to a large extent, and the remaining whites tended to be of lower status than the Negroes who remained.

The analysis of the question of poverty and race, then, establishes the context in which the riot occurred. The nonwhite segment of the Detroit population, as is the case with nonwhites nationally, were disproportionately poor, and disproportionately residents of poverty areas. The specific areas of the violence were areas of racial change in which a lower status white population resided compared to the nonwhite residents of the areas.

Riot Participation: Negro and White

Governor Romney's assertion that the Detroit riot included both Negro and white participation in the violence lends a somewhat unique nature to this disturbance. As previously indicated, the current racial violence has primarily involved Negro violence against white-owned property. To establish an accurate analysis of the Detroit riot of 1967, it is thus necessary to attempt documentation of the extent of white involvement.

A situation of mass civil violence is by its very nature a condition of tremendous confusion. Events may be recorded simply because of the accidental presence of a news reporter or the precision of a police report. At the same time, significant occurrences may be lost in the rubble or forgotten amidst the countless individual acts comprising the total violence. Perhaps an approximation is the best that can be hoped for in any attempt to piece together what happened in a riot such as occurred in Detroit. In identifying who participated in the violence, we must consult many different sources in the hope that these different perspectives will yield a fairly accurate picture.

One of the first essential considerations is whether the context of the Detroit riot was significantly different from that of other recent disturbances. The previous analysis of the areas of Detroit where the violence occurred indicates that they were areas undergoing significant racial change. By 1960, over 75 percent of the population of the West Side Riot Area was Negro, and close to 55 percent of the population of the East Side Riot Area. The direction of racial change within these areas undoubtedly continued after 1960. Assuming that the sample from the TALUS study accurately reflects the racial distribution of the area of civil disturbance (the West Side Riot Area), by 1965, approximately 80 percent of the residents of the area were nonwhite. While the amount of racial changeover in the East Side Riot Area was somewhat smaller, the Negro percentage of the area in 1967 was undoubtedly larger than 55 percent.[32]

In 1965, racial violence occurred in both the Los Angeles area of Watts and the Cleveland area of Hough. In the same year, the Bureau of the Census conducted special censuses in each of these areas.[33] Some significant differences are notable between these areas and the scenes of the Detroit riot.

First, the areas of the Watts and Hough riots contained a more solidly Negro population. Of the 29,990 residents of Watts in 1965, 26,900 (90 percent) were Negro, while only 2,900 (9.7 percent) were white. Of the 58,979 residents of Hough in 1965, 51,861 (87.9 percent) were Negro, while only 6,808 were white. Secondly, the areas of both Watts and Hough are considerably more confined than the areas of violence in Detroit. The Watts and Hough areas each contain only ten census tracts. The two areas of Detroit analyzed here together contain 50 census tracts. Thus, the wider area and corresponding larger population of the Detroit riot areas indicate that even if the percentage of white residents was smaller here than in Watts and Hough, a larger total number of white individuals would most likely have been residents of the relevant areas.

Current analysis has indicated that racial violence is being contained largely within Negro "ghettos." The percentage of white residents within the Detroit areas of violence, and the extent of the areas of violence in Detroit, demand that we consider the Detroit riot an exception to this general observation.

That white individuals were present within the riot areas is insufficient evidence to conclude that they "participated" in the violent activity. One of the most thorough accounts of the Detroit riot is found in the *Detroit Free Press.*

Free Press reporters document two instances of white looters being killed.[34] The first, Walter Grzanka, was shot shortly after midnight,

---

32. To note the amount of racial changeover was greater in the West Side Riot Area can be substantiated by pointing out that this area was the first of the two to contain an invasion tract, and consequently the first to contain a succession tract. Further, by 1960, only the West Side Riot Area contained census tracts with a Negro population of 90% or more of the total population and, by 1960, there were 5 such tracts in the West Side Riot Area.

33. Bureau of the Census, U.S. Dep't of Commerce, Characteristics of the South and East Los Angeles Areas, November 1965, Series P-23, No. 18 (1966); and, Bureau of the Census, U.S. Dep't of Commerce, Characteristics of Selected Neighborhoods in Cleveland, Ohio: April 1965, Series P-23, No. 21 (1967).

34. The Gzanka incident was first reported in the *Detroit Free Press,* July 25, 1967, § A, at 3 (Metro Edition). The Lust incident was first reported in the Detroit Free Press, July 27, 1967, § A, at 1 (Metro Edition). Both incidents are more thoroughly researched and reported in: *The 43 who Died: An Investigation into How and Why Detroit's Riot Victims Were Slain,*" Detroit Free Press, Sept. 3, 1967, § B, at 1 and 4.

July 24 by a store manager who saw Grzanka come through the broken window of the looted grocery. The second white looting victim was Julius Lust who was shot by police while caught stealing in an automobile junkyard. Two white companions of Lust left the junkyard before the police arrived.

The overview gained by the reporters offers valuable insights. George Walker summarized his interpretation of the violence:

> It is easier to say what the riot is not than it is to say what it is. . . . It is not a sharp, deadly conflict in a small, contained area. It is not a civil rights disturbance. Most important of all, it is not a race riot—and from this simple fact may emerge the only ray of hope in an otherwise totally dismal setting. It is not a race riot because there has been almost no conflict between whites and Negroes. Negroes and whites loot together, stand side by side to watch buildings burn, go to jail together.[35]

A *Free Press* editorial expressed this same sentiment:

> One thing the riots were not. They were not a massive Negro uprising against white people. . . . There were Negro and white looters and snipers fought by Negro and white policemen and soldiers. It wasn't basically race against race. This needs to be emphasized because some terms used to describe what happened—Negro riots, ghetto uprising, Negro rebellion—don't really describe what occurred in Detroit.[36]

In addition to reporting specific instances of white participation, the general feeling obtainable from reading the *Free Press* is that the Detroit riot did involve white participation, and, in this regard, differed significantly from earlier "racial" disturbances.

A second relevant source of information involves arrest and prosecution data.[37] During the July disturbance, a total of 6,528 adults were arrested. Of these, 5,747 (88 percent) were nonwhite, and 781 (12 percent) were white. Subsequently a total of 4,881 (74.8 percent of all adults arrested) were prosecuted. Of those prosecuted, 4,292 (90 percent) were nonwhite, and 489 (10 percent) were white.

The arrest and prosecution statistics do indicate that a number of white individuals were involved in the riot. However, simply being arrested and prosecuted (perhaps for minor offense) does not indicate

35. G. Walker, *The Riot: A Quiet Look, at What It Is,* Detroit Free Press, July 26, 1967, § A, at 5 (Metro Edition).

36. Editorial, *Sift Ashes for Reasons Behind Ghetto Outbreak,* Detroit Free Press, July 27, 1967, § A, at 4 (Metro Edition).

37. Statistical Report on the Civil Disorder Occurring in the City of Detroit: July, 1967, a report submitted by Governor George Romney to the U.S. Senate Committee on Government Operations, Permanent Subcommittee on Investigations.

actual participation in the violence itself. To determine the extent of white participation we must examine the cause of arrest and the substance of the prosecution. Looting was one of the major activities of the riot participants. A total of 152 white adults were arrested for looting-related offenses (various breaking and entering or larceny charges); this represented 19.5 percent of all whites arrested. Of these, 110 were subsequently prosecuted for the offense they were charged with; this represented 22.5 percent of all prosecutions of white individuals. The only other major categories of white arrests and/or prosecutions involved carrying a concealed weapon, violation of the emergency proclamation (curfew), and "miscellaneous" offenses. Whether these offenses indicate actual participation in riot activity or merely presence in the riot area is not certain.

There are serious limitations, however, to the arrest and prosecution data. Sniping was one of the major reported activities of the violence. There were only 26 successful prosecutions (all Negro) for sniping activities. A total of 552 separate fires were reported during the riot.[38] However, there were only 13 successful prosecutions (all Negro) for arson. These findings would provide strong evidence for concluding that the arrests during the riot tended only to apprehend "surface" offenders. Nearly one-fourth of all arrests made during the riot were for violation of the emergency proclamation and "miscellaneous" offenses.

At the same time, the information from both the *Free Press* and the arrest-prosecution data does indicate an element of white participation in the riot activity. The data rather firmly confirms white participation in the looting. White participation in arson and/or sniping cannot be confirmed one way or the other.[39] Unfortunately, the majority of both arsonists and snipers were most probably not known or apprehended. The available data leads to the conclusion that white individuals were present within the riot areas and that they did participate in the riot activity.

---

38. *Id.*

39. On July 25, the Free Press reported the slaying of a supposed white sniper, Clifton Pryor. Pryor was shot by a National Guardsman. In its subsequent investigation, the Free Press attempted to discredit earlier reports. The police claimed that police and guardsmen investigating the sniping where Pryor was killed found Pryor with a shotgun in his hand, ordered him to halt, and shot when he refused to do so. Those with Pryor at the time claim he was holding a broomstick and that no warning was shouted before the guardsman shot. The reports remain contradictory. *See* Detroit Free Press, July 25, 1967, *supra* note 34, and Detroit Free Press, Sept. 3, 1967, *supra* note 34 at 2. The Kerner Commission also discusses a wire service report of the killing of another alleged white sniper. In a similar fashion, the Commission discredits the report. NATIONAL ADVISORY COMM'N ON CIVIL DISORDERS, *supra* note 3 at 102-104.

Historical Perspective and Theoretical Implications

Widespread racial violence has created a national crisis—a crisis in terms of the doubt it casts upon the ideals of a nation which claims equality for all and a rational system of government to provide equally for all—a crisis in terms of chaos, death, and destruction. This crisis has lead to national concern with current racial violence.

This concern over racial violence, however, runs the risk of falling victim to the difficulties of myopia. If we are truly to understand the significance of white participation in the Detroit riot, we must see current racial violence (and the Detroit riot of 1967 as a specific instance) within its historical and theoretical context.

Current ghetto "uprisings" are not the only instance of violence in the history of American racial relations. Nor, in fact, are such disturbances the only type of American racial violence. A number of distinguishable types of violence have emerged in our history. The following analysis identifies the "patterns" or "types" of violence which have occurred.[40] The violent incidents noted within this analysis are intended to be examples of the type of violence they illustrate.

Suppression and Insurrection

In 18th century America, as slavery became more and more accepted, the master-slave relationship as a dominant-subservient relationship also became more and more established. Inherent within this situation was the assumption that a master had the "right" to resort to physical force in dealing with his slaves. As Myrdal notes:

> The social pattern of subduing the Negroes by means by physical force was inherent in the slavery system. The master himself, with the backing, if needed, of the local police and, indeed, of all white neighbors, had to execute this force, and he was left practically unrestricted by any formal laws.[41]

The Negro did not universally resign himself to this subjugation. There are noted attempts at slave rebellion.[42] However, these rebellions were universally unsuccessful. Ultimately, these revolts led to the reassertion of the dominant form of violence—the suppression of Ne-

---

40. For a more thorough discussion of the patterns of American racial violence, see J. Corsi, *American Racial Violence: A Step Toward Comprehension*, 2 Case Western Res. J. of Sociology (June, 1968).

41. G. Myrdal, An American Dilemma 558 (1944).

42. The insurrections of Gabriel in Richmond, Virginia (1800), Denmark Vasey in Charleston, South Carolina (1822), and Nat Turner in Southampton County, Virginia (1831) are notable examples of slave revolts. *See* E. Frazier, The Negro in the United States 87-93 (1949) and B. Brawley, A Social History of the American Negro 86-90, 132-48 (1921).

groes by whites in the attempt to maintain the master-slave relationship. However, after the threat of a slave revolt became recognized, another element was added to this suppression: violence directed toward removing all possibility that the slaves would risk continued insurrection.

Lynching

A second major pattern is that of lynching. In general, lynching refers to group violence directed toward an individual or small group which results in the illegal death of one or a few victims. The Tuskegee Institute, perhaps the most complete source on lynching, has established four criteria which may be used to judge that an event constitutes lynching:[43]

1.) There must be legal evidence that a person was killed;
2.) The person must have met death illegally;
3.) A group must have participated in the killing;
4.) The group must have acted under the pretext of service to justice, race, or tradition.

Lynching in the United States was quite common in the late 19th Century. As the years went on and the number of lynchings became smaller, it became quite apparent that lynching was of significance mainly in the South and was serving predominantly as a form of white violence against Negroes. As Myrdal emphasizes:

> Since the early 1890's, the trend has been toward fewer and fewer lynchings. . . . The decrease has been faster outside the South, and the lynchings of whites has dropped much more than that of Negroes. Lynching has become, therefore, more and more a Southern phenomenon and a racial one.[44]

In 1953, the Tuskegee Institute (which had been collecting lynching data since 1882) decided to stop publishing lynching data. The Institute had made the decision that there were so few lynchings that they no longer served as a meaningful index of racial relations.

White-Dominated, Person-Oriented Rioting

Distinct from lynching, white-dominated, person-oriented rioting is not an attack upon specified individuals or limited groups of individuals. Rather, the violence is directed upon whole communities of individuals. The normal course of the violence is as follows: the attackers are whites; their victims are Negroes; the violence originates

43. Tuskegee Institute, 1947 Negro Year Book 303 (1947).
44. Myrdal, *supra* note 41 at 560-561.

with, and is directed and controlled by whites; the whites aim to inflict personal injury upon the Negroes; the Negroes, as victims, have historically done little to defend themselves.

Perhaps most typical of this form of violence is the race riot of 1908 in Springfield, Illinois.[45] Enraged by two alleged rapes of white women by Negroes, the white community of Springfield, Illinois launched two days of rioting, burning, and lynching aimed at the Negro residents of the city. The Negro reaction was mainly one of terror and flight. Approximately 2,000 Negroes gathered for protection within the Springfield Arsenal. Others left their homes and fled to safety. Before the riot ended, 5,000 militia were patrolling the streets of Springfield.

Other examples of this type of one-sided rioting are notable in the late 1890's and early 1900's. They include riots in Wilmington, North Carolina (1896); East St. Louis, Illinois (1917); Washington, D.C. (1919); and Tulsa, Oklahoma (1921).

Racial Warfare, Person-Oriented Rioting

Negroes did not always remain passive in rioting. The next pattern would involve each race engaged in attacks upon the members of the other race. However, the attacks still remained oriented toward inflicting physical harm upon members of the opposite race.

The model for this type of violence is the 1919 riot in Chicago, Illinois.[46] On July 27, 1919, a 17 year-old Negro would be drowned during an inter-racial fight at the Twenty-ninth Street Beach in Chicago. This event would touch off thirteen days of racial warfare. Those days of violence saw countless physical attacks and accompanying property damage. The casualty statistics alone, however, serve as a compelling indication that physical harm remained the major objective. A reported total of 38 persons were killed (23 Negroes and 15 whites), while a reported total of 537 were injured (342 Negroes, 178 white, 17 undetermined). Even with national guard units in the city, the violence did not begin to seriously quiet down until Chicago was faced with rain and falling temperatures.

The same type of racial violence was evident in the 1943 riot in Detroit, Michigan.[47] Here, in less than three full days of rioting, 710 individuals were killed or injured. Once again, persons of both races participated in the violence; the major form of violence involved physical attack.

---

45. For a more detailed account of this riot, see CHICAGO COMM'N ON RACE RELATIONS, THE NEGRO IN CHICAGO 67-71 (1922); and the N.Y. Times, Aug. 16-18, 1808.

46. For a very thorough discussion of the events of this riot see *Id.* at 1-52.

47. For a detailed account of this riot see A. LEE & N. HUMPHREY, RACE RIOT (1943); and R. SHOGAN & T. CRAIG, THE DETROIT RACE RIOT (1964).

Negro-Dominated, Property-Oriented Rioting

A further pattern of American racial violence has been the Negro-dominated, property-oriented riot. A riot of this type is distinguished by the fact that Negroes initiate the violence and direct their hostilities toward property rather than toward persons. Most of the property is white-owned, but located within the Negro ghetto. This violence seldom spreads outside the Negro neighborhoods to white residential areas or to such neutral areas as downtown locations. White individuals are rarely involved except for their membership in police or other units (national guard, federal troops, etc.) which may become involved in controlling the riot.

The first major appearance of this type of violence occurred in Harlem in 1935.[48] On March 19, an incident occurred involving a Negro youth caught stealing from a dime store in the middle of Harlem. A crowd which gathered outside the store got the impression that the boy had been murdered by the white store personnel. The rumor which followed led to the formation of Negro mobs which roamed the streets of Harlem, breaking store windows and looting. Incidents between Negroes and whites were at a minimum—with the exception of confrontations between the police and the looters. The looting continued through the next day, but was finally brought under control through the efforts of police and local Negro leaders.

The patterns have occurred in historical sequence: suppression and insurrection, lynching, etc. However, there is a considerable overlap between the individual types. When the first major Negro-dominated, property-oriented rioting occurred in Harlem, for instance, this did not mean that the racial warfare, person-oriented pattern would not occur again. It did in Detroit in 1943. What is indicated, however, is that each pattern was, for a time, barely noticeable, then, gradually more important, and, finally, the dominant pattern of racial violence, only to be replaced by the emergence of another dominant pattern.[49]

In many respects, the Detroit riot of 1967 differs from the expected pattern of Negro-dominated, property-oriented rioting: it did not occur in a narrowly-defined Negro ghetto, rather it occurred over a wide area recently undergoing racial change and yet retaining a significant num-

---

48. For a detailed account of this riot see H. Orlansky, The Harlem Riot: A Study in Mass Frustration (1943); and J. Boskin & F. Feldman, Riots in the City: An Addendum to the McCone Commission Report 6-7 (1967).

49. Further analysis indicates that at first the white element was the dominant factor in the violence. It is entirely possible to demonstrate that this role changeover in violent behavior is entirely consistent with the development of Negro-white relations in general. This relationship argues for consideration of racial violence as a product of, and a reflection upon, the general overriding pattern of racial relations prevalent at the time the violence occurs. *See* Corsi, *supra* note 40.

ber of white residents; it was not strictly Negro-dominated rioting, it included significant white participation in the riot activity (in fact, there were reported instances of white looters helping Negro looters in a co-operative effort);[50] the attacks were not directed solely at white-owned property, Negro business establishments were also looted and burned.[51] If the Detroit riot was strictly a typical Negro-dominated, property-oriented riot, the element of white participation would be totally inconsistent. Given the degree of white participation in evidence, the evaluation of the Detroit riot becomes considerably more complex.

To comprehend the significance of this riot, we must examine the riot participation in more detail. Many popular theories have developed to explain why people take part in a riot situation. One applicable field of social scientific thought on the subject is the sociology of collective behavior. Both the popular and collective behavior explanations essentially postulate two theories of riot participation: reasoned participation and emotional response.

If riot participation is reasoned behavior, the assumption is that the participating individuals have a rational motivation, and so their behavior can be seen as oriented toward the achievement of specific goals. One of the most thorough of the collective behavior analysts, Neil J. Smelser, argues that instances of collective outburst are aimed toward change. In the specific instance of a violent outburst, Smelser argues that after a number of conditions are present (a general situation in which violence will be permitted, some definite sources of tension which create dissatisfaction, a precipitating event, etc.), a generalized belief that violence will result in a beneficial change can prompt the individuals into a riot situation.[52]

One of the most thorough studies conducted of Negro attitudes concerning a riot situation was conducted by UCLA following the Watts riot of 1965.[53] This study lends support to the reasoned participation argumentation. Of the Negroes questioned, 56 percent thought the disturbance in Watts had a goal, and 62 percent felt that the riot was a Negro "protest." Of those who thought that the riot had a goal, 41 percent felt the goal was to call attention to Negro problems, 26 percent felt the riot would serve as an instrumentality in improving con-

50. For documentation of Negroes and whites looting side by side see Detroit Free Press, July 25, 1967, A, 8 (Metro Edition).

51. For discussion of the destruction done to Negro-owned business establishments see *"Brother" Signs Ignored by Looters,* Detroit Free Press, July 25, 1967.

52. N. Smelser, Theory of Collective Behavior (1962), especially pp. 222-269.

53. The survey of Negro attitudes in the Los Angeles Riot Study involved the interviewing of 596 Negroes in the Watts "curfew zone," and 124 arrestees. The data cited here is taken from the curfew zone sample. T. Tomlinson & D. Sears, *Negro Attitudes Toward the Riot,* Los Angeles Riot Study (1967) .

ditions and ending discrimination, and 33 percent felt that the riot served to express hostility.

Further, the Negroes interviewed felt that the Watts riot had "targets of attack." Of those responding, 38 percent felt the targets were stores and merchants, and 28 percent felt the targets were white people in general. The Negroes interviewed saw justification behind the attack. A total of 31 percent of those interviewed felt the targets were attacked because of mistreatment of Negroes, 19 percent felt the targets were attacked because of economic exploitation of Negroes (overcharging, selling inferior goods, etc.) or because of the Negroes' inferior economic position (unemployment, poverty, etc.). Only ten percent of those interviewed felt that specific targets were attacked by chance. Finally, of those interviewed, 64 percent felt that the targets of the riot deserved attack.

When interviewed about the expected outcome of the riot, a considerable number of Negroes indicated they expected beneficial effects. When asked what the main effects of the riot would be, 58 percent of the Negroes responded "very or somewhat favorable," 12 percent indicated that they expected neutral effects, or that they were not sure. When asked if the riot would help the Negro's "cause," 38 percent indicated that they felt the riot would help. Thirty percent indicated that the riot would make no difference or they were not sure what the effect would be. Only 18 percent expected "very or somewhat" unfavorable effects, and only 24 percent felt that the riot would "hurt" the Negro's cause.

In analyzing what this data signifies, Tomlinson and Sears observe:

> Much of this no doubt represents a rationale constructed after the fact for a violent series of events that almost certainly had no single cause and was not deliberately planned. Nevertheless, the riot was a widely-based outburst of Negro hostility, and fed upon reservoirs of resentment and hatred that had not been perceived earlier or understood well by white people. It had a clear focus on racial antagonisms; the objects of hostility were not other Negroes, but white people, primarily merchants, and almost any symbol of constituted authority. Even if the "purposeful" quality of the riot was rationalization, it described a moderately "rational" series of events.[54]

This data supports the position that the Negroes involved in the Watts riot perceived a rational process. However, to truly uncover the motivation behind riot behavior, we need to analyze one further factor —causation. If once the riot got going, the Watts Negroes saw it as

---

54. *Id.* at 17.

purposeful, target-oriented, and likely to produce a beneficial change, then it implies an attempt to change an undesirable situation.

The dissatisfaction constituting this undesirable situation is a complex phenomenon. That the Negro in the United States has suffered as a result of racial discrimination is undeniable. The President's National Advisory Commission on Civil Disorders had begun to explore the subtle meaning of racial discrimination.[55] The Commission charged that white racism has created a second-class position for the Negro American. The result is that the Negroes' "life style" expectations in American society become drastically reduced once reality is faced. The impact upon the Negro is two-fold: psychologically, in the sense that the Negro must face a situation where he is constantly regarded (by whites and as a result by Negroes also) as inferior; socially and economically, in the sense that the Negroes' share of the wealth of America is limited. The economic aspect of the deprivation has been documented in this article with the thesis that Negroes are disproportionately poor and residents of poverty areas.

These conditions, and not the immediate precipitating events, are the ultimate cause behind the rioting. The Negroes surveyed in Watts verified this conclusion. Specific grievances (discrimination, poverty, mistreatment, inadequate services, etc.) were cited as the "cause" of the riot by 38 percent of the respondents; general anger and hostility was cited as the cause by 26 percent. Only 11 percent of those surveyed felt that the Frye Incident truly "caused" the Watts riot.

Thus, even for the Negro rioter, social and economic factors contribute to building the dissatisfaction which "cause" a riot. Undoubtedly, racial prejudice is the ultimate factor determining this situation of inferior social and economic class status for the American Negro. However, as was the case with the consideration of race and poverty, the issues of racial prejudice and inferior class status become intrinsically interconnected.

The Urban League's study of the Negro attitudes in the Detroit riot indicate the same preoccupation with class considerations as the situation of dissatisfaction which ultimately "caused" the Detroit riot.[56] The following is a list of specific causes, and the percentage of Negroes interviewed, who felt that these factors had "a great deal" to do with causing the riot in Detroit: policy brutality, 57 percent; overcrowded living conditions, 55 percent; poor housing, 54 percent; lack of jobs, 45 percent, poverty, 44 percent; dirty neighborhoods, 44 percent; anger

55. NAT'L ADVISORY COMM'N ON CIVIL DISORDERS, *supra* note 3.

56. In the Detroit survey, a total of 437 Negroes living in the East and West Side Riot Areas were interviewed. MEYER, *supra* note 28.

with local business people, 43 percent; too much drinking, 40 percent; broken political promises, 39 percent; failure of parents to control children, 39 percent. These conditions indicate both mental anger and a real situation of social and economic deprivation.

The question of white participation can be analyzed from this point of view. The white individuals in the area have been shown to be lower-status white individuals than even the majority of Negroes within the area. The logic of the reasoned participation analysis would argue that a similar state of social and economic deprivation could constitute the requisite dissatisfaction needed to promote riot activity. A riot situation need not have a single motivation. There is no reason why whites near a riot situation, and capable of identifying with the general grievances of Negro rioters, should not also participate in the violent activity.[57]

The second general theory of riot participation, emotional response, must also be considered. This approach argues that the riot situation is one of near-anarchy where traditional behavioral restraints break down. Within this context, individuals may find themselves involved in the emotion of the moment and participate in the riot activity without any elaborate rational justifications. As the President's National Advisory Commission notes:

> The chain we have identified—discrimination, prejudice, disadvantaged conditions, intense and pervasive grievances, a series of tension-heightening incidents, all culminating in the eruption of disorder at the hands of youthful, politically-aware activists—must be understood as describing the central trend in the disorders, not as an explanation of all aspects of the riots or of all rioters. Some rioters, for example, may have shared neither the conditions nor the grievances of their Negro neighbors; some may have coolly and deliberately exploited the chaos created by others; some may have been drawn into the melee merely because they identified with, or wished to emulate, others.[58]

The emotional response analysis can be traced in the theory of collective behavior back to early theorists such as Gustave Le Bon.[59] Le Bon

---

57. Further support for this analysis is available in the preliminary data of the Social Psychological Study of Detroit's Civil Disturbance, under the direction of Robert A. Mendelson of the Lafayette Clinic. This study interviewed arrestees from the Detroit riot. Unfortunately the sample was not able to be stratified for race, however, 28 white individuals did appear among those interviewed. A total of 23 of the 28 white individuals were working; their average wage was approximately $90.00 a week. The average weekly wage for the employed Negro arrestees (17 years of age or over) was approximately $115.00. On the basis of this data, the economic situation of the whites interviewed was somewhat less promising than the economic status for the Negroes in the sample.

58. NAT'L ADVISORY COMM'N ON CIVIL DISORDERS, supra note 3 at 112.

59. G. LE BON, THE CROWD: A STUDY OF THE POPULAR MIND 30 (1903).

contended that the essence of such collective outbursts was the transformation which occurred in men participating in crowds. In this context, a man tends to act in a manner different than his usual behavior. There are fewer restraints and inhibitions which limit his activities.

The logic of this argumentation would lead to the conclusion that the white individuals who participated in the riot activity were an incidental element of the riot. These individuals merely were taking advantage of the general disorder, and, as such, were not the main element of the riot.

It should be noted that these two approaches to the analysis of riot participation need not be thought of as competing theories. Most probably, the construction of a situation of disorder was conducive to the participation of many Negroes who did have very detailed and specific grievances and who viewed the riot situation as an opportunity to register their protest. At the same time, the general disorder may also have given whites an opportunity to engage in behavior which served as a release of pressures or, perhaps, an expression of grievances similar to those of the Negroes in the area.

That racial considerations predominate the violence seems relatively clear: the incident prompting the violence was of such a nature that it specifically angered the Negro community, the majority of arrests and prosecutions were Negro. However, the evidence of white participation compels us to consider the Detroit riot as substantially different than the traditional Negro-dominated, property-oriented riot.

Perhaps if whites had not been present within the riot areas, the violence would have followed the expected pattern. It is uncertain whether similar riots can occur again in integrated areas; or, rather, whether a riot area demands a certain minimum Negro percentage of population. The Detroit riot does however indicate that should a riot situation develop in an area similar to the Detroit riot areas of 1967, white participation as well as Negro participation can be expected.

Conclusion

That the element of white participation in the Detroit riot has been ignored is significant in and of itself. The available evidence compels consideration of this element. For some, analysis is simpler without concern for the white rioters. Certainly, with this element absent, the Detroit riot seems to more closely fit the current Negro-dominated, property-oriented pattern. Perhaps others have ignored or suppressed consideration of white participation. However, whether avoiding the issue has been a result of ease of analysis or some sense of guilt or, perhaps, even subtle prejudice is essentially an unanswerable question.

This analysis of the Detroit riot leads to a number of conclusions. There was a racial element involved in the violence; however, even for Negro rioters class considerations were very important in constructing an attitude of dissatisfaction demanding expression. The further evidence of white participation yields strong support to the class as opposed to the racial aspect of the violence.

Undoubtedly, future Negro-dominated, property-oriented rioting will continue. Whether future racial violence will become concentrated on more and more high-value white property or, perhaps, become person-oriented is not within the scope of this article. What Detroit does demonstrate is that a hostile outburst can simultaneously include both Negro and white participation, and that such an outburst cannot be analyzed strictly along racial considerations.

The Corporation and the Ghetto:

An Analysis of the Effects of Corporate Retail Grocery Sales on Ghetto Life

MARY C. SENGSTOCK*

FOLLOWING the 1967 Detroit riot, the Detroit Urban League conducted a survey of attitudes of Negro residents of the city of Detroit to determine their attitudes toward the riot, the white community, the black community, and related topics. One of the topics considered was the degree to which members of the black community felt that anger with local business people was a factor contributing to the discontent which precipitated the riot. Forty-three percent of the respondents interviewed replied that they felt this factor had "a great deal" to do with the disturbance; thirty-one percent more thought it had something to do with it; and only eighteen percent felt this factor was unrelated to the riot.[1] Apparently then, dissatisfaction with the merchants who provide them with needed services is, at least in the minds of the majority of members of the black community, a matter of some importance in causing unrest. The present article is an attempt to examine one type of service required by the black ghetto, and the degree to which the service provided in non-white areas is equivalent to that provided the white community.

The service selected for analysis is the relative availability of low-cost foodstuffs in the lower-income and non-white areas of the city versus middle income and predominantly white areas of the city. The provision of this service is an especially crucial one to the understanding of unrest in the black ghetto, for food merchants, the Urban League survey found, were the group of merchants most disliked by the respondents. Fifty-four percent of them stated they felt that grocery stores treated them unfairly.[2] This was higher than the percentage of respondents expressing distrust of any other category of merchant. It seems relevant, therefore, in an analysis of unrest in the black community, to consider the degree to which such alleged exploitation may be accurate, and, if it is, the reasons why the phenomenon exists.

A recent study in New York City has suggested the lower income

---

* Ph.B. 1958, University of Detroit; A.M. 1960, University of Michigan; Ph.D. 1967, Washington University (St. Louis); Assistant Professor, Wayne State University, Detroit, Mich.

1. *How 23 Possible Riot Causes Were Ranked in Survey*, The Detroit Free Press, Aug. 20, 1967, § B, p. 4, col. 5.

2. *The Businesses Residents Think Are Least Fair*, The Detroit Free Press, Aug. 20, 1967, § B, p. 4, col. 3.

consumer, who very frequently is non-white, generally tends to pay more for all the merchandise he buys than do middle and upper class consumers for similar types of merchandise.[3] The persons surveyed in this research reported paying extremely high prices, often for goods of inferior quality. The means by which such exorbitant prices were extracted from the consumer were many. The low income consumer frequently must buy on time; hence he pays interest because of his inability to pay cash. He has a poor credit rating; hence he must buy from companies which will deal with high risk customers;[4] such companies are also those which make up their losses with exceptionally high interest rates. These rates are usually "hidden" within the purchase price, so that the consumer really never knows the price of the article versus the cost of the loan. Many were the victims of smooth-talking salesmen, who induced them to sign contracts for merchandise, often sight unseen, and without informing them of the terms of the contract.[5] The merchandise sold is often shoddy and poorly made; sometimes second-hand merchandise is even sold for new.[6] It is not unreasonable to suggest that a likely factor contributing to the unrest and dissatisfaction of the urban poor may very reasonably be their realization that they do pay exorbitant prices for goods of inferior quality while the wealthier classes, who can better afford the extra expense, acquire better merchandise at a bargain. It has also been noted that the poor exhibit a preference for shopping near their homes in familiar surroundings, which makes them, in effect, a "captive audience," unable or unwilling to go elsewhere if the goods and services are not to their liking.[7]

The types of purchases considered in the work cited above are chiefly durable goods—furniture and various types of appliances. The author notes, however, that some of the families studied bought food on credit also. These credit food purchases included purchases from milkmen, and other items from small independent food stores near the respondents' homes. Thus the question arises: If the poor buy their food like their other purchases, are they also victimized in this regard? To date there has been no systematic study made of this question.

It would seem that the poor would pay unusually high prices for food, especially if they follow the practice of doing their food shopping near their homes, as they do when they buy appliances. For lower

3. D. Caplovitz, The Poor Pay More (1963).
4. *Id.*, ch. 7.
5. *Id.* ch. 10.
6. *Id.* at 28.
7. *Id.* at 50; President's Committee on Consumer Interest, The Most for Their Money 6 (1965).

class neighborhoods appear to have a higher concentration of independent grocery stores than middle class ones, as was suggested by the 1965 President's Committee on Consumer Interest.[8] In the course of a previous research project, the present author had occasion to interview Negroes who frequented the independent grocery stores owned by members of a particular ethnic group.[9] These persons, most of whom lived in lower income sections of the City of Detroit, complained bitterly of the fact that the stores near their homes were predominately small independently-run stores, rather than the chains with their traditionally lower prices. As has been noted, a frequent complaint reported by participants in the Detroit riot of July, 1967, was the lack of availability of low-priced merchandise in their neighborhoods.[10] Food merchants themselves seem to view the lower class Negro neighborhood as the domain of the small independent store owner. A chain store executive and several independent food merchants interviewed commented that these businesses could succeed only in such areas.

Additional evidence which suggests that lower class Negro neighborhoods are served by independent grocers rather than chains can be gained from an analysis of the types of stores which sustained greatest damage during the 1967 Detroit riot. The *Fire Damage Study* conducted by the Detroit Fire Department during the aftermath of the riot indicated that 60 food stores (including grocery stores; supermarkets; meat, poultry or fish markets; and party stores; but not including exclusively beer or liquor stores) sustained some type of fire damage, ranging from partial burning to total demolishment.[11] Of these, however, only four (6.7%) were owned by chains; the rest were all independently owned.

It appears, therefore, that there is a widespread belief, supported by some evidence, largely of an impressionistic nature, which suggests that the lower income neighborhoods are deprived of the opportunity to purchase food at low cost in chain-owned food stores, and are forced to purchase in higher priced independently owned stores. This article will be an attempt to determine whether the accusation that few chain stores are located in lower income areas has a basis in fact. It is suggested that several questions remain concerning food-buying practices in the lower-class Negro neighborhood. Do such areas actually have a

---

8. *Id.* at 5.

9. M. Sengstock, Maintenance of Social Interaction Patterns in an Ethnic Group, 1967, (unpublished Ph.D. thesis, St. Louis: Washington University.) The study is an analysis of a group of Iraqi immigrants and their descendents.

10. *Supra*, note 2.

11. Detroit Fire Dep't, *Fire Damage Study*, The Detroit News, Aug. 5, 1967, § A, p. 3.

higher concentration of independent food stores than middle-class white neighborhoods, or does this only appear to be true? Are there actually fewer chain stores in these areas, or is this too a fiction? If these beliefs are borne out, what is the reason? Is it because the chains have deliberately left the lower-class Negro area? Or do the shopping patterns of the lower class Negro tend to favor the independent versus the chain store? In succeeding pages I shall attempt to provide answers to some of these questions.

The Grocery Chain Store—a Middle-Class Phenomenon

In an attempt to determine the validity of the claims that there are few chain-owned grocery stores in lower-class Negro areas, a list of all chain-owned grocery stores doing business in the Detroit metropolitan area in June, 1967, was obtained from the regional offices of each of the nine chains in southeastern Michigan. Every effort was made to assure the inclusion of all such chains. Once the address of each chain-owned store had been obtained, the type of neighborhood in which the store was located could be determined by a comparison of the address of the store with known socio-economic data for that area.

For the purposes of this study, the Detroit Metropolitan Area has been broken down into 93 units. Forty-four of these units are civil divisions outside the City of Detroit, each of which is taken as an entire unit. The remaining 49 units are subdivisions of the City of Detroit, known as subcommunities. These subcommunities are artificial constructs made up of contiguous census tracts which exhibit somewhat similar social and economic characteristics. They have been established by the Research Department of the United Community Services of Metropolitan Detroit and have been in use for some years as a convenient technique for dividing the City into relatively homogeneous parts.[12] Since important demographic data, including percentage of Negroes and median income, are available for these subcommunities, I shall make use of these divisions in an attempt to determine the regularity of placement of chain-owned stores throughout the Detroit Metropolitan Area. The demographic characteristics of the population presented here have been taken from analyses of Detroit population figures compiled and published by the United Community Services.[13]

---

12. United Comm'y Services of Metropolitan Detroit, Social Rating of Communities in the Detroit Area 3 (1965).

13. *Id.* at 2-9, 18-21. The reader will note that 1960 census figures have been used throughout this analysis. These figures are somewhat out of date in 1967. The reader will also note, however, that the comparisons being made are in the nature of gross differ-

The Chain-Operated Grocery Outlet and the Racial Composition of Communities

The first question concerns the degree to which chain-owned grocery outlets are located in areas which are of varying racial composition. Is it true, as has been suggested, that the chain-owned stores are located primarily in predominately white neighborhoods? Do they avoid areas with a large non-white population? Or is this an inaccurate impression? The results of data-analysis, as presented in Table I, suggest that it may be somewhat inaccurate.

TABLE I. PERCENT OF COMMUNITIES SERVED BY CHAINS AND SELECTED INDEPENDENT GROCERY MERCHANTS BY RACIAL COMPOSITION OF COMMUNITY

TYPE OF GROCERY MERCHANT	Total # Stores	PERCENT OF COMMUNITIES SERVED RACIAL COMPOSITION OF COMMUNITY 40% or More Non-white (21 communities)	Less Than 40% Non-white (72 communities)
A. *Major Categories of Store Types:*			
Chain Store (total–all chains)	**344**	85.7%	93.1%
Large Chains (more than 20 stores)	**301**	71.4 *	88.9 *
Small Chains (20 stores or less)	**43**	23.8	43.1
Discount Chains	137	33.3	63.9
Selected Independent Stores	**152**	81.0 *	31.9 *
B. *Breakdown for Specific Chains:*			
1. Large Chains			
Chain A (R) (regular line of Chain A)	44	19.0	41.7
Chain A (D) (discount line of Chain A)	15	14.3	16.7
Chain B (R) (regular line of Chain B)	31	14.3 *	27.8 *
Chain B (D) (discount line of Chain B)	42	9.5 *	38.9 *
Chain C (R) (regular line of Chain C)	44	19.0 *	43.1 *
Chain C (D) (discount line of Chain C)	26	4.8	22.2
Chain D	69	52.4	41.7
Chain E (discount chain)	30	-0- *	29.2 *
2. Small Chains			
Chain F	15	4.8	16.7
Chain G (discount chain)	20	4.8	23.6
Chain H	4	19.0 †	-0- †
Chain I	4	-0- †	5.6 †

* Indicates a pair of percentages which are significantly different from each other, in a statistical sense. That is, the difference between the two ratios would occur by chance less than 5 times out of 100, as computed by the x^2 method.

† Total number of cases too small to compute x^2.

ences: above and below a specific percentage of non-whites. While it is recognized that some of the communities considered may have been "borderline cases" in 1960 and have since crossed into the other major category, this has probably not occurred in so many instances as to have had an appreciable effect on the validity of the data.

The data in Table I indicate the type of communities served by outlets of each of the major chain-owned supermarkets in the Detroit area by the racial composition of the community in which the store is located. Communities are divided into two major types: predominately white, and predominately non-white. Of the 93 communities in the Detroit metropolitan area, 21 were classified as non-white because they had a racial composition which was 40 percent non-white or more. Seventy-two communities with less than 40 percent non-white population were classified as predominately white communities.

The percent of communities of each type which are served by each of the major food chains was then computed. Also computed are the percent of communities served by various types of food chains: all chain-owned stores considered together; all of the largest chains (those with more than 20 outlets in the Detroit metropolitan area); all of the smaller chains (those with 20 or fewer stores in the Detroit area); and all of the chains which advertise themselves as "discount" food outlets.[14] For comparison purposes, a group of independently owned stores has also been included. These stores are all owned and operated by a single ethnic group; they are, however, all owned and operated independently of each other.

As the table indicates, there does not appear to be a general pattern of non-service to the non-white communities by the chain-owned supermarkets. When all chains, of large and small size, discount and otherwise, are considered together, there is no significant difference in the percentage of communities of white and non-white populations served. Ninety-three percent of the white communities and 86 percent of the non-white communities are served. This difference is small enough to have occurred by chance. In breaking down these figures into various types of chains, some greater differences appear, but in most cases these differences are also not statistically significant. Hence, the chains with less than 20 stores serve 24 percent of the non-white communities, and 43 percent of the white communities, again a difference which is not significant. Chains which advertise as being discount food stores appear slightly more likely to serve white neighborhoods, as they serve 64 percent of the white communities, and only 33 percent of the non-white communities; but again, this difference is one which could occur by chance.

---

14. Where a chain operated two lines of stores in the area, a discount line and a regular line, the *total number* of stores operated by the chain, not the number of each specific type, was used to determine the size of the chain. Hence if a chain operated 15 discount stores and 15 non-discount stores, a total of 30 stores altogether, the chain was considered to be one large chain, not two small ones. For some purposes, however, the analysis will consider the two lines separately.

The one type of chain which appears most unlikely to serve the Negro area is the very large chain, with more than 20 outlets in the Detroit metropolitan area. Here it may be noted that there is a statistically significant difference between the percentage of non-white areas served (71 percent) and the percentage of white areas served (89 percent). Apparently then the largest chains do tend to serve the white communities to a greater extent than they serve the non-white neighborhoods. This difference becomes especially noticeable when it is compared to the relative percentages of communities of each type served by the group of selected independents in our sample. These independently owned food stores serve 81 percent of the non-white areas, as opposed to only 32 percent of the white neighborhoods, this difference being statistically significant at better than the .05 level. Thus it appears, at least in comparing the very largest chains to the independently owned stores, the white communities are more likely to be served by the largest chains, the non-white communities by the independently owned stores.

In Section B of Table I, the percentages of communities of each type served by each of the various chains individually is computed. Here it becomes clear that certain chains are more likely than others to concentrate on the white neighborhoods. As the table indicates, three chains (B, C, and E), are significantly less likely to serve the non-white areas as are the other chains, where the differences in percentages of white and non-white communities served by the chain are not statistically significant. Chain B, which operates a regular and a discount line of grocery stores, serves only 14 percent of the non-white communities with its regular line, and 10 percent with its discount line. At the same time, it serves 28 percent of the white communities with its regular line, and 39 percent with its discount line. Both of these differences are statistically significant at the .05 level. Similarly, Chain C is significantly more likely to serve white neighborhoods with its regular line, 43 percent of such communities being served, while only 19 percent of the non-white communities are served. This chain serves only 4 percent of the non-white communities with its discount line, 22 percent of the white communities; but this difference might fairly frequently occur by chance. It should be noted that Chain E, which is widely advertised as a discount chain, serves *none* of the predominately non-white communities, and 30 percent of the white neighborhoods. This difference is statistically significant.

Nearly all of the other chains indicate slight tendencies, not statistically significant, to serve the white rather than the non-white areas. Thus Chain A serves 19 percent of the non-white communities with its regular line, and 14 percent with its discount line; at the same time its service includes 42 percent of the white communities in its regular line, and 17 percent in its discount line. Similarly, Chains F and G each serve only 5 percent of the non-white communities, but 17 and 24 percent, respectively, of the white areas. (Again, while these differences may be suggestive of a trend, they cannot be considered conclusive because of their lack of statistical significance.) Chain I, a very small chain with only 4 stores, also appears to concentrate its efforts in all-white neighborhoods, none of its stores being located in predominately non-white neighborhoods.

Only two chains, Chain D, a very large chain with 69 stores, and Chain H, a very small one with only 4 stores, appear to concentrate a great deal of effort on serving the non-white areas. Chain D serves slightly more of the non-white than the white communities (52 percent as opposed to 42 percent), a difference which is, however, not statistically significant. And Chain H has all of its stores in non-white areas, serving 19 percent of the non-white communities and none of the predominately white areas.

Thus it appears that the allegation that the chain stores do not tend to locate their stores in predominately non-white communities has some validity: several of the chains in the metropolitan Detroit area were found to provide service to a greater percentage of the white communities than to the non-white communities. However, the picture becomes even clearer when we turn our attention, not to the *percentage* of communities of each type served by the chains, but to the *extent* to which they serve the communities of different racial composition. That is, in the analysis just completed, a chain was considered to have served a community if it had located any number of outlets in that community. It is possible then that the results of the preceding analysis may be somewhat misleading; for a chain with one outlet in a community would be considered to have served that area to an equal extent with a chain which had two, three, or more outlets in that area. I have, therefore, attempted, in Table II, an additional form of analysis, in order to determine whether the *number* of chain outlets is equivalent in the communities of each type.

In order to determine whether the *extent of service* of the chain stores to the non-white communities is also less than the extent of its service to the white areas, a ratio of stores to total number of communities has been computed for each of the major types of chains and for each chain individually. Again the group of selected independent food stores was used for comparison purposes. The ratios which appear

TABLE II. Extent of Service to Communities by Chains and Selected Independent Grocery Merchants by Racial Composition of Community

TYPE OF GROCERY MERCHANT		RATIO OF STORES PER COMMUNITY RACIAL COMPOSITION OF COMMUNITY 40% or More Non-white		Less Than 40% Non-white	
A. *Major Categories of Store Types:*					
Chain Store (total-all chains)		1.81	*	4.26	*
Large Chains (more than 20 stores)		1.33	*	3.72	*
Small Chains (20 stores or less)		0.29		0.54	
Discount Chains		0.57	*	1.58	*
Selected Independent Stores		4.62	*	0.76	*
B. *Breakdown for Specific Chains:*					
1. Large Chains					
A(R)	(N = 44)	0.19	*	0.56	*
A(D)	(N = 15)	0.14		0.17	
Total A	(N = 59)	0.33	*	0.72	*
B(R)	(N = 31)	0.14		0.39	
B(D)	(N = 42)	0.10	*	0.56	*
Total B	(N = 73)	0.24	*	0.94	*
C(R)	(N = 44)	0.19	*	0.56	*
C(D)	(N = 26)	0.05	*	0.35	*
Total C	(N = 70)	0.24	*	0.90	*
D	(N = 69)	0.67		0.76	
E (discount)	(N = 30)	–0–	*	0.42	*
2. Small Chains					
F	(N = 15)	0.05		0.19	
G (discount)	(N = 20)	0.05		0.26	
H	(N = 4)	0.19	†	–0–	†
I	(N = 4)	–0–	†	0.06	†

* Indicates differences which are statistically significant at the .05 level.
† Total number of cases too small to compute x^2.

in Table II were computed very simply: to obtain the ratio of stores of a particular chain for white communities, the total number of stores of that chain located in predominately white areas was divided by the total number of predominately white areas. The resulting ratio is then considered to be the ratio of stores of that chain for white areas. The same formula was then used to determine the ratio of stores of each chain for non-white communities, and to determine the ratio of stores of each category (large, small, discount, et cetera) for each type of community.

As Table II indicates, the pattern of greater service to the white areas than the non-white areas on the part of the chains appears even more clearly when the extent of service, rather than simply the percentage of communities served, is considered. The data clearly show that, among the largest chains at least, the service to the non-white areas is much less than that to the white areas. In Table II no significant differences appear between the extent of service to the two types of communities on the part of the small chains, with 20 stores or less. The ratio of service of all small chains taken together for non-white areas is 0.29 stores per community; that for white areas is 0.54 stores per community. While this suggests that these chains provide greater service to the white areas, the difference is too small to be statistically significant. When each of the small chains is considered individually, 3 of the chains (F, G, and I) are seen to provide slightly greater service to the white areas than the non-white areas. Chain F exhibits a ratio of 0.19 for the white areas, 0.05 for non-white areas; for Chain G the ratios are 0.26 and 0.05, respectively; and for Chain I they are 0.06 and 0.00, respectively. But with the small total number of stores operated by the chains as a whole, these differences are not significant.

A totally different picture arises, however, when we turn our attention to the service ratios of the large chains. When all chains, large and small, are considered together, the ratio of service to the white communities is 4.26; that is, there are more than four chain-owned food stores for each predominantly white community. In the non-white areas, on the other hand, the ratio of service by the chains as a whole is only 1.81; that is, in non-white areas there are fewer than two chain-owned food stores per community. This difference is significant at the .05 level. For the large chains alone, the pattern of offering over twice as much service to the white as to the non-white communities appears. The ratio of service for the large chains to the white areas is 3.72; that to non-white areas only 1.33. In contrast, the ratio of service of the selected independent stores is 4.62 for the *non-white* areas, and only 0.76 for the white areas. Hence a pattern continues to emerge of chain stores being concentrated in white neighborhoods, and non-white areas being served predominantly by independent food merchants.

Turning our attention to Section B of Table II, in which each individual chain is considered separately, it can be seen that in only *one* of the large chains is there relatively equal service to the white and non-white areas. Chain D has a ratio of service to white areas of 0.76, and 0.67 to non-white areas, the difference being much too small to be of any import whatsoever. Chain A, however, has a ratio of service to white areas of 0.72, when all of its stores of both discount and regular type are considered together; in non-white areas the ratio 0.33. Chain B's ratio of service to white areas is 0.94, to non-white, 0.24; and Chain C's ratio to white areas is 0.90, to non-white, 0.24, all of these differences being significant at the .05 level. The absence of stores of Chain E in the non-white areas is of special concern because of the nature of the E Chain, a topic which will be considered next.

A particularly interesting datum which appears in Table II is the paucity of discount stores in the non-white areas. Since non-whites tend to be clustered in the lower income brackets,[15] they stand in greatest need of those types of food markets which provide foodstuffs at discount prices. Do the stores which advertise themselves as providing this type of service also tend to locate their outlets in areas where persons having the greatest need of their services reside?

As the table shows, this is indeed not the case. When all discount chains (both the discount lines of the large chains with two lines of outlets, and the chains which operate only a discount line) are considered together, discount chains are found to provide services to the white neighborhoods in the ratio of 1.58 stores per community. For non-white communities, on the other hand, the ratio of service of the discount chains is only 0.57. Taking each discount chain individually, only one of the chains, the discount line of Chain A, provides relatively equal service to white and non-white areas—the ratio of service to white areas being 0.17, to non-white areas, 0.14. Chain B, in contrast, provides 0.56 discount stores per white community, and only 0.10 stores per non-white community, a difference which is significant at the .05 level. Chain C is also more likely to locate its discount stores in the white areas, its service ratio in these areas being 0.35, and in the non-white areas, only 0.05. Most interesting again is Chain E, also a discount chain, which provides 0.42 stores per community in white areas, and none at all in non-white areas. Finally, Chain G, a small discount chain, provides 0.05 stores per community in non-white areas, and 0.26 stores per community in white neighborhoods, this is, however, not statistically significant. Hence it appears that the non-white areas are especially ignored by those chains which specialize in providing lowest cost foodstuffs to their customers.

Of course, one might argue that the chains would be forced, by the demands of good business practice, to locate their stores where they would obtain the largest clientele. Hence it would be unwise for them to locate their stores in any area, regardless of its racial composition, if that area did not have a large enough population to support a supermarket. We would expect the chains to locate their stores in proportion to the population of the communities. Hence, if a community had only 6000 residents, we would expect it to have fewer stores than one with two or three times the population. Can we, therefore, explain the dearth of chain-owned food stores in non-white areas on the basis of population density? One's immediate impression would be that this is an unlikely explanation, for the density of population in non-white areas is

15. M. Harrington, The Other America 190 (1962).

usually higher than that in white areas. Therefore, this would not appear to be a valid explanation of the observed phenomenon. In order to test the proposition, we refer to the data in Table III wherein the size of the community together with the number of chain-owned stores located therein is considered.

TABLE III. Ratio of Chain-Owned Grocery Stores to Population of Community by Racial Composition of Community

	RACIAL COMPOSITION OF COMMUNITY					
RATIO OF CHAIN STORES TO POPULATION	40% or More Non-white		Less Than 40% Non-white		Totals	
A. 1 store/8000 population or less	5.0%	(1)	31.3%	(21)	25.3%	(22)
B. 1 store/8001–1/14,000	30.0	(6)	46.3	(31)	42.5	(37)
C. 1 store/14,001–1/20,000	25.0	(5)	11.9	(8)	14.9	(13)
D. 1 Store/20,000 population or more	40.0	(8)	10.4	(7)	17.2	(15)
TOTALS	100.0	(20)	99.9	(67)	99.9	(87)

$x^2 = 14.86$, significant at .01 level.

In this table, the dependent variable is a ratio of chain-owned food stores to the population of the community. For each of the communities in the Detroit metropolitan area[16] a fractional ratio was obtained by placing the number of chain-owned food stores in the community over the total population of the community. The resulting fractions were divided into the four categories which appear in Table III: Category A, communities in which there is a ratio of one store for every 8000 or fewer persons residing therein; Category B, in which there is a ratio of one store for every 8001 to 14,000 persons residing therein; Category C, in which there is a ratio of one store for every 14,001 to 20,000 persons residing therein; and Category D, in which the ratio of stores to population is less than 1/20,000. In this last category there are some communities in which the ratio is equal to 0.00, that is, there are no stores for the population of these communities.

Clearly then, the communities with the greatest amount of chain store service would be those in categories A and B, where there is at least one store for each 14,000 persons. The least amount of service would be found in those communities in categories C and D, in which there are fewer stores than one for each 14,000 persons resident in the community. As Table III indicates, over three-fourths of the predominantly white communities (78 percent) are in categories A and B, indi-

16. Six Communities have been omitted from consideration in Tables III and VI. These communities are known to have experienced phenomenal population growth during the 1960-1967 period; and it was felt that a ratio of stores/population based on 1960 census figures would be totally inaccurate and might substantially bias the results of the present study.

cating the greatest amount of service per population. In contrast only 35 percent of the non-white communities are in these two categories. Sixty-five percent of the non-white communities fall into either of the latter two categories, indicating the lowest ratio of service per population, as opposed to only 22 percent of the predominantly white communities. In addition, the most extreme situation, in which service is provided at the rate of less than one store per 20,000 residents, pertains in only 10 percent of the white communities, but 40 percent of the non-white communities. It might also be noted that some of the most extreme cases are in predominantly non-white communities. One community, with a population which is 90 percent non-white, had no chain-operated food store to serve its population of 48,000 persons; another 60 percent, non-white, had only one chain operated store to serve its population of 51,000 persons; and a third, 90 percent non-white, had only one store to serve its population of 34,000 persons.

It is obvious, therefore, that *the chain stores tend to locate their outlets in areas which are predominantly populated by whites.* Non-white communities are less likely to be served by chain-owned super markets, and considerably less service is provided by the chain stores to those non-white communities which have chain store food outlets. The question which arises at this point is, of course, why this pattern appears. Is it due to a policy of deliberate racial prejudice on the part of the chain stores? Or might there be some other reason for the appearance of the pattern? One explanation which might be suggested is the possibility that the food chains are not deliberately locating their outlets in *white,* as opposed to *non-white,* residential areas, but that they are locating in predominantly *middle income,* as opposed to *lower income,* communities. Since non-whites are more likely to be clustered in lower-income residential areas, the pattern just described would of necessity appear. What should be determined, however, is the extent to which the food chains tend to be located in middle income areas, regardless of their racial composition. I turn now to an analysis of this phenomenon.

The Chain-Operated Grocery Outlet and the Economic Level of Communities

Limited incomes are not solely the domain of the non-whites. Although the percentage of non-whites with limited incomes is higher than the percentage of whites with limited incomes, the fact remains that the majority of persons with limited incomes are whites.[17] The

17. HARRINGTON, *supra* note 15 at 190.

question thus arises: Do the grocery chains serve the white lower class to a greater extent than they serve the non-white lower class? Or is their service to this group also limited? In short, do we find that the chain store supermarket is essentially a middle and upper class phenomenon, to the same extent that it is a phenomenon of white society?

In order to answer this question, the median family income for the communities and subcommunities considered in the preceeding section was calculated. All communities with a median family income of $6000 per year or above were considered to be "middle income" communities. Those with median family incomes of less than $6000 per year were considered to be "lower income" communities. Fifty-nine communities in the Detroit area were found to be middle income communities; thirty-four were classified as lower income communities. The results of this analysis are presented in Tables IV, V, and VI.

TABLE IV. Percent of Communities Served by Chains and Selected Independent Grocery Merchants by Median Family Income of Community

TYPE OF GROCERY MERCHANT	Total # Stores	PERCENT OF COMMUNITIES SERVED MEDIAN FAMILY INCOME OF COMMUNITY: Less Than $6,000/yr. (34 communities)	$6,000/yr. or more (59 communities)
A. *Major Categories of Store Types:*			
Chain Store (total–all chains)	344	85.3%	93.2%
Large Chains (more than 20 stores)	301	76.5 *	91.5 *
Small Chains (20 stores or less)	43	20.6 *	49.2 *
Discount Chains	137	41.2	64.4
Selected Independent Stores	152	70.6 *	27.1 *
B. *Breakdown for Specific Chains:*			
1. Large Chains			
A(R)		17.6 *	40.7 *
A(D)		17.6	15.3
B(R)		11.8 *	32.2 *
B(D)		17.6 *	40.7 *
C(R)		17.6 *	49.2 *
C(D)		5.9 *	25.4 *
D		61.8 *	33.9 *
E (discount)		8.8 *	30.5 *
2. Small Chains			
F		5.9	18.6
G (discount)		2.9 *	28.8 *
H		11.8 †	–0– †
I		2.9 †	5.1 †

* Differences which are significant at .05 level.

† Total number of cases too small to compute x^2.

The data clearly indicate that the pattern which appeared when the communities were divided into predominantly white versus non-white in racial composition also appears here. But the pattern is even more pronounced in the case of the economic level of the community.

The reader will recall that most chains gave at least limited services to the predominantly non-white neighborhoods (a single store perhaps); what they failed to provide was the same *extent* of service, measured by the ratio of stores per community and the ratio of stores to population (see Tables I, II, III). In Table I it was shown that only three chains (B, in its regular and discount lines; C, in its regular line; and E, a discount only line) exhibited a statistically significant tendency to be confined to white rather than non-white areas. As Table IV shows, however, five chains (A, in its regular line; B, in both its lines; C, in both its lines; E, the discount only line; and G, a relatively small discount chain) exhibited a statistically significant tendency to be confined to areas in which the median family income was $6000 or over. Chain D, which, as was noted earlier, was the only large chain which appeared to be fairly equally distributed between white and non-white areas, appears in Table IV as the only chain to serve more low income areas than middle income areas. As Section B of Table IV shows, 62 percent of the lower income communities were served by this chain, as opposed to only 34 percent of the middle income communities.

As the summary data in Section A of Table IV indicate, all the major types of chain stores show a slight tendency to serve the middle rather than the lower income neighborhoods; in only two instances, however, are these differences large enough that we may feel certain they are not attributable to sample error. Thus the large chains, with more than 20 stores, serve 92 percent of the middle income communities, but only 77 percent of the lower income communities. The small chains serve 49 percent of the middle income communities, but only 21 percent of the lower income communities. It appears that the independent stores serve the lower income areas more than the middle income areas. The group of selected independents served 71 percent of the lower income areas, and only 27 percent of the middle income areas.

In the analysis of the chain store service to white versus non-white areas, the pattern of greater chain store service to white areas become clearer when the extent of service rather than simply the percent of communities served was considered. A similar situation exists with the lower versus middle income communities.

As Table V indicates, chain stores tend to maintain a ratio of 4.58 stores per community in middle income areas, while providing, only 2.18 stores per community in lower income areas. The large chains maintain a 3.97 ratio in middle income areas, but only a 1.85 ratio in lower income areas. Similarly, for small chains the ratios are 0.61 and 0.21, respectively. Here, as with the white-non-white comparisons, a most interesting fact is the relative absence of discount food chains in the lower income areas. Middle income areas have a ratio of 1.93 such stores per community, whereas lower income areas have a ratio of only 0.68.

TABLE V. Extent of Service to Communities by Chains and Selected Independent Grocery Merchants by Median Family Income of Community

TYPE OF GROCERY MERCHANT	RATIO OF STORES PER COMMUNITY MEDIAN FAMILY INCOME OF COMMUNITY: Less Than $6,000/yr.	$6,000/yr. or more
A. *Major Categories of Store Types:*		
Chain Stores (total–all chains)	2.18 *	4.58 *
Large Chain (more than 20 stores)	1.85 *	3.97 *
Small Chains (20 stores or less)	0.21 *	0.61 *
Discount Chains	0.68 *	1.93 *
Selected Independent Stores	3.85 *	0.29 *
B. *Breakdown for Specific Chains:*		
1. Large Chains		
A(R)	0.18 *	0.64 *
A(D)	0.18	0.15
Total A	0.35 *	0.80 *
B(R)	0.12 *	0.44 *
B(D)	0.18 *	0.61 *
Total B	0.29 *	1.05 *
C(R)	0.18 *	0.64 *
C(D)	0.06 *	0.41 *
Total C	0.24 *	1.05 *
D	0.94	0.63
E (discount)	0.09 *	0.46 *
2. Small Chains		
F	0.06	0.22
G (discount)	0.03 *	0.32 *
H	0.12 †	-0- †
I	0.03 †	0.05 †

* Differences significant at .05 level or better.
† Total number of cases too small to compute x^2.

As Section B of the Table indicates, all of the large chains except one give a significantly higher ratio of service to the middle income areas than to the lower income areas. The sole exception is Chain D, which, as has been shown, exhibits a consistent tendency to serve the non-white and lower income areas. It should also be noted that the discount line of Chain A maintains a relatively equal ratio of service in the lower and middle income areas.

Among the small chains, both Chain F and Chain G have higher ratios of service to the middle income areas; but only with Chain G is the difference sufficiently large to be significant. Chains H and I are extremely small, and firm conclusions concerning them are impossible. It appears, however, that Chain H is more likely to serve lower income rather than middle income areas, while Chain I maintains an equal ratio in both types of neighborhoods. It is, of course, a moot question whether the chains which tend to locate in lower income areas have done so because of a willingness to provide low cost foodstuffs to the residents of these areas, or whether they seek to exploit the presumed greater gullibility of the lower class consumer. The present data provide no clue to this question. Further research concerning the relative prices of the chains which serve the lower income consumer versus the middle income consumer would be necessary in order to answer this question.

In the lower income areas it is also clear that the stores/population ratio is considerably lower than it is in the middle income neighborhoods. As Table VI shows, over 77 percent of the middle income

TABLE VI. Ratio of Chain-Owned Grocery Stores to Population of Community by Median Family Income of Community

	MEDIAN FAMILY INCOME OF COMMUNITY					
RATIO OF CHAIN STORES TO POPULATION	Less Than $6,000/yr.		$6,000/yr. or more		Totals	
1 store/8000 population or less	11.8%	(4)	34.0%	(18)	25.3%	(22)
1 store/8001–1/14,000	41.2	(14)	43.4	(23)	42.5	(37)
1 store/14,000–1/20,000	17.6	(6)	13.2	(7)	14.9	(13)
1 store/20,000 population or more	29.4	(10)	9.4	(5)	17.2	(15)
TOTALS	100.0	(34)	100.0	(53)	99.9	(87)

$x^2 = 9.30$, significant at .05 level.

areas have a store ratio of one store per 14,000 population or better; in contrast, only 53 percent of the lower income communities have so high a ratio. However, more of the lower income areas fall into the category having the fewest chain food stores for the size of the population. Twenty-nine percent of the lower income areas, as opposed to only 9 percent of the middle income areas, have a ratio of stores/population which is equal to one store/20,000 or more persons. In addition, the most grossly underserved communities were predominantly non-white and lower income areas. For example: one non-white, lower income area had no chain-operated store to serve its 48,000 persons; another had no store to serve its 26,000 persons; two others had only one chain-operated food store to serve their 34,000 and 51,000 persons, respectively. Only one white middle income area had such a dearth of chain-owned stores.

It appears clear, therefore, that the chain-owned food stores are predominantly a white, middle-class phenomenon. They do not tend to be located in lower income and non-white neighborhoods. The effect which this fact has upon the service which the non-white, lower income areas receive with respect to the availability of low cost foodstuffs, and the reasons why this pattern exists, are problems next to be considered.

Consequences of the Observed Pattern

It has frequently been noted that the poor pay higher prices for food than do middle income consumers.[18] One authority reports: "The average small grocery store . . . charges a median 10 per cent more than large middle income area chain stores . . . ."[19]

At least in the grocery-type items, the customer who patronizes a small, independently-owned store will probably pay a higher over-all price for the merchandise he buys than will the customer who patronizes a chain store. One chain executive reported on comparative pricing of selected items from the various Detroit-based chains which his company periodically conducted. The regular, non-discount lines tended to show a mark-up of 15 to 19 percent of the wholesale price. Discount chains, which usually avoid costly mass media advertising and eliminate such added frills as trading stamps, sometimes lowered their prices to as little as 11 to 14 percent of the wholesale price. In contrast, one medium-sized independenly-owned store reported a mark-up of about 25 percent of the wholesale price. A second, and smaller store, reported a mark-up of over 50 percent of the wholesale price. There was, however, one very large independently-owned store which reported a mark-up of only 18 percent, about equivalent to that of the non-discount chains. According to one of the owners of this store, the very large independent supermarkets are often accorded the same favorable rates on their wholesale supplies as are the chains. They are, therefore, in a position to offer their merchandise at comparable prices. No attempt has been made to compare the mark-up on produce and meats because of the extreme variability in quality possible in foodstuffs of this kind. Further research in this area is obviously needed; it is suggested that this would be a fruitful area for research by professional home economists or food merchandisers. Food merchants interviewed have men-

18. Ridgeway, *Segregated Food at the Supermarket, New Republic,* Dec. 5, 1964 at 6-7; Bureau of Labor Statistics, A Study of Prices Charged in Food Stores Located in Low and Higher Income Areas of Six Large Cities (1966); Note: *Consumer Legislation and the Poor,* 76 Yale L. J. 745, 755-57 (1967).

19. *Supra* note 15 at 755-56.

tioned, however, that market conditions often place the independent in a better competitive position with regard to these items than to grocery items.

Another complaint which residents of low income areas frequently voice against the independent businessmen is the accusation that they pursue a systematic policy of cheating their customers: over-charging; giving dishonest weights on such items as meats and produce; selling below-standard foods, such as rancid meats; and returning less change than the customer is entitled to receive. However, this complaint is not one which would necessarily be alleviated by the introduction of a larger number of chain-owned food outlets into the lower-class and non-white neighborhoods.

Persons interviewed in the course of the present study accused the chain-owned stores of engaging in practices which tend to undermine the concept of "equal service for equal payment." Some chains were accused of distributing their freshest and best merchandise to middle-class areas, the remainder to their lower-income area stores. All food chain executives interviewed denied that their chains engaged in such activities. One executive took a practical approach explaining, "Even if we wanted to, it's too dangerous, too easy to get caught." Another means by which the chains were said to discriminate between various areas is the technique of "zone pricing." This refers to practice that some chains pursue of charging different prices to customers in different zones of their operation. If there are several "discount type" food stores in an area, all of the chains in the area pursue the policy of lowering their prices, but if it is an area with few discount food stores, it is contended that they charge higher prices in that area. Executives of Detroit chains claimed that, while they do engage in zone pricing, all of the Detroit metropolitan area is in the same price zone, and any price variations between various Detroit area stores is purely accidental. It is not unknown, however, for different parts of the same city to be in different price zones, as studies in other cities have indicated.[20] It should also be noted that, while the executives insisted that *their* chains did not have different price zones within the Detroit area, executives from two of the five largest chains claimed that *other* chains in the area engaged in this practice.

It is possible, therefore, that the movement of chain-owned food outlets into non-white and lower income areas would not necessarily lead to the disappearance of dishonest and discriminatory merchandis-

---

20. Ridgeway, *supra* Note 15 at 67; *Hearings on H. R. 7179 Before a Subcommittee of the House Committee on Government Operations*, 89th Cong., 2d Sess. at 172 (1966), (statement by David Borden).

ing practices in these neighborhoods. Only a vigilant attitude on the part of the consumer and of neighborhood agencies and governmental commissions, working together, can prevent the widespread use of such practices. What the wider distribution of chain-owned food outlets can do, however, is provide the lower income and non-white areas with lower cost foodstuffs due to the use of more efficient business practices and the lower overhead on the part of the retail merchant—a service the independent merchant is in no position to do effectively.

While there can be no doubt that some independent businessmen do engage in dishonest business practices, it is also true that there are many independent store owners who are falsely accused of such activities. Three independent store-keepers reported instances of having been investigated by various agencies, from informal neighborhood grievance committees to formal governmental pure food and health agencies, and having been cleared of all charges against them. Hence it is apparent that at least some of the charges of cheating leveled against the independent food merchants are probably groundless. Even with the most honest independent grocer, however, the customer is bound to pay a higher price than he will at a chain-owned store for several reasons.

First of all, due to the fact that he must pay a higher price for his wholesale supplies, the independent merchant must necessarily charge higher prices for his merchandise than the chain store, which buys in such large volume that it can obtain a very low mark-up on its supplies from the wholesaler. The smallest of the independents reported paying a mark-up of 6 percent over the wholesaler's cost, while the largest independents paid only a 5 percent mark-up, and the chains even less. The wholesale suppliers, of which there are three major ones in Detroit, at least one of which is financially linked to one of the major retail chains, were also known to receive "special deals" from the major grocery packing houses.[21] Thus, one of the major packing companies would offer a special on a particular type of commodity, at several cents less per can than the usual wholesale price. The wholesale supply companies, the independents reported, always passed these savings on to the best of their wholesale customers, viz. the chains and the very largest independents. Conversely, the smaller independent retailers received the benefit of these "bargains" only infrequently, putting them at a considerable disadvantage in competitive pricing.

Secondly, small stores are further disadvantaged by the delivery policies of the wholesalers which provide delivery and unloading

21. That chains, especially the large national ones, enter into such agreements with manufacturers has been noted in *The Clorox Case*, 32 Consumer Reports, 362 (July, 1963).

services for only the largest wholesale customers. Small stores, which usually buy less than $750 worth of groceries per week, are often forced to purchase on a "cash and carry" basis. That is, they must pick up their own supplies at the wholesale supply center themselves, instead of receiving delivery to their stores, thus necessitating that the owner leave his business to make the pick-up, pay a delivery service, or employ a driver to make these pick-ups for him. If the wholesaler does make deliveries to a small store, there is frequently an extra service charge. Again, this is an expense which the chain store is spared. Thirdly, the chains, with a greater amount of capital at their disposal, frequently buy their canned goods in very large quantities at harvest time, when they are at their cheapest. They are then stored until needed for sale. Often they own and operate their own processing factories, producing grocery items under their own brand names; usually they can sell these items at a few cents cheaper than the nationally known brands. The independent grocer has neither the capital nor the storage room necessary to pursue these policies. Hence he must buy as he needs and can afford the supplies, often when they are out of season and most expensive.

Clearly then, a major reason for the higher retail prices charged by most independent food merchants is the higher wholesale price which such merchants must pay for their own supplies. Not only their foodstuffs but also their other supplies, such as linens, butcher paper, et cetera, come higher, due to the smaller quantities in which they purchase or rent these items. Hence the independent grocer must charge more because he himself has paid more.

Furthermore, the unbelievable inefficiency of the small grocery store operation makes it somewhat more difficult for the small store owner to price his merchandise in an accurate manner. Rationally speaking, it would be most efficient for the store owner to determine the cost of all of his supplies, together with the cost of carrying on his operation, include a calculated percentage of profit, and determine the retail price of his merchandise on the basis of the mark-up which would be required in order to achieve this result. However, this process requires, that the store owner have accurate knowledge of the amount he has spent for each of the items involved: utilities, rent, insurance, wholesale supplies, paper and linen needs, and so forth. In talking with the independent grocers interviewed it became apparent that the majority of them had no accurate knowledge of these costs. As a bill arrived, most of the grocers pursued a policy of paying the bill out of their own pockets, keeping no record of the amount spent for each item. They had, therefore, no real knowledge of the costs of these items over time, and could not use these figures in calculating their actual operating costs and arriving at a fair mark-up figure.

Because they had no accurate knowledge of either their wholesale or overhead costs, the independent merchants tended to have personal formulas for arriving at their retail prices. One man claimed that he ". . . divided the price per dozen by ten and added two." This applied, however, only to less expensive items, of ten or fifteen cents apiece or less. For more costly items he used another formula. A second store owner explained that he used the wholesaler's suggested retail price as a guide: if the suggested retail price for an item ended in a nine, he left it alone; if it ended in some other digit, he added two cents to the suggested retail price. He could give no reason for using this formula, but claimed that "most small stores do it that way." Doubtless both retailer and customer would benefit from a more efficient and rational method of pricing, but small store owners seem to lack either the ability or the interest in developing such procedures. As one put it, "The nice thing about our store is it's so relaxed."

Another factor which made an accurate estimate of their costs difficult to obtain was the procedure generally followed with regard to "sale pricing." Like most stores, they tended to place certain items on sale, sometimes at retail prices which were below the wholesale price paid by the grocer himself. Most larger stores place such items on sale for a limited time only and can, therefore, give a fairly accurate estimate of the number of these items they will sell within that period of time, and the amount of money they stand to lose on the item. The small store owners interviewed used no such procedures. Sales were for an indefinite period of time. One store owner explained that his extremely low price on one item had been in effect for "about a month," and was likely to last "until someone gets around to taking the sign down." The cost of the sale is, therefore, inestimable.

The price patterns which result from these manipulations tend to be somewhat difficult to interpret. A sample of prices for selected items were obtained from two independent stores located in lower class non-white neighborhoods in Detroit. For comparison purposes, the prices of similar items in a chain store were used. In each case, the price listed is that charged for the cheapest item of that type offered in the store; hence no judgment as to quality is made. While the small number of cases studied drastically limit the conclusions which may be drawn from the analysis, one fact may be gleaned from the data: the presumed pattern of higher prices in independent stores is by no means clearcut. As Table VII shows, the chain store did tend to have the greatest number of lower prices for the selected items considered. Of

TABLE VII. Relative Prices for Selected Items in Independent versus Chain Stores**

FOOD ITEM	TYPE OF STORE Independent #1	Independent #2	Chain Store
Canned Goods (cheapest brand offered):			
fruit cocktail (#303 can)	.23*	.37†	.263
green peas (#303 can)	.19*	.29†	.22
tomatoes (#303 can)	.22	.23†	.18*
chicken (10½ oz. can)	.185	.195†	.15*
Dairy Foods:			
milk (½ gal.)	.49	.49	.47*
eggs (grade A, Large, doz.)	.49	.49	.445*
cheese (Amer. process, 6 oz.)	.31*	.39	.39
Meats:			
frankfurters (1 lb.)	.49*	.59	.59
bologna (1 lb.)	.59	.69	.69
Other (cheapest brand offered):			
corn flakes (12 oz.)	.31	.35†	.28*
white flour (5 lb.)	.59	.59	.45*
diced beans (1 lb.)	.19	.23†	.155*
sugar (5 lb.)	.59	.67†	.49*
coffee (1 lb.)	.89†	.69	.69
Total (14 items)	$5.775	$6.265	$5.463

** Prices current as of the second week of August, 1967, in three Detroit area food stores.

* Indicates the lowest price at which the item could be obtained in any of the three stores studied.

† Indicates the highest price on any single item for any of the three stores studied.

the 14 items considered, the chain store price was lowest for 8 of them, and tied with one of the independents on another item. On 5 of the items, however, one of the independents had lower prices than the chain. The second independent generally tended to charge higher prices than either of the other two stores. If a customer had purchased all 14 of the items listed, he would have paid a total of over $0.31 more at the first independent than at the chain, and over $0.80 more at the second independent.

As has been suggested, among the reasons for the generally lower prices in the chains are their lower overhead, their cheaper wholesale prices, and the fact that they often market products under their own brand names, most of these brands being cheaper than the standard national brands. When an independent offers an item at a lower price than the nearby chain store, it may be for any of several reasons: the independent may be selling an extremely poor brand of the product, for which he himself pays very little; or he may be offering the item as a "special," for a limited or perhaps an unlimited time; or, strangely enough, he may not really have accurately calculated the price of the article and be aware of the fact that this item is priced lower than the chain store item (and perhaps lower than even his own wholesale price). In the course of interviews concerning their prices, one independent store owner commented: "I didn't realize that price was so low—I'll have to raise it—we're losing money!" But he apparently had not been aware of it until that minute.

In cases where the prices of the independents were appreciably higher than the chain store prices for similar items, the independent grocers often explained their higher prices as being payment for extra services: for the extremely long hours they were open (often from 7 a.m. to midnight); for the fact that they frequently ordered whole cases of special items for only one or two customers, necessitating extra storage space; and for the fact they often "charged" groceries. This last characteristic is one which often leads to considerable loss, as some of these debts are never paid. One grocer called his store a "convenience store," and therefore felt justified in charging a higher price.

This, of course, does not help the very limited budgets of those persons who must patronize these stores. Persons with limited incomes, more than anyone else, must obtain the most for their meager food dollars. And apparently the most certain manner in which to obtain the most for their food dollars is to shop at stores which have *consistently* lower prices, largely due to a more efficient management of their businesses: they are open a standard number of hours per day, so that overtime payments to employees are unnecessary; they obtain their wholesale supplies at the lowest possible prices; and they sell in such large volume that they do not have a sizeable inventory to be concerned about at any one time. Yet, as has been shown, stores of this type are grossly underrepresented in the lower income and non-white areas of Detroit. A major solution to the food budget problems of the lower income family would be the provision of chain store super markets more conveniently located in their areas. This fact was noted by Mary Gardiner Jones, a member of the Federal Trade Commission, in an address to the National Association of Food Chains in October, 1967.[22] Why are the chain stores so inadequately represented in these areas? Is it a deliberate plan on the part of the chain store managements? If so, what are their reasons? Or is there some other explanation for the phenomenon?

---

22. *FTC Member Urges Food Chains to Give Special Services in Slums,* 2 LAW IN ACTION, 4-7 (no. 8, Nov. 1967).

Reasons for the Observed Pattern

Interviews with regional executives of the five major Detroit area chains revealed that for the most part they are not unaware of the problem. Executives of four of the five recognized the existence of a service differential between outlying communities and what they frequently referred to as the "core city." The fifth failed to recognize the differential rate of service until the factual data were laid before him. On the other hand, one executive even spontaneously mentioned the concern of his company with the problem of serving these areas, before the topic was brought up by the interviewer.

Several reasons were given by the respondents for the lack of service by the chains to the lower income and non-white areas. One explained that studies conducted by his company had shown that chain stores as a whole tend to draw less of the food business in lower income areas of the core city than in outlying upper and middle income areas. Thus while the chain stores in outlying areas draw from 65 to 85 percent of the food dollars spent in these areas, they expect to draw only about 28 percent of the food dollars spent in core city areas. These chain-store directed dollars are, of course, divided among *all* of the chain store outlets in the neighborhood. Hence the chains are more reluctant to locate an outlet near a competing chain in a lower income than a higher income area, since they feel that the already existing chain has captured whatever market there is in the area for the chain store service.

Whether his allegation is accurate, and if so, why the chains get less of the food business in low income areas are, of course, other questions. Chain executives tend to believe it is due to a preference, on the part of the lower income and non-white consumer for the type of service the independents provide, especially the availability of liquor and easy credit. It may, however, also be due to the fact that chain-owned food outlets are not as readily available in these areas as in other neighborhoods. Were there as many chain stores, conveniently located, in lower income areas as in higher income sections, the proportion of the business they garner might be equally as large.

Fear of the high crime rate in such areas was also mentioned by executives of three chains as a reason for their hesitance to exert more effort to capture the market in lower income areas. This fear affected the chain management in two respects. First, three reported that stores in such areas tended to have a higher rate of damage and pilferage than stores in middle income neighborhoods, resulting in greater economic losses to the company. An executive of one particularly conservative chain explained that the directors of his company tended to take the position that stores in these areas were not worth the risk of high losses due to damage, pilferage, and high insurance premiums, that investment of their money into "safer" areas was more prudent. Second, two executives reported that their chains had trouble staffing such stores: employees, even Negro employees, often feared to take positions in these stores, especially at the managerial levels and during evening hours. These were by no means unanimous opinions among the executives, however. One respondent from a chain which had few stores in low income areas but claimed to want more, disagreed with both these positions. He claimed his chain had no trouble staffing its core city stores. Further, he indicated that one of the stores in his chain with the highest rate of shoplifting was in a middle class suburb with an exclusively white clientele.

Hence there is some disagreement over the effect that the traditionally held difficulties of doing business in lower income non-white neighborhoods has upon the chain store operations in these areas. While the management of some chain stores seems to believe that these elements are relevant, others see them as little or no problem. Most agree, however, that they are not the crucial reason for the relative absence of chain-store operations from these areas. All agreed that their main reason for being in business was to make a profit; and four of the five felt that if they could profitably operate in these areas, they would seek solutions to any other problems which the situation presented.

Executives from all of the five largest chains, felt, however, that certain basic elements essential to their manner of doing business were absent from such areas. The entire operation of the chain food stores is based upon a philosophy of a low price mark-up coupled with a high volume of sales. Chain stores have developed a highly complex system of bureaucratic procedures which have been found, through experience, to lead to a lowering of overhead, thus enabling them to lower prices. They have found, for example, that unless the store sells a very large number of items, it cannot long maintain its low prices without soon showing a loss. This high volume of business, in turn, requires the existence of a large stock of many varying items, a fact which they claim requires a considerably larger amount of space than is true of a low volume, high mark-up operation.

They have also found that certain physical features of the store and its surroundings contribute to producing the necessary high volume. Thus a store with a large parking area in front of the store will have a higher sales volume than one with a smaller lot or a lot in the rear. Placement of items within the store is also important; certain items will sell better near the entrance, others near the exit.[23] The maintenance of the low-price character of the chains is based upon the simultaneous retention of their high volume character. And this, in turn, is based upon the assumption that their proven high-volume-producing characteristics can be maintained. Apparently, many of these high-volume-producing characteristics can be reproduced in the core city areas only at great expense or with great difficulty.

The major factor inhibiting the large-scale entry of the chains into the core city areas appears to be the difficulty of obtaining sufficient land for the large modern super market. As noted above, the chains have found they can obtain the necessary high business volume with large stores and large parking lots visible from the street. Most executives estimated the minimum adequate lot size to be 60,000 square feet. In a new undeveloped suburban area, such a lot could be obtained with ease and at reasonable cost. In well-developed core city areas the cost and difficulty can well become prohibitive. Core city land, especially that which is zoned for commercial use, is frequently so expensive that the chains feel the rental figures alone would be so high as to prevent the store from being profitable. Hence they hesitate to enter such ventures. Two executives mentioned having considered such extremely radical proposals as building a super market with underground or overhead parking in areas where a large plot of land is unavailable or extremely expensive. Most chains are, however, quite reluctant to take such radical action, since the cost of such a building would be much greater than that involved in the construction of the traditional single-story super market with adjoining parking lot. In such a radical venture, the company's loss, in case the store proved unsuccessful, would be substantially greater.

An even greater problem, the respondents reported, stemmed from the difficulty of *obtaining* the required land. A 60,000 square foot area in the core city is almost inevitably broken up into several lots, each owned by a separate individual. The difficulty involved in convincing all of them to sell is enormous; the entire deal can fail because of the refusal of any one of the individual owners. After a few such incidents, the real estate managers of most chains become discouraged about making further attempts.

The executives also complained that, once an appropriate site were found, with the present owners willing to sell, they frequently encountered governmental opposition to their plans. Core city sites of this size nearly always involved at least some footage which was zoned

23. V. PACKARD, THE HIDDEN PERSUADERS 94-95 (1957).

for non-commercial use. City Planning Commissions, in Detroit and elsewhere, have tended to be reluctant to change the zoning, again preventing entry of a chain food store into the core city. The higher-priced independent merchants are, however, content with much less land, since their higher prices permit a much lower volume; they are happy, therefore, to settle in the relatively small commercially-zoned sites which exist.

The obvious solution to the problem would appear to be the use by the food chains of the core city urban renewal lands available through the city government. Such lands are usually somewhat cheaper than other core city property, and lots of the appropriate size would be easier to obtain. Several chains reported having negotiated for the purchase, or for lease from developers, of areas of this type. Again, however, they frequently encountered discouraging problems, for here too they were often required to engage in practices which worked against accepted principles of super market management. The chief complaint revolved around the attempts of urban renewal directors to dictate various aspects of the physical plant of the businesses entering urban renewal lands. They would require, for example, that the parking area be in the rear rather than the front. This placement may be more esthetically pleasing to the eye, but, as has been noted, it may not lead to the development of an adequate volume of business. So again, most chains become discouraged and turn to other market areas.

It might be suggested that the food chains could be *required*, by legal action, to provide a certain level of service to core city areas, in spite of the difficulties involved. Hence each chain would be expected to open a specified number of core city stores which are smaller in area than the optimum size, or which have their parking areas inappropriately located. This would appear to be a self-defeating proposition. For such a requirement would, in a very real sense, be requiring the chains to violate their own principles of good management, quite possibly leading to the operation of the store at a loss. Such losses could only be recouped by charging higher prices, thus, defeating the original purpose for desiring the entry of the chains into these areas. As an alternate, it is proposed that a system be devised by which the good management principles which have proved so effective elsewhere may be allowed to operate, unhampered, in the core city also. I shall detail shortly some suggested ways in which this might be accomplished.

The reader will recall that one of the large chains (Chain D) was quite unlike the others, in that it exhibited a much higher tendency to serve the lower-income and non-white areas than did most other chains. For purposes of comparison, it is interesting to consider the differences between the majority of food chains, on the one hand, and this company, on the other, in order to determine whether the management of this company has developed any procedures of business management which are particularly suited to the conduct of business in core city areas. Three major distinctions can be uncovered.

Perhaps the most important is that this chain is involved in other operations besides its retail food sales. Chain D, one of the largest national chains, operates its own food processing plants, producing grocery items under its own brand labels. It is not the only chain operating in the Detroit area which engages in ventures other than retail food sales; chains A, B, and C do so as well. It is, however, the only chain which determines the profit level of the company on a *joint* basis; that is, the profits and losses of its retail and manufacturing operations are *computed together*. Chain D seeks only to make an overall profit from all of its several operations of all types. The other chains with diverse operations compute the relative profitability of *each unit of operation separately*, and each unit is expected to show a profit of its own.

This method of profit determination produces a second difference between Chain D and the others, in that the management of Chain D is willing to operate any single unit at a small loss if they feel it is making a substantial contribution to the entire operation. Thus, if a particular store is selling adequate amounts of Chain D's private label items, the Chain feels justified in retaining the store, even if it shows a small annual loss as a necessary cost of the distribution and sale of its manufactured goods. Other chains, which operate their various enterprises as separate operations, feel pressed to close any retail outlets which do not pay their own way. And local chains, such as E, F, and G, which lack manufacturing operations cannot, of course, afford to retain outlets which are unprofitable. Such losses could only be recouped by a rise in overall retail prices, and this would eliminate the value of the chain store for the consumer.

Lastly, Chain D has exhibited a greater willingness to accommodate itself to the requirements of urban renewal directors and zoning officials than have the other chains. While the management of the other large chains generally took the approach that they *must* be permitted to operate according to their own rules of store design and management or they did not care to enter the area, Chain D officials were more willing to accommodate their management principles to governmental stipulations, as evidenced by the fact that five *new*, modern outlets of Chain D have been constructed in core city areas since 1961. Again, this greater tendency toward risk-taking on the part of Chain D may also be due to the fact that its management feels somewhat "protected" against a possible failure of the new retail outlet, knowing that the manufacturing profits are available to offset the losses of an unprofitable retail store.

It appears, therefore, that the greater willingness of Chain D to do business in core city areas is largely due to the fact that the management does not depend upon its retail operation alone to show a profit. The existence of a manufacturing unit which offsets retail losses enables the management to take greater risks in its retail operation. Consequently, they are more willing to retain a store which shows a small loss, or to open a store which has questionable chances of success.

An Eye to the Future

It has been suggested in the present article that the chain-operated retail food stores tend to be clustered in middle income, white neighborhoods, based on data collected in the City of Detroit and surrounding suburbs. Further, the lower income and non-white areas of Detroit tend to be served largely by independently owned food stores which tend, often as a result of market conditions and not because of a deliberate policy of customer exploitation, to charge higher prices. Hence the non-white and lower income consumer is placed in the position of having to travel long distances to purchase food, or pay a premium price to feed his family.

It is suggested that a possible solution to the problem of providing low-cost foodstuffs to the lower income and non-white populations of the core city would be a concerted policy designed to attract the chain-owned super markets back into these areas in greater numbers. Such a program might be built around the following three measures:

1) Urban areas could make greater use of condemnation procedures in core city areas to provide the large blocks of land which chain store managers have found to be necessary for the type of high volume-low price operation they conduct.

2) Greater flexibility should characterize the governmental agencies charged with zoning and urban renewal. In order to obtain the desired result of low cost food for core city residents, it is suggested that city governments should establish a setting which allows the unhampered operation of the management principles which have proven successful in more affluent neighborhoods. (The reader should note that I do not propose a return to a total *laissez-faire* philosophy of trade regulation. The grocery chains are, and should remain, under governmental supervision. What is suggested is that some governmental regulatory activities have tended to hamper the advantageous, rather than the disadvantageous aspects of chain store operations.)

3) Lastly, it is suggested that the type of operational procedures which make Chain D more willing to risk core city retail operations should be encouraged. Because it combined its retail and manufacturing operations in computing its profit-loss statement, Chain D management appeared less fearful of a losing retail operation, and was even willing to operate small stores on a low-volume, low-mark-up basis. Were the other chains to follow the same procedure, their managements might be equally willing to take such a risk. Hence government might encourage the use of such accounting procedures, possibly through the allowance of tax credits for losing operations carried on the books in such instances.

Consumer Legislation and the Ghetto

ELLIOT B. GLICKSMAN* AND VERA MASSEY JONES*

> The deep resentment of those who take advantage of the slum dweller's lack of sophistication in handling money, in selling shoddy goods, in overcharging for what he gets is a source of discontent. A consumer service and consumer protection program is required to eliminate this injustice.[1]

These words of Detroit's Mayor Jerome P. Cavanagh spoken on August 15, 1967, before the President's National Advisory Commission on Civil Disorders, only 18 days after the occurrence of one of this country's worst civil disorders, expresses one of the major problems of the poor that thus far has been given little or no attention.

To date, however, with rare exceptions, federal, state, and local governmental agencies have emphasized job training programs, and wage legislation to alleviate the multitude of problems which beseige the economically disadvantaged citizen of today.[2] In addition to these governmental programs, the private sector has recently instituted recruitment programs designed to relieve the hard-core unemployment problems.[3]

These programs, which have, to a large extent, concerned themselves with increasing the income of the poor, should not be minimized. However, such efforts fail to consider a major factor of poverty: how the poor spend, not earn, their money, and what they receive in return.[4] They do not spend their money in the same way, nor pay the same prices, nor receive the same quality of merchandise for similar moneys spent by middle class consumers. It is this factor of spending which aggravates and perpetuates poverty.[5]

The services, and particularly the goods, sold to the ghetto resident by the private sector have been of very poor quality and most

---

* Students, University of Detroit School of Law.

1. Speech by Mayor Jerome P. Cavanagh, City of Detroit, Before the President's National Advisory Committee on Civil Disorders, August 15, 1967, Washington, D.C.

2. Note, *Consumer Legislation and The Poor*, 76 YALE L.J. 745 (1967).

3. Arjay Miller, Ford Motor Company President, announced at a meeting, of the New Detroit Committee, that the Company would seek to help alleviate some of the hard core unemployment in Detroit by launching a special Inner City recruitment program. This program is designed to recruit approximately 6500 employees for its Southeastern Michigan Plants from the hard-core unemployment sector in Detroit.

Mr. Miller went on to say that trained Company recruiters would be located at the various Total Action Against Poverty Centers (TAP) located in the Detroit Area. Source: Ford Motor Company News Release, News Department, Dearborn, Michigan, October 26, 1967.

4. *Supra* note 2, at 745.

5. *Id.*

expensive. Retail stores, which sell large consumer items such as appliances and other household furnishings, often use mark-ups of 300-400 percent on the price of merchandise, and add on excessive service charges for time payments.[6] Indeed, it is not unusual to find different service charges used in the same store.[7] Even public utilities penalize the ghetto resident by requiring that he pay a large deposit to assure payment of bills.[8]

Society's failure to institute significant legislation to curb exploitation of the poor consumer in the form of exorbitant credit charges, excessive pricing, poor quality merchandise and service bears considerable responsibility for the civil disorders which have plagued our urban areas during the recent sixties. Such conditions might have been responsible for the arson and looting in the Detroit disorder, since many of the businesses so destroyed were those which allegedly engaged in unethical, sometimes illegal, practices.

> One columnist writing for the *Detroit News* claimed that: "A Negro woman on relief set fire to a furniture store because she felt she would never be able to pay the bill she owed there. Due to the interest rate she was being forced to pay $910.12 to satisfy an original debt of $285."[9]

What has been done to alleviate this situation? Very little, unfortunately. There is, however, a growing effort to promote various means and devices, legal and educational to protect the ghetto consumer.

To appreciate the impact of these efforts, it must be realized that there was never a problem until the innovation, in the 1930s, of the so-called time payment. Up until then, the consumer simply saved up his money and purchased for cash—or did without. With the introduction of comparatively low-priced, massed produced, durable goods, and the pressures upon the consumer to buy (familiar to all of us), the buy-now, pay later philosophy became ingrained in the American way of life. At first installment buying was limited to certain classes, but in time it became readily accessible to—perhaps forced upon—the poor consumer. What began as an aid to the purchaser became, in time, an economic chain binding and imprisoning him so much so that it became apparent, that government curbs on time payment sales was necessary.

---

6. *Id.* at 756, note 61.
7. *Id.* at 756, note 77.
8. Case studies from the University of Detroit Urban Law Clinic.
9. *Hearings on* H.R. 11601 *Before the Subcomm. on Consumer Affairs of the Comm. on Banking and Currency,* 90th Cong., 1st Sess. 803, 804 (1967).

In spite of such legislation, the poor consumer was still without adequate protection, for the general assumption underlying the legislation was that the consumer and the seller were dealing on equal terms, *i.e.,* that:

1. the model purchaser was free to shop for the best buys;
2. the model purchaser was able to judge quality; and
3. the model purchaser knew his rights and liabilities under the purchase agreements.[10]

But such is not the case with the poor consumer.

One of the essential reasons that this model cannot be applied to the poor is that the poor consumer shops for credit rather than for goods.[11]

The poor consumer has not escaped the mass media's bombardment of messages to buy now and pay later. Faced with various cultural pressures for the accumulation of durable goods, the poor consumer by virtue of his extremely low income, poor credit record, and unstable sources of income is precluded from making his purchases at established large national or local retail firms. The result is that the poor consumer is compelled to patronize the local neighborhood merchant who will extend him credit.[12]

Being apprehensive about shopping in areas which are unfamiliar to him, the poor consumer becomes a captive of the local credit-advancing merchant. He thus fails to seek out competitive prices.[13]

The second attribute of the consumer-model, the ability to judge the value of the goods offered, likewise cannot be applied to the poor consumer. In fact it is rare that he ever has the opportunity to make judgmental decisions, being in essence a member of a captive market for the ghetto merchant.

The third attribute of the consumer-model, a supposition of knowledge of one's legal rights cannot be applied to the poor consumer. Indeed most laymen, ignorant of their rights seek professional help, but the poor consumer lacks even this rudimentary knowledge.

An examination of the various instalment sales acts and the manner in which they are applied brings the realization that even the middle class consumer, who is presumed to possess the attributes of the consumer-model, is afforded no real consumer protection.

Virtually all of the retail instalment sales acts contain rate ceiling

---

10. *Supra* note 2, at 748.
11. *Id.* at 750.
12. U.S. Riot Comm'n Report, Report of The National Advisory Comm'n on Civil Disorders 274-75 (Bantam Books, 1968)
13. *Supra* note 2, at 750.

provisions, expressed in terms of either percentage per year, or dollars per year per hundred dollars of debt. However due to the various methods used by retail merchants to compute the service charges, it is almost impossible for the average consumer to determine whether or not he is in fact being charged the legal rate as per statute. Indeed, he often does not even know the rate!

The confusion which besieges the average consumer when he attempts to calculate the legal rate of finance charges in an instalment contract, coupled with the contract theory that one is presumed to know what he signs, defeats the disclosure purpose of the acts and limits valid litigation under the acts.

In addition to the disclosure features, many of the instalment sales acts contain provisions which prohibit the sales agreement between the merchant and the consumer to contain: (1) acceleration clause of the amount owing in the absence of the buyer's default. (2) power of attorney to confess judgment or assignment of wages, (3) waiver of buyer's legal remedies for illegal act committed in collection or repossession procedure.

Virtually all of the instalment sales acts prohibit the signing of contracts with blank spaces in relation to essential terms of the contract.

The underlying philosophy of consumer legislation is the attempt to equalize the bargaining power between the parties to a consumer-credit transaction.

Full disclosure of credit information may only be a partial answer to the problem of equalizing the bargaining power. To effectively equalize this relationship, the law must step in and remove the parties' control over some of the items normally left to bargaining, thus the justification for those limitations on the freedom to contract between merchant and consumer.[14]

This reflection of consumer problems and the existing legislation leads to the necessary conclusion that the present retail instalment sales acts when applied to given situations do not accurately or totally inform the consumer. Therefore, the major purpose, disclosure, is defeated.

President Johnson stated this very simply in his 1967 Message to the Congress on consumer protection:

> The consumer has the right to know the cost of this key item [credit] in his budget just as much as the price of any other commodity he buys . . . . The consumer should not have

---

14. *See, e.g.*, MASS. GEN. LAWS ANN. ch. 255D, § 9d (Supp. 1966); ORE. REV. STAT. § 83:060 (1963); NEB. REV. STAT. § 45-303 (1959); MICH. STAT. ANN. § 19.416 (101) - (122) (Supp. 1968).

to be an actuary or mathematician to understand the rate of interest that is being charged.[15]

This situation could be corrected by explicit provisions for a uniform method of computing interest or service charges in the retail instalment sales acts. By requiring every lender and every merchant to state the true interest rate in a uniform manner as per the proposed changes in the retail instalment sales acts, it would be possible "to break the endless chain of misleading claims and shabby deceptions which now characterize too large a segment of the credit industry."[16] Such provisions when applied to the average consumer would truly fulfill the legislative intent. But even these proposed changes will not provide the poor consumer any greater protection than that afforded by the present statutes.

As stated by Mr. Sargent Shriver, Director of the Office of Economic Opportunity (OEO):

> Disclosure alone will not solve the credit problems of the poor. Disclosure presupposes the ability to choose, which is just what the poor do not have, disclosure does not protect the consumer from abuses connected with repossession, and quality merchandise to which the poor are particularly susceptible.[17]

To combat effectively this situation the poor consumer must be given the type of information which will enable him to decide whether the benefits received from the purchase are worth the price which he must pay.

The information given must contain an explanation in his own terms of the consumer's legal rights and obligations which arise under an instalment sales contract.

In addition, the uneducated consumer must be given adequate information which will allow him to judge the quality of the goods offered. In this manner, the consumer will be able to determine the probable benefits which he will derive from the contemplated purchase.

To effectuate the dispersement of consumer information the existing governmental, and private anti-poverty centers could be utilized, adding consumer counselling services.

In order that this educative process be effective it is imperative that professional experts from the urban universities as well as the

15. Special Presidential Message, *Consumer Protection, H. Doc.* No. 57, 90th Cong., 1st Sess. 205, 207 (1967).
16. *Supra* note 9 at 804-05.
17. *Hearings,* Supra note 9, at 242.

existing social institutions be available and utilized by the neighborhood agencies to disperse this consumer education.

The problem of alerting the community of the probable benefits to be gained from participation in this educative program is one that must be solved before the program can effectively operate. In discussions held with a labor economist in the Detroit area,[18] who has been directly involved with advising neighborhood self-help agencies, this problem of communications was vividly demonstrated. One of the self-help agencies which this economist advises, undertook the operation of a grocery co-operative, but due to the communication problem the successes of this venture were less than expected. A suggested means to alleviate this communication problem would be the use of advertisement leaflets circulated among the residents of the community to inform them of the services provided by this co-op, and the savings to be realized by their patronage. The use of these leaflets would likewise be a valuable communication device to inform the neighborhood residents of the existence, location, and services provided by consumer counselling centers.

Another method of changing the present unbalanced relationship between the local merchant and the captive consumer is the selective boycotting of merchants who practice unethical credit practices.

The argument most often advanced by local merchants in support of their pricing practices is that the cost of operating in deprived areas necessitates the higher pricing of their goods. The chief factors of the higher operating costs cited are the costs of insurance and the risk involved in allowing credit purchases.[19]

According to a recent Federal Trade Commission Study in Washington D.C. cited by the U.S. Riot Commission Report on Civil Disorders, merchants doing business in ghetto neighborhoods charge higher prices than those doing business in other parts of the city. The FTC identified a number of stores specializing in selling furniture and appliances to low income households. About 92% of the sales of these stores were credit sales involving instalment purchases. Definitely catering to a low-income group, these stores charged significantly higher prices than general merchandise outlets in the Washington area and while higher prices are not necessarily exploitative in themselves, many merchants in ghetto neighborhoods take advantage of their superior knowledge of credit buying by engaging in various exploitative tactics-high pressure salesmanship, bait advertising misrepresentation of

18. Interview with Joe Guggenheim, Economic Research Department International Union UAW AFL-CIO, March 22, 1968.

19. *Supra* note 2, at 756 *see* note 60.

prices, substitution of used goods for promised new ones, failure to notify consumers of legal actions against them, exorbitant prices for credit charges and use of shoddy merchandise.[20]

A consumer boycott some time ago was used to force down prices at an East Harlem grocery store; had there been any justification for the price levels the store soon would have gone into bankruptcy, yet the store did better than ever before.[21]

Still another method of altering the existing unbalanced relationship between the local merchant and the poor consumer is the introduction of meaningful competition into the neighborhood. Within the framework of our given economic system and our preference for local self-help programs, consumer co-operatives could be a most desirable manner of achieving this end. The establishment of such co-operatives would of course involve certain administrative and financial problems, but such problems could be overcome.[22]

The goods offered would be of better quality or at least at qualities commensurate with their price. In addition, the member consumer would not be subjected to the abusive practices which are very prevalent in the ghetto neighborhood stores. Thus he would have real choices both as to price and quality. These choices will place the poor consumer in relatively the same position as the average buyer, and thus the retail instalment sales acts could afford both classes of consumers equal protection.

It is clear that the unethical, often illegal, credit practices, frequently found in local neighborhood stores, had a significant relationship to the recent civil disorders, experienced in our country's major cities. According to a recent report:[23]

> "practices of white merchants and brutality of the police . . . seem to be the most salient forms of white exploitation perceived by the Negro Community. Among those questioned in the study . . . the most highly discontented with the practices of the merchants were most likely to give moral support to, and become involved in, the riot."

In Detroit's recent catastrophic rioting the victims of looting and arson included thirty-two furniture, appliance and hardware stores,

---

20. *Supra* note 12, at 278.

21. *Supra* note 2, at 756 *see* note 60.

22. The formation of co-operative associations comes under MICH. STAT. ANN. § 21.99-248 (1948). Under these sections the basic fundamentals for the establishment of a co-op are set forth. Co-operatives needs for capital are largely determined by the time lag between paying for products it handles and being reimbursed for them.

An important source of raising the necessary capital in most co-ops is by selling common stock in stock associations or charging membership dues or fees.

The management functions of a co-operative are generally shared by many people.

23. Department of Sociology, University of California at Los Angeles, Structure of Discontent (June 1, 1967).

and twenty-three clothing and jewelry stores.[24] Numerous stories on the riots appeared in the Detroit press alluding to the systematic burning of stores which were believed to engage in excessive credit practices.

While our society cannot tolerate the existence of violence, steps must be taken to eradicate such business practices which lead men to frustration and outright rebellion.

It is also clear that the existing consumer legislation although intended to provide consumer protection; whatever its value to the middle class consumer, its intended protection for the poor is almost nonexistent.

It is the writers' contention that the ideal remedy, or at least the ideal goal is to introduce meaningful competition into the neighborhood by expanding the already existing co-operatives to deal in retail sales of durable goods. In this manner the local merchant will be economically compelled to compete both in credit services, as well as the quality of goods offered.

Though the co-operative programs will be slow in developing it is imperative that meaningful consumer counselling be instituted and ongoing, in order that the poor consumer be given an equal opportunity to participate, equitably and justly in our consumer economy.

24. *Supra* note 9, at 804.

State Riot Laws:
A Proposal

GERALD D. DUCHARME* AND EUGENE H. EICKHOLT*

Introduction

Although the problem of quelling a riot is primarily one for the police, it must be called to mind that the police can only enforce the laws as they exist. The more clear and unambiguous a law is, the more effective can be its enforcement. The state can best deal with a riot situation and with those who cause that situation through clear and strict riot laws. However, riot laws themselves do not stop riots from happening. Because riots are not caused by criminal minds, their solution cannot be found solely within the criminal law.

Riot laws focus themselves upon a riot already begun. They provide definitions for riot, penalties for rioting as well as for associated crimes, and procedures for quelling a riot. With the ever-increasing threat of riots, some of these laws will find themselves subject to enforcement on a large scale. To be prepared therefore, it is necessary to study, to compare and contrast these laws in order that an effective model riot control law can be constructed.

We begin, then, with an examination of the Michigan riot laws followed by a look at the riot laws of all American state jurisdictions and conclude with an outline of a model riot control provision.

Michigan Riot Laws

Michigan has its riot laws, as does every other state in the union.[1] The Michigan statutes are taken, to some extent, from their English predecessor, the famous Riot Act of 1714, which commanded the local magistrate to read the Riot Act in the case of a riotous, unlawful assembly:

> Our Sovereign lord the King chargeth and commandeth all persons, being assembled, immediately to disperse themselves, and peaceably to depart to their habitations or to their lawful business, upon the pains contained in the Act made in the first year of King George, for the prevention of tumults and riotous assemblies. God save the King.[2]

Throughout, the authors give their own opinions for there is little written authority in this field.

* Students, University of Detroit School of Law.

1. MICH. COMP. LAWS § 750.521 (1948); MICH. STAT. ANN. § 28.789 (1954).
2. GEO. I, Stat. 2, c. 5 (1714).

Under Michigan law, a disturbance constitutes a riot when twelve or more persons armed and/or thirty or more persons unarmed are tumultuously assembled. The local magistrate or mayor is ordered by the statute to enter into the assembly and to disperse the crowd[3] and to command the assistance of all assembled to aid him in his task, and those who remain so unlawfully assembled are also deemed to be rioters.[4] Those magistrates or mayors who refuse or neglect to "immediately proceed to the place of such assembly" are guilty of a misdemeanor, carrying a sentence of not more than six months in the county jail or a fine of not more than two hundred and fifty dollars.[5] The magistrates or local officials are given the authority to call others to their aid and to use necessary force to quell the riot.[6] If anyone is killed or injured in the process of dispersing the riotous crowd, the magistrates and officers and those assisting them are guiltless of the offense.[7] If a dwelling house or other building is damaged during the riot, those responsible are held as felons.[8]

The effectiveness of the Michigan riot laws was indicated by Mr. William Cahalan, Wayne County Prosecuting Attorney, who commented:

> . . . Michigan's riot act imposes absolutely no penalty on the rioters. The legislation dated back to 1846, and we suspect the penalty clause was left out through an oversight.
>
> * * *
>
> Our office has no policy regarding the enforcement of the statutory riot act, because it is ineffective. . . . However, we do prosecute under 1948 Compiled Laws, Sec. 750.505, which incorporates all common-law offenses not otherwise spelled out in the statutes. In these cases we charge the common-law offense of inciting to riot, and/or riot, depending on the facts of the case.[9]

According to the testimony of the City of Detroit before the President's National Advisory Commission on Civil Disorders, only 11 juveniles, 43 adult males and 5 adult females were charged with inciting to riot after the Detroit riots of 1967 and no one was charged with riot, either under the statute or under common law.[10] Apparently those

---

3. *Supra* note 1.
4. MICH. COMP. LAWS § 750.522 (1948); MICH. STAT. ANN. § 28.790 (1954).
5. MICH. COMP. LAWS § 750.524 (1948); MICH. STAT. ANN. § 28.792 (1954).
6. MICH. COMP. LAWS § 750.525 (1948); MICH. STAT. ANN. § 28.793 (1954).
7. MICH. COMP. LAWS § 750.527 (1948); MICH. STAT. ANN. § 28.795 (1954).
8. MICH. COMP. LAWS § 750.528 (1948); MICH. STAT. ANN. § 28.796 (1954).
9. Letter from William L. Cahalan to Gerald D. Ducharme, November 13, 1967.
10. Appearance of the City of Detroit before the President's National Advisory Comm'n on Civil Disorder (August 15, 1967, Washington, D.C.) [hereinafter referred to as

charged with inciting to riot were charged with the common law offense. Thus 59 people were charged with a violation of a riot law out of a total of nearly 7,200 who were arrested in the largest riot this country has yet known.

Recently a committee of lawyers and judges in Michigan was appointed to reevaluate the Criminal Code and to revise the riot law—this time giving it a punitive clause. The proposed section reads:

> Sec. 5510(1) A person commits the crime of riot if, with 5 or more other persons, he wrongfully engages in tumultuous and violent conduct and thereby intentionally or recklessly causes or creates a grave risk of causing public terror or alarm.
> (2) Riot is a Class C felony.[11]

In attempting to determine whether this new riot provision was adequate, the authors wrote a letter to the Hon. Horace W. Gilmore [Wayne County Circuit Judge and Chairman of the Revision Committee] asking whether, in the light of the Summer-1967 Detroit riots, his committee was considering making a revision in its proposed code. The Judge commented:

> At the present time there are no plans for revising Section 5510. I think it is the judgment of the Committee that this section and the others in the chapter covering Public Order and Decency are adequate to cover riot situations.[12]

The proposed riot law contains a penalty clause, thus allowing the state prosecutors to make charges under it, rather than under the common law. The number required to constitute a riot is reduced from twelve armed and/or thirty unarmed to a straight five persons. As far as laying out any new procedure that a mayor or magistrate is to follow during times of civil disturbance, the revised code concerns itself with only criminal law, ignoring procedural provisions.

There is no modern case law interpreting the provisions of the existing Michigan riot law, so to define "riot" we must look to other jurisdictions. Although all derivative in substance from the Riot Act of 1714, some of the riot statutes do have their own peculiar characteristics and some have case law definitions. It should be kept in mind that the laws we are concerned with here deal primarily with an embryo riot which must be stopped from developing into the uncontrollable chaos which occurred in Watts, Newark and in Detroit.

Detroit Appearance]. Common-Law crimes may be charged in Michigan under MICH. COMP. LAWS § 750.505 (1948), MICH. STAT. ANN. § 28.775 (1954).

11. MICH. REV. CRIM. CODE § 5510 (final draft, 1967).

12. Letter from Hon. Horace W. Gilmore to Gerald D. Ducharme, November 8, 1967.

Riot

At common law two elements were necessary before an assembly became an actual riot. An assemblage of three or more persons for an unlawful purpose was simply an unlawful assembly. When that assembly performed an act leading toward the perpetration of an unlawful objective, such as walking to the prospective scene, then it was a rout. When the actual unlawful act was committed, then the assembly was deemed a riot.[13] A few states have statutes which make the distinction between unlawful assembly, rout, and riot, e.g. South Dakota.[14] Such statutes are for the purpose of affording the local authorities a means by which they might identify a riot in the making thus providing a legal means by which it can be quelled before an uncontrollable outbreak of violence occurs.

Although the statutes of the several states are similar in many respects, the case law interpretation of them is sometimes varied. In *Feinstein v. City of New York*,[15] the New York Court outlined the elements of a riot. At least three persons with a common intent who begin the execution of that common purpose or intent and who have the intent to aid each other in the execution of the common purpose and who exercise such force and violence as to alarm those reasonable people who are not participants of the disturbance are guilty of riot. A Pennsylvania court has said that a riot consists of three broad elements: unlawful assembly and intent to act in violation of and against lawful authority in such a way as to be accompanied by acts of violence.[16] A Minnesota court among other state courts has said that no actual force or violence is necessary to constitute a riot, but only a threat to do violence accompanied with the power of immediate execution which results in an actual disturbance of the peace.[17] In order that there be a riot, there must be a public act and an act done "secretly away from public view is not a 'riot', though there is terror or disturbance at the time the damage is discovered."[18] Concert of action seems to be a necessary element but the rioters need not act toward a common cause such as the perpetration of one singular illegal act.[19]

---

13. 2 Holdsworth, History of English Law 450.
14. S.D. Code § 13.1402 (1939).
15. Feinstein v. City of New York, 283 N.Y.S. 335, 157 Misc. 157 (1935).
16. State v. Hoffman, 199 N.C. 328, 154 S.E. 314 (1930); Commonwealth v. Ray, 177 Pa. Super. 154, 110 A.2d 764 (1955).
17. State v. Winkles, 204 Minn. 466, 283 N.W. 763 (1939).
18. Int'l Wire Works v. Hanover Fire Ins. Co., 230 Wis. 72, 283 N.W. 292, 293 (1939); State v. Winkles, 204 Minn. 466, 283 N.W. 763 (1939); Walter v. Northern Ins. Co. 370 Ill. 283, 18 N.E.2d 906 (1939); Commonwealth v. Paul, 145 Pa. Super. 548, 21 A.2d 421 (1941).
19. Trujillo v. People, 116 Colo. 157, 178 P.2d 942, 944 (1946); Commonwealth v. Ray, 177 Pa. Super. 154, 110 A.2d 764, 766 (1955).

Just as in criminal law, where it is the effect of men's acts which most concerns the law, so it is with riot. Private acts are not the subject of riot laws; riot is what may be termed a public offense—it is a direct offense against society which a segment of the public actually can witness and experience. The Wisconsin Supreme Court brings out the necessity for actions to be of a public nature:

> [I]f . . . the assembly . . . attempted or made a move toward blocking the sidewalk or the street, or both, or blockading the entrance to the Milwaukee Club, such assembly became an unlawful assembly and if it was violent and tumultuous and resulted in terror, or in a serious disturbance to those who were the object of the demonstration and protest, it became such an assembly as amounted to a riot . . . .[20]

The court made a clear distinction between unlawful assembly and riot by equating riot with unlawful assembly plus terror to those against whom the assembly was directed. Terror is the key and this terror is that of the public not of one individual, nor one small set of individuals.

A Utah court has stated that in proving the existence of a riot, it is only necessary to have testimony showing that a general feeling of alarm existed as a consequence of the acts complained of. It is not necessary to show any actual physical damage but only a threat of imminent damage to the public at large.[21]

Four different classes of persons may be charged with the offense of riot. One who incites,[22] one who participates,[23] one who fails to disperse upon command,[24] and, in some instances, one who fails to render assistance upon lawful order.[25]

---

20. Koss v. State, 217 Wis. 325, 258 N.W. 860, 863 (1935).

21. People v. O'Loughlin, 3 Utah 133, 1 P. 653 (1882). For instance, the destruction of an individual dwelling by a riotous mob may not be physical damage to the public at large but it certainly constitutes a sufficient cause of terror and alarm for those who occupy dwellings nearby.

22. The following is a list of those states that have a special statutory provision prohibiting inciting to riot with the maximum penalty indicated therefore: ALA. CODE tit. 14, § 407(2) (1961), defendant held as a principal for any crime committed during the riot; ALASKA STAT. § 11.45.010(2) (1962), 3-15 yrs.; CAL. PEN. CODE § 404.6 (West 1956), 1 yr. and/or $1000; CONN. GEN. STAT. ANN. § 53-44 (1960), 10 yrs. and/or $5000; D.C. has very recently passed an inciting statute; GA. CODE ANN. § 26-904 (1953), 5-20 yrs.; ILL. ANN. STAT. ch. 134, § 10 (Smith-Hurd 1961), 10 yrs.; NEV. REV. STAT. § 203.040 (1965), 6 mo. and/or $500; N.H. REV. STAT. ANN. § 609-A:6 (Supp. 1965), defendant held as principal; N.Y. PEN. LAW § 2091.2 (McKinney 1944), 2 yrs. and/or $500.; N.D. CENT. CODE § 12-19-04(4) (1960), not less than 3 yrs.; OKLA. STAT. tit. 21, § 1312(4) (1961), 2-20 yrs.; ORE. REV. STAT. § 166.050(2) (1960), 15 yrs.; S.D. CODE § 13.1404(4) (1939), 3 yrs.; WASH. REV. CODE § 9.27.050(2) (1956), 2 yrs. and/or $1000.

23. See Appendix A.

24. *Id.*

25. The following states charge those who do not assist in the quelling of a riot upon lawful demand as rioters: FLA. STAT. ANN. § 870.04 (1965); IDAHO CODE ANN. § 18-6406

The number of people necessary to constitute a riot differs from state to state. The minimum number necessary ranges from two in some jurisdictions to twelve armed and/or thirty unarmed in others.[26] It should be noted that better than eighty percent of the states require either two or three persons to constitute a riot. One would expect that a state, not heavily urbanized, would demand a lesser number of persons to constitute a riot as its police facilities may not be as great as that in a more completely urbanized state. But such is not the case. New York, for example, requires only three, New Jersey requires twelve armed and/or thirty unarmed, Minnesota requires three and Missouri twelve armed and/or thirty unarmed.[27]

Also varying from state to state are the penalties for riot, ranging in jail terms and fines from 30 days and/or $100 to three years and/or $2000.[28] These penalties refer to what may be termed "simple riot," meaning a disturbance where there is no loss or injury to person or property but merely a public disturbance causing fear and terror to the citizens of the community. Over one half of the states provide for six months to one year maximum jail terms and up to $500 in fines.[29]

Although many states have small maximum penalties for riot, just as many have large maximum penalties and although probably seldom imposed, are in the discretion of the trial judge.

Aggravated Riot

Although the penalties for what may be termed "simple riot," that is, riot not accompanied by any other violation of the law amounting to more than a misdemeanor, are in most cases similar, if not identical, to the penalties for a common misdemeanor, the law is more stringent in dealing with the offender when his riotous acts are ac-

(1947); Iowa Code § 743.6 (1962); Ky. Rev. Stat. § 377 (1962); Me. Rev. Stat. Ann. ch. 136, § 9 (1964); Mass. Ann. Laws ch. 269, § 2 (Supp. 1966); Mich. Stat. Ann. § 28.791 (1962); Mo. Rev. Stat. § 542.200 (1959); N.D. Cent. Code § 12-19-10 (1960); Okla. Stat. tit. 21, § 103 (1961); Ore. Rev. Stat. § 145.020(2) (1960); S.D. Code § 14.1403 (1939); Utah Code Ann. § 77-5-5 (1953).

These states impose a lesser fine or jail sentence: Ill. Ann. Stat. ch. 38, § 31-8 (Smith-Hurd 1961), $100 fine; Kan. Gen. Stat. Ann. § 21-1002 (1963), $100 fine; Neb. Rev. Stat. § 28-805 (1943), $25 fine; N.H. Rev. Stat. Ann. § 609-A:5 (Supp. 165), 3 mo. and/or $50; N.Y. Pen. Law § 2095 (McKinney 1944), Misdemeanor; Ohio Rev. Code Ann. § 3761.99(D) (Baldwin 1964), $50 fine; R.I. Gen. Laws Ann. § 11-38-3 (1956), $30 fine; V.I. Code Ann. tit. 14, § 1824 (1967), 90 days and/or $100; Wis. Stat. Ann. § 946.40 (1965), $100 fine.

26. See Appendix B.
27. *Id.*
28. See Appendix A.
29. *Id.*

companied by acts destructive of person or property.[30] Exemplar of such statutes is that of West Virginia:

> If any person engaged in a riot, rout or unlawful assemblage, pull down or destroy, in whole or in part, any dwelling house, courthouse, jail, prison, asylum, hospital, school or college building, or any public building of any character, or assist therein, shall be guilty of a felony, and, upon conviction, shall be confined in the penitentiary not less than one year nor more than ten years . . . .[31]

Many states have provisions increasing the riot penalty for those who wear disguises during a riot or carry dangerous weapons.[32] Although all the crimes handled by these provisions, e.g. arson, are generally covered in seperate provisions in the respective state codes, it would seem that the primary reason why they are again covered in riot provisions is evidentiary. When a riot takes place, it would appear to be difficult to gather sufficient evidence to convict any one individual of a distinct crime. Thus the West Virginia statute, and those similar to it, treat such crimes as arson, looting, etc., as mass crimes, enabling the police to arrest groups of people charging them with a felony without bringing forth separate evidence against each individual offender. In short, those who riot and who, in the process of rioting, damage person or property are jointly liable for a felony.

Unusual Riot Felonies

Indiana has a statute making it a felony to participate in a simple riot in the nighttime. Such persons are charged with "Riotous Conspiracy" and may be sentenced from two to ten years.[33] Recognizing the danger of retaliation by those rioting against those sent to suppress them, North Dakota has this statute:

30. The following is a representative list containing citations to state provisions covering such topics as destroying buildings while rioting, injury to persons, property, wearing disguises and carrying dangerous weapons. The penalties for such crimes done while rioting are given after the respective citation. ALASKA STAT. § 11.45.010(2) (1962), 3-15 yrs.; FLA. STAT. ANN. § 870.03 (1965), 5 yrs.; ILL. ANN. STAT. ch. 38, § 25-1(c) (Smith-Hurd 1961), 1-5 yrs. and/or $1000; IND. ANN. STAT. § 10-1506 (1956), 2-10 yrs. and/or $2000; IOWA CODE § 743.9 (1962), 1-5 yrs. and/or $500; MINN. STAT. ANN. § 609.71 (1963), 5 yrs. and/or $5000; N.H. REV. STAT. ANN. § 609-A:3 (Supp. 1965), 1-3 yrs. and/or $1000; N.H. REV. STAT. ANN. § 609-A:6 (Supp. 1965), defendant held as a principal for any crime committed during the riot; N.Y. PEN. LAW § 2091.1 (McKinney 1944), 5 yrs. and/or $1000; N.D. CENT. CODE § 12-19-04(3) (1960), 2-10 yrs.; OKLA. STAT. tit. 21 § 1312(3) (1961), 2-10 yrs.; ORE REV. STAT. § 166.050(2) (1960), 15 yrs. (max.); S.D. CODE § 13.1404(3) (1939), 2-10 yrs.; VT. STAT. ANN. tit. 13, § 905 (1959), 5 yrs. and/or $1000; WASH. REV. CODE § 9.27.050(1) (1956), 5 yrs. and/or $1000; W. VA. CODE ANN. § 61-6-6 (1961), 1-10 yrs.

31. W. VA. CODE ANN. § 61-6-6 (1961).

32. *Supra* note 30.

33. IND. ANN. STAT. § 10-1506 (1956).

> A person who after the publication of a proclamation by the governor, or who after lawful notice to disperse and retire, resists or aids in resisting the execution of process in a county declared to be in a state of riot or insurrection, or who aids or attempts the rescue or escape of another from lawful custody or confinement, or who resists or aids in resisting a force ordered out by the governor or any civil officer to quell or suppress an insurrection or riot, is guilty of a felony, and shall be punished by imprisonment in the penitentiary for not less than two years.[34]

In an attempt to protect its national guard from physical assault in the quelling of a riot, the West Virginia legislature makes it a felony to interfere with the national guard in the performance of its duty.[35]

A statute such as this is broad enough to cover fire departments, police departments, ambulance crews and other persons assisting these. They represent a lawful means enabling the enforcement agencies to arrest people at the first sign of resistance to lawful authority during a riot.

Rioting with a dangerous weapon is recognized by many jurisdictions to constitute a felony.[36] Minnesota has gone to an apparent extreme by providing a penalty of imprisonment for not more than five years for someone participating in a riot with the knowledge that someone in the riot is armed, although he himself is not.[37]

INCITING TO RIOT

Under the Riot Act of 1714, one who incited others to riot was guilty of simple riot, a felony with the same penalty as riot.[38] Modern American statutes have lessened the penalty for simple riot, making it generally a misdemeanor,[39] though some jurisdictions make inciting to riot a felony.[40] Penalties for inciting to riot range from one year in California to a maximum of 20 in Oklahoma.[41] A Pennsylvania court has distinguished riot from inciting to riot:

> Inciting to riot and riot are legally separate and distinct offenses and . . . the former is not necessarily a constituent element of the latter, and . . . one may incite a riot and not participate in it, or may be concerned in a riot without having incited it. . . .[42]

---

34. N.D. CENT. CODE § 12-19-23 (1960).
35. W. VA. CODE ANN. § 15-1D-6 (1961).
36. *Supra* note 30.
37. MINN. STAT. ANN. § 609.71 (1963).
38. *Supra* note 2.
39. See Appendix A.
40. *Supra* note 22.
41. *Id.*
42. Commonwealth v. Apriceno, 131 Pa. Super. 158, 198 A. 515, 517 (1938).

The gist of inciting to riot is the inciter's tendency to provoke a breach of the peace, even though the parties may have assembled in the first instance for an innocent purpose. It encompasses conduct, words, signs, language, or any other means by which one can be urged to action, or such other actions as would naturally lead or urge other men to engage in such conduct which, if completed, would constitute a riot.[43]

Some jurisdictions have diverged from the common law in this area and have passed statutes specifically dealing with inciting to riot. Typical of those states which affix a higher maximum penalty than for riot is New York:

> ... if the offender directs, advises, encourages, or solicits other persons, present or participating in the riot or assembly, to acts of force or violence, by imprisonment for not more than two years, or by a fine of not more than $500 or by both such fine and imprisonment.[44]

Other jurisdictions define inciting to riot in the same way as New York but affix a heavier penalty. Such states are Alaska, Connecticut, Georgia, Oklahoma and Oregon with maximums ranging from 10 to 20 years.[45]

The Connecticut statute, which deems one who praises riotous activities guilty of inciting to riot,[46] has been specifically held to be constitutional in the case of *Turner v. LaBelle.*[47] Although the mere praising of a riot or a riotous disturbance may seem to be too slight an infraction of the law as to warrant a serious sentence, the United States District court in *Turner* upheld the constitutionality of the Connecticut statute:

> To encourage an assault on a policeman or individual is likely to produce a clear and present danger of a serious substantive evil that rises far above public inconvenience, annoyance, or unrest.[48]

---

43. State v. Cole, 249 N.C. 733, 107 S.E.2d 732, 742 (1959).
44. *Supra* note 22; N.Y. PEN. LAW § 2091.2 (McKinney 1944).
45. N.Y. PEN. LAW § 2091.2 (McKinney 1944).
46. CONN. GEN. STAT. ANN. § 53-44 (1960) states:

Any person who, in public or private, orally, in writing, in printing or in any other manner, advocates, encourages, justifies, praises, incites or solicits the unlawful burning, injury to or destruction of any public or private property or advocates, encourages, justifies, praises, incites or solicits any assault upon any organization of the United States . . . or the police force of this or of any other state or upon any officer or any member thereof, or the killing or injuring of any class or body of persons, or of any individual, shall be fined not more than five thousand dollars or imprisoned not more than ten years or both.

47. Turner v. LaBelle, 251 F. Supp 443 (D. Conn. 1966).
48. *Id.* at 446.

Being the broadest of inciting statutes, this Connecticut statute covers both oral and printed inflammatory remarks which would tend to incite a riot.

Of a more limited scope is the Georgia statute which covers only printed or written inflammatory material, and its minimum punishment for inciting to riot is 5 years.[49] In contrast to the Georgia statute, the very narrow Illinois statute on inciting to riot restricts the offense to merely the transmission of inflammatory statements by the telegraph which incite a riot.[50]

The crime of inciting to riot both at common law and by statute is concerned with the most crucial stage of a riot. It is well known that the causes of the modern mass urban riot are widely existant and that the spark is many times the only missing factor. Often the inciter is that necessary spark. The inciter is the actor who moved intentionally—he is the one who spoke, who encouraged and solicited. Many of the follower rioters were merely caught up in a mad hysteria becoming part of an unthinking crowd. Is not the inciter more guilty than those who did not think or intelligently choose to be in a riot?

In pondering over the state statutes listed above, it is questioned whether the strict penalties offered in them will act as sufficient deterrents to inciters. Is the solution to riots an inciting to riot statute with a 20 year penalty clause? The answer is probably NO but certainly the penalty should be proportionate with the crime and it does not seem equitable to hold a follower equally as guilty as his leader (the inciter).

Recently, the Minnesota legislature has chosen to repeal its inciting-to-riot statute, which had a higher penalty than did the statute covering simple riot, and has put the inciter and the rioter on the same punitive level saying: "Inherent in the concept of unlawful assembly or riot is the encouragement of and assistance to others. Additional punishment should not, therefore, be imposed on this ground."[51] Although riot and inciting to riot were equated under the Riot Act of 1714, both were treated as felonies and thus, even though inciting to riot seemed to be the more evil of the two offenses, it was punished with riot to the full extent of the law. Under the theory suggested by the Minnesota legislature, inciting to riot is to be treated on an equal level

---

49. GA. CODE ANN. § 26-904 (1953) states:

If any person shall bring, introduce, print, or circulate, or cause to be introduced, circulated, or printed, or aid or assist, or be in any manner instrumental in bringing, introducing, circulating, or printing within this State any paper, pamphlet, circular, or any writing, for the purpose of inciting insurrection, riot, conspiracy, or the resistance against lawful authority of the State, or against the lives of the inhabitants thereof, or any part of them . . . shall be sentenced in the State penitentiary for not less than 5 nor more than 20 years.

50. ILL. ANN. STAT. ch. 134, § 10 (Smith-Hurd 1961).

51. MINN. STAT. ANN. § 609.71 (1963); *see* Advisory Comm. Comment.

with riot, as a misdemeanor. This liberal attitude adopted by the Minnesota legislature does not constitute a trend in the law.

In the light of the 163 riots during the summer of 1967, with the experts predicting even a longer, hotter summer of 1968 and possibly even a winter riot season,[52] it would seem to be a necessary task for the various states to produce a definition of inciting to riot so that an act of inciting can readily be recognized by the police. It should be incumbent upon police departments to instruct its officers on exactly what length one may go before he is deemed to be an inciter. It is a relatively simple task to point out an inciter after a riot has already taken place, but in order to be most effective, the law must go to the immediate cause and it must swiftly exercise its arm of enforcement to bring an inciter to justice before he can cause the harm which he intends. It is not an easy task for an officer to determine whether a speech is inflammatory and, in fact, contains inciting statements. George M. Gelston, Adjutant General of the State of Maryland, said recently at the federal anti-riot bill hearings:

> Inciting a riot would seem to be one of the most difficult things to indict a man on. It is difficult for police officers to notice something dangerous is happening, to grab a speaker off the stand before he is finished, and the judge says, was there a riot? And he says, no, there was not. There was not a riot.[53]

Basically, the police officer must apply the Supreme Court's clear and present danger test. Although its terms sound deceptively simple, in practice it has been proven to be difficult of interpretation. As the Supreme Court in *Bridges v. California* has enumerated:

> What finally emerges from the "clear and present danger" cases is a working principle that the substantive evil must be extremely serious and the degree of imminence extremely high before utterances can be punished. Those cases do not purport to mark the furtherest most constitutional boundaries of protected expression, nor do we here. They do no more than recognize a minimum compulsion of the Bill of Rights. For the First Amendment does not speak equivocally. It prohibits any law "abridging the freedom of speech, or of the press." It must be taken as a command of the broadest scope that explicit language, read in the context of a liberty-loving society, will allow.[54]

52. *Hearings on H.R. 421 Before the Committee on the Judiciary*, 90th Cong., 1st Sess. 786-88 (1967), [hereinafter cited as 1967 Hearings]; *see also*, U.S. NEWS & WORLD REPORT 62 (Jan. 8, 1968).

53. 1967 Hearings 746.

54. 314 U.S. 252, 263 (1941).

In summarizing the court's stand on this problem, Mr. Justice Brandeis in *Whitney v. California* in his concurring opinion stated:

> This Court has not yet fixed the standard by which to determine when a danger shall be deemed clear; how remote the danger may be and yet be deemed present.[55]

Thus the question as to what is inciting to riot is an open one, subject to a shifting unsettled constitutional test which in practice is difficult to apply, especially by a layman.

A legislature in considering the passage of an inciting to riot statute thus must consider a three-fold problem. The statute must be broad enough to cover oral and written inflammatory statements; it must meet the clear and present danger test required by the interpretation of the first amendment; and it must be clear and precise enough to enable local enforcement agencies to enforce it effectively. Admitted, the third problem is a matter of police training and experience more than a legal problem. The reasons for enacting such riot legislation are obvious for such laws are necessary to enable the local enforcement agencies to quell a riot at its inception. Serving in some manner as a deterrent measure, they have the purpose of giving notice to rioters caught up in a mob hysteria that superior force will be used which could endanger their lives.[56] Further, riot provisions also provide the procedure by which higher authority may be called in to furnish assistance. Inciting to riot laws provide some means by which an inciter may be identified as such and also a legal process by which he may be stopped before his activities actually precipitate a riot.

---

55. 274 U.S. 357, 374 (1927). The Supreme Court has commented on the history and development of the "clear and present danger" test and expressed approval of the concurring opinions of Justice Holmes and Justice Brandeis in the *Whitney v. California* case. The court in *Dennis v. U.S.,* 341 U.S. 494 (1951), stated at page 507:

> In their concurrence they repeated that even though the legislature had designated certain speech as criminal, this could not prevent the defendant from showing that there was no danger that the substantive evil would be brought about.

56. The following is a representative list of statutes that require a command to disperse before the local officials can move in to quell a riot: ALA. CODE tit. 14, § 407(1) (1958); ARIZ. REV. STAT. ANN. § 13-634 (1956); CAL. PEN. CODE § 409 (West 1956); FLA. STAT. ANN. §870.04 (1965); IOWA CODE § 743.4 (1962); KAN. GEN. STAT. ANN. § 21-1002 (1963); ME. REV. STAT. ANN. ch. 136, § 9 (1964); MINN. STAT. ANN. § 609.715 (1963); MO. REV. STAT. § 542.150 (1959); MONT. REV. CODES ANN. § 94-35-5304 (1947); NEB. REV. STAT. § 28-804 (1943); N.H. REV. STAT. ANN. § 609-A:4 (Supp. 1965); N.J. STAT. ANN. § 2A:126-4 (1952); N.Y. PEN. LAW § 2093 (McKinney 1944); N.D. CENT. CODE § 12-19-08 (1960); OHIO REV. CODE ANN. § 3761.14 (Baldwin 1964); OKLA. STAT. tit. 21, § 1316 (1961); ORE. REV. STAT. § 145.020 (1960); PA. STAT. ANN. tit. 53, 16620 (1957); R.I. GEN. LAWS ANN. § 11-38-1 (1956); S.D. CODE § 34.0201-0202 (1939); TEX. PEN. CODE art. 8.04 (1948); UTAH CODE ANN. § 77-5-3 (1953); VT. STAT. ANN. tit. 13, § 901 (1959); V.I. CODE ANN. § 4021 (1967); VA. CODE ANN. § 18.1-247 (1960); W. VA. CODE ANN. § 15-1D-4 (1961). New Jersey and Rhode Island still require the magistrate or local official to read a prescribed "Riot Act" to the rioters before they move in to quell them. The script to be read resembles somewhat the famous English Riot Act of 1714.

A Model Provision

From the examination of the various state riot statutes, it appears that many states have retained the basic elements of the English Riot Act of 1714. A riot in 1967 is considerably different from a riot in 1714—the causes, probably, and certainly the size and scope have been altered by time. In contrast to a riot of the Eighteenth Century, today's riots can spread faster due to the modern advances in travel and communication making such a riot potentially more dangerous. Our rapidly exploding population makes it very possible that some day urban areas will stretch for hundreds of miles, running from state to state. Riots will not stop at the state borders and some interstate cooperation is required.

Because of these factors it would appear that some sort of uniformity among the various state riot statutes would be desirable. In the preparation of such uniform acts, the various legislatures should consider:

a) Definitions for riot, inciting to riot and aggravated riot.
b) Penalties for riot, inciting to riot and aggravated riot.
c) Provisions providing for an order to disperse and call for the aid of the citizenry.
d) Provisions prohibiting the interference with the police or national guard.
e) Provisions exempting enforcement officials for personal injuries caused in the performance of their duties in quelling a riot.
f) Provisions providing criminal liability for a mayor or other local official who is negligent or guilty of nonfeasance in the performance of his duty in quelling a riot.
g) Provisions granting immunity to witnesses so to aid in the prosecution of rioters.
h) Provisions enabling the mayors to proclaim a local curfew during a riot and to assume emergency powers.
i) Provisions enabling the governor to make reciprocal agreements with neighboring states to lend aid in suppressing a riot.
j) Provisions defining the conduct of the national guard in suppressing a riot.

Definitions for Riot, Aggravated Riot and Inciting To Riot

Probably it would be more efficient if the common law distinctions between unlawful assembly, rout, riot, and affray were replaced by the term "mob action."[57] The minimum number of persons requisite for a riot should be carefully considered in the light of the type of police force prevalent in the various towns in the particular state along with the adequacy of the state police. Probably most relevant would be the number of large urban areas in the state, for the recent riots seem to have had them as their center. Thus, the minimum number is better placed at two or three, for a violent seed may quickly spread in an urban area.

A state riot act should provide for crimes causing serious injury to person or property committed during the process of a riot. Such a provision could be termed "aggravated riot."[58] Such sections should contain clauses covering the wearing of disguises and the carrying of dangerous weapons.[59] An aggravated riot provision would enable the courts to entertain mass trials, saving much time and expense. Some of the existing state statutes in this area provide excellent language for a proposed aggravated riot statute.[60]

A broad definition of inciting to riot, such as that of Connecticut, would seem to be the most adequate in this area as it can cover almost any possible means by which a riot may be incited.[61] Because a broad definition should be given, the question as to whether to take action in certain cases must, of practical necessity, be left to the judgment of the local law enforcement officials.

Penalties for Riot, Inciting to Riot and Aggravated Riot

The great majority of jurisdictions make riot a misdemeanor with penalties ranging from 6 months to one year imprisonment and fines

57. ILL. ANN. STAT. ch. 38, § 25-1 (Smith-Hurd 1961); N.H. REV. STAT. ANN. § 609-A:1 (Supp. 1965), which reads:

609-A:1 Mob Action. Mob action consists of any of the following:

I. The use of force or violence disturbing the public peace by two or more persons acting together and without authority of law; or

II. The assembly of two or more persons to do an unlawful act; or

III. The assembly of two or more persons, without authority of law, for the purpose of doing violence to the person or property of any one supposed to have been guilty of a violation of the law, or for the purpose of exercising correctional powers or regulative powers over any person by violence.

58. *Supra* note 34; exemplar is that of New Hampshire, N.H. REV. STAT. ANN. § 609-A:3 (Supp. 1965):

Any participant in a mob action which shall by violence inflict injury to the person or property of another shall be fined not more than one thousand dollars, or imprisoned for not less than one nor more than three years, or both.

59. IND. ANN. STAT. § 10-1506 (1956) provides an example:

Riotous conspiracy. If three [3] or more persons shall unite for the purpose of doing any unlawful act in the nighttime, or for the purpose of doing any unlawful act while wearing white caps, masks or being otherwise disguised, they shall be deemed guilty of riotous conspiracy, and, on conviction, shall each be imprisoned in the state prison not less than two [2] years nor more than ten [10] years, and each be fined in any sum not exceeding two thousand dollars [$2000].

60. ALASKA STAT. § 11.45.010 (1962).

61. *Supra* note 46.

ranging from $500 to $1000.[62] The penalty for inciting to riot, however, should be more severe for the reasons listed earlier.[63] But it is also desirable to leave a good deal more room for discretion because of the very broad terms defining a riot. A boistrous beach party may fall into the category of a riot or mob action and certainly, in such a case, neither the inciter nor his followers have real punishable criminal intent.

As now existing, the penalties for aggravated riot are those for a felony.[64] Although there is an overlap with separate criminal offenses, it is desirable to have an aggravated riot provision in order to alleviate the prosecutor of much of his evidentiary burden against the individual offender and to enable him to make a mass charge against groups of people breaching the law as per a conspiracy statute. Still, sentences seem to reflect the fact that mass destruction of person and property is a most dangerous and serious threat to the life and safety of the community and that its commission should be punished severely. Some states provide for liability as a principle for both inciters and rioters for any offense committed during a riot.[65]

It may be argued that more severe penalties for riot, inciting to riot, and aggravated riot would serve as effective deterrent measures but Professor Jerome Hall has discounted the effectiveness of any such position:

> Recent German apologists of retroactivity ridiculed the notion that a lawbreaker is entitled to notice of the penalty he may incur. Although they wished to strike terror into the hearts of criminals, they argued that experience and observation amply demonstrate that penal laws do not deter, that it is a vestage of a rationalistic age to believe that the prospective offender will weigh the advantage of his crime against the evil of his punishment.[66]

It can be said on behalf of deterrence, however, that Jerome Hall may be primarily concerned with individual crime and not with the mass riot situation as experienced in Detroit. The individual criminal mind may not be deterred from crime by a strict penalty once that mind has initiated itself towards a goal. The mass mind, i.e. the mind

62. *See* Appendix A.

63. *Supra* note 22.

64. *Supra* note 30. The penalties range from one to fifteen years.

65. Typical of these statutes is that of New Hampshire, N.H. REV. STAT. ANN. § 609:8 (1955):

> Liability as Principal. Any person who shall promote, aid or encourage a riot or mob, or take any lead or direction of such mob, by word or act, or attempt to do so, or who shall be armed or disguised therein, shall be liable criminally as a principal for any crime or offense which may be committed by the mob, or any of them.

66. HALL, PRINCIPALS OF CRIMINAL LAW 30 (1960). *See also* MERCIER, CRIMINAL RESPONSIBILITY (1926).

of those involved in a riot, could seemingly be deterred from rioting by an announcement of the penalty for such action or, as often said, by a reading of the "Riot Act." Once the penalty was announced by an official, it would be very possible that the average man would join in a general dispersal and return peaceably to his home or business. However, such a penalty announcement would be totally useless if it was believed by the rioters that it was really not intended to be enforced and was really only a bluff.

Provisions Providing for an Order to Disperse and Call for Aid of the Citizenry

A state statutory provision should provide for the local officials to give the rioters an order of dispersal and a majority so do.[67] This type of provision acts to advise the rioters that they are acting in violation of the law and also operates to give them the opportunity to disperse peaceably without criminal liability. Such provisions allow for a "cooling off" period which, in many cases, would bring an end to the disturbance. It is not recommended, however, that a set formula be read to the rioters as is required in Rhode Island and New Jersey,[68] but that simply the information—that if dispersal is not forthcoming, those rioting will be arrested—be relayed by some mass media. Under such statutes, one who fails to disperse would be treated as a rioter and so charged.[69]

A state statute should contain a provision for a command to the citizenry to aid the local officials in the suppression of a riot. The basic purpose of such a provision is to insure the cooperation of citizens rather than to have them act as a supplement to the police force. Under this provision, those who would not cooperate could be charged either with riot or fined from $25 to $100.[70]

Provisions Prohibiting the Interference with the Police, Fire Department or National Guard

The 1967 summer riot in Detroit has given testimony to the fact that rioters assault firemen in the performance of their duties and that hospitals have been laid siege to and police and national guard fired upon. Such serious interference, of course, requires a criminal penalty. One of the few states that specifically includes such a provision in its riot laws is West Virginia, making it a felony to "assault, fire upon, or

---

67. *Supra* note 56.
68. *Id.*
69. *See* Appendix A.
70. *Supra* note 25.

throw any missile" at enforcement authorities quelling a riot or anyone assisting them such as the fire department or ambulance or hospital authorities.[71] Indeed, such a provision should find its place in a complete riot act.

Provisions Exempting Enforcement Officials for Personal Injuries Caused in the Performance of Their Duties in Quelling a Riot

Many states have provisions within their respective riot acts explicitly exempting enforcement officials and those assisting them from liability for the injuring or killing of rioters when their arresting efforts are resisted by rioters.[72] The basic reason behind such a provision, it seems, is to make it known to those who are suppressing a riot that they are not to be inhibited in the lawful execution of their duties. A typical statute of this type is that of New Jersey.[73]

Provisions Providing Criminal Liability for a Mayor or Other Local Official Who is Negligent or Guilty of Nonfeasance in the Performance of His Duties in Quelling a Riot

Some jurisdictions have provisions within their riot acts making it a misdemeanor for any mayor or other local official to neglect to attempt to quell a riot after having notice of its existence. These provisions put an affirmative duty upon the local official to proceed to the place of the riot, or as near thereto as he can safely go, in order that he attempt to

---

71. *Supra* note 35. The statute reads:

> Assaults on national guard or persons aiding it. It shall be unlawful for any person to assault, fire upon, or throw any missile at, against or upon any member or body of the national guard, or civil officer, or other person lawfully aiding them, when going to, returning from, or assembled for performing any duty under the provisions of this article; and any person so offending shall be guilty of a felony, and, on conviction, shall be imprisoned in the penitentiary for not less than two or more than five years.

72. The following is a representative list of state statutes which exempt state officials and those assisting them in the suppression of a riot from liability for the killing or injuring of one who is rioting: CONN. GEN. STAT. ANN. § 53-171 (1960); ME. REV. STAT. ANN. ch. 136, § 11 (1964); MASS. ANN. LAWS ch. 296, § 6 (Supp. 1966); MO. REV. STAT. § 559.040(3) (1959); NEB. REV. STAT. § 28-807 (1943); N.H. REV. STAT. ANN. § 609-A:4 (Supp. 1965); N.J. STAT. ANN. § 2A:126-6 (1952); OHIO REV. CODE ANN. § 3761.15 (Baldwin 1964); PA. STAT. ANN. tit. 53, § 16624 (1957); VA. STAT. ANN. tit. 13, § 904 (1959); V.I. CODE ANN. tit. 5, § 4023 (1967); VA. CODE ANN. § 18.1-251 (1960); WASH. REV. CODE § 9.48.160 (1956); W. VA. CODE ANN. 15-1D-5 (1961).

73. N.J. STAT. ANN. § 2A:126-6 (1952):

> Persons killing rioters held guiltless. If, in the dispersing, seizing or arresting of any persons so unlawfully, routously, riotously and tumultuously assembled, or in endeavoring to disperse, seize or arrest such persons, any of them are killed, hurt or wounded, by reason of resisting the persons endeavoring to disperse, seize or arrest them, then every such magistrate, sheriff, undersheriff, police officer or constable, and any person assisting them, or any of them, shall be held guiltless and be absolutely indemnified and discharged.

disperse the rioters.[74] Such provisions are to insure that a riot will be quelled even though the mayor is a member of or has leanings toward the rioting group. This kind of provision is a type of safety measure to protect that group under physical attack be it the majority or minority.

Provisions Granting Immunity to Witnesses so to Aid in the Prosecution of Rioters

A few states provide for the immunization of witnesses in riot prosecution when the witness himself was a rioter. Typical of such statutes, the New Hampshire provision states:

> Any person participating in a riot who shall be called by the state to testify as a witness upon the trial of any person for taking part therein, who shall testify in relation thereto, shall not be liable to prosecution for such participation.[75]

Obviously, such provisions constitute an important tool in the hands of the prosecutor which could alleviate much of his difficulties in obtaining evidence in a mass trial.

Provisions Enabling the Mayor to Proclaim a Local Curfew During a Riot and to Assume Emergency Powers

A few states have provisions providing for emergency powers to be assumed by the mayor or common council of first class cities during a time of civil unrest or riot. A Wisconsin statute provides the authority for the common council of a first class city to pass ordinances or resolutions declaring an emergency and to pass certain emergency orders to assist to bring the city under the control of lawful authority. The statute also provides that, in the absence of the common council, the mayor may assume the same emergency powers. It is a misdemeanor for anyone to disobey such a lawfully executed order.[76] Such a statute

---

74. MASS. ANN. LAWS ch. 269 § 3 (1956); MICH. COMP. LAWS § 750.524 (1948), MICH. STAT. ANN. § 28.792 (1962):

> Any mayor . . . having notice of any such riotous or tumultuous and unlawful assembly . . . who shall neglect or refuse immediately to proceed to the place of such assembly . . . or shall omit or neglect to exercise the authority with which he is invested by this chapter, for suppressing such riotous or unlawful assembly . . . shall be guilty of a misdemeanor, punishable by imprisonment in the county jail not more than six [6] months or a fine of not more than two hundred fifty [250] dollars.

75. N.H. REV. STAT. ANN. § 609:10 (1955), *also see* N.D. CENT. CODE 12-19-27 (1960).

76. WIS. STAT. ANN § 66.325 (1965) provides:

> Emergency powers, cities of the first class. (1) . . . the common council of any city of the first class is empowered to declare by ordinance or resolution, an emergency existing within such city whenever conditions rise by reason of . . . riot or civil commotion. . . .
>
> (2) . . . the common council may provide penalties for violation of any emergency ordinance or resolution, not to exceed the maximum penalty of $100 fine

proved to be very useful to the mayor of Milwaukee during that city's disturbance in the summer of 1967, by allowing him to order a 24 hour curfew. In many other states, such as Michigan, the governor is the only official authorized to issue such emergency orders.[77] Emergency powers, such as those for Michigan and Wisconsin, allow the issuing official to close businesses, restrict the sale and distribution of gasoline, and prohibit the sale of firearms. Again, this is a useful tool in the hands of the local officials to restrict the spread of a riot and, it would seem, that such a tool would best be placed and be most effective on the local level.[78]

Provisions Enabling the Governor to make Reciprocal Agreements with Neighboring States to Lend Aid in Suppressing a Riot

Although an Oregon statute authorizing its Governor to enter into agreements with other governors for mutual assistance in the enforcement of the criminal law was not intended to be a vehicle allowing the borrowing of troops to aid in the suppression of riots, there is no obvious reason why it cannot be so used.[79] At the very minimum, this provision could provide for reserve emergency fire protection for cities boardering on the state line. However such statutes constitute a study in themselves and are without the scope of this comment.

Provisions Defining the Conduct of the National Guard in Suppressing a Riot

A few states go beyond merely directing the national guard to use whatever force may be required in their discretion to quell a riot. These states provide that first every effort consistent with the preserva-

---

> or, in lieu of payment thereof, 6 months imprisonment for each separate offense.
>
> (3) In the event because of such emergency conditions the common council shall be unable to meet with promptness, the mayor or acting mayor of any city of the first class shall exercise by proclamation all of the powers herewith conferred upon the common council which within the discretion of the mayor are necessary and expedient for the purposes herein set forth. . . .

77. MICH. COMP. LAWS § 10.3 (1948), MICH. STAT. ANN. § 3.4 (1961).

78. *Supra* note 79. *See also* MO. REV. STAT. § 542.220 (1959) which gives the mayor or magistrate of any city the power to proclaim a curfew for minors when there is an apprehension that a riot will take place. It is suggested, however, that this power be extended by further statutory enactment.

79. ORE. REV. STAT. § 145.060 (1960) provides:

> Governor's power to enter into agreements with other states for crime prevention purposes. The Governor of Oregon may enter into agreements or compacts with the Governor of any or all the states of Washington, Idaho, California, and Nevada, each acting on behalf of his own state, in order to effectuate cooperative effort and mutual assistance in the prevention of crime in those states and in the enforcement of their respective criminal laws and policies.

tion of life must be used to induce or force the rioters to disperse before an attack can be made which will endanger the rioters' lives.[80] Provisions such as this one provide for a restraint upon the over-diligence of over-enthusiastic authorities by demanding the use of persuasion before force and should, therefore, be included in a state riot act.

CONCLUSION

Riot laws are *not* a solution to riots. They are useless unless enforced. That riots occur is indeed an unfortunate situation but it is more unfortunate that they are allowed to continue once started due to lack of preparedness or diligence on the part of local and state authorities. Once rioters are captured and the commotion is quelled, those who have broken the law should be punished and the law should be such that this is a feasible end, even when thousands find themselves charged with crimes at the same time and the courts are overcrowded.

Due to the pressures generated from the riots of the 1960's, riot law is emerging from its relatively static position into a phase of dynamic change and modification. With predictions being made that serious riots can be expected to be an annual event in many of our cities in the next ten to twenty years, it can be safely estimated that ever more pressure will be exerted upon the state legislatures to review the condition of their respective riot laws. But, again these laws are not the solution to riots:

> The peace of the people is a fundamental function of our democracy. When it becomes evident that the deliberate conduct of a person tends to disturb a great number of people to a breach of the peace, it becomes a duty to restrain such person and hold him accountable. In these days of stress and social unrest the law must effectively act to prevent rioting or mob activity.[81]

---

80. MONT. REV. CODES ANN. § 94-5311 (1947); N.D. CENT. CODE § 12-19-22 (1960) which provides:

> Officers must endeavor to disperse riot before endangering life. Every endeavor must be used, both by the magistrate and civil officer and by the officer commanding any troops, which can be made consistently with the preservation of life, to induce or force the rioters to disperse before an attack is made upon them by which their lives may be endangered.

81. Chicago v. Lambert, 47 Ill. App. 2d 151, 197 N.E.2d 448 (1964).

Appendix A

The Following Is A List Of The Maximum Criminal Penalties Attached To Simple Riot Or Failure To Disperse

State Citation	Time and/or	Fine
Ala. Code tit. 14, § 407 (1958).	6 mo.	—
Alaska Stat. § 11.45.010 (1962).	1 yr.	$500
Ariz. Rev. Stat. Ann. § 13-631 (1956).	2 yrs.	$2000
Ark. Stat. Ann. § 41-1402 (1947).	1 yr.	$500
Cal. Pen. Code § 405 (West 1956).	1 yr.	$1000
Colo. Rev. Stat. Ann. § 40-8-6 (1963).	6 mo.	$200
Conn. Gen. Stat. Ann. § 53-174 (1960).	6 mo.	$100
Del. Code Ann. tit. 11, § 361 (1953).	6 mo.	$200
D.C. Code Ann. § 22-1121 (Supp. 1967) [Disorderly].	90 da.	$250
Fla. Stat. Ann. § 870.01 (1965).	6 mo.	$500
Ga. Code Ann. § 26-5302 (1953).	Misdemeanor	
Hawaii Rev. Laws § 305-2 (1955).	2 yrs.	$1000
Hawaii Rev. Laws § 305-3 (1955) [Failure to disperse].	1 yr.	$500
Idaho Code Ann. § 18-6402 (1947).	6 mo.	$300
Ill. Ann. Stat. ch. 38, § 25-1(b) (Smith-Hurd 1961).	30 da.	$500
Ill. Ann. Stat. ch. 38, § 25-1(d) (Smith-Hurd 1961) [Failure to disperse].	1 yr.	$500
Ind. Ann. Stat. § 10-1505 (1956).	3 mo.	$500
Iowa Code § 743.1 (1962).	30 da.	$100
Kan. Gen. Stat. Ann. § 21-1001 (1963).	—	$200
Ky. Rev. Stat. § 437.010 (1962).	50 da.	$100
La. Rev. Stat. § 103A(7) (Supp. 1962) [Disturbing the Peace].	90 da.	$100
Me. Rev. Stat. Ann. ch. 136, § 6 (1964).	1 yr.	$500
Mass. Ann. Laws ch. 269, § 2 (Supp. 1966).	1 yr.	$500
Michigan, Common-Law	90 da.	$100
Minn. Stat. Ann. § 609.71 (1963).	1 yr.	$1000
Mo. Rev. Stat. § 562.160 (1959).	Misdemeanor	
Mont. Rev. Codes Ann. § 94-35-182 (1947).	2 yrs.	$2000
Neb. Rev. Stat. § 28-804 (1943).	3 mo.	$100
Nev. Rev. Stat. § 203.070 (1965).	6 mo.	$500
N.H. Rev. Stat. Ann. § 609-A:2 (Supp. 1965).	1 yr.	$500
N.J. Stat. Ann. § 2A:126-5 (1952).	3 yrs.	$1000
N.M. Stat. Ann. § 40A-20-4 (1952).	6 mo.	—
N.Y. Pen. Law § 2091 (McKinney 1944).	1 yr.	$250
North Carolina, Common Law	Misdemeanor	
N.D. Cent. Code § 12-19-04(5) (1960).	Misdemeanor	
Ohio Rev. Code Ann. § 3761.99(C) (Baldwin 1964).	30 da.	$500
Okla. Stat. tit. 21, § 1312 (1961).	Misdemeanor	
Ore. Rev. Stat. § 166.050(3) (1960).	1 yr.	$500
Pa. Stat. Ann. tit. 53, § 16620 (1957).	2 yrs.	—
R.I. Gen. Laws Ann. § 11-38-4 (1956).	1 yr.	$1000
S.C. Code Ann. § 16-113 (1962).	30 da.	$100
S.D. Code § 13.1404 (1939).	Misdemeanor	
Tex. Pen. Code art. 466 (1948).	1 yr.	$1000
Utah Code Ann. § 76-52-3 (1953).	2 yrs.	$1000
Vt. Stat. Ann. tit. 13, § 902 (1959).	6 mo.	$100
V.I. Code Ann. tit. 14, 1822 (1967).	1 yr.	$100
Va. Code Ann. § 18.1-252 (1960).	1 yr.	$500
Wash. Rev. Code § 9.27.050(3) (1956).	1 yr.	$1000
W. Va. Code Ann. § 61-6-6 (1961).	1 yr.	$500
Wis. Stat. Ann. § 947.06 (1965).	1 yr.	$500
Wyo. Stat. Ann. § 6-108 (1957).	3 mo.	$100

Appendix B

The Following Is A List Of States And Territories Showing The Minimum Number of Persons Necessary To Constitute A Riot

State Citation	Number of Persons
Ala. Code tit. 14, § 407 (1958).	(3) Riot
Alaska Stat. § 11.45.020 (1962).	(3) Riot
Ariz. Rev. Stat. Ann. § 13-631 (1956).	(2) Riot
Ark. Stat. Ann. § 41-1402 (1947).	(3) Riot
Cal. Pen. Code § 404 (West 1956).	(2) Riot
Colo. Rev. Stat. Ann. § 40-8-6 (1963).	(2) Riot
Conn. Gen. Stat. Ann. § 53-169 (1960).	(3) Riot
Del. Code Ann. tit. 11, § 361 (1953).	(3) Riot
Fla. Stat. Ann. § 870.02 (1965).	(3) Riot
Ga. Code Ann. § 26-5302 (1953).	(2) Riot
Hawaii Rev. Laws § 305-1 (1955).	(6) Riot
Idaho Code Ann. § 18-6401 (1947).	(2) Riot
Ill. Ann. Stat. ch. 38, § 25-1 (Smith-Hurd 1961).	(2) Mob Action
Ind. Ann. Stat. § 10-1505 (1956).	(3) Riot
Iowa Code §§ 743.2, 743.4 (1962).	(3) Riot
Kan. Gen. Stat. Ann. § 21-1001 (1963).	(3) Unlawful Assembly
Ky. Practice & Forms, pt. 4, tit. X, ch. 1, § 375 (Russell, 1960).	(20) Riot
La. Rev. Stat. §§ 103, 103.1 (Supp. 1962).	Breach of the Peace
Me. Rev. Stat. Ann. ch. 136, § 6 (1964).	(3) Riot
Maryland, Common-Law	(3) Riot
Mass. Ann. Laws ch. 269, § 1 (Supp. 1966).	(5) armed, (10) unarmed unlawful assembly
Mich. Comp. Laws § 750.521 (1948).	(12) armed, (30) unarmed
Minn. Stat. Ann. § 609.71 (1963).	(3) Riot
Mississippi, Common-Law	(3) Riot
Mo. Rev. Stat. § 562.160 (1959).	(12) armed, (30) unarmed
Mont. Rev. Codes Ann. § 94-35-181 (1947).	(2) Riot
Neb. Rev. Stat. § 28-804 (1943).	(3) Riot
Nev. Rev. Stat. § 203.070 (1965).	(2) Riot
N.H. Rev. Stat. Ann. § 609-A:1 (Supp. 1965).	(2) Mob Action
N.J. Stat. Ann. § 2A:126-1 (1952).	(5) Mob
N.M. Stat. Ann. § 40A-20-4 (1952).	(3) Unlawful Assembly
N.Y. Pen. Law § 2090 (McKinney 1944).	(3) Riot
North Carolina, Common-Law	(3) Riot
N.D. Cent. Code § 12-19-03 (1960).	(6) Riot
Ohio Rev. Code Ann. §§ 3761.13, .14 (Baldwin 1964).	(3) Riot
Okla. Stat. tit. 21, § 1311 (1961).	(3) Riot
Ore. Rev. Stat. §§ 145.020, 166.040 (1960).	(3) Unlawful assembly
Pa. Stat. Ann. tit. 53, § 16620 (1957).	(12) Riotous assembly
R.I. Gen. Laws Ann. § 11-38-1 (1956).	(12) armed, (30) unarmed riotous assembly
South Carolina, Common-Law	(3) Riot
S.D. Code § 13.1402 (1939).	(3) Riot
Tenn., Common-Law	(3) Riot
Tex. Pen. Code art. 439 (1948).	(3) Unlawful assembly
Utah Code Ann. § 76-52-2 (1953).	(2) Riot
Vt. Stat. Ann. tit. 13, § 902 (1959).	(3) Riot
V.I. Code Ann. tit. 14, § 1821 (1967).	(3) Riot
Virginia, Common-Law	(3) Riot
Wash. Rev. Code § 9.27.040 (1956).	(3) Riot
W. Virginia, Common-Law	(3) Riot
Wis. Stat. Ann. § 947.06 (1965).	(3) Unlawful assembly
Wyo. Stat. Ann. § 6-108 (1957).	(3) Riot

Riots, Congress and Interstate Commerce:

The History of the Commerce Clause and Its Relation to the Cramer Amendment

KENNETH IRA SOLOMON* AND STEPHEN R. YATES**

PROPOSED FEDERAL ANTI-RIOT LEGISLATION

Legislative "History" of the Cramer Amendment

ON August 8, 1966 Representative Cramer of Florida introduced an amendment to Title Five of the Civil Rights Act of 1966.[1] The Cramer Amendment[2] was proposed during a summer of violent racial disturbances. Major ghetto violence had occurred in Chicago and Cleveland, and there were minor disturbances in many other cities. These riots obviously weighed heavily on the minds of the congressmen. There was substantial evidence of a growing "white backlash" and the elections were fast approaching. The purpose of the Cramer Amendment was to provide federal penalties for those who actively took part in the riots or helped to instigate the disturbances.

The legislative history of the Cramer Amendment is clear. Congressional intent was most directly stated by Representative Cramer himself:

> Mr. Chairman, fires, looting, vandalism, violence, and death —these have become the bywords of the American summer. Sections of this country's great cities have been turned into battlefields. Numerous individuals, many of them innocent bystanders, have lost their lives and their fortunes as a result.
>
> With these events in mind, I am proposing an amendment which would make it a Federal offense to use interstate commerce with the intent of inciting riots and other forms of violent disturbance and violent civil disobedience.

---

* B.S., C.P.A. 1963, M.A. 1964, University Illinois; J.D. 1967 University Chicago; Assistant Professor of Law, Case Western Reserve University.

** B.A. 1964, J.D. 1967 University of Chicago; Clerk to Judge Henry Burman, Illinois Appellate Court.

1. Section 502, H.R. 14765, 89th. Congress, 2d Session.

2. *Protection of Rights*

Section 502. Whoever moves or travels in interstate or foreign commerce or uses any facility in interstate or foreign commerce, including the mail, with intent to—
(1) incite, promote, encourage, or carry on, or facilitate the incitement, promotion, encouragement, or carrying on of, a riot or another violent civil disturbance; or
(2) commit any crime of violence, arson, bombing, or other act which is a felony or high misdemeanor under Federal or State law, in furtherance of, or during commission of, any act specified in paragraph (1); or
(3) assist, encourage, or instruct any person to commit or perform any act specified in paragraphs (1), (2), and (3), shall be fined not more than ten thousand dollars or imprisoned not more than five years, or both.

> This amendment is the result of evidence which supports the contention that this violence is the work, in part, of well-trained outside agitators who come into these communities for the express purpose of inciting violent civil disobedience.[3]

Representative Edwards of Alabama had a somewhat more extreme view of the evil which the amendment was intended to alleviate:

> Mr. Chairman, I support the Cramer amendment. It gets at the individual action of those who would travel across State lines for the purpose of stirring up civil disobedience . . . . Unfortunately, over the last few years, many of us from the South have asked for help as the hordes descended upon us crying for civil rights, but leaving violence in their wake. At any rate it took riots in the big northern cities before the people of this nation finally woke up to the fact that what we had been saying all along was really true; that there are those who travel from State to State stirring up trouble; that there are those who use the mails and the telephone lines of this country to incite people in troubled areas; that Communists are involved in these riots.[4]

On the other hand, Representative Edwards of California expressed a different view as to the appropriateness of the amendment:

> I say that it is wrong to include in this bill a new Federal law concerning riot control in our cities. The matter of law and order and keeping of the public peace in our cities has always been traditionally a matter of local control.[5]

Representative Corman of California agreed with Edwards as to the inadvisability of Congress legislating over areas traditionally of local concern:

> I do not believe it is proper for the Federal Government to assume responsibility for criminal law which is entirely intrastate when there is not a shred of evidence any one of the 50 states has had a breakdown of law and order or that there has been a reluctance on the part of the states to enforce laws against this condition.[6]

The Cramer Amendment passed the House on August 9, 1966, by a vote of 389 to 25. However, the Senate failed to act on the Civil Rights Bill or the Cramer Amendment. Representative Cramer has resubmitted the amendment in bill form to the first session of the

3. 112 CONG. REC. 17652 (remarks of Rep. Cramer).
4. *Id.* at 17654 (remarks of Rep. Edwards).
5. *Id.* at 17659 (remarks of Rep. Edwards).
6. *Id.* at 17669 (remarks of Rep. Corman).

90th Congress. The bill, HR 421, was passed by the House and Senate Judiciary Committee. Hearings have been held on the bill.[7]

Obviously, the purpose of the Cramer Amendment is to punish those who incite riots and participate in them. However, as pointed out by Representatives Corman and Edwards, control of breaches of the peace has traditionally been the concern of the states through the exercise of their police power. Congress is limited in the subjects over which it may legislate by the enumeration of powers in the Constitution. "General police power" is not one of the enumerated powers possessed by Congress;[8] therefore, it would *prima facie* appear that Congress possesses no power to prohibit by criminal sanction activity already dealt with by the states through the exercise of their police powers.

Relevance of the Commerce Clause

The preceding argumentative impression, though perhaps logically sound, does not take into account Supreme Court interpretation of congressional power and implied power under the commerce clause of the Constitution. It is the purpose of this article to investigate the scope of congressional power under the commerce clause within the context of a federal anti-riot bill. This, in turn, requires an analysis and investigation of Supreme Court decisions concerning congressional power to regulate commerce, because congressional power can only go so far and touch only as much regulatory subject matter as the Supreme Court finds "necessary and proper."

The Cramer Amendment provides the focus for our study of the commerce power and we are starting our inquiry where, as some may argue, it should end—with the presumptive conclusion that there exists no legitimate legal theory available to the Supreme Court for the purpose of restraining congressional exercise of its power under the commerce clause, as long as Congress is willing to comply with certain arid formalities in drafting legislation. It seems that this paucity of legal theory, in an area where control is necessary in the interests of both federalism and individual rights, is the result of a complete surrender by the Court to political pressures culminating in the "court-packing plan" when less than complete surrender was necessary.[9]

---

7. *Hearings Before the Committee on the Judiciary of the Senate*, 90th Cong., 1st Sess. (1967).

8. U.S. CONST. art. I, § 8.

9. President Roosevelt's much publicized attempt to "pack" the Supreme Court involved his proposal to the Senate in February of 1937 for court reform which the Judiciary Committee eventually rejected after almost 5 months of hearings. [SEN. REP. No. 711, 75th

The Social Need

We must leave to the sociologists and psychologists the study of the actuating motivational spark which touches off racial rioting and corresponding community unrest and civil turmoil. This group of analysts represents the proper expertise segment of our society for determining whether federal anti-riot incitement legislation is an effective means for preventing future racial violence. Legal scholars cannot, of course, close their eyes to the social inequities perpetrated upon the American Negro, overtly in the South and in a more subtle manner in the Northern ghettoes. Likewise, the perverse combination of "white guilt" and lower class ethnic white resentment of Negro "intrusion" into previously "lily-white" job markets and neighborhoods cannot be ignored in any examination of federal legislation which would propose to severely punish those who travel from state to state for the purpose of inciting riotous activity. Despite our apparent disclaimer earlier in this paragraph, we have reached certain conclusions regarding the wisdom (or lack thereof) of anti-riot legislation, federal or state. Such legislation may be subject to attack as useless surplusage since it is the eventual manifestations and consequences of riots—fires, looting, vandalism and serious bodily harm to innocent parties—which the legislature would seek to curb, yet in the face of the existence of *specific* criminal sanctions providing punitive measures for such *specific* acts of criminal violence.

Further, a broad anti-riot legislative enactment would open up a wide avenue of manipulative possibilities to the police by conveying an ability to discriminate through selective enforcement. For example, such a criminal sanction would permit one individual among many to be arbitrarily singled out by the law enforcement officials "as an example," resulting in great harm to the specific individual flowing from the overly-broad police discretion.

Both the deterrent effect and the sociological and psychological impact at the present time of such legislation on the Negro segment of the population are matters which cannot, and must not, be over-

Cong., 1st Sess. (1937)]. The proposal, in essence, provided that for any judge, who has sat on any federal court for at least ten years and attains age seventy and does not resign or retire within six months thereafter, the President should appoint one additional judge to Cong., 1st Sess. (1937)]. The proposal, in essence, provided that for any judge, who has sat the court on which the septuagenarian sits. The proposal set fifteen members as the maximum for the Supreme Court. It is interesting to note that at the time six of the justices were over seventy years of age: Brandeis (81), Butler (71), Hughes (75), Sutherland (75), and Van Devanter (78). *See* JACKSON, THE STRUGGLE FOR JUDICIAL SUPREMACY (1941); BURNS, ROOSEVELT: THE LION AND THE FOX ch. 15 (1956). Although the attempt by Roosevelt to appoint his own ideology to the Court failed, its impact on the character of the Court's subsequent commerce clause decisions is indisputable. *See*, Frankfurter, *Mr. Justice Roberts*, 104 U. PA. L. REV. 311 (1955).

looked. It is quite probable that the enactment of anti-riot legislation may have what we choose to call a "reverse backlash" effect. The promulgation of such legislation, at the present time, might easily be interpreted by a vast segment of the Negro community as a reflection of legislative abdication or "opting out" from the subsumed responsibility for the betterment of social conditions, with a concomitant loss of confidence by that group of citizenry in its Federal or State legislature.[10] In other words, such a legislative enactment could easily be viewed as a legislative failure to seek solutions and make inroads into remedies for the social and economic ills which cause and precipitate riots. We submit that a cancer is cured by the elimination of its *cause* at the very root of the matter—the social cancer which precipitates riots and civil turmoil will not be eliminated by the enactment of anti-riot legislation. We venture to say that such legislation will not even have a significant deterrent effect on riots themselves.

The Constitutionality of the Cramer Amendment

The Cramer Amendment would probably be sustained against constitutional objections. The only objections which could possibly

---

10. This "reverse backlash" effect was defined and analyzed by Kenneth I. Solomon in testimony before the Ohio House of Representatives' Judiciary Committee on November 17, 1967. The following account of these events appeared in the Cleveland Press, Nov. 18, 1967, p. 3, Enforce Present Laws, Anti-Riot Hearing Told:

> Cleveland Negroes want stricter enforcement of laws already on the books rather than a new set of anti-riot legislation.
>
> That's the message six Negro leaders want delivered to Columbus by the House Judicial Committee which is studying riots in Ohio.
>
> Kenneth Solomon, an assistant professor at the Case Western Reserve University Law School, told committee members in a one-day hearing at Lakeside Courthouse yesterday that a "broad-based anti-riot bill could start a reverse backlash" among Negroes here. "I think the feeling in the Negro community would be: 'Oh, boy, they can't solve the real problems, but they sure can pass an anti-riot bill."

Evidence of what the authors label a "reverse backlash" effect of anti-riot legislation further comes from the testimony of Miss Carol Gibbons, a New York City Welfare Department caseworker, before the United States Senate Judiciary Committee on Wednesday, August 23, 1967:

> Personally, I do not believe that the anti-riot legislation that you are now considering is the kind of legislation that will prevent these riots.
>
> I believe that it is basically repressive, and therefore will be very ineffective.
>
> I think it will further simply convince people that the American society does not really care about them, and that it is not willing to attempt to solve their problems, because this doesn't deal with them in any way at all.
>
> Riots in American Negro ghettos are not caused by a few men. They are caused by problems that are very, very deep seated. And if you want to stop the riots, you have to deal with these causes.
>
> * * *
>
> I think that if you really want to stop riots, you have to begin with an attack on the causes, and you have to do it, as I said previously, basically just with a commitment. You have to convince the American Negroes in this country that they are truly regarded as human beings, that their problems are understood by the society at large, that the society wants to change them, and that if they are to be responsible citizens of America, America also has a responsibility to them, and it is quite a responsibility of giving them not a partial and a piecemeal equality, but a very full and complete equality. *Hearings Before the Committee on the Judiciary, United States Senate*, 90th Congress, 1st Sess.; H.R. 421, Pt. 2, p. 709.

be sustained would be those of a first amendment or fifth amendment due process[11] nature concerning over-breadth and vagueness resulting from the "advocacy," "incitement," and "instruct" language of the amendment. However, these objections are beyond the scope of our study. It is significant to note in considering the constitutionality of the amendment that its constitutionality was not questioned in the rather lengthy debate on the floor of the House in so far as congressional power under the commerce clause was concerned. Indeed, the amendment is patterned after 18 U.S.C. § 1952,[12] which was constitutionally sustained in *United States v. Zizzo.*[13]

The question, therefore, is not whether the Cramer Amendment would be sustained as a valid exercise of the commerce power, but rather why there is such a dearth of legal theory which might have been advanced to attack the validity of the amendment. The answer to this query necessitates a study of the abdication by the Supreme Court of its duty to review the validity of legislation supposedly enacted under the commerce power. During the course of this article we shall attempt to analyze the reasons for this abdication and offer suggestions as to how it might have been avoided so that the constitutional relationship between state and national government could have been maintained.

---

11. *See, e.g.,* Abrams v. United States, 250 U.S. 616 (1919), upholding the Espionage Act of 1917, as amended in 1918 ("intended to incite, provoke and encourage resistance to the United States"); and, Dennis v. United States, 341 U.S. 494 (1951), sustaining the constitutional validity of the Smith Act against a first amendment attack and a fifth amendment challenge based upon "vagueness and indefiniteness."

Of even more modern vintage, note carefully the language in Edwards v. South Carolina, 372 U.S. 229 (1963); Note, *Due Process Requirements of Definiteness in Statutes,* 62 HARV. L. REV. 77 (1948); and Amsterdam, *The Void for Vagueness Doctrine in the Supreme Court,* 109 U. PA. L. REV. 67 (1960).

12. 18 U.S.C. 1952, (enacted September 13, 1961), reads as follows:

§ 1952. Interstate and foreign travel or transportation in aid of racketeering enterprises.

(a) Whoever travels in interstate or foreign commerce or uses any facility in interstate or foreign commerce, including the mail with intent to—

(1) distribute the proceeds of any unlawful activity; or

(2) commit any crime of violence to further any unlawful activity; or

(3) otherwise promote, manage, establish, carry on, or facilitate the promotion, management, establishment, or carrying on, of any unlawful activity,

and thereafter performs or attempts to perform any of the acts specified in subparagraphs (1), (2), and (3), shall be fined not more than $10,000 or imprisoned for not more than five years, or both.

(b) As used in this section "unlawful activity" means (1) any business enterprise involving gambling, liquor on which the Federal excise tax has not been paid, narcotics, or prostitution offenses in violation of the laws of the State in which they are committed or of the United States, or (2) extortion or bribery in violation of the laws of the State in which committed or of the United States.

(c) Investigations of violations under this section involving liquor or narcotics shall be conducted under the supervision of the Secretary of the Treasury.

13. 338 F.2d 577 (7th Cir. 1964), *cert. denied,* 381 U.S. 915 (1965).

The Scope of the Commerce Power

Climate of the Convention

At the Constitutional Convention there was little debate over the scope of the commerce power. However, certain conclusions about the Framers' intent may be drawn by indirection. The commerce clause was the only enumerated power developed at the Convention by which Congress was given any broad powers over commercial activities.[14] The use of the term "commerce" probably denotes only economic transactions. According to the dictionaries of that time, commerce primarily denoted trade, traffic, buying and selling, or the exchange of goods, and the movement of goods was only one of its connotations.[15] Indeed, it would seem that the Convention was concerned primarily with one problem, *viz.*, rivalry among states for economic predominance. When the Framers considered the need for regulating "commerce with foreign nations and among the several states," they were thinking only in terms of the national control of trade with the European countries and the removal of barriers obstructing the physical movements of goods across state lines.[16]

Early Judicial Interpretations

The most significant interpretation of congressional power under the commerce clause reasonably contemporaneous with the tenor of the Convention was that of Chief Justice Marshall in *Gibbons v. Ogden*.[17] In the course of his opinion, Justice Marshall dealt specifically with the problem of defining the three aspects of the commerce clause that provide the pivotal key to all subsequent commerce clause litigation. Those three aspects, essentially terminological, are: the meaning of "commerce"; "among the several states"; and "regulation."

In *Gibbons*, the specific problem before the Court was the question whether navigation is comprehended within "commerce." The Court decided that it was. Of greater significance, however, was Marshall's dicta concerning the objects that were subsumed within congressional powers of regulation:

> Commerce, undoubtedly, is traffic, but it is something more: it is intercourse. It describes the commercial intercourse between nations, and parts of nations, in all its branches, and is

---

14. Stern, *Which Concerns More States Than One*, 47 Harv. L. Rev. 1335 (1934).

15. *Id.* at 1346, citing The American Encyclopedia (1798), Samuel Johnson's Dictionary (6th ed. 1785), and Perry's Royal Standard Dictionary (4th Am. ed. 1796).

16. Stern, *supra* note 14, at 1344, there citing Hamilton, Jay, Madison, The Federalist nos. VII, IX, XLII, and 3 Elliott's Debates 260.

17. U.S. (9 Wheat.) 1 (1824).

> regulated by prescribing rules for carrying on that intercourse.[18]

This definition by a Chief Justice who had himself been a member of the Virginia Ratifying Convention is important for what it does not say. While stating that the commerce power is an economic one dealing with commercial intercourse, the opinion does not state that any kind of social and basically non-economic activities are to be included within the scope of the power. It would seem, therefore, that the original conception of these activities to be subsumed within the meaning of "commerce" were strictly economic transactions and events. Endless searching by the writers, at least, has failed to uncover even one source contemporary with the Constitutional Convention that would indicate otherwise.[19]

The next question dealt with was one of federalism: which activities occurring exclusively within the boundaries of a state could be reached by the federal commerce power? Completely internal commerce was excluded from congressional regulation.[20] However, activities exclusively intrastate could be regulated if they affected other states. Unfortunately, the scope of the crucial term "affecting" was not defined.[21]

Finally, the Court dealt with the scope of the power to regulate, assuming that the activity to be regulated had already been determined to be an article of commerce which in some as yet undefined manner "affected" interstate commerce. The power to regulate, that is, the means to be applied to enforce the regulatory power, was found to be "complete in itself, may be exercised to its utmost extent, and acknowledges no limitations, other than are prescribed by the Constitution."[22] Justice Marshall, in comparing the power to regulate com-

---

18. *Id.* at 84-5.

19. Our inability to resurrect any non-economic interpretation of "commerce" is not surprising in light of the view of semantics experts contemporary with the period and has plagued other legal scholars as well, As evidence of the former, see Samuel Johnson's definition of "commerce" in SAMUEL JOHNSON'S DICTIONARY (6th ed. 1785), and 3 ELLIOTT'S DEBATES 260. As for the latter assertion, carefully examine Stern, *supra* note 14, at 1344; STORY, COMMENTARIES ON THE CONSTITUTION (4th ed. 1873); and 1 CROSSKEY, POLITICS AND THE CONSTITUTION, ch. 8 (1953).

20. Gibbons, *supra* note 17 at 85, where Chief Justice Marshall stated: "The completely internal commerce of a State, then, may be considered as reserved for the State itself."

21. *Id.* at 86, where Marshall only peripherally attempted to enunciate an "affectation" theory in the following manner:

> The genius and character of the whole government seem to be, that its action is to be applied to all the external concerns of the nation, and to those internal concerns which affect the states generally; but not to those which are completely within a particular state, which do not affect other states, and with which it is not necessary to interfere, for the purpose of executing some of the general powers of the government.

22. Gibbons, *supra* note 17 at 86.

merce to other congressional powers, stated that all such powers were governed by the same general rules. He also made clear that though the commerce power is "plenary," the means to implement it would be subjected to the same scrutiny as the means to implement any other enumerated power. "Limitations . . . prescribed by the Constitution" certainly included the necessary and proper clause and "pretext" limitations that had already been formulated and articulated in *McCulloch v. Maryland,*[23] along with those implicit in due process and the tenth amendment.

The Lottery Case and Its Dangerous Precedent

The most significant Supreme Court decision bearing upon the Cramer Amendment is the *Lottery Case,*[24] which established plenary congressional police power over commerce. The case questioned the constitutionality of the Federal Lottery Act of 1895 which prohibited importing, mailing, or transporting lottery tickets from one state to another. In a 5-to-4 decision the Supreme Court opined that "lottery tickets are subjects of traffic and therefore are subjects of commerce, and the regulation of the carriage of such tickets from State to State, at least by independent carriers, is a regulation of commerce among the several states."[25] Relying on the necessary and proper clause, the Court held that prohibition of an article from commerce was an "appropriate" method of regulating commerce in that article. The Court justified this viewpoint by asserting that lotteries were "confessedly injurious to the public morals." In essence, the Court decided that congressional authority over commerce had the same attributes of sovereignty as a state's authority through its police power over its own internal concerns (such as public health, safety, morals, and general welfare). Congress was effectively held to be akin to a state legislature with respect to its enumerated power to regulate commerce. The Court, however, overlooked the fact that a state government exercises its authority over its citizens through the police power ostensibly, at least, with the consent of the governed, whereas congressional control over commerce is a plenary power not subject (except in an indirect way) to political controls but only to whatever controls the Constitution itself exercises over all of the enu-

---

23. U.S. (4 Wheat.) 316 (1819). Chief Justice Marshall enunciated the famous "pretext" argument, in the following manner:

> . . . or should Congress, under the pretext of executing its powers, pass laws for the accomplishment of objects not entrusted to the government; it would be the painful duty of this tribunal, should a case requiring such a decision come before it, to say that such an act was not the law of the land.

24. Champion v. Ames, 188 U.S. 321 (1903).
25. *Id.* at 354.

merated powers. Congressional control over commerce is, in substance, autocratic, not democratic. The danger of equating a state's control over its citizens through the police power with congressional control over activities in interstate commerce through its commerce power is that the political and constitutional structure of the two sovereignties is different.

The *Lottery Case* Court felt that there were some controls and limitations upon Congress in its use of the "police power" over commerce to protect commerce from pollution,[26] even though the Court earlier in its opinion,[27] had already sanctioned exclusions from commerce based solely on the moral judgment of Congress. This conclusion, of course, is the same as that made by Justice Marshall in *Gibbons*. The Court also relied on Marshall's statement that the plenary nature of the power to regulate was subject only to political controls. However, it failed to point out that Justice Marshall was referring to the regulation of *economic* affairs and *economic* judgments by Congress solely with respect to interstate *economic* activities. Justice Marshall was not referring to *moral* judgments about *social* activities related tangentially, at best, to interstate commerce. It would seem that Marshall was referring to an "economic police power," not to a broadly-based social or socio-economic police power.

The dissent in the *Lottery Case* accurately called attention to the inconsistencies in the majority opinion. The dissenters pointed out that the suppression of lotteries was a problem for the states under the police power.[28] It was further noted by the dissenters that though prohibiting transportation to all lotteries would be an effective method of regulating lotteries or enforcing a general police power, they felt that this was not an appropriate way of utilizing the commerce power.[29] Congress had not been given general police power by the Constitution, and to sustain the Lottery Act would be tantamount to permitting Congress to attain objects not entrusted to it by the Constitution in violation of the tenth amendment.[30]

The dissent pointed out that the Act could be sustained only if:

---

26. *Id.* at 356, where the Court did qualify, to some extent, its recognition of congressional "police power," as follows: "We may, however, repeat, in this connection, what the court has heretofore said, that the power of Congress to regulate Commerce among the states, although plenary, cannot be deemed arbitrary, since it is subject to such limitations or restrictions as are prescribed by the Constitution."

27. *Id.* at 355.

28. Fuller, C. J., dissenting, *Id.* at 364-6.

29. *Id.*

30. The tenth amendment declares: "The powers not delegated to the United States by the Constitution, nor prohibited by it to the States, are reserved to the States respectively, or to the people." U.S. CONST. amend. 10.

1.) the lottery tickets were articles of commerce, and 2.) if Congress could prohibit the transportation of anything or anybody in interstate commerce.

Since the ticket itself was not an article of commerce, as conceded by even the majority, the dissenters properly asked how the shipment of a non-commercial article across state lines could "transform" that article into one of interstate commerce, and thereby render it subject to regulation. Chief Justice Fuller ably pointed to the dangerous expanse of the majority's open-ended commerce clause "police power":

> An invitation to dine, or to take a drive, or a note of introduction, all become articles of commerce under the ruling in this case, by being deposited with an express company for transportation. This in effect breaks down all the differences between that which is, and that which is not an article of commerce, and the necessary consequence is to take from the states all jurisdiction over the subject so far as interstate communication is concerned.[31]

The dissent went on to state that no matter how great a local problem lotteries might represent, neither the Court nor Congress could "ease the shoe where it pinches."[32] Congress was not executing one of its granted powers, it was only operating under the "pretext" of doing so. They distinguished Congressional legislation that had previously been upheld to prohibit the transportation of diseased animals and infected goods by the railroads: "for they [diseased or infected commodities] would be in themselves injurious to the transaction of interstate commerce, and moreover, are essentially commercial in their nature."[33] The dissent hypothesizes as an assumed impermissible exercise of the commerce power that a person could not be excluded from commerce just because he was going from one state to another to engage in the lottery business.[34] Ironically, in view of the Cramer Amendment, the day when such exclusion is possible may certainly be at hand.[35]

The *Lottery Case* dissent is based upon principles of constitutional interpretation basic in any case involving the questioning of congressional action under its enumerated powers. The basic question in all such cases must, of necessity, be whether congressional regulation has been appropriately exercised within the purview of substantive con-

31. The Lottery Case, *supra* note 24 at 371.
32. *Id.* at 372.
33. *Id.* at 374.
34. *Id.*
35. And indeed may have been reached long ago with the enactment of the Mann Act. See text accompanying notes 43-47.

gressional power; this is an inquiry, in turn, which involves the scope of the necessary and proper clause.[36] A corollary to this inquiry must be whether or not Congress has passed a law for "objects entrusted to the government" by the Constitution, which requires an examination of congressional motive or purpose.

In addition to these related principles of constitutional adjudication, the *Lottery Case* dissenters dealt specifically with the scope of congressional power under the commerce clause. Most importantly for purposes of this study, that opinion draws a necessary line around what might be called the "police power" of Congress over commerce; *i.e.*, the power of Congress to protect the facilities of commerce themselves from injury. The dissent limits the protection of commerce from those injuries which might fairly be considered economic or those of a directly ascertainable physical nature. Diseased animals and goods may be excluded for they would be injurious in themselves to transactions in interstate commerce, and are *commercial* in nature. An attempt was made to draw a line past which the commercial police power of Congress could not go. In other words, Congress could protect commerce from harmful *economic* transactions involving more states than one, but the protection extended only to those activities harmful in an economic sense.[37] It seems to these observers that this was a line that should have been drawn, and the failure to draw it in the *Lottery Case* accounts for the failure of the Court today to draw any meaningful restrictions on congressional power to reach any and all activities related in any way, shape or form to interstate commerce. Today, indeed, Congress possesses police power like any state,[38] in spite of the fact that

---

36. U.S. CONST. Art. I § 8: [T]o make all Laws which shall be necessary and proper for carrying into Execution the foregoing Powers, and all other Powers vested by this Constitution in the Government of the United States, or in any Department or Officer thereof."

37. Examine United States v. E. C. Knight Company, 156 U.S. 1, 13 (1895), where the Court, per Chief Justice Fuller, stated:

> It is vital that the independence of the commercial power and of the police power, and the delimitation between them, however sometimes perplexing, should always be recognized and observed, for while the one furnishes the strongest bond of union, the other is essential to the preservation of the autonomy of the States as required by our dual form of government; and acknowledged evils, however grave and urgent they may appear to be, had better be borne, than the risk be run, in the effort to suppress them, of more serious consequences by resort to expedients of even doubtful constitutionality. It will be perceived how far reaching the proposition is that the power of dealing with a monopoly directly may be exercised by the General Government whenever interstate or international commerce may be ultimately affected. The regulation of commerce applies to the subjects of commerce and not to matters of internal police.

38. To illustrate the scope and ubiquity of congressional "police power" under the commerce clause, examine Kentucky Whip and Collar Co. v. Illinois Central R. Co., 299 U.S. 334 (1934), sustaining the validity of the Ashurst-Sumners Act which prohibited the transportation of convict-made goods into States whose laws restricted trade in such goods; Gooch v. United States, 297 U.S. 124 (1936), The Federal Kidnapping Act; Hermans

the sovereignty of a state exercised through its police power and the ability of Congress to devise reasonable means to carry out its enumerated powers are not the same processes, be the measuring stick constitutional or political.

Simply restated, our primary concern is with the use by Congress of commerce-prohibiting methods to solve local community social problems having a national impact. However, Congress has attempted to deal legislatively with economic evils as well as social ones, and at times, the problems have contained both social and economic evils. The approaches taken by the Court in all of these disparate cases have tended to use interchangeably the same legal concepts. Whether or not this approach was correct, and we submit it was not, a proper understanding of the Court's interpretation of congressional power to legislate under the commerce clause against purely social evils such as prostitution or racially-incited rioting requires an understanding of the congressional power to legislate against purely economic problems. Therefore, in dealing with post-*Lottery Case* decisions, it is necessary to deal with congressional legislation where economic or social activity or both are involved. In any event, the majority opinion in the *Lottery Case* has had a profound effect upon all subsequent commerce clause decisions.

Subsequent Extensions of the Lottery Case Expansion

Hipolite Egg Co. v. United States[39] was another case dealing with congressional prohibition of a commercial commodity. The problem dealt with—trade in adulterated foodstuffs—was both social and economic in that it focused upon commercial intercourse but with the concomitant desire to protect the public health and safety. The case presented a question as to the application of the Pure Food and Drugs Act of 1906, involving the propriety of confiscation of adulterated preserved eggs even after their junket in interstate commerce had been completed. The Court concluded that since the eggs were "outlaws" of

v. United States, 163 F.2d 228 (6th Cir. 1947), The Fugitive Felon and Witness Act; FPC v. Natural Gas Pipeline Co., 315 U.S. 575 (1942), natural gas price regulation; Currin v. Wallace, 306 U.S. 1 (1939), Tobacco Inspection Act of 1935; Sunshine Anthracite Coal v. Adkins, 310 U.S. 381 (1940), coal price fixing by Congress; and 21 U.S.C. 347 (1961) (intrastate sales of colored oleomargarine—1950), and 21 U.S.C. 360 (1967 Supp.) (drug producer registration—1962). Examples of congressional police power enactments under the auspices of the commerce clause which have not as yet been enacted involve a federal business corporation statute and a federal sales act. *See*, Wickersham, *Federal Control of Interstate Commerce*, 23 HARV. L. REV. 241, 258 (1910); Morawety, *The Power of Congress to Enact Incorporation Laws and to Regulate Corporations* 26 HARV. L. REV. 667, 672 (1913); Llewellyn, *The Needed Federal Sales Act*, 26 VA. L. REV. 558, 561 (1940); and *A Symposium: The Proposed Federal Sales Act*, 26 VA. L. REV. 537 (1940).

39. 220 U.S. 45 (1911).

commerce they could be confiscated anywhere at any time. The reasoning of the *Lottery Case* is much in evidence in *Hipolite Egg's* conclusion that issues of federalism are not involved where the commodity is banned from commerce because of its inherently evil qualities.

The Court decided that the necessary and proper clause enabled Congress to employ any "appropriate" means to enforce its denial of the avenues of commerce to the proscribed product. Such a conclusion smacks of an unholy analytical alliance of hindsight and question—begging.

In *Hoke v. U.S.*,[40] the Supreme Court sustained the constitutionality of the Mann Act. This case certainly is very much in point in a discussion of the Cramer Amendment because although there is an economic element ever present in prostitution, it has been played down in the Mann Act decisions subsequent to *Hoke*.[41] The Act prohibited the transportation of a woman in interstate commerce for prostitution or "other immoral purposes." The Court drew no distinction between the different kinds of articles that had previously been excluded from interstate commerce by congressional regulation. Whether the regulations concerned transportation *in the course of* commercial transactions or were designed to *protect* commercial transactions *from harm* was of no importance to the Court in *Hoke*.[42] No line was drawn to limit the scope of the congressional police power over commerce although lip service was paid to the necessary and proper clause:

> [I]t must be kept in mind that we are one people; and the powers reserved to the states and those conferred on the Nation are adapted to be exercised, whether independently or concurrently, to promote the general welfare, material and moral. This is the effect of the decisions, and surely if the facility of interstate transportation can be taken away from the demoralization of lotteries, the debasement of obscene literature, the contagion of diseased cattle or persons, the impurity of food and drugs, the like facility can be taken away from the systematic enticement to and the enslavement in prostitution and debauchery of women, and, more insistently, of girls . . . . The principle established by the cases is the

---

40. 227 U.S. 308 (1913).

41. *See e.g.*, Cominetti v. United States, 242 U.S. 470 (1917), where the Mann Act was upheld in its application to "non-commercialized vice."

42. This absence of a commercial v. noncommercial distinction, in terms of the specific "evil" article, is highlighted by the fact that, in addition to the *Lottery Case*, the Court relied upon United States v. Popper, 98 F. 423 (N.D. Cay. 1889), which involved an 1897 statute prohibiting the "carrying of obscene literature and articles designed for indecent and immoral use from one State to another."

> simple one, when rid of confusing and distracting considerations, that Congress has power over transportation "among the several states": that the power is complete in itself, and that Congress, as an incident to it, may adopt not only means necessary but convenient to its exercise, and the means may have the quality of police regulations.[43]

This overly broad interpretation of the commerce power, when coupled with the *Lottery Case* and *Hipolite Egg* marked the end, for all practical purposes, of any limitation upon congressional power to regulate activities having no relation to commerce, if that term is to be understood in a business sense, *i.e.*, within the wide (yet constrained) context of economic exchanges. Activities that were traditionally (and one might add, constitutionally)[44] subject to local control could now be regulated by Congress as soon as they approached a public highway. All Congress would have to do would be to ban the use of the facilities of interstate commerce to the persons or property involved in the activity and, as an appropriate means of enforcing the ban, proceed to regulate the local activity. This device has not been questioned as long as the particular activity is traditionally one considered socially undesirable; *e.g.*, gambling, prostitution, kidnapping.

The necessity of there being any relationship between the "evil" itself and economic factors was completely destroyed in *Caminetti v. United States*,[45] another Mann Act case, which upheld the Act's prohibition against transporting a woman for "an immoral purpose." In the course of a somewhat muddled opinion, the Court held that all that was necessary to enable Congress to utilize its police power was the presence of an element of travel between states by the "evil" parties or properties. The limitation of the commerce power to the presence of some degree of economic activity involving commercial intercourse was completely discounted—the offense was the furnishing of transportation for an evil purpose, and Congress could protect commerce from all such evil uses. *Caminetti* made it clear that the freedom to travel interstate was, therefore, subject to the social and moral judgments of Congress.

---

43. Hoke *supra* note 40 at 322-3. The Court further cited Gloucester Ferry Co. v. Pennsylvania, 114 U.S. 196, 215 (1885), in support of its proposition that means employed by Congress are nonetheless "necessary and proper" because they may have the quality of police regulations.

44. The term "constitutionally" is intended to convey adherence to the social attitude and expressed policies of the Framers at the Convention. *See* THE WORKS OF THOMAS JEFFERSON IX, at 398 (Federal ed. 1904-5); I. CROSSKEY, POLITICS AND THE CONSTITUTION ch. 8 (1953). *See generally*, Cushman, *National Police Power Under The Commerce Clause of the Constitution*, 3 MINN. L. REV. 289 (1919).

45. 242 U.S. 470 (1917).

An Awkward Effort of Limitation—The Child Labor Case

The *Child Labor Case, Hammer v. Dagenhart,*[46] presents an interesting example of an attempt by the court to limit congressional power to regulate commerce after the cat had already gotten out of the bag. Whether the limits imposed were judicially or politically motivated, the Court attempted to provide some viable limits to the open ended principles announced in the *Lottery Case*. Without directly overruling the *Lottery Case,* the reasoning of the Court appeared to be setting up limits that could not be sustained by virtue of the prior decision. That the decision in the *Child Labor Case,* and those invalidating much of the New Deal legislation enacted in the mid-1930's, was politically motivated is quite possible.[47] But it is equally reasonable that in *Hoke* and the *Lottery Case* the Court had already gone too far in removing restrictions from the commerce power and could not impose restrictions at a later date without appearing to be unprincipled in its decisions.[48]

The act invalidated in the *Child Labor Case* prohibited the shipment in interstate commerce of goods that had been produced by child labor. There were important economic considerations involved because of the nation-wide effect of competition between goods manufactured by child labor and hence costing less to produce with goods produced in states which had already enacted statutes banning child labor. Such considerations were simply not involved in the *Lottery Case,* and could not even remotely be thought to have influenced the *Lottery Case* Court. The *Child Labor Case* Court, however, overlooked this distinction. It chose instead to distinguish the *nature of the goods involved* from those in the *Lottery Case*. This was an unhappy choice, since the Court was enforcing a distinction without a difference. In the previous commerce clause cases, "the use of interstate transportation" was not "necessary to the accomplishment of the harmful results."[49] "Or, at least it was not any more necessary than in the *Child Labor Case*.

---

46. 247 U.S. 251 (1918).

47. Examine Panama Refining Co. v. Ryan, 293 U.S. 388 (1935); Perry v. United States, 294 U.S. 330 (1935); Railroad Retirement Bd. v. Alton R. Co., 295 U.S. 330 (1935); Schecter Poultry Corp. v. United States, 295 U.S. 495 (1935); and Carter v. Carter Coal Co., 298 U.S. 238 (1936). *See, e.g.,* Wechsler, *Toward Neutral Principles of Constitutional Law,* 73 HARV. L. REV. 1 (1959); and Stern, *The Commerce Clause and the National Economy,* 1933-46, 59 HARV. L. REV. 645 (1946).

48. This argumentative possibility must assume that the Court did not realize that it was engaging in a futile effort to close the barn door after the horse was long gone.

49. To illustrate, let us return to the evil of organized prostitution which Congress sought to curb by the enactment of the Mann Act, sustained by the Court in *Hoke, supra* note 40. It can hardly be questioned that "the use of interstate transportation" was not "necessary to the accomplishment of the harmful results" of organized prostitution. In fact, few would disagree that such interstate movement was less essential, or most certainly

The Court also stated that the "prohibition of commerce" technique utilized in the Child Labor Act was a *necessary* legislative devise in the previous cases[50] but not in the case of goods produced by child labor.[51] This use of the necessary and proper clause was not explained and would seem in retrospect to have been logically unsound. The Court felt that the *Lottery Case* could be distinguished because these goods *themselves* (even though produced by child labor) were harmless.[52] But what is the great harm from lottery tickets themselves?

Some statements made by the Court would have been sound given their overruling of the *Lottery Case*—but when read in conjunction with the *Lottery Case*, it can only be viewed as spurious legal reasoning:

> The maintenance of the authority of the States over matters purely local is as essential to the preservation of our institutions as is the conservation of the supremacy of the federal power in all matters entrusted to the Nation by the Federal Constitution.
>
> * * *
>
> To sustain this statute would not be in our judgment a recognition of the lawful exercise of congressional authority over interstate commerce, but would sanction an invasion by the federal power of the control of a matter purely local in its character, and over which no authority has been delegated to Congress in conferring the power to regulate commerce among the states.[53]

The argument is an impossible one to legitimately construct because of the broad prohibiting powers granted to Congress in the *Lottery Case*. It is an opinion, perhaps, which should have held sway in the *Lottery Case* and other early commerce clause cases in which Congress could prohibit interstate travel to persons and commodities involved in purely local activities. In any event, the *Child Labor Case* Court invalidated the act on the grounds that it was in violation of

---

not any more essential, to the achievement of the evil purpose in connection with organized prostitution than in the case of goods produced by child labor. The same can be said of the evil consequences stemming from adulterated foodstuffs, the regulation of which was upheld in *Hipolite Egg, supra* note 39. Yet, there existed profound economic consequences in the *Child Labor* case *resulting from the use of interstate transportation.* This economic evil flowed from the fact that the more cheaply made goods resulting from the employment of child labor possessed a distinct advantage over locally-manufactured commodities in those jurisdictions where statutory enactments prohibited the use of child labor by local producers. Such an *economic* evil was not directly presented by the organized prostitution which was the object of congressional power in its enactment of the Mann Act.

50. The Court noted that *prohibition* was a "necessary" legislative device in both Hipolite, *supra* note 39, and Hoke, *supra* note 40.

51. *The Child Labor Case, supra* note 46 at 271-2.

52. *Id.* at 272.

53. *Id.* at 275-6.

both the tenth amendment and the "enumerated powers-pretext" argument of *McCulloch v. Maryland.*[54]

In effect, the opinion established that economic affairs are subject only to the local police power (although, undoubtedly, a social component may be present in the problem), while purely social affairs such as prostitution and lotteries are subject to Congressional regulation. Congress must prove its case when it attempts to prohibit commerce as a means to regulate local economic activities, and motive is unimportant when some recognized "social evil" is involved. There is little doubt that if a social practice in one state allows that state to produce goods more cheaply than a neighboring state, that practice has an effect upon commerce. In these instances Congress may call upon its plenary power to regulate the local social evil producing generalized economic effects. This can be done either by prohibition or any other means logically related to that evil. For this reason it would seem that the *Child Labor* decision is backward, or "upside down," in its emphasis on and distinction between economic and social activities. Transporting a girl across state lines to engage in the future in some sexual act does not "affect commerce" and is not "in commerce." On the other hand, disparity in state child labor laws may have a substantial effect upon commerce. Yet the *Child Labor* Court would allow Congress to regulate the former activity but not the latter under the commerce power.

The Anti-New Deal Cases—The Non-Economics of Economics

In the series of cases overruling various New Deal emergency economic measures, the same distinction in judicial scrutiny between cases involving economic activities and social activities continued.[55] Economic legislation was subjected to tests that would better have been applied in evaluating congressional police measures that dealt with local social evils. When these cases were overruled in *United*

---

54. *Id.* at 276, where Mr. Justice Day writing for the majority reached the following conclusion on the basis of the McCulloch v. Maryland, *supra* note 23, "pretext" argument:

> In our view the necessary effect of this act is, by means of a prohibition against the movement in interstate commerce of ordinary commercial commodities to regulate the hours of labor of children in factories and mines within the states, a purely local authority. Thus the act in a two-fold sense is repugnant to the Constitution. It not only transcends the authority delegated to Congress over commerce but also exerts a power as to a purely local matter to which the federal authority does not extend. The far reaching result of upholding the act cannot be more plainly indicated than by pointing out that if Congress can thus regulate matters entrusted to local authority by prohibtion of the movement of commodities in interstate commerce, all freedom of commerce will be at an end, and the power of the states over local matters may be eliminated, and thus our system of government be practically destroyed.

55. *See* cases cited in note 47, *supra.*

States v. Darby,[56] the valid principles they had enunciated but applied too vigorously were thrown out, which was like throwing the baby out with the bath water. Would it not have been better to have transferred the tests to the social field where they properly belonged? Since the relationship between purely social activity and interstate commerce is tenuous, and the exercise of congressional power must be looked into with extreme care by the reviewing courts, scrapping the tests altogether cannot help but lead to confusion because of a lack of any standards. For in its violent reaction to the misapplication of valid standards to the wrong set of cases, the *Darby* Court overreacted. They removed any chance of limiting the commerce power which, as we have observed, is subject to misuse in certain non-economic areas. Nevertheless, an examination of the anti-New Deal cases is warranted since the standards they enunciated may have been valid, although misapplied to the particular factual contexts then before the Court.

In *Railroad Retirement Board v. Alton Railroad Co.,*[57] the Supreme Court relied primarily on the necessary and proper clause to overturn a compulsory retirement and pension plan for all carriers subject to the Interstate Commerce Act. The Court held that Congress could not legislate for the peace of mind of railroad employees under the commerce clause, but rather had to limit its enactments to providing for an efficiently run railroad. The regulation of social welfare had nothing to do with the regulation of commerce. Social welfare was "outside of the orbit of congressional power."[58] The act was therefore faulty on two counts: 1.) The means adopted were not related to the power to regulate commerce in violation of the necessary and proper clause; and 2.) Congress possessed no substantive power to provide for the general welfare of railroad employees—the act was void on the strength of the "pretext" argument. The second fault found by the Court merely meant that Congress sought to exercise a power it did not possess.

In *Schecter Poultry Corp. v. United States,*[59] part of the National Industrial Recovery Act of 1933 was invalidated. The case itself dealt with the fixing of hours and wages in the poultry industry in New York. The basic question was whether the activities sought to be regulated were sufficiently related to interstate commerce to be subject to congressional regulation. The Court distinguished between "direct" and "indirect" effects upon interstate commerce as a means of further

---

56. United States v. Darby, 312 U.S. 100 (1941)
57. Alton R. Co., *supra* note 47.
58. *Id* at 368.
59. *Supra* note 47.

defining the traditional limit upon the ability of Congress to reach local affairs (that traditional limit being phrased in terms of whether the activities "affected" interstate commerce.).[60] The purpose of this new distinction was obviously to mke the phrase "affecting interstate commerce" more exclusive as to which activities might be reached by Congress. The Court dwelt at length upon the need to prevent Congress from reaching activities which were local and subject only to control by the states. *Schecter* gave the Court an opportunity to decide whether a *local activity* was subject to congressional regulation, but judicial prudence prevailed and the Court obviously intended to use the discretion with strict care.

In *Carter v. Carter Coal Co.*,[61] the Court invalidated the Bituminous Coal Conservation Act of 1935 that sought to regulate collective bargaining and wage and hour agreements in the coal industry. The Court held that the activities sought to be regulated were not "commerce" and therefore not subject to the commerce power, and that Congress possessed no general police power. Commerce was defined in the strictest sense as intercourse for the purposes of trade, and the local wages of workers and the production of goods were not part of the "trade" subject to congressional regulation.[62] But could Congress reach these local activities because they directly affected commerce? The Court felt that this question had been practically answered by the previous finding that the activities sought to be regulated were not commerce within the meaning of that word as used in the Commerce Clause—Congress cannot regulate that which is not commerce.[63]

The Court emphasized that the police power was not one of the enumerated powers that had been granted to Congress by the Constitution; in effect, that the ability to legislate for the "general welfare" was left exclusively to the states. Only in so far as it acts legitimately to carry out a granted power may Congress legislate for the general welfare since the Constitutional Convention had rejected giving Congress the power to legislate in all cases where the separate states were "incompetent."[64]

---

60. *Id.* at 544-8.
61. Carter Coal Co., *supra* note 47.
62. *Id.* at 303-4.
63. *Id.* at 304, 308-9.
64. *Id.* at 291-2, where the Court not only cited Mr. Justice Story's caveat in Martin v. Hunter's Lessee, U.S. (1 Wheat. 304), 326 (1816) that the general government "can claim no powers which are not granted to it by the Constitution, and the powers actually granted, must be such as are expressly given, or given by necessary implication," but also cited United States v. Butler, 297 U.S. 1, 64, and suggested for comparison Jacobson v. Massachusetts, 197 U.S. 11, 11. *See also*, Kansas v. Colorado, 206 U.S. 46, 89-90 (1907), and Munn v. Illinois, 94 U.S. 112, 124 (1877).

These cases invalidating New Deal legislation are not directly in point with the Cramer Amendment because the legislation in those cases was not commerce-prohibiting in nature, while the regulation of local transactions encompassed by the Cramer Amendment could be considered a necessary and proper step to effectuate a ban on transportation. In addition, the regulations in *Alton Railroad, Schecter* and *Carter* were aimed at activities more economic than social in nature. Nevertheless, the three cases do demonstrate the use of limitations by the Court to restrain congressional power under the commerce clause. The limits were valid regardless of one's feelings as to the rationality of their application. Even further, it seems to these observers that the pronounced limits should at least have been retained in the "repertoire" of the Supreme Court.

The Darby Case—An Unfortunate Retributive "Sledge-Hammer"

United States v. Darby[65] represented a complete return to the *Lottery Case.* In overruling the *Child Labor Case,* the *Darby* Court spoke of the powers of Congress in unnecessarily broad terms. Many of the valid limits on congressional power which had been developed just years before were discarded and those limits that were retained were given little more than lip service. At issue was the Fair Labor Standards Act which prohibited the shipment in interstate commerce of goods manufactured by employees whose wages were less than a national standard, and also prohibited the employment of workmen to expend efforts on the goods thus prohibited or tainted.

The plenary police power over all individuals and commodities traveling in interstate commerce was asserted as it had been in the *Lottery Case.*[66] In this exclusion of harmful articles Congress could follow its own conceptions of public policy, in no way being limited to economic considerations. The Court also held that the motive or purpose of Congress in enacting commerce clause legislation could not be inquired into by the reviewing courts.[67] This claimed inability to look at congressional motives would seem to represent the abandonment of the pretext argument advanced in *McCulloch v. Maryland.* After *Darby,* the Supreme Court could no longer properly inquire into whether

65. Darby, *supra* note 56.
66. *Id.* at 113.
67. *Id.* at 115, where Mr. Justice Stone, writing for the majority, limited the reviewing court's scope of inquiry into Congressional motive in the following manner:

> The motive and purpose of a regulation of interstate commerce are matters for legislative judgment upon which the Constitution places no restriction and over which the courts are given no control . . . . Whatever their motive and purpose, regulations of commerce which do not infringe some constitutional prohibition are within the plenary power conferred on Congress by the Commerce Clause.

Congress was actually acting in pursuance of one of its enumerated powers. The *Darby* decision, viewed in the context of federal anti-riot legislation, means that the question of whether congressional purpose was to regulate commerce or merely to stop local rioting is no longer for the courts to determine. Is this wise in a system under which Congress is constrained by the Constitution to act only in furtherance of its enumerated powers? It would seem that Congress after *Darby* might call any of its legislation a "regulation of commerce," and thereby assure its constitutionality.

This abandonment of an intensive search into congressional motive has its effect on the necessary and proper clause as well as upon due process. The examination of congressional motive falls within the sphere or penumbra of "constitutional limitations" that cannot be "infringed," to use the words of the Court in *Darby*. The necessary and proper clause has been interpreted to mean that the means employed by Congress must be appropriate to the ends involved.[68] It would be difficult, if not impossible, for the Court to decide whether the means are appropriate if it has no idea what the ends of the legislation are, unless the appropriateness of a particular regulation is only something to be conjectured upon. An even more substantial objection to this abandonment of an investigation of congressional motive is raised by the due process clause, which is certainly a "constitutional limitation." To satisfy due process the relationship or *nexus* between means and ends in legislation must not only be "necessary and proper" but must also be based on a rational decision on the part of Congress.[69] It would be immensely difficult, at best, to ascertain whether this requisite element of a rational nexus is present without looking into congressional motive or purpose.

Furthermore, it seems that *Darby* removed the "affecting interstate commerce" limitation upon the power of Congress to deal with purely local matters.[70] In defining the power of Congress to prevent produc-

68. McCulloch v. Maryland, *supra* note 21 at 421. *See* VI WRITINGS OF JAMES MADISON 141-406 (Hunt ed. 1906).

69. The post-1937 due process requirement of a rational nexus between means and end is well illustrated by Olsen v. Nebraska, 313 U.S. 236 (1941); Lincoln Federal Labor Union v. Northwestern Iron & Metal Co., 335 U.S. 525 (1949); Day-Brite Lighting, Inc. v. Missouri, 342 U.S. 42 (1952); Railway Express Agency v. New York, 336 U.S. 106 (1949); and Ferguson v. Skrupa, 372 U.S. 726 (1963). Examine further, McCloskey, ECONOMIC DUE PROCESS AND THE SUPREME COURT: AN EXHUMATION AND REBURIAL, 1962 SUP. CT. REV. 34 (1962); and Hetherington, *State Economic Regulation and Substantive Due Process of Laws*, 53 NW. U.L. REV. 13 (1958).

70. It may be arguable that Wickard v. Filburn, 317 U.S. 111 (1942), reinstated the "affectation doctrine." In *Wickard*, the Court sustained the wheat marketing quota and atendant penalty provisions of the Agricultural Adjustment Act of 1938 as applied to wheat not intended in any part for commerce but wholly for consumption on the farm against an attack of unconstitutionality based upon the commerce clause. The Court

tion of goods that could not be shipped in commerce, a new concept was introduced:

> The power of Congress over interstate commerce is not confined to the regulation of commerce among the states. It extends to those activities intrastate which so affect interstate commerce or the *exercise of the power of Congress over it* as to make regulation of them appropriate means to the attainment of the legitimate end, the exercise of the granted power of Congress to regulate interstate commerce. (Emphasis added).[71]

The above-emphasized language apparently gives Congress plenary power over intrastate affairs as well as over interstate commerce. It is no longer essential that an activity affect more states than one; it is only necessary that a purely local activity unrelated to interstate commerce affect congressional power as a precondition for Congress to act. The *Darby* opinion represents a clear attempt to give Congress as wide a power over "commerce" as possible. The legitimate end of the commerce power is no longer the regulation of interstate commerce, but has become the very exercise of the granted power *itself.*

The Court's goal of giving Congress the widest possible power over commerce has also been achieved by an expansive reading of the necessary and proper clause in connection with the regulation of local activities. The clause now allows congressional regulation of all local activities by a two step device: 1.) prohibition of the fruits of the activity from commerce; and 2.) regulation of any and all local activities connected with the prohibited goods as an appropriate means to protect congressional exclusionary policy. Indeed, the concept of "affecting commerce" as a limit upon congressional incursion into local activities can no longer be considered an absolute prohibition. After *Darby,* any local activity completely unrelated to interstate commerce can be directly regulated by Congress as a necessary and proper means of congressional exercise of its power over commerce.

---

made the following statement, which unquestionably possesses "affectation doctrine" overtones:

> It can hardly be denied that a factor of such volume and variability as home-consumer wheat would have a substantial influence on price and market conditions. This may arise because being in marketable condition such wheat overhangs the market and, if induced by rising prices, tends to flow into the market and check price increases. But if we assume that it is never marketed, it supplies a need of the man who grew it which would otherwise be reflected by purchases in the open market. Home-grown wheat in this sense *competes with wheat in commerce.* The stimulation of commerce is a use of the regulatory function quite as definitely as prohibitions or restrictions thereon. This record leaves us in no doubt that Congress may properly have considered that wheat consumed on the farm where grown, if wholly outside the scheme of regulation, would have a *substantial effect* in defeating and obstructing its purpose to stimulate trade therein at increased prices [emphasis added]. *Id.* at 128-9.

71. Darby, *supra* note 56 at 118 [emphasis added].

Darby Revitalized?

Four justices in *United States v. Five Gambling Devices*[72] felt that it was unnecessary that the local activity sought to be regulated have any "effect" upon interstate commerce. In their view, if the local activity had some relationship to congressional power over commerce generally, Congress could regulate the activity to protect and sustain its authority over interstate commerce.[73]

The Civil Rights Act of 1964—Further Commerce Clause Expansion Coupled With Modern Judicial Ambiguity

The most recent litigation involving the power of Congress to regulate commerce involved the Civil Rights Act of 1964. In *Heart of Atlanta Motel v. United States,*[74] the Court upheld, as a legitimate exercise of the commerce power, Title II of the Act which forbade discrimination in places of public accommodations. The Court found that discrimination impeded and burdened interstate commerce because it reduced the travel of Negroes into the South. The Act was sustained on the basis of practically every one of the previous congressional exercises of the commerce power that had been sustained by the Court. The cases used as authority included commerce regulations and prohibitions, intrastate and interstate activities, and economic and social exercises of the "police power." All of these cases were reconciled as having been exercises of the congressional power to protect commerce itself. In other words, all of the cases represented congressional use of its police power over commerce and it was of no consequence that the activity regulated was not economic.[75] Any and all distinctions between moral and economic activities and between direct and indirect effects upon commerce were skillfully avoided in the decision. Whether or not Congress in-

---

72. 346 U.S. 441 (1953).

73. The unusual result in the Five Gambling Devices case, *Id.* arose because Mr. Justice Black, joined by Mr. Justice Douglas, concurred in the invalidation of the Attorney Generals' application of the Act of January 2, 1951, prohibiting the shipment of gambling machines in interstate commerce along with attendant reporting and registration provisions, because of the vagueness of the Act's reporting provision without reaching the commerce clause question. Mr. Justice Clark, joined by Chief Justice Warren, and Justices Reed and Burton, dissented based upon their view that the Act was not vague or indefinite as applied and that Congress had not exceeded its power under the commerce clause in seeking to regulate admittedly *local* activity where necessary to protect Congress' own power and authority over interstate commerce. Had Justices Black and Douglas reached the commerce clause question, their view would presumably have coincided with that of the dissenters, effectually meaning that six Justices in 1953 would have favored the broad sweep of Justice Clark's *Darby*-oriented dissent.

74. 379 U.S. 241 (1964).

75. *Id.* at 256, where the Court cited Caminetti as authority for the declaration that it is of no consequence to Congressional exercise of the commerce power that the activity regulated is not an *economic* one.

tended to regulate interstate commerce was a question not asked, let alone answered, by Mr. Justice Clark's opinion for the Court.[76]

Under the "economic nexus" approach to the commerce power, advocated by the writers, it is vital to any meaningful analysis of the legal consequences of an anti-riot legislative enactment such as the Cramer Amendment: 1.) that it be contrasted with Title II of the Civil Rights Act of 1964; and 2.) that both be subjected to the somewhat spurious test established by the Court in *Heart of Atlanta.* Our contrast of the two legislative enactments must initially proceed along the lines of their end result upon the regulated parties. Both contain a measure of deterrence. The proponents of the anti-riot bill hope to deter "rabble-rousers" and inflamatory racial agitators from moving from place to place for the purpose of "rousing their rabble" on a massive nation-wide scale,[77] while the Civil Rights Act as applied to

---

76. It is interesting to note that Mr. Justice Clark also authored the dissent in Five Gambling Devices, *supra* note 72.

77. Quite instructive on the attitude of those who actively demand anti-riot legislation are the following excerpts from the opening statement of Senator Strom Thurmond before the Senate Judiciary Committee on Wednesday, August 2, 1967 (*Hearings*, Part I, page 19):

> These riots demonstrate that human rights can only be protected by safeguarding property. Looting, arson, and murder are the fundamental enemies of freedom. Therefore it is hard to understand the callous disregard of the authorities who are reluctant to order police and troops to take the necessary action to bring the matter under control, and to fire and use as much force as necessary to quell this disturbance.
>
> The measures must be proportionate to the gravity of the situation. Looting and arson are not mere property damage but they are the collapse of civil order. They are the collapse of civilized society. The police and troops must be allowed to use the necessary force to restore order immediately.

Those who wonder about the genesis of such an outcry might examine some provoking comments put to a Cambridge, Maryland crowd on the evening of July 24, 1967, by H. Rap Brown, Chairman of SNCC:

> Brothers, you've got to get some guns. I don't care if it's B-B guns with poisoned B-Bs. He's [the white man] done declared war on black people. He don't mind killing them. It might be your son he kills next. Or it might be your daughter. Or it might be you. So, wherever you go, brother, take some of them with you. That's what you do, brother. An eye for an eye; a tooth for a tooth. Tit for tat, brother, that's the only kind of war that man knows. That's the only thing he recognizes. Ain't no need in the world for me to come to Cambridge and I see all them stores sitting up there and all them honkies owns them. You got to own some of them stores. I don't care if you have to burn him down and run him out. You'd better take over them stores. The streets are yours. Take 'em. They gave you the streets a long time ago; before they gave you houses. They gave you the streets. So, we own the streets. Take 'em. You've got to take 'em. They ain't going to give them to you. Freedom is not a welfare commodity. It ain't like that old bad food they give you. They can't give you no freedom. You got to take your freedom. You were born free. You got to exercise that right though, brother, cause the honkey got you where he wants you.
>
> You making money for him. If you make money for that honkey, you don't make money for yourself. . . . He wants you to go home and suffer the whole summer. He wants you to sit in them hot houses and say, see what we can do to you when we get ready. He controls you niggers. That's what he's been telling you and you been sitting back there saying, "Yassuh, Yassuh." You been sitting back there telling him: "Yassuh, y'all control us." They gave you 5 nigger cops who can't whip nothing but black heads.
>
> You've got to understand, that's part of that man's trick. Ye ain't making

Heart of Atlanta Motel was intended to deter the proprietors of such motels from engaging in racial discrimination in the letting of public accomodations. On the one hand, the evil sought to be curbed by the Civil Rights Act—discrimination—more directly affected interstate commerce by impeding travel in the South by Negroes. But even this evil itself was not an *economic* one, it merely produced an effect upon one manifestation of interstate commerce.

On the other hand, the evil sought to be eliminated by the Cramer Amendment—riots—only remotely touches interstate commerce when severe enough to economically isolate a metropolis like Detroit or Newark for more than one day, even though riots, like discrimination, do not represent an *economic* evil. Interstate transportation, while being the very manifestation of interstate commerce impeded by the evil of racial discrimination, is only an incidental vehicle for the justification of Congressional legislative jurisdiction needed to curb the evil of riots and resultant civil turmoil.

This distinction is crucial, not so much to justify the legitimacy of Title II as applied to Heart of Atlanta Motel while attacking the validity of the Cramer Amendment, but for the purpose of illustrating our conclusion that, *in both instances,* the legislative enactments are impermissible exercises of the commerce power since the problem or evil sought to be eliminated is not itself an *economic* one. Even further, this critical distinction supports our assertion that congressional passage and Court affirmance of the Cramer Amendment would be an even more drastic departure from the *Lottery Case* dissent than was the decision in *Heart of Atlanta.* At first, this might not be seen at all, if one is content to merely superficially read the Court's language in *Heart of Atlanta,* to the effect that Congress possesses the power to enact measures necessary to protect that very commerce power itself. The reader can conveniently fit Title II, the Cramer Amendment or *any other*

---

no progress cause them niggers ain't walking but in a car. They think they're making progress, brother. They ain't making no progress. Not when they can't whip no honkies.

* * *

Ain't got no reason for white folks to be leisurely walking up and down your community. He's got no business coming over, talking about taking black women out of your community. You ain't a man if you let that animal come over here and take a black woman out of your community. To do what he want to do with her. And that's what he's doing. He doing what he want to do with her. Brother, it's up to you to stop that. . . .

He's been running around here letting them do everything they want. I mean, don't be trying to love that honkey to death. Shoot him to death. Shoot him to death, brother. 'Cause that's what he's out to do to you. Like I said in the beginning, if this town don't come around, this town should be burned down. It should be burned down, brother. They're going to have to live in the same stuff I live in 'cause I ain't going to make it no better for them." (*Hearings, supra* note 7, Pt. I, pp. 33-34, 36.

Congressional legislation within its scope by showing any relationship, however insignificant, between a desired local activity and the Congressional power. In fact, because of the compact interlocking nature of our modern society, one can find *economic* consequences in almost any social problem. Unfortunately, however, an economic relationship today can never be a satisfactory test or limitation upon the commerce power but can serve only as an *excuse* for Congressional action.

In *Katzenbach v. McClung*,[78] the lack of any effective limits upon congressional action under the commerce power was apparent. The relevant part of the Civil Rights Act placed a restaurant under the purview of the Act "if . . . it serves or offers to serve interstate travelers or a substantial portion of the food which it serves . . . has moved in commerce."[79] The restaurant involved, Ollie's Barbecue, did not serve interstate travelers but did serve some food that had at some point moved in interstate commerce.[80] Thet Court reviewed at length evidence to the effect that discrimination in restaurants which purchased food that had moved in interstate commerce "affected" that commerce. The Court found that "commerce" included any and all economic effects whether casually proximate to the racial discrimination or not. Any activity that affected commerce in any way provided a pretext for congressional action. The term "affecting interstate commerce" was deprived, in the course of the opinion, of all substantive meaning:

> The fewer customers a restaurant enjoys the less food it sells and consequently the less it buys. . . . In addition, the Attorney General testified that this type of discrimination imposed an artificial restriction on the market and interfered with the flow of merchandise. . . . In addition, there were many references to discriminatory situations causing unrest and having a depressant effect on general business conditions in the respective communities.[81]

As was true with respect to our preceding analysis of *Heart of Atlanta* as contrasted with the Cramer Amendment, the end result of the Civil Rights Act of 1964 as applied in *McClung* must be drawn through a similar comparison with the consequences of the Cramer Amendment upon the regulated parties. In our view, *McClung* goes further than *Heart of Atlanta* in departing from the *Lottery Case* dissent but not as far as would Congressional enactment of the Cramer

---

78. 379 U.S. 294 (1964).

79. Civil Rights Act of 1964, tit. II, §§ 201(b) & (c).

80. In the 12 months preceding the passage of the 1964 Act, Ollie's Barbecue purchased approximately 46% of its food (in the form of meat) from a local supplier who had procured it from outside the State. *See*, McClung, *supra* note 78 at 296. Query: was not this meat, when purchased by Ollie's Barbecue, just like the chickens in *Schecter*?

81. McClung, *supra* note 78 at 299-300.

Amendment. This conclusion is based upon the fact that the non-economic evil sought to be prohibited in *McClung*—discrimination—is the same as that sought to be prohibited by the Act in *Heart of Atlanta.* However, while it is a direct manifestation of interstate commerce—interstate transportation and travel by Negroes—sought to be protected in *Heart of Atlanta,* there is no such preservation of interstate commerce in *McClung* since Ollie's Barbecue *served no interstate travelers,* white or black. In effect, there was no direct link between the evil of discrimination and interstate commerce in *McClung.* The link was "twice removed," at best, since it involved a connection between interstate commerce and some meat served by the restaurant. This link is significantly different than the *direct* connection in *Heart of Atlanta* between racial discrimination and interstate travel by Negroes. Thus, *McClung* is more like the Cramer Amendment than its sister case, *Heart of Atlanta,* since interstate commerce in *McClung,* as in the Cramer Amendment, is not itself burdened by the evil sought to be curbed but acts only as a convenient handle or bootstrap by which Congressional power over a non-economic evil can be justified.

In both *Heart of Atlanta* and *McClung,* due process and necessary and proper clause objections were rejected. The two concepts are, of course, interrelated due to the fact that whenever Congress acts outside of the bounds of constitutional power established by the necessary and proper clause its action may be considered "arbitrary" in due process terms. The necessary and proper limitation was summarily expressed in *McClung* as follows:

> But where we find that the legislators, in light of the facts and testimony before them, have a rational basis for finding a chosen regulatory scheme necessary to the protection of commerce, our investigation is at an end.[82]

The due process limitation was similarly treated by the Court in *Heart of Atlanta Motel:*

> The only questions are: (1) whether Congress had a rational basis for finding that racial discrimination by motels affected commerce, and (2) if it had such a basis whether the means it selected to eliminate that evil are reasonable and appropriate.[83]

However, the *McClung* opinion discounted a "nexus to commerce" contention that seems to the writers to be relevant to both standards:

> The absence of direct evidence connecting discriminatory restaurant service with the flow of interstate food, a factor on

82. *Id.* at 303-4.
83. Heart of Atlanta Motel, *supra* note 74 at 258-9.

> which the appellees place much reliance, is not, given the evidence as to the effect of such practices on other aspects of commerce, a crucial matter.[84]

The *McClung* decision is an example of the bankruptcy of commerce clause doctrine in the Supreme Court. Congressional legislative power over commerce is for all practical purposes not subject to any meaningful control. This does not mean that certain commercial regulations *happen* to partake of certain aspects of the police power supposedly retained by the states; rather, it is our contention that *the commerce power is now a complete police power over all local activities,* and traditional concerns of federalism, where the federal legislative exercise of the commerce power is concerned, are no longer of any importance. The tenth amendment does not protect any local activity from federal regulation, for as the Court stated in *Darby:* "The Amendment states but a truism that all is retained which has not been surrendered."[85] It must be remembered, considering the fact that the state police power and congressional power under the commerce clause are so similar, that state exercise of its police power is no longer subject to any practical restraint because of the demise of the due process clause as an effective restraint upon police regulations.[86] Indeed, there is a great similarity in the processes utilized within the Court by which state legislative police power and congressional commerce power have been completely unbridled from all judicial restraint.[87]

Riots, Congress and Interstate Commerce—Future Prospects and Recommendations: Police Power v. Economic Check

General Considerations

In the course of decisions by the Supreme Court interpreting the breadth of congressional power of regulation under the commerce clause and formulating various limits upon that power there have been three pivotal decisions: *The Lottery Case; The Child Labor Case;* and *United States v. Darby.* These three decisions are intimately related, and it seems that the mistakes made by the Court in the course of the three decisions account for resultant cases like *McClung,* where the Court obviously just went through the motions in its reference to restraints upon the police power of Congress over local activi-

84. *Id.* at 304-5.
85. Darby, *supra* note 56 at 124.
86. *See* note 69.
87. Excellent illustrations of this similarity of judicial modus operandi are Day-Brite Lighting v. Missouri, *supra* note 65, and Railway Express Agency v. New York, *supra* note 65.

ties. These three cases constructed two kinds of mistaken analyses. In the first place, the Court failed to draw reasonable lines of limitation *within* the police power of Congress over commerce. Secondly, the Court failed to adequately define gestalt constitutional limitations upon congressional power.

We stated earlier in this study our belief that the Cramer Amendment would be sustained as a constitutional exercise of the congressional power to regulate commerce. Solely on the basis of precedent this decision would be correct. However, that the amendment is not a proper constitutional exercise of federal legislative power and its probable success in the courts results from certain basic mistakes that have been made in previous cases. Our task at this point is to present our case for the unconstitutionality of the Cramer Amendment, along with a more intensive elaboration upon the mistakes made by the Court in interpreting the breadth of the commerce power, and how these mistakes might still be corrected.

Line-Drawing Within *the Police Power*

In discussing the first kind of mistaken analysis—the failure of the Court to draw lines within the police power—the *Lottery Case* is of great importance. The basic mistake made in that case, which had bedeviled all subsequent decisions, was its conclusion that *non-economic* items or transactions when they move in interstate commerce, even though this movement is not commercially motivated, become subject to congressional regulation under the commerce power. In other words, anything that moves at some time between two states was found to be subject to congressional regulation. This meant that the phrase "regulating commerce" encompassed the power to regulate activities in which no business or commercial motive was present. Justice Marshall's definition of commerce as "commercial intercourse" in *Gibbons v. Ogden* certainly did not go this far; and it is probable that his use of the word "traffic" connoted an inherent economic component clearly lacking in the social activity sought to be regulated in the *Lottery Case*. From the standpoint of semantics, if not one of legal theory, there is something illogical about calling the elimination of discrimination in a restaurant, for example, a regulation of *commerce*. Thus, extending the congressional police power over commerce to non-economic transactions with non-economic effects was a major error of the Court in the *Lottery Case*.

Limitations On *the Police Power*

The second major mistake in the *Lottery Case* opinion lies in the breadth it gave to the police power it had simultaneously created. Assuming that commerce itself is a concept that can be protected from activities that harm it, the protection should have been limited both in terms of activities subject to regulation and means applied to regulate. In order to protect commerce from burdens and interferences, Congress should have been allowed to regulate only commercial activities, and the concept that commerce could be harmed by moral evils which possessed no economic factor should not have been accepted. Prohibition of commercial techniques should have been allowed only for the purpose of protecting economic transactions between states, since most articles harmful to the public health are transported with some kind of trade in mind. It is our contention that a fair reading of the commerce clause would have limited the congressional police power to "protect" commerce to economic burdens and obstructions, and that the power to prohibit should have been limited to *economic* commodities involved in *economic* transactions. The power to prohibit people from commerce because of some non-economic characteristic that a particular Congress might consider to be evil should not have been considered to be either necessary or appropriate to the granted power. The power of Congress is to regulate commerce not public morals. The power of Congress is to protect commerce (an *economic concept*) from *economic* activities that cause *economic* harm.[88] This position, which for the most part is that of the dissenters in the *Lottery Case,* would have provided reasonable limits upon the police power of Congress over commerce and would have precluded Congress from the area of public morals.

The writers offer an "economic nexus" standard against which Congressional exercise of its commerce power should be measured. Lest one be misled by associative terminological theory, "economic nexus" means far more than the "affect interstate commerce" rationale. It requires that the object of Congressional regulation be an economic problem or involve purely economic activities or evils. Legislative enactments, such as the Cramer Amendment and Title II of the Civil Rights Act of 1964 as applied in *McClung,* which prohibit or seek to curb non-economic evils that *do not directly impede or burden interstate commerce,* as well as those, such as Title II as applied in *Heart of Atlanta,* directed at non-economic evils that *do produce a burdening effect upon one or more manifestations of interstate commerce* would be struck down under our "economic nexus" test. Only where the evil or problem sought to be regulated is itself *economic,* does there exist a sufficient nexus between commerce and Congressional legislative purpose, so as to justify the invocation of the commerce power.

88. *See* Chief Justice Fuller's dissent in *The Lottery Case, supra* note 24 at 367, 371.

We submit that there is a basic policy error in equating the police power of the states with the commerce power of the federal government, and subjecting both powers to the same constitutional tests of validity. The commerce power is purely an economic power while the police power of the states extends to moral problems as well as economic ones. Randolph's proposal at the Constitutional Convention to give Congress general police power was rejected, and this rejection is reflected in the tenth amendment.[89] The congressional sovereignty over commerce and the state's sovereignty over its citizens are not the same. The only "citizens" of commerce are those who may travel or trade in it, whereas a state in the exercise of its police power is responsible to *all* of its citizens. The political implications of this difference in responsibility are apparent. The state in the exercise of its police power is subject to the political pressures of all of its citizens, while Congress in the exercise of its police power over commerce is subject to the political pressures of only part of its citizenry. If the Court had kept these objections in mind and had limited congressional police power over commerce the Cramer Amendment (and the Mann Act as well) would now be found unconstitutional because "Congress, under the pretext of executing its powers, . . . [had passed] . . . laws for the accomplishment of objects not entrusted to the government . . . ," à la *McCulloch v. Maryland*.[90]

The other basic mistake the Supreme Court had made rests in its interpretation of congressional power under the commerce clause in relationship to constitutional limitations. This overly broad interpretation of congressional power in relation to principles of constitutional limitation is not a feature unique to commerce clause litigation. The "specific prohibitions of the Constitution" have been given little attention in recent due process cases challenging state or federal economic regulation.[91] The tenth amendment also, which represents the constitutional sanction for both federalism and the "affecting commerce" rationale, has been stripped of any substantive force and effect.[92]

The failure of the Court to meaningfully apply these constitu-

---

89. Examine CROSSKEY, *supra* note 44, at 206-14, 221; Dunlop's American Daily Advertiser (Philadelphia), Feb. 8 & 15, 1791; and MADISON'S DEBATES at 117, where the following resolution proposed by Randolph is reported:

> . . . that the National Legislature ought to be impowered to enjoy the Legislative Rights vested in Congress by the Confederation & moreover to legislate in all cases to which the separate States are incompetent, or in which the harmony of the United States may be interrupted by the exercise of individual Legislation.

90. McCulloch v. Maryland, *supra* note 23, where Chief Justice Marshall first made the "pretext" argument.

91. *See* note 69.

92. *See* Darby, *supra* note 56 at 123-4 for an emasculation of the tenth amendment. Examine STORY, COMMENTARIES ON THE CONSTITUTION, §§ 1907-1908 (4th ed. 1823).

tional prohibitions is in large part due to the violent executive and legislative reaction to the *Child Labor Case* decision and those cases which invalidated other New Deal legislation. As pointed out earlier, the *Child Labor Case* applied valid constitutional limits but in a discriminatory fashion to the wrong set of facts (social rather than economic). The Court felt that in regulating the production of goods Congress was not acting in furtherance of its delegated power to regulate commerce and for that reason was in violation of the tenth amendment. The Court concluded that it had a legitimate right to look at congressional motive in order to assess the real reason Congress was exercising its commerce power. These valid principles were misapplied to the facts of the case, however, because the production of goods by methods of child labor (an economic activity) did have an effect on the national economy in the sense that the same goods made without child labor would have to be higher priced. If the local activity sought to be regulated was not essentially economic in nature or did not have a substantial effect on the national economy, the utilization of the principles enunciated in the case might have been a *proper* application. Of course, the *Child Labor Case* opinion also suffered from either the failure to distinguish between police power regulation of economic activities for economic ends and regulation of social activities for social ends, or, if the two were distinguished, the Court's undoubted possession of a perverse conviction that social regulation (the Mann Act) was within the scope of the commerce power while regulation that was primarily economic (the Child Labor Act) was not. The *Child Labor Case,* in our view, involved valid but *misapplied* constitutional principles coupled with a commendable and valid attempt to limit the police power of Congress but in a *misguided* way.

The *Darby* decision, on the other hand, represents a correct substantive decision which unnecessarily stretched valid principles in order to demonstrate that the era of the *Child Labor Case* was at an end. The *Darby* Court should have properly recognized the validity of the constitutional limitations enunciated in the *Child Labor Case,* and simply have stated that those principles were improperly applied to the wrong set of economic facts. *Darby* could alternatively have been decided on traditional commerce clause grounds, in reliance upon the theory that the production of goods where the workers had been paid below a stated minimum had a destructive effect on commerce in other states. The Court decided, however, to attack not only the decision of the *Child Labor Case,* but also what it conceived to be the political motivation of the restraints applied. In so doing the Court effectively emasculated the misapplied but valid "necessary and proper" and "pretext" principles enunciated in the *Child Labor Case* decision. The valid efforts of the Court in the *Child Labor Case* to draw lines *within* the penumbra of the congressional police power was completely overruled so that the power took on an unlimited scope. A proper principle was thereby overruled because of a mistaken earlier application. The pretext principle requiring that Congress must act only in such a manner as to carry out the powers delegated to it was erased *sub-silentio* because the motive behind congressional regulation of interstate commerce could no longer be examined by the Court. The necessary and proper clause which had served as the philosophical basis behind the phrase "affecting interstate commerce" was stretched so that the prohibition of any commodity or activity in interstate commerce could lead to the regulation of local activity which did not even affect interstate commerce. Indeed, the necessary and proper clause was extended to allow congressional regulation where the regulated local activity *affected the power of Congress over commerce* rather than commerce itself. Finally, the tenth amendment, a sound yet misapplied principle of the *Child Labor Case,* was deprived of all substantive force as a possible limitation upon Congress.

At the present time, it is highly dubious that a due process contention would be sustained against any economic regulation, either state or federal.[93] This is largely the result of a reaction against early opinions which had invalidated state attempts through the police power to regulate economic activity. In essence, for a legislative pronouncement to fulfill the due process requirement, it must be shown that the legislature has not acted arbitrarily. Due process effectually includes the necessary and proper clause since the legislative body must have 1.) a rational basis for concluding that a problem exists and that one of its granted powers is applicable to that problem, and 2.) a rational basis for its choice of means to serve the valid legislative end. In early cases the Supreme Court itself decided whether the state or federal government had exercised legislative judgment in a rational manner.[94] The more recent cases, however, require only that the legislative body could *possibly* have a rational basis for its legislative judgment as to what the problem is and what means will best achieve a solution to that problem.[95]

---

93. See the cases cited in note 65 which illustrate the modern post-1937 "hands-off" trend.

94. *See* Lochner v. New York, 198 U.S. 45 (1905).

95. An ideal illustration is Railway Express Agency v. New York, *supra* note 69. It no longer matters whether the Court believes the legislature has chosen the *wrong* alternative if its action was *reasonable.*

Due process objections, as such, have not presented a significant problem in the commerce clause cases. Due process is relevant, however, in two respects. In the first place, the history of Supreme Court interpretation of the clause in the economic area shows an increasing willingness to assume that legislative action has not been arbitrary— and this finding almost certainly will sustain the legislative action, when subjected to necessary and proper clause attack. Secondly, considering the fact that the commerce power is now virtually identical to the police power of the states, one might expect future attacks upon commerce clause legislation to shift from questioning whether a local activity affects commerce to questioning the due process of legislative action. This is the legal ploy which, along with equal protection arguments, has been used to attack state police power regulations.

Various techniques have been used by the Supreme Court during its history to limit the attempts by Congress to expand its power under the commerce clause. We have seen above that these techniques have included the invocation of the due process clause, the necessary and proper clause, the "pretext" argument of *McCulloch v. Maryland,* the tenth amendment, the direct v. indirect effects upon commerce dichotomy, and attempts to limit the police power theory developed in the *Lottery Case.* None of these limits, unfortunately, have any substantive qualities remaining. However, the enumerated limits are all valid; and, indeed, all emanate from the Constitution itself. Each could *and should* receive more than lip service from the Supreme Court. But the Court has, in essence, over-reacted to a set of cases which misapplied these valid principles and, along with overturning and disregarding the cases, has unnecessarily disregarded the principles as well. Commerce clause cases of recent origin talk of how the commerce power is subject to the "prohibitions" of the Constitution, yet the aforementioned limits have no force in commerce clause litigation.

The same limits that have been emasculated in the commerce clause area have retained their vitality in the civil liberties area.[96] One might wonder whether the civil liberties of a person convicted under the Cramer Amendment are any less threatened than are those of a civilian subjected to military court martial.[97] A revitalization in commerce clause litigation of those limiting principles which have maintained their vitality in the civil liberties area would be a salutary

96. *See, e.g.,* Trap v. Dulles, 356 U.S. 86 (1958); and Kinsella v. United States ex. rel. Singleton, 361 U.S. 234 (1960).

97. Examine Reid v. Covert, 354 U.S. 1 (1957), which is further illustrative of the vitality in civil liberties cases of the same constitutional limitations which are virtually today dead in commerce clause litigation.

development. In addition, we believe the Court would reassume its role of upholding the Constitution as an integrated whole—a role which it has not properly played in this area. There is no reason why constitutional limitations on the enumerated powers of Congress should be applied differently when the Court is dealing with different enumerated powers; the Constitution certainly makes no provision for this kind of "legislative" judgment on the part of the Supreme Court.

The Cramer Amendment As A Vehicle for Reinstatement of Some Limitations: An Uneasy Recommendation

A proper application of constitutional principles would result in the Court withholding its stamp of approval from the Cramer Amendment. This would, of course, require limits being placed on the congressional police power over commerce, as well as a revitalization of both the "pretext" theory and the tenth amendment in the commerce clause area. As previously asserted in this study, the police power of Congress over commerce should be limited to *protecting commerce from economic evils* and should not extend to moral ones. Only economic transactions that occur in commerce with economic motives should be regulable. This would simply entail a return to the *Gibbons v. Ogden* definition of commerce as being "commercial intercourse," and would require the overruling of the primary "villain" in the commerce area, the *Lottery Case,* in turn placing *McClung* on its proper foundation *viz.* the fourteenth amendment. In other words, Congress cannot regulate commerce unless that is in reality what it is doing: it cannot attempt to control local rioting and claim it is regulating commerce. This judicial review process, of course, requires a close examination by the Court of the congressional motive, something which *Darby* said the Court could not do. However, it would seem that where a government can act only in furtherance of its enumerated powers, the reviewing court must be charged with the responsibility of assuring that the legislature has so acted within those powers. The corrollary to the "pretext" theory must be the proposition that when Congress does not act in furtherance of its delegated powers it violates the tenth amendment—surely the two operate together.

A close look at the legislative history of the Cramer Amendment demonstrates that the majority of Congressmen supporting it were not interested in protecting commerce at all.[98] They wanted to punish

98. *See* notes 3 through 6. The writers also wish to acknowledge the assistance of Representative Sidney Yates (D, Ill.) in an informal assessment of the Congressional mood in the 2d session of the 89th Congress.

those who instigated riots or took part in them,[99] thereby contributing to the recent civil turmoil. If the commerce power were interpreted properly so as to be an economic power, then certainly Congress in the Cramer Amendment is using its power over interstate Commerce not to regulate commerce but to punish offenders against local laws. The writers assert that such action on the part of Congress should be considered a violation of the tenth amendment.

Our suggestion is that the commerce power be returned to its proper *economic* role in our society and that the limiting principles upon the other enumerated powers of Congress be given the same interpretation in the commerce area as they have been given in the civil liberties area. Steps such as these would have a beneficial effect upon the prestige of the Court as a disinterested upholder of the Constitution, for when a press conference roars with laughter after a President, asked about the public accommodations coverage of the Civil Rights Act of 1964, has stated, "The question would be, it seems to me, whether Mrs. Murphy had a substantial impact on interstate commerce,"[100] it is the Supreme Court at whom they are laughing. Should not the upholding of the Cramer Amendment, if and when enacted and challenged, engender the same breed of laughter?

---

99. 112 CONG. REC. 17652-9.

100. President John F. Kennedy at 1963 press conference, in response to question from May Craig.

Police Brutality and Racial Prejudice:
A First Close Look

VINCENT J. RINELLA, JR.*

> *The Commission has found and discussed throughout this report many needs of law enforcement and the administration of criminal justice. But what it has found to be the greatest need is the need to know.*†

INTRODUCTION[1]

FROM California to New Jersey and everywhere in between police misbehavior towards Negroes has consistently been singled out as

* B.A. 1963, Brown University; LL.B. 1966; Assistant Professor of Law, Wayne State University, Detroit, Mich.

† PRESIDENT'S COMM'N ON LAW ENFORCEMENT AND ADMINISTRATION OF JUSTICE, THE CHALLENGE OF CRIME IN A FREE SOCIETY 273 (1967).

1. Unfortunately, the highly acclaimed *Report of the National Advisory Commission on Civil Disorders*, Bantam Books (1968) [hereinafter cited as *Report*] was released after completion of the article for publication. In chap. 11/ "The Police and the Community," pp. 299-322 the commission examines and recommends solutions for five basic problem areas in the general field of "Police brutality" and "racial prejudice": [1] "The need for change in police operations in the ghetto to ensure proper individual conduct and to eliminate abrasive practices. [2] The need for more adequate police protection of ghetto residents to eliminate the present high sense of insecurity to person and property. [3] The need for effective mechanisms through which the citizen can have his grievances handled. [4] The need for policy guidelines to assist police in areas where police conduct can create tension. [5] The need to develop Community support for law enforcement." (*Report*, p. 301).

Drawing heavily on the reports of the President's Commission on Law Enforcement and Administration of Justice (See note 2, infra), the present commissions' analysis of these "problem areas" is as lucid as could be expected in light of their massive task and the limited space specifically devoted to police-Negro community relations. However, the "problem areas" are far from exhaustive, and by formulating the issues as essentially general political ones, rather than Sociological, or psychological ones, the examination finally fails as a careful and probing analysis.

The Commissions' recommendations for solutions to the problems, are, again, largely abstract and political, although, even with this caveat, they are far superior to most proposed solutions to police-Negro community problems, in both depth and scope. (See, note 94, infra). For example, in dealing with the problem of ensuring assignment of well-qualified police to ghetto areas, the Commission recommends, among other things, that: "Screening procedures should be developed to ensure that officers with superior ability, sensitivity and the common sense necessary for enlightened law enforcement are assigned to minority group areas. We believe that, with proper training in ghetto problems and conditions, and with proper standards for recruitment of new officers, in the long run, most policemen can meet these standards" (*Report*, p. 306). As this paper attempts to show, "sensitivity" and "common-sense" (or their opposites) rarely exist in a policeman at the point where he can be screened out of or into a ghetto neighborhood. Rather, these behavioral patterns seem to exist by virtue of a commingling of the policeman's perceptions (of himself and others), his assigned tasks and roles, the institutional framework of which he is a part with its own definitions of rewards and punishments and also, the various ways that the community itself defines "enlightened law enforcement."

Despite this tendency to deal with an incredibly complex subject in a simplified manner—a tendency no doubt influenced by the urgency of its task, at least as defined

one of the major causes of America's recent civil crises.[1A] In Los Angeles the arrest of two "drunken" Negroes, coupled with the manhandling of a pregnant Negro girl, is said to have "caused" the Watts conflagration.[2] Newark's civil crisis, according to some reports, was "caused" by the arrest of a Negro cabbie for a traffic offense and a post-arrest rumor that the police had murdered the misdemeanant.[3] In Detroit, an early Sunday morning raid on a crowded "blind pig," resulting in the mass arrest of almost one hundred Negroes, was the apparent "cause" of ten days of looting, arson, sporadic sniping, and sheer terror.[4] When the visible smoke had cleared from all three cities, the cry of "police brutality" hung heavy in the acrid air, as wise men found a reason and those less wise a scapegoat for what may accurately be viewed as an overdetermined nightmare.

Racial prejudice is commonly alleged to be the cause, and core, of police misbehavior toward the Negro citizen. Indeed, to equate such misbehavior with stupidity, sadism, or a host of more complicated factors, would, at least theoretically, serve to alleviate the antagonism between whites and blacks that has become visible once again in the past few months. Arguably, police abuse of all citizens, regardless of color, might forge a common bond between white and black citizen-victims—a bond which would encourage both integration and a collective effort at reform. Unfortunately, America's recent urban up-

---

by the National Community, as well as its "action-orientation"—the Commission *Report* is by far one of the most useful and intelligent discussions of the causes and cures of "police brutality" and "racial prejudice" extant.

1A. The term "civil crisis" has been defined as "the situation in which parties at issue no longer 'find it possible to resolve their disputes within informal sanctioning, private adjudication, and civil law.' In such a crisis, each party tends increasingly to act with 'an intent to destroy 'the enemy' rather than . . . to defeat him, but (to) keep him in the (political) game, thus indicating a context in which the moral order has been disrupted, or has never been created.' " Blake, Holden, Mendelsohn, & Sigel, Research Memorandum on the Civil Crisis of Detroit 3 (1967) (unpublished, Dept. of Political Science, Wayne State University), quoting Holden in THE ALLOCATION OF JUSTICE, *Politics, Public Order, and Pluralism,* (Klonoski and Mendeloshn, eds., forthcoming).

For this article's purposes, the terms disturbance, riot, rebellion, and such, are deemed to possess the same meaning as "civil crisis" defined above, and such terms are used without reference to their legal meaning. Further, the use of such terms is not meant to attribute any particular purpose to the participants, nor is it meant to imply any factual knowledge on the author's part concerning the event referred to in the text.

As to the racial overtones of our nation's civil crises, see note 5, *supra.*

2. COHEN & MURPHY, BURN, BABY, BURN: THE WATTS RIOT 23-58 (1967). *See also* JOHN F. KRAFT, INC., ATTITUDES OF NEGROES IN VARIOUS CITIES 2 (1966) which was quoted in THE PRESIDENT'S COMMISSION ON LAW ENFORCEMENT AND ADMINISTRATION OF JUSTICE, TASK FORCE REPORT: THE POLICE 147 (1957) [hereinafter cited as TASK FORCE REPORT]. *See* GOVERNOR'S COMMISSION ON THE LOS ANGELES RIOTS, VIOLENCE IN THE CITY—AN END OR A BEGINNING? 12 (1965) as cited in TASK FORCE REPORT 147-148.

3. *Life,* July 28, 1967, p. 18.

4. *Snipers Prolong Emergency. Death Toll Climbs To 23,* The Detroit News, July 25, 1967, p.1, cols. 1-8.

heavals have provided little motivation for such a coalition. Taking a cue from the racial overtones of the conflicts[5] and the behavior of white policemen in quelling them, the Negro citizen in particular, as well as a number of whites, has concluded that the police are, for the most part, a collection of racially prejudiced people who express their prejudice by "brutalizing" Negroes.

This is not, of course, a new complaint. It has been bruited about the Negro communities of most major cities for a number of decades: it was simply reactivated by the recent civil crises.[6] For this reason alone it would probably be more profitable to examine police behavior patterns and prejudices toward Negroes over the last few decades, rather than to examine only their behavior during, or immediately prior to, an urban riot.

There is an even more compelling reason for focusing primarily on police behavior throughout the recent past if we seek meaningful clues to the riddle of "police brutality" and racial prejudice. Police activity during, or immediately before, a riot is rarely reflective of normal police behavior. Such activity is a specifically determined phenomenon, motivated largely by the peculiar stresses of an intense and open conflict which the community demands be immediately stopped,

---

5. Despite the fact that a plethora of politicians and commentators have been careful to characterize various of these crises as a colorless conflict between the "lawless" elements in the community and the "law-abiding" citizen, rather than as a violent confrontation between the Negro and the white man, it is clear that in terms of act and result, if not because of motive, the predominant tone of most conflicts was a racial one. The fact that some whites engaged in unlawful activities pales in significance beside the post-crisis charges of prejudicial action by white policemen against Negro participants, the anti-white sentiment now prevalent among large segments of the Negro population, and the burgeoning backlash among America's white middle-class. From the vantage point of the ordinary citizen, the upheavals are perceived as unambiguous racial conflicts. No amount of *ex post facto* empirical investigation, it seems, will convince either Negroes or whites that such was not the case.

6. For a compilation of polls concerning Negro attitudes toward police behavior in the past, see TASK FORCE REPORT 146. It is clear that, generally, police-Negro community relations in most cities where riots have occurred have never been optimal. The results of a 1965 poll of Detroit's Negro population are representative of the prevailing sentiments in most urban areas. That poll "found that 58 percent of Negroes did not believe that law enforcement was fair, and an earlier poll in 1951 found that 42 percent of Negroes believed that it was 'not good' or 'definitely bad.'" TASK FORCE REPORT 146, citing Ouderlugs, "How Citizens Rate Police Department on Racial Fairness," Detroit News, Feb. 3, 1965, sec. A, p. 1, col. 3.

In a recent Louis Harris poll, a sample of Negro adults were asked what they thought might be the two or three main reasons for the Negro riots. Thirty-six percent replied that prejudice, promises unkept, and bad treatment were a major cause, while 49 percent of the Negroes interviewed cited police brutality against Negroes as a major cause of the rioting. *Newsweek*, August 21, 1967, p. 19.

In any search to locate the elements giving rise to these attitudes, one is sure to stumble upon the reality of racial prejudice and, perhaps, never regain the balance to continue. Racial prejudice on the part of the police, like police brutality in general, is not an element in itself, but is rather an umbrella term which must be teased apart so that its components may be examined.

combined with the average policeman's inexperience in dealing with the unusual situations which occur within the framework of both the initial conflict and a mass rebellion. The latter consideration, police inexperience, was obvious throughout the recent civil crises. Unlike the riots of years past, these crises were characterized by a sophisticated sort of urban guerilla warfare, rather than a mere tactical use of bricks and bottles. Often caught off guard, and consequently embarrassed or placed in unusually dangerous positions, the police probably reacted by expressing more hostility and aggression toward "lawbreakers," both Negro and white, than they normally do.[7]

Observation of police brutality toward Negroes during, and immediately prior to, a riot may mislead citizens into believing either that such behavior is the norm or that specific recent incidents of police brutality "caused" the civil disorder. Neither is quite correct. If we are concerned with the causal relationship between police misbehavior toward Negroes and a racial disturbance within a particular community, it would be most efficacious to examine the history of "brutality" in that community, rather than focus on specific recent incidents of police conduct. The failure to separate long-term, habitual police activity from police conduct during a civil crisis is likely to result in the asking of wrong-headed or irrelevant questions about police brutality and its relation to riots. It may also make unreliable the answers to suitable questions. Although a number of immediate conditions or circumstances may trigger off a large scale racial disturbance,[8] the origins of most riots lie in the prior existence of prejudice or brutality, strengthened and released by these later, more obvious factors.[9] Examination of most riots reveals a pattern of intense previous hostility between the participants, including the police and the Negro citizen. A prolonged period of verbal abuse and discrimination by the police toward the Negro generally precedes an outbreak of individual or collective physical violence.

---

7. Once a disturbance or riot is in progress, of course, the dominant consideration must be to end it . . . . For example, the common police technique in controlling riots is to use a massive amount of force to break up the rioters into small groups as soon as possible. Snipers are generally answered in kind; batons, dogs, and tear gas may be used. TASK FORCE REPORT 193.

8. "[M]ost riots are at least triggered by police action." TASK FORCE REPORT 193. Other exciting causes of riots include wildly circulating rumors, hot weather, and some rapid change in the prevailing social situation. G. ALLPORT, THE NATURE OF PREJUDICE 56-63 (abr. ed. 1958). See also Dahlke, *Race and Minority Riots—A study in the Typology of Violence*, SOCIAL FORCES 30, 419-425 (1952).

9. "[P]oor police-community relations has contributed to the disturbances and riots which have increasingly afflicted our cities for the last three years . . . In addition, more often than not, riots were set off by some quite ordinary and proper action by a policeman." TASK FORCE REPORT 145. *See also* ALLPORT, *supra* note 8 at 59.

Racial Prejudice

To accept racial prejudice as the heart of "police brutality" toward Negroes is to encounter an idea whose dimensions have rarely been defined.[10] In his classic work on the subject of ethnic prejudice, Gordon Allport attempts at least three definitions before he arrives at one which is functional for the purposes of his inquiry. Says Allport:

> [Racial] prejudice is an antipathy based upon a faulty and inflexible generalization. It may be felt or expressed. It may be directed toward a group as a whole, or toward an individual because he is a member of that group.[11]

Although this characterization contains the necessary ingredients of all definitions (i.e. reference to a feeling-tone and unfounded judgment), it is too broad for the purposes of our present analysis. Prejudice as an element of police brutality toward Negroes is significant only as it manifests itself, either subtly or notoriously, in action. If an officer has a belief in the inherent criminality of Negroes, such belief would not be included in the concept of brutality unless it were translated into some policy, action, word, or gesture. Hence, this article will examine the "acting out" of prejudice by the police in its varying degrees of intensity, rather than any antipathy toward Negroes which an officer may feel, but which is neither directly nor indirectly expressed. With slight modifications, Allport's prejudice-intensity scale of 1.) Antilocution, 2.) Discrimination (including avoidance and segregation), and 3.) Physical attack, will serve as a guide for our inquiry.[12] Even using these guidelines, however, the issues may be clouded not only by the close interrelationships among the concepts the guides purport to represent, but also by a host of epistemological problems inextricably related to the objective actions which make up the concepts of prejudice and brutality.[13]

---

10. Where the issue of either "brutality" or racial prejudice," however that action or attitude be defined, is seen as a continual and pervasive phenomenon, it may fairly be viewed as a matter of "bad" or "deteriorating" relations between the police department and the Negro community. The focus of discussion, then, will necessarily shift from the specific problem of the policeman's interaction with the Negro individual or small group to the more general problem of the police department's interaction with the Negro community as a whole.

11. Allport, *supra* note 8 at 10.

12. Allport suggests a scale of intensity resulting in five types of rejective behavior: 1) Antilocution, 2) Avoidance, 3) Discrimination, 4) Physical Attack, and 5) Extermination. He later simplifies the five steps into three: 1) Verbal rejection (antilocution), 2) Discrimination (including segregation), and 3) Physical attack (of all degrees of intensity). *Id.* at 48.

13. Racial prejudice as a component of police brutality may, of course, be analyzed within a more traditionally legal framework, since certain police procedures, *e.g.*, arresting,

Antilocution

Verbal discourtesy, abuse, and rejection by the white policeman toward the Negro citizen is, in many ways, the aspect of brutality which is most dangerous to the mental and physical health of the total community. Although "allegations of excessive physical force receive the most attention, verbal abuse and discourtesy [are] probably greater irritants to community relations."[14] Furthermore, if officers are "abusive, insulting or condescending, the most insignificant contact can become an occasion which arouses hostility against the police,"[15] leading to physical attack by either the officer or the abused victim. Finally, discriminatory statements, perhaps more so than violent forms of prejudice and brutality, produce not only anger, but also strong counterprejudices among minority groups.[16]

Contrary to the beliefs of most policemen, "the overwhelming majority of the public has a high opinion of the work of the police";[17] but Negroes are "significantly more negative than whites in evaluating police effectiveness in law enforcement."[18] Most interesting is the fact that the greatest attitudinal difference between Negroes and whites revolves around the issue of police discourtesy. In one survey of Negroes in the general area of Watts, the highest percentage of respon-

---

searching a suspect, seizing his property, or interrogating, have evolved into recurring patterns of behavior either constitutionally prohibited or surrounded by other legal rules and regulations. It is doubtful, however, that prejudice or brutality are rooted in these procedures, although they may be expressed by them. Rather, prejudice and brutality cut across all procedures and are better analyzed by examining their social and psychological roots and more general modes of expression. In examining the charge that the police are racially prejudiced toward Negroes it is most relevant, I think, to inquire whether particular police conduct is unprofessional or detrimental to good police-Negro community relations, rather than illegal or unconstitutional. Some conduct described in the text is clearly illegal, *e.g.*, the unauthorized use of deadly force, some may be unconstitutional. But here the sole focus is on the racial prejudice and brutality exhibited in these activities, regardless of legal or constitutional issues.

14. TASK FORCE REPORT 180, citing Galvin & Radelet, A NATIONAL SURVEY OF POLICE AND COMMUNITY RELATIONS 17 (1967). *See also* Reich, *Police Questioning of Law Abiding Citizens*, 75 YALE L.J. 1161, 1164 (1966):

> I have read that when Negroes complain of "police brutality" in areas like the Watts section of Los Angeles, they are as much concerned with verbal tone as with physical violence. And this is understandable; incidents like those described cause a sense of injury to the person in a direct, visceral sense. Members of a minority group are likely to be especially sensitive to such address. There is something deeply offensive in familiarity which is deliberately used by a person in authority for the purpose of causing humiliation.

15. TASK FORCE REPORT 180.

16. *Id.*, citing WILLIAMS, STRANGERS NEXT DOOR: ETHNIC RELATIONS IN AMERICAN COMMUNITIES 46-48, 253, 257-258, 283, 301 (1964).

17. TASK FORCE REPORT 145.

18. *Id.* 146. The Commission relied for this point primarily upon a survey by the National Opinion Research Center. A National Sample Survey Approach to the Study of the Victims of Crimes and Attitudes Toward Law Enforcement and Justice (Unpublished, 1966).

dents cited lack of respect or use of insulting language as the sort of police misconduct which they personally experienced; activities such as beatings while in custody and the use of unnecessary force in making arrests were experienced by a much smaller percentage of the subjects.[19] Recognizing the possible unreliability of surveys in general and the particular questionability of this survey, which lacked a white control group for comparison purposes, there is little question that the Negro citizen does perceive and experience a great deal of verbal abuse, and that antilocution is a common activity among policemen. However, a number of factors, often obscured or ignored, may somewhat mitigate the harsh accusations against the police in this particular area.

First, many observers have noted that, although "The use of racial epithets such as 'nigger,' 'coon,' [and] 'boy' appears to be widespread [among individual officers], their use is condemned by responsible police administrators . . . ."[20] Indeed, various departments have issued specific policy directives prohibiting certain forms of address by officers, while the police manuals of other departments contain the same prohibitions.[21] Though such institutional action reaffirms the existence of a serious problem, it also indicates that racial prejudice is not an institutionally supported norm[22] and that if conformity to departmental standards is a factor motivating police behavior,[23] a decrease in verbal abuses of the Negro may be anticipated. Naturally, any departmental position on a critical social issue may be viewed by both the public and the policeman as little more than a public-relations gesture. Unimplemented by enforceable sanctions, it may become a shield of false security for the citizenry and a badge of freedom for the officer, behind which he may secretly release his personal prejudices. But, if taken in good faith, these recent executive regulations will exert a controlling influence on the antilocutions of individual officers and do reflect an awareness of a disease which is not endemic to the police department as a representative institution.

Second, certain forms of antilocution often perceived as racially

---

19. Raine, Los Angeles Riot Study: The Perception of Police Brutality in South Central Los Angeles Following the Revolt of August 1965 (1966), cited in Task Force Report 147.

20. Task Force Report 180.

21. *Id.* 181. In addition to the examples given there, see The Detroit Police Manual, ch. 10, § 10 (Supp. 1965).

22. This is not to imply, however, that such prejudice is not normative behavior among policemen within a particular department. See, for example, Skolnik, Justice Without Trial: Law Enforcement in Democratic Society 81 (1966).

23. ". . . [P]olicy directives of a department, if enforced, can affect the actions of individual officers." Task Force Report 164.

prejudiced comments against Negroes may, when objectively viewed, reflect a general discourtesy on the part of policemen toward members of all races. Some Negroes have informed this author that white police officers in Detroit, when stopping them for suspected traffic offenses, accost them with the word "boy" and, after examining their license, address them by their first name only. These citizens have uniformly interpreted the refusal of officers to address them by their last name, prefixed by an appropriate title (e.g. Dr., Mr., Mrs.) as a sign of racial prejudice. In fact, since the author and several white acquaintances have, in similar circumstances, often been victims of the same insensitivity, these verbal habits may stem from bad manners rather than any sort of racial prejudice. This conclusion, of course, will not bind the wounds or stifle the resentments of many Negroes, but it does contribute to our understanding of what may or may not be part of "umbrella" terms like racial prejudice and police brutality.

Other factors which may dilute the accusation that verbal abuse of Negroes is always equivalent to racial prejudice as we have defined it are located in that shadowy corner where the policeman's professional role is dovetailed into a series of specific environmental influences as well as certain habits of speech and perception common to most citizens. For example, the policeman's well-known penchant for stereotyping and categorizing all Negroes, regardless of individual physical and personality differences,[24] may not evidence actual racial prejudice, but may reflect a number of more complicated and, perhaps, excusable traits. Jerome Skolnik has noted that officers stereotype all minority groups because their "culture is that of the masculine workingman," who speaks of the black man as a "nigger" rather than a member of an underprivileged minority just as he refers to Joe DiMaggio as a great "wop" centerfielder, rather than a ballplayer of "Italian extraction." This antagonism toward "euphemisms" of any sort, common among most men of action, is, for the policeman, part of a social world that tends to be constructed along ethnic lines in general. Thus, "although hostile feelings toward the Negro are characteristic of white policemen in general, these dispositions are also linked to a broader pattern of racial and ethnic stereotyping . . .," making the disposition to stereotype the Negro "an integral part of the policeman's world . . . ."[25] This broader pattern of racial stereotyping may exist within most forces largely because police recruits are "substantially working class, of high school education or less, who are

24. *Id.*, citing Westley, The Police: A Sociological Study of Law, Custom and Morality 168 (1951) (unpublished).

25. Skolnik, *supra* note 22 at 82, 83.

more likely to have the stereotypes . . . ."[26] Indeed, some observers have found less prejudice and stereotyping among "professional" police forces, which require that many of their officers obtain a college education (often unobtainable for the underclass members of our society), than among other forces.[27] Or, again, stereotyping may simply be due to the lack of Negro representation on most police forces.[28] Finally, some assert that the pattern of stereotyping exists for more complicated psychological reasons.[29] Most important for our discussion, however, is the fact that underlying all these theories is the conviction that stereotyping is not a trait peculiar to the police and that, although many officers appear to possess an antipathy toward Negroes or other minority groups, they may actually be acting out a professional role that is incompatible with their true feelings. As one officer put it: ". . . I don't think I'm prejudiced—not the way some guys here are. Sure, I call them niggers around the department—everybody does it, so I do it too. But I don't let my kids say nigger at home."[30]

Antilocutions may also stem not from racial bias, but from a natural response to the second environment inhabited by most officers—the street. Skolnik notes, for example, that:

> Unlike most whites, the policeman has some sort of social contact with lower-class Negroes. He has learned that in the Negro community the term "nigger" is not necessarily taboo, and that it refers to impoverished and illiterate Negroes, usually of Southern origin. While the use of the term "nigger" by "Negroes"—itself a term stemming from slavery—expresses the inevitable self hatred of the oppressed, the policeman is not a student of culture and personality.[31]

26. Beasley, *Cop in the Ghetto*, The South End [newspaper], Nov. 14, 1967, p. 4, col. 2, quoting Dr. Burt Levy of the Michigan Civil Rights Commission.

27. Task Force Report 163, citing Williams, *supra* note 16 at 54.

28. "The mere lack of contact between white and minority group officers on the force will make other measures to end prejudice and discrimination less effective. Studies of prejudice show that stereotypes tend to be modified and prejudices reduced when whites have contacts with Negroes on an equal footing . . . . [Another] study found that the more white officers worked with Negro policemen, the less they were prejudiced against them." *Ibid.* 174, citing, respectively, Williams, *supra* note 16 at 156-159, 167-168, 185, 191, 217, 220, and Kephart, Racial Factors and Urban Law Enforcement 98-99, 188-189 (1957).

29. "The hostility directed toward minority groups, expressed as discrimination based on prejudice, is an example of displaced aggression." Coville, Costello, & Rouke, Abnormal Psychology 53 (1960).

"According to psychoanalytical interpretation, ethnic hostility is a projection of unacceptable inner strivings onto a minority group." Bettelheim & Janowitz, Dynamics of Prejudice: A Psychological and Sociological Study of Veterans 45 (1950). *See also* Allport, *supra* note 8 at 28-45, 194.

30. Skolnik, *supra* note 22 at 81.

31. *Id.* at 82. For the proposition that use of the term "nigger" by Negroes expresses the inevitable self-hatred of the oppressed, Skolnik cites Sarnoff, *Identification With the Aggressor: Some Personality Correlates of Anti-Semitism Among Jews*, 20 J. of Personality 199-218 (1952).

However, it is not just an unthinking imitation of those speech patterns abounding on a policeman's particular beat which produces the verbal abuse so often construed as expressing a deeply held antipathy. It is also the very nature of that beat as it impinges on the officer's professional role as protector of the community. For instance, Michael Banton suggests that, "If policemen meet members of any one social category chiefly in situations which spell trouble for the officer, they are likely to react by expressing disapproval of the whole category."[32] There is little doubt that a similar generalized reaction occurs when an officer encounters members of a particular *racial* category in the ghettos of urban America, where the surroundings alone "spell trouble" for the ordinary policeman. His "disapproval of the whole category" (of Negroes) is likely to be expressed in words, although his use of antilocutions may reflect not a degree of personal prejudice against Negroes, but rather a professional distaste for what are perceived as "troublemakers."

Similarly, Skolnik has noted that, because the main environmental influence on police work is a sensitization to potentially violent or dangerous behavior, most policemen develop a "perceptual shorthand to identify certain kinds of people as symbolic assailants, that is as persons who use gesture, language, and attire that the policeman has come to recognize as a prelude to violence."[33] The policeman's tendency to be suspicious of all social deviance will often undermine the judicious use of his authority, especially as it affects those Negroes whose life-style deviates from the white majority's in terms of speech and action. Moreover, an officer's suspicion may be directed not only to unusual actions or excited speech, but also to appearances alone. As Skolnik notes:

> Hostility toward Negroes is apt to be revealed on the street, especially in situations inviting stereotyping. If police are looking for a robbery assailant, and have "nothing to go on" but a vague description of a Negro male, innocent Negro males will easily be assimilated to the policeman's stereotype of the suspect.[34]

Seeing all Negroes as symbolic assailants, the officers are threatened by their mere presence; the perceived threat may even lead officers to "defensive" abuse of the citizen, verbal or otherwise.

In his social relations inside or out of the department, the white policeman usually has no contact with Negroes, but many Negroes

32. Banton, The Policeman in the Community 179 (1964).
33. Skolnik, *supra* note 22 at 45.
34. *Id.* at 86-87.

may inhabit the areas the officer must patrol—areas where a lack of money, jobs, education, and adequate housing may contribute to a high crime rate. Thus the policeman is likely to "live in a world straining toward duality and suggesting danger when 'they' [Negroes] are perceived."[35]

Naturally, signs of deviance vary from area to area. The mere presence of an unknown, non-resident Negro in a predominantly white neighborhood is more likely to spell danger to an officer than would the presence of that same Negro in a neighborhood inhabited largely by Negroes. Within a predominantly Negro neighborhood, however, an officer may view *all* the inhabitants as deviant in the sense that none conform to the behavioral norms of the larger, middle-class white society. It should be emphasized that such a perception will not be a consciously chosen one for most policemen, but it will be inherent in the structural and cultural conditions of their professional rule. Likewise, although the officer may feel no antipathy toward Negroes as persons, his involvement in situations which he perceives as threatening may encourage his use of antilocution or some other, and perhaps harsher, defensive reaction, (e.g. unnecessary physical force) in his dealings with Negro citizens. Such a response might be caused, once again, by the policeman's professional personality, as formed by his distinctive occupational role, rather than by actual "prejudice."[36]

Finally, it is an accepted social fact that the white, ghetto policeman operates within an environment whose inhabitants are bitter and hostile, either toward him personally or toward what he represents. Although one recent survey found that "Most Negroes, regardless of their feelings do not physically or verbally react with hostility in routine situations . . .,"[37] nonetheless, "A uniformed policeman is a conspicuous and visible target for subtle but unmistakable forms

35. *Id.* at 47. "Officers see the worst side of life and, in view of the higher crime rate, especially the worst side of the ghetto. As a result, their stereotypes of Negroes, as well as of other minority groups, may be strengthened." TASK FORCE REPORT 164.

36. The precise extent to which prejudice affects the conduct of the officer on the street is not known. Social scientists, however, believe that discriminatory action is influenced not only by individual attitudes, by the social structure, and by the views of the rest of the group, but also by the policies of the organization. . . . On the other hand, the seriousness of strongly held prejudices by numerous officers should not be minimized. . . . Whatever bias an officer has when he joins the force, without adequate training it will often get worse. . . . And such prejudices are likely to become increased by virtue of the large number of other officers who express prejudice.

TASK FORCE REPORT 164, citing WILLIAMS, *supra* note 16 at 96, 345-348. *See also* SKOLNIK, *supra* note 22 at 80-90 and text accompanying notes.

37. TASK FORCE REPORT 148, discussing Black and Reiss, Police and Citizen Behavior in Routine Field Encounters: Some Comparison According to the Race and Social Class Status of Citizens (unpublished, 1966).

of insult such as sidelong glances, pursed lips, or loud sniffs."[38] Also, as novelist James Baldwin, discussing the plight of the white policeman in Harlem, comments: "there are few things under heaven more unnerving than the silent, accumulating contempt and hatred of a people."[39] Hostilities—mute, subtle, or vocal—are minor irritants which may evoke an unjudicious verbal response by the policeman—a response expressing fear and counterhostility rather than an authentic prejudice.

Antilocution is a complex phenomenon which exists in varied forms. It may include not only the habit of using the word "boy" when speaking to Negroes, but may also encompass the tendency on the part of some white officers to employ a condescending or abrupt tone or a haughty gaze when dealing with Negroes. In there more subtle cases of gestural, tonal abuse, as in the clearer cases of verbal abuse, police behavior may indeed indicate actual prejudice and a degree of brutality. More often, however, they reflect a set of unthinking responses to a series of complicated pressures and, although perceived or felt by Negroes to be "brutal" or prejudiced, are neither intentional harms nor expressions of antipathy toward the Negro *qua Negro.*

Discrimination

Police discrimination against Negroes, if a less pervasive and potentially dangerous type of rejective behavior than antilocution,[40] is more energetic and actually dangerous in terms of the indignities inflicted on the Negro citizen.

Discrimination is more easily described than defined. It occurs when the policeman treats individuals or groups unequally; and it is a prejudicial action based on distinctions of a relatively obvious sort, e.g. color. Because discrimination involves unequal treatment, and the distinctions underlying the inequality are obvious, it is often more visible than antilocution. Its impact on the individual or group is more intense, and the resentment it engenders is often more powerful than that caused by verbal abuse.

However, what discrimination is, how often it occurs, and to what extent it affects the various kinds of discretion delegated to policemen depends largely on the vantage-point from which it is examined. From the vantage point of the Negro, discrimination by the police is primarily felt as selective enforcement or non-enforcement of the laws

---

38. SKOLNIK, *supra* note 22 at 87.
39. BALDWIN, NOBODY KNOWS MY NAME 62 (1962).
40. ALLPORT, *supra* note 8 at 55.

which favors the white man and harasses the black. It is not a discrimination among classes, since poor, middle, and upper class Negroes are stopped, arrested, searched, physically or verbally abused and charged more often than are their white counterparts in the corresponding class.[41] However, from the vantage point of the observer of police conduct, it appears that police do not discriminate *primarily* between Negroes and whites of the same social or economic class, but rather that police behavior depends on a potential arrestee's socio-economic status, as well as whether he is labeled as one of the law's "undesirables," such as "homosexual," "drunk," or "vagrant."[42]

Other less visible criteria also seem to influence the discretionary powers formally or informally delegated to the policeman. Banton noted that in deciding whether to arrest a drunken offender, officers consider such factors as whether the offender is near his home, and whether he lies when asked if or what he is drinking.[43]

The criteria employed by policemen in exercising their discretion are not the only clues to the nature and extent of racial discrimination. Skolnik has made it clear that such discrimination cannot be adequately discussed without reference to the policeman's assignment, which both defines the extent of his discretion and determines the parameters of his various criteria.[44] Focusing on the traffic warrant policeman who, after writing up an arrest warrant, has the discretion to free a defendant who cannot post bail but assures the policeman he will do so at a later date, Skolnik found that racial discrimination, although it appeared to be a factor in this decision, was most often a spurious variable. The traffic warrant policeman operates according to general standards, such as the apparent stability of the defendant's residence and whether the defendant is steadily employed. Although many Negroes find these standards more difficult to meet than whites, there was a "notable tendency for traffic warrant police to respond

---

41. TASK FORCE REPORT 183, citing Lohman & Misner, 1 THE POLICE AND THE COMMUNITY 78, 107 (1965); LOHMAN & MISNER, 2 THE POLICE AND THE COMMUNITY 105, 153 (1966). and BUREAU OF SOCIAL SCIENCE RESEARCH, SALIENT FINDINGS ON CRIME AND ATTITUDES TOWARD LAW ENFORCEMENT IN THE DISTRICT OF COLUMBIA 13B (1966). *See also* TASK FORCE REPORT 178-190.

42. Werthman & Piliavin, *Gang Members and the Police, The Police* 56-98 (ed. Bordua 1967). TASK FORCE REPORT 183, citing BLACK & REISS, *supra* note 37 at 9-10, 14-17.

43. BANTON, *supra* note 32 at 57.

44. Skolnik, *op. cit. supra* note 22 at 84. At pp. 71-90, the author focuses solely on *delegated* discretion, that is discretion clearly given the police officer, as opposed to *unauthorized* discretion, that is discretion which the officer exercises but for which he may not have been given authority. For a discussion of how the exercise of largely *unauthorized* discretion within the context of various assignments may lead to discrimination, see Goldstein, *Police Discretion Not to Invoke the Criminal Process: Low-Visibility Decisions in the Administration of Justice,* 69 YALE L.J. 543, 573-580 (1960).

favorably to Negroes appearing to possess the middle-class virtues of occupational and residential stability."[45] This particular type of policeman "may . . . appear to be discriminating against the Negro, when, in fact he may be mainly implementing departmental goals by deciding against the poor, the unemployed, and the residentially unstable, many of whom are black."[46]

The uniformed officer with a gun on his hip, rather than an arrest warrant in his pocket, does not use the same criteria in deciding how to deal with a suspect or arrestee.[47] Even in that assignment bracket, however, it is clear that racial discrimination has broader social and economic implications. For example, surveys have shown that although Negroes and various other minority groups are indeed stopped, frisked, and arrested in disproportion to their numbers,[48] such groups often live in high crime areas and hence, "normal, completely fair police work would doubtless produce the arrest or stopping of larger numbers of these groups."[49]

There are two final related phenomena that are at least apparent components of the general concept of *discrimination* as it operates against the Negro: the social isolation of the police from both the community at large and the Negro community in particular, and the lack of adequate police protection provided for members of minority communities.

---

45. SKOLNIK, *supra* note 22 at 85.

46. *Id.* at 86.

> This analysis suggests that, as in so many other sectors, especially employment and housing, the problem of "bias" is not merely racial, but has broader social and economic implications. At the same time, a cool and objective analysis provides little comfort to those Negroes who face the existential problem of being poor, unemployed, and residentially unstable.

See also note 13, *supra*.

47. *See* section on *Physical Attack*.

48. For a comprehensive look at police misbehavior toward minority groups in the areas of field interrogation, arrest for investigation, arrest for harrassment, and arrest for minor crimes, see TASK FORCE REPORT 183-188. Most of the mitigating factors attaching to the charge of police brutality and prejudice toward Negroes in these areas are touched upon in this general discussion.

> It might be noted that the President's Commission, like the American Law Institute, believes that there is a definite need to authorize the police to stop suspects and possible witnesses of major crimes, to detain them for brief questioning if they will not voluntarily cooperate, and to search such suspects for dangerous weapons when such a precaution is necessary.

TASK FORCE REPORT 184, ALI MODEL CODE OF PRE-ARRAIGNMENT PROCEDURE 95-97 (Tent. Draft No. 1 1965). It is impossible to predict whether the granting of such clear authority to the police would result in an even greater number of Negro stoppings, or whether the number of Negro stoppings would remain constant while whites, stopped less often when police were unsure of their authority, would be stopped more often. Whites will be stopped more often under the new authority only if they have not been stopped in the past for some reason other than racial bias, *e.g.* the policeman's fear of their objection or retaliation against his uncertain authority.

49. TASK FORCE REPORT 183.

Skolnik has pointed out that although James Baldwin and others have analyzed racial discrimination in law enforcement in terms of the isolation or alienation of the police from the Negro community,[50] it is "in many respects simply a special case of the alienation of the police from the whole community—so that what Baldwin sees as a function of race appears in important degree to be a function of police-civilian relationships in general."[51] The most cogent evidence Skolnik cites for this proposition is the fact that when the police in his studied community were asked to rank the most serious problems police have, "the category most frequently selected was not racial problems but some form of public relations: lack of respect for the police, lack of cooperation in enforcement of law, lack of understanding of the requirements of police work."[52]

Banton, though recognizing that "a gulf may arise between the police and the public where . . . the police feel alienated from society," focuses on the separate situation where the police "see a section of the population as not belonging to their own society."[53] He notes the consequences of this particular gulf may be much more serious. Recording his observations of police work in the American South, he states:

> At no time did I get the impression that white police officers felt the same involvement in the rights and wrongs of life in the Negro district as they did in the white districts. An officer who came across a Negro woman who had been badly beaten by her lover showed none of the feelings of indignation and sympathy he might have revealed had she been white. There were some exceptions, of course, as there usually are, but generally speaking, the white policeman saw beatings and stabbings as customs of the Negro sections, like shooting craps.[54]

In the same vein, another commentator has noted that, "Some policemen feel that assault is an acceptable means of settling disputes among Negroes, and that when both assailant and victim are Negro, there is no immediate discernable harm to the public which justifies a decision to invoke the criminal process."[55] The variety of forms such discriminatory behavior may take was noted by the President's Commission:

> Lack of protection can take the form of police being slow to respond to calls, having inadequate personnel, or tending to

50. SKOLNIK, *supra* note 22 at 49.
51. SKOLNIK, JUSTICE WITHOUT TRIAL: LAW ENFORCEMENT IN DEMOCRATIC SOCIETY (1966), 34 U. CHI. L. REV. 226, 233 (1966).
52. SKOLNIK, *supra* note 22 at 50 & n.13.
53. BANTON, *supra* note 32 at 172.
54. *Id.* at 172-173.
55. GOLDSTEIN, *supra* note 44 at 575.

> ignore offenses by one minority person against another in contrast to those by members of minority groups against whites or whites against whites. While the lack of attention paid to investigating violations against others of the same race is probably decreasing, it still exists in many localities.[56]

The most important result of the white policeman's alienation and isolation from the Negro community, then, is not simply his lack of empathy with Negro victims or his stereotypical view of Negro life, but the fact that such subjective states and private values are rapidly translated into policy-shaping factors which create a situation where tendencies toward criminal behavior are aggravated within the Negro community, while that same community is provided grossly inadequate police protection.

Where this lack of protection exists, stemming from either a departmental policy of selective non-enforcement of some or all laws within the Negro community, or from the individual officer's passivity or conscious omission to enforce the law in certain recurring situations, it tends to corrode the quality of police-Negro community relations in general.[57] In addition, because it assumes a variety of undetectable forms,[58] it doubtless causes as much or more psychic and

---

56. TASK FORCE REPORT 183, relying upon SKOLNIK, *supra* note 22 at 172; *Report to the U.S. Commission on Civil Rights, Delaware Advisory Committee*, 50 STATES REPORT 92 (1961); SIMPSON & YINGER, RACIAL AND CULTURAL MINORITIES 511-512 (rev. ed. 1958); and LAFAVE, ARREST: THE DECISION TO TAKE A SUSPECT INTO CUSTODY 110-114 (1965).

57. The Negro is aware of "the law" only as an agent of the white community. The police act directly upon the Negro to keep him "in his place." The effect has been that many southern Negroes . . . continue to regard the policeman as a natural enemy. The only manner in which the confidence of all groups can be won is by impartial and vigorous enforcement of the law. Absolute impartiality requires that the law be enforced against all violators. The idea that race, creed, or nationality are extenuating factors, permitting of different applications of the law, must be abandoned . . . . The police officer who is tempted to vary his role according to personal notions as to the worth of various groups is himself in violation of the law. An officer has a capacity for delivering equal justice only to the extent that he has this problem under control.

LOHMAN, THE POLICE AND MINORITY GROUPS 5 (1947) (manual prepared for use in the Chicago Park District Training School), cited in GOLDSTEIN, *supra* note 44 at 576 n.69.

58. [P]olice decisions not to invoke the criminal process, except when reflected in gross failures of service, are not visible to the community. Nor are they likely to be visible to official state reviewing agencies, even those within the police department.

GOLDSTEIN, *supra* note 44 at 552.

It should be noted that the selective non-enforcement of the law by officers, when applied to *all persons* may, in fact, be justified.

> The police have a duty not to enforce the substantive law of crimes unless invocation of the process can be achieved within bounds set by constitution, statute, court decision, and possibly official pronouncements of the prosecutor. *Total enforcement,* were it possible, is thus precluded, by generally applicable due-process restrictions on such police procedures as arrest, search, seizure, and interrogation. *Total enforcement* is further precluded by such specific procedural restrictions as prohibitions on invoking an adultery statute unless the spouse of one of the parties complains, or an unlawful-possession-of-firearms statute if the offender surrenders his dangerous weapons during a statutory period of amnesty.

physical harm to the individual Negro than do those active, aggressive forms of verbal or physical discrimination, which, being more visible, are more highly publicized. And as such, this lack of protection is possibly a more significant component of the "police brutality" concept, especially when it appears to the Negro to be rooted in avoidance.

In the selection, assignment, and advancement of police personnel, discrimination as a type of rejective behavior not only manifests an avoidance of the Negro by the white policeman, but also makes visible various patterns of segregation[59] which may produce an increase in police "brutality." Despite the complaints of numerous police officials that it is impossible to locate Negroes who are willing or able to become policemen,[60] it is clear that discrimination in the selection and advancement of officers exists in many cities. In this area alone, perhaps, the statistics tend to speak for themselves:[61] the gross discrepancy between the number of Negroes who apply for jobs or promotions are those whose ambitions are fulfilled can only be explained plausibly by reference to a discriminatory policy.[62]

> Such restrictions of general and specific application mark the bounds, often ambiguously, of an area of *full enforcement* in which the police are not only authorized but expected to enforce fully the law of crimes. An area of *no enforcement* lies, therefore, between the perimeter of *total enforcement* and the outer limits of *full enforcement*. In this *no enforcement* area, the police have no authority to invoke the criminal process.
>
> Within the area of *full enforcement*, the police have not been delegated discretion not to invoke the criminal process. . . .
>
> *Full enforcement*, however, is not a realistic expectation. In addition to ambiguities in the definitions of both substantive offenses and due-process boundaries, countless limitations and pressures preclude the possibility of the police seeking or achieving *full enforcement*. Limitations of time, personnel, and investigative devices—all in part but not entirely functions of budget—force the development, by plan or default, of priorities of enforcement. Even if there were "enough police" adequately equipped and trained, pressures from within and without the department, which is after all a human institution, may force the police to invoke the criminal process selectively.

GOLDSTEIN, *supra* note 44 at 554 & n.20, 555-560. *See also* notes 29, 30, 32.

It is impossible, however, to justify selective non-enforcement as applied *only* to minority group members. Moreover, such racial discrimination, verging on avoidance, makes police discretion even more unreviewable than non-enforcement in general. (For an explanation of why the non-enforcement decision is unreviewable in general, *see* GOLDSTEIN, *supra* note 44 at 552-553.) This is so because, with respect to Negroes, an added factor enters into the problem. Since the Negro is generally hostile to the police and often reluctant to report violations of law, even when a full enforcement policy exists, he will no doubt never report instances of non-enforcement. This is especially true where nonenforcement is based upon racial bias, for in such a case the Negro, whose charge is one of *patently unjustifiable* nonenforcement, is likely to fear future police retaliation.

59. "*Segregation* is a form of discrimination that sets up spatial boundaries of some sort to accentuate the disadvantage of members of an out-group." ALLPORT, *supra* note 8 at 52.

60. INT'L ASS'N OF CHIEFS OF POLICE AND CONFERENCE OF MAYORS, POLICE-COMMUNITY RELATIONS POLICIES AND PRACTICES 8 (1965), cited in TASK FORCE REPORT 169.

61. TASK FORCE REPORT 167-174 and tables therein.

62. Other factors contributing to the gross under-representation of minority group

The impact of such a policy on the existence of real or apparent police brutality is complex and powerful. Most abstractly, the very existence of a discriminatory or segregationist policy in these areas exerts a demoralizing influence on the Negro community. It undercuts its respect for the department and creates a resentment in the Negro citizen that may, if expressed, provoke an officer into responding in a prejudicial or "brutal" manner. A discriminatory policy in the area of promotions, moreover, is likely to engender resentment among those Negro officers within a department and perhaps encourage them to behave abusively or prejudicially toward not only white citizens, but Negroes as well. More concretely, such a policy makes it particularly difficult to recruit qualified Negroes into the police force. The result—a predominantly white police department—helps maintain the stereotypes and prejudices of many officers, which would probably be modified and reduced if there were frequent contact between members of both races on an equal footing.[63] Since the stereotypes and prejudices are often expressed via antilocutions or other prejudicial actions, perceived by the Negro as examples of police misbehavior, even this institutional discrimination aids in filling out the contours of "brutality."

In examining racial prejudice as a component of police brutality, it may be even more important to note that discrimination and segregation exist within most police departments even after some Negroes (no matter how few) are accepted into the force. Negro officers are segregated from white officers both socially and professionally.[64] Most notably, they are either assigned exclusively to patrol Negro areas, or are never assigned to Negro neighborhoods when white policemen are patrolling them.[65] The result of such a discriminatory policy is often more harmful to police-Negro community relations than having a police force with no Negroes whatsoever. If only white policemen are assigned to patrol Negro communities, the residents may conclude

---

members on police forces include educational deficiencies and low scores on department intelligence tests designed for the middle class white. Usually, all three factors operate to interfere with increased recruitment of Negroes. With respect to the inequities in promotions, discrimination seems to be the primary factor responsible. TASK FORCE REPORT 168-171.

63. WILLIAMS, *supra* note 16 at 156-159, 167-168, 185, 191, 217, 220, cited in TASK FORCE REPORT 174.

64. For examples of social segregation *see* TASK FORCE REPORT 170-71 and BANTON, *supra* note 32, at 54.

65. U.S. Civil Rights Commission, Administration of Justice Staff Report ch. 11, 24, ch. 12, 10-11; THE 50 STATES REPORT, submitted to the U.S. Comm'n on Civil Rights by the Mass. Advisory Comm. 253-254 (1961) [hereinafter cited as STATES REPORT]; RUDWICK, THE UNEQUAL BADGE: NEGRO POLICEMEN IN THE SOUTH 13-14 (1962); all cited in TASK FORCE REPORT 174.

that their "protector" is merely a symbol installed in their midst for the purpose of affirming the status quo. If the officer exhibits prejudicial tendencies of any intensity, these same residents, already possessing an accumulated resentment and prejudices of their own, may provoke the white policeman into being far more "brutal" than he normally would be, even in an all Negro environment. Conversely, if segregation takes the form of assigning only Negro officers to predominantly Negro neighborhoods, the residents may actively express their resentment of such a discriminatory policy, which they may perceive as demeaning, by making the officer's life on the beat more difficult. This, of course, makes more likely a "brutal" response by the officer. Furthermore, the Negro officer in such a situation may resent his superior's prejudicial actions regarding assignments and become less effective and more "brutal" in performing his designated functions.

Fortunately or not, in some instances these same segregationist policies may prevent the occurrence of certain forms of brutality. For example, the assignment of only Negro officers to predominantly Negro neighborhoods may deter brutality by lessening tensions between residents and the patrolling officer. Both patrolmen and police officials have reported that Negro policemen are especially competent and effective in Negro neighborhoods. For example, they are more respected than white officers and "are in a better position to control their districts due to the knowledge of their own people, personal acquaintance, hangouts, permanent residents and transients."[66] Putting aside the ethical and practical questionability of sacrificing the principle of equal treatment for a preventive measure which might tend to reduce the likelihood of brutality, it is clear the efficacy of the tactic is too often diluted by the actual behavior of the Negro policeman in the ghetto, behavior which is often more harsh and abusive than that of his white counterpart.[67] This fact, in turn, engenders a preference in many low-income Negroes for white policemen as protectors of their respective communities.[68] To give weight to this preference and assign only white officers to Negro neighborhoods might, as we have noted, create equal or greater hostility than assignment of those Negro officers who are especially abusive, in which case the game would hardly be worth the candle.

On balance, discrimination, avoidance, and segregation are significant elements of police brutality. They are not simply factors

66. U.S. Civil Rights Commission, *id.* 24, quoted in TASK FORCE REPORT 167.

67. *See* 1 LOHMAN & MISNER, *supra* note 41. at 93, 101, vol. 2, 116, 132-133; KEPHART, *supra* note 27 at 118; A. REISS, JR., THE PHYSICAL FORCE IN POLICE WORK 10 (1966); all cited in TASK FORCE REPORT 167.

68. RUDWICK, *supra* note 65 at 11.

which tend to either diminish its impact or fall outside the ambit of actions the concept itself circumscribes. Even if this were not the case, if these particular expressions of prejudice were pragmatically useful in reducing "brutality" to some extent, and were desired by both officers and citizens, their existence and employment would be indefensible as incompatible with values underlying all theories of democracy.

Physical Attack

Within the context of our discussion, physical attack may be most usefully described as an unjustified, excessive or unnecessary use of force by an officer against a Negro. Like antilocution and discrimination, physical attack has been seen by many as another expression of prejudice by policemen toward Negroes. However, the problem is a more complicated one.

Any violent physical attack upon a Negro is usually the outgrowth of a milder state of mind or action, such as antilocution or a nonviolent discrimination,[69] but physical misconduct probably occurs less frequently than those preceding activities. Numerous civil rights leaders have stated that verbal abuse and harassment, not excessive use of force, is the major police-community relations problem today.[70] Moreover, although the statistics are sparse, recent studies suggest that violent physical attack by the police of members of any race is a less serious problem than it has been in the past.[71]

Nonetheless, unjustified physical attacks of Negroes and other racial groups do occur today, especially in the South.[72] Although the problem may not be extensive enough to fire the consciences of Negro leaders, its existence may wreak more immediate havoc on the community than decades of verbal abuse and subtle discriminations. This is especially true when it results in death or serious bodily harm, whether the victim be an officer or citizen. Furthermore, the integrity of the body is a deeply held societal value which when violated, even by minor touchings, becomes the potential exciting cause of a collective community retaliation, perhaps culminating in a genuine civil crisis.

---

69. ALLPORT, *supra* note 8 at 56.

70. GALVIN & RADELET, *supra* note 14 at 66; Raspberry, "Physical Violence May Be Gone, But Police Brutality Still Exists," The Washington Post, May 27, 1966, B, p. 1, cols. 1, 2, 3, cited in TASK FORCE REPORT 181. *See also* GELLHORN, WHEN AMERICANS COMPLAIN 176-177 (1966).

71. TASK FORCE REPORT 181.

72. Roberts, *Police Seize 11 in Rights March*, New York Times, June 24, 1966, § 21, col. 4; 175 *Negroes Are Pursued and Clubbed*, The Washington Post, July 11, 1966, p. 1, col. 3; *Court Told How Police Ignored Negro Beatings*, The Washington Post, Sept. 16, 1966 A, p. 6, cols. 1, 2; U.S. COMMISSION ON CIVIL RIGHTS, LAW ENFORCEMENT: A REPORT ON EQUAL PROTECTION IN THE SOUTH 174-175 (1965); STATES REPORT, 1, 29-44, 105-109 (1961), all cited in TASK FORCE REPORT 181-182.

For evidence that the problem still exists in the North as well, *see* REISS, *supra* note 67 at 16-17, and STATES REPORT 687.

In examining physical attack as an expression of police prejudice and a component of police brutality toward Negroes in particular, it is crucial to distinguish it from abusive use of physical force by the police in general. If police physically abuse proportionate numbers of non-Negro citizens, as well as Negroes,—and this has not been proved —then the charge of racial prejudice and police brutality toward Negroes must be re-examined. Most important, the solution to this particular problem may turn out to reside in something other than a racial re-education of policemen.

Recent studies make it fairly clear that the unjustifiable use of force by officers is based on factors other than race. For example, a team of Presidential Commission observers witnessed over five thousand police contacts in a number of major cities and reported that in the twenty cases in which officers used force where none was clearly required or where its use was plainly excessive, racial prejudice was rarely the basis for abuse. Rather, a series of interrelated factors, such as the victim's economic status, his actual or imagined character or condition, and his particular response to the officer's authority seemed to activate the policeman's aggression.[73] Other surveys reveal that the primary cause of physical attack, is, again not a person's skin color, but the policeman's misconceptions about when he is in fact justified in using force. In a survey of one midwestern city's force policemen were asked what reasons they felt justified "roughing a man up." The largest percentage of officers answered that a citizen's disrespect for the policeman was the best reason.[74] However, in later in-depth interviews, most of these same respondents asserted their belief that "the only way to treat certain *groups* of people, *including Negroes* and the poor is to treat them roughly." [Emphasis Added][75] In light of good evidence that Negroes as a group are no more verbally hostile to officers than are whites,[76] the suspicion remains that factors such as "lack of respect" may be rationalizations for the physical expression of racial prejudice. However, it is important to discover whether many Negroes, perhaps because of their social isolation from and lack of identification with white officers, manifest their resentment in a nonverbal manner more often than do whites, e.g. through passive resistance, flight, initiative

---

73. REISS, *supra* note 67 at 16-17, cited in TASK FORCE REPORT 182.

74. Westley, *Violence and the Police*, 59 AM. J. SOC. 38.
Only one reason was counted—either that first mentioned or that given most heatedly or at greatest length—for each officer. Dr. Westley believed that the officers were cautious with him because of recent criticism by the chief of police and the community about the use of violence.
TASK FORCE REPORT 183 at n.340.

75. TASK FORCE REPORT 183.

76. BLACK & REISS, *supra* note 37 at tab. 3, cited in TASK FORCE REPORT 148.

physical contact, and so forth. If the Negro does tend to make the policeman "work harder" to take him in, physical attack, based not on prejudice but on impatience and ignorance, is likely to result.[77]

The unauthorized use of *deadly* force by officers (e.g. unnecessary use of firearms) to apprehend and arrest Negroes, whether or not it results in death, is probably the most explosive single factor behind a civil crisis. The unwarranted use of such force exists within many large police forces,[78] and is very closely associated in the public consciousness with the phrase "police brutality." As with the use of force in general, this particular sort of force is rarely exercised against a person because of his color. First, many of those factors which are inherent in the officer's professional role such as oversensitization to danger, and which cut across all forms of misbehavior perceived as prejudicial or "brutal," operate to motivate the unwarranted use of deadily force by policemen against members of all races. However, the primary cause of this particular abuse probably lies in the refusal or inability of most police departments to articulate a clear, concrete, and understandable policy on the matter.

As one national survey of forty-five large cities showed, few departments provide their officers with careful instruction on the circumstances under which the use of a firearm is permissible.[79] Some departments did issue comprehensive policy statements, while many had oral policies which "normally developed through customary practices that rarely are the product of careful analysis and are usually not well understood by patrolmen."[80] Similarly significant are the results of a recent

---

> 77. The "uncooperative" white delinquent will be treated just as roughly as the black. And woe to the white demonstrator who goes "limp" with others during a protest demonstration. For the policeman, this form of protest generates physical labor, hard and, in his view, unnecessary. When a citizen *makes* a policeman sweat to take him into custody, he has created the situation most apt to lead to police indignation and anger.

SKOLNIK, supra note 22 at 88. However:

> [A]s a result of the civil rights movement, white policemen sometimes seem *more* color conscious in an interesting fashion. They perhaps used to unconcernedly push a black man around—the suspect was just another "nigger." Now, the policeman may think twice—a Negro suspect may appear to him not only as a man with rights, but one with exceptional political power as well. . . . In an earlier period (but less than twenty years ago) the police used outright violence to maintain respect. It is now more difficult for them (at least in . . . most . . . northern urban areas) to maintain control through these techniques because of the operation of civil rights groups, and the increased knowledgeability of the citizens most likely to talk back—the younger males.

SKOLNIK, *id.* at 86, 88.

If the latter observations are true, they may, of course, affect all aspects of police behavior toward Negroes, especially in the area of physical attack.

78. TASK FORCE REPORT 189 and nn. 416-418. *See also* note 72, *supra.*

79. CINCINNATI POLICE DEPARTMENT, POLICE REGULATIONS GOVERNING USE OF FIREARMS SURVEY 1 (1964), cited in TASK FORCE REPORT 189.

80. TASK FORCE REPORT 189, citing Chapman & Crockett, *Gunsight Dilemma: Police Firearms Policy*, POLICE, May-June, 1963, 22.

survey of Michigan police forces which revealed that many departments in that state have no firearms policies at all.[81] In light of his qualifications and the exigencies of his professional task, it is foolish to allocate to the policeman the role of ethicist and decision-maker and expect anything less than disaster.

The probable reason for the lack of standards and criteria in this area is neither racial prejudice nor inertia on the part of police administrators. An articulaton of the circumstances under which the use of deadly force by an officer should be allowed is an extremely difficult task, requiring a reconciliation of important values which are often irreconcilable and the ability to foresee a variety of unforeseeable situations.[82] Abstract formulations, if they do manage to balance the values satisfactorily, usually fail to have an impact on actual police conduct, while detailed manifestoes, if formulable, are useless to the officer in an emergency situation that requires a split-second decision. Furthermore, since the legal rules on the subject are often predicated on obsolete distinctions,[83] the drafting of new policies must usually start from scratch. Fortunately, some intelligent and useful criteria have recently been proposed,[84] providing some hope that this manifestation of "police brutality" toward all citizens may soon be reduced.

---

81. *Id.*, citing Chapman & Crockett, *supra* note 80 at 54.

82. For an excellent discussion of the problems involved in articulating the circumstances under which deadly force should be allowed, see ALI MODEL PENAL CODE § 3.07, comment at 52-64 (Tent. Draft No. 8., 1958).

83. An example is the traditional rule distinguishing the force to be applied in apprehending felons and that to be used in apprehending misdemeanants.

> The common law approach to a solution of the problem . . . is based on the distinction between felony and misdemeanor; deadly force is authorized where necessary to prevent the escape of one fleeing from arrest for felony, but not for misdemeanor. . . .
>
> This distinction, whatever its virtues for the period in which the rules of justification were formulated, seems manifestly inadequate for modern law. Such rational justification for the common law rule as can be adduced rests largely on the fact that virtually all felonies in the common law period were punishable by death. Though effected without the protections and formalities of an orderly trial and conviction, the killing of a resisting or fleeing felon resulted in no greater consequences than those authorized for punishment of the felony of which the individual was charged or suspected.
>
> Today, the significance of the distinction between felony and misdemeanor has wholly altered. Relatively few crimes are punishable by death. A very small percentage of arrests actually made are for offenses which are capitally punishable. . . . Of these, the number in which capital punishment is likely to be imposed is very substantially smaller. Moreover, under modern legislation, many statutory misdemeanors involve conduct more dangerous to life and limb than some felonies. Compare, for example, such felonies as the distillation of alcohol in violation of the revenue laws, on the one hand, and such misdemeanors as reckless and drunken driving, on the other. Even a felony which often is committed in such a way as to endanger life, may in many particular cases be committed in a fashion which creates no such peril. Accordingly the felony-misdemeanor distinction is inherently incapable of separating out those persons of such dangerousness that the perils arising from failure to accomplish immediate apprehension justify resort to extreme force to accomplish it.

Id. at 56-57.

84. *See,* for example, *Id.* at § 3.07(1)(2)(3).

The Epistemological Problems

The validity or invalidity of the charge that police are prejudicial or brutal toward Negroes is often determined by the accuracy of perception and judgment of those people who observe or hear about police behavior. There are, in fact, a host of implied epistemological questions underlying certain of our assumptions and cutting across all three of our alleged components of "police brutality," viz. antilocution, discrimination, and physical attack. The answers to those questions may cause a radical revision of our tentative conclusions regarding the composition of that concept. Indeed, a careful examination of the questions themselves may reveal that the problems we have been considering are finally matters of misperception and ignorance, rather than prejudice or brutality. It is useful at this juncture to articulate and comment on a few of the most important and representative epistemological questions surrounding the concept of police brutality toward Negroes, in order to clarify various central assumptions which have been implicit in our discussion.

Both critics and defenders of police behavior agree that Negroes, especially those residing in the urban ghettos, have little respect for white officers. Members of both groups, in fact, would go so far as to posit a feeling of hate on the part of Negroes for white policemen. The bases for these feelings have never been explored. However, it is important to discover whether the Negro's hatred, assuming it exists, stems from a personal experience of having been abused by the police, or whether it is based on an observation of a fellow Negro's plight at the hands of an officer. In light of modern discoveries concerning the inherent unreliability of both memory and perception,[85] it may be that the correlation between the Negro's feelings and the existence of an actual stimulus of police abuse is lower than most observers believe. Indeed, if certain other conditions obtain, there may be no positive correlation at all. It is possible, for example, that most Negroes who "hate" white officers have neither experienced nor been an eye witness to any police abuse at all, but have taken on faith what others have reported. It is important in that case not only to discover *who* did the reporting, but also to locate the bases for *his* assertions, and to assess his ability to relate facts honestly and accurately. An epistemological exploration of modest proportions would at least inform us whether those Negroes who do experience "police brutality" ever talk about it at all, and whether, irrespective of their proclivities to communicate their experiences, they are the same people who possess those feelings of

85. Marshall, Law and Psychology in Conflict 5-82 (1966).

hatred for the policeman, feelings so often attributed to the entire Negro community.

These epistemological problems are compounded when we examine the role that "rumor" plays within the Negro community. It is apparent that although "rumor" is a popular source of both information and misinformation for the general public, it is especially potent within the Negro community as a transmitter of experience, including experience at the hands of the policeman. This occurs partly as a reaction against the mass media of the general community, which concentrate heavily upon crimes committed by Negroes and give little publicity to the achievements of the Negro citizen.[86] More generally, however, the Negro's retaliatory motives are rooted in his basic mistrust of the mass media and their information sources. When for many years numerous public information agencies, financed, administered and controlled by various white power structures, have arrogated unto themselves the task of defining, often erroneously, the Negro's needs and aspirations without consulting Negroes themselves, there is justification for such mistrust. With respect to police behavior, particularly, it is well known that the mass media's characterizations of the quality of police-Negro relations in some major cities have been inaccurate and incomplete, and have been viewed as a "snow-job" by a majority of the Negro community.[87] Unfortunately, however, rumors of police misbehavior that circulate wildly among Negro citizens are equally unreliable and misleading.

In their continual search for "newsworthiness," the mass media may at times overplay and publicize alleged incidents of police misbehavior more than enough to offset their frequent whitewashings of the department in general. What is reported may slightly exaggerate the actual abuse occurring within a particular community. It would be interesting in such a situation to discover whether the Negro's posited "mistrust" of "white" information sources is maintained or shedded.

To locate answers to this and similar questions, however, it is important to determine precisely the epistemological relation existing between the ghetto community and the mass media. The search will necessitate a host of further inquiries. Does the partial isolation of this particular community from the "white" world and its informal chan-

86. Lee, *The Press in the Control of Intergroup Tensions*, 244 ANNALS 144-151 (1946), cited in ALLPORT, *supra* note 8 at 195. *But see* ALLPORT, *supra* note 8 at 196.

87. Police-community relations programs within many police departments suffer the same fate. LOHMAN & MISNER, *op. cit. supra* note 41 at vol. 1, 58, vol. 2, 82-83. Since police-community relations personnel are often assigned to prepare press releases, it may be that the mass media's inaccurate characterization of police-Negro relations stems not from deceptive motives or rank irresponsibility, but rather from the "public relations" motives of their sources. TASK FORCE REPORT 153.

nels of public opinion compel it to "take on faith" whatever the mass media report as true? Or does this isolation remove most ghetto inhabitants from the effects of the mass media? Does either isolation from, or undue reliance upon, these formal information transmitters distort the concept of police brutality for the underclass Negro? Or does it clarify it? Again, does either isolation or undue reliance tend to foster oversensitivity to certain forms of police behavior in the mind of the Negro, or does one or the other condition minimize a realistic sensitivity? In view of our "objective" examination of the label "police brutality" toward Negroes, and the behavioral complexities it revealed, the injection into our discussion of inter- and intra-subjective questions of knowing and perceiving will hopefully result in a more lucid observation between that "brutality" and racial prejudice in general.

To return to the Negro's alleged "hate" for the white policeman, it is useful to determine whether that feeling is directed toward *individual* policemen in response to their actual misbehavior, or whether it is leveled at officers not because they have *done* something, but because they *are* something: the most visible representatives of the total "white" establishment, which the Negro commonly identifies as an oppressive phenomenon. Is the policeman a "symbolic assailant" for the Negro in much the same way that the underclass Negro seems to be a symbolic assailant for the white officer?[88] If so, police brutality toward Negroes, like Negro criminality, may be based primarily on the Negro's expectations rather than on the policeman's conduct.

In a similar manner, one may inquire whether the Negro's concern with police brutality is somehow a surrogate for an abiding concern with deeper and more frustrating problems, such as the denial of jobs, housing, and equal educational opportunities for the majority of Negro citizens. As the President's Commission noted:

> To a considerable extent, the police are victims of community problems which are not of their making. For generations, minority groups . . . have not received a fair opportunity to share the benefits of American life. They suffer from bad housing, inferior education, unemployment, underemployment, or low wages. They have been discriminated against and abused by welfare and public housing officials, private landlords and businessmen. Their frustrations and bitterness are taken out, at least in part, on the policeman as the most visible symbol of a society and its law which have often treated them so unjustly.[89]

---

88. *See* text accompanying notes 33-35, *supra*.

89. Task Force Report 150.

Immediately after the 1967 Detroit riot, the author interviewed several Negro citizens displaced by the crisis. When asked who or what was to blame for the riot, all

"Brutality" is also a surrogate for the white men. Many white critics of police brutality toward Negroes may, like the Negro, blame the wrong culprits. It is all too easy for the white citizen, ambivalent or negative about extending equal rights and opportunities to Negroes, to resolve his ambivalences or deny his prejudices by deceiving himself, and using the police as a scapegoat for all the ills the Negro suffers. Conveniently, he shifts blame for the past and responsibility for the future from himself and society to the policeman.

Sometimes simple misjudgment and ignorance, rather than self-deception or denial, are the essence of "scapegoating." If the police are often blamed for the abuses and prejudices that society as a whole heaps on the Negro citizen, they are even more maligned because of the injustices suffered by many Negroes within the confines of the rest of the criminal justice system, especially in the criminal courts of the cities. While it strains the imagination to consistently equate unfair educational opportunities with police prejudice, it takes little mental effort to associate the entire criminal process with the policemen who set it in motion. Again, the President's Commission provides an apt description of the situation that prevails in most urban areas:

> When a suspect is held for long periods in jail prior to trial because he cannot make bail, when he is given inadequate counsel or none at all, when he is assigned counsel that attempts to extract money from him or his family even though he is indigent, when he is paraded through the courtroom in a group or is tried in a few minutes, when he is sent to jail because he has no money to pay a fine, when the jail or prison is physically dilapidated or its personnel brutal or incompetent, or when the probation or parole officer has little time to give him, the offender will probably blame, at least in part, the police officers who arrested him and started the process.[90]

Naturally, it is not only the Negro whose opinion of the police is jaundiced by the rest of the process. However, insofar as most of these indignities are the result of a lack of money on the part of the defendant or convicted offender, it is the Negro, often economically discriminated against by society long before arrest, whose view of the policeman is sure to be warped most severely.

---

interviewees responded by saying it was a lack of money, time, and effort spent by the community at large on improving the slum areas in the city, and getting the Negroes better jobs and homes. No one pointed the finger at police brutality as a primary reason for the crisis. This leads one to inquire whether the apparent concern with police brutality in Detroit is somewhat a surrogate for much deeper problems. It is quite possible, of course, that verbal concern with money and housing, based on simple material issues, covered deeper psychological problems, such as relations with policemen as individual human beings and/or as symbols.

90. *Id.*

The evils imbedded in the post-arrest process also exert a critical and often degrading influence on police attitudes and behavior patterns, especially as they impinge on the lives of minority groups. It is well known that for most policemen the conviction of an arrested defendant is a confirmation that they are performing their task correctly and efficiently.[91] Since the series of deprivations and discriminations in the lower criminal courts probably results in a large number of convictions of minority group members, the policeman will continue perceiving those people as "symbolic assailants" and will arrest them as frequently as ever. More importantly, because the court's confirmation of an officer's efficiency is uninfluenced by the quality of his conduct, the officer who has been abusing minority group members while apprehending them will probably continue to do so, mistaking a confirmation of his efficiency for an approval of the methods used to attain it. Of course, if the courts openly condone police misbehavior—and there is reason to believe they sometimes do—the officer will persist even more readily in his previous behavioral patterns. Conversely, it should be noted that if the quality of our judges, prosecutors, bail bondsmen, and prison personnel were improved, police treatment of Negroes might improve considerably. If, for instance, the number of convictions of such citizens fell, either because the police had abused an individual, violated one of his constitutional rights, or simply been wrong about his probable guilt, the policeman might react by abusing the members of that group less frequently, reducing his perception of those group members as "symbolic assailants" and, finally, invoking the rest of the criminal process against them less often than he does.

Finally, as Skolnik has observed, policemen themselves are acutely aware of at least one particular issue which they feel is primarily responsible for the false accusation that they are racially prejudiced toward Negroes. That issue is located in the vast area between epistemology and semantics. Although most officers will admit that they dislike Negroes, they will rarely confess that they are prejudiced against them. This is so, according to Skolnik, because:

> To say of somebody that he is *biased* against another is to make an *accusation* rather than a descriptive report of feelings. The policeman knows what it means to hate or fear or merely dislike. But he finds it difficult to accept a term which transforms an explicit emotion—hatred—into a fuzzy and condemnatory abstraction. To say of somebody that he *hates* another is a statement of fact—there may be good reason for hating. However, to accuse somebody of bias is to put him

91. "The organized form of confirmation is the handing down of convictions by the public courts." HAZARD, *supra* note 51 at 228.

> clearly in the wrong, since there is never a justification for bias. Moreover, the term racial bias implies something exceptional about the policeman's attitude toward the Negro; it distinguishes the policeman's antipathy from the run-of-the-mill community attitude. From the policeman's point of view, an accusation of racial bias tends to make a scapegoat of him, when as a rule he is probably no more prejudiced than his fellow citizens who lead lives isolated from Negroes.[92]

Conclusion

In order to formulate intelligent solutions to the puzzle of police brutality toward Negroes in contemporary urban America, we must define our objectives with precision; recognize exactly what the problems are; and admit that certain limitations, may exist, inherent in our efforts, which are presently unknown. As our analysis has shown, the phrase "police brutality toward Negroes" describes a variety of undesirable activities brought about and motivated by an interrelated series of numerous complicated factors, most of which owe their existence not to racial prejudice, but to the professional role the policeman must play, the nature of the institution he is a part of, and the often impossible and conflicting tasks we have charged him with performing. For this reason alone, there exists no overall solution which will eradicate all the components of such "brutality" at the same time. To deal with verbal abuse, a group of solutions may recommend themselves, while to reduce the incidence of physical attack or discrimination, a number of separate and discrete reformative methods may be required. In short, different diseases with different causes call for different cures.

By and large, most recently suggested solutions to the problems under discussion, although varying and comprehensive, are doomed to failure. In neglecting to analyze carefully the meaning of either racial prejudice or "police brutality toward Negroes," proponents of those solutions have ignored the need to deal with each component of the problem according to its particular requirements. As Hubert Locke, former Administrative Assistant to the Detroit Commissioner of Police, put it:

> Of primary importance is some basic concensus [*sic*] on what the term "police brutality" means or ought to mean . . . [M]uch of the current confusion concerning this issue (how to deal with "brutality") stems from attempts to create a single, problem-solving mechanism that will deal effectively with dozens of situations which are different, both in kind and

92. Skolnik, *supra* note 22 at 81-82.

> in degree. . . . [L]ittle clarity is brought to the discussion of these practices when [they] are recited under the rubric—police brutality, especially when this leads to a search for a single procedure that will resolve [all] problems. . . . Each infraction . . . has to be viewed for what it is, factually and accurately, and then dealt with accordingly.[93]

Furthermore, even those reformers who recognize this need, seem to be unaware of the behavioral and epistemological complexities inherent in each component. While intelligently questioning the wisdom of creating a civilian review board or an ombudsman to handle complaints of police brutality on the grounds that they must, by their very nature, operate "post-facto," Locke himself proposes some preventive solutions that, in light of our discussion, offer only the slimmest chance of effectiveness.[94]

If the central component and cause of police brutality toward Negroes were, in fact, racial prejudice, a "single, [effective] problem-solving mechanism" might not be hard to concoct: "Persons with relatively slight prejudices will probably control them if properly trained and supervised."[95] But, because of the institutional and professional pressures imposed on policemen, most expressions of brutality toward Negroes or other minority groups may be impossible to eliminate without a total restructuring of the police department and a redefinition of the officer's role in society. Such a step requires that the community reorder its expectations regarding the functions an officer should perform, as well as the values which the law has been charged with affirming. The failure of reformers to come to grips with the more difficult and complicated realities of police work and their insistence

---

93. Locke, *Police Brutality and Civilian Review Boards: A Second Look*, 44 U. DET. J. URBAN L. 625 (1967).

94. [I]n-service training for police officers in human relations, special concern for the "kind and quality of applicants that are recruited" into departments, and an "emphasis on training and professionalization" (Locke, *id.* at 631,633) are, of course, laudable objectives to be pursued by any effective police department. If attained, they may even contribute to a reduction of the most obvious sorts of brutality, defined by Locke as "any situation in which a police officer *physically and with intent*, whether with or without provocation abuses a person in his custody. *Id.* at 626. But do they really grapple with the daily situational behavior problems which confront the policeman in his assigned role and performing his assigned tasks within an institutional framework which may, by its committment to those tasks and that role, foster more subtle but equally abhorrent forms and patterns of brutality, and also preclude the exercise of a "human relations" approach?

Another abstract, and probably ineffective, proposed solution to the general problem is found in Terris, *The Role of the Police*, 374 ANNALS 58-69 (1967). Terris suggests that what is needed to cure our diseased state of police-community relations is a radical alteration in both the policeman's and the community's conception of what police work is all about. He advises both parties to develop a conception of police work as a "service role."

95. TASK FORCE REPORT 164.

on dealing with only the most obvious aspects of brutality is, perhaps, excusable. But a community's failure to be honest with itself about what is demanding of their police force is not excusable. When we direct the policeman to "protect the community" without explaining what we mean by this phrase, and without clearly describing how he should perform the task, we should not be surprised if most officers take the directive to heart, view all Negroes as "symbolic assailants," and follow up this perception by abusing such "potentially dangerous" individuals.

If the community, through the mechanisms of denial and "scapegoating," continues to avoid confronting its own deepest prejudices, the policeman, like the Negro, will become victimized and, finally, demoralized or rebellious. In these times of exceptional tension, the policeman, like the criminal and the Negro, has become a scapegoat—a target for the community's frustrations and aggression. And his existence has allowed both Negroes and whites to "blame someone else" for the antipathies they themselves feel and express for each other. Because the police, like the Negro and the criminal, are not a "vocal, scholarly group that devotes much time to presenting in a favorable light the facts that bear on the problem,"[96] the realities of brutality, like the realities of prejudice within the community, are necessarily obscured. And once again the policeman serves to reflect the values and deflect the perceptions of society as a whole.

Finally, although upon objective consideration it seems that racial prejudice is rarely a component or cause of police brutality toward Negroes, still, from the Negro's vantage-point, police abuse is inexcusable and is usually perceived as a manifestation of prejudice. As Fanon comments in his classic work on colonialism and revolution, "For the native, objectivity is always directed against him."[97]

Furthermore, if it is true that prejudice rarely motivates abuse, it is also true that the policeman's attitude toward Negroes in general does not differ significantly from the attitudes of the wider white community from which he has been recruited, and the values of which he has introjected.[98] That this wider community is, economically, socially and institutionally, an unconsciously racist society is, I think, easier to prove than to refute.[99] In this light, it is surprising that racial prejudice

96. Wilson, *Police Arrest Privileges in a Free Society: A Plea for Modernization*, POLICE POWER AND INDIVIDUAL FREEDOM: THE QUEST FOR BALANCE 25 (Sowle ed. 1962).

97. FANON, THE WRETCHED OF THE EARTH 61 (English ed. 1966).

It should be understood that the term "native," although possessing a degrading connotation for many white Americans, is used by Fanon and this author to refer simply to the Negro exploited by any white majority.

98. WESTLEY, *supra* note 74 at 39-40.

99. Although it is difficult or impossible to prove the truth or falsity of this propo-

plays so minor a role in the occurrence of police brutality toward Negroes, and that the policeman *qua* scapegoat is not called upon to quell more violent demonstrations against our society.

---

sition, it is not difficult today to find those, both black and white, who believe in its truth. *See* FANON, *supra* note 97.

"Racism in America has become institutionalized," Joyce says, to point [sic] that "it is not just that white people—though that's certainly true too—but that racism is an unstated premise of every institution. It has become an unconscious thing for most people.'" Askins, A Middle-Class Youth and Racism, Detroit Daily Press, Dec. 3, 1967, § A, p. 3, col. 1-6, quoting Frank Joyce, founder of People Against Racism.

Riot Response:

The Police and the Courts

HUBERT G. LOCKE*

INTRODUCTION

BY 7 a.m. on the morning of July 23, two platoons of police officers consisting of twenty-two patrolmen and two sergeants had been dispatched to 12th Street with orders to begin clearing the streets. The sergeants in command of those platoons made a decision upon their arrival at the scene which was confirmed several hours later at Police Headquarters. That decision became one of the most bitterly contested aspects of the riot and was the subject of endless debate thereafter. In brief, the issue was, and in the minds of many still is, one of whether police action was firm enough at the outset.

Many citizens, both Negroes and whites, were outraged that the police did not take firmer action. The *Michigan Chronicle*, the most widely circulated Negro weekly in Detroit, headlined its July 29 issue: "It Could Have Been Stopped!" and entitled its head story for the same issue: "Did Police Just Write Off 12th?" The story itself quoted the paper's editor as describing police "just standing around" while looting took place and carried his observation that "if police had stopped looting when it was centered on one 12th Street block early Sunday when the mood was allowed to become a 'Roman Holiday,' the riot could have been prevented."[1] The editorial, however, drew a widespread criticism and in the following week's edition, in a front page editorial, the *Chronicle* pointedly noted that their call for firmer police action the week previous was not a recommendation that police "should use undue force or shoot to kill."[2] However, in spite of the *Chronicle*'s subsequent moderation of its position, a great many Detroiters felt that the police action on 12th Street that morning was wholly inadequate and inappropriate.

What the appropriate and adequate police action might have been, no one has ever been willing or able to suggest, although in the confusion of that first day, all sorts of advice was being given, from using

---

* Director of Religious Affairs and Research Associate, Center for Urban Studies, Wayne State U. Former Administrative Assistant to Commissioner of Police, Detroit.

1. Michigan Chronicle, July 29, 1967, at 1.
2. Michigan Chronicle, August 5, 1967, at 1.

police dogs (which the Department does not have) to using fire hoses. The latter suggestion came from a very prominent, militant civil rights leader, to whom it was explained that in addition to potentially triggering an outrage as great as that which was experienced when the infamous Bull Conner used the same technique in Birmingham, the pressure from fire hoses would have left a carnage of broken bones and battered skulls lying in the street.

For the two sergeants who were first on the scene, the issue of appropriate police action was less dramatic but crystal clear. Both men are quite explicit in saying that at the time of their assignment, they were neither given orders to shoot or to refrain from shooting looters; they were instructed to use whatever force they deemed necessary to quell the disturbance.[3] As they recount the scene after their arrival, they describe crowds of well over one thousand people on the street, many of whom were standing on the sidewalks watching the calamity while others in the crowd would dart in and out of broken store windows or doors. To have used firearms in that situation, they insist, would have inevitably meant the risk of shooting women with small children in their arms. The police officers did attempt to clear the streets and they did make arrests[4] but they did not shoot, and according to the police officers who were there at the time, they have no regrets about their decision—they can sleep with their consciences at night!

Later that morning, Commissioner Girardin confirmed that decision with a statement to a group of community leaders who met in his office. He stated firmly that while the Department would employ every legitimate means at its disposal to quell the disturbance, it would consider the value of human life above that of property and would accordingly seek to restrain the rioters with a minimum loss of life. It was undoubtedly one of the most humane judgments ever made by a police official in the midst of any such civil disturbance, but in a society as materialistic and as property-oriented as in America, the response to it was understandably and tragically appalling. The post-riot critics—"armchair generals" as they came to be called at Police Headquarters—never quite found a comfortable way to quarrel with the Commissioner's judgment. After all, who would say publicly that property is worth more than human life! When, however, the Commissioner later reiterated his stand in a post-riot article in the *Saturday Evening Post,* the *Detroit Free Press* launched a screeching editorial attack. In the *Post* article, the Commissioner made the observation that "any riot

---

3. The statements of the two sergeants are from private conversations.

4. Between 5 a.m. and noon on Sunday, July 23, 1967, a total of 44 arrests were made in connection with the disorder.

can be crushed. But this would be an invitation to revolution."[5] To this, the *Free Press*[6] responded:

> *It would not* . . . of course any riot can be crushed and of course any riot must be crushed and beyond this any potential riot ought to be nipped in the bud, and still beyond this conditions which provide the climate for a riot ought to be quickly changed.
>
> The alternatives of crushing a riot and causing a revolution, or not crushing a riot and permitting widespread destruction may be Mr. Girardin's alternatives but they are not ours. Laws must be enforced. Implicit permission for lawbreaking, the sort of permission which Mr. Girardin's police force gave Detroit's looters in the early hours of our disturbance, produces just what was produced here—widespread lawbreaking and escalating lawbreaking to more serious crimes. Nor does there need to be any choice between shooting child looters and permitting massive looting, another false alternative Mr. Girardin set up in his article. Reasonable and sufficient force to maintain law must be applied . . . Negroes and whites alike, have a right to expect official assurances that their persons and their property will be protected.[7]

What constitutes "reasonable and sufficient force" was never made clear, either by the *Free Press* or anyone else. Most of the critics failed to grasp the significance of one basic fact. When the riot began on Sunday morning, a total of three hundred eleven police officers were on duty in Detroit, of which one hundred ninety-three were on street patrol.[8] The Headquarters Command Post Activity Log records that shortly after 5:00 a.m. that morning, District Inspector Anthony Bertoni, the weekly duty officer whose responsibility it is to be available on a 24-hour basis for whatever command decisions that must be made during the afternoon and midnight platoons, gave instructions to the Control Center Inspector to secure sufficient cars from other precincts to quell the disorder. As it turned out, those cars were involved in a near-frantic response to an incredible number of calls that began to pour in to police headquarters around 5:00 a.m.—"12th and Clairmount—man shot"; "14th and Gladstone—trouble"; "12th and Clairmount—officer needs help"; "Linwood and Clairmount—all stores being broken into." By the time executives in the Department had been alerted and mobilization orders given, crowds on 12th Street were already numbering in

5. *After the Riot: Force Won't Solve Anything*, Saturday Evening Post, Sept. 23, 1967, at 10.
6. Detroit Free Press, Sept. 13, 1967, at —.
7. *Id.*
8. Detroit Police Department Memorandum, August 1, 1967 (unpublished).

the hundreds.[9] Unlike the Kercheval incident of a year earlier, there simply was not a sufficient number of police personnel available to respond in force.

The reason for the tragically small complement of men available that Sunday morning is simple, if not adequate. For over a year prior to the riot the Police Department had repeatedly indicated that it was over 500 men short of its authorized strength. As it entered the summer of 1967, the Department had slightly over 3300 patrolmen in its ranks, a number which must be divided between three platoons (shifts), distributed between thirteen precincts and 12 bureaus, and then reduced by some forty percent to allow for the number of officers normally on furlough, on leave days or sick days during the months of July and August. Finally for every two police officers on street duty, one officer is required in a support assigned (i.e., communications, prisoner processing and detention, etc.). This normal distribution of manpower is further determined by the fact that from 4:00 a.m. Sunday until Monday morning is usually the quietest period in the week as far as crime and law enforcement are concerned. And although the public may not believe it, police officers have those human frailties that the rest of the citizenry is heir to; although they are theoretically on duty seven days a week, they enjoy days off (leave days) and go to church and have families that they like to take to the beach or the cottage or camping. And that happens to be where a number of off-duty, Detroit police officers were on Sunday morning, July 23: at early Mass or at the beach or spending the weekend at the cottage. The simple truth is that Sunday morning, from a police perspective, is a bad time to have a riot!

The manpower situation on Sunday, July 23, is also one of the basic differences between the police response that morning as contrasted with the highly lauded police action during the Kercheval incident a year earlier. The Kercheval incident had erupted on the sultry night of August 9, a few minutes after eight in the evening. For a number of reasons, there was an unusually large force of police officers on the streets of Detroit that night. It was, for example, a Tuesday evening as contrasted with the Sunday morning hour when the 12th Street riot began. It also broke during the third platoon when police strength, because of traditional crime patterns, is at its highest. In addition, not only had the Tactical Mobile Unit just come on duty an hour before—in ironic contrast with 12th Street where they had just gone off duty an hour before the disorder began—there was also, on the night of August 9, an End-the-Viet-Nam-War Rally at Central Methodist Church in downtown Detroit. These rallies had become the frequent target of

9. From eyewitness reports, the number of persons on 12th Street was well over 500 by 6 a.m. At 9 a.m. I personally observed crowds in excess of 2,000 on 12th Street.

a group of right-wing extremists in the city and were therefore a potential place of conflict. A special unit of police officers was on the scene near the church, in case trouble arose. They happened also to be the first contingent of officers dispatched to Kercheval Street when the first alert was given.

The other principal difference between Kercheval and 12th Street was the type of conflict situation the police faced. Kercheval was primarily a teenage disturbance, consisting of relatively small crowds of youths whose primary activity was limited to pelting passing cars with bricks and tossing poorly made Molotov cocktails, most of which never ignited. In contrast, 12th Street was a man's war, the participants were much older,[10] the crowds right from the start were incredibly larger, and once it was underway the 12th Street riot became an awesome experience of widespread, well-accomplished arson and gun sniper activity. The police, or no one else, had any indication at the outset that the pattern of the 12th Street riot would be any different from that of Kercheval, except that the crowds were larger and the available police strength smaller. The police strategy that had worked so well a year earlier, and which was providentially assisted by a generous summer rain on the second night, proved futile on 12th Street. There also lingers the suspicion in the minds of some, whether any type of police action on 12th Street, given the nature of the disturbance, would have proven effective.

Some citizens also harbour the suspicion that a series of internal difficulties in the Detroit Police Department might have contributed to a low morale among the patrolmen and consequently resulted in a markedly slow response of police officers to the mobilization orders that were issued shortly after six a.m. on July 23. There is ample evidence that the Department had been through an incredible two year period prior to the riot; veteran officers describe it as the worst two years in their careers. It had been under intensive scrutiny by two Wayne County Grand Jurys, whose efforts were sparked by a conviction, amply fanned by the press, that a major scandal of bribery and corruption existed in the Department. The personnel problem had also begun to take on serious dimensions, with more men resigning, primarily for economic reasons it should be noted, than could be replaced by new recruits. Simultaneously, the crime problem was beginning to attract major attention among the citizenry, with "crime in the streets" becoming the most frequently discussed and debated issue in town. This in turn had brought on the inevitable political feuds, but in this instance they had mounted to an intensity sufficient to spawn

10. Fifty percent of the 7800 arrestees were between the ages of 17-19, according to police records.

a recall movement against the Mayor and a demand for the firing of the Police Commissioner. The Kercheval incident also, while successfully handled, was simply an added strain on an already tense, undermanned, overtaxed Department. Finally the spiraling wage scale in Detroit had triggered a demand by the Detroit Police Officers Association for a significant salary increase in a fiscal period when all indications were that the city budget would incur its first sizable deficit in several years. The inability of the city and the Police Officers Association to resolve this dispute had led to what became known as the "blue flu" incident in which during a ten-day period close to one thousand officers failed to report for duty on the grounds of illness. The Police Department was just beginning to recover from this crisis when the riot broke.

What effect all of this had on the police response to the riot, no one really knows, but what evidence there is would suggest that if there was any effect at all, it was relatively little and apparently insignificant. No officer failed to report for duty when called, and once on the job, many of the men worked three and four hours beyond their required twelve-hour shifts. Many are the stories of men who became ill or were injured and who reported back for duty without medical permission. Ironically, after the "blue flu" incident, police officers, half-jokingly reflecting on the series of crises which the Department had undergone, frequently expressed the opinion that matters had to get better because they could not conceivably be any worse. That opinion, of course, died swiftly on the morning of July 23.

Courts, Prisons and the Administration of Justice

Of the many incredible problems that arose during the riot, none was more massive than that of the detention of the 7800 persons arrested[11] from July 23-31 and their processing through that maze which is the administration of justice in American society. The magnitude of the problem is symbolized by the fact that as many persons were arrested and processed through the courts in six days as would be processed in six months under normal circumstances. In contrast to the police, however, who at least during the first three days were somewhat uniformly praised for their action, the courts and those responsible for prisoner detention facilities came under almost immediate fire from segments of the public and were accused of having suspended the Constitution by exacting excessive, punitive measures against those arrested. Unlike the criticism of the police which developed in the latter stages and the aftermath of the riot and which came from people who were angry, hostile toward or outraged by

11. Statistical Report on the Civil Disturbance Occurring in the City of Detroit, July, 1967 (compiled and printed by the Record Bureau, Detroit Police Department).

police action but who had in most instances little if any technical or practical knowledge and experience on which to base that criticism, the critics of the courts came from the ranks of the legal profession itself: the bar associations, the dean of one of the city's three major law schools and ACLU attorneys.[12]

If the courts did not respond to the riot within the best tradition of American jurisprudence, at least it must be acknowledged on their behalf that the juridical situation which they confronted would have put even the best court systems to the test. At the outset of the riot, the criminal court was opened around the clock,[13] and though a majority of the judges worked in six-hour shifts, at least the mechanism for speedy arraignments was provided. In the minds of some, however, that mechanism was far too speedy. On Tuesday, July 25, the Dean of the University of Detroit Law School assembled a staff of volunteer attorneys to assist the Neighborhood Legal Services Center, an arm of the city's poverty program, in providing legal counsel for arrestees at the time of arraignment. The attorneys concentrated initially on interviewing and the arraignment-bail release process for female prisoners, the majority of whom had been abruptly separated from families and children. It was considered to be both humane and of minimal risk to the continuance of the riot to assist those women in returning to their families as soon as possible.

Initially, a significant portion of the judges apparently decided that it would be in the best interests of restoring law and order to prevent arrested rioters from returning to the streets too easily. With one exception therefore, the judges uniformly set bonds ranging from $10,000 to $200,000.[14] This, in turn, meant not only the temporary detainment of prisoners until their arraignment but also the problem of detention after arraignment, a problem technically under the jurisdiction of the county sheriff. The county jail was filled to capacity within 36 hours after the riot began. At one point, the jail which has a maximum capacity of some 1200 prisoners was crammed with over 2200 arrestees. It fell to the police department to make the hasty arrangements for transportation and detention of prisoners to six other penal facilities in the state, including the state prisons at Jackson and Ionia, the federal penitentiary at Milan, and county jails in Monroe, Washtenaw and Ingham counties. When these were filled to capacity, the Police Department with the aid of the Detroit Department of Streets and Railways, hastily converted the women's bathhouse on Belle Isle,

---

12. *For Example*, address by Professor F. Sengstock, 1967 American Association of Law Schools Convention, in Detroit, December, 1967.

13. Order of the Detroit Recorder Court Executive Judge, Vincent Brennan.

14. *Supra* note 11.

one of the city's principal recreation facilities, into a detention center. Because of its situation on the shore of an island in the Detroit River and its rather comfortable appointments when compared to most county jails, the police and prisoners quickly dubbed it "Belcatraz," and there were a significant number of its inmates who inquired if they could serve out their entire prison sentences within its walls.

By far the sharpest criticism of the courts was directed at its judicial posture during the riot.[15] In the minds of many attorneys, the court became an extension of the police department, rather than an independent arbiter of guilt or innocence. The court in exercising judgment upon police decisions and practices seemed in many instances to assume the guilt of those brought before it and imposed high bond as an improper security measure. In a number of cases, prisoners were arraigned *en masse* and in several instances only after some judicially intemperate remarks were made from the bench. By Wednesday, July 26, the Detroit branch of the American Civil Liberties Union had become sufficiently alarmed to convene an extraordinary session of its Executive Board which unanimously issued on the following day a statement calling for certain actions to be taken immediately "to remedy some of the injustices that have inevitably occurred as a result of the impossible burdens to which our police and our courts have been subjected."[16]

Viewed in retrospect, the statement was remarkably restrained in its criticism of the police, ironically during a period in which police action was beginning to come under heavy fire. The courts, however, did not escape as easily. In part, the statement read:

> In calling for remedial measures, the Metropolitan Detroit Branch of the ACLU wishes to place no blame upon any of our city officials who, on the whole, have served the public interest with remarkable devotion. At the same time the constitutional rights of those who have been accused of participating in the rioting cannot be left unattended if we are to restore the respect for law and order which has broken down so completely in the last week. Order has apparently been restored. It is essential that law be restored as well. The first was fundamentally the job of the police and the military, the second is the primary responsibility of the Courts. Persons arrested have almost without exception been held under excessive bond without respect for their personal circumstances or the nature of the charges against them. . . . Normal facilities for obtaining information to enable the Courts to make a reasonable and

15. *Id.*

16. American Civil Liberties Union, Press Statement of Executive Board, July 26, 1967.

> individual evaluation of the circumstances of the accused have been totally inadequate to deal effectively with the massive problems presented to them. . . . To the extent that these and other breakdowns in the system are the result of a shortage of judicial manpower, the stand-by offer of the Wayne Circuit Bench to assist the Recorder's (i.e., criminal) Court made last Monday . . . should be accepted and implemented immediately.[17]

The ACLU statement then recommended a number of steps to remedy the situation, including an immediate inventory of the names and location of all arrestees; an acceptance by the Courts of assistance offered by public agencies concerned with securing information "of and to the Court for the purpose of setting reasonable bond; a review of bonds already set; access by attorneys to all persons in custody; the early release of female prisoners; the request and acceptance by the Juvenile Court of assistance from social workers and community agencies; and the disqualification of any judge from handling riot cases who had engaged in prejudicial conduct on the bench."

Summary

In essence, the police and the courts were not prepared for the enormous pressures that the civil disorder created. The police were prepared for a civil disturbance in which the main tactical problem was one of crowd control and dispersal, but they were not prepared, in numbers, training or equipment to handle the kind and size of disorder that erupted on 12th Street. Neither the courts nor the prison system were equipped to process the massive number of persons arrested during the disorder. The ACLU statement reflects a sensitivity to this incredible strain that the police and the courts were placed under during Detroit's episode of "America's summer madness." If the riot demonstrated anything at all in this area, it reflected how fragile are the restraints that hold a social order together and how even the majesty of the law can break down in an appalling fashion in the midst of such a massive civil crisis.

---

17. *Id.*

Bail and Civil Disorder

F. PHILIP COLISTA* AND MICHAEL G. DOMONKOS**

Introduction

THE only recognized justification of the use of bail in the pretrial stage of judicial proceedings has been to provide a means of insuring the appearance of the defendant for trial. Courts in many cities during the recent massive civil disorders have expressly rejected this traditionally accepted notion in order to "keep the defendants off the streets."[1] Although the exigencies of such crises might seem to demand a different standard for the determination of bail, there appears to be no legal precedent for the use of high bail or an outright denial of bail, in an emergency situation for the purpose of preventive detention. The purpose of this article is to examine the use of bail during the Detroit riot, to discuss the widespread use of bail for preventive detention during civil disorders and to suggest a controlled and fair mechanism to deal with the great numbers of persons arrested during such times.

The Recorder's Court and Bail During the Civil Disorder

The sole criterion for the determination of bail, has been that it should be set no higher than necessary to insure the presence of the accused at trial. Typical constitutional provisions, however, permit the denial of bail in certain instances such as in the cases of murder and treason.[2] In implementation of its constitutional provision the Michigan statute relating to bail provides:

> [except in cases of murder and treason] . . . the person accused shall be entitled to bail. The amount of the recognizance shall be fixed with consideration of the seriousness of the offense charged, the previous criminal record of the defendant and the probability or improbability of his appearing at the trial of the cause.[3]

---

* Wayne State University, B.A., 1957; LL.B., 1960. Assistant Dean, University of Detroit School of Law; Director, Urban Law Program.

** Wayne State University, B.A., 1958; J.D., 1960. Assistant Prof., University of Detroit School of Law; Associate Director, Research Division, Urban Law Program.

1. *See e.g*, Detroit News, July 31, 1967, 20c.

2. MICH. CONST. art. I, § 15 (1963):

"No person shall be subject for the same offense to be twice put in jeopardy. All persons shall, before conviction, be bailable by sufficient sureties, except for murder and treason when the proof is evident or the presumption great."

And at art. 1 §16: "Excessive bail shall not be imposed . . . ."

3. MICH. COMP. LAWS § 765.6 (1948), MICH. STAT. ANN. § 28.893 (1954).

Despite the use of the word "and" in the statute, in view of the historical context of the bail system, the seriousness of the crime and the previous record would appear to be part of the consideration of the probability of the defendant's appearing at the trial rather than separate considerations. It would make no sense to say that the former two considerations relate to a determination of whether the defendant if released would commit a crime, because the only logical remedy in such case would be to deny bond altogether. That is to say, such construction would result in a determination that the defendant would likely commit a crime if released but if he can afford the bail he will be free to do so.

The extraordinary use of bail during the week of July 23 in Detroit can be illustrated by data gathered by the Urban Law Program of the University of Detroit School of Law from riot arrestees at Jackson prison.[4] The data obtained related to factors ordinarily taken into account in the setting of bail but which were almost entirely ignored by the Detroit Recorder's Court during that week in July. The figures reveal that the Court practiced preventive detention by use of the bail system during that time.

It might be argued that the court did set bail but that it was merely high. It has been stated that courts, *sub rosa*, practice preventive detention of dangerous criminals by use of the bail system merely by setting bond too high for the defendants to meet.[5] In Detroit during

4. See Appendix *infra*.

These statistics were gathered by the Urban Law Program of the University of Detroit during the week of July 23rd, 1967, the week of the Detroit riot. This data was not originally gathered for purposes of sociological or legal analysis but rather was the result of an effort on the part of the Urban Law Program staff and law students to obtain bond reductions on behalf of riot arrestees.

Immediately following the first days of the Detroit riot, it became obvious that many of those arrested were not being accorded the usual hearing on bail held at the arraignment on the warrant and that high bonds were being uniformly exacted. Program staff in conjunction with other legal services agencies in the city decided that it was imperative to obtain information relative to bail in order to pursue bond reductions. On Wednesday, July 26, on behalf of those arrested, the Program, pursuant to this decision, sent its associate director in charge of its clinic and twenty of its students to the Michigan State Prison in Jackson where more than 1000 riot arrestees were being held due to lack of detention facilities in Detroit. These students, using prepared questionnaires, interviewed 1014 prisoners in a period of two and one half days. At the end of each day one of the students would drive back to Detroit from Jackson with completed interviews. Program staff began to classify the arrestees according to those believed to be entitled to Personal bond or a lower surety bond. On others not falling into either of the above classifications we made no recommendations. Using program/clinic facilities, the staff with the assistance of law students and VISTA volunteers, engaged in the process of verifying the interviews on an ongoing basis, *e.g.*, calling relatives, employers, etc. of the arrestees. This procedure was followed through Wednesday, August 2, 1967. Subsequently the information so gathered was coded and tabulated by Prof. Joseph Althoff of the University of Detroit Department of Sociology.

5. 79 HARV. L. REV. 1489 (1966); *cf. Task Force Report, President's Comm'n on Law Enforcement and Administration of Justice* 39-40 (1967).

the civil disturbance there was no pretense in such use of the bail system. The court clearly was denying bail. For a substantial period, bonds were not accepted even when the money was raised.[6]

During more normal times it appears that many of the arrestees interviewed at Jackson prison would have been entitled to a personal or nominal bond.[7] That many would ordinarily be entitled to a much lower bond is evident. An examination of whether the usually relevant criteria were considered follows.

All of the 1014 defendants interviewed at Jackson Prison were male having a median age of twenty-four years.[8] Forty-four percent were married[9] with seventy-six percent of those married living with his spouse[10] and having one or more children.[11] Seventy-three percent had a length of present residence of one year or more[12] and, about thirty per cent had lived at their present residence for five years or more.[13] The median length of residence at their present address for all of the defendants interviewed was one year and eight months.[14] The median length of former residence was even greater, two years and five months.[15] Thus far we can conclude that the defendants were rather young but many were married with children and obviously had financial responsibilities.

Further, their length of present residence seems to reflect a considerable amount of stability in the community. These criteria are normally considered by the courts in setting bond for the accused.[16]

Another and highly relevant criterion is the employment status of a defendant.[17] The information under consideration indicates that the Recorder's Court did not consider the employment status of the accused in making a determination on bond. Significant is the fact that eighty per cent of those interviewed were employed[18] and of these, forty-one per cent were employed by one of the three major automobile

---

6. Otto Kerner, U.S. Riot Comm'n Report, Report of the National Advisory Comm'n on Civil Disorders 341 note 7 (Bantam, 1968) [hereinafter referred to as 'Kerner Report'].

7. Between 26 and 30 percent of the persons arrested during normal times are released on personal recognizance. During the riot, the figure was two percent. Kerner Report at 341. Also interview with Bail Project personnel of the Bail Project release program, Detroit, Michigan, May, 1968.

8. Appendix, Table 1.

9. Appendix, Table 2.

10. *Id.*

11. Appendix, Table 3.

12. Appendix, Table 4.

13. *Id.*

14. *Id.*

15. Appendix, Table 5.

16. Annot., 72 A.L.R. 801 (1931).

17. *Id.*

18. Appendix, Table 6.

firms in the City.[19] Further, of the eighty per cent who were employed, forty-nine per cent had been with their present employer from 1 to 5 years while fourteen per cent were so employed from 5 to 10 years or more.[20]

Courts in criminal cases traditionally have inquired into the accused's past criminal record in evaluating the level of bond to be set in the cases before them.[21] When one examines the statistics relating to those persons detained at Jackson prison, there appears to be no consistency between prior criminal record and the amount of bond. Of those interviewed, forty-seven per cent had never experienced a previous arrest while an additional twenty-seven per cent had only one arrest.[22] Sixty-seven per cent of the defendants had no prior convictions, nineteen per cent had one conviction and only fourteen per cent had two or more convictions.[23] Seventy-nine percent of these defendants had no arrests and/or convictions for the perpetration of a felony.[24]

The table entitled "Extreme Prisoner Characteristics and Bond Size" reveals the almost total disregard for the foregoing criteria ordinarily thought relevant to the setting of bond amount. Arrestees who were married, employed and without prior criminal records were treated virtually the same as defendants who were single, unemployed and had previous convictions and/or arrests.[25] Usually used in determining bond level is the severity of the crime charged.[26] In order to draw any conclusions with respect to this criterion we will comment on a few of the many crimes charged against persons arrested during the Detroit disorder of July, 1967.

The most frequent crime charged was entering without breaking with the intent to commit larceny.[27] This charge was commonly used against those accused of "looting," and fifty-four per cent of the defendants at Jackson prison were held accused of this offense.[28] Michigan law makes this offense a felony punishable by imprisonment for a maximum of four years.[29] Violation of the curfew ordered by the Governor of Michigan was the next most frequent charge against those imprisoned. Fifteen per cent were detained on a charge of curfew vio-

---

19. Appendix, Table 7.
20. Appendix, Table 8.
21. *Supra* note 16.
22. Appendix, Table 10.
23. Appendix, Table 11.
24. Appendix, Table 13.
25. Appendix, Table 19.
26. *Supra* note 16.
27. MICH. COMP. LAWS § 750.110 (1948), MICH. STAT. ANN. § 28.306 (Supp. 1968).
28. Appendix, Table 14.
29. *Supra* note 27.

lation, a misdemeanor punishable up to a maximum of 90 days.[30] The amount of bond showed little relation to the severity of the crime charged. For example, twenty-four percent of those charged with entering without breaking had bonds set under $3000 and forty-three percent had bond from $8000 to $12,000.[31] Twenty-five percent of those charged with violating curfew had bonds of under $3000 and thirty-five per cent had bonds of $8000 to $12,000.[32] Similar percentages hold true for the crime of breaking and entering, a ten year felony.[33] Therefore it is clear that the court made little effort to set bond according to the severity of the crime charged, for little distinction was made between felony and misdemeanor offenses.

The preceding represents an examination of the breakdown of the right to bail during a civil disorder which has been characteristic of recent court response across the country in the face of rioting.[34]

There are probably a number of contributing factors to this reaction by the courts. It is clear that they assumed a law enforcement posture in that they felt that keeping the arrestees off the streets would help break the back of the rioting. Further, public pronouncement by the judge that rioters would be locked up and that prohibitively high bail would be set was thought to provide a threat to potential riot participants and hence a deterrent to continued rioting. Undoubtedly anger at the rioters and fear and uncertainty at the apparent apocalyptic condition of their city provided a part in the behavior of the courts. Perhaps such judicial action and statements were in part a communication to the rest of the community that the courts were doing something to end the rioting. The pervasiveness and tenacity of this judicial behavior and attitude seems to reflect a state of mind that this was the "natural" thing to do.

Bail and Civil Disorder— The Scope of the Crisis

Civil disorder in our cities represents a new and complex problem for our courts and legislatures. Threatened are individual rights and civil liberties as well as social and political structures. The lack of a thought out and structured judicial response to such massive arrests during civil disorders has caused and could continue to cause individual injustice and community bitterness toward the legal system. The ab-

30. Appendix, Table 14. *See also* MICH. COMP. LAWS § 10.31 (1948), MICH. STAT. ANN. § 3.4 (1) (1961) and MICH. COMP. LAWS § 10.33 (1948), MICH. STAT. ANN. § 3.4(3) (1961).
31. Appendix, Table 17.
32. *Id.*
33. *Id.*
34. See text accompanying notes 65-69 *infra*.

sence of constitutional and statutory standards governing such situations must be dealt with by the lawyers and lawmakers of this nation.

Conceptually there presently exist only two apparent and absolutist positions on the subject of right to bail during civil disorders. The response of the courts thus far under such conditions represents a de facto, although unarticulated position that no riot arrestees should be released during the pendency of a riot. The other view is that all such arrestees should be accorded the right to reasonable bail set only in consideration of the risk of possible non-appearance at trial.

It is submitted that neither of the aforementioned positions afford an adequate or just system for dealing with the problem of massive arrests during civil disorders.[35] There have been virtually no alternative solutions suggested.

The report of the National Advisory Commission on Civil Disorders[36] (hereinafter called the Kerner Report) deals with the massive arrest and bail problem in a chapter devoted to the administration of justice under emergency conditions. It reports that in both the Detroit and Newark riots, the initial response of most judges was to set inordinately high bail so as to prevent or frustrate release.[37] Bail review hearings or preliminary examinations which principally served as bail review hearings were conducted after the disorders were under control.[38] Also noted was the general lack of any attempt to individualize the bail setting process.[39]

The Kerner Report is critical of such practices and recommends that the

> . . . riot defendant should receive an individual determination of bail amount. He should be represented by counsel and the judge should ascertain from counsel, client and bail interviewer the relevant facts of his background, age, living arrangements, employment, past record. Uniform bail amounts based on charges and riot conditions alone should be shunned as unfair.[40]

---

35. The technique of mass arrests has characterized law enforcement during the recent disorders. Kerner Report at 339. There are alternatives such as ticketing minor offenders which are discussed in the Kerner Report at 347-8.

36. *Supra* note 6.

37. *Id.*

38. *Id.* at 341 note 9 and 842. In an action which cannot be denominated an action resulting from a hearing, the presiding judge of the Detroit Recorder's Court on July 28, reduced to personal bond approximately 1500 persons after their records had been flown back from Washington, D.C. where their records and fingerprints had been checked against the FBI files.

39. *Id.* at 341.

40. *Id.* at 353.

The Commission states that it is "... fully aware that some rioters, if released, will commit new acts of violence."[41]

The report notes that the traditional purpose of bail is to prevent confinement before trial and to insure appearance of the defendant for trial.[42] Then the Commission states that "[t]he purpose [of the bail system] has not been to deter future crime. Yet some [members of the commission?] have difficulty supporting a puristic adherence to the doctrine when it results in releasing a dangerous offender back into the riot area."[43] The Commission rejects a scheme of preventive detention[44] even for "dangerous offenders" and advocates alternatives along the lines previously recommended by the President's Commission on Law Enforcement and Administration of Justice.[45]

> We point out that, as to the dangerous offender, there already exists a full range of permissible alternatives to outright release as a hedge against his reentry into the riot.
>
> These include: release on conditions that forbid access to certain areas or at certain times; part-time release with a requirement to spend nights in jail; use of surety or peace bonds on a selective basis. In cases where no precautions will suffice trial should be held as soon as possible so that a violator can be adjudicated innocent and released; or found guilty and lawfully confined pending sentencing. Finally, special procedures should be set up for expedited bail review by higher courts, so that defendants' rights will not be lost by default.[46]

In short the Kerner Report recommendations parallel those of the President's Commission on Law Enforcement. The latter commission found that the present bail system operates harshly on the poor, is not even well designed for its avowed purpose of protecting against flight from trial and is particularly ill-designed to prevent future crimes by detaining persons under the mechanism of inordinately high bail.[47]

---

41. *Id.*
42. *Id.* at 354
43. *Id*
44. *Id.* at 344, *cf.* 354 note 24.
45. *Id.* at 354 note 24 citing *Challenge of Crime in a Free Society-A Report* 131-2 [hereinafter referred to as 'Challenge'].
46. *Id.* In the summary of recommendations the following appears although such release to custodians is not discussed in the text!

> That communities and courts plan for a range of alternative conditions to release, such as supervision by civic organizations or third party custodians outside the riot area, rather than to rely on high bail to keep defendants off the streets.

Id. at 357. Release to the "custody of a designated person or organization" is provided in the Federal Bail Reform Act of 1966, 18 U.S.C. § 3146(a) (1).

47. The President's Comm'n on Law Enforcement recommended the following:

> Bail projects should be undertaken at the State, county, and local levels to furnish judicial officers with sufficient information to permit the pretrial release without

There has been much concern and comment about the money bail system. Growing evidence is tending towards the conclusion that very few persons if released would flee or commit other crimes let alone serious crimes during pretrial release.[48] The President's Commission poses the following dilemma:

> If a satisfactory solution could be found to the problem of the relatively small percentage of defendants who present a significant risk of flight or criminal conduct before trial, the Commission would be prepared to recommend that money bail be totally discarded. Finding that solution is not easy. Empowering magistrates to jail defendants they believe to be dangerous might well create more of a problem than the imposition of money bail, in the light of the difficulty of predicting dangerousness. Such a system also might raise issues under State and Federal constitutional grants of a right to bail, issues that have not been determined by the Supreme Court.[49]

Because of the difficulties of prediction, the constitutional issues and the very real possibility that judges will err very heavily on the side of caution and thus detain a large percentage of defendants as posing a threat of committing a crime, the President's Commission and many commentators have been inclined to oppose a system of preventive detention at least until less drastic alternatives have been given a trial and until predictive science is more advanced.

The authors are inclined to the view that under normal circumstances a system of pretrial preventive detention is not advisable if only because little is known about predicting future criminal activity. The President's Committee on Law Enforcement and Administration of Criminal Justice and the writing upon the subject have been concerned with normal times and do not deal with the crisis of a civil disturbance or riot. It is submitted that the Kerner Report in adopting recommendations written with normal conditions in mind did not adequately consider whether riot conditions require different solutions. In normal times, as mentioned above,[50] the incidence of serious crimes committed by persons during pretrial release has not been great. Because prediction of future crimes during normal times is so difficult and because of the presumption of innocence,[51] society must take the "cal-

---

> financial condition of all but that small portion of defendants who present a high risk of flight or dangerous acts prior to trial . . . . Each state should enact comprehensive bail reform legislation after the pattern set by the Federal Bail Reform Act of 1966.

Challenge note 45 at 132.

48. *Supra* note 5.
49. Challenge note 45 at 131.
50. *Id.*
51. Perhaps more accurately "due process" and the concept that one should not be

culated risk"[52] of release because of the harm[53] that would be suffered by the innocent or non dangerous defendant in a system permitting pretrial preventive detention.

In a riot situation, is a recalculation of risk permissible? First less is known and likely will ever be known about the probability that riot arrestees if released would engage or reengage in the riot. Statistics might be obtained during normal times relating to persons released on bail information projects and to persons raising money bail. What would such statistics say about the conduct of such persons when released back into a riot situation. Their applicability would certainly be debatable. The variety[54] and relative infrequency of riots, the difficulty of obtaining statistics, and the understandable reluctance of judges to experiment would militate against obtaining the same quantum of information about released defendants during riot situations. There is some evidence that persons released during riots are not likely to be rearrested.[55] This evidence must be viewed in the light of the fact that even the most lenient judges released only the very best prospects (particularly those accused of minor crimes) and by the low crime-to-arrest ratio prevailing in riot situations. That is to say, that a released defendant during a riot situation might, despite reentry into the riot, escape arrest in the vastness and general lawlessness of the situation.[56]

Further, an ongoing riot or civil disturbance is a present and continuing threat to society. If it were determinable that an individual might only pose a one in ten possibility of committing a crime during release, this might arguably require his release in normal times in that detaining all such persons would result in nine harmless persons being penalized for the one who presented a danger to society. However, during a riot situation because of the sheer numbers of persons arrested

---

jailed before one is found guilty of a crime and *a fortiori* before one commits a crime. Presumption of innocence refers to the burden of proof at the trial. *Supra* note 5, at 1497.

52. Justice Jackson in *Stack v. Boyle*, 342 U.S. 1, 7-8 (1951) said that the spirit of the bail procedure is to enable defendants to stay out of jail until a trial has found them guilty and the possible danger to society "is a calculated risk which the law takes as the price of our system of justice."

53. For a typical catalog of the harm or prejudice commonly observed to accrue to defendants who are subject to pretrail detention *see* 36 GEO. WASH. L. REV. 178, 185-6 (1967).

54. There are no "typical riots." The disorders of 1967 were unusual, irregular, complex and unpredictable social processes. Kerner Report at 5, 109-110.

55. Kerner Report at 342 note 9. A Detroit Recorder's Court Judge who had permitted release on personal recognizance of approximately 10% of the riot defendants coming before him revealed to one of the authors that he knew of only two rearrests of those he released. It is estimated that he released 100 persons. This would mean that only 2 percent were rearrested. Interview with a Detroit Recorder's Court Judge in Detroit, Michigan, April, 1968.

56. Offsetting this in some measure would be the possibility that a released defendant though innocent of the second charge, might be rearrested in the dragnet type arrests that prevail in riot situations.

and because of a possible multiplier effect of a handful of incorrigible types keeping a riot going, perhaps a different standard should be imposed.

The authors suggest that there appear to be a great number of arrested persons who pose little risk of entry (or perhaps reentry) in the riot. Doubtless many of those arrested during riots are completely innocent of any crime.[57] Many of those who in fact are guilty of some of the crimes prevalent in riots, such as looting, are ordinarily responsible citizens—the mere contact with authority or arrest would likely suffice to shake them back into the reality of the danger of future criminal conduct.[58] It is submitted that normal bail procedures including extensive use of release on recognizance, should be applicable with respect to these persons.

There are others whose criminal records reveal a consistent lack of respect for law and who might reasonably be thought to be persons who would take advantage of a riot situation. There are still others arrested, accused of serious crimes which would tend to promote or continue a riot such as sniping, inciting to riot or arson. Assuming there is substantial evidence of such activity, the risk in the release of such persons during an actual and ongoing civil disorder is apparent.

A Proposal

The authors suggest that during riots or other serious civil disorder that some form of limited preventive detention be authorized for the poorer risks. Under such system many, perhaps more than two-thirds of the persons arrested, would not be detained because of posing little threat of future misconduct.

Federal constitutional questions would be raised by the operation of such a preventive detention system. For example: Does the prohibition against "excessive bail" in the eighth amendment apply to the states? Does the amendment create a right to bail and, if so, are there

---

57. Concerning the possibility that great numbers of persons arrested were completely innocent, the following from the Kerner report is of interest:

> For whatever reasons—policy or evidentiary problems—in the Watts riots, 43 percent of adult felony arrests and 30 percent of adult misdemeanor arrests did not result in convictions. In Detroit, 25 percent of all arrests and 24 percent of the felony arrests were not prosecuted, including 57 percent of the homicide arrests, 74 percent of the aggravated assault arrests, 83 percent of the robbery arrests, 43 percent of the stolen property arrests, and 62 percent of the arson arrests. Only 29 percent of the curfew arrests were not prosecuted. Reportedly, plea bargaining in Detroit was based almost entirely on a defendant's past record. Kerner Report at 356 note 25, *see also* 339.

58. One of the authors interviewed several defendants who had good jobs, families and homes who admitted their participation in the rioting. They were ordinarily good citizens and expressed real concern about their jobs and appeared to have achieved real recognition about the foolishness and risk of their participation in the looting.

any qualifications or exceptions? These points have not been resolved by the United States Supreme Court. The problems and the state of the law have been exhaustively discussed elsewhere.[59] Suffice it to say that there is a good likelihood that a carefully devised state system of preventive pretrial detention, at least during massive civil disturbances, would not be held violative of the eighth and fourteenth amendments of the United States Constitution. It would almost certainly have to be non-discriminatory towards the poor[60] and reasonably calculated to detain only those persons who could reasonably be expected to pose a threat of serious criminal conduct before trial.[61]

An additional constitutional basis for a system of preventive detention may be *Moyer v. Peabody*.[62] *Moyer,* in effect, permits preventive detention by state military forces of a person not even accused of a crime when the Governor has declared a state of insurrection.[63] Although it appears that the breakdown of law and order was more complete in portions of Detroit than in Colorado in 1904, it is nevertheless true that the Michigan Governor had not proclaimed an "insurrection"[64] but rather a state of emergency. It is undecided whether the

---

59. *See e.g.*, Foote, *The Coming Constitutional Crises in Bail*, 113 U. PA. L. REV. 959 *et. seq.* (First part); 113 U. PA. L. REV. 1125 *et. seq.* (Second part) (1965). 79 HARV. L. REV. 1489-1505 (1966).

60. *Cf.* Griffin v. Illinois, 351 U.S. 12 (1956).

61. If the eighth amendment prohibition of excessive bail were held applicable to the states through the fourteenth amendment and if it were held to imply a right to bail, the authors believe it unlikely that it would be interpreted to provide an absolute right to bail in all cases. The court could easily recognize reasonable exceptions such as the prevalent and historical exception "for murder and treason when the proof is evident or the presumption great." MICH. CONST. art. I § 15 (1963). "Due Process" is perhaps the most potent obstacle. *See Foote supra* note 22, at 1182 where the author concludes that "detention is only consistent with the due process demand of fundamental fairness only in situations of extraordinary risk."

62. 212 U.S. 78 (1909).

63. Moyer, a Colorado labor leader, during the turbulent mining disputes at the turn of the century, was imprisoned for two and a half months while the courts were open, with no complaint having been filed against him. *In re Moyer* 35 Colo. 159, 85 Pac. 190 (1905) had held that the militia could properly detain Moyer pending the suppression of the disorder. The conduct of the arresting officers who had ignored a writ of habeas corpus from a lower civil court was thus determined proper. *Moyer v. Peabody* was an action for damages against the Colorado governor, then out of office, who had ordered the detention. The Court in an opinion by Holmes held that absent a showing of a lack of good faith there was no cause of action against the ex-governor. In the course of the opinion, Justice Holmes said:

> . . . [I]t is familiar that what is due process of law depends on the circumstances. It varies with the subject matter and the necessities of the situation . . . when it comes to a decision by the head of the state upon a matter involving its life, the ordinary rights of individuals must yield to what he deems the necessities of the moment. Public danger warrants the substitution of executive process for judicial process. This was admitted with regard to killing men in the actual clash of arms; and we think it is obvious, although it was disputed, that the same is true of temporary detention to prevent apprehended harm. *Id.* at 85.

64. *Cf.* RANKIN, WHEN LAW FAILS 77-84 (1939). *See also* In re Moyer, 35 Colo. 159, 85 Pac. 190 (1905). Aside from the problem of whether the facts fit the definition of insurrec-

martial law precedents such as *Moyer* are applicable to a declaration of emergency pursuant to a state statute where the National Guard is called out to suppress a civil disorder.

The *Moyer* decision could be used to support a limited preventive detention system during "an emergency" proclaimed by the Governor on the following theory: *Moyer* holds that preventive detention by the military is constitutionally permissible during an insurrection and martial law even when those detained are not accused of a crime. Should not a limited preventive detention system then be possible for persons accused of crimes and determined by a judicial hearing to pose a serious threat of entry or reentry into an ongoing civil disorder, when the civil disorder has necessitated a gubernatorial declaration of an emergency and the calling out of the state military forces? In short, while due process standards are probably higher for emergencies than for insurrections, a judicially administered limited preventive detention system affords "more" due process than does outright military detention.

It is submitted that an insistence upon bail and release on recognizance procedures "as usual" for all persons might bring on a declaration of insurrection and martial law by a governor under pressure to prevent the release of arrested persons. The detention of persons and interference with the liberties of persons under a martial law situation would be far more subject to abuse than a judicially administered statutory system of limited preventive detention.

The absence of any alternative system no doubt was a factor in the indiscriminate preventive detention by use of excessive bail, as shown time and time again in the recent disorders in Chicago,[65] Detroit,[66] Los Angeles,[67] Newark[68] and Washington, D.C.[69]

A limited system of judicially administered preventive detention could, in summary, 1) prevent release of accused persons likely to engage or reengage in the disorder, 2) provide a mechanism for the release of perhaps 80% of the arrestees [presently the courts, being without guidelines or alternatives, break down and practice nearly total detention], and 3) make less likely a gubernational declaration of insur-

---

tion, it was clear that a declaration of insurrection would have possibly jeopardized tens of millions of dollars in insurance claims whose exclusion of coverage turned on that phrase.

65. A.C.L.U., Report and Evaluation on Bail Procedures in Chicago's Looting cases, August, 1967 (unpublished work on file at the University of Detroit School of Law). This work deals with bail and looting cases in the Chicago snow storm of Jan., 1967.

66. Kerner Report at 340-41.

67. *See also* BAIL & SUMMONS: 1965, *Proceedings of the Institute on the Operation of Pretrial Release Projects* (N.Y. 1965) *and Proceedings of the Justice Conference on Bail and Remands in Custody* 116 (London, 1965).

68. *Supra* note 66.

69. Wash. Post, April 7, 1968, at 14A, col.3.

rection and martial law with consequent wholesale suspension of civil liberties by offering a workable and less drastic alternative.

The Kerner recommendations with respect to conditional release of dangerous offenders (i.e. part-time release with requirements to spend nights in jail, forbidding access to certain areas, peace bonds, and release to third persons)[70] seem to the authors to be unrealistic except for some possible use of the recommendation that arrestees be released to custodians outside the riot area. For example, rearrest for failure to return to jail at night would probably not be feasible due to the record keeping and follow-up required of an otherwise well occupied police force. Also rearrest would be impossible in situations such as the Detroit riot where police for a time abandoned control of whole sections of the city. Daytime release from detention facilities perhaps 100 miles from the city required by inadequate local jail facilities would be impracticable.[71]

These inadequacies make it unlikely that the courts would adopt the Kerner recommendations and alter in the face of a riot their practice of detaining almost all of those arrested.

The Kerner Report suggestion of early trial for those possible dangerous offenders, detained presumably on excessive bail, merely avoids the Constitutional issue of the legality of their detention and a speedy trial might be a disaster during the pendency of a riot.[72]

Some would argue that there should be no bail during a riot situation,[73] but this position clearly leads to a harsh and unjust result. The authors were witnesses to events at the Detroit Recorder's Court and were distressed at the fact that persons charged with minor curfew violations, mothers with children at home and twenty-year employees at local motor companies were, for the most part, given uniformly high and unreasonable bail without any differentiation from persons such as the three-time felon with no employment history. Most judges would not even entertain the most compelling argument for release.

The authors offer a statutory alternative permitting limited riot

---

70. See text accompanying note 46 *supra*.

71. *E.g.*, more than 1000 arrestees were sent to the state penitentiary at Jackson, Michigan in July, 1967 due to inadequate facilities in or around Detroit. Jackson is about 80 miles from Detroit.

72. If the trial were held during or very shortly after the riots, the defendant could be prejudiced by the animosity of judges and juries created by the riot conditions. In respect to this recommendation for a speedy trial, the Kerner Report makes no reference to its finding earlier in the Report that "[t]rial and sentencing proved vulnerable to the tyranny of numbers. Sentences meted out during the riots tended to be harsher than in those cases disposed of later. Some judges in the early days of the riots openly stated that they would impose maximum penalties across the board as deterrents." Bantam Ed. p. 343.

73. Obviously the position of most of the judges that have been sitting in the criminal courts in the riot affected cities. *See also*, BAIL AND SUMMONS *supra* note 67, at 115-6.

pretrial detention from a pessimistic view that unless clear guidelines are formulated, the courts would again detain nearly everyone. Further, we should recognize that those most critical of the high bonds set by the court, including the staunchest advocates of civil liberties, were invariably concerned about the persons charged with minor crimes, the jailed substantial citizen, or the wife and mother. Few were concerned about immediate bail for the accused sniper, arsonist or the hardened criminal.[74] But the greatest wrong done by the legal system in Detroit in those days in July was its refusal to treat individual defendants as such; its denial of humanity, not its denial of bail. Lawyers who felt this could not articulate and react to it, because they were paralyzed by their ambivalence toward the release of the truly dangerous offenders.

It is suggested that legislative consideration be given to a statute which would provide for a limited preventive system to go into effect upon the declaration of an emergency by the Governor.[75] The system should only be operative during an actual and continuing civil disorder (not when such disturbance is merely threatened).[76] The fact of actual and continuing civil disorder should be judicially determinable. Assuming the preceding conditions are met, the following procedures would be required by law:

1) That an individual determination of bail be made.[77]

2) That a reasonable bail amount be set in all cases,[78] but

3) That if, in a given case, a judge determines that one or more of the circumstances in which detention is permitted by law do exist, the accused may be detained and the operation of the order of bail suspended until—

(A) The Governor rescinds the proclamation of a State of Emergency; or

---

74. Bail and Summons, *supra,* note 67, at 63 where comment is made that those bail projects which automatically exclude habitual criminals are perhaps following a kind of acceptance of preventive detention for certain persons.

75. A number of states provide for such a declaration of emergency by the governor. *See e.g.* MICH. COMP. LAWS § 10.31 (1948), MICH. STAT. ANN. § 3.4 (1) (1961); FLA. STAT. ANN. § 14.021 *et. seq.* (1961); GA. CODE ANN § 40-211 *et. seq.* (1957); S.C. CODE ANN. § 1-128 *et. seq.* (1962).

76. After Dr. Martin Luther King's death the Michigan Governor, admitting that there was over-reaction, declared a state of emergency in the Detroit metropolitan area. The system suggested by the authors should not be operative during periods of mere threat of disorder or when there are only sporadic incidents.

77. It was clear that in Detroit despite the thousands of arrests there was ample time for careful and individual bail determination. Address by Judge Geo. W. Crockett, Jr., Detroit Recorder's court, at the conference of the A.C.L.U. at Detroit, Michigan, April 20, 1968.

78. Except in cases where bail may be denied under existing laws, e.g., for "murder and treason where the proof is evident and the presumption great." MICH. CONST. art. I, § 15.

(B) A judicial determination is made, that a continuing actual civil disorder does not obtain, or

(C) A judge declares the accused eligible for release or bail;

Such detention shall end upon the happening of any one or more of these three conditions.

4) An accused may be detained and the operation of the order of bail suspended if there is substantial evidence that—

(A) he participated in inciting a riot or rebellion; or

(B) he has a criminal record that evidences violent or destructive antisocial behavior,[79] or

(C) he committed or attempted a serious crime against the life or physical safety of others, or arson, or illegal destruction of buildings or property by explosives or other violent means.

The above criteria are admittedly imprecise and undoubtedly would present difficulties.[80] However, they do provide some reasonable guidelines and if fairly applied would have resulted in the release of the better risks during the Detroit riots.

The merit of the above proposal is that automatically at the end of the actual emergency the bail order would become operative with respect to those detained. There would have been no ritual of setting bail that cannot be made. There would be no hasty bail review.

Such a system would in Michigan as in many other states require a constitutional amendment. The Michigan Constitution could be amended to read (the new language being in bold type) as follows:

> Sec. 15 . . . all persons shall, before conviction, be bailable by sufficient sureties, except for murder and treason when the proof is evident or the presumption great AND EXCEPT AS

79. The availability of the actual criminal records of the police department would not be essential in all cases. The arrestee's own testimony about his record as well as verification performed by bail information project personnel might be sufficient in many cases. The Detroit experience of July, 1967, revealed that high bail set at speedy arraignments where the criminal record was not available resulted in detention for as long as two weeks before the preliminary examinations were held and which preliminary examinations were, in part, bail review hearings. Priority in record checking might be given to those arrestees claiming no previous record or a less serious record. Under the present record checking system it has been estimated that it might be possible to check the records of 1000 arrestees at Detroit Police Headquarters within a 24 hour period. (Interview with Detroit Police I.D. Bureau Personnel.) Absent computerization of the criminal records or other major efforts to speed up the record checking operation, there is no way to prevent lengthy pre-arraignment detention for some arrestees assuming the court requires the actual police records in front of it. The authors suggest that it would be better to delay arraignment during a reasonable time required to search records in view of the numbers arrested than to set excessive bail in the absence of such a record for fear of what it would contain. *Cf.* Kerner Report, *supra* note 6, at p. 351 n.21.

80. See *Bail and Summons, supra* note 67, at 42-3 where Daniel J. Freed, Assoc. Dir., Office of Criminal Justice, U.S. Dept. of Justice indicates the difficulty of drafting a fair and precise preventive detention provision.

MAY BE PROVIDED BY LAW FOR PERSONS REASONABLY DEEMED BY INDIVIDUAL DETERMINATION BY THE COURT TO PROVIDE A SERIOUS THREAT TO THE COMMUNITY DURING A RIOT, REBELLION OR INSURRECTION AND THEN ONLY SO LONG AS SUCH CIVIL DISORDER SHALL CONTINUE.

Conclusion

The authors do not favor a system of preventive detention during normal times. They believe that the utilization of a limited system of pretrial detention during a riot does however deserve consideration. The lack of certainty and guidelines in this area has contributed to a wholesale denial of bail by the courts by the indiscriminate setting of high bail. The proposal of the authors seeks to outline a workable system which would provide due process of law for all those arrested during civil disorder. The authors do not argue for mass arrests and detention as a technique to deal with civil disorder. They merely assume that this pattern of law enforcement will continue to be used in such times with the consequent pressure on the courts to deal with the release or detention of hundreds or thousands of arrested persons. Release on bail or personal recognizance should be provided for the great majority of persons who do not appear to provide a risk of subsequent serious criminal conduct.

The recent conduct of the courts in the face of civil disorder must be considered by lawyers and lawmakers and workable recommendations made. Whether the suggestions in this article are the answer or not, it is hoped that they will stimulate constructive debate by the legal profession which must be committed to the protection of individual dignity and constitutional standards no matter how unpopular the defendant or difficult the time.

APPENDIX

The information on the following tables was gathered by interviews at Southern Michigan State Prison, Jackson, Michigan, of persons allegedly involved in the Detroit Riot of July, 1967. The number of respondents totalled 1014 and all were male adults.

Of the 1014 interviews taken, 238 were verified by the interviewers. Of this 238, 10% needed major corrections. The remaining 776 probably contain a similar percentage of error. The tables should be viewed with this in mind.

TABLE 1
Age (In Years)†

Category	N		%
16 years	5		*
17-20	283		28%
21-24	224		22%
25-28	160		16%
29-32	107		11%
33-36	84		
37-40	52		
41-43	35		
44-47	22	231	23%
48-51	11		
52-55	13		
56-60	8		
61 & Over	6		

† Median age = 24 years

TABLE 2
Marital Status*

Category	N	%
Married	*437	44%
Single	460	46%
Divorced	43	4%
Separated	49	5%
Widowed	14	1%

* 76% are living together

TABLE 3
Number of Children*†

Category	N		%
None	79		15%
One	133		25%
Two	108		20%
Three	97		18%
Four	43		
Five	34	113	21%
Six	19		
Seven†	17		

* 484 of sample = unknown
† Median number of children approx. 2.5

TABLE 4
LENGTH OF PRESENT RESIDENCE†*

Category	N		%
1-3 mos.	110		13%
4-6 mos.	66		8%
7-11 mos.	52		6%
1 yr.	114		14%
2 yrs.	104		13%
3 yrs.	79		10%
4 yrs.	50		6%
5 yrs.	40		
6-10 yrs.	99		
11-15 yrs.	56	243	30%
16-20 yrs.	30		
21+ yrs.	18		

† Median length of present residence approx. 1 yr. 8 mos.
* 196 unknown

TABLE 5
LENGTH OF FORMER RESIDENCE†*

Category	N		%
1-3 mos.	19		4%
4-6 mos.	22		5%
7-11 mos.	19		4%
1 yr.	81		17%
2 yrs.	69		15%
3 yrs.	62		13%
4 yrs.	31		7%
5 yrs.	30		
6-10 yrs.	74		
11-15 yrs.	19	160	35%
16-20 yrs.	23		
21+ yrs.	14		

† Median length of former address approx. 2 yrs. 5 mos.
* 551 unknown

TABLE 6
EMPLOYMENT STATUS*

Category	N	%
Employed	792	80%
Unemployed	203	20%

* 16 unknown

TABLE 7
MAJOR EMPLOYERS*

Category	N		%
Auto Manufacturer "A"	148		
Auto Manufacturer "B"	118	325	41%
Auto Manufacturer "C"	59		
Other	467		59%

* 16 unknown

TABLE 8
YEARS WITH PRESENT EMPLOYER*†

Category	N		%
Less than a year	263		36%
1 yr.	146		20%
2 yrs.	104		14%
3 yrs.	84		11%
4 yrs.	29		4%
5 yrs.	18		
6-10 yrs.	29	106	14%
10+ yrs.	59		

* 60 unknown
† Median length of employment approx. 1 yr. 11 mos.

TABLE 9
SIZE OF BOND†

Category	N	%
To $1,500	80	9%
$1,501-$2,500	132	14%
$2,501-$3,000	46	5%
$3,001-$4,000	2	*
$5,000	183	20%
$7,000	2	*
$10,000	404	44%
$15,000	6	*
$23,000	1	*
$25,000	58	6%
$100,000	2	*

† 98 unknown
* less than 1%

TABLE 10
PREVIOUS ARRESTS*

Category	N		%
None	455		47%
One	264		27%
Two	96		
Three	44		
Four	32		
Five	24	226	23%
Six	14		
Seven	8		
Eight	8		
Nine+	25		3%

* 44 unknown

TABLE 11
PREVIOUS CONVICTIONS*

Category	N		%
None	611		67%
One	173		19%
Two	73		8%
Three	29		
Four	14		
Five	6		
Six	0	55	6%
Seven	1		
Eight	1		
Nine+	4		

* 102 unknown

TABLE 12
ARRESTS AND/OR CONVICTIONS FOR MISDEMEANORS*

Category	N		%
None	687		79%
One	119		14%
Two	33		
Three	9		
Four	9		
Five	3	59	7%
Six	0		
Seven	1		
Eight	2		
Nine	2		

* 149 unknown

TABLE 13
ARRESTS AND/OR CONVICTIONS FOR FELONIES*

Category	N		%
None	692		79%
One	117		13%
Two	48		
Three	12	67	8%
Four	5		
Five	2		

* 138 unknown

TABLE 14
Type of Crime†

Category	N	%
Entry without Breaking	447	54%
Breaking and Entering	89	11%
Breaking w/o Entering	4	*
Larceny	91	11%
Receiving Stolen Goods	48	6%
Concealed Weapon	16	2%
Assault w/ intent	1	*
Arson	3	*
Curfew	120	15%
Loitering	3	*
Other	3	*

† Undetermined = 189
* Less than 1%

TABLE 15
Judges Handling Cases and Number*

Category	N	%
Judge A	49	11%
B	77	18%
C	38	9%
D	29	7%
E	9	2%
F	49	11%
G	51	12%
H	29	7%
I	14	3%
J	25	6%
K	20	5%
L	49	11%

* 575 unknown

TABLE 16
Size of Bond by Judge

Judge	To $2,999		$3,000 to $7,000		$8,000 to $12,000		$13,000 to $17,000		$23,000 to $27,000		$100,000	
A	3	6%	3	6%	42	86%	—		1	2%	—	
B	3	4%	6	8%	38	49%	—		28	36%	2	3%
C	22	58%	14	37%	2	5%	—		—		—	
D	9	41%	7	32%	5	23%	1	5%	—		—	
E	6	67%	2	22%	1	11%	—		—		—	
F	1	2%	44	94%	1	2%	—		1	2%	—	
G	16	32%	15	30%	17	34%	—		2	4%	—	
H	12	41%	5	17%	10	34%	—		2	7%	—	
I	2	15%	—		11	85%	—		—		—	
J	4	16%	8	32%	11	44%	1	4%	1	4%	—	
K	2	10%	16	80%	1	5%	—		1	5%	—	
L	13	28%	11	23%	22	47%	1	2%	—		—	

TABLE 17
CRIME AND BOND SIZE

Crime Bond Size	Entry w/o Break	Breaking and Entering	Break w/o Entry	Larceny	Re'd Stolen Goods	Concealed Weapon	Assault w/Intent	Arson	Curfew	Loitering
To $2,999	105 24%	24 28%	1 25%	23 26%	4 9%	5 31%	0	0	28 25%	0
$3,000-$7,000	115 27%	18 21%	1 25%	19 22%	13 30%	2 13%	0	0	43 39%	0
$8,000-$12,000	187 43%	36 42%	2 50%	35 40%	24 55%	9 56%	0 0	0 0	39 35%	3 21%
$13,000-$17,000	2	0	0	1	0	0	1 100%	1 33%	0	1 7%
$23,000-$27,000	21 5%	8 9%	0	10 11%	3 7%	0	0	0	0	10 71%
$100,000	0	0	0	0	0	0	0	2 67%	0	0

TABLE 18
COMPARISON—THE PRISONERS WITH NO PREVIOUS ARRESTS AND THE PRISONER WITH ARREST AND CONVICTION RECORD

	Bond Size					
	To $2,999	$3,000 to $7,000	$8,000 to $12,000	$13,000 to $17,000	$23,000 to $27,000	$100,000
No Arrest— (N = 385)	85 22%	85 22%	185 48%	3 1%	26 7%	1
Arrest(s) and Conviction(s)— (N = 275)	60 22%	83 30%	109 40%	2 1%	20 7%	1

TABLE 19
"EXTREME" PRISONER CHARACTERISTICS AND BOND SIZE

	Bond Size					
	To $2,999	$3,000 to $7,000	$8,000 to $12,000	$13,000 to $17,000	$23,000 to $27,000	$100,000
Prisoners who were married, employed, no arrests and no convictions— N = 164	36 22%	38 23%	75 46%	2 1%	13 8%	0
"Neutral" characteristics— N = 718	167 23%	186 26%	316 44%	4 1%	43 6%	2
Prisoners who were single, unemployed and had a record of previous arrests and convictions— N = 32	9 28%	9 28%	10 31%	0	4 13%	0

TABLE 20
NUMBER OF PREVIOUS ARRESTS AND BOND SIZE

Bond	Number									
	None	One	Two	Three	Four	Five	Six	Seven	Eight	Nine or More
To $2,999	94	59	23	12	5	4	4	1	1	4
	23%	25%	25%	28%	17%	18%	33%	14%	13%	19%
$3,000-$7,000	90	59	25	11	11	11	2	5	3	5
	22%	25%	27%	26%	38%	50%	17%	71%	38%	24%
$8,000-$12,000	192	103	38	18	11	5	5	1	3	10
	47%	43%	42%	42%	38%	23%	42%	14%	38%	48%
$13,000-$17,000	3	2	0	0	0	0	0	0	0	0
	1%	1%								
$23,000-$27,000	28	14	5	2	2	2	1	0	1	2
	7%	6%	5%	5%	7%	9%	8%		13%	10%
$100,000	1	1	0	0	0	0	0	0	0	0

TABLE 21
NUMBER OF PREVIOUS CONVICTIONS AND BOND SIZE

	Number of Convictions				
Bond	None	One	Two	Three	Four or More
To $2,999	132 24%	37 24%	15 22%	5 17%	3 14%
$3,000-$7,000	126 23%	43 27%	17 25%	15 52%	8 38%
$8,000-$12,000	258 46%	63 40%	31 46%	6 21%	9 43%
$13,000-$17,000	3 1%	2 1%	0	0	0
$23,000-$27,000	37 7%	11 7%	5 7%	3 10%	1 5%
$100,000	1	1	0	0	0

Recorder's Court and the 1967 Civil Disturbance*

JUDGE GEO. W. CROCKETT, JR.**

A United States Senate Committee recently suggested that Detroit's Recorder's Court was too lenient in its handling of cases growing out of Detroit's civil disturbance last summer.[1] I assume the Committee had reference to the fact that the large bulk of the 1967 riot cases on our docket have been and are being disposed of as simple misdemeanors instead of felonies; and the sentences generally are limted to the time spent by the defendant in jail while awaiting reasonable bail or the final disposition of the case.

I disagree with the Senate Committee. Instead, I suggest that we judges (perhaps subconsciously) are belatedly endeavoring to make amends for the wholesale denial of the constitutional rights of virtually everyone who was arrested during that disturbance. And I include myself in this indictment. As the report of the President's Commission on Civil Disorders points out,[2] the bails fixed by me were the lowest in the Court; but they still were much higher than they should have been.

Nor am I convinced that there is general appreciation even now of the full extent of the injustices we committed by our refusal to recognize the right to immediate bail and our objection to fixing reasonable bail. Some of the cases which have come before me as a result of the curfew imposed following the death of Dr. King, suggest that the prosecutor's office and the policemen in the street have learned nothing from last summer's experience; and this has serious implications for the coming summer.

The situation we faced last summer is authoritatively summed up in the recent Report of the President's National Advisory Commission on Civil Disorders:

> In all, more than 7,200 persons were arrested. Almost 3,000 of these were picked up on the second day of the riot, and by midnight Monday 4,000 were incarcerated in makeshift jails. Some were kept as long as 30 hours on buses. Others spent days in an underground garage without toilet facilities. An uncounted number were people who had merely been un-

* Portion of remarks prepared for delivery to the American Civil Liberties Union conference at Detroit, Michigan, April 20, 1968.

** B.A., Morehouse, 1931; L.L.B. University of Michigan, 1934; Judge, Recorders' Court, City of Detroit, Michigan.

1. Otto Kerner, U.S. Riot Comm'n Report, Report of the National Advisory Comm'n on Civil Disorders (Bantam, 1968) [hereinafter referred to as 'Kerner Report'].
2. *Id.* at 342 note 9.

fortunate enough to be on the wrong street at the wrong time. Included were members of the press whose attempts to show their credentials had been ignored.[3]

People became lost for days in the maze of different detention facilities. Until the later stages, bail was set deliberately high, often at $10,000 or more. When it became apparent that this policy was unrealistic and unworkable, the prosecutor's office began releasing on low bail or on their own recognizance hundreds of those who had been picked up. Nevertheless, this fact was not publicized for fear of antagonizing those who had demanded a high-bail policy.[4]

At least eighty-three percent of these 7,200 arrestees were Black citizens. I suggest that this fact accounts in large measure for the unconstitutional procedures uniformly followed by the authorities after their arrest—the exceedingly large number of unjustifiable felony charges (which have since been reduced to misdemeanors; the insistence upon routine time-consumming clerical and identification procedures as a pretext for holding people in custody; the refusal to utilize the judges and staffs of other courts so as to expedite the processing of cases and afford time for individual examination at arraignments; and, of course, the assessment en mass of exorbitantly high bail which resulted in wholesale imprisonment and the exhaustion of our conventional detention facilities.

The Curfew Cases

The bulk of the over 7,000 arrestees were arrested for being on the streets after the curfew hour. A large portion of these were juveniles whose cases came before the Wayne County Juvenile Court. Three thousand of these arrests occurred on the second day of the riot when the initial curfew proclamation was in effect. Each of the curfew arrests made under the initial curfew proclamation was illegal because the proclamation failed to provide that its violation would constitute a misdemeanor. The statute makes such a provision mandatory.[5] Notwithstanding this omission, our court enforced the initial proclamation as written. Later this "error" was detected and a new proclamation was issued.

This curfew misdemeanor was punishable by a fine of not more than $100 and/or a jail sentence of not more than 90 days.[6] As such, it was the equivalent of a traffic violation for which a traffic ticket

3. *Id.* at 106.
4. *Id.* at 107.
5. Mich. Comp. Laws § 10.33 (1948), Mich. Stat. Ann. § 3.43(3) (1961). See also Mich. Comp. Laws § 10.31 (1948), Mich. Stat. Ann. § 3.4.(1) (1961).
6. *Id.*

normally is given and the defendant is not detained. There was then, in my judgment, no justification whatever in *detaining* these curfew violators any longer than the time required to obtain and verify their names and correct addresses. Either they should have been 1.) issued a summons (on the spot or at the precinct station) to appear in magistrates court; or 2.) simply ordered the individuals to disperse and go immediately to their homes. Those who failed to appear on the appointed court date could be prosecuted by warrant later; and those who disobeyed the order to go to their homes would then be arrested and charged with the high misdemeanor of failing to obey the arresting officer—a prison offense.

Had this procedure been followed the number of arrestees would have been greatly reduced, the processing of cases involving serious charges would have proceeded more expeditiously, our detention facilities would have been more adequate for the demand, the rights of all citizens could have been secured, and, most importantly, the fears and tensions in the Negro community would not have been nearly as great nor the aftermath of bitterness so potentially threatening.

Instead, the arresting officers, the prosecutors, and the judges made a critical situation worse by their indiscriminate and prolonged detention of all curfew violators before bringing them before a judge. Almost without exception these people did not come before a judge until 24-48 hours after their arrest and detention in city buses parked in the blazing sun. In most instances they admitted their guilt or they were tried by the judge and found guilty. In either event the usual result was a suspended sentence or a sentence equal to the time already spent waiting to be arraigned. In any event, the net result is that they were punished by "cruel and inhuman treatment" even before they reached court.

To claim then that our disposition of the curfew cases was too lenient overlooks completely the injustices already visited upon these defendants as well as the fact that the magnitude of the arrests made any other final disposition impossible in these cases.

The Felony Cases

The real complaint about "the leniency" of Recorder's Court seems to concern our disposition of the felony cases. The publicity credited to the prosecutor's office and the police department at the time of the 1967 disturbance left the public impression that an unusually large number of major crimes were being committed, and there were repeated assurances that "these felons will be prosecuted to the full extent of the law."

When, as it later appeared, the evidence was not forthcoming to support these serious charges, the judges were criticized and the complaint is now heard that Recorder's Court judges are too lenient.

The truth of the matter is that in the overwhelming majority of the cases the police and the prosecutor simply charged more than they could possibly prove. And I am of the view that much of this was racially motivated that it was done for the purpose of having a prohibitive bond placed against the black defendants so they could be detained in prison pending their examination and trial.

The report of the President's Commission states that twenty-four percent of those arrested for felonies in the Detroit riots were never prosecuted.[7] That is, they never became court cases. Also, of the seventy-six percent who were prosecuted, about half of these, (forty-nine percent) were dismissed at the preliminary examination for lack of evidence.[8] This report further points out that twenty-six persons were charged with sniping, but twenty-three of these charges were dismissed;[9] thirty-four persons were arrested for arson, but twenty-one of these were never prosecuted;[10] twenty-eight persons were arrested for inciting to riot but twenty-two of these were not prosecuted;[11] and of the 253 assault arrests, 184 were discharged, eleven were convicted, and 58 are still pending.[12]

The statistics from our own court records are most revealing. Of the 7200 persons arrested, our records show that only 4260 were brought to Recorder's Court.[13]

Of the cases brought to our court, seventy-five percent of the persons were charged with a felony. With few exceptions, the charge was looting—entering without breaking with intent to steal—a five year felony. This means that each of these 3230 persons is entitled to counsel, an arraignment on the warrant, a preliminary examination, and an arraignment on the information—a total of three court appearances for each person before his trial date. And since virtually all of those charged with felonies were indigents, each of these felony cases costs Wayne County taxpayers an average of $150.00 in assigned counsel fees in addition to the usual cost of processing a felony file for six or more months.

In these felony cases, as in the curfew cases, the prosecutor de-

---

7. Kerner Report 339.
8. *Id.* at 340.
9. *Id.* at 339.
10. *Id.*
11. *Id.*
12. *Id.*
13. Records on file, Recorder's Court, Detroit, Michigan (1967).

manded, and our court imposed, unconstitutional bail ranging from $10,000 to $200,000! And we did it routinely and without making any individual inquiry whatever to determine if such bail could be justified. The asserted justification for this unusual procedure was: "We have to keep *these people* locked up and off the streets so they won't go out and do the same thing again"! Or "The prosecutor and the police department are waiting for an FBI check on each felony defendant so we won't allow any wanted criminals or "outside conspirators' to escape"!

The prosecutor knew or should have known—and certainly we judges should have remembered—that reasonable bail before conviction is a matter of constitutional right under both our state and federal constitutions. As the United States Supreme Court said in *Stack v. Boyle*:

> This traditional right to freedom before conviction permits the unhampered preparation of a defense, and serves to prevent the infliction of punishment prior to conviction . . . . Unless this right to bail before trial is preserved, the presumption of innocence, secured only after centuries of struggle, would lose its meaning.[14]

There are other principles set forth in *Stack v. Boyle* which should have been binding upon us in fixing bail and which we ignored. Thus the Court pointed out:

> [T]he fixing of bail for any individual defendant must be based upon standards relevant to the purpose of assuring the presence of that defendant.[15]
>
> * * *
>
> If bail in an amount greater than that usually fixed for serious charges of crimes is required. . . , that is a matter to which evidence should be directed in a hearing so that the constitutional rights of each petitioner may be preserved."[16]

And Mr. Justice Jackson's opinion points out:

> Each defendant stands before the bar of justice as an individual. Each accused is entitled to any benefits due to his good record, and misdeeds or a bad record should prejudice only those who are guilty of them.[17]
>
> [I]t is not the function of the grand jury [the prosecuting authority] to fix bail, and its volunteered advice is not govern-

14. Stack v. Boyle, 342 U.S. 1, 4 (1951).
15. *Id.* at 5.
16. *Id.* at 6.
17. *Id.* at 9.

> ing. Such recommendations are better left unmade, and if made should be given no weight.[18]

The unconstitutional conduct of our court in fixing prohibitive bail in a uniform en masse manner and without any inquiry into the defendant's family, employment, or community ties, was further compounded by an oral order to the sheriff to refuse to release even those who offered our high bail unless and until the court could re-examine and determine if their bail should not be made higher still! However, this provision went too far for several members of our court, and they each gave specific orders to the sheriff and to the bonding clerk to release immediately anyone who posted the bond initially fixed by them.

This "high bail policy" in our court was followed from Sunday, July 23, until Friday noon, July 30. As a result, hundreds of presumably innocent people, with no previous record whatever, suddenly found themselves separated from their unknowing families and jobs and incarcerated in our maximum security detention facilities at Jackson and Milan; and all of this without benefit of counsel, without an examination, and without even the semblance of a trial.

As should have been anticipated, racial tensions mounted to something approaching the explosion point. By Friday noon the prosecutor was so disturbed that he requested authorization to countermand our court's bail orders and to use his uncontrolled discretion in releasing prisoners of his choice. Also by Friday noon the Governor, the Mayor, and the President's personal representative were sufficiently apprehensive that they demanded and received a special audience with our court and asked that we expedite the release of as many arrestees as possible.

Again by Friday afternoon, a sizable delegation representing Detroit's Black community demanded and received a hearing with our bench and they lodged a vigorous protest against the flagrant denials of their civil rights and liberties, the killing of some thirty-three Negros by police and guardsmen, and the indiscriminate kicking in of doors and the searching Black people's homes.

It was not until these encounters occurred that we judges returned to our judicial senses. Within a matter of a few hours orders were entered releasing the overwhelming bulk of these defendants on personal bond. But the damage had been done.

Conclusion

In the five or six years preceeding our 1967 disturbance, much progress was made in Detroit in improving police-community relations.

---

18. *Id.* at 9, 10.

No police commissioner in the past 25 years enjoyed the respect and confidence in the Negro community that Commissioner Girardin enjoyed prior to the summer of 1967. Commissioner Girardin is still highly regarded; but not so his department, nor the Wayne County Prosecutor's Office, nor the Recorder's Court.

Black citizens of Detroit find it difficult to understand a system of criminal justice that charges 3230 persons with felonies and then, after imprisonment for days and the payment of thousands of dollars in attorney fees, disposes of the first 1630 of these felonies with 961 dismissals, 664 pleas to misdemeanors (trespass, petty larceny, and curfew violations) and only *two* convictions after trial on the original charge![19]

It is not surprising that police-Negro tension in our City today is almost as high as it was immediately after last summer's events. The simple truth is that Detroit's black community has no confidence in the administration of justice in their city; they believe that the temple of criminal justice is sagging, is tottering. They feel the beams resting upon their necks. What is particularly disturbing is the refusal of the Establishment to open its eyes to the fact and take corrective measures before it is *too late*.

---

19. *Supra* note 13.

The Efficient Use of Military Forces to Control Riots:

Some Proposals for Congressional Action

ALLEN SULTAN* AND RICHARD A. HOWARD**

> If men were angels, no government would be necessary. If angels were to govern men, neither external nor internal controls on government would be necessary. In framing a government which is to be administered by men over men, the great difficulty lies in this: you first enable the government to control the governed; and in the next place oblige it to control itself.†
>
> James Madison

INTRODUCTION

THE riots of last July raise serious questions concerning the ability of state and/or federal government to respond in an effective and timely manner so as to minimize loss of life and property during such outbreaks. There is, obviously, a need to examine whether we have succeeded in our efforts to ". . . enable the government to control the governed."

In retrospect it is clear that there existed two basic problems. The first, and perhaps most important, was the demonstrated lack of training and leadership of the national guard to deal with this type of civil commotion or riot. Secondly, was the delay involved in dispatching federal troops to assist local authorities. A study of existing statutes has resulted in a determination that some added legislation is needed if these problems are to be solved.

THE NATIONAL GUARD

On July 26, 1967, President Johnson said in a radio and television address to the nation ". . . Law enforcement is a local matter. It is the responsibility of local officials . . . . The Federal Government should not intervene—except in the most extraordinary circumstances."[1] This statement is, of course, consistent with the concept of sovereignty of the various states. However, the control of riots at

* Assistant Professor, School of Law, University of Detroit

** J.D., University of Detroit Law School. Mr. Howard is substantially responsible for the statutory suggestion relating to the National Guard.

† The Federalist, No. 51.

1. Weekly Compilation of Presidential Documents, vol. 3, No. 30 p. 1051 (1967)

state level, like those of last summer, requires the availability of a well trained and highly disciplined national guard capable of being mobilized and deployed on a timely basis under effective leadership. It seems clear that the Michigan National Guard was not properly trained to handle this type of riot.

Over 90 percent of the operating expense of the guard is provided by the federal government; aid to the states that is subject to specified conditions. Thus, congressional enactment provides for the forfeiture of federal aid to any state failing to fulfill or enforce any regulation prescribed by the President[2]—an effective tool for the upgrading of the guard training programs. On July 27, 1967, in another address to the nation, President Johnson, pursuant to his power to regulate the guard,[3] reported that he had directed special training courses to be added to the existing guard training programs.[4] Orders to train are, however, ineffective absent prior provision for both adequate duty time to carry them out and adequate inspection procedures to assure they are in fact being carried out. It is submitted that existing statutory commands as to both training time[5] and inspection routines[6] are inadequate. It seems highly probable that the annual inspection is, in reality, an audit of equipment and record keeping activities. There are five specific points to be reviewed during the annual inspection: whether the amount and condition of property are satisfactory; whether the guard is properly organized; whether the members meet prescribed physical and other qualifications; whether the guard is properly uniformed

2. 32 U.S.C. § 108 (1965)

3. 32 U.S.C. § 110 (1965); These regulations prescribe that: "The President shall prescribe regulations; and issue orders, necessary to organize, discipline, and govern the National Guard."

4. *Supra* note 1, at 1056.

5. 32 U.S.C. § 502 (1965)

6. 32 U.S.C. § 105 (1965)

(1) the amount and condition of property held by the Army National Guard are satisfactory;

(2) the Army National Guard is organized as provided in this title;

(3) the members of the Army National Guard meet prescribed physical and other qualifications;

(4) the Army National Guard and its organization are properly uniformed, armed, and equipped and are being trained and instructed for active duty in the field, or for coast defense; and

(5) Army National Guard records are being kept in accordance with this title.

The Secretary of the Air Force has a similar duty with respect with the Air National Guard.

(b) The reports of inspections under subsection (a) are the basis for determining whether the National Guard is entitleed to the issue of military property as authorized under this title and to retain that property; and for determining which organizations and persons constitute units and members of the National Guard.

and equipped and is being trained for active duty in the field or coast defense; and whether the records are properly kept.[7] Only one deals with training and it is limited to combat training or active duty in the field and to coast defense.

Certainly, an inspection routine concerned with availability and accountability of materials and equipment is necessary; but it ought to be a separate activity. Accordingly, it is submitted that a separate inspection ought be established for audit purposes, and that additional semi-annual inspections that concentrate on training functions also be undertaken by the Pentagon. Ideally, one training inspection would occur during the "encampment" period, and another during a regularly scheduled drill session or sessions. Expanding the scope of these inspections to include review and analysis of the actual training in "controlling and subduing domestic violence of all types" should become part of their "standard operational procedure."

In addition to the above measures there should be a means of demonstrating proficiency in military occupational specialties on the part of commissioned and non-commissioned officers as well as enlisted men.[8] This training inspection should be conducted by a team of not less than four qualified regular army commissioned officers, at least one of whom should be a general grade officer in order to mitigate the possibility of the inspections lacking substance.

The foregoing inspection procedures should all be predicated upon a realistic threat of withdrawal of federal aid with respect to any unit failing inspection.

It is also submitted that additional training time must be provided. The present statute provides that the minimum drill period be one and one-half hours per week.[9] This should be doubled to three hours a week to allow sufficient time for training after allowing time for roll call, issuance of equipment, etc. It is to be noted that many units now train only one week-end a month. While this provides an opportunity to obtain a full day of training, weekly meetings would allow more frequent exposure to military discipline. This should result in more desirable means of preparation from the military point of view, and consequently, a better trained, better led guard capable of handling most civil disturbances.

---

7. *Id.*

8. McWhirter, *Favorite Haven for the Comic Soldier*, Life, October 27, 1967, at 85. The author joined several guard units across the country to gather information for this article. On page 94 he states: "[S]ome members of the units were taking MOS (Military Occupation Specialty) tests, although most of them had no idea what their specialties were."

9. 32 U.S.C. § 502(d)(2) (1965).

The necessary statutory amendments to Title 32 of the United States Code would appear to be as follows:

> *32 USC § 105* Inspection [*of equipment and records*].
> (a) The Secretary of the Army shall have an inspection made at least once a year by inspector general, or, if necessary, by any other commissioned officer of the Regular Army detailed for that purpose, to determine whether:
>> (1) the amount and condition of property held by the Army National Guard are satisfactory;
>> (2) the Army National Guard is organized as provided in this title;
>> [(3)] the Army National Guard and its organization[s] are properly uniformed, armed, and equipped[;] and are being trained and instructed for active duty in the field, or for coast defense; and
>> [(4)] Army National Guard records are being kept in accordance with this title.

The addition of the words "of equipment and records" to the existing title of this section is intended to reflect the intent to restrict the scope of this inspection to essentially audit type activities. Accordingly, provisions in the original statute for determining that members of the guard meet prescribed physical and other qualifications and that they are being properly trained for active duty in the field and for coastal defense have been deleted. Subsection (b) has been retained without change because of its purpose to make passing the inspections the basis for determining whether the unit being inspected will qualify for the issuance of military equipment.

The only relevant modification with respect to required drills and field exercises is as follows:

> *32 USC § 502* Required drills and field exercises.
> (a) ****
> (b) ****
> (c) ****
> (d) No organization may receive credit for an assembly for drill or indoor target practice unless—
>> (1) the number of members present equals or exceeds the minimum number prescribed by the President;
>> (2) the period of military duty or instruction for which a member is credited is at least ~~one and one half~~ [three] hours; and
>> (3) the training is of the type prescribed by the Secretary concerned.

This change is suggested in order to extend the minimum required drill period from the present one and one-half hours to three hours. As indicated earlier it is believed that this additional period is necessary in order to provide adequate time for assembly and roll call, issuance of equipment, and a meaningful training section.

A new proposed section is as follows:

> *32 USC §* Inspection [*of training and physical fitness*].
> (a) The Secretary of the Army shall have an inspection made at least twice a year by a team of not less than four commissioned officers of the Regular Army, detailed for that purpose, one of which must be of General Officer rank to determine whether:
>
> (1) commissioned and non-commissioned officers and enlisted men of the National Guard meet prescribed physical qualifications;
> (2) commissioned and non-commissioned officers and enlisted men of the National Guard have achieved acceptable proficiency within their military occupational specialty;
> (3) that the National Guard unit is being trained and instructed for active duty in the field, or for coast defense; and in handling, controlling, and subduing all types of domestic violence;
> The Secretary of the Air Force has similar duty with respect to the Air National Guard.
>
> (b) The reports of inspectors under subsection (a) are also the basis for determining whether the National Guard is entitled to the issue and retention of military property as authorized under this title and for determining which organizations and persons constitute units and members of the National Guard.

This section is added in order to emphasize the importance of training, and to insure that training in the handling and controlling of all types of domestic violence is being accomplished. Previously the inspection of training was done in conjunction with audit type activities and was limited to determining whether the guard was adequately trained for active duty in the field and for coast defense. There was no specific requirement that members of the guard demonstrate profiency in their assigned military occupational specialty. This is, of course, essential if a unit is to function smoothly.

The Use of Federal Forces

Notwithstanding the availability of a better trained and led guard, situations will arise requiring the use of federal troops and/or guard units from sister states under federal control. The possible uses of military force by the federal government to quell domestic disturbances are provided by title 10, section 331-333 of the federal code.[10] Contained in chapter 15, entitled "Insurrection", and promulgated August 10, 1956, this legislation was not effectively utilized during the Detroit riots. A review of these sections will do much to explain the hesitancy of local political leaders to request federal aid. If aid is requested under Section 331, the riot or disturbance must be characterized as an insurrection; under section 332 a rebellion; and, finally, section 333 requires that the state be regarded as having denied equal protection of the laws secured by the Constitution. If a constitutionally valid amendment of the present law can serve to mitigate the possibility of such delays in the future, such changes would appear to demand serious consideration due to the present potentially explosive composition of urban America.

The first impression one is likely to gain in perusing the existing legislation is an attitude of extreme caution or limitation. This is perhaps due to the fact that early authority suggests a judicial sensitivity to extensive federal activity.[11] Thus section 331,[12] implementing article IV, section 4 of the United States Constitution,[13] is designed to have the federal government play a "back-up" role to the recognized authority of state and local officials. This approach reflects traditional American values of federalism and Jeffersonian democracy.

As indicated earlier, the basic problem in using section 331 as a basis for deployment of federal troops centers around the definition of the term "insurrection" which is not defined anywhere in chapter 15 and is the very subject matter of the legislation. Further problems involve the assumption in the statutory language that information available to state officials will permit them to request sufficient forces to be at the command of the President, and that action by the President

---

10. 70 Stat. 15 (1956). One should also note the existence of 18 U.S.C. § 1385 (20 stat. 152 (1878)) known as the "Posse Comitative Act," it was amended on June 25, 1959 (73 stat. 144 (1959)) following congressional debate regarding the use of the federal troops in the South. Although it forbids forces to engage in ordinary police activities, if requested for that purpose by local officials, it does not affect the implementation of sections 331-33 of Title 10, herein discussed. *See* Sutherland, Constitutionalism in America 450 (1965).

11. *See, e.g.*, Martin v. Matt, 6 U.S. (12 Wheat) 19 (1827); Luther v. Borden 48 U.S. (7 How.) 1 (1849).

12. 10 U.S.C. § 331 (1965). Federal aid for State governments
Whenever there is an insurrection in any State against its government, the President may, upon the request of its legislature or of its governor if the legislature cannot be convened, call into Federal service such of the militia of the other States, in the number requested by that State, and use of such of the armed forces as he considers necessary to suppress the insurrection.

13. Section 4. The United States shall guarantee to every State in this Union a Republican Form of Government, and shall protect each of them against Invasion; and on Application of the Legislature, or of the Executive (when the Legislature cannot be convened) against domestic Violence.

after request by local officials is discretionary rather than mandatory.

The generality of presently obtaining dictionary definitions[14] of "insurrection" indicates the need for an exacting characterization of the term, should Congress desire it to be applied to contemporary circumstances of group lawlessness. Also, presently obtaining dictionary references to the term "rebellion" as a synonym suggest characterizing an "insurrection" as an uprising with intent to overthrow legally constituted governments,[15] and not merely a situation of temporary resistance by a group of citizens to that government's proper exercise of police authority. With respect to the public law of the federal government, this limited definition of the term "insurrection" is supported by early congressional activity: on February 28, 1795, Congress enacted the first precursor to the present section 331[16] when it "authorized the President to call out the militia in case of insurrection against the government of any state."[17]

In seeking a precise definition, one must recognize that the term "rebellion" does not possess a more exacting characterization than does "insurrection"—either in the dictionaries[18] or in the public mind. Thus one may well conclude that use of the term "insurrection" was "rebellion" to the status of a legal limbo. For example, one finds "insurrection" defined as "the open and active opposition of a number of persons to the execution of law in a city or state". Following this definition one discovers the clear and categorical statement that "a mere mob is not an insurrection; neither is a riot."[19] And following the

14. *E.g.*, BLACK, LAW DICTIONARY 946 (3d. ed. 1951): "A rebellion or rising of citizen or subjects in resistance to their government." WEBSTERS, THIRD NEW INTERNATIONAL DICTIONARY 1173 (1961): "1. An act or instance of revolting against civil or political authority or against an established government. 2. An act or instance or rising up physically, Syn.: Rebellion." WEBSTER, COLLEGIATE DICTIONARY 523 (5th ed. 1948): "A rising up against civil or political authority. Syn. *See* Rebellion."

15. *See, e.g.*, BOUVIER, LAW DICTIONARY 1636 (1914):

> Insurgents. Rebels contending in arms against the government of their country who have not been recognized by other countries as belligerents. Insurgents have no standing in international law until recognized as belligerents.

Yet, on the next page, 1637, the term "insurrection" is defined not only as a "rebellion," but in addition as:

> Any open and active opposition of a number of persons to the execution of the laws of the United States of so formidable a character as to defy, for the time being, authority of the government, constitutes an insurrection, even though not accompanied by bloodshed and not of sufficient magnitude to make success possible.

16. 1 Stat. 424 (1795)

17. Library of Congress Ann. *Constitution of the United States*, 88th Cong. 1st Sess. No. 39 p. 796 (1964).

18. *See e.g.*, WEBSTER, THIRD NEW INTERNATIONAL DICTIONARY 1892 (1961): "1. open opposition to a person or thing in a position of authority or dominance. 2. open defiance of or armed resistance to the authority of an established government.": BOUVIER, *supra* note 15, at 2819: "The taking up arms traitoriusly against the government. The forcible opposition and resistance to the laws and process lawfully issued."

19. BALLENTINE, LAW DICTIONARY 667 (1930).

term "rebellion," one finds the caution that "insurrection, sedition, rebellion, revolt, and mutiny express action directed against government or authority, while riot has this implication only incidentally, if at all."[20]

Since section 331 as presently defined is of little use, "if at all", we must seek elsewhere for clear authority to deal with our present urban disturbances to the public tranquility. However, other operative sections of Title 10, chapter 15, do not offer any greater assistance—again—"if at all." Section 332 deals with challenges to federal authority;[21] section 333 is designed for situations that result in the deprivation "of a right, privilege, immunity, or protection named in the Constitution and secured by law"— meaning federal law.[22] Enacted pursuant to jurisdiction established in various parts of the Constitution,[23] these latter provisions are, in the words of the United States Supreme Court, indicative of the fact that:

> The entire strength of the nation may be used to enforce in any part of the land the full and free exercise of all national powers and the security of all rights entrusted by the Constitution to its care. The strong arm of the national government may be put forth to brush away all obstructions. . . . If the emergency arises, the army of the Nation, and all its militia, are at the service of the Nation to compel obedience to its laws.[24]

---

20. BOUVIER, *supra* note 15, at 2819 (emphasis added).

21. 10 U.S.C. § 332 (1965). Use of militia and armed forces to enforce Federal authority

> Whenever the President considers the Unlawful obstructions, combinations, or assemblages, or rebellion against the authority of the United States, make it impracticable to enforce the laws of the United States in any State or Territory by the ordinary course of judicial proceedings, he may call into Federal service such of the militia of any State, and use such of the armed forces as he considers necessary to enforce those laws or to suppress the rebellion.

22. 10 U.S.C. § 333 (1965). Interference with State and Federal law

> The President, by using the militia or the armed forces, or both, or by any other means, shall take such measures as he considers necessary to supress in a State, any insurrection, domestic violence, unlawful combination, or conspiracy, if it—
>
> (1) so hinders the execution of the laws of that State, *and* of the United States within the State, that *any part or class* of people is deprived of a right, privilege, immunity, or protection named in the Constitution and secured by law, and the constituted authorities of that State are unable, fail, or refuse to protect that right, privilege, or immunity, or to give that protection; or
>
> (2) opposes or obstructs the execution of the laws of the United States or impedes the course of justice under those laws. In any situation covered by clause (1), the State shall be considered to have denied the equal protection of the laws secured by the Constitution. [Emphasis added]

23. In addition to the preamble declaring one purpose of our national fundamental law to be the insurance of "domestic tranquility," the operative provisions of the Constitution with respect to section 331 and 332 are the first militia clause (art. I, § 8, cl. 15), the "necessary and proper" clause (art. I, § 8, cl. 18); and amend. XIV, § 5 grants Congress jurisdiction for the promulgation of section 333. For a recent expression of this congressional power, *see* United States v. Guest, 338 U.S. 745 (1966), especially the concurring opinion of Mr. Justice Brennan.

24. *In re* Debs, 158 U.S. 532, 582 (1895). The decision held, *inter alia*:

To apply these latter sections, therefore, one must seek out a federal law that is being violated. This is a most questionable undertaking in situations involving mob challenges to local police authority.

It is submitted that this basic distinction between section 331 vis-a-vis sections 332 and 333, upheld in recent executive implementations of chapter 15,[25] should be retained in any legislative attempts to utilize the chapter in resisting subsequent domestic strife. Amendments that do not respect the basic statutory "scheme" may well result in both an additional confusion of implementation and the unnecessary posing of constitutional issues. Consequently, the proper legislation to be considered for amendment is title 10, chapter 15, section 331 of the United States Code. In addition the chapter title should be amended to reflect the additional circumstances the chapter is intended to cover.

It is respectfully suggested that the Congress of the United States should consider amending chapter 15 to read, *inter alia*:

> CHAPTER 15—INSURRECTION [AND RIOT].
> *10 USC § 331* Federal aid for State governments.
> Whenever there is an insurrection [*riot or uncontrollable civil commotion*] in any state ~~against its government,~~ the President ~~may~~ [*shall*] upon the request of its legislature or of its governor if the legislature cannot be convened, call into Federal service such of the militia of the other States ~~in the number requested by that State,~~ and use such of the armed forces, as he considers necessary to suppress the insurrection [*riot or uncontrollable civil commotion*].

It is submitted that the term or expression *uncontrollable civil commotion*[26] is more limited, and therefore more exactly characterizes the

---

> [T]he government of the United States is one having jurisdiction over every foot of soil within its territory, and acting directly upon each citizen; that while it is a government of enumerated powers, it has within the limits of those powers all the attributes of sovereignty; [. . . and] that the powers thus conferred upon the national government are not dormant, but have been assumed and put into practical exercise by the legislation of Congress.: 2 ed. at 599.

See also Dunne v. United States, 138 F.2d 137 (1943).

25. Little Rock, Arkansas: Exec. Order No. 10730, Sept. 24, 1957 (22 F.R. 7628); Proc. No. 3204, Sept. 24, 1957 (22 F.R. 7628). Mississippi: Exec. Order No. 11053, Sept. 30, 1962 (27 F.R. 9693); Proc. No. 3497, Proc. No. 3497, Sept. 30, 1962 (27 F.R. 9681). Alabama: Exec. Order No. 11111, June 11, 1963 (28 F.R. 5709) and No. 11118, Sept. 10 1963 (28 F.R. 9863); Proc. No. 3542, June 11, 1963 (28 F.R. 5707) and No. 3554, Sept. 10, 1963 (28 F.R. 9861).

26. It is noteworthy that the use of the term or expression "civil commotion" was the result of one of the writers (Mr. Sultan) inspecting the exclusionary provisions of his insurance policy with State Farm Insurance Company. The coverage, which exempted property damage resulting from "riots" as well as from "civil commotion" was in force prior to the Detroit riots of July, 1967. Since the exclusions were part of the standard form used in home owner fire-liability coverage by one of the major national underwriters, one may well question the validity of the justification given by the Governor for not calling for federal troops at an earlier date.

group behavior under consideration the term "riot."[26a] Its use thus tends to avoid any possible attack on fifth amendment due process "void for vagueness" grounds—a distinct possibility with the utilization of the term or expression "riot."[26b] In addition, since "civil commotion" appears in conjunction with "insurrection," the definitions of both new terms or expressions would tend to be exactingly characterized by the application of the maxim *noscitur a sociis.* The two terms or expressions will be "associated with and take color from each other."[27] Thus, their use should be construed to apply to all group behavior in open and manifest contravention of established civil authority, to any collective contumacy against duly constituted officialdom.

Delection of the words "against its government" is dictated by the fact that an "insurrection" is no longer the sole concern of the statute. Not only do the deleted terms tend to be surplusage in the existing statute in light of the accepted definition of "insurrection,"[28] but the remainder of the section tends to render its "plain meaning" quite clear, viz., that the assistance is to be granted to the state law enforcement officials be they state police, the national guard, or members of other local enforcement units duly created under state authority.

Finally, replacement of the term "may" in the existing statute with the term "shall" is designed to render *mandatory*[29] the President's

---

26a. *Compare* 7 Words and Phrases 381-82 (1961) *with* 37 Words and Phrases 457-69. *See also* Wong Chow v. Transatlantic Fire Ins. Co., 13 Hawaii 160, 162 (1900) where "civil commotion" is characterized as being the wild or irregular action of many persons assembled together, or the mass uprising of people resulting in prolonged serious disturbance. While it is the wild and irregular action of a large assembly of individuals, it does not possess the status of armed insurrection. The Court quotes Lord Mansfield's interpretation of the riot acts of 1870 as authority for its characterization.

26b. Connally v. General Construction Co., 269 U.S. 385, 391 (1926); Lanzatta v. New Jersey, 306 U.S. 451 (1939). It is noteworthy that Title X, Section 1002 of the 1968 Civil Rights Act, promulgated April 11, 1968, characterizes a "civil disorder" (new 18 USC § 232(1)) as "any public disturbance involving acts of violence by assemblage of three or more persons, which causes an immediate danger of or results in damage or injury to the property or person of any other individual." Since "three or more persons" is traditionally used to define a "riot" (*see supra* notes 19 and 26a), both "riot" and "civil disorder" can also be challenged as being too broad, and therefore "arbitrary, capricious, or unreasonable." *See, e.g.,* Schneider v. Rusk, 377 U.S. 163 (1964); Bolling v. Sharpe, 347 U.S. 497 (1953).

27. Black *supra* note 14, at 1209.

28. *Id.*

29. The entire need for statutory amendment of section 331 could well have been alleviated if President Johnson, through his advisors, had conformed with a hundred year old precedent of the United States Supreme Court. In *Supervisors v. United States* 71 U.S. (4 Wall) 735 (1866) the Court, after citing early common law cases construing the term "may" and "shall," declared as follows (at pp. 446-47):

> The conslusion to be deduced from the authorities is, that where power is given to public officers, in the language of the act before us, or in equivalent language—whenever the public interest of individual rights calls for its exercise—the language used, though permissive in form, is in fact peremptory. What they are empowered to do for a third person the law requires shall be done. The power

reaction to a request for aid from a member state of the union, the only requirement being that the call for assistance comes from the proper organ of the state government. Since the President has the power to federalize the national guard for use in enforcement of federal law,[30] certainly both federal units as well as federalized units of sister-states not needed in their home state should be available to a member state for use in an emergency situation. The authors submit that the concept of a "federal union", with each state being a member of the same governmental "family", demands no less than a timely response to a call for aid. Mandatory executive response by the federal government should be considered *a matter of right,* and not be dependent upon possible ancillary factors. This proposition should be accepted as being fundamental, and not affected by the validity or invalidity of claims that politics was a factor in past decisions to use federal forces, as have been advanced with regard to the July, 1967, Detroit riots.

The basic consequences that will result from replacing "may" with "shall" requires consideration of possible contentions of the unconstitutionality of this new approach to the disposition and the use of federal military power. One can also envision some claiming it will result in the possible premature or improper use of such forces by state officialdom. Regarding the latter possibility, one can advance a dual response: separate but distinct political considerations obtaining on the level of state government will operate to strongly mitigate any possibility of improper use of the newly vested powers; and the proposed statute not only enlarges the existing Presidential power to determine the amount of all forces to be alerted for use in the requesting state (a point not clear in the existing statute), but also maintains Presidential discretion with respect to the "use," including numbers, of forces to be dispatched. The consequence of the change, therefore, is to tend to remove possible political considerations in the use of federal forces coming to the aid of a member state temporarily finding

---

is given, not for their benefit, but for his. It is placed with the depositary to meet the demands of right, and to prevent a failure of justice. It is given as a remedy of right, and to prevent a failure of justice. It is given as a remedy to those entitled to invoke its aid, and who would otherwise be remediless.

In all such cases it is held that the intent of the legislature, which is the test, was not to devolve a mere discretion, but to impose "a positive and absolute" duty.

The line which separates this class of cases from those which involve the exercise of a discretion, judicial in its nature, which courts cannot control, is too obvious to require remark.

Such response to the Detroit riot by President Johnson would have rendered moot the constitutional issue discussed below, at least until he or a subsequent president posed the issue.

Cf: United States ex rel. Siegel v. Thoman, 156 U.S. 353 (1895); Farmers and M. Bank v. Federal Reserve Bank, 262 U.S. 649 (1923).

30. *See, supra* note 21-23.

itself unable to control a riot situation, whether or not *in terrorem pupuli.* Yet, consistant with his constitutional powers as Commander-in-Chief,[31] the federal executive retains the power of disposition with respect to both number and use of the out-of-state military response. Moreover, once federal troops are committed, the probability of their being sent in sufficient numbers is very great because the safety of the troops as well as the general population are a matter of presidential concern; indeed, one may well contend that the safety of federal troops are his more immediate concern, since they are under direct federal military control.

The most important issue, as well as the greatest barrior to realization of the above proposals, is the constitutional problem presented by a congressional command to the President regarding any disposition of federal troops in the light of his constitutional powers as Commander-in-Chief of the armed forces. Traditionally, the United States Supreme Court has been most sensitive to any encroachment by one of the three federal organs upon the constitutionally vested powers of the others. Since this "balance of power" structure was clearly intended by the Federalists with their adoption of the proposals of the French jurist and philosopher Montesquieu,[32] the Court has persistently upheld the integrity of this division of authority. Moreover, this has consistently been done notwithstanding any particular "political" attitudes that may have obtained with respect to the majority of the tribunal.[33]

It has thus been held that Congress, under its powers to "raise and support Armies, provide and maintain a Navy" or even "To declare War,"[34] may *not* impair the distinct presidential powers of Commander-in-Chief.[35] Although Congress may authorize the President to fulfill certain legislative functions,[36] as it has done in sections 331-33,

---

31. U.S. CONST. art. II § 3. *See infra* for discussion of constitutional ramifications.

32. The Federalist Papers No. 47; *see, also* No. 48:

It is agreed on all sides, that the powers properly belonging to one of the departments ought not to be directly and completely administered by either of the departments. It is equally evident, that none of them ought to possess, directly or indirectly, an overruling influence over the others in the administration of their respective powers. It will not be denied, that power is of an encroaching nature, and that it ought to be effectually restrained from passing the limits assigned to it. After discriminating, therefore, in theory, the several classes of power, as they may in their nature be legislative, executive, or judiciary, the next and most difficult task is to provide some practical security for each, against the invasion of the others. What this security ought to be, is the great problem to be solved.

33. *Compare* Bailey v. Drexel Furniture Co., 259 U.S. 20 (1922) with Baker v. Carr 369 U.S. 186 (1962).

34. U.S. CONST. art I § 8.

35. Swain v. United States, 28 Ct. Claims 173, 165 U.S. 553 (1897). *See also* Street v. U.S. 24 Ct. Claims 247 (1889).

36. Edwards v. U.S. 286 U.S. 482 (1932). When Congress does so authorize the President to act in this capacity, his powers in this capacity are limited to those delegated to him in the legislation: Blair v. U.S., 19 Ct. Claims 541 (1884).

its regulatory powers over the military may not compromise the efficiency of the President to act as the Commander-in-Chief.[37]

Authority of a more general nature does, however, suggest that a congressional command to the President regarding the disposition of federal military forces to quell domestic violence does not violate this division of power. In 1849, the United States Supreme Court held in the leading case of *Luther v. Borden*[38] that Congress possessed the power to ascertain the proper method to be utilized in guaranteeing member states of the union their constitutional right of protection against domestic violence. Thus Congress had the power to *authorize* the President to call out the militia should an insurrection challenge the established government of any member state. Indeed, the act construed in *Luther v. Borden*[39] *was the precursor* to section 331 discussed herein.

It may be contended that further support for the extensive congressional power to promulgate the above proposals can be found in the 1943 Court of Appeals decision in *Dunne v. United States.*[40] There the Eighth Circuit held *inter alia,* that various constitutional provisions, including the "necessary and proper clause," established a constitutional "expression" that Congress has the power to utilize the armed forces of the United States to preserve the "life of the Nation and of the States and the liberties and welfare of their citizens."[41]

Attempts to predict subsequent decisions by the United States Supreme Court, especially on issues of constitutional interpretation, are questionable undertakings under any circumstances. Where the existing authority is not only so meager but also so divided as to provide authority for a decision either way, prudence dictates one should hesitate to declare any firm conviction of eventual Court action.

This is not to say that there is any basis for a forlorn attitude with respect to the above proposal. Rather, one can seek comfort in the constitutional history surrounding the vesting in the President the powers of Commander-in-Chief of the military forces. Back in March of 1788, Alexander Hamilton indicated that this power was designed specifically for *wartime* situations:

> The propriety of this provision is so evident in itself, and it is, at the same time, so consonant to the precedents of the State constitutions in general, that little need be said to explain or enforce it. Even those of them which have, in other respects coupled the chief magistrate with a council, have for

37. Blair v. U.S. 19 Ct. Claims 541 (1884).
38. 12 (7 How.) 1 (1849).
39. 1 Stat. 424 (1795).
40. 138 F.2d 137 (8th Cir. 1943).
41. *Id.* at 140 [emphasis added].

> the most part concentrated the military authority in him alone. Of all the cares or concerns of government, the direction of war most peculiarly demands those qualities which distinguish the exercise of power by a single hand. The direction of war implies the direction of the common strength; and the power of directing and employing the common strength, forms a usual and essential part in the definition of the executive authority.[42]

While it is true that some past Presidents have interpreted this power very broadly,[43] at least one attempt to do so was effectively stymied by the United States Supreme Court.[44] One can thus hope that the utilitarian nature[45] of our fundamental law, the Constitution, will once again rise to the occasion of public necessity, and that the Supreme Court will hold that it is not an invasion of presidential power as Commander-in-Chief when the Congress acts under its legislative jurisdiction to do whatever is "necessary and proper" to "insure domestic tranquility." Moreover, Congress' specific power "to make rules for the government and regulation of the land and naval forces" could also be a source of support for its direction to the President that the *peacetime* use of the national military force to help quell domestic disturbances shall be placed into operation upon a duly authorized call for help by one of the member states of the American Union: the concept of Union demands no less.

Should this prove not to be the case, should the Court declare that dispositon of the military as outlined above is not permitted by the Constitution, the need for amendment is clearly apparent. Given this eventuality, one can take heart from the fact that recent experience has proven the possibility of rapid amendment.[46] The emergency situations presently obtaining in urban America should guarantee its prompt ratification. Indeed, we have even recently witnessed amendment for a less necessary purpose.[47] Should it prove necessary, it will in all probability be rapidly forthcoming, so that the law of the land will meet the challenge of the time.

---

42. Federalist No. 74.

43. *See, e.g.* ROSSITER, THE AMERICAN PRESIDENCY 24-25 (2d Ed. 1960).

44. Youngstown Sheet & Tube Co. v. Sawyer 343 U.S. 710 (1952). *See* argument of Mr. Holmes Baldridge, Assistant Attorney General of the United States before Judge Alexander Hortzoff in the United States District Court for the District of Columbia on April 9, 1952, exerpts can be found at West in THE ANATOMY OF THE CONSTITUTIONAL LAW CASE 38 (1958). The government subsequently withdrew the claim.

45. Martin v. Hunter's Lessee, 3 U.S. (1 Wheat) 562 564-65 (1816) Heart of Atlanta Motel v. United States, 379 U.S. 241 (1964) at 251.

46. Amendment XXV (1967) following the assassination of President Kennedy on November 22, 1963.

47. *Cf.*: Amendment XXIV (1964) with Harper v. Virginia Bd. of Elections, 383 U.S. 663 (1966). Thus, this amendment has been characterized as dropping an atom bomb on a mouse.

The National Guard and Riot Control:
The Need for Revision

COL. L. J. CRUM * †

INTRODUCTION

FROM a purely academic point of view, the events of recent summers (we will be concerned here basically with the Detroit riots) will provide material for treatises for years to come. Many questions have already been raised and more will be. Which of the problems in our society were the underlying causes of the discontent? Alternately some have asked, were the riots just sheer lawlessness? What event or events brought the unrest to the surface? What can be done to prevent further outbreaks? Why have the riots taken place in certain localities but not in others? Are future outbreaks predictable? Are the riots a local or a national phenomena? Are they organized or spontaneous?

The answers to all of the above questions may never be satisfactorily supplied; too many are purely speculative. However, control of a riot situation presents an area where speculation cannot suffice. The Detroit riot left in its wake further conflicts because of the manner in which it was handled. The purpose here is not to analyze causes, etc., but to examine what has already happened, with particular reference to necessities in the future should similar situations arise. With this goal, the following questions form the guidelines:

I. What are the interests of the state and federal governments in preventing and/or controlling riot situations?

II. What procedures are presently required to bring state or federal action in riot situations?

III. What rights and liabilities does the National Guardsman have if under state control? Under federal control?

IV. Is the reciprocal agreement (currently proposed by the Governors' Conference) an enforceable or workable solution?

V. What statutory or procedural reforms are needed to eliminate problems within the National Guard during civil disturbances?

These topic headings are used primarily for convenience.

* Kalamazoo College, B.A., 1931; Detroit College of Law, LL.B., 1936. National Guard 1926; Infantry Officer 1932-1946, Staff Judge Advocate, 46th Division, National Guard, 1948-1958; State of Michigan, Judge Advocate General with rank of colonel, 1958 to present.

† Assisted by James T. Brignall, Harvard, B.A.; University of Michigan, J.D.

Federal and State Interest in Riot Control

Protection against civil disorder is an area, where federal interest had been minimized until last summer. The state interest is the more obvious of the two; it is on this level that the primary responsibility for law enforcement is carried out. It is beyond our scope to investigate the differences between state enforcement policies, and therefore the Michigan provisions will be used for illustration.

Law enforcement is an executive function; that is, the constitution provides that the Governor is responsible for execution of the laws. In *State v. McPhail,*[1] the court pointed out that constitutional language requiring the Governor to see that laws are executed has no obscure or technical meaning; neither was it intended for a mere verbal adornment of the office. The constitutions of the various states provided the means along with the duty. The means is the organized state militia. Article 5, Section 12 of the Constitution of the State of Michigan provides: "The Governor shall be commander-in-chief of the armed forces and may call them out to execute the laws, suppress insurrection and repel invasion." The militia, by constitution, is also to be provided for by law (various provisions of state statutes will be cited throughout). Apparently the framers of the constitution felt that at some point the normal local authorities would be unable to enforce the law. The extraordinary military powers which the governor has at his disposal are, therefore, provided for one purpose only; that is, the enforcement of law where ordinary procedures have broken down.

The legislature, following the constitutional mandate, has outlined the executive powers. In Michigan, these are found in Act 302 of the Public Acts of 1945.[2] The Governor may, during the time of great emergency or public crisis, disaster and rioting, or when he may have reasonable apprehension of the immediate danger therefrom, either upon his application or that of the mayor, sheriff, or commissioner of the State Police, proclaim a "state of emergency." Moreover, the United States Supreme Court has decided that "the declaration by the Governor of a State that a state of insurrection existed is conclusive of that fact."[3]

The Michigan statute further provides that with such a proclamation or declaration, the Governor will promulgate reasonable orders, rules and regulations to protect life and property and to bring the emergency situation within the affected area under control. These rules and regulations may provide for control of traffic, public and private

1. 182 Miss. 360, 180 So. 387 (1938).
2. Mich. Stat. Ann. § 3.4(1) (1961).
3. Moyer v. Peabody, 212 U.S. 78, 83 (1909).

transportation within the area or any section thereof, and designate specific zones within the area in which occupancy and use of buildings and ingress or egress of persons and vehicles may be prohibited or regulated. They may control places of amusement and assembly; control persons on public streets and thoroughfares; establish a curfew; control sale and transportation of alcoholic beverages and liquors; control possession, sale, carrying and use of fire arms or other dangerous weapons and ammunition; and control the use, storage and transportation of explosives or inflammable material or liquids deemed to be dangerous to public safety. Such orders and regulations are effective from the date and in the manner described in such orders and regulations, and they must be made public. They may also be modified and amended until the Governor proclaims that the emergency no longer exists. Implementation of many of the above rules and regulations may be seen in the Detroit rioting. For example, a curfew was established; the sale of gasoline was regulated because of its inflammable nature; traffic, including air traffic, was restricted from the affected area. And the regulations were constantly modified according to the developing situation. For example, a curfew was originally instituted on Sunday, July 23, covering the hours between 9:00 p.m. and 5:00 a.m.; on Saturday, July 29, the curfew was extended to 11:00 p.m.; on Monday, July 31, the curfew was revised to 12 midnight to 5:30 a.m.; and on Tuesday, August 1, the curfew restrictions were lifted.

The modifications of the curfew restrictions are illustrative of a point made above. It was stated earlier that the emergency powers of the Governor are provided for the enforcement of law. Important in this respect is reestablishment of the ordinary patterns of enforcement. By statute, the flexibility was provided to achieve this end. The early, severe restrictions could be gradually lifted as the stability of the situation was tested. The same gradual lifting could also be illustrated in both the sale of gasoline and the sale of alcoholic beverages.

In order to enforce the above emergency regulations, the Governor may use the services of both the organized and unorganized militia. Act No. 150 of the Public Acts of 1967 gives the Governor authority to order out "such troop of the organized militia as he believes necessary to meet the emergency."[4] He may also order into the defense any members of the "unorganized militia."[5]

---

4. MICH. STAT. ANN. § 4.678(151) (1968 Supp.).

5. MICH. STAT. ANN. § 4.678(155) (1968 Supp.). The unorganized militia consists of all other able-bodied citizens of this state and all other able-bodied citizens who are residents of this state who have or shall have declared their intention to become citizens of the United States, who shall be age 17 or over and not more than age 60, and shall be subject to state military duty as provided in this act. MICH. STAT. ANN. § 4.678(109) (1968 Supp.).

Thus far, no need has arisen for calling of unorganized militia. However, the calling of the organized militia, i.e., the National Guard, has been the executive's chief weapon in controlling emergency situations.

As the Detroit riots will attest, however, the states are not always able to control civil disorders with their own resources. At this point, the federal interest comes to our attention. Beginning with the "Buckshot War" in 1838 and up through the Detroit riots of 1967, the states have requested federal assistance in suppressing domestic violence 16 times. Federal help was given in 12 of the requests.[6]

The federal intervention has constitutional and statutory basis. Article IV, Section 4 of the United States Constitution provides:

> The United States shall guarantee to every State in this Union a Republican Form of Government and shall protect each of them against invasion; and on Application of the Legislature, or of the Executive (when the Legislature cannot be convened) against domestic Violence.[7]

It should be noted that all appeals for aid against "domestic violence" have come from the Executive.

The statutory provisions are found in Title 10, United States Code, Chapter 15:

> § 331. Federal aid for State governments
>
> Whenever there is an insurrection in any State against its government, the President may, upon the request of its legislature or of its Governor if the legislature cannot be convened, call into Federal service such of the militia of the other states, in the number requested by that state, and the use of such of the armed forces, as he considers necessary to suppress the insurrection.
>
> * * * * * *
>
> § 334. Proclamation to disperse
>
> Whenever the President considers it necessary to use the militia or the armed forces under this chapter, he shall, by proclamation, immediately order the insurgents to disperse and retire peaceably to their abodes within a limited time.

The federal government has therefore the ultimate responsibility for halting civil disorder. However, the first request for federal assistance in the Buckshot War of 1838 set the requirement that State authorities be proven inadequate to quell the rioting.

---

6. *See*, Report of Special Subcommittee to Inquire into the Capability of the National Guard to Cope with Civil Disturbances, 90th Cong., 1st Sess., 5645 (1967) [hereinafter cited as *Report*].

7. U.S. CONST. art. IV § 4.

Moreover, the federal government influences all situations requiring state militia because of the dual nature of the National Guard. Manpower allotment, for example, is subject to two federal controls. First, the National Guard is a part of the reserve forces system of the United States Army, and, as such, is subject to the overall, federal defense scheme. Because of this federal interest, troop strengths are determined at that level.[8] Second, the Congress has the "power of the purse." 90% of the funds used by the National Guard are provided by the federal government.[9] This power has been one of the most influential in determining governmental action in many areas; the National Guard is no exception.

Other federal control must be mentioned in passing because of implications important later. One important control is over the use of weapons. Standards that are applicable to the regular army are applicable to the National Guard as well. Where the United States is involved abroad, as at present, the materials available to the Guard are limited because of defense priorities. The federal government is also concerned with the type and amount of training received by the Guardsmen. Since the Detroit riots, the Acting Chief of Staff of the U.S. Army issued a directive to the Chief of the National Guard Bureau requiring immediate implementation of a more intensive training program to train National Guard personnel in civil disturbance and riot control techniques.[10]

The dual interest in controlling riot situations is thus twofold. Both the state and federal governments have a duty to the citizens for protection. The state's duty is primary; the federal government's is ultimate. And the state and federal governments exert concurrent control over the National Guard (in which the primary responsibility for riot control rests). In this area, the state interest has been readily apparent; the federal government's role, however, controls the situation due to the national defense interest.

Procedural Requirements

Undue hesitation resulted during the Detroit riots due to uncertainty over the necessary procedures in activating both state and federal forces. Too much time was wasted in debating semantics. We can never be sure how many lives or how much property damage could have been saved if the officials involved had not delayed so long over choice of terminology. It was the action, not the phraseology, that was important.

8. *See*, Levantrosser, Congress and the Citizen-Soldier, 1967.
9. *Id.* at 4.
10. *Report*, *supra* note 6, at 5655.

The first step is the declaration by the Governor (or the mayor, sheriff, or commissioner of the State Police) of a "state of emergency." As was noted above, this declaration is conclusive as to that fact. At this point, the governor may promulgate the reasonable orders, rules and regulations for controlling the situation. Up to this point (largely covered above), there has been a factual determination and administrative orders have been put in force.

The next step is equally important; setting in motion the forces necessary to enforce the governor's orders and restore peace to the area. The governor must exercise his power to activate the organized militia. The necessity for this was pointed out in an exchange between Congressman F. Edward Hebert of Louisiana and General Clarence Schnipke, the Adjutant General of the State of Michigan. General Schnipke advised Mr. Hebert that some 380 Guardsmen were in Detroit at 8:00 a.m. Sunday. When asked if they were "available" to the Mayor, Schnipke replied: "Well, they were in a drill status, Mr. Chairman. Now before they are available they must be requested and put into a mobilization status. We have to get them out of that status into a State status."[11] General Schnipke further testified that these troops were not requested until 4:15 p.m. Sunday. This delay could have been critical. Schnipke summarized by saying: "Our opinion is the Guard got into Detroit too late. The thing was at its maximum by the time we arrived there."[12]

These proclamations and requests by the governor are not subject to mystic phrases to make them enforceable. "Such an order does not have to contain any particular recitals. It is enough that it was an order and that the facts de hors justified its issuance and its execution."[13]

If state action is inadequate, federal assistance may be requested. Attorney General Ramsey Clark advised all of the governors by letter on August 7, 1967, of the prerequisite for the use of federal troops:

> (1) That a situation of serious "domestic Violence" exists within the state. While this conclusion should be supported with a statement of factual details to the extent feasible under the circumstances, there is no prescribed wording.
>
> (2) That such violence cannot be brought under control by the law enforcement resources available to the governor, including Local and State police forces and the National Guard. The judgment required here is there is a definite need for the assistance of Federal troops, taking into account the remaining time needed to move them into action at the scene of violence.

---

11. *Id.* at 5664.
12. *Id.* at 5665.
13. State v. McPhail, *supra* note 1.

(3) That the legislature or the governor requests the President to employ the Armed Forces to bring the violence under control. The element of request by the governor of the state is essential if the legislature cannot be convened. It may be difficult in the context of urban rioting, such as we have seen this summer, to convene the legislature.[14]

Attorney General Clark asserted that the request must be in writing (a telegram would suffice). Upon receipt of the request, the President still has discretion as to the use of troops and to the timing and the size of the force to be sent.[15]

The Attorney General's choice of terms brings up one very important concept if last summer's events are repeated. That is, in determining whether or not state resources are inadequate to control the situation, due consideration must be given to the additional time required to move the federal troops into action. This is the same problem cited by General Schnipke in activating National Guard troops. Neither the procedure for activating the Guard nor the procedure for requesting federal assistance are particularly time consuming. However, the decision-making process often is. This was apparently true in Detroit. If unnecessary aggravation of already serious disturbances is to be prevented in the future, the proper officials must be alert to the requirements so that these details can be quickly met. The problem of timing in the decision-making process will be the only remaining factor in taking action.

Rights and Liabilities of Guardsmen

A recent issue of *Life* magazine carried an article that was written on the apparent premise that "It's fun to be a Guardsman." The author must never have been a Guardsman in a riot situation, nor suffered the consequences after one. It is beyond the scope of this article to discuss individual cases arising from the riots (some are still pending), but it must be noted that many Guardsmen have been subject to civil and/or criminal actions as a result (one civil action demands $300,000.00 in damages). It should be noted that this refers to actions against individuals, not the National Guard or any branch of the government.

In discussing the rights and liabilities of individual Guardsmen, I will separate the criminal from the civil aspects. The criminal discussion, of course, centers around defenses to various charges. Whether the Guardsman is charged with assault and battery or with murder (assuming the event in question has occurred), the Guardsman must find his defense in his status. What that status is, and what it means in

14. *Report, supra* note 6, at 5669.
15. *Id.* at 5670.

terms of justifying his actions, are subject to conflicting state decisions and statutes.

One fundamental point is useful as a beginning; that is, that the military is subordinate to the civil authority.[16] The Michigan case of *Bishop v. Vandercook*[17] contains an extensive discussion on this point. The Court declared that while civil law was in operation, it was supreme. The constitutional language in this area must be given a meaning. None of the cases seem to disagree on this basic point. However, from here on, there is a split.

The status of the activated Guardsman illustrates the problem. In Michigan, he is an "aid."

> When proper civil authority invokes military aid, it is extended as an aid, and must act within, and in accordance with, the civil law, and while soldiers are subject to military law, that fact does not take away from the citizens the rights and remedies for injuries arising through wrongful exercise of military law or power.[18]

The status under such a decision is most unsatisfactory. Without arguing with the fact that civil remedies remain available, giving an activated Guardsman the status of a mere "aid" can leave him virtually ineffective. He does not have the ordinary powers of police officers, and, with the more limited claim of authority, would be subject to more actions for abuse. It should also be noted that the result is contrary to the majority in states with similar statutes. The case is notable, however, in the fact that it reflects a desire to limit the rights of the activated Guardsman and in the fact that it has not been overruled in Michigan.

Other jurisdictions have reached other results. One illustrative case would give the Guardsman the same rights as a peace officer. In this case the Court decided that:

> The militia was established for the use of the civil power, when necessary, and the Governor is a civil officer and the militia, under his control, are civil agencies in the execution of laws.[19]

The Court carried this further by saying that the Guardsman thus gets "executive authority" in the enforcement of law. In this way, the Guardsman is not made a peace officer himself, but when on duty and resisting lawlessness, he has the rights of a peace officer. This is of considerable importance in making the arrest of an offender.

---

16. MICH. CONST. art 1 § 8 (1963).
17. Bishop v. Vandercook, 228 Mich. 299, 200 N.W. 278 (1924).
18. *Id.* at 306.
19. *See*, State v. McPhail, *supra* note 1, at 390.

A peace officer may arrest without a warrant for (1) a felony committed in his presence or (2) a person whom he has probable cause to believe has committed a felony (even if there was in fact no offense against the peace in his presence).[20]

A third set of decisions are at extremes with the Michigan view. These interpretations would allow the Guardsman greater rights than a peace officer. A lead case is *Herlihy v. Donohue*.[21] In this case, one defendant, Donahue, was a major in the Guard. Acting on the assumption that the plaintiff was violating restrictions set upon the sale of alcohol, he ordered two other Guardsmen to remove and destroy the liquor. These other Guardsmen were also joined as defendants. The Supreme Court of Montana ruled that the plaintiff should have received notice and an opportunity to show that he was not violating the restrictions. However, the Guardsmen on the scene were exonerated; only the Major was liable. Such a ruling gives the individual Guardsman greater rights than a peace officer.

Herlihy also leads to the next area of concern in assessing the rights and liabilities of the Guardsmen. That is, how far does a defense based on obedience to an order of a superior extend in protecting those Guardsmen on the scene.

> A subordinate officer of the state militia may defend his acts against civil liability by reference to the order of his superior officer, unless it is so palpably illegal or without authority that a reasonably prudent man ought to recognize its invalidity or want of authority, in which event obedience furnishes no excuse for a wrongful act even though disobedience may subject the offender to punishment at the hands of a military tribunal.[22]

Here is the famous "reasonably prudent man" of tort law once again. In his new face, our "man" is not expected to know all of the details of a given situation. So in *Herlihy*, where the Guardsmen knew that restrictions were imposed on the sale of alcohol and that it was their duty to enforce these restrictions, they were justified in obeying an order of a superior that was valid on its face, although it was subsequently shown to be in excess of authority.

The reasoning behind such a holding is sound both from the standpoint of the military and from that of the civilians. Such a view is necessary for the military in order to keep discipline within the ranks. Challenges by individual Guardsmen to each superior order would prevent

20. 5 Am. Jur. (2d) "Arrest," pp. 715-717.
21. Herlihy v. Donohue, 52 Mont. 601, 161 Pac. 164 (1916).
22. *Id.* at 167.

any cohesive action in enforcing and restoring law. Even hesitation in order to investigate the order would result in a breakdown of efficiency in military strategy. The civilians would also benefit from the above holding because of the nature of their interest; i.e., restoration of order. If Guardsmen could not rely on the apparent lawful orders of their superiors, discipline would break down, and the Guard without discipline would be nothing more than a mob.

Nor would the above mean that civilians would be subject to capricious or malicious whims of the National Guard. All statutes and decisions recognize the fact that each individual disorder necessitates its own orders toward solution.

> But necessity can never require obedience to an order manifestly illegal or beyond the authority of the superior to give, and therefore reason and common sense seems to justify the rule that the inferior military officer may defend his acts against civil liability by reference to the order of his superior, unless such order bears upon its face the marks of its own invalidity or want of authority.[23]

Even though the above privileges certain actions, the civilian is not stripped of his rights, for at least the officers of the military forces "are liable to be tried for any excess . . . of power, not by the martial code, but under common and statute law."[24] So in *Herlihy*, although the Guardsmen at the scene were held not liable, the Major who had given the order was held.

All of the above is based on the premise that civil authority continues functioning concurrently with the military (such was the condition in Detroit). A somewhat different situation would arise if martial law were declared. Such a declaration is not unknown in this country.

One of the more direct discussions of martial law is contained in *State ex rel., O'Connor v. District Court.*[25] In this situation martial law had been declared by the Governor, and orders were issued by him for correcting the situation. Pursuant to these orders, investigative tribunals were established and arrests made without warrants. After the emergency situation was ended, several of the military officials were sued by individuals who had been arrested and questioned under martial proceedings. The decision was rendered upon an application for a writ of prohibition against the District Court's continued hearing of the case. The defendants admitted at the outset that if the arrests were made maliciously, they would be civilly liable.

---

23. *Id.*
24. O'Connor v. District Court, 219 Iowa 1165, 260 N.W. 73 (1935).
25. *Id.* at 83.

The Court began by pointing out that the Governor had certain immunities in the exercise of his office, and that martial law had been legitimately declared by him. The members of the militia, in acting within the Governor's orders, acquired his immunities. They also held that during a period of martial law the supervisory authority has greater latitude in operation than civil authorities in peace time.

The Michigan Court has delved into the same area but with a less direct relationship. In *Bishop v. Vandercook*[26] the defense argued against liability on principles applicable to martial law. The Court however, noted that civil authority had never ceased activity. From this fact, they held that there is no such thing as "qualified martial law;" that is, martial rule cannot coexist with civil authority. Constitutionally the military is subordinate to civil authority, and this means that while civil law is acting, it is supreme. In order to supersede the civil, martial law must be declared.

> The effect of martial law, therefore, is to put into operation the power and methods vested in the commanding officer by military law. So far as his power for the preservation of order and security of life and property are concerned, there is no limit but the necessities and exigencies of the situation. And in this respect, there is no difference between a public war and domestic insurrection.[27]

There is no apparent contradiction between *O'Connor* and *Bishop* in their holdings. Both recognize the greater latitude of action under martial law.

But the Michigan decision is interesting because of a recent statutory attempt in favor of the militia. Act No. 150 of the Public Acts of 1967 of the State of Michigan provides in part:

> Sec. 105(j) "Martial law" or "martial rule" means the exercise of partial or complete military control over domestic territory in time of emergency because of public necessity.[28]

Such a statute would seem to bring the greater latitude contemplated in *O'Connor* into force even in situations like the Detroit riots, since there was at least partial control over domestic territory. However, the *Bishop* decision has not been overruled in Michigan, and in so far as it makes the constitutional determination that while civil authority is functioning, it is supreme, the above cited definition is invalid at least in part. As long as *Bishop* stands, there cannot be the "qualified martial law" that would result with only partial military control. It is the opin-

26. *Supra* note 17.
27. *Supra* note 16, at 313.
28. MICH. STAT. ANN. § 4.678(105)(j) (1968 Supp.).

ion of this writer, therefore, that the recent statute does not alter the case law. This would require a constitutional amendment which is not foreseen.

A different sort of statutory attempt has been more successful; i.e., immunity statutes. Michigan provides as follows:

> No member of the state military establishment is subject to prosecution by civil courts for any military act done in obedience to the lawful orders of the governor.[29]

This is basically a codification of *State ex rel. O'Connor v. District Court.*[30] Thorough understanding of this case would be the greatest aid in determining how cases under the new statute should be decided.

New York, and other states, have been more direct. "Members of the militia ordered into the active service of the state . . . shall not be liable civilly or criminally for any act or acts done by them in the performance of their duty."[31] Crucial under the above statute are the words "in performance of their duty." Once this is established, however, the personal immunity applies. In *Dorr v. Gibson*[32] the Court held the driver in a military convoy not liable in a negligence action on the basis of the statute. Under a similar statute in the State of Louisiana,[33] the question again was active duty. The Court defined two types of active service: first, when on call by the governor (as in an emergency); second, by being a member of the organized militia. If the individual were seeking immunity under the first type, it would be granted; under the second, it would not.

A Minnesota decision qualifies the others in respect to immunity.[34] This is a qualification that we have seen before—excess of authority. Immunity does not extend to such excess. Agreeably, this can be justified on one of two theories. First, immunity is granted because it is the performance of a *duty,* whereas if authority is exceeded, it is beyond the scope of that duty. Second, to grant immunity to cases beyond the limits of authority would be to violate the spirit of the law. Merely having the status in the military cannot be enough to justify malicious or capricious action, and the legislature could not have intended to include such acts in its grant of immunity.

Before proceeding to final considerations on the rights and liabilities of Guardsmen, a brief summary of the above points is in order. First, when the Guardsman is called into active service, his status should

---

29. MICH. STAT. ANN. § 4.678(179) (1968 Supp.).
30. *Supra* note 23.
31. New York Statutes, "Military Law," Sec. 235.
32. Dorr v. Gibson, 145 N.Y.S.2d 48, 208 Misc. 262 (1955).
33. LA. REV. STAT. § 29.31 (1950).
34. Nixon v. Reeves, 65 Minn. 159, 67 N.W. 989 (1896).

be determined vis-à-vis the preexisting civil order. There seems to be a split on this point, but the most satisfactory solution appears to be that expressed in *State v. McPhail*;[35] that is, he should have the rights of a peace officer. If states continue to disagree, however, the individual Guardsman should be advised of his status within his state's framework. And whatever the status received above, it is necessarily broadened under a *declaration* of martial law. Once the status is determined, the boundaries of authority take shape. If the Guardsman is then charged civilly or criminally, he may show any of the following (depending on applicable statutes) : he was within the authority of his position; he had relied on the legitimate order of a superior; or he was immune from prosecution.

We might suppose, however, that a given act was in excess of authority and was not defensible as under a legitimate superior order or immune. What then becomes of our defendant and injured plaintiff? Currently, and especially if the action was not under federal control, recovery depends on the individual assets of the Guardsman. This is generally unsatisfactory to both parties. Moreover, the New York Court has enforced the state's immunity along with the Guardsman's, leaving the plaintiff remediless.[36]

If the Guard has been federalized, claims could be brought under the Federal Tort Claims Act.[37] This act is the exclusive remedy if the proper qualifications are met.

> "Employee of the government" includes officers or employees of any federal agency, members of the military and naval forces of the United States, . . . temporarily or permanently in the service of the United States, whether with or without compensation.[38]

As with the problem of immunity, the "employee" must be in the active service of the United States.[39] And further, to be within the scope of his employment, he must be acting in "the line of duty." As with so many federal statutes, the F.T.C.A. relies on state law for definition, since "line of duty" merely invokes the state law of respondeat superior.[40] It has been argued that the doctrine is expanded in governmental cases, but the prevailing view is that "line of duty" is no greater than in nongovernmental respondeat superior cases.[41]

---

35. *Supra* note 1.
36. Dorr, *supra* note 32.
37. 28 U.S.C. 2671 et seq. (1964) (hereinafter cited as F.T.C.A.).
38. F.T.C.A., Sec. 2671.
39. United States v. Prager, 251 F.2d 266 (5th Cir. 1958), *cert. denied*, 356 U.S. 939 (1958).
40. McCall v. United States, 338 F.2d 589 (9th Cir. 1964), *cert. denied*, 380 U.S. 974 (1964).
41. Keener v. Jack Cole Trucking Co., 233 F. Supp. 181 (E.D. Ky. 1964).

The above code provisions and interpretive decisions are much in line with the developing state law discussed in reference to Guard responsibility. That is, he must be activated (achieve his status); he must be acting under *apparently* legitimate orders (the "reasonably prudent man" test?); and he is not covered if he exceeds his authority.

The F.T.C.A. could provide many of the answers to the problem of personal liability. However, certain deficiencies must be overcome. First, Sec. 2680(h) of the F.T.C.A. exempts certain types of claims from coverage. Among the exemptions are several which may reasonably be foreseen after a riot situation, e.g., false arrest and false imprisonment. If, during an emergency situation, executive orders were issued relevant to detaining rioters, and, pursuant thereto various persons were arrested, Guardsmen should be protected. In no case would they be covered if the actions were malicious. Nor would recovery be allowed if the arrests were proper under the circumstances. But if the individual Guardsmen were carrying out executive orders valid on their face, but contrary to law in the particular situation, the plaintiff would have a source of recovery other than the individual. Moreover, in ill-founded cases, the government would be the defendant, and thus the defense costs would be borne at this level. There is a more serious deficiency, however. The F.T.C.A. provides a fine basis for solution, but only if the Guard is in active federal service. The individual states or the National Guard Bureau need similar coverage when the Guardsman is called into active state service. At present the possibilities for recovery are represented by two extremes. In New York, the immunity precludes all recovery.[42] In Michigan, Guardsmen are realizing the threat of personal, financial disaster. In both cases, a civil wrong is left without chance of recovery. Moreover, the individual Guardsman may be required to engage his own counsel. This is especially true of the civil matters.

A favorite law school cliche is "the problem is just a matter of insurance." This is at least partially true here. The state has the responsibility in restoring order in an emergency. It must also carry a further responsibility if innocent parties are injured pursuant to its executive orders. And the Guardsman deserves the protection as well, not as a license for wrongdoing (for that would not be covered), but for carrying out his duties within the military.[43]

---

42. *Supra* note 30.

43. For a more complete discussion aimed at tort liability, *see*, Shaw, William Lawrence, "Tort Liability and National Guard Personnel," *The Judge Advocate Journal*, Bulletin No. 39, pp. 7-25 (1967).

Reciprocal Agreements

During its October, 1967 meeting, the National Governors' Conference proposed a National Guard Mutual Assistance Compact.[44] The concerned response of the governors to the summer of 1967 is encouraging; however, the solution in this writer's opinion, is unsound.

In one respect the solution is unsound because it does not help eliminate the basic problem; i.e., speed of response. One factor in achieving optimum speed of response is distance. The Department of the Army prepared a table based on a 100 miles distance from certain metropolitan areas. In the case of Detroit, for example, there are 7,140 men available within 100 miles, or 71.9 per cent of total state strength. The Department points out that the others are of course available, but there would be a longer period of response.[45] Mobilization of the forces of other states would require not only the additional distance, but the additional time required to request and have approved the assistance desired. For a state to call up Guardsmen and commit them to duty in a sister state cannot be accomplished as quickly or efficiently as a request from the federal government. The Active Army has seven task forces, each of brigade size, available for civil disturbance duties. These task forces represent a total strength of over 15,000 men.[46] And they are already active and so immediately available.

The solution is also unsound because it is unnecessary. The President may already call into federal service the militia of other states when proper request for assistance has been made by a governor or the legislature. The relevant section (Title 10, United States Code, Chapter 15, Sec. 331) is set out in full above. The forces of a sister state have not been unavailable therefore, in such numbers as may be required. To date, however, the necessity of added National Guard troops has not been present. For example, in the Detroit riots of 1967, 85.0 per cent of the total state strength was used, and the Army advises that 20 to 25 per cent of the forces sent were held in reserve and never actually committed to control the disturbance.[47] Moreover, there are the 15,000 federal troops specifically designated for civil disturbances, and additional Army and Marine forces should they be needed.

Finally, the solution is unsound because of its questionable enforceability. Under the U.S. Code cited above, the President may com-

---

44. Copies available through the Council of State Governments, 1313 East 60th St., Chicago, Illinois 60637.

45. *Report, supra* note 6, at 5651.

46. *Report, supra* note 6, at 5649.

47. *Id.* at 5649.

mit Guard troops to other states in an emergency. His power is constitutional, derived from Article IV, Section 4. What conceivable power, however, does a governor have to send citizens of his state to enforce the laws of a neighbor. Understandably, each state is concerned with events in the others, but the duty with regard to keeping the peace is with the state itself or with the federal government. There could be several proper parties to challenge the orders. For example, a citizen of Detroit injured by an Ohio Guardsman could challenge his status. The mutual compact purports to give him the same rights as the Guardsman of the state to which he was sent. However, assuming the requesting state gave the rights of a peace officer, the out-of-state Guardsman would have more difficulty in proving the legality of his status. Arguably at least, one state does not have the right to interfere with the internal affairs of another. Another proper party to challenge the compact would be the Guardsman himself. If he were ordered to a sister state by the governor, he would be bound under military law to obey and failure to do so would subject him to prosecution by the military. However, as discussed above, the Guardsman may only defend actions under orders which are valid on their face. Can such a compact give one state the right to enforce the laws of another, even when requested, although no constitutional duty or sanction is given? What would the reader answer as "a reasonably prudent man?"

In conclusion, let's consider under what circumstances aid from other states would be sought. The Detroit riots would make a useful illustration. We have seen that troops were available for use at 8:00 a.m. Sunday; they were not called, however, until 4:15 p.m. the same day. We must assume that up to this point, assistance would not have been sought elsewhere. The first Guardsmen appeared on the streets at 6:57 p.m. At this point, we must also assume (from the actions of officials) that the situation was not considered out of hand. At 8:30 a.m. Monday, the first telegrams were sent by the Governor to the President "recommending" immediate deployment of 5,000 federal troops to the area. Now we can assume that mutual assistance would also have been requested. At 6:36 p.m., federal troops were available at Selfridge Air Base. At 12 midnight, the troops were put under federal control. At 8:30 Monday morning, when the President was first requested, the need for help was urgent. It had been only 16 hours since the first Guard troops were committed, but the situation was rapidly worsening. The state was also fortunate in mobilizing since many of the Guardsmen were in Camp Grayling for summer training. The prospect of receiving aid from other states at 8:30 a.m. could not have been as immediate as from the federal government. The utility of aid from other states would be in a prolonged situation *after* the primary emergency had been met and contained. Before this point, if state resources were inadequate, the federal government would be contacted for help. If such were the situation, the federal government should retain control over the determination of forces needed from other states. This power already exists. A cooperative effort between the states is an unsound and unnecessary measure.

Substantive and Procedural Reforms

While the Governor's proposal is unsatisfactory, there are many areas in which the law should be revised before another summer like the last. Both the state and the federal governments have an interest in the revisions.

First, give the Guardsman a definite status when on active duty. This is a subject not generally covered by statute. It is, however, a proper subject for the legislature. If the Governors wanted to encourage uniformity, the establishment of the Guardsman with the rights of a peace officer would be a positive step.

Second, the crimes involved in rioting should be specified. Most riot provisions are merely rewrites of the old English riot act and rely extensively on the common law to define the offense. In view of the past summer, the various offenses that the Guardsmen will be called on to enforce should be clearly spelled out. In Michigan the Governor's Crime Commission has made various recommendations that deserve comment. Among them were proposals to give mayors, sheriffs and the State Police director the power to declare states of emergency and impose temporary restrictions; to outlaw interference with on-duty firemen and to make it a felony to do so with a dangerous weapon; to outlaw certain incendiaries; and to provide units within police departments to detect and prevent organized elements from operating. These, along with others, are working in the right direction. Many are already included within the Governor's emergency powers, e.g., control of incendiaries, but their specification in statute is still desirable.

Third, the state should provide immunity for the Guardsman while on active duty and should waive its own immunity in regards to civil suits brought as a result of state action. That is, provide a state version of the F.T.C.A. that would cover Guardsmen in active service. In this respect, the F.T.C.A. should be strengthened by reducing the number of exemptions in coverage. Situations that can be reasonably foreseen, e.g., false arrest, should not be exempted.

Fourth, the federal government should go forward with its proposed legislation aimed at controlling the "carpetbagger" type of agitator, traveling from state to state with intent to foment violence and incite riots. The bill, H.R. 421,[48] must be carefully worded to avoid conflicting with the Bill of Rights, but the idea is sound and can be justified as a legitimate federal interest under Article IV, Section 4 of the Constitution.

Conclusion

If the past summer's events taught anything, they should suggest that adequate preparation is essential if there are similar occurrences in the future. Efficiency is the essential point of operation. This means that each person must know his duties during the emergency. Hesitancy can cause as much damage as organization within the mob. Our law must keep pace. This is as much a part of future preparation as the condition of the enforcement units themselves.†

---

48. H.R. 421, 90th Cong., 1st Sess. (1967).

† The following in an Act recently passed by the Michigan Legislature to amend the Military Law in the State. This Act was written as a result of "lead" sheets on this article being submitted to the State military authorities:

An Act to Amend Section 179 of Act 150 of Public Acts of 1967 . . . .

Section 1. Section 179 of Act No. 150 of the Public Acts of 1967 is amended to read as follows:

Sec. 179. (a) No civilian person, except the governor, may command personnel of the state military establishment.

(b) Whenever any portion of the Originized Militia is called into active state service or into the service of the United States to execute the laws, engage in disaster relief, suppress or prevent actual or threatened riot or insurrection, or repel invasion, any commanding officer shall use his own judgment with respect to the propriety of apprehending or dispersing any snipers, rioters, mob or unlawful assembly. Such commander shall determine the amount and kind of force to be used in preserving the peace and carrying out the orders of the governor. His honest and reasonable judgment under the circumstances then existing, in the exercise of his duty, shall be full protection, civilly and criminally, for any act or acts done while in line of duty; and no member of the Originized Militia in active state service or in the service of the United States shall be liable civilly or criminally for any act or acts done by him in the performance of his duty.

(c) A member of the Originized Militia in active state service or in the service of the United States, while acting in aid of civil authorities and in line of duty shall have the immunities of a peace officer.

(d) The Attorney General of Michigan shall defend any civil action or criminal prosecution brought in any court, state or federal, against any member of the Originized Militia or his estate arising from any act or omission alleged to have been committed while in active state service or in the service of the United States.

When Will the Troops Come Marching In?:

A Comment on the Historical Use of Federal Troops to Quell Domestic Violence

RUTHANNE GARTLAND* AND RICHARD A. CHIKOTA*

INTRODUCTION

During the Detroit Riot of 1967, Governor George Romney became the twenty-fourth governor of a state to request that a President assist in quelling domestic violence with the aid of federal troops.[1] Three urgent requests for federal troops were made by the Michigan governor and still the federal officials merely debated the propriety of intervention. In response, Governor Romney charged that President Johnson "played politics in a period of tragedy and riot."[2]

In order to dispel future confusion concerning the respective duties of a governor and the President during a domestic uprising, this comment will explore every request made by a governor for federal troops to determine why troops are or are not deployed by the President, and, in particular, what is the relevance of the manner of application. On the basis of this research, we have constructed a model request conforming to historical and statutory standards.

STATUTORY HISTORY

On Wednesday, July 18, 1787, Colonel Mason said at the Constitutional Convention:

> If the General Government should have no right to suppress rebellions against particular States, it will be in a bad situation indeed. As Rebellions against itself originate in and against individual States, it must remain a passive Spectator of its own subversion.[3]

In response to this argument, the Convention passed resolution sixteen, which became Article IV, § 4 of the United States Constitution:

> The U.S. shall guarantee to every State in this Union a republican form of government and shall protect each of them

* Students, University of Detroit School of Law.

1. This comment will not explore requests by governors of territories, state legislatures, or federal officials. See generally, Note, *Riot Control and the Use of Federal Troops*, 81 HARV. L. REV. 638 (1968).
2. N.Y. Times, July 26, at 28.
3. 2 M. FARRAND, THE RECORDS OF THE FEDERAL CONVENTION OF 1787 47.

against invasion, and, on application of the legislature, or of the executive (when the legislature cannot be convened), against domestic violence.

The particular responsibility for protecting the states against domestic violence has been entrusted to the Chief Executive. Article II, § 3 reads, "He shall take care that the laws be faithfully executed." While all other officers of the government are required to swear only "to support the Constitution," the President must swear to "preserve, protect, and defend" it.[4]

So that the President may perform this duty, the land and naval forces are under his orders as their commander-in-chief,[5] but his power is to be used only in the manner prescribed by the legislature.[6]

The constitutional authorization given to Congress[7] to provide for settlement of domestic violence was executed in 1795, when an act was passed: "to provide for calling forth the Militia to execute the laws of the Union, suppress insurrections, and repel invasions."[8] In 1807, this act was expanded so that in all cases of domestic disorder where it was lawful under the statute of 1795 to call forth the militia, it would also be lawful for the president to employ "such part of the land or naval forces of the United States, as shall be judged necessary, having first observed all the prerequisites of the law in that respect."[9] The statutes of 1795 and 1807 were combined and revised in the Act of 1861[10] and have remained essentially the same.[11]

---

4. Presidential Oath, U.S. CONST. art. II, § 1.
5. U.S. CONST., art. II, § 2.
6. 9 OP. ATT'Y GEN. 517 (1860).
7. U.S. CONST., art. I, § 8.
8. Act of Feb. 28, 1795, ch. 36, 1 Stat. 424.
9. Act of Mar. 3, 1807, ch. 39, 2 Stat. 443.
10. Act of July 29, 1861, ch. 25, 12 Stat. 281. These statutes were later reprinted as Revised Statutes 5297, 5298, and 5299. After codification, the 1861 statute became § 201, 202, and 203, Title 50, U.S. Code, before being republished as §§ 331, 332, and 333, Chapter 15, U.S. Code.

Statutory requirements are based upon the Acts of 1795, 1807 and 1861, now 10 USC, §§ 331, 332, and 333. Section 331 authorizes the use of federal troops when there exists:

1. an insurrection against a state government
2. a request by the state legislature or the governor if the legislature cannot be convened

The power of the President under this section cannot be exercised except upon the application of the legislature or executive of a state.

Section 332 authorizes the use of troops:

1. whenever the President considers that unlawful obstructions, combinations, or assemblages, or rebellion against the authority of the U.S.
2. make it impracticable to enforce the laws of the U.S. . . . by the ordinary course of judicial proceedings.

As this section relates only to the enforcement of federal laws, the President's action is not conditioned upon an appeal from state authorities. It was thus possible under this section for President Eisenhower to order troops int Little Rock, Arkansas, and President Kennedy into Mississippi.

Section 333 provides that:

Article IV, § 4 of the Constitution and the statute of 1861 have two basic requirements which must be met to the satisfaction of the President:[12] 1.) the existence of domestic violence or an insurrection against the state government, and, 2.) a request by the state legislature (or the governor if the legislature cannot be convened in time).

Analysis of Governors' Requests

To determine why requests for federal troops are or are not granted, we constructed a chart detailing relevant factors, procedural and substantive, surrounding each request (See Chart A). We further charted those factors present when troops were sent (See Chart B), and the reasons given when troops were not sent (See Chart C). In the body of the article, each even is categorized as to type: political racial, economic, or racial-economic, and an analysis made to determine what relationship, if any, exists between the character of the disturbance and the factors which must be present before troops will be deployed.

Disturbances by Type

Over the years, governors have requested federal troops in four distinguishable types of disturbance. The first requests made in 1838, 1842, and 1856, were for troops to quell disorders of a political character. Racial violence was involved in uprisings during 1874, 1876, and 1943. Between 1877 and 1921 the disturbances were basically economic in nature, chiefly strikes at railroads and mines. The violence of the present decade, however, combines racial and economic overtones.

The President, by using the militia or the armed forces, or both or by any other means, shall take such measures as he considers necessary to suppress, in a State, any insurrection, domestic violence, unlawful combination, or conspiracy, if it—

(1) so hinders the execution of the laws of that State, and of the United States within the State, that any part or class of its people is deprived of a right, privilege, immunity, or protection named in the Constitution and secured by law, and the constituted authorities of that State are unable, fail, or refuse to protect that right, privilege, or immunity, or to give that protection; or

(2) opposes or obstructs the execution of the laws of the United States or impedes the course of justice under those laws

In any situation covered by clause (1), the State shall be considered to have denied the equal protection of the laws secured by the Constitution.

11. One remaining statute dealing with the President's suppression of rebellion is 15 USC § 334, previously 50 U.S.C. § 204. This act, in effect since 1792, requires that whenever the President considers it necessary to use the militia or the armed forces, he "by proclamation, immediately order the insurgents to disperse and retire peaceably to their abodes within a reasonable time." This condition precedent probably derives from the common law duty of magistrates, in the event of a riotous or tumultous assembly, to go to the scene of the riot and make a proclamation by reading the Riot Act and commanding the rioters to disperse.

12. Martin v. Mott, 6 U.S. (12 Wheat.) 19 (1827).

CHART A

Incident	Size of Mob at Time of Request	Amount of Violence At Time of Request	Whether Militia Put into Action	Manner of Application	Reasons Given for Granting Request	Reasons Given for Refusing Request
1. Political controversy in Pa. (Buckshot War) 1838	several hundred	Mob invaded House of Representatives; prevented Congress from functioning. None injured; no damage	No	Governor Ritner wrote President Van Buren stating: A.* B.		2. 3. 4. **
2. Political Rebellion in R.I. (Dorr Rebellion) 1842	1st—0 2nd—0 3rd—200 4th—1000	1st—none 2nd—none 3rd—Mob tried to seize arsenal 4th—4 citizens injured	No	Governor King made three requests and the Legislature made one. 1st—State "threatened" by domestic violence B. 2nd—A. 3rd—State "threatened." 4th—Violence "imminent."		1st—1. 2nd—2. & 3. 3rd—1. & 3. 4th—1. & 2.
3. Vigilantee Rebellion in California. 1856	6,000-7,000	Prisoners taken, houses searched, two men hung, militia joined the Vigilantees	Yes	Governor Johnson wrote President Pierce stating: "existing conditions required aid" C.		1. 2. 5. & 8.
4. Racial uprising in New Orleans, La. 1874	10,000	Mob took over city, posse and police surrendered, 32 killed, 48 wounded, Militia joined mob	Yes	Governor Kellog wrote President Grant stating: A. B. C.	Suff. evidence of violence; Leg. cannot be convened in time	

CHART A (*continued*)

Incident	Size of Mob at Time of Request	Amount of Violence At Time of Request	Whether Militia Put into Action	Manner of Application	Reasons Given for Granting Request	Reasons Given for Refusing Request
5. Ku Klux Klan riots in S.C. 1876	300	Gunfire between white mob & Negro Militia, All Negro homes broken into, 25 captured, 6 killed	Yes	Governor Chamberlin wrote Pres. Hayes, stating: A. B.	Satisfactorily shown the violence exists, Leg. cannot be convened in time, state can't control sit., Gov. has made due application	
6. Railroad strike riots. 1877 W.Va.	1,000	Strikers drove away scabs, police powerless, Militia joined rioters	Yes	Governor Matthews wrote Pres. Hayes, stating: A. B. C.	Gov. has represented that domes. vio. exists; Leg. cannot be convened in time; State can't suppress vio.; Gov. has made proper application	
7. Md.	few thousand	Railroad station burned, trains wrecked, state militia attacked, 9 killed, 30-40 injured	Yes	Gov. Carroll wrote Pres. Hayes, stating: A. B. C.	Gov. has represented that domes. vio. exists; Leg. cannot be convened in time; State author. unable to suppress vio.	
8. Pa.	several thousand	All freight traffic stopped, railroad cars burned, Militia stoned by mob, $8-10 million prop. dmg., 53 killed, 109 wounded	Yes	Gov. Hartranft wrote Pres. Hayes, stating: "I call upon you for troops to assist in quelling mobs."	Gov. has represented that domes. vio. exists; State author. unable to suppress vio.; Leg. cannot be convened in time	
9. Ill.	25-40 thousand	Factories shut down, looting and rioting, 19 killed, 100 wounded	Yes	Gov. Cullom wrote Pres. Hayes, stating: A. C.	(Troops sent in only to protect property of U.S.)	

CHART A (*continued*)

	Incident	Size of Mob at Time of Request	Amount of Violence At Time of Request	Whether Militia Put into Action	Manner of Application	Reasons Given for Granting Request	Reasons Given for Refusing Request
10.	Mich.	none	Unsettled and threatened conditions	No	Adjutant General wrote Sec. of War, stating: unsettled & threatened conditions existed		1.
11.	Ind.	3,000-4,000	Rioters running rampant in city	Yes	Gov. Williams wrote Pres. Hayes, stating: domestic violence threatened	(Federal troops eventually sent at the behest of a fed. judge, the Pres.'s military advisor & others)	Failure to call upon Pres. under Con. & stat.
12.	Cal.	none	None	No	Gov. Irwin wrote Pres. Hayes, stating: a riot is apprehended; local forces will be insufficient		1.
13.	Wis.	none	Danger threatened	No	Gov. Ludington wrote Pres. Hayes, stating: there is danger of a disturbance, Militia will be insufficient		1.
14.	Mining riots in Idaho. 1892	400-500	Mill dynamited, much property dmg., people killed & injured	Yes	Gov. Willey wrote Pres. Harrison, stating: riot has commenced B. C.	Gov. has represented that an insurrection exists, & Leg. cannot be convened	

CHART A (*continued*)

Incident	Size of Mob at Time of Request	Amount of Violence At Time of Request	Whether Militia Put into Action	Manner of Application	Reasons Given for Granting Request	Reasons Given for Refusing Request
15. 1894	several hundred	Strikers attempted to dynamite buildings	Yes	Gov. McConnell wrote Pres. Cleveland, stating: A. B. C.	(Proclamation not issued)	
16. 1899	1,000	Mill dynamited, train seized, 2 killed	No (none available)	Gov. Steunenberg wrote Pres. McKinley, stating: A. B. C.	(Proclamation not issued)	
17. Railroad strike riots in Mont. (Coxey Rebellion) 1894	600	Train stolen, miners clashed with 65 deputy marshals	Yes	Gov. Rickarts telegraphed Pres. Cleveland, stating: C.	(Proclamation not issued)	
18. Mining riots in Colo. 1903	several thousand	Armed pickets took possession of mine property, intimidations and threats	No	Gov. Peabody telegraphed Pres. Cleveland twice: 1st—great emergency exists 2nd—described violence C.		1st—3. 5. 7. 2nd—1. 3. 5.
19. Mining riots in Nevada. 1907	3,000	Dynamiting, threats, 1 killed	No (none available)	Gov. Sparks wrote Pres. T. Roosevelt, stating: A. C.	Troops were sent but were never used because vio. not great enough	

CHART A (*Continued*)

	Incident	Size of Mob at Time of Request	Amount of Violence At Time of Request	Whether Militia Put into Action	Manner of Application	Reasons Given for Granting Request	Reasons Given for Refusing Request
20.	Mining riots in Colo. 1914	several thousand	Miners' camp burned to ground, much property dmg., a number of people were killed or wounded	Yes	Gov. Ammons wrote Pres. Wilson, stating: A. B. C.	Domestic vio. exists; Leg. cannot be convened; state unable to control situation	
21.	Mining riots in W. Va. 1921	5,000 4,000 several thousand	300 state troopers fired on by miners Mob ready for invasion 2 killed, 2 injured	No (none available)	Gov. Morgan wrote Pres. Harding, stating: A. C. A. C. A. C.	3rd request granted because investigators verified need for troops	1st—3. 2nd—3.
22.	Race riots in Detroit, Mich. 1943	10,000	Rioting, looting, 5 killed, thousands injured	No (none available)	Gov. Kelly wrote Pres. F. D. Roosevelt, stating: A. B. C.	Gov. has made due application representing that domestic vio. exists, Leg. is not in session, and the state is unable to suppress the vio.	
23.	Riots in Detroit Mich. 1967	several thousand	250 major fires, $100 million prop. dmg., 4 dead, 500 injured	Yes	Gov. Romney made one oral request and two requests by telegram: 2nd—A. 3rd—A.	3rd request granted because Gov. had represented that domes. vio. existed & that state forces were unable to suppress vio.	1st—9. 2nd—Must use word "insurrection"

* Code
A—Domestic violence (or an insurrection) exists within the state
B—The Legislature is not in session and cannot be convened in time to meet the emergency
C—State forces are unable to suppress the violence
** For meaning of numbers—See Chart C.

CHART B

Factors Present When Requests Were Granted

Incident	Considerable Violence Had Already Occurred	Evidence That State Forces Inadequate	Gov. Alleged That Domestic Violence Existed	Gov. Alleged That Leg. Could Not Be Convened	Gov. Alleged That State Forces Were Inadequate
1. Racial uprisings in New Orleans 1874	X	X	X	X	X
2. Ku Klux Klan riots 1876	X	X	X	X	
3. Great Riots 1877: W. Va.	X	X	X	X	X
4. " Md.	X	X	X	X	X
5. " Pa.	X	X			
6. " Ill.	X		X		X
7. Mining riots in Idaho 1892	X		X	X	X
8. " 1894			X	X	X
9. " 1899	X	X	X	X	X
10. Coxey Rebellion 1894	X	X			X
11. Mining riots in Nevada 1907	X	X	X	X	X
12. Mining riots in Colo. 1914	X	X	X		X
13. Mining riots in W. Va. 1921	X	X	X		X
14. Race riots in Detroit 1943	X	X	X	X	X
15. Riots in Detroit 1967	X	X	X		X

CHART C
Reasons Given When Requests Were Refused

Incident	1. Violence Only Threatened	2. No Evidence That Legis. Cannot Be Convened	3. No Evidence That State Forces Are Inadequate	4. Disturbance Not in Opposition to Laws of the State	5. No Allegation That Legis. Cannot Be Convened	6. No Allegation That State Forces Inadequate	7. No All. That a State of Insurr. Exists	8. Troops Not Spec. Reques.	9. Request Not In Writing
1. Buckshot War—1838		X	X	X					
2. Dorr Rebellion—1842	X	X	X						
3. Vigilantee Rebellion—1856	X	X			X			X	
4. Great Riots of 1877—Mich.	X								
5. " Ind.	X				X	X			
6. " Cal.	X								
7. " Wis.	X								
8. Mining Riots in Colo. 1903	X		X		X		X		
9. Mining riots in W. Va. 1921			X						
10. Detroit, 1967							X		X

Political Disturbances

The Buckshot War of 1838 broke out when a meeting of the Pennsylvania Legislature was disrupted by a mob disputing the results of a recent election. Governor Ritner sent a letter to President Van Buren requesting troops because of the state of domestic violence and the inability of the legislature to convene.[13] This request was refused by the War Department because, 1.) the commotion was a "political contest" and the federal government did not feel it ought to interfere in such grave and delicate affairs; 2.) the legislature was apparently then in session and, thus, should have made the request, and, 3.) there was no indication that state forces were employed or were inadequate.[14]

At the time of the Dorr Rebellion in 1841 numerous non-freeholders and some freeholders drew up a constitution extending suffrage to all adult male citizens. Although not authorized by the legislature, the constitution was adopted by a majority of the people. Meanwhile another party, the charter party, with the approval of the legislature, submitted a second constitution in March of 1842, but it was defeated.[15] Still the opposition called for an election. Governor King, expecting trouble, requested the aid of federal troops;[16] however, the request was refused because violence had not yet erupted.[17] Subsequent requests were made on May 25 and June 23, but President Tyler again denied them because of the absence of actual violence, the failure to use state facilities, and because the legislature was in session.[18]

During the summer of 1856, a San Francisco Vigilantee Committee was formed of 6,000 to 7,000 well-armed men, including members of the militia.[19] The objective of this committee was to check the spread of lawlessness in Califoria, but in so doing they perpetrated lynchings and killings. Governor Johnson requested "assistance in arms and ammunition" on June 19, 1856.[20] This request was refused by Secretary of State Marcy because the violence had diminished, a request solely for arms and ammunition had been made, and there had been no allegation that the legislature was not in session or that it could not be convened.[21]

---

13. H. R. Doc. No. 28, 25th Cong., 3d Sess. 6-7 (1838).
14. *Id.* at 8-9.
15. *See generally,* H. Doc. No. 225, 28th Cong., 1st Sess. 1-49 (1844) [Hereinafter cited as H. Doc. 225]; *Federal Aid in Domestic Disturbances,* 19 S. Doc. No. 19, 67th Cong., 2d Sess. 54-60 (1922) [Hereinafter cited as 19 S. Doc.].
16. *Id.* at 54.
17. *Id.* at 54-55.
18. *Id.* at 226-27; H. Doc. 225 at 40-41.
19. 19 S. Doc. at 71-78.
20. *Id.* at 75-76.
21. *Id.* at 76.

It can thus be seen that when the disturbance has been political in character, the President has been very unwilling to interfere and very particular as to the manner of application. The reluctance of the Chief Executive to intervene in this type of disturbance is understandable. If the President did act, he would be forced to become the final arbiter. He would be required to "take sides" and then enforce his decision with federal troops. To so meddle in state affairs would do violence to the federal system. Furthermore, in this type of conflict the participants are not attempting, as such, to violate state or federal law. They are attempting, instead, to assert their right to a political office or to enforce the law themselves. Of course, the situation can deteriorate to the point where federal intervention is required, but the President should avoid involvement until it is absolutely necessary.

Racial Disturbances

The second type of disturbance for which federal forces have been requested is racial in nature. In each instance of this type (New Orleans, 1874;[22] South Carolina, 1876;[23] and Detroit, 1943[24]) large roving mobs of whites attacked Negro men, women, and children.

The violence prior to the dispatch of federal troops on these occasions was great. In New Orleans[25] a mob of 2,000 to 3,000 armed men clashed with armed police; at least thirty-two men were killed and forty-eight wounded.[26] During the riots in several South Carolina counties, "Rifle Clubs" killed approximately twenty-one persons.[27] In Detroit, during 1943, two died and thousands were injured; looting and burning were common; thousands roamed the streets in search of prey.[28]

In each instance, the respective governor, in requesting troops, stated that domestic violence existed, that the legislature was not in session and could not be convened in time, and that federal aid was

---

22. *See generally, id.* at 120-39.
23. *See generally, id.* at 156-57.
24. *See generally, A. Lee & N. Humphry, Race Riot* (1943) [Hereinafter cited as RACE RIOT].
25. It should be noted that a political hassle was also involved in the Louisiana Riot. However, several months before the riot near New Orleans, President Grant had issued a proclamation for disorderly persons to disperse. He recognized Governor Kellog as the present executive of the state in light of Kellog's certification by the Louisiana Supreme Court and his tacit recognition by Congress. 19 S. Doc. at 128-29.

The reader should also realize that the disturbances in Louisiana had occurred sporadically for several years, coming to a head in 1874.

26. *Id.*
27. *Id.* at 156-57.
28. RACE RIOT 11-18.

necessary,[29] thus fulfilling statutory requirements. When the violence has been racially motivated, troops have always been sent. However, in each of these instances state forces were also inadequate and statutory application was made.

Economic Disturbances

During the period from 1877 to 1921, a number of bitter labor strikes arose throughout the country involving hundreds of thousands of strikers. Sixteen appeals were made for federal aid to quell these labor disputes; the Chief Executive responded with troops twelve times.

The Great Riots of 1877 followed a nationwide railroad strike. Federal troops were sent into West Virginia, Maryland, Pennsylvania, Indiana, and Illinois. Federal military aid was unsuccessfully requested in California, Michigan, and Wisconsin. Because all of these states requested federal aid as a result of the same disturbance, the reasons for denial of some of the requests are highly significant.

Where troops were sent considerable violence had actually occurred. In Martinsburg, West Virginia, strikers stopped the movement of trains completely. The police were powerless and the state militia wholly inadequate to the task.[30] Maryland Governor Carroll, anticipating trouble, sent the state militia to Cumberland, Maryland, to protect railroad property. In an ensuing pitched battle between strikers and the militia, nine people were killed and thirty-four wounded; railroad property was burned.[31] In Pittsburgh, Pennsylvania, a large mob held the state militia at bay in a roundhouse. The militia retreated when strikers burned them out. An estimated fifty-three people were killed, over one hundred were wounded, and eight to ten million dollars worth of railroad property was burned.[32]

Mobs numbering 25,000 to 40,000 roamed Chicago, Illinois. Factories were shut down, looting and burning occurred, nineteen persons were killed and over one hundred wounded.[33] However, the troops sent were not to be used except for the protection of federal property unless another emergency arose. Apparently the violence had abated because the troops were never actively engaged.[34]

29. New Orleans: 19 S. Doc. 128.
South Carolina: *id.* at 156-57.
Detroit: 57 Stat. pt. 2 at 742-43; Race Riot 42.

30. 19 S. Doc. 164-65; *see generally,* E. McCabe, the History of the Great Riots 17-27 (1877) [Hereinafter cited as McCabe].

31. 19 S. Doc. 164-65; *see generally,* McCabe 50-65.

32. 19 S. Doc. 166-70; *see generally,* McCabe 76-128.

33. 19 S. Doc. 172-73; *see generally,* McCabe 369-402.

34. 19 S. Doc. 173.

In Indiana, even though a mob of from 2,000 to 4,000 had gathered, federal troops were sent in only after repeated requests by a federal judge, a military advisor, and other leading citizens, and their use was restricted to the protection of governmental property.[35] However, the Governor's request had been rather informal:

> In view of the threatened domestic violence growing out of the railroad strike, I request that authority be at once given to the commandant of the arsonal to render me all the aid possible in preserving the peace.[36]

It is difficult to discern any pattern for this limited intervention by federal troops since it occurred only twice. In Illinois the reason for intervention was the rather severe violence that had already arisen and the potential threat of further violence of a marked degree. In Indiana the urgency and number of requests from several sources appears to have been the catalyst.

Another possible answer is the fact that the strikes were nationwide and spreading. Given this fact, it could be argued that the President will be more readily disposed to dispatch troops to check further spreading of a national disorder. Such an explanation also seems plausible when one considers the extreme caution exercised by President Johnson in Detroit, and his apparent readiness to send troops when rioting broke out in several major cities throughout the country following the assassination of Dr. Martin Luther King.

Requests were made in 1877 by the governors of California,[37] Michigan,[38] and Wisconsin;[39] however, troops were not dispatched. Two reasons can be given in explanation: 1.) insufficient domestic violence to warrant intervention and 2.) defective applications. In California, Michigan, and Wisconsin, although conditions were unsettled and threatening, no mobs had formed.[40] In addition, the requests did not state that domestic violence existed, or that the legislature was not in session or could not be convened in time. Only Governor Ludington of Wisconsin alluded to the insufficiency of his state militia.[41]

The successful requests by the governors of West Virginia,[42]

35. *Id.* at 171-72.
36. *Id.* at 177.
37. *Id.* at 287.
38. *Id.* at 286.
39. *Id.* at 287.
40. *Id.* at 175.
41. *See* notes 36, 37, and 38. The state militia was not called out by these governors.
42. 19 S. Doc. 162.

Maryland,[43] and Illinois[44] conformed substantially to statutory requirements. The request of Pennsylvania Governor Hartranft is an apparent exception:

> I call upon you for troops to assist in quelling mobs within the borders of the State of Pennsylvania. Respecfully suggest that you order troops from adjoining States, and prepare to call for volunteers authorized by act of Congress.[45]

It appears that the form of the request is not (at least in 1877) an overriding consideration when, as in Pennsylvania, the worst riot at that time in our history was occurring,[46] and the governor was sojourning outside the state.[47]

However, the President may, as he did in Indiana and Illinois, limit the use of federal forces to the protection of federal property when the violence has abated but the situation remains highly volatile, or in a doubtful situation when he defers to requests from several reliable sources. When the violence is only threatened, any form of request will be denied.

Between 1892 to 1900, a series of bloody strikes by Colorado miners erupted. Troops were dispatched in 1892,[48] 1894,[49] and 1899.[50] In these instances, roving bands of armed strikers dynamited mills and kept various mining areas in a state of insurrection. Numbering between 400 and 1,000, the mobs killed several individuals and injured many.

The three Colorado requests fulfilled statutory requirements. It was asserted on each occasion that state forces were inadequate to handle the situation.[51] These outbreaks closely paralleled the disturbances in West Virginia and Maryland in 1877 when troops were promptly sent following outbreaks of violence and a formal application by the Governor.

On April 24, 1894, a contingent of 600 men belonging to Coxey's Army under the leadership of one General Hogan stole a train in Montana to aid in their march on Washington. They clashed with

43. *Id.* at 165.

44. *Id.* at 172. Governor McCullum, however, did not assert the inability to convene the legislature. Because of the rather informal nature of the request, as in Indiana, the use of troops was limited to the protection of federal property. *Id.* at 172.

45. *Id.* at 167.

46. *See* chart A.

47. 19 S. Doc. 167.

48. *Id.* at 190-91.

49. *Id.* at 199-200.

50. *Id.* at 210-13. *See also,* H. Rep. No. 1999, 56th Cong., 1st Sess. 6-7, 22-23.

51. State forces had been sent to quell the strikers in 1892 and 1894. However, no forces were available in 1899.

sixty-five deputy marshalls on April 19. Governor Richarts telegraphed the President to send troops because the state militia was ineffective. After talks with his military advisor, the President sent troops on April 25.[52]

"Teddy" Roosevelt, through Secretary of War Elihu Root, refused to aid the Governor of Colorado in 1903. Though several thousand strikers took possession of mine property and made repeated intimidations and threats, no eruption of massive violence occurred.[53] The requests of November 16[54] and 18[55] failed to fulfill the statutory requirements. Furthermore, state forces were not mobilized. This situation differs from the California-Michigan-Wisconsin disturbances only in so far as a mob had actually congregated. However, this factor was not deemed relevant. Domestic violence of sufficient magnitude must be evidenced.

Four years later, Governor Sparks of Nevada requested federal assistance in controlling disorders in Goldfield.[56] President Roosevelt dispatched nine companies, but instructed General Funstan not to take sides. The troops were only to be used to "prevent riot, violence, and disorder." However, when no occasion arose necessitating their intervention, Roosevelt required the Governor to convene the Nevada legislature so it could request the contingent to remain.[57] Federal troops

---

52. B. RICH, THE PRESIDENTS AND CIVIL DISORDER 88-89 (1941); Clinch, *Coxey's Army in Montana*, 15 MONT. W. HIST. 2 (no. 4, 1965).

53. S. DOC. NO. 122, 58th Cong., 1st Sess. 9-14 (1905).

54. Industrial troubles in Colorado are assuming more dangerous proportions every day; coupled with the stand of the Western Federation of Miners comes the American Mine Workers' Association, and has closed practically all of our coal mines. Demands for State troops to protect life and property are of daily occurrence. The welfare of our people and their property must be protected and coercion and violence prohibited. The emergency is great. Will you instruct General Baldwin, commanding the Department of Colorado, to furnish me such aid as I may call for?

JAMES H. PEABODY,
Governor of Colorado.

Id. at 9.

55. Unauthorized armed pickets have taken possession of property in San Miguel County, Colo., prohibiting owners, operators, or workingmen from continuing business. Mining, milling, and other business is suspended there by intimidations, threats, and violence of an unlawful, armed organization. The sheriff reports inability to cope with situation, and the State has exhausted every means at its command to enforce the law, suppress lawlessness, and protect life and property there and elsewhere in the State, and, in accordance with the law in such case provided, I, as governor of the State of Colorado, do respectfully request that you instruct the commander of the Department of Colorado to furnish me such aid, immediately, as I may call for.

JAMES H. PEABODY,
Governor of Colorado.

Id. at 10.

56. 19 S. DOC. 310-11; H. REP. DOC. NO. 607, 60th Cong., 1st Sess. 4-7 (1908).

57. 19 S. DOC. at 311.

were also sent to Colorado again to assist in dispersing rioting coal miners in 1914.[58]

The final instance in which the President granted a request relating to an economic disturbance took place in 1921. President Harding at first balked at intervening in a West Virginia mining strike on May 12 and again on August 25. However, when 5,000 strikers assembled, 300 armed, and clashed with state forces, he granted the August 29th request of the Governor. Even then, further requests on August 30 and 31 were required and federal advisors had to concur on the need for troops.[59] Though at first blush this situation appears similar to that of Detroit in 1967, the President here did not object to the form of the request, but rather to the lack of evidence that state forces were inadequate. In Detroit, President Johnson objected not only to a lack of evidence that an insurrection was present, but also to the manner in which the request was made. When one compares the amount of violence present in these two situations, it is obvious that the violence in Detroit exceeded that in West Virginia.

Large-scale violent strikes represent another type of incident in which the Chief Executive is willing to intervene upon proper request by the Governor. He may also send in troops to protect federal property if the violence is substantial though the request is somewhat informal. And when the violence is only threatened, troops will not be mobilized regardless of the form of the request.

Racial-Economic

The violence which has arisen during the past several years has had a distinct racial-economic overtone. The recent riots in Watts, Cleveland-Hough, Detroit, Washington, D.C., Chicago, Baltimore, and elsewhere have been directed at both people and property. As in the race riots in New Orleans, South Carolina, and Detroit, bands have gathered to inflict bodily injury, and snipers have killed a number of people. However, as in the economic disturbances of the previous century, numerous rioters are protesting their economic plight.

During the Detroit riot Governor Romney was required to make three requests, and even then the troops were not sent into Detroit until almost eleven hours after their arrival at nearby Selfridge Field Air Base.

Shortly after a blind pig was raided by police on Sunday, July 23,

58. *Id.* at 312-15; 1 STONE, HISTORY OF COLORADO, 874-75 (1918); H.R. DOC. No. 1630, 63d Cong., 3d Sess. 4-30 (1915).

59. *Id.* at 320; E. BERMAN, LABOR DISPUTES AND THE PRESIDENTS OF THE U.S. 210-13 (1924).

a crowd began to gather. By 7:50 a.m. the crowd had grown to 3000 people, and to 9000 by 9.00 a.m. Sporadic looting had broken out by late afternoon. A large contingent of state militia and the state police were brought in. By Monday morning a curfew had been imposed, at least four persons were dead and hundreds injured, millions of dollars in property damage had occurred, and numerous major fires blazed.[60]

On July 24, 1967, at 2:40 a.m. Governor Romney orally requested of Ramsey Clark that federal troops be sent to Detroit. He was informed that a written request would be required.[61] Most regrettably, Governor Romney then proceeded to draft telegrams for over four hours.[62] Finally, at 8:30 a.m. Romney again called Clark and read him a second request in which he "recommended" the use of troops and excluded the term "insurrection". This request was also refused.[63] In his final request at 10:56 a.m., the Governor used the word "request," but wrote around the word "insurrection."[64]

Troops arrived at nearby Selfridge Field Air Base at 4:00 p.m. However, it was not until 10:00 p.m. that presidential assistant, Cyrus Vance had the troops brought into the Detroit area; and they were not actually used until 2:30 a.m., July 25.[65]

Admittedly using hindsight, the authors submit that Governor Romney and President Johnson permitted politics to enter the decisional process. At the time Romney made his first request, the situation was such that the use of federal troops was necessary. However, Romney took over four more hours to compose a telegram which would not make him appear to be incapable of handling the situation. Conversely, Ramsey Clark could have accepted use of the words "recommend" and "domestic violence". Granted that the Chief Executive must not hastily intervene and usurp state functions, a squabble over the use of a term while a riot of the magnitude Detroit witnessed is to be regretted and avoided. The constant reference to the Michigan Governor's inability to control the situation by the President in dispatching forces, also demonstrates the interjection of politics.[66] This fact is further substantiated when one looks at the willingness and swiftness of the President in sending troops into Chicago, Washington, D.C., and

---

60. Det. News, July 24, 1967, § A at 1, 9.

61. Because of the unavailability of the telephone in the past, prior requests were written or teletyped. However, the authors feel that if intervention is warranted, an oral request followed by a written request should be sufficient in order to permit the swiftest possible deployment of troops.

62. N.Y. Times, July 30, 1967 at 1, col. 3, & at 50, cols. 2-6.

63. *Id.*

64. *Id.*

65. Det. Free Press, July 25, 1967, § A, at 2, col. 2.

66. N.Y. Times, July 26, 1967, at 38.

Baltimore, during the disturbances following the assassination of Dr. Martin Luther King. If one compares the amount of violence present in Detroit on July 25 with that in Pennsylvania, Indiana, and Illinois in 1877, at least a limited intervention to preserve federal property was justified by historical precedent.

Relevant Factors in General

Altogether there are nine separate reasons which have been given by past presidents for refusing to grant state requests for federal troops. Four of these are substantive, relating to the nature of conditions: 1.) the violence was not actual, but only threatened, 2.) there was no evidence that the legislature could not be convened, 3.) there was no evidence that state forces were inadequate, and 4.) the disturbance was not in opposition to the laws of the state or nation. The remaining reasons given are procedural, relating to the manner of application; 5.) there was no allegation that the legislature could not be convened, 6.) there was no allegation that state forces were inadequate, 7.) there was no allegation that a state of insurrection existed, 8.) troops were not specifically requested, and 9.) the request was not in writing.[67]

Of the procedural reasons for refusal, numbers five and seven are based upon the statutory requirements in the Act of 1861. These requirements, however, are not always insisted upon; no allegation was made that the legislature could not be convened, and yet troops were sent. (See Chart B). The two reasons which most frequently have been given for refusing to send troops are *substantive*: number one, the violence was only threatened, and number three, there was no evidence that state forces were inadequate. The existence of actual violence and of evidence that the state is unable to quell the disturbance are also the two conditions most often present when troops *are* granted; thus, they appear to be more important factors than the statutory requirements.

We have seen that the manner of request is very important when

67. It may be noted that there is a remarkable similarity between the factors relevant in a presidential determination to interfere with federal troops and those factors relevant in the Supreme Court's determination to hear a case appealed from a state court of last resort. In the latter situation, the Supreme Court considers whether 1.) the case is ripe for adjudication (violence must be actual and not threatened), 2.) the standing requirement has been met (request must come from the legislature if it is in session or can be convened), 3.) there exists an adequate state remedy to dispose of the case (state forces must be inadequate to handle the situation), 4.) the controversy involves a question under the Constitution or laws of the United States (disturbance must be in opposition to the laws of the state or nation), and 5.) it had been alleged in the petition that a case or controversy exists, that the person appealing is a proper party, that the state remedy is inadequate, and that a federal question is involved (governor must also allege factors one-four in his request.

the disturbance is political, when the disturbance is economic and violence is only threatened, and, predictably, when the disturbance is racial or racial-economic and violence is only threatened.

It may further be noted, referring to Chart C, that there have actually been just four occasions when the method of application was criticized (Vigilantee Rebellion of 1856, Indiana Riot of 1877, Colorado Riot of 1903, and the Detroit Riot of 1967). In all but one of these instances (Detroit, 1967) when formal requests were demanded, there was *no actual violence.* The 1967 cataclysm in Detroit was apparently the only time in our history when the manner of application was criticised while actual violence of such magnitude was occurring.

We conclude that when the substantitive conditions of actual violence and evidence of the state's inability to handle the disorder are present, a formal request is not absolutely necessary. Yet a wise governor should not risk the chance of his request being denied because it was improperly worded.

Model Request

Based upon our analysis, we have constructed a model request which a governor could use in requesting federal troops.[68] In every instance the governor should formally request that the President intervene with federal troops. He should assert 1.) that domestic violence or an insurrection exists, 2.) which state forces are incapable of controlling, and 3.) that the legislature is not in session and cannot be convened in time to make the request.

> Pursuant to the United States Constitution and applicable federal statutes, I, Governor ―――――――― of the State of ――――――――, call upon the President of the United States to send federal troops to quell domestic violence [an insurrection] against the laws of the State in ――――――――.
>
> All available state forces have been mobilized and they are unable to control the domestic violence [insurrection].
>
> The State Legislature is not now in session and cannot be convened in time to make this request.

This request fulfills every constitutional, statutory, and historical requirement evinced from Chart A. The request should be accompanied by a statement of the conditions existing at the time of the request. The Governor should also include clear evidence of the

68. The same model and procedure can be used by a legislature by merely striking out the sections dealing with the fact that they are not in session and cannot be convened.

amount of violence. He should support and document the statements that the legislature cannot be convened in time and that state forces are incapable of controlling the situation.

Hopefully, this information will preclude the necessity of first sending a presidential advisor to determine the validity of the request. Once troops have initially been sent, the President can then place greater reliance on a military advisor. However, we submit that the Chief Executive should be able to make an initial determination based upon the request and the accompanying evidence. Should the President have any doubts, he could limit the use of federal troops to the protection of federal property, or merely send troops to be used upon a further showing of the need for their intervention. Having witnessed the potential havoc which can emerge in an urban center, any doubts should be resolved in favor of granting the request.

This procedure should adequately preserve the federal system and yet provide an orderly and efficient manner of application upon which the President could initially act. Finally, the use of a uniform request by virtually all the governors would clarify any doubts as to the proper form and would minimize the possibility that political factors would be determinable.